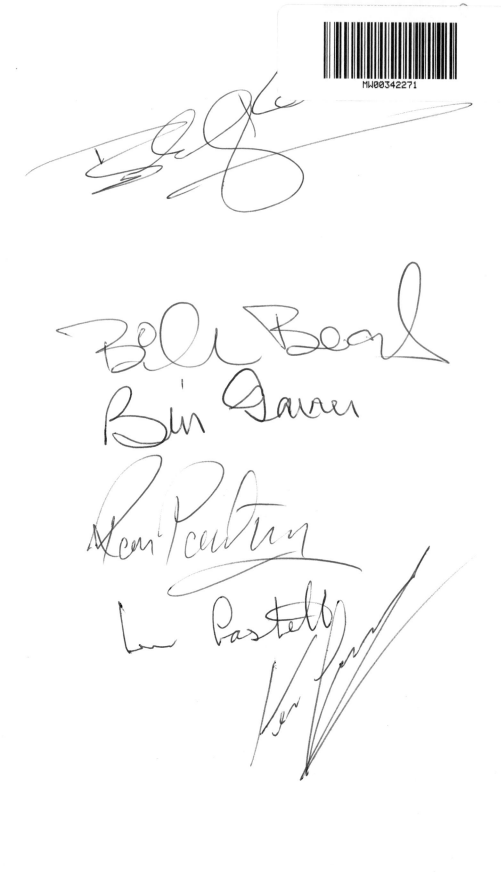

The Southend United Chronicles
1906-2006

DESERT ISLAND FOOTBALL HISTORIES

The
Southend United
Chronicles 1906-2006

A Century of Local Press Reports

Series Editor: Clive Leatherdale

Edited by
Keith Roe

DESERT ISLAND BOOKS

First published in 2006
by
DESERT ISLAND BOOKS LIMITED
7 Clarence Road, Southend-on-Sea, Essex SS1 1AN
United Kingdom
www.desertislandbooks.com

© 2006 Southend Standard and Echo Newspapers

British Library Cataloguing-in-Publication Data
A catalogue record for this book is available from the British Library

ISBN(13) 978-905328-18-5
ISBN(10) 1-905328-18-4

Printed in Great Britain
by
Biddles Ltd, King's Lynn

Photo Credits: The Phil Cox Collection; The Roger Wash Collection;
The Desert Island Books Collection

Contents

Introduction

by Clive Leatherdale

When Keith Roe showed me his bulky, spiral-bound record of Southend United's first 100 years it was quickly apparent that this was more than just another privately researched football book. He had called it 'Southend United: Press On – A Look at The Blues through the eyes of the local press.' And that is exactly what it is.

But it is also much more than that. For four years Keith had spent every spare hour at the microfilm reading machines at Southend Library, whirring the handles back and forth through the pages on Southend United, spending a small fortune on photocopies, then laboriously typing them up on his computer at home. It was a monumental undertaking, the fruits of which can now be seen in *The Southend United Chronicles*.

Anyone who has ever used a microfilm reader knows they are both a blessing and a curse. Prior to the 1970s, those wishing to research national or local newspapers in this country would sit at a desk and wade through thick volumes of huge broadsheet pages. By 2006 broadsheet newspapers have largely disappeared, in favour of user-friendly smaller formats.

Irrespective of the page-size, by the 1970s libraries faced mounting problems. Newsprint naturally yellowed and crumbled with age. The archive was literally rotting away, and the dust inhaled deterred some researchers while forcing others to turn up with pockets stuffed with Kleenex. Storing newspapers also took up so much space that some alternative had to be found. When microfilm technology allowed a page of newsprint to be reduced to an inch of film, then viewed through a lens, it seemed a perfect solution. Months of newspapers could now be transferred to a single reel of film and stored in a small box.

Sadly, the 'solution' was far from perfect. In the same way that e-books have been slow to replace real books, reading from film is more tiring on the eye than reading actual newspapers. Just imagine the job of photographing every page of every newspaper in the country. It took years. But people and machines are fallible. Sometimes pages would be overlooked. Should the camera be slightly out of focus or set to the wrong exposure, the resulting page was unreadable. The 'gutter' presented particular difficulties. The hefty volumes needed to be pressed flat to allow those text columns nearest the spine to be filmed. Often that proved impossible, with predictable consequences. One might think that missing, unreadable or blurred pages could be revisited and photographed again. But once filmed, the original newspapers were often destroyed to save space. That was why they were filmed in the first place.

This gives some idea of the problems Keith faced as he sought to retrieve the 100-year archive of Southend United. Sometimes the reports he hoped to reproduce were, for whatever reason, indecipherable, forcing him to switch his attention to other matches and other reports. While initially intending to cover the Blues in as many competitions as possible and use 'important' games and events as his yardstick, on occasions he had to compromise these ideals, resorting instead to lesser matches where at least the text was clean.

Despite this minor qualification, what Keith has achieved deserves the gratitude of all those who follow Southend United. Local newspapers are the first port of call for historians of all football clubs. The first-hand reports by local correspondents are the primary source, often the only source, particularly concerning a club's early years.

This does not mean a newspaper archive is wholly reliable or presents an unblemished record. When journalists go on strike, matches go unreported, their record lost for ever. Over Christmas, New Year and Easter, clubs traditionally played matches back to back, coinciding with Bank Holidays when newspapers often did not get published or did not have space to cater for extra matches or compressed deadlines.

Besides, there existed no videos to check what really happened against what was scribbled down at the time, often in haste, and without the benefit of slow-motion replays to verify what was written. If goals stemming from goalmouth scrambles defeat us today (without TV help), what price correctly identifying them a century ago from a vantage point on the halfway line while peering through fog or a blizzard! Mistakes? of course there were, and plenty of them too. The lot of the football correspondent was a taxing one, and it still is.

Errors in match reports – whether the responsibility of the correspondent or sub-editor – are common even today, in national newspapers as well as locals, despite the array of technological aids which assist the harassed sports reporter no less than the cosy TV viewer. Prior to the video age, once an error appeared in print it was likely to be cast in stone, incapable of correction, and would be passed on through every book that revisited the same source.

Keith Roe attempts no mediation, assessment or correction. What you read in this book is exactly what readers of the Southend local press have read over these past 100 years.

Today's football fan is bombarded with factual overload. Southend United have spawned several websites, official and unofficial, updating the latest news or gossip almost hourly. All matches are filmed. ITV shows the goals on Sunday morning and club videos compress seasonal 'highlights' for the delectation or despair of diehard supporters.

Yet widespread use of the internet has been with us a mere ten years, personal computers barely twenty. Video recorders only became fashionable in the late 1970s. Hard to believe, but prior to the Premiership revolution in the early 1990s the football authorities insisted that televised matches fostered lounge lizards and was the root cause of dwindling attendances. Whereas today's satellite or cable viewer can be rendered goggle-eyed by football most days a week, back in the 1980s – apart from BBC's *Match of the Day* and ITV's *The Big Match* (or regional variations) – there was nothing.

Radio followed a similar path. Radio 5 Live, with its sports-obsessed agenda, is a newcomer to the soundwaves. There was a time, not so long ago, when it was necessary to tune into Radio 2 on the hour for sports updates and at 10pm for the evening's football results. Should you miss them, or the results which followed *The News at Ten* on ITV at 10.30, it was necessary to wait for the following morning's newspapers to learn your team's fate.

Local press coverage of the Blues' first 100 years is similarly uneven. We are familiar today with the daily *Southend Echo*, which recently changed its name from the *Evening Echo*. But the *Echo* only arrived in 1969. The first 63 years of United's existence were recorded solely by the weekly *Southend Standard* (and to a lesser extent the *Southend Telegraph* and *Pictorial*. From 1922 to 1964 there was also a *Southend Times*, not related to today's weekly of the same name).

Published in midweek, the indispensable *Southend Standard* offered the only detailed report of the past weekend's action and next weekend's prospects. Whereas daily coverage, as supplied by the *Echo*, self-evidently means fresher reports and more frequent transfer talk and news updates, this is somewhat offset by the huge wordage previously offered by the weekly *Standard*. It was not uncommon in pre-television times for match reports in the *Standard* to run to several thousand words. Correspondents in bygone times were expected to paint graphic word-pictures for their readers. For some, this makes their reports somewhat Dickensian and prolix, hard to digest; for others, like myself, they demonstrate a mastery of language that makes for gripping and often hilarious reading. The years immediately prior to the First World War, for example, saw Southend United despatched to Welsh outposts like Mardy and Treharris in the Southern League, and readers in search of side-splitting footballing escapades are recommended to seek out the relevant sections.

Then as now, football writers resorted to popular clichés and metaphors. Instead of 'crunching challenges' and 'sick as a parrot' we learn that the ball was 'the sphere' or 'the leather', the opposing goal was a 'citadel', tussles for the ball, like rugby, were a 'scrimmage', forwards attacked in 'a rush', players would head the ball with their 'cranium', each 45 minutes was 'a moiety', injured players were '*hors de combat*', and scoring a goal was 'a point'.

Other Blues historians, of course, have consulted these same newspapers. Devotees of Southend United have already enjoyed excellent histories by Peter Mason, Dave Goody and Peter Miles, but the earliest of these – Mason's pioneering official history – was published as recently as 1993.

From the outset, Keith Roe intended his record to be impersonal, not to pay homage to this or that correspondent. None are mentioned by name. In any case, bylines in British journalism are comparatively recent. Flipping through the sports pages of *The Times* – both before and immediately after the

Second World War, for example – one commonly finds match reports filed by 'our special correspondent'. Yet from the earliest years of Association Football in the late 19th century, many local publications gave specific pen-names to their football correspondents. The Lancashire hot-bed of professional football featured reports penned by 'The Rambler', 'The Grumbler', 'Free Critic'. The *Coventry Evening Telegraph* tagged its chief Coventry City reporter 'Nemo'. Nemo's match reports appeared for over half a century and only ceased in the 1960s. Needless to say, Nemo was not one man, but several, each new incumbent succeeding upon the retirement of his predecessor.

In the case of Southend United, early correspondents included 'The Ref' and 'Centre-half'. The identity of these individuals, or sequence of individuals, is unknown to me or to Keith Roe, or perhaps to anyone else. That is especially poignant, for our knowledge of the early years of the club is almost entirely down to their efforts. They reported on the Blues from near and far, often perched on precarious gantries exposed to Arctic blasts or Atlantic gales, notepad pressed on saturated or shivering knees with pen or quill clutched in gloved hand. Our debt to them is immense, and it seems ungracious to deny them a tribute by name.

More recently, readers of the *Standard* and the *Echo* have been able to put a name and usually a face to sports reporters on Southend United. Followers of the club have been wonderfully well served in this respect, for the coverage of Alf Smirk in the 1960s, through Howard Southwood, Nigel Fuller, Bernie Friend and currently Chris Phillips has been of a consistently high order.

As Keith's labours gradually took shape, he began arranging reports by topic. These have been retained in these chronicles, so we find chapters – among others – on Big Wins and Losses, Finals, Semi-finals, Internationals, and even a chapter specifically devoted to Brighton & Hove Albion. Thanks Keith, that's a real kick in the teeth! Everything in the chronicles builds, however, towards a logical dramatic climax, the home victory over Bristol City in May 2006 which clinched the championship of what is now called League One, but which old hands like me still think of as Division Three. The book is rounded off by the kind of statistical detail that only anoraks like Keith could lovingly prepare.

Despite Keith's effort and enterprise in compiling this precious archive, it was not originally intended for a wider audience. Historians employ a wide range of sources, and providing they quote sparingly and acknowledge those sources, no offence is normally taken by the original publication. But *The Southend United Chronicles* is different. Every word has been taken from the *Standard, Telegraph, Pictorial* or *Echo*, who obviously own copyright. This book, in other words, could not have been published except for the generous permission of the newspapers involved. When I sought to persuade Editor-in-Chief Martin McNeill that Keith's archive was so important that it deserved to be publicly available, he kindly granted permission for a small print-run.

Southend United were conceived and born in 1906. The period from 1906 to the outbreak of the First World War in 1914 has come to be seen as the Golden Age of English football. Players took centre-stage, managers influenced little that happened on the field, and matches were watched by vast crowds. The Golden Age would be destroyed by the Great War, and the newspapers that recorded those huge football crowds would soon be recording similar daily battle casualties.

It might seem quaint to mention Southend United and Golden Age in the same breath. Admittedly, our newborn club was rather on the fringes of the action, but it was there nevertheless, and one of her players – Harold Halse – would soon be in the thick of it. By that time, of course, he had left Roots Hall for Manchester United.

Centenaries of the great and famous are normally dictated by their greatness and fame. Which leaves the position of Southend United somewhat anomalous. This little football club in the south-east corner of Essex in the south-east corner of England has not achieved anything very much in national terms, no big Cup finals or Championships or anything close. Its glories have been small and fleeting. Astronomers are fond of telling us that our sun is a perfectly ordinary star, feebler than most, in fact, and they are right. But it is our star – where would we be without it? – and it is our club, whether it be ever so feeble or ever so mighty. Some hanker that one day it might rub shoulders with the mighty. In the meantime we just wait, and wait. 'Only wait very hard; wait when others have stopped waiting, forgetting their yesterdays.' Konstantin Simonov was writing of the siege of Leningrad during the Second World War, but supporters of the Blues know the feeling.

And while we wait, what better way to relive the highs (few) and lows (many) of our beloved Southend United than through the pages of Keith Roe's archive. To my knowledge, no club of comparable size has ever benefited from a record as comprehensive as this, and Keith deserves our thanks.

CLIVE LEATHERDALE
DESERT ISLAND BOOKS

PUBLISHER'S NOTE

Desert Island Books gratefully acknowledge the permission granted by Martin McNeill, Editor-in-Chief of *Echo Newspapers*, to publish this archive.

Publishers usually try to impose order and consistency on the terms and styles they employ. In this case, dealing with reports written across 100 years, to do so would create more problems than it solved, and in some cases substantially change the tone of what was written. As far as possible, therefore, reports are included in this volume verbatim.

CHAPTER ONE

The Beginning

This article appeared in the *Southend Standard* during August 1906

SOUTHEND'S PROFESSIONAL FOOTBALL TEAM.
ITS INTENTIONS AND PROSPECTS.

When the idea of a professional football team was mooted some months ago, it was little thought that by the end of August matters would be in such shape that the promoters of Southend United Football Club were not only able to command a very capable combination, but had also made certain of a uniformly good quality of football by securing admission into the Second Divisions of the Southern League and the South-Eastern League.

The prospectus issued a week or two back inviting applications for shares will have made many of our readers acquainted with the aims and intentions of Southend United Football Club, Ltd. The directors are: Messrs. C.A. Stein (chairman), O. Trigg, G.H. Hogsflesh, F. England and T.S. Tidy.

A lease has been secured for seven years of the ground situate in West Street, and at the present moment active steps are being taken to transform it into a proper playing arena. Mr. Ducat has been entrusted with the work of erecting a grandstand of wood, situate on the eastern side of the ground, and capable of holding 600 people. This will be certain to be ready for occupation when the opening match takes place on September 1st. There will be a reserved enclosure in front of the stand. The field is being enclosed all round with a new ten feet fence and between this and the rope separating the playing field, the ground will in due time be sloped as to afford all the spectators a view of the game. It is estimated that accommodation will be found for 6,000 people. Entrance will be secured on payment of 6d. at the new entrance gates which are being erected in West Street. Another sixpence will admit to the grandstand or enclosure. Season tickets are being issued at 12s. 6d. for the stand and 10s. for the other parts of the ground.

The playing pitch, it is interesting to note, is 111 yards 1 foot long and 74 yards 1 foot broad, a ground about the size of that of Bolton Wanderers and quite as large as the majority of those of other clubs. The goals will be situated at the north and south ends of the ground.

The Second Division of the Southern League represents a very good standard of football, for our town will be visited by the reserve elevens of Southampton, Portsmouth, Fulham, Swindon, Reading, West Ham and the first elevens of the R.E. Aldershot, Tunbridge Wells Rangers, Southern United, Hastings and St. Leonards, Salisbury City and Wycombe Wanderers.

The South-Eastern League includes Clapton Orient, Depot Batt. R.E., East-bourne, Tunbridge Wells, Tunbridge Wells Rangers, Hastings and St. Leonards, Chesham Generals, Grays United, Redhill, Chesham Town and West Hampstead. Southend United, by entering the two Leagues will thus be able to provide their supporters regularly with good matches right throughout the season and we anticipate, when the fixture cards are published, it will be found that most of the Southern League engagements will take place on Saturday and those of the South-Eastern League on Wednesday. It is also hoped that arrangements will be completed which will allow of friendly matches being played on Wednesday, with first class combinations.

The directors have engaged as their Secretary and Manager, Mr. Robert Jack, late Manager of Plymouth Argyle Football Club. Mr. Jack has a good record both as a manager and a player. We notice that the *Western Weekly News* said of him last year 'The Argyle directorate have appointed Mr. Jack manager, and although he has had to follow in Mr. Frank Brettell a man thoroughly conversant with all that pertains to the managerial department, Jack has given ample proof of his ability to obtain players. In this department, a particularly difficult and onerous one for a man stepping into a new position, the Argyle manager has been eminently successful and there is every reason to anticipate, judging from the results already achieved, that the present season of the Argyle club will be satisfactory from a playing as well as from a financial point of view. Jack has the full confidence of the directors and the loyalty of the players, two essentials in the making or marring of a club.'

As a footballer, Mr. Jack has been very successful. He is a native of Alloa, Scotland, and played for a time for Alloa Athletic. At 17 years of age he migrated to England and played for six years as outside left with Bolton Wanderers; then a year each with Preston North End and Glossop. For the last three years he has turned out for Plymouth Argyle. It deserves to be noted in respect of the engagement of professionals for Southend United, that they were all signed on prior to Mr. Jack's arrival.

The 'uniform' will be royal blue jerseys with black collars and cuffs and white knickers.

The trainer is Mr. Arthur Norris, who has done similar work in connection with Tottenham Hotspur.

The players have been in training since August 3rd – as long a time as any team in the South. They are showing very good form.

Taking the men individually, we start with:

C. Cotton, the goalie, he is a Plymouth man, stands 5ft. 10ins., scales 11st. 11lbs. and is 25 years of age. He has played for Reading for three seasons, with West Ham two and a half, finishing up the remainder of one season with Liverpool.

G. Molyneux, captain of the team and left back, was born at Liverpool. He played as an amateur with Kirkdale Juniors and was then signed on by Wigan

City of the Lancashire League. Everton got hold of him and he was there for two seasons. Southampton secured him for five years and last year he played for Portsmouth. He was a member of the Southampton team when they were finalists for the English Cup in 1901 and 1902 and he received his cap in the latter year for England v. Scotland and was at Ibrox Park on the day of the disaster caused by the collapse of a stand. The year following he was honoured by three international caps for England. He is 5ft. 10ins., 12st. 7lbs. in weight, and 27 years of age.

W. Thomson, right back, is well known to Southenders as one of the pluckiest players in the district, and his value to Southend Athletic's defence in the past has been very considerable. He has played for Essex and earned the commendation of the County experts. He is 24 years of age, 5ft. 8ins. high, and weighs 11st. 7lbs.

A. Perry, who can conveniently play right or left back, 'commenced his career at Forest Gate. He then captained Manor Park, was leader of Leytonstone team for three years, and for the last two seasons has captained South Weald. He has played for Essex four times, and is the possessor of 14 football medals. He has assisted occasionally teams like Woolwich Arsenal and Tottenham Hotspur. He is 27, 12st., and 5ft. 10ins. in height.

A.J. Johnson is a Grays lad, regularly played right half for Grays United, and has been in the ranks of Queen's Park Rangers. He is only 20, weighs 12st., and is 5ft. 9½ins.

Harry Owen, the centre half, late skipper of the Southend Athletic, is known to every local footballer of the game as a sterling, determined player, always cool, and in the right place.

Ben. Freeman, also a half back, belongs to Birmingham. He is 27, 5ft. 11ins. high, and 12st. in weight. He first turned out as a professional for Small Heath (now Birmingham F.C.), he was one year with Queen's Park Rangers, and has been with Grays United two years, from whom he comes to Southend.

A. Holden is capable of filling either the outside right or outside left positions. He is a native of Portsmouth, and has played for the team of that town three years. He is only 24, stands 5ft. 9ins., and scales 11st. 4lbs. He is also a professional cricketer of merit, and is fulfilling an engagement this season at Virginia Water, Surrey.

H. Mitchell, inside or outside right, was born at Brimington, near Chesterfield. He played for the local team there and Derby County, noticing his ability, signed him on. He is 22 years of age, 5ft. 10ins. high, and 11st. 10lbs. in weight.

H.J. Halse, centre forward, is also well-known locally and in the County as a forward of exceptional promise. He stands 5ft. 7ins., is 10st. 10lbs., and only 20 years of age, so that he has great possibilities before him. He played for Wanstead last year and has assisted Clapton Orient in League matches. He has played for the county several times, and is a goalgetter of exceptional ability.

J. Axcell, who can play inside left or half back, is, as is well known, a son of Leigh. He stands 5ft. 6½ins., is 11 stone, and 20 years of age. He has rendered fine service for Leigh Ramblers and has played for Fulham Reserves and Grays United.

A.E. Watkins can play inside or outside left. He is a Welshman standing 5ft. 9ins., weighing 12 stone, and 27 years of age. He has appeared for Aston Villa and Leicester Fosse, and for the past five years has turned out for Millwall. He possesses 13 international caps for Wales.

In addition to these, Mr. Jack is available as a forward.

The season will begin in real earnest on Saturday next, when the local team will be hosts in a Southern League fixture with Swindon R. On the following Wednesday they are at home to Depot Batt., R.E. in the South Eastern League; on September 15th, they meet R.E. Aldershot, at home; and on Wednesday, September 26th, Clapton Orient will be the guests.

CHAPTER TWO

'Southend Standard' Football Memories

SOUTHEND UNITED REMINISCENCES 1906-1920

'Football Memories – Southend United Reminiscences'
was published in the *Southend Standard* during the 1939-40 season.
This extract covers the non-League seasons – 1906-07 to 1919-20.

PART TWO *(Part One is not reproduced, as it only previewed what was to follow)*

Probably what did more to create a movement for the inauguration of a professional side in Southend was the fact that Andrew Ducat, the local born player, was transferred to Woolwich Arsenal, then playing at Plumstead, in 1905. The inauguration of a professional organization was a matter of local discussion for a long period. In those days Southend Athletic, who had their ground at the Kursaal and did great things in the South Essex League, was the chief football organization in the town. At a meeting of the members of Southend Athletic Club on May 16th, 1906, the question was raised as to whether that team should be converted into a professional one, or whether it should continue to preserve its amateur status. After a lengthy discussion, it was ultimately decided that the Athletic should preserve its amateur status. A suggestion that they should return to their old ground in Prittlewell was also negatived, it being argued that the worst season at the Kursaal was considerably ahead of the gate receipts at Prittlewell. This decision largely influenced those who were in favour of starting a professional team to go forward with the scheme.

It may be said that it was on May 19th, 1906, that Southend United, as a professional club, was born. Amongst the pioneers of its inauguration were Messrs. Oliver Trigg, G.H. Hogsflesh, A. Howard, John Holton, C. Auger, Josiah Sellar, A. Ducat, Sen., A. Whybrow, C. Sewell, C. Anderson, A. Budd and many others. Most of those gentlemen have now passed away, though Messrs. Hogsflesh and Howard still remain with us. The name of the club was changed from Prittlewell United to Southend United, and it was decided that a limited liability company should be formed in order that the capital necessary to finance the launching of the new professional club could be raised. A lease of Roots Hall field in West Road (adjoining the garden of St. Mary's Vicarage and at present a disused sandpit) was obtained for a period of seven years as from September 1st, 1906, and it was stated that it was capable of accommodating 6,000 spectators, and that a grandstand to seat 500 people, together with dressing rooms, and other accommodation, was to be erected. An agreement dated July 30th, 1906, was entered into with Mr. Robert Jack, who had been previously with Plymouth Argyle Football Club, as manager, secretary and player. The club was successful in obtaining admission to both the Southern League (Division II) and South Eastern League (Division II).

The idea of a professional football club in the town was not at first received with the acclamation which was expected, and there was considerable opposition from the followers of Southend Athletic and also in the western district – Leigh was not then within the Borough – by supporters of the old Leigh Ramblers club. Amateurism was fairly strong in the district at that time, as represented by these clubs and the old Leigh Rectory Yard club, while Rayleigh and many of the outlying villages also possessed capable amateur organizations. In the prospectus issued on August 6th, 1906, the capital of the company was stated to be £2,000, divided into 8,000 shares of 5s. each. The original directors as announced in the prospectus were Mr. Charles Albert Stein, Mr. Oliver Trigg, Mr. G.H. Hogsflesh, Mr. Frederick England and Mr. T.S. Tidy. Mr. Arthur Buxton subsequently joined the board. The response to the appeal to take up shares was disappointing, and the late Mr. Oliver Trigg had a very substantial deficit to face before the company went to allotment. He, in fact, retained a large proportion of the shares until his death in 1919.

On Wednesday, July 5th, 1906, a meeting was held at the Masonic Hall in furtherance of the new club, when Mr. G.H. Hogsflesh occupied the chair. The then Secretary of the Football Association, Mr. E.J. Wall (later Sir Frederic Wall), sent a message wishing the club success in its efforts and hoping that they would prove capable of taking a prominent position in Southern football. In the meantime, preparations continued apace for the opening on September 1st, 1906, at Roots Hall. Time was short, money was scarce, and yet everything had to be accomplished within the short space of three months. No transfer fees were payable at that period by Southern League clubs for players who left Football League clubs. There was a wide choice in those days for those organizers of Southern League clubs who were able to pay the wages demanded and numbers of famous players migrated South. The colours of the Southend club were decided upon as royal blue, with black collars and cuffs and white shorts, and the colours remain the same to-day, except that the black facings have given way to white.

As trainer, the club engaged Arthur Norris, who had for some time been assistant trainer to Tottenham Hotspur and was an old long-distance runner. Among the players who were engaged by Mr. Jack and Mr. Anderson were Charles Cotton, a goalkeeper with considerable experience at West Ham and Reading; George Molyneux, formerly of Portsmouth, Southampton and Everton, who had several international caps to his credit as a full-back for England, including his appearance in the memorable match when the Ibrox Park disaster took place, and who is at the present time still resident in the Borough; W. (Jerry) Thomson, a former Southend Athletic back; A. J. Johnson, of Grays; Harry Owen, a centre-half, of Southend Athletic; Bert Freeman, formerly of Birmingham; S.P. (Prince) Blott, half-back or inside forward, a Southend lad; Arthur Holden, of Portsmouth; H. Mitchell, of Derby County; Harold J. Halse, formerly of Wanstead and Clapton Orient, who had played cricket for Prittlewell in the previous season; James Axcell, of Leigh; A.E. Watkins, who had assisted Millwall, Aston Villa and Leicester, and secured thirteen international caps for Wales, and, of course, the Secretary-Manager, Mr. Jack, formerly of Bolton, Plymouth, Preston North End and other clubs.

Southend was at that time wealthy in promising amateur talent, and Mr. Jack was not slow to take advantage of this fact. He obtained five or six splendid local amateurs in his side and kept adding to them and developing amateur talent in a manner in which no succeeding manager has equalled. Many think there is plenty of local talent to be developed now. Amongst other players signed on were Alfred Frost, from Southend Corinthian, Prince Blott, from Southend Athletic, Ernest Emery, from Leigh, and Peter Wilson, from Tilbury.

The season opened on September 1st with a match in the Second Division of the Southern League against Swindon Reserves, and the first team to represent Southend was: Cotton; Thomson and Molyneux; Johnson, H. Owen and Freeman; Holden, Mitchell, Halse, Watkins and Jack. George Molyneux, one of Nature's gentlemen, a great full-back and a fine general, was Southend's first captain. Though Southend monopolized nearly the whole of the play in their initial game, they were beaten 1-0. In the *Southend Standard* at that time, it was remarked that they seemed literally to be fighting against fate. Three times that season the Southend United scores ran into double figures, and when close time came they had scored 222 goals against 54. The club headed both the Second Division of the Southern League and the Second Division of the South-Eastern League, and Halse headed the goalscorers for the season with 91. Even goalkeeper Cotton was included in those who found the net, when he was brought in to take penalty kicks.

The total record was: Southern League – Played 22, won 14, drawn five and lost three; goals for 58, against 23; points, 33. South-Eastern League – Played 18, won 17, drawn 0 and lost one; goals for 85, against 6; points, 34. Friendlies – Played 25, won 19, drawn three and lost three; goals for 79, against 25. The gate receipts for the season did not come up to anticipation, the total aggregate being 47,768 spectators, which, spread over 43 home games, averaged little more than 1,000 a game. The total gate receipts were £875 4s. 8d. (a sixpenny gate was then charged and there was no Entertainment Tax), but with a wages bill of £1,443 12s. and various other heavy outgoings, it is not surprising that at the end of the season there was a loss of £1, 142 10s. Of this sum, Mr. Oliver Trigg advanced as a loan to the club £861 5s. 4d.

The following letter, from John Budd of 'Mentone,' Beresford Gardens, Thundersley, was received following publication of the above:

'Sir, Respecting Football Memories in last week's *Southend Standard*, the first kick-off in starting the Southend United Football Club was after the late Mr. Oliver Trigg gave me the entrance fee for the Second Division of the Southern League and authorized me to make application for admittance. I then received a letter from the late Mr. N. Whittaker, Secretary of the Southern League, inviting us to meet the delegation at the George Hotel, Strand, which I and Mr. Trigg did. We laid our views before the delegates, intending to run an amateur team in the Southern League, but under those conditions they would not accept us but persuaded us to try to get a few professionals, giving us a month to think it over. I then, under the advice of Mr. Trigg, sent letters to the gentlemen you have mentioned, inviting them to a meeting to be held at the Blue Boar (date I have forgotten) where they then decided to call a town's meeting held at the Victoria Hall, Alexandra Street.'

PART THREE

At the very outset of their career, Southend had to win the championship of the Second Division of the Southern League twice before the Southern League clubs promoted them to Division I. Automatic promotion and relegation had not then been adopted by the Southern League, and when Southend finished up champions in 1907, Bradford Park Avenue were preferred to them on a vote by the First Division clubs. This was the first Northern club to be elected to the First Division of the Southern League. At the end of the 1908 season, however, Southend reaped a just reward and were promoted to Division I. Not dismayed by the experiences of the first season, the club signed on practically all the old players for 1907-08, but in order to meet some of the expenses of the closed months, Arthur Holden was transferred to Plymouth Argyle, subsequently going on to Chelsea, A.J. Johnson went to Sheffield United and S.P. Blott to Bradford Park Avenue. Several local amateurs, including M.A. Cantor, of Southend Athletic, George Harrod, of the Corinthians, Anderson and Bombardier Newland (now Inspector Newland of Shoeburyness) gave their assistance. The season started with nine victories off the reel, Queen's Park Rangers Reserves (2-1) being the club to stop the United's victorious career.

For the first time in their existence, the United were able to take part in the F.A. Cup, and they were drawn against Clapton, at the Spotted Dog, where they won by 1-0. A well-known Westcliff doctor of the present day, Dr. A.W. Holthusen, was at that time playing for Clapton, though not that day, and C.S. Rance and H.J. Eastwood were in the team. The United subsequently defeated Ilford at Roots Hall by 3-1. A severe test awaited them in the third stage, when they were destined to meet the Second Division League club, Clapton Orient, at Homerton, on November 2nd, 1907. The United fought a wonderful battle there, and after Routs, their outside-right, had scored the first goal, Whittaker equalized for the Orient and the game ended in a draw of 1-1. The tie was memorable for a wonderful display of goalkeeping by Cotton, the United custodian, who on his day was one of the best goalkeepers the Blues have ever had. The teams met again on the following Wednesday at Roots Hall before a most enthusiastic crowd, and at half-time there seemed little hope of the United surviving the ordeal, for Clapton Orient were leading by 1-0. In the second half, however, Halse scored a brilliant equalizer, which was followed by a second by Robert Jack, while Wilson tapped the ball into the net for the third time after Whittaker had gone full length in saving a remarkable shot from Halse. The United thus won by 3-1, amid tremendous scenes of enthusiasm, and the victory was acclaimed in Southern England as an outstanding one for a Second Division Southern League club over a Second Division Football League side. The gate at Roots Hall that day was a record for Southend, the receipts totalled £84 – sixpence being the price of admission. However, this did not prove the best gate of the season, for on Easter Monday £93 was taken, when the United beat Woolwich Arsenal reserves by 3-0 in the South Eastern League.

There were then hopes that the United would secure admission to the first round proper of the F.A. Cup, but in the final qualifying round they were drawn to meet Carlisle (of the Lancashire Combination, First Division). When they arrived at Carlisle station they found a large welcoming crowd awaiting them. Southend, however, gave one of their worst displays of the season there on the following day, and were beaten 4-0. The first eleven again won the Southern League (Division II) championship, thirteen matches being won and three drawn. Goals scored totalled 47, with 16 against. In the South Eastern League, 17 matches were won and five drawn. In all, the club took part in 74 games; 44 were won, 18 lost and 12 drawn. In these encounters, 167 goals were obtained and 102 conceded. The reserve team competed that season in the South Eastern League, Division II, and met with fair success. They were eighth in the table.

The Directors again applied formally before the end of the season 1907-08 for admission to the Southern League, Division I, and they themselves offered a guarantee of £150 towards the extra expenses. They resolved at a later date to call a town's meeting to launch the project. After scoring five goals against Swindon Reserves at Swindon, Harold Halse came further into prominence, and it was known that several clubs were seeking his transfer. Halse was a fine centre forward and a terrific shot. He could drive the ball home knee high and had many remarkable scoring feats for the United. He played his last match for Southend at Maidstone on March 21st, 1907, and he was later that night transferred to Manchester United. At that time there was in existence a League rule which limited players' wages to £4 a week and also laid down at the same time that a club could not receive more than £350 for one player's transfer fee. Very soon clubs overcame this difficulty by disposing of a player required with another player as makeweight. Therefore, if two players were taken, £700 would be paid, and if three players were taken, the club received £1,050. This was frequently done. In the case of Southend, it was agreed that both Halse and James Axcell should go to Manchester United, and the United, therefore, received approximately £700.

The transfer of Halse caused a good deal of heartburning and resentment among the club supporters, but the directors issued a statement in which they set out that the transfers were necessary owing to lack of funds, and that they had to take steps to clear off debts which had been hanging over the club. Harold Halse walked straight into the Manchester United team and scored his first goal for his new club against Preston North End. In April, 1909, he won an English Cup medal by assisting Manchester United to beat Bristol City in the F.A. Cup Final, and he also secured a further one, in 1913, when he helped Aston Villa to beat Sunderland. The directors secured the transfer, in the last three weeks of the season, of A. ('Nutty') King, centre-forward, and Cotterill, two players from Maidstone United, who considerably strengthened the team. The number of spectators who attended the home matches had increased to 68,571, and receipts were £1,434 1s. 1d., or nearly £600 more than the previous period. At the end of the season, mainly through the sums received for the transfers of Halse and Axcell, and the sporting action of Mr. Oliver Trigg in waiving his claim for the sum of £877, the directors were able to report a net profit on the season of £305 11s. 8d.

PART FOUR

In order to establish a claim to Division I status of the Southern League, as champions of Division II, Southend United had to beat Wycombe Wanderers at Wycombe in the last match of the 1907-08 season. It was the day of the Football Association Final at the Crystal Palace, when Wolverhampton Wanderers beat Newcastle by 3-1. When, however, the United arrived at the centre of the basket chair-making industry, it was snowing so hard that it was impossible for the match to take place. It had to be postponed until the following Tuesday, when the United won 4-1, and so secured the championship. Shortly after the close of the season a public meeting was held at Southend to promote a fund to assist the Club in its fight to obtain First Division membership. The then Mayor (Ald. J.C. Ingram, J.P.) occupied the chair and a sum of £400 was guaranteed. It is to be remembered that money values were entirely different in those days, and that £400 would probably represent about twice as much of the present time. In the meantime, the position in the Southern League had become somewhat involved and strained.

The Southern League had passed a rule that any club leaving the League and not having given notice by December 31st previously was liable to a fine of £500. The Southern League having refused automatic promotion and relegation for so long a period, that competition was the subject of severe criticism in the Press and many of the clubs in membership had shown dissatisfaction with its policy. The climax was reached when Bradford Park Avenue, who had evidently used the League simply as a stepping stone for twelve months, announced their intention of withdrawing to make application to the Football League for membership of Division II, and they were followed by Tottenham Hotspur and Queen's Park Rangers, who also stated they were applying for admission to the Second Division of the Football League. The Rangers abandoned their proposition, but it was too late, and they were apparently left without a competition, for the Southern League had decided to exclude both the Spurs and the Rangers from its membership. The two bottom clubs of Division I had also to withdraw and apply for re-election according to rules, and, therefore, with the defection of Bradford Park Avenue, the Spurs and the Rangers, there were five vacancies in the League.

The annual meeting was held on Friday, May 29th, 1908, and Ald. A. Prevost, J.P., who had been elected Chairman of the Directors, and Mr. G.H. Hogsflesh stated the claims of Southend United for admission, while a booklet had also been published on behalf of the Club, emphasizing its prospects and advantages, also giving a list of the men signed on. Among the other applicants were Exeter City, a club which had only come into existence that year, Coventry City, an ex-Birmingham League club, Croydon Common, another combination formed that year on the Selhurst ground at South Croydon, and Hastings and St. Leonard's.

The latter club did not pursue its application, and the final vote resulted as follows: Exeter City 33; Leyton 32; New Brompton 31; Southend 26; Coventry 25. Not elected, Croydon Common. Mr. Sidney King, the West Ham manager at that time, was one of the first to congratulate Southend on assuming First Division status, and hoped that they and the West Ham Club, who were then members of the Southern League, would have many happy meetings. Queen's Park Rangers were subsequently taken back into the fold. The one topic of conversation during the closed season was the prospects of the United in Division I of the League. It was with pleasurable anticipation that the town welcomed the advent of first-class football in its midst, and the stock of the Club rose considerably.

Practically all the Southend previous season's players were re-engaged, including Cotton, Thomson, Molyneux, Emery, Owen, Harrod, Frost, A. Haggar (a local goalkeeper), P. Wilson and B. Freeman, while S.P. Blott, who had been for a season at Bradford, re-joined the Club. Among the new players obtained were A. Birnie, a Sittingbourne outside-right; D. Ronaldson, a centre-forward from Brighton and Hove Albion and Norwich; J. Wright (Watford); E. Anderson (Woolwich Arsenal Reserves); T. Caldwell (West Ham and Clapton Orient), W. Leslie, of Finchley (a centre-half, whose name subsequently transpired to be Askew), H. Styles (a goalkeeper from Kettering), B. Shinner, full-back (Bristol City), C. Axcell, half-back, formerly of Leigh and Burton United, and E.G. Fincke, forward (Walthamstow), while among the amateurs signed were T.S.C. Little, the Ilford centre-forward, D. Cairns, of Rochester, and W. Nash (Grays Athletic). Following the departure of T.S.C. Little, for Bradford, after assisting the United in a few matches, the Blues obtained the services of Walter Smith, a Liverpool reserve, to take the centre-forward position, and he did well in a number of matches, but did not maintain his form. Andy Clark, a Plymouth back, was also signed later to take the place of Thomson, who was injured, and he did good service for the Club during that season. Financial troubles still beset the United, and, after the away match at Brighton in February, 1909, Alec Birnie was transferred to Bury.

In their initial season in the First Division of the Southern League, Southend United created something of a record at Roots Hall. They played until Christmas morning there without a defeat and without a goal being scored against them in the Southern League. On that Christmas morning, 1908, Portsmouth were the visitors, and surprised them by beating them 6-2. The United's first match in the Southern League, Division I, was at New Brompton (now known as Gillingham), where they lost by the only goal scored, Reynolds netting for the winners in the second half. The team that did duty for that match was: Cotton; Thomson and Molyneux; Emery, Owen and Blott; Birnie, Ronaldson, T.S.C. Little, Wright and Caldwell.

On the following Saturday, at Roots Hall, there was a record crowd of 6,000 to witness the United play their first Division I match at home, their opponents being the great Millwall Club, who then had their headquarters on the Isle of Dogs, in East Ferry Road. It was a great contest, and will always be remembered by all those who witnessed it. There were long odds laid on Millwall winning, but the United confounded all their critics by beating their visitors by 3-0. The first goal was scored by 'Jocky' Wright, father of the United half-back, D. Wright, who is now assisting Newcastle United, and who in his day was one of the cleverest inside-forwards who ever kicked a ball. 'Jockey' Wright could make a pass with deadly accuracy, and he has had few superiors as a creator of openings.

At half-time the large crowd of Millwall supporters who were present were still optimistic that stamina and pace would settle the United in the second half. The latter forty-five minutes were, however, electric. Playing up into the West Road end, Alec Birnie twice netted grand goals from his wing, which enabled the United to win by 3-0. The victory was acclaimed throughout the country as a great one for the youthful United. As this match was somewhat of a historic one, it is perhaps interesting to recall the teams on that day. Southend United: Cotton; Thomson and Molyneux; Emery, Leslie and Blott; Birnie, Frost, T.S.C. Little, Wright and Caldwell. Millwall: Joyce; Stevenson and Jeffrey; Frost, Comrie and Blythe; Dean, Cunliffe, Tellum, Twigg and Hunter. In the Football Association Cup that year the United were drawn away in the final qualifying round to Luton, and, thanks to a fine exhibition of goalkeeping by Cotton, they managed to draw there. The re-play took place at Southend on the following Wednesday, and at one time it appeared the United would win comfortably, for they were leading 2-1 with only a few minutes to go, both home goals being scored by Ronaldson, their centre-forward.

Just before the end, however, Luton equalized, and the end of 90 minutes saw a score of 2-2. Extra time was played, and Luton scored twice during that period, to win by 4-2. Once again the first round of the F.A. Cup had dodged the United. It is a peculiar fact that Luton and Southend met three times within a fortnight, for on the following Saturday, they were at Roots Hall in the League, the United winning by 2-0.

PART FIVE

The first victory achieved by Southend United away from home in the Southern League was at Coventry on September 26th, 1908, when they beat the representatives of the cycle industry by 5-2. In those days telephones were a luxury and there were few grounds in the country on which a telephone was installed, telegrams being regarded then as generally the quickest means of communication. At half-time the score was 2-1 in favour of the Blues, and I well recall the late Mr. R.A. Jones sending a telegram from the ground at half-time giving the scores and stating that Southend were sure to win. He was certainly an optimist, for up to that period the exchanges had not been predominantly in favour of the United, but in the second half there was a great rally, in which Bob Jack and 'Jockey' Wright, who are still residents in the Borough, played a great part.

The following week the United were drawn away against Leyton in the second round of the qualifying stages of the F.A. Cup, having beaten London Caledonian in the previous round by 4-0. At Leyton they had to meet the then strong Leyton professional side, who in those days were members of the First Division of the Southern League. It was a tremendously exciting game and the United won a great victory by a goal to nil, the point being scored by Ronaldson. Leyton pressed almost without cessation in the closing quarter of an hour, but the United defence held out. Another great victory which the United achieved in those early days was against the famous Southampton club (the Sotons), whom they vanquished at Roots Hall by 2-0, while their other away League victory was on the slopes of Sydenham, where they beat Crystal Palace 3-1.

In subsequent stages of the Football Association Cup they overcame Shoebury Garrison by 4-0, and Ilford by 3-1, to be finally beaten by Luton, as was related last week. The initial meeting of the first eleven and West Ham in the Southern League ended in a goal-less draw at Roots Hall, but in the return encounter the Hammers succeeded by 4-0. The first United double in the Southern League was achieved against Coventry, when the latter were defeated in the return match by 4-0. The United wound up the season well by beating Swindon 6-2 at Roots Hall and drawing with Queen's Park Rangers 0-0.

Looking back, it could be said that the game made remarkable strides in the Borough during that season and that interest in the doings of the club materially increased. For a long time the United occupied a lowly position in the League table, but this was chiefly due to their having taken part in fewer games than other clubs, caused by the interferences of their fixtures by F.A. Cup-ties. They, however, finished up the season twelfth on the list, with the same number of points as Millwall, but having a little inferior goal average.

To gain this place out of 21 clubs was very creditable and, therefore, from a playing point of view it could be said that the season had quite realized anticipations. It was pleasing to note that Southend United finished above five out of the six London clubs in the competition, and in view of the support which the Metropolitan teams could command and the wage bills they paid, this was eminently satisfactory. Queen's Park Rangers, the previous season's champions, West Ham (with the most expensive team in the League), Brentford, Crystal Palace and Leyton were no mean opponents to get the better of, while Norwich, Watford, Brighton and Coventry all failed to gain as many points as the Blues.

Southend's home record was distinctly good, for only two League games were lost at Roots Hall; a performance which Norwich and Watford alone excelled. Brighton were the other eleven to win at Southend, viz., by 2-0. Also, only Leyton and West Ham had fewer goals scored against them at home, and, had it not been for Portsmouth's half dozen on Christmas morning, United would have been an easy first. Of the 20 clubs who visited Roots Hall in the Southern League, only six obtained goals there. These privileged ones were Portsmouth (6), Brighton (2), Northampton (2), Swindon (2), Plymouth (1) and Bristol Rovers (1).

Southend's Southern League record showed that they won 14 games, lost 16 and drew 10, with 52 goals for and 54 against. Of these, 12 were won at home, two lost and six drawn. The away account showed two victories, four draws and 14 reverses. Thirty-three goals were scored at home and 19 away, while the Blues' opponents registered 14 goals at Roots Hall and 40 away. Some of the performances in order of merit throughout the season were: Swindon, 6-2; Crystal Palace, 3-1 (away); Millwall, 3-0 (home); Coventry City, 5-2 (away); Southampton, 2-0 (home) and 1-1 (away); Coventry, 4-0 (home); Reading, 0-0 (away); Leyton, 0-0 (away); Norwich, 3-0 (home); Watford, 2-2 (away); New Brompton, 1-0 (home); Luton, 2-0 (home); Watford, 2-0 (home) and Brentford, 1-0 (home). The team participated in draws at home against Northampton (2-2), West Ham, Queen's Park Rangers, Exeter, Leyton and Reading (the last five all being goal-less), but while they should have won against the three former, the last-named two did not find the Roots Hall brigade at their best.

One of their best away exhibitions was at Northampton on Boxing Day, when they had the misfortune to lose by a penalty. Their other reverses included (away from home): New Brompton, 1-0; Queen's Park Rangers, 2-1; Brentford, 4-1; Swindon, 4-2; Millwall, 3-1; Plymouth, 2-1; Exeter, 2-1; West Ham, 4-0; Reading, 2-1; Brighton, 2-0; Bristol Rovers, 1-0; Portsmouth, 2-0; Norwich, 2-0 and Luton, 3-0. At Plymouth, Exeter, Park Royal and Bristol they had hard luck to lose. The club also competed in the now defunct United League, but they never took this competition seriously. In this they defeated Brentford 4-3 and Croydon 5-0, but lost to Hastings 2-1 and New Brompton 7-0. They also drew with New Brompton, 2-2 (home), Brentford, 1-1 (away), and Hastings, 1-1, at home.

Towards the end of the 1908-09 season there was further dissatisfaction expressed with the then Management Committee of the Southern League and in April, 1909, strong efforts were made to form a Third Division of the Football League. It was proposed that a Third Division should be formed, consisting of 20 clubs, of which 18 were to be selected from the Southern League. The Football League was somewhat enamoured of the new proposal, because previously players migrating to the Southern League could do so without the payment of transfer fees, and the new proposal laid down that the embryo Third Division of the League clubs should pay transfer fees for League players upon a basis to be agreed.

The upshot of the proposal, which was the result of a conference at Birmingham between the Football League and representatives of the Southern League, was that 16 clubs of the Southern League held a private meeting, at which they decided to incorporate themselves as the Third Division, with the addition of Brentford and Coventry. The remaining clubs they most unfairly left in the lurch. It was subsequently stated that at the vote taken the 16 clubs, in deciding to increase the number to 18, voted: Eleven for Coventry; nine for Brentford; six for Croydon; four for New Brompton; two for Watford and nil for Southend. The effect of the new proposal, therefore, was that in the composition of the new Third Division, Southend United, New Brompton, Watford, and Croydon Common, which was then a Second Division club, but was due for promotion, would have been excluded. Brentford and Coventry City, it might be mentioned, were the two bottom clubs in the final Southern League table.

The Southend United club and the three other clubs who were excluded from the League immediately took action and called a meeting at the Holborn Restaurant, London. At that meeting a resolution was passed protesting in the strongest possible manner against the treatment which had been meted out to them by the other 16 clubs of the Southern League meeting in secret and attempting to control the nomination of the 18 clubs to the proposed Third Division of the Football League. The resolution went on to suggest that the action was unauthorized and illegal, for at a meeting of the Southern League it was agreed that 20 Southern League clubs should be nominated for the proposed Third Division, or that negotiations with the Football League should be abandoned. Those who represented the Southend club at that meeting at the Holborn Restaurant were the late Ald. A. Prevost, J.P., and Messrs. J.W. Davies, T. Cooper and Robert Jack, with Mr. John W. Burrows, J.P., and Mr. T. Byford representing the Supporters' Club. The United directors also sanctioned the terms of a circular to be sent to the meeting of the Football League on the following Friday.

PART SIX

Feeling in Southend was intense over the action of the Southern League clubs, for it was felt that just as Southend had got on to its feet as a first-class club it was likely to be deprived of its status by the action of the sixteen clubs of the Southern League. A large and enthusiastic meeting of protest was held on Friday, April 23rd, 1909, at the Hotel Victoria, where Mr. T. Byford presided and addresses were given by the late Canon F. Dormer Pierce, Mr. O.M. Howard, Mr. John W. Burrows, J.P., Mr. H.S. Rogers and Mr. G.H. Hogsflesh. It was decided that a circular should be drafted, in the strongest possible terms, protesting against the action of the clubs.

On the following day, after the United had beaten Swindon 6-2 at Roots Hall, a protest meeting was held on the ground, with Mr. T. Byford as chairman. The late Canon F. Dormer Pierce moved a resolution in the following terms: 'That this meeting of supporters of Southend United expresses its deepest dissatisfaction at the very unfair and unsportsmanlike action which has been taken by sixteen Southern League clubs in meeting in secret and endeavouring to control the nomination of the eighteen clubs to form part of the proposed Third Division of the English League. This meeting, believing that the directors will take every possible step to vindicate the claims of Southend United F.C., assures the directors that it will do everything in its power to support them in any action they make take to support Southend's just cause.' The late Mr. John H. Burrows, J.P., C.A., seconded, and the late Rev. A.E. Whitham supported, and the resolution was carried unanimously.

An appeal issued by the Southend United Club was incorporated in a circular, together with articles and cuttings from the *Southend Standard*, including interviews with the Gillingham directors and Secretary. In their protest Southend were strongly supported by Mr. J. Barnes, Chairman of Gillingham, and Mr. W.I. Groombridge, the Secretary, and representatives of Watford and Croydon. Southend United directors also circulated to all the League clubs a printed copy of an article by myself entitled 'Save me from my friends.' At the meeting held at the Midland Hotel, Manchester, the proposal of the Southern League clubs came before a special meeting of the Football League clubs.

Southend United's interests were excellently managed by the late Ald. A. Prevost, the late Messrs. J.W. Davies, R.A. Jones and Oliver Trigg, and Mr. Robert Jack, the manager. A good deal of lobbying and canvassing took place with representatives of League clubs before the meeting, and on the morning of the important assembly it was a recognized fact that the support obtained for the cause of the ostracized clubs had damned the proposal. In fact, when the meeting commenced no one attempted to justify the proposal, and long before the session ended it was a dead-letter. The only question ever put to the meeting was whether there should be a Third Division or not, and though a resolution was carried in favour of a Third Division, it did not receive the requisite three-fourths majority, and was, therefore, declared not carried.

Among the most keen critics of the proposal was Mr. Houghton, of Preston, who paid striking tribute to the sportsmen of the South, while the late Sir Henry Norris, of Fulham and later of the Arsenal, supported the Third Division proposal on the condition that it should be thrown open to the country. Capt. Wells Holland, of Clapton Orient, was another great critic of the sixteen clubs, and his suggestion was that the matter should be adjourned for twelve months. It is safe to say that had the proposal for a Third Division been carried by the League clubs by the requisite majority it would have been thrown open to the country and would not have embodied the scheme of the sixteen clubs. The voting in favour of a Third Division was 25 votes to 13.

It was stated in the *Southend Standard*, with almost prophetic accuracy, that this step by the sixteen Southern League clubs had set back the formation of a Third Division for a generation. This proved to be true, for it was not until 1920-21 that the Third Division became an accomplished fact, with the whole of the Southern League clubs then taken over. The news of the defeat of the scheme was received with great satisfaction in Southend and was conveyed to the public by means of a special edition of the *Southend Pictorial Telegraph*.

The United, therefore, were able to proceed with their arrangements for the second season in Division I of the Southern League, and they were saved much worry in the early rounds of the Cup owing to the Football Association exempting them until the first qualifying round. A new rule was passed that year making two qualifying rounds instead of one, and Southend were one of the 24 clubs exempted until that stage, and it was ordained that they should go into the hat with the 24 winners of the preliminary rounds. The United played only one friendly match in the 1908-09 season, and that was against Reading, when they lost 2-1. Therefore, the sum total of the season's work was: Played 56, won 21, lost 21, drawn 14, goals for 84, against 79. Included in this total was the United League match with Hastings on a Wednesday, in which only a reserve team took part.

The Reserves started the season well, but did poorly afterwards and occupied a lowly position in the South-Eastern League, to which they were elected at the beginning of the season. They were also fourth in the now defunct United League. Several friendlies were played and most of them won.

Players supported the Club in a most loyal manner, and one could not speak too highly of their services. They were a good set of professionals and treated the local spectators to some excellent football throughout the season.

Cotton, in goal, was at the top of his form and gave a most consistent and safe exhibition between the sticks, which played no small part in the Club's success. Thomson performed better than ever and had few equals in his class at right back. Skipper Molyneux's services to the Club could not be over-estimated. Early in the season, and especially again at the latter end, he displayed form which reminded one of his palmist days. He always played that clean, resourceful and safe game of which he was a great exponent. His judgement proved a boon to the side. 'Andy' Clark also played some grand games for the Blues, but his accident towards the end of the season kept him out of the team.

The Southend half-back line was one of the features of the side. The temporary loss of Harry Owen was severely felt during the fourteen or fifteen games from which he was absent through injury, but when in the team his cool, calculating methods and his brainy touches to members of his front rank made him of great value. Emery was, perhaps, the most improved man in the team, and his success as a half-back was strikingly demonstrated, especially in the second moiety of the season. Blott, in his day, had no superior as a left half. Clever, he could almost play football on the proverbial sixpence, while he was frequently as good as a sixth forward.

It was among the front line that the most difficulty arose. In Birnie the Club had a fine right winger, but after his departure for Bury the honour was divided between Cotterill and Barrett. Both did well at times, but the position was never really satisfactorily filled after Birnie left. Frost occupied the inside-right position throughout and did well on the whole. He was the most successful shot in front of goal.

The position of centre-forward, also, was by no means adequately filled. Little was doing extremely well, when he decided to leave for Bradford Park Avenue, and this brought in Ronaldson. He played successfully for a time, but did not maintain his form, and this led to the introduction of Smith, from Liverpool. For a while he did splendidly, but he failed to reproduce his early prowess, and this led to the reintroduction of Ronaldson, who played most creditably throughout the holiday matches and in the closing games of the season. W. Peake, a local amateur (now, as then, a respected member of the Southend Borough Surveyor's Department), also assisted several times and rendered the Club useful service.

At inside-left 'Jockey' Wright played in nearly all the matches. He was a very clever footballer, and adept in the art of passing. Jack and Caldwell divided the outside-left position between them pretty equally, and though Jack proved not so young as he used to be and also had the cares of manager, he demonstrated he could hold his own with most half-backs and often outpaced them. He played some splendid games for the Blues, especially in the early portion of the season. A pleasing feature of the last few matches was the improved exhibition of Caldwell. In the reserve team Styles did wonderfully well until he met with an unfortunate accident at Norwich. Haggar was most useful at back, and

Harrod very consistent at half. Johnson, however, failed to reproduce his previous good form when with the United two seasons previously. Harrod and Axcell often played in the first eleven, when Owen was injured, and proved very capable substitutes. Fincke and Anderson also assisted.

Several of the other reserve men were hardly the success that it was hoped they would be. Some promising local talent, however, was discovered, including M.A. ('Dot') Cantor, whom I met in the town only the other day, on his annual holiday in the Borough, and who did excellent service in the half-back line.

Part Seven

Blott and Cotton took part in most matches, each of them having missed only one in the season 1908-09. Blott was the only player to participate in every Southern League engagement. Frost headed the list of goal-scorers with twenty, Ronaldson being second with nineteen, and the others being: Smith eleven, Caldwell seven, Wright seven, Birnie six, Jack six, Emery two, Peake two and Barrett, Blott, Cotterill, Johnson and Leslie one each. In the Southern League the scorers were: Frost thirteen, Ronaldson seven, Smith seven, Birnie five, Caldwell five, Jack three, Emery two and Barrett, Blott, Leslie and Peake one each. During the summer of 1909 a Supporters' Club was formed, with the late Mr. T. Byford as Chairman, Mr. O.M. Howard as Hon. Secretary and Mr. John W. Burrows, J.P., as Hon. Treasurer. Efforts were made to raise the sum of £200 towards the provision of summer wages. This was done and the Supporters' Club also subsequently had erected the western stand on the sixpenny side of the ground, and helped in subsequent seasons to raise sums to assist the Club in carrying on.

A deserved compliment was paid to the Supporters' Club when three of their number – Messrs. T. Byford, O.M. Howard and J.A. Faers – were elected to the Board. At the end of the season Mr. George Radford, who had taken charge of the reserve team in 1908-09, also qualified and was elected a director. To further assist the finances of the Club S.P. Blott was transferred a second time, on this occasion to Manchester United, where he went to join Harold Halse and Jimmy Axcell. At the third annual meeting of shareholders on August 9th, 1909, the directors, in their report, stated: 'It will be seen that the improved fixture list attracted a considerable increase in the attendances at Roots Hall during last season, a total of 105,334 spectators patronizing the matches – 36,763 more spectators than in the previous year, and the match receipts increased by over £1,000. The average attendance at the Southern League matches was 3,168.

'The shareholders must, therefore, feel satisfied that the step taken in obtaining promotion to the First Division of the Southern League has been fully justified. The best gate of the year was secured on Easter Monday for the Northampton match, the attendance being 7,200 and the receipts £191 14s.

3d. The fixture with Reading was responsible for the lowest return – £29 5s. Undoubtedly the fact that the team had to take part in all the preliminary rounds of the Association Challenge Cup competition, thus being forced to accept mid-week dates for four attractive Southern League games, accounts for a loss of at least £200 in match receipts, and a sum of £104 5s. 7d. was also disbursed in compensation to the Brentford and Brighton and Hove Albion clubs for the alteration of Southern League dates.

'The directors are also glad to report the Club will not be similarly handicapped in the coming season, as exemption has been granted from the early round of the qualifying ties. The directors consider that the position attained by the team in its first venture in the Southern League First Division is one for congratulation, especially considering the limited number of players engaged and the necessarily moderate wages bill as compared with those of other members of that League.

'The defeat in the English Cup sustained from Luton, after a drawn game, proved a great disappointment, and the Reserve eleven did not acquit themselves with any great success in the South-Eastern League, although it may be remarked that accidents kept a few of the most useful reserve players off duty in many of the matches. Generally speaking, the loss of over £746 incurred is only what might be expected from a first year's working in First Division football. Many more players had to be engaged than in the previous season, and, as already stated, the upset caused through the rearrangements of a number of the Southern League fixtures very adversely affected the match receipts. At the same time it must be admitted that the attendances at Roots Hall hardly came up to reasonable expectation.

'The directors are sanguine, however, that the Club is assured in the coming season of further and more consistent support. Each season, as compared with its forerunner, shows considerable increase in income, and the directors are justified in expecting that the forthcoming term will be found profitable.

'A number of the Club's professionals of last year have been re-engaged, namely: C. Cotton, W. Thomson, G. Molyneux, D. Cairns, E.W. Emery, H. Owen, A.W. Frost and J. Wright, and Robert Jack has again been fixed up as secretary and player. The directors have also signed T. Murray (Partick Thistle), J.H. Bigden (Bury), A. McLellan (King's Park), James Harrower (King's Park), Norman L. Brown (Luton) and A. King (Woolwich Arsenal), all players of proved ability, and to their number will shortly be added other capable professionals.'

In reviewing the proceedings of the League meeting at Manchester, the writer stated: 'I should like also to express my admiration for the excellent way in which the opposition was organized towards the proposals for a Third Division. Anyone who was up in Manchester must have been struck with the astuteness and practical manner in which the directors manoeuvred their case, backed up by the gentlemen behind them. I firmly believe that it was Southend who killed the Third Division proposals, and the Southern League has thus found that Southend are a stronger force in football than they at first thought. Watford certainly did all they could to back Southend up, but it would have been a feeble protest had Southend not taken the matter in hand in earnest at the start.

The thanks of the Southend public are due to these gentlemen who have gone to so much trouble in the matter, and in this connection I must couple the name of our friend, Mr. Robert Jack. One could easily perceive that he possesses a lot of influence among North Country sportsmen and that he is universally respected by all who have any connection with football. At the same time, it is, perhaps, opportune here to give a word of praise to him for the way he has steered the Southend ship through the troublous water of the first season in the Southern League. It says much for his discretion and judgement that he got such a good side together at the beginning of the season at such a moderate cost.'

The Board of Directors was strengthened for the season 1909-10, and the late Mr. R.A. Jones succeeded the late Ald. A. Prevost as Chairman, with Mr. Donald Taylor as Vice-Chairman. In addition to the players mentioned above, the following were also signed on: Parke, left winger (Tunbridge Wells Rangers); T. Crews, outside-left (Woolwich Arsenal and Everton); S. Sugden, inside-forward (Notts. Forest, Queen's Park Rangers and Brentford) and E.W. Meare (Woolwich Polytechnic).

Thus Southend United settled down to their second season in Division I, and this season of 1909-10 witnessed the abolition of the transfer limit and also the provision that players could take a share of the transfer fee. The Southern League now included 22 clubs. Brighton finished at the top of the table, Croydon Common and Reading being the bottom two clubs, and the first victims of the automatic promotion and relegation rule. The United started off the season well by winning on the opening day of the season, at the old Millwall ground at East Ferry Road, by 3-1. They then lost at home to Queen's Park Rangers, and things never went smoothly throughout the season.

The death of Charles Cotton, the United goalkeeper, on January 3rd, 1910, threw a gloom over the season. He was taken ill in November with Bright's disease, and died when only thirty years of age. He had played many fine games for the United, and the present writer, in penning an appreciation of him, said, 'When the history of the Southend United Club comes to be inscribed on the roll of fame – and I sincerely hope it will – those who remember the early inception of it will always have a kindly remembrance for the name of Charles Cotton, and it will be cherished by the youths and sportsmen of our town for years to come.'

Following him, first A. Haggar, a local man whom I now frequently meet in everyday life and who had previously signed on as a full-back, played in goal, and then at Christmastide P.E.S. Toone, an amateur from Woolwich Arsenal, was signed on, and he made his initial appearance at Northampton on December 30th, 1909, when the United were defeated 11-1, the heaviest reverse they ever sustained in the whole of their history. However, Toone never played a finer game than he did that day.

The late Billy Sutherland, who fell in the early days of the last war, scored the only goal for the United, whose ranks were sadly depleted by injuries, Owen being off the field for a considerable period. As the United had lost 6-2 on Boxing Day, they had the unenviable distinction of having conceded seventeen goals in two away matches. However, they started 1910 a little better, with a draw of 2-2 against Queen's Park Rangers at Park Royal. Although not achieving a great success, they managed to maintain their position in the Southern League at the end of the season.

PART EIGHT

For the first time in their history the United reached the competition proper of the Football Association Cup in 1909, beating Barnet Alston 5-2 and Hastings 4-1 in the two qualifying rounds, and they were then drawn in the first round to meet Gainsborough Trinity on the latter's pitch. This was on the Saturday fixed for the first polling day of the January General Election of 1910 – elections lasted nearly three weeks in those days – and the team stayed on the Friday night at the Saracen's Head, Lincoln, the headquarters of the Conservative candidate for the borough of Lincoln at that election. As the evening progressed a great crowd assembled outside the hotel and began to wait somewhat impatiently for the arrival of the candidate to deliver a final message to the electors.

M.A. Cantor, the United amateur half-back, who was always one of the humorists of the party, was persuaded to go out on to the balcony, and for about twenty minutes he addressed the crowd on the Conservative candidate's behalf, and he received a most enthusiastic reception and the cordial thanks of the local Conservative Party. However, Mr. Cantor's oration was all in vain, for the Liberal candidate was returned on the following evening, though with a much smaller majority! The United put up a great fight at Gainsborough and succeeded in effecting a draw of one goal each. King scored for Southend and Stevens equalized. The gate was a poor one, the United only receiving £21 3s. as their share, including travelling and hotel expenses. The match was replayed at Roots Hall on the following Wednesday, and the United succeeded by 1-0. King registering the only goal eighteen minutes from the end.

The United were then drawn against Queen's Park Rangers at Roots Hall in the second stage, and an extra-ordinary encounter was witnessed. The home team pressed almost continuously, but Shaw, the Rangers' Scottish International goalkeeper of that day, was seemingly unbeatable and gave one of the most marvellous exhibitions of goalkeeping ever witnessed, the game ending in a goal-less draw. The replay was at the old Park Royal ground (now the site of Guinness' brewery) on the following Wednesday, and after a very rough encounter, in which at one time a free fight nearly developed, the Rangers won by 3-2. One player from each side was ordered off the field, but after the passage of all these years I do not think it necessary now to give their names.

At half-time the United led by 1-0, the point being scored by the late Sidney Sugden, but after Toone had saved a penalty taken by Steer, the Rangers' amateur centre-forward, he made a couple of mistakes which allowed Steer and Travers to score for the Rangers. After the ordering-off incident, Steer got a further goal for the Londoners and Frost scored again for Southend. On the day's play Southend were distinctly unfortunate to lose, for they were the better footballing side.

In consideration of the transfer to Manchester United of Harold Halse and Axcell, the late Mr. J.J. Bentley, Chairman of Manchester United and at that time President of the Football League, brought the Manchester full Cup-winning team to Southend to play an exhibition match, and the result was a draw of two each.

The season of 1909-10 was not a very satisfactory one, either from a playing or revenue point of view. Many of the new players engaged at the beginning of the season did not realize expectations; several matches were inexcusably lost; there were spells of atrocious weather, and the gates suffered severely in consequence.

It was satisfactory that Southend avoided relegation, but it was not very pleasing to notice that they were twentieth in the League table, whereas in their first season in the competition they were twelfth. In the 1908-09 season Southend obtained 38 points for 40 games in the League, whereas in the 1909-10 campaign they only secured 33 points for two games more. This decline was chiefly due to the loss of so many home matches.

Whereas in 1908-09 Southend were only defeated twice at home, in this season they suffered reverses before their own spectators on no fewer than seven occasions, and with four draws this left a record of only half the home matches won. The away results were very similar to those of the previous campaign, but showed an advance of one point, for the United registered two away victories and five draws, as against two wins on foreign soil and four draws in the previous season. The goal average was far from pleasant reading, and, with the exception of Croydon and Luton, Southend sacrificed more goals than any other Southern League team, while only Millwall and Bristol Rovers found the net on fewer occasions.

The United's defence was pierced 90 times, while the credit total was only 51. The home goal account revealed that the United found the net 26 times and 17 goals were registered against them, and the away record showed that whereas the United had netted 25 times, they had 73 goals notched against them, an average of practically three to one. On eight occasions at home the Blues were unable to score, and six times away, while visiting clubs at Roots

Hall were not able to penetrate the defence on eleven occasions. Coventry and West Ham were the only sides to fail to score against them away.

The Club was seriously affected by injuries, for, in addition to Cotton's death, Bigden was hurt in the initial training before the opening of the season and was only able to assist the first team twice. Thomson was laid up from November 13th to late in February, while Molyneux's accident at Portsmouth at the end of February deprived the United of his services for the remainder of the season. This was a serious loss, especially in the holiday matches. King was kept out of the team for two months owing to rheumatic fever, and at Easter he was again incapacitated for a couple of weeks at the most important part of the season. Brown made somewhat irregular appearances on the extreme right owing to an injury to his groin and a dislocated shoulder in the Queen's Park match. Owen was injured early in the season and his appearances were few and far between after the beginning of December. Sutherland, Frost, Crews, Wright and several others had to stand down owing to injuries. Most of the heavy scores obtained against the United were in the first four months of the season, before Toone was secured, when Cotton was often too ill to show his best.

A feat upon which the Southend team could congratulate themselves was that they obtained three points from the champions. They were the first team to administer defeat to the Brightonians, and, with a rather scratch team, they secured one point on the Hove ground. Four points were extracted from Millwall, three from Luton, two each from Leyton, Reading, Exeter, Southampton, Coventry, Croydon, New Brompton, Crystal Palace and Portsmouth (two draws), while Queen's Park (away), Bristol Rovers, Plymouth, West Ham (away) and Swindon furnished one point each. Southend's best victories were Luton 4-1, Crystal Palace and New Brompton 3-0, Coventry 2-0 (away), Millwall 2-1 and 1-0, Croydon 3-1, Exeter 2-0, Leyton and Reading 1-0, and Southampton 2-0.

It was not satisfactory, however, to note that Watford, Norwich and Brentford took four points from the United by substantial margins. Brentford defeated them 4-1 and 3-0, and Watford 3-1 and 1-0. Norwich won at Roots Hall by 5-2 and followed up with a 3-0 success at the Nest. Northampton were the other team to take four points from the United, and they did so by 11-1 and 2-1.

Other substantial scores against Southend were Crystal Palace 6-0, Leyton 7-3, New Brompton 5-0, Southampton 6-2 and Swindon 6-1. Plymouth, West Ham, Bristol Rovers, Queen's Park Rangers and Swindon secured three points from the Blues.

It was fortunate that Southend made their position absolutely unassailable before the last game of the season, for, with Croydon winning their final two home fixtures, only a couple of points saved them, especially as the Blues came a severe cropper at Plymouth in the final encounter in April.

Southend United also took part in the Southern Counties Charity Cup Competition and reached the second round. In the first stage they were opposed to New Brompton, whom they defeated 4-1, but Park Royal was again the scene of their exit. As was their usual custom, Southend scored first at Park Royal, and to within half a minute of time the game was a draw. In the closing darkness, with Molyneux off the field, the homesters got the deciding point.

The United League Competition was dropped this season. West Ham and Southend played mixed sides at Roots Hall for the benefit of Charlie Cotton's widow, and Southend won by 5-2. The Reserves occupied a moderately good position in the South-Eastern League, being thirteenth in the list, with the following record: Played 34, won 11, lost 16 and drawn seven. In addition to their League games the Reserves indulged in several friendlies, winning eight and losing two.

The success of the season was undoubtedly Murray, who assumed the reins of captaincy after Molyneux's injury. Murray proved himself to be the most valuable of the United's captures, and the safe position which they attained was in no small measure due to him. As a right-back he had few equals in the South. The goal-scorers for the first eleven were: King 25, Frost 14, Brown and Sugden seven each, McLellan and Sutherland five each, Wright four, Jack three, Anderson and Emery two each and Parke one.

A the close of the season, on May 2nd, 1910, the United went for a tour of Germany. They first met Hertha F.C. at Berlin and lost 3-1, but in their second match they beat Berlin Union 4-0, King doing the hat-trick and Harrod scoring the fourth. Next they met Victoria F.C., 1896 at Magdeburg and beat them 8-2, the scorers being King (three), Harrod (two), Emery, Frost and Sutherland (one each). At Halle they won 3-1, Anderson and Sutherland netting. During their stay in Berlin the United met Oxford City (amateurs, also on tour). The Germans arranged an exhibition between the two teams, and the United won 10-1. On the following day they opposed Combine at Hamburg and won 4-1. Throughout the tour the team were received with the utmost courtesy, and the game was played by both English and German teams in true football spirit. The United players who made the tour were: Toone, Murray, Thomson, Emery, Frost, Harrower, Parke, Sutherland, King, Harrod, E.E. ('Dits') Anderson, M.A. Cantor and R. Jack.

PART NINE

After the close of their second season in Division I of the Southern League, Mr. Robert Jack received a tempting offer to return to his former club at Plymouth and he decided to accept it. The Directors of the United reluctantly agreed to release him, and George Molyneux was appointed team manager and Mr. O.M. Howard became hon. Secretary. At the annual meeting of the shareholders in 1910, the Vice-Chairman (Mr. Donald Taylor), presiding in the absence of the Chairman (Mr. R.A. Jones), said he was very sorry that they had to report a loss of £450 3s. 9d. on the year's working, although the bulk of the loss had been from the reserve team. In fact, he might say that every penny had come from that source. There were a few more shares than the previous year, and the liabilities were heavier. There was nothing which called for any particular comment on the asset side, but on the profit and loss account he would like to point out a few facts.

The players' wages were a big item; they had gone up by £400, which was due to signing on a strong reserve team, with which they hoped to do better. Unfortunately, the gates of the reserve team had gone down. The travelling and hotel expenses of the first team had gone up by £37 as compared with the previous year, and those of the reserve team had gone up £10. Advertising expenditure and postages had increased by £61, owing to more bills being posted. As compensation they had received £73.

On the other side, with reference to the Southern League and English Cup, the first eleven receipts had increased by £207, which was a good deal due to the success in the English Cup ties; the receipts of the second eleven had gone down £42, and they had received £35 compensation, which was the first time such a thing had happened. Season tickets went down £15, whereas they ought to have gone up about twice that amount. Sundry receipts, which were £152 6s. had increased by £77; most of that money had come from the Supporters' Committee, while the transfer fees for the players had gone up £300. The previous year they made a loss of £706 2s. 9d.; that year it was £450 3s. 9d.; and next year they hoped to save at least £700 or £800 on players' wages. They had withdrawn the reserve team from the South-Eastern League and entered them in the South Essex League, and, as they would not pay big wages for the second eleven, they would not be playing at a loss.

As for the first eleven, they hoped it would pay its way in the coming season, and they wanted the second eleven to be a financial success. Dealing with the matches which had been played, the speaker said they had not done so well as they had hoped, but they had to take into consideration the fact that they had a good many injuries among the players to contend with, while they suffered a great blow from the loss of their goalkeeper, Charles Cotton, whose death affected them a great deal. Thomson, Molyneux, Owen, King and Brown were all laid up from various causes, which had handicapped them a great deal, and now they were losing their secretary and manager, Mr. Jack, who was going back to Plymouth as manager of the team he was previously with before coming to Southend. They were sorry they were losing him and wished him all success in his new sphere of work at Plymouth.

He (the speaker) thought the directors had made a popular move in appointing Molyneux as team manager for the ensuing season, while they would be pleased to learn that Mr. O.M. Howard had accepted the Hon. Secretaryship of the Club for the coming season. He was sacrificing a great deal of his time in undertaking the work, but he was an enthusiast in sport, and they hoped he would have a very successful season in the position he had taken up.

Many tributes were paid to the four years service to the Club by Mr. Robert Jack, who was wished every success in his appointment at Plymouth. Mr. Jack, in reply, said that he had thoroughly enjoyed his stay in Southend and his association with the Club, and he had been highly pleased to see it rise from a small concern to the decent club it now was. He added that in the previous season their gates had averaged £82 per match, though that was not large enough to run a first-class team. So ended Mr. Jack's association with the United. A sum of £300 was asked for by sale of tickets, and a bazaar was arranged to start the next season free of debt for summer wages. Mr. Donald Taylor succeeded Mr. Jones as Chairman of the Directors, with Mr. T.A. Buxton as Vice-Chairman, while Dr. J.R. Tombleson followed Dr. Hopkins as Medical Officer.

The season 1910-11 was started with great hopes, but finished in despair, for the Club was relegated at the end of April after a most sensational finish. Most supporters imagine that the United's colours have always been royal blue jerseys, with black facings, and white knickers since the inception of the Club, but that is not so, for in the season 1910-11 someone had a brainwave that these jerseys did not make the players look sufficiently imposing, so the colours were changed to red and yellow hooped jerseys. At some places these colours caused great amusement, and the players were likened to beer barrels, while at others one heard the cry, 'Go on the Beef and Mustards!' So much ridicule was, however, poured upon these jerseys during this season that at the end of February, with permission, they reverted to the original royal blue.

The United had obtained for goalkeeper David Clark, a former West Ham Reserves' custodian, while much was hoped of Jack Harwood, a centre-half obtained by Mr. Jack at the end of the previous season, McKenna and Dunn, from Newcastle, and Craig, from Reading. The new shirts of yellow and red were worn for the first time at Boleyn Castle, against West Ham, and I can well recall seeing Ken Duncan, the present local band leader and amateur golfer, then a small boy, dressed up in these striking colours as the Club's mascot. Those who favoured the change early proclaimed it as lucky, for, after West Ham had scored thrice in twelve minutes and led 3-1 at the interval, the United pulled the game out of the fire and drew 3-3.

This was in the great days when the Hammers' front line included Ashton, Shea and G.W. Webb, and Kitchen was in goal. George Lavers, who was deaf and played many fine games for Southend, was at centre-half. Lavers often did not hear the whistle sound and would go on playing after the other players had stopped. He was a whole-hearted half-back and was a favourite with the crowd. Losses followed the West Ham match too frequently, and, despite the fact that the United vanquished Millwall 7-0 at Roots Hall on Boxing Day, 1910, long before the end of the season the Club was in danger of relegation.

The directors subsequently obtained the services of new forwards in Curtis (Chelsea), Archie Wilson (Tottenham Hotspur), Joe Bradshaw (Queen's Park Rangers and Chelsea), Hodgkinson (Southampton) and J. Holman, a London postman and Somerstown amateur. During April they made a great rally and they secured five victories in eight matches and drew one game, but consecutive losses against Norwich (away), and Queen's Park Rangers (home) 2-1, at Easter, practically sealed their fate.

The position in the final match of the season was that the United, to escape relegation, had to win at New Brompton, and Bristol Rovers had to lose at Brighton. Supported by a large body of enthusiastic followers, the United won at Gillingham, a thing they had never done before, by 2-1, but Bristol Rovers made a goal-less draw at Brighton and so saved themselves from relegation. So, as Southend United played their first match in Division I of the Southern League at New Brompton, so they also played their last for some time to come.

The United were relegated with Portsmouth to Division II of the Southern League, then comprised mostly of Welsh clubs. In an interview the writer had with Mr. Harry Bradshaw, the Secretary of the Southern League, he said Southend were unlucky to be relegated on the football he had seen them play, but it appeared to him Southend started to build up their team too late in the season. In the Southern League they played 38 matches, won 10, lost 19 and drew nine; goals for 47, against 64.

PART TEN

January, February and March, 1911, were three black months for Southend, and during those thirteen weeks they obtained but one victory, and that at the expense of Portsmouth, the third week in the New Year. Then for six consecutive matches Southend never scored a goal and four matches in succession were lost by the only point registered. It was at the end of February that the directors at long last, after repeated warnings in these columns, took steps to secure new blood, as stated in last week's instalment.

The first match which was won for nearly three months was on April 1st, a month which brought Southend five victories, one draw and two defeats. Though Southend eventually went down into Division II, old supporters will always remember the gallant fight which the players made to save the club in the final fixtures. But for an unfortunate accident to Holman, which incapacitated him for two games, they might have accomplished it, but it is worth noting that in their last month's play they obtained as many victories as they did in the previous three months.

One great handicap which Southend felt, however, in the closing games and which told heavily against them, was that they sacrificed home points earlier in the season to three or four clubs who were struggling to escape relegation. Southend's away record was superior to anything they had accomplished in the previous two seasons in the Southern League. They won three matches away from home, viz., at Plymouth, Southampton and New Brompton, while they drew at Northampton, Crystal Palace, West Ham, Park Royal and Leyton.

At home, their victories were against Millwall, Northampton, Coventry City, Norwich, Plymouth, Portsmouth and Watford, while drawn games were played with Bristol Rovers, New Brompton, Leyton and Crystal Palace. Thus eight matches were lost at home and eleven away, and from the fact that twenty points were sacrificed to opposing teams at Roots Hall and only eighteen were obtained by Southend, their lowly position could easily be understood.

Among the best performances of the team were the three points obtained from Northampton without a goal being scored against them. Southend won at home by 2-0 and with rather a scratch side the locals effected a draw on the County ground. Plymouth were the only team to yield all four points to Southend, and Northampton and New Brompton were the two clubs from whom the United captured three points.

A notable victory was the 7-0 win over Millwall on Boxing Day. One of the best home games was seen against Plymouth, but, on the other hand, there were several poor displays, notably against Exeter, New Brompton, Bristol, Brighton, Swindon, Southampton, Brentford and West Ham. Swindon, Brighton, Brentford, Luton and Exeter all captured four points from the United, while Queen's Park Rangers, West Ham and Bristol Rovers succeeded in taking three points each from the Blues.

It was a peculiar fact that the only Southern League teams which Southend had up to that date been unable to defeat were Queen's Park Rangers and West Ham, and, although they were able to effect a draw in both away matches, curiously enough, they lost the encounters with these two clubs at Roots Hall. League goal scorers were: King, 10; Bradshaw, 7; Holman, 6; Harwood, 5; Sutherland, 4; Chalkley, 3; Murray, 3; Dunn, Hodgkinson and McKenna, two each; Craig, Curtis and Frost, one each.

Southend's progress in the Football Association Cup did not extend as far as it did in the previous year, chiefly owing to the fact that the management decided to journey to Blackburn for the tempting bait of £400 which was offered them at the time. They were drawn against the Rovers at Southend, but accepted the Lancashire club's offer to change the venue to Ewood Park. Southend put up by no means a bad show there, but lost by 5-1. The teams playing that day were: Southend – Clark; Thomson and Molyneux; Emery, Harwood and Chalkley; F. Ward, Frost, Curtis, Sutherland and Dunn. Blackburn Rovers – Ashcroft; Crompton and Suttie; Walmesley, Smith and Stevenson; Garbutt, Latheron, Davis, Aitkenhead and Bradshaw. They did not visit Ewood Park again until January 21st last, when they put up a great fight against the Rovers, who beat them 4-2 in the fourth round of the F.A. Cup.

The performance of Southend in the two qualifying rounds of the competition in 1910-11 was, however, somewhat of a criterion of how badly the side were playing at the time and what a poor team they were in the early part of the season. It was only after a struggle which gave the Southend supporters several frights that the professionals managed to draw at Enfield, thus obtaining the right to replay against the clever Middlesex amateur club at Roots Hall, where Southend were successful by 3-1.

In the final qualifying round Tunbridge Wells Rangers were encountered, and it was only in the final five minutes that Southend obtained the winning goal. At that time the Kent club had a poor side and had lost several of their South-Eastern fixtures by upwards of five goals.

That season the Southend second string appeared in the South Essex League, and the competition proved an attractive one at Southend as far as gates were concerned. It was imagined at the start that Southend Reserves would win the championship fairly easily, but in the end they had to occupy third place to South Weald and Custom House, the last-named being the League leaders. A home defeat at the expense of Custom House, a sound thrashing at South Weald and a home draw against Grays Athletic all militated against their chances.

The Southend first team again reached the second round of the Southern Counties Charity Cup, which was eventually won by Swindon. In the first round Southend drew at home against Crystal Palace, but managed to win the replay, after extra time, on the slopes of Sydenham by 2-1. The match was played in a deluge of rain. In the next stage of the competition they were opposed by their old rivals, Queen's Park Rangers, but, as in the two previous years, the Rangers were successful, for after a drawn game at Roots Hall, the Rangers won the replay at Park Royal by the curious score of 5-3. The record of Southend's first team for all matches this season was, therefore: Played 46, won 13, drawn 12 and lost 21; goals for 68, against 81.

Clark was the only man who played in every first team match, and no one could deny that he served the club well. His displays at Norwich, Northampton, Crystal Palace, Plymouth and Bristol were wonderful. For a greater part of the season, Murray and Molyneux were the backs, but towards the end of February, Molyneux's years of service began to tell on him and Thomson came in at left-back, and it must be admitted that it was a strengthening of the defence. Murray again proved himself a great defender and Thomson appeared to have quite recovered from his accident.

Of the half-backs, the weakness was on the left. Emery kept up his form, while Jack Harwood proved one of the captures of the season, and, next to Clark, took part in the most number of matches. Craig started well at left-half, but did not maintain his early form, and, although Chalkley played some useful games, he was uncertain. Until the advent of Wilson, the outside-right position was never satisfactorily filled. Ward, the young Highgate teacher, played some really good games, and Lloyd Evans also assisted. Sutherland was clever but his fault was his lack of shooting ability. King started the season in great style, and, though he headed the list of first team scorers, he appeared to lose much of his old form. The transfer of Frost to West Ham in the first half of the campaign was a mistake and his bustling tactics were much missed. When he went to West Ham, Curtis, the reserve pivot for the Hammers, came to Southend in part exchange.

On the left wing there was always a perceptible weakness, and Dunn and McKenna never realized expectations. The last-named was just getting into form when he met with an unfortunate accident at Millwall, and he was not seen again in the first team until the Watford game, when he reappeared at out-side-right in place of Wilson, who was injured, and he did very creditably in the last three matches.

Dunn also had the misfortune to break his jaw. Bradshaw and Hodgkinson proved one of the best wings that the club has ever had, the former being a clever and experienced player. Several of the reserve men were hardly the success it was hoped they would be. Other local players who assisted were H. Childs, R. Chapman, A.H. Layzell and W.W.T. Whistler. In the latter months of the season the Reserves had the assistance of King, Curtis, Molyneux, Dunn, etc. Loyal help was again given by the Southend Supporters' Club.

PART ELEVEN

The season 1911-12, therefore, saw the United competing in Division II of the Southern League, which necessitated trips to South Wales nearly every fortnight, for the majority of the clubs in Division II were recruited from the Principality. The five years valuable association of George Molyneux with the club also came to an end. He was a great player, an astute skipper, and one of Nature's gentlemen, on and off the field. Southend started their fight to regain their lost status under the management of Mr. Joseph Bradshaw. Three of the directors paid a visit to several of the Welsh grounds during a walking holiday before the season opened and returned with rather alarming stories of what the Welsh pitches were like.

These were not a trifle exaggerated and certainly some of the Welsh grounds in those days were not fit to play on. The players retained by Mr. Bradshaw were few owing to the poor financial position of the club and were: Murray, Thomson, Emery, Harwood, Wilson and J. Holman. Among the new players signed on were George Arnold, H. Wileman (Chelsea), McNaught (Queen's Park Rangers), H.W. Nurthen and Griffiths (goalkeepers), etc. The fixture list disclosed a heavy programme of 82 matches in the Southern League, Division II, South Eastern League and South Essex League, in addition to F.A. Cup-ties.

After the previous disastrous season the finances of the club were in a very low condition and on May 22nd, 1911, a meeting was held in the Park Hotel, Southend, where the Southend United Supporters' Committee met for the purposes of considering the position of the club and of rendering assistance, if necessary. The forward policy of the directors in retaining the best players was endorsed and the appointment of Mr. Bradshaw as manager received cordial endorsement. Mr. John H. Burrows, J.P., presided and announced that to date the Supporters' Club had handed over to the football club over £250, in addition to £60 guaranteed upon the western stand.

The United's exchequer, however, was very depleted. Speeches were also delivered by Mr. Donald Taylor, Chairman of the Directors, Mr. Bradshaw, Mr. O.M. Howard, and Mr. A. Howard, Secretary of the Supporters' Committee. Several suggestions were made for raising money, including the continuance of the Shilling Fund and the arrangement of a carnival and fete. In June, 1911, it was announced that the management of the Football League had postponed for twelve months the suggestion for the formation of a Third Division.

Southend opened their campaign in Division II with a match against Chesham, which they won by 7-0, and then they were at home to Treharris, whom they beat 2-0. They won 2-0 at Croydon against the Common, but lost on the following Saturday at Kettering by 3-1. On October 21st they made their first visit to South Wales and beat Treharris 3-1 on a small and bumpy ground. On one side of this pitch there was barely sufficient room for the players to take corner kicks; in those days it more resembled a marine store dealer's yard than a football ground.

Soccer was, however, quite a novelty in most districts of South Wales in those days and the visit of the United proved very popular amongst the inhabitants of the town. Afterwards they were taken down the Oceanic coal mine, that proved the one and only time on which the writer has had any first hand association with coal mines and pit ponies. This victory at Treharris smashed a four years old unenviable record that the United had not won a game after the first goal had been scored against them. For this trip the United made their headquarters at the King's Head Hotel, Newport, and on the following Monday they were due to play Cwm Albion.

After a journey through one of the many valleys of South Wales, they met something of an unknown quantity in Cwm and the sight which presented the team on arrival was somewhat dispiriting. Rain was teeming down and the field was almost bare, except that the touch-lines were roughly marked out, while the playing pitch was full of miniature valleys and dells. The only building on the ground was the dressing room for the visiting team. It was a rough shed, the roof and walls of which did not keep the wet out. The match was played in heavy rain and there was no shelter for spectators or Pressmen, but Southend won easily, piling up a score of 8-0 against their Welsh opponents. English teams were regarded somewhat in the nature of football missionaries in South Wales in those days and it was stated after the game that Southend had given the local spectators an education in football.

One of the most important fixtures bearing on promotion that season was at Roots Hall on Christmas morning against Portsmouth, and it ended in a goal-less draw. The return match should have been played at Fratton Park on Boxing Day, but the ground was under water when Southend arrived and the game had to be postponed. Early in the New Year another player was obtained in H. Cane, from Chelsea.

Though at one time Southend appeared likely to make a great bid for promotion, defeats at Portsmouth, Ton Pentre and Walsall seriously jeopardized their chances and the final blow was at Merthyr on March 16th, 1912, when they were beaten by 5-0. They won at Aberdare on the following Monday by 2-0, but it was too late and the chance had passed for that season.

The game at Aberdare was the one occasion on which I officiated as linesman for the United, as, owing to the absence of one of them the referee, Mr. I. Baker, asked me to take the flag, which I did. In their earlier matches the United had suffered from poor goalkeeping, but matters improved with Nurthen under the bar. Ultimately, Portsmouth and Merthyr were promoted, with Cardiff City and Southend in next places on the list.

At Mardy, in the final Southern League game, on the worst of all the bad grounds in the Second Division, Southend lost by 3-2, after leading until nearly the end. From the Mardy pitch there was a sheer drop on to the railway station and it was quite usual for the team that was leading to wait many moments while a small army of boys was kept busily employed in retrieving the football from the railway line below. In the fourth qualifying round of the F.A. Cup, the United beat London Caledonian by 3-1, but lost to Brentford in the fifth stage at Southend by 1-0. As consolation for their non-success in the Southern League, the United won the Southern Counties Charity Cup by beating Coventry City in the final, at Tottenham, by a goal to nil scored five minutes from the end of the game by Bradshaw.

PART TWELVE

In 1911-12 the Southern League Management Committee, of which Mr. Radford was a member representing the Second Division clubs, held several meetings to attempt to strengthen Division II, but it was nearly hopeless, as many of the English clubs, including Walsall, Kettering and Chesham, notified that they were not competing again. Luton and Leyton were relegated from Division I to Division II and this blow proved to be the end of the Leyton professional club.

Meanwhile, at the end of February, another financial crisis beset the club and a circular, dated February 22nd, 1912 was sent to all shareholders, signed by the manager, Mr. J. Bradshaw, stating that the Company could not by reason of its liabilities continue its business, and it was desirable that it should be wound up voluntarily. A meeting of shareholders was held on Friday, March 1st, 1912, at which Mr. D. Taylor, Chairman of Directors, presided. It was stated that the liabilities of the club were heavy, and one creditor, a director, had served the club with a writ for £90. Their liabilities, without the sum owing to directors, amounted to £456. Speeches were delivered by Messrs. G. Radford, T. Byford, John W. Burrows, J.P., A.J. Walker, A. Howard, A.H. Smith, J.P., and others. The meeting was adjourned to allow the directors to propose a scheme for the £456 to be raised. A subscription list of £185 was announced. A public meeting followed, with Mr. John W. Burrows, J.P., in the chair, and the then Mayor (Coun. Chalton Hubbard, J.P.) was present, both gentlemen speaking of the value of the club to the town. The Mayor promised to open a Mayor's Fund for the club to wipe off the debts, and Mr. Burrows was elected Treasurer.

The first list announced in the *Southend Standard* on March 7th was £263 16s. 6d., including donations from all the directors and £30 from the Supporters' Committee. The fund aroused great enthusiasm in the Borough and the late Mr. T.A. Mead ('Tarn,' of the old 'Morning Leader'), Mr. E.J. Grant and others rendered valuable assistance. The progress of the fund was shown by large clocks at Victoria Circus and in High Street. By the following week it had risen to £469 8s. 9d., and on March 14th a further meeting was held at the Blue Boar Hotel to enhance the success of the scheme. By March 21st the total was £614 7s. 2d., a splendid response, looking to the difference of money values at the present day. Eventually, the total was £629, raised in a little over a fortnight — a wonderful effort. Promises unfulfilled reduced the sum to about £600, but this great town's response undoubtedly saved the club from extinction.

In the Southern League, Division II, that season Southend played 26 games, 16 of which were won, nine lost, and one drawn, scoring 73 goals against 24, the same number that Portsmouth registered though the Hampshire men had four less marked against them. At home the Blues won ten games, lost two and drew one, and it is significant to note that on each occasion upon which they dropped points they failed to score. Probably the United's best performances in the competition were their away victories against Croydon, Cardiff, Treharris and Aberdare, while the worst undoubtedly were against Kettering, Merthyr, Ton Pentre and Walsall.

Four points were obtained from Aberdare, Chesham, Cwm Albion, Croydon and Treharris, two against Cardiff, Pontypridd, Walsall, Ton Pentre, Kettering and Mardy, while Merthyr captured all four points from the United and three were secured by Portsmouth. It was this loss of points to clubs who were rivals with the seasiders for promotion that so greatly injured their chances of success. As it was, the United finished eight points behind both Merthyr and Portsmouth, the promoted clubs. To add to the difficulties of the season a coal strike was in progress during the season and the lack of trains made many of the journeys tedious.

The South-Eastern League was used by the United as a sort of 'stop-gap' to fill up dates when there were no Southern League games, and there is no doubt that the galaxy of matches which this competition involved, together with the Southern League, the F.A. Cup, and the Southern Counties Charity Cup, accounted, to a large extent, for the staleness of many of the United players, and their inability to win matches after Christmas.

Little notice was taken of the United's doings in the South-Eastern League, for on many occasions a wholly reserve eleven were played, while at the best, it was generally a mixed team of reserves and first eleven men who carried through these fixtures. Under the circumstances, it was a somewhat creditable achievement that Southend should finish up in exactly the halfway position in the League table, with sixteen wins, sixteen losses and six draws, for on thirteen occasions an absolutely second string was turned out.

One of the smartest performances which Southend brought off during the season was their victory at Chelsea, when they defeated a very strong team of the Pensioners by 3-2, after at one time being two goals in arrear. Another signal victory was against Tottenham Hotspur Reserves at Roots Hall, when the Spurs brought down virtually a Football League eleven with a £5,000 forward line — a large sum in those days – but Southend were at that time bang on top of their form, and they followed up victories at Treharris and Cwm by defeating the Spurs by 2-1.

In this competition, two clubs won at Roots Hall, viz., Chelsea Reserves and Peterborough, the last occasion being when Southend had a reserve team out; while four clubs drew, viz., Brighton Reserves, Clapton Orient Reserves, West Ham Reserves and Watford. The remaining thirteen games at home were won. Four points were obtained against Swindon Reserves, Norwich City Reserves and Leyton Reserves, and to Peterborough belonged the distinction of being the only club to take four points from the United, though on each occasion they had reserve teams to meet. Brighton, Clapton Orient and Watford secured three points each. West Ham Reserves and the United played two draws of two goals each. The attendance at the South-Eastern League matches at home was rather disappointing, and pointed to the fact that the public did not take them very seriously.

It was unfortunate for the United also that this season they made an early exit from the Football Association Cup. In fact, after reaching the competition proper in the two previous seasons, they were this year dismissed in the final qualifying round. They were first drawn against the London Caledonians at Tufnell Park, and after the game had to be postponed once on account of the ground being under water, Southend won by 3-1. They then had to meet Brentford at Southend, and, after a hard game, they were defeated by the only goal scored, Southend missing, among many fine chances, a penalty.

The Cup-ties were of little financial assistance to the Club, and this proved a serious loss compared with the previous season, when they had the £400 plum for travelling to Blackburn. The winning of the Southern Counties Charity Cup competition was a much pleasanter topic, and it was a notable performance on the part of Southend, for they defeated four First Division

Southern League clubs, including the champions of the Southern League, Queen's Park Rangers. Considering only one match was played at home, this is an achievement to be proud of, and the Rangers were the only team to score against them in the competition. In the first round, Southend defeated New Brompton, at Gillingham, by 3-0; in the second round Queen's Park Rangers succumbed at Roots Hall by 5-4; in the semi-final Reading were beaten by a goal to nil, and in the final Coventry bowed the knee by a similar score.

In addition to assisting in several of the first team fixtures in the South-Eastern League, the Reserves competed in the South Essex League and managed to obtain a respectable position, after a very poor start, in fact, four victories in December placed them in the running for the championship, but they did not maintain the improvement and finished half-way up the table. Until he met with an accident, D. Adams was scoring many goals for them, and his continued absence made a great difference to the eleven.

The South Essex League was at the time an interesting competition and provided good sport. The Southend first team played three friendly games, losing to Brentford 3-0 and Ilford (for Molyneux's benefit) and winning against Shaftesbury Athletic. The Reserves defeated Southend Amateur 1-0 and Plumstead 1-0, losing to Waltham by seven to nil.

PART THIRTEEN

In the Southern League, South Eastern League, F.A. Cup, Southern Counties Charity Cup and the three friendly games in the season 1911-12, Southend scored in all 145 goals in 73 matches, or practically an average of two goals per contest, while the debit side showed 112 goals against.

Wileman was easily the most consistent goal-scorer for the United in all competitions, and his total for the season was 35, of which 17 were registered in the Southern League. Manager Bradshaw came next with a total of 27, of which 14 were Southern League goals. Holman was third with 23, McNaught fourth with 14, and, Wilson fifth with 13, while Parke was sixth with half a dozen. Other scorers were: Arnold, 5; Adams, 3; Harwood, 3; Emery, 2; Murray, 2; Bowles, 2; Jack Bradshaw and Hooton, two each; Baker, Preston, P. Chapman, Johnson, Curry and Childs, one each.

In addition to being the most consistent scorer, Wileman was also one of the most consistent players. He appeared in all 58 games for the first team and one for the Reserves, and, considering his dash and energy, it was wonderful that he never had to lie by on account of injuries. He shared with Bradshaw and Harwood the distinction of being the only players who did not miss a Southern League match.

Next to Wileman in the number of games played were Thomson and Harwood, with 48 each, while Bradshaw appeared in 47, and Emery in 43. Murray might have almost tied with Wileman's record had he not broken down some six weeks before the end of the season, but injuries affected both Wilson and Arnold, who, otherwise, played in a large percentage of the fixtures. Nurthen proved the best of the men tried in goal, and Boyd, of Redhill, showed great promise when he was snapped up by Crystal Palace. Kebbell, a local player, revealed real capabilities as a custodian in three or four games.

Winter, a Naval man, also assisted, and Chinnery, another local, did useful work for the Reserves. For a considerable portion of the season Southend were fortunate with their backs, for Murray and Thomson played without injury until the middle of March, and then the muscles of Murray's right thigh gave way, and he was placed hors de combat for the remainder of the season, while Thomson was also damaged in the final two weeks.

Emery kept up his excellent form, but Harwood, though being a great defender, did not give sufficient assistance to his forwards. A local player who proved very useful during the season was Layzell, who was the emergency standby of the team. Others who were tried in the rear division were Crutchington, Harrod and Preston, the last-named being a good substitute for Harwood.

On his best day there was no more brilliant winger than Archie Wilson, and, though he lost his form in the early part of the year, he fully recovered it before the end of the season. Knee trouble kept him out of the team for a period. The centre-forward position was a continual source of trouble. The lack of a first class centre-forward probably cost Southend promotion, as, though numerous experiments were made to fill the position, scarcely any were successful. Sentence, of Shaftesbury, was tried, as was also Hooton, while McNaught was given a run in the position, yet the need still remained.

The most successful experiment of the series was when Wileman led the vanguard, but this caused a rearrangement of the remainder of the front line. C.H. Curry, formerly of Bronze Athletic, who occupied the position in the closing game against Aberdare, created a good impression. Bradshaw played in every position on the field, including that of goalkeeper at Norwich, where the United won a South Eastern League match 1-0, and at full back at Swindon, and proved himself a very clever player. Parke proved a valuable substitute on either wing. McNaught (Queen's Park Rangers) and Cane and Bowles, who were obtained from Chelsea, also rendered assistance.

In the following season, to the relief of all supporters, Southend United secured promotion and regained their status in Division I of the Southern League. They were second in the League table to Cardiff City. Among the new players signed on were: Clarke, late of Cwm Albion, and Kebbell, a local, who formerly played for Garon's as a goalkeeper; Spencer, a promising full back from the North; Moon (centre-half); A. Hobson, a full-back from Everton; A.J. Chapman and Jack Bradshaw (amateur forwards) and Tommy Stott, a centre-forward. In addition to competing in the South-Eastern League, the United also took part in the Southern Alliance. Jerry Thomson was skipper this year. In their first journey to Wales they obtained three points, winning at Aberdare

2-1 and drawing against Mid-Rhondda at Tonypandy 1-1. Owing to having to play throughout all the preliminary stages of the F.A. Cup this season – the necessary application for exemption was omitted to be made – the United had only fulfilled eight League fixtures up to Christmas time of which four had been won, two lost and two drawn. They had harvested only 10 points, compared with 19 by Cardiff and 16 by Luton. The last-named clubs had played ten fixtures.

The New Year, however, started with successes over Croydon and Newport and prospects appeared more promising. A serious setback to their chances of promotion was received at Llanelly in a remarkable match on January 25th, 1913. The ground was in a terrible condition on account of continuous rain, but the United appeared likely to win, for they were leading 1-0 until midway through the second half, when a blunder gave the homesters a chance to equalize, which they did.

An unfortunate incident then occurred, when Llanelly's Welsh international goalkeeper was ordered off the field on the ground that he fouled Parke, the United outside-left. Things now looked easy for Southend to force home their footballing advantage and win, but the crowd started singing 'Land of my Fathers' and some Welsh hymns. The effect was electrical, for the home players seemed to be inspired and they went through the tired Southend defence with the utmost of ease and won in the end by 4-1. At the rate of scoring in those last few minutes they would have made it a dozen if there had been much longer to play.

PART FOURTEEN

Early in February, 1913, at Roots Hall, Swansea surrendered their previously unbeaten certificate to Southend by 3-1, and hopes of promotion reigned once more. Llanelly again proved a thorn in the side of the Blues on the next Saturday, for they stopped their previously unbroken winning record at Roots Hall by drawing 2-2, and they nearly won. Thus Llanelly took three points from Southend, whereas they should have sacrificed four.

On the following Saturday the United travelled to Newport, where the newly made ground was a mass of uncovered clinker and stones following heavy rain. Mr. E.J. Grant, on behalf of Southend, called the attention of the referee (Mr. E.E. Small) to it and some time before the match was due to start he declared the ground unfit and the match was postponed until a later date. Hundreds of Cardiff City supporters accompanied their team to Southend for the needle championship match on February 21st, but instead of a Titanic struggle as was anticipated, a poor game ended in a draw of one goal each, a similar result to the match at Roots Hall against Luton on the following Saturday.

At this stage, Southend were ten points behind Cardiff, four behind Luton, with two games in hand of each, and two points in front of Swansea, who had three games more to play. How slender Southend's chances of promotion appeared at this stage may be gauged from the fact that they had but two fixtures at home against Mardy and Aberdare and away encounters at Treharris, Ton Pentre, Mardy, Newport, Pontypridd and Swansea. They started with a draw at Treharris and then completed their home Southern League programme by beating Mardy and Aberdare at Eastertide.

Then they had to visit Ton Pentre on the last Saturday in March and the match was played in a downpour of rain, which in the Welsh valleys has to be seen to be believed. The ground, which was approached by a small bridge over a mountain torrent, was flooded and quite unfit for play, liquid mud and coal dust being several inches deep. Players could not dress on the ground, but had to do so at a hall close by and then to cross the bridge in mackintoshes and coats.

Mr. R.R. Crump, the referee, decided to get the game through if possible and a start was made. The black coal dust with which the pitch was faced was churned up into a perfect sea of inky mud and made the players look more like niggers than white men. The contest was a farce, though fraught with grave consequences to the United. Even the coin which the skippers tossed fell into a pool of slush and was not recovered. Players attempting to head the ball were rendered unconscious through concussion and men on the wings or who were not always in the thick of the fight were practically frozen, for the icy rain continued to descend in bucketsful and there was a keen easterly wind blowing. All lines on the pitch were obliterated.

The United eventually won by 2-0 by goals scored by Wilson and Wileman, but not before the team had had some shocks. Ton Pentre were awarded a penalty when the United were leading 1-0 and the referee had to step out the 12 yards to discover the distance of the penalty spot. Before the kick was taken, a United player surreptitiously scraped up a lot of mud in front of the ball, and when Clarke, of Ton Pentre, took his shot the ball and mud flew high into the air and went over the crossbar. All the visiting players were in a state of collapse at the end of the encounter and had to receive special treatment, including hot whisky.

Meanwhile, in Division II of the Southern League, Luton, Croydon and Swansea had been taking points from one another, and by two victories during the first week-end in April, first at Pontypridd (where a tanned running track ran across the ground) by 1-0 and at Newport by 2-0, Southend's chances of promotion became bright. These two successes were obtained during one week-end, which was one of the most cheerful I can recall in the many visits to South Wales.

Then the United had to visit Mardy on the same Saturday as Aston Villa beat Huddersfield in the F.A. Cup (April 19th), and Swansea and Croydon looked on anxiously, for Luton, by a defeat at Ton Pentre, had lost their opportunity. As previously stated, the ground at Mardy was situated on top of a hill, with a sheer drop at one corner into the railway station below. This was a convenient place to send the ball into touch when hard pressed and boys used to be kept running up and down to the station to fetch the lost footballs. This ground was in a terrible state and was one mass of ploughed up mud, with great ridges in places.

Mr. John Goodall, the former English international, Derby County and Watford forward, was manager of Mardy at the time, and he was most anxious for the match to be played, as the Mardy club was in poor financial condition and he had sold £100 worth of tickets for the game. It was a question as to whether the United directors would lodge a protest against the state of the ground, looking to the important issues involved, but they decided not to do so. There was a crowd of about 3,000 present, and after a nerve-testing contest Southend won 3-1. They led 2-0 at half-time, but Crales reduced the deficit early on the resumption. Batchellor, the United outside-left, was injured and was carried off the field and the United were left to complete the struggle with ten men. Stott got the third goal for the Blues and this was how they said farewell to Division II of the Southern League.

The news of their success was hailed with great enthusiasm when recorded in the windows of the *Southend Standard* office. A special illustrated supplement of the *Southend Standard* set out in detail the United's progress to promotion, for, although they lost the final match of the season at Swansea, it did not matter, for they finished second, seven points behind the champions, Cardiff City, but two points in front of Swansea.

PART FIFTEEN

In this season, 1912-13, through an oversight in not making the customary application for exemption, Southend United had to play through all the qualifying rounds of the Football Association Cup; moreover, they were drawn away from home on six successive occasions and most of the ties resulted in heavy financial losses through the poor gates and heavy travelling expenses. In the fourth qualifying round they beat Clapton at the Spotted Dog ground at Upton Park 2-1, and then in the final qualifying stage, had to visit Cardiff City at Ninian Park. On December 14th, 1912, they achieved one of the best Cup victories of their career.

This was one of the dozen 'finest' games in which the United have ever taken part. It is interesting to recall the team that did duty on that day, viz.: Kebbell; Thomson and Spencer; Emery, Moon and J. Axcell; Wilson, Wileman, Frost, Bradshaw and Stott. Bradshaw scored in the first half and Frost and Wilson obtained further goals in the final ten minutes. The day was a very wet one and the attendance far below expectations. The following week, the United had to visit Ninian Park again in the League and lost 1-0.

The prospect of sharing in a bumper gate was hailed with delight when they were drawn to meet Chelsea at Stamford Bridge in the first round of the competition proper. Had it been a fine day, they would have shared in a £1,000 gate at least (a large sum in those days with a sixpenny admittance), but the conditions were terrible, with rain, wind, sleet and mud predominant. Half the cup-ties set down for decision were not concluded and six of those that were completed ended in drawn games. Chelsea eventually won 5-2. They early obtained a lead of 2-0, but the United fought back, and, playing much better football, reduced the deficit before the interval. At the commencement of the second half, the referee awarded Chelsea two penalties, the justice of which will always be hotly disputed by Southend supporters, and Whittingham converted both. United reduced the lead once more, but Chelsea registered a further point through Vivian Woodward. Southend played pluckily and well, but the two penalties were their undoing. The gate was only £525, and Southend's share was about £240.

Excluding a friendly match against West Ham played for Emery's benefit on a Wednesday afternoon, Southend's full record for the season 1912-13 was as follows: Southern League – Played 24, won 14, lost four and drawn six. Southern Alliance – Played 16, won five, lost seven and drawn four. English Cup – Played seven, won six, lost one and drawn nil. Southern Counties Charity Cup – Played one, won nil, lost one and drawn nil. Friendlies – Played five, won three, lost nil and drawn two. In the Southern League, the goal average was: For 43, against 23; Southern Alliance: For 19, against 32; Football Association Cup: For 24, against 8; Charity Cup: For nil, against two; friendlies: For 12, against 6. Total: 98 goals for, against 71.

The goal-scorers for the season were: Wileman, 24; Frost, 19; Stott, 15; Bradshaw, 13; Wilson, eight; Curry, five; Moon, three; Parke and Emery, two each; Mason, Batchellor, Axcell, Layzell, Church, Bradshaw, jun., and F. Hawkes (Luton), one each. The following were the Southern League scorers: Frost, nine; Wileman, seven; Bradshaw and Stott, six each; Wilson, five; Curry, three; Emery, two; Batchellor, Parke, Axcell, Church and Hawkes (Luton), one each. Moon, the centre-half, who greatly improved during the season, held the record for the most appearances for the club during the season, for he played in 51 out of 53 games, while he was the only Southender who played in every Southern League match. Next to him was 'Jerry' Thomson, the skipper, who participated in 44 games, and only missed one Southern League match, while Spencer's 42 appearances included 22 Division II games. Wileman's injury kept him out of the team for six weeks, but he appeared 41 times, of which 19 were Southern League games.

The directors reported a loss of £73 2s. on the season, mainly due to the payment of £60 in bonuses subsequent to the players gaining promotion. The directors congratulated the shareholders on the increase in gate receipts, which was all the more commendable as there was no reserve team as at Roots Hall in previous years. The directors were also pleased to report they had re-signed the majority of last season's players, including Kebbell, Clarke, Thomson,

Spencer, Emery, Moon, Axcell, Wilson, Wileman, Stott, Frost, Cairns and Bradshaw, and newcomers were Barnes (outside-left) from Queen's Park Rangers and Hanks (centre-forward), Woolwich Arsenal, while several amateurs had promised to assist, including A.J. Chapman, J. Bradshaw, J.W. Batchellor, L.V. Mason, Church, Wales, Rogers, Caley, Fuller, F. Shrier, P. Garon and others.

Mr. Donald Taylor resigned from the Board, having taken up a position in Ontario, Canada, and his resignation was received with regret by the directors. One would like to pay tribute after all these years to the wonderfully loyal way in which Messrs. Radford, Byford, Oliver Trigg and Grant served the United during the two years in the wilderness of the Second Division.

The return of the club to Division I of the Southern League was greeted with enthusiasm and a fairly satisfactory season was enjoyed, for the club not only made a small profit, but maintained their position in the League. Among the new players signed were Robson, a full back, from the North Eastern district, Alec Steel, a brother of the Robert and John Steel of 'Spurs' fame, L.A. Louch, an international amateur centre-forward from Portsmouth, Frost, forward (who had returned from West Ham), and Barnes, winger (formerly of Queen's Park Rangers).

They started off the season with an away victory at Watford (2-1) and a home success against Reading by a similar margin. At the opening of the New Year they were in a good position, but the second half of the season was disappointing, and it was another few weeks before they won again, while a further month went by before they tasted the sweets of victory once more against Cardiff City at Roots Hall.

Then three matches were lost and three drawn, and when the United visited Plymouth on April 18th they required a point to make their position safe in the League. They won at Plymouth 1-0 and drew the final home game against Southampton, eventually finishing up fifth from the bottom; Merthyr Town and Coventry were relegated and Luton and Brentford promoted. Southend's record was: Won 10, lost 16 and drawn 12; goals for, 41; against, 66; points, 32.

PART SIXTEEN

Two outstanding victories of the season 1913-14 were those in the Southern League against Swindon and West Ham. Swindon Town, the ultimate champions, remained undefeated until November 15th and had only been held to a draw once when they visited Roots Hall on that date.

The United always had a habit in those days of rising to the occasion when they were opposed to good teams, and amid tremendous enthusiasm they won 2-0. By this victory Southend United riveted the attention of the British football public upon their doings, and frequently their players were watched by representatives of other clubs. The defence which did duty for the United on that day was the youngest in the whole of the three Leagues, Kebbell and Probert being but 20 years of age and Robson 19. Southend had all the better of the play in that contest and after a blank first half, Bradshaw and Frost scored the goals. Swindon were at that time in the hey-day of their prosperity and the teams on view on that occasion were: Southend – Kebbell; Robson and Probert; Emery, Liddell and Steel; Wilson, Frost, L. A. Louch, Bradshaw and Barnes. Swindon – Skiller; Kay and Giles; Tout, Silto and Lockhead; Jefferson, Fleming, Wheatcroft, Bown and Bolland.

Two weeks later the United also astonished West Ham followers at Boleyn Castle by winning there 1-0. L.A. Louch scored the only goal from a corner taken by Wilson. In 1913-14, Southend again reached the first round of the competition proper in the F.A. Cup. They beat Tunbridge Wells Rangers 3-0 at Southend (the game was played at Roots Hall by arrangement) in the fourth qualifying round, and then after drawing at Brentford 1-1, they vanquished the Bees at Roots Hall 2-0.

They were drawn to meet Birmingham at St. Andrew's in the first round on January 10th, 1914, and after a splendid and plucky struggle, on a rain-swept ground, they went under 2-1. Never does the writer remember two colder and bleaker days than this day and the Sunday which followed it. Rain fell incessantly throughout the match and Southend were somewhat unlucky to lose. Jerry Thomson, the skipper, was injured on November 8th, 1913, and lost his place in the first team, never to regain it. Ned Liddell, Southend's future manager, was transferred from Clapton Orient and played his first game for the United on the same day. The United's failures were chiefly at home. Six teams won at Roots Hall.

The club's ill-luck in draws in the F.A. Cup was proverbial about this time, and the one at Birmingham was their eleventh in succession away from home. To Emery belonged the distinction of having played in every first-class match during that season, for he appeared in all 38 Southern League games and the four English Cup-ties. The next on the list was Archie Wilson, for he made 37 Southern League appearances – missing only the match at Southampton – and four cup-ties. Kebbell was third with 33 League games and four cup-ties, and Steel and Frost were bracketed fourth with 31 Southern League matches and four cup-ties. Probert, who never missed an encounter after he was loaned to Southend by Portsmouth, participated in 30 League games and four cup-ties, while Robson represented the Blues in 28 League games and four cup-ties. Wileman was next with 28 League and three cup games, while L.A. Louch donned the club's colours in 27 League and four cup matches.

Liddell also never missed a first team game after he joined the United's ranks and he appeared in 26 League and four cup matches. Mr. Bradshaw, the manager, though not on the playing list, proved a valuable stand-by, and he turned out in 24 League matches and three cup-ties. Other appearances with the first team were: Barnes, 16 League and two cup-ties; McKay, 13 League; Thomson, 13 League; Axcell, 9 League; Batchellor, 8 League and one cup-tie.

During the season 1913-14 the United tried in their first team 25 players, made up in their respective positions as follow: Two goal-keepers, five backs, five half-backs and thirteen forwards. In the Southern League matches Frost was top scorer with eleven to his credit, while Wileman and L.A. Louch were second with nine each. Then came the two wingers, Wilson and Barnes, with four each, while McKay scored twice, and Bradshaw and Emery once each. Mixed teams were played in the Southern Alliance and the United finished at the bottom of the table with four wins, three draws and nine losses.

Every match away from home in that competition was lost, while at home four were won, three drawn and one lost, the latter being against Brighton, who were champions of the competition. The scorers were: Frost, 7; Wileman, 2; Tosswill, Wilson, McKay, Plumb, Clever and Todhunter, one each. Three friendly matches were arranged with mixed teams of first eleven players and reserves, Luton were beaten by two to none, while Grays Wednesday were beaten 3-2 at Roots Hall, and a draw of one goal each was played at Grays.

The second eleven started off well in the Kent League, but finished rather disappointingly, for they only occupied eighth position with twelve wins, 11 losses and seven draws, total 31 points, their goal average also showing a debit balance of 45 to 51. It was at first thought that the Kent League would prove an attraction, but the poor performance of the second team discouraged spectators, and the crowds for reserve matches dwindled to small dimensions before the finish.

The chief goal scorers for the reserves were: J. Todhunter, 11; Jack Bradshaw, 10; Hanks, 7; Stott, 6; Clover, 4; Moon, 3; Axcell, 2; Clarke, Young and Jones, one each. During this season there were, unfortunately, frequent dissensions among some members of the Board, which ended in Mr. G. Radford resigning his position as Chairman of the Company. He had previously purchased the lease of the Roots Hall ground to save it for the club.

At the close of the season the United directors transferred Archie Wilson to Middlesbrough for the highest transfer fee they had ever received up to that date. Mr. R. McIntosh, the then Middlesbrough manager, watched Wilson play against Coventry on Easter Monday, and ultimately arranged terms for his transfer to that club. In view of the club's insecure position in the League, Wilson was allowed to remain at Southend until the end of the season's engagements. The news of Wilson's impending departure was published in the *Southend Standard* on the Thursday following Easter and denied by the directors, but at the end of the season Wilson went to Middlesbrough. The balance sheet presented on May 11th, 1914, showed total gate receipts amounting to £3,575 9s. 4d., and a profit on the year of £12 10s. 8d.

PART SEVENTEEN

The season of 1914-15 opened under the shadow of the commencement of the Great War, and by the time the fixtures started, great numbers of the young men had joined the Army. While the Football Association and the Football League decided to carry through to the end of the season, it was a very depressing and disheartening business. Gates were small and were insufficient to meet players' wages and travelling expenses, and clubs like Southend were in a bad way before many months had passed.

In the hope of materially strengthening the side and making it really first-class – in the closed season and before the war was thought of – Mr. Bradshaw had signed on several new players, including E.H. Leahy, goal-keeper (Leicester Fosse and West Ham), K. Bennett, forward (Cardiff), S. Bassett, centre-half (Swansea), F. Burrill, forward (West Ham), George Marshall, full back (Shankhouse), A.W. Hamilton, centre-half (Portsmouth), T.S. Lonsdale, goal-keeper (Grimsby Town), D. McWhirter, an amateur international from Kent, J. Neil, full back (Bradford City), M. Woodward, half-back (Leicester Fosse), Jack Young, forward (South Shields), S. Eltringham, Jack Burton, forward (Cardiff City), H. Longstaffe, winger (Brighton), S. Rodgerson, centre-forward (Huddersfield), H.A. Flanders (Sutton Town) and many amateurs.

Though the League programme opened with home victories against Southampton (4-0) and Bristol Rovers (2-0) at Roots Hall, the team did badly and the club got into arrears with players' wages, and those with families were soon in want. It was hoped that a substantial sum would be paid to each player on Christmas Day out of the gate of the Christmas morning match against Croydon Common, but ill-luck still dogged the United, for fog descended and it was impossible to play the match – a great disappointment to players, directors and all concerned. In order to provide the players with a little cheer over Christmas a whip-round was made and a sum handed over to them. That morning, also, a German Taube aeroplane sailed over Southend Pier and proceeded as far as Purfleet, just as the sun was beginning to chase the fog away about one o'clock. It turned back and was soon out to sea again.

Things went from bad to worse in the late part of 1914 and early 1915, but the Southend United directors hoped to get a little money out of the F.A. Cup, in which they were that season excused until the first round proper. They were drawn to meet Bristol Rovers at Stapleton Road, where a fortnight previously they were beaten 4-1 in a League match. Much rain had fallen about this time, and, to add to the United's financial embarrassments, after staying the Friday night at Bristol they found the Rovers' ground at Eastville on Saturday morning, January 9th, 1915, under water and unfit for play. Thus another week passed, with added expenses, no income and no players' wages.

Down to Bristol they travelled again on the following Saturday, and, thanks to a wonderful display of goalkeeping by Tommy Lonsdale, who was the best custodian Southend ever had, they were enabled to effect a goal-less draw after a most exciting match. The replay was at Roots Hall on the following Wednesday and the United won 3-0 and qualified to meet the then Cup-holders, Burnley, at Turf Moor, on January, 30th. Burnley, however, outclassed them and beat them 6-0. Players had hoped to receive some of their back pay as the result of this tie, but they did not obtain it, so heavy were the club's other commitments, including advances by all the directors. While up in the North, Mr. J. Bradshaw, the manager, was taken ill, and when the club had to go to Watford on the following Wednesday in a postponed League match, there was no one to take them there and no money for expenses, so Mr. Percy Garon went with the team and paid the expenses. Leading 1-0 until five minutes from time, they lost 2-1.

So everything seemed to go wrong for the club, and, in addition to the anxiety of the national situation, players and all connected with the club became depressed and dispirited. After a home reverse in February, the directors announced that the club would have to disband and not fulfil the remaining League fixtures owing to their inability to carry on. It was then that the late Mr. George Radford offered to continue the club until the end of the season, paying out all outgoings and receiving what income there was. It was the action of a great sportsman, and but for that spontaneous offer, Southend United would probably, like Croydon Common, have ceased to exist and would not have been resuscitated.

Match after match was lost during the latter part of February, March and early April, and when Reading and Crystal Palace won at Roots Hall and Swindon and Reading beat them away, they were left with but three matches to produce five points, which were necessary to save the club from finishing in the bottom pair. They first drew at home against Queen's Park Rangers, and the position looked hopeless, for they then had to visit Millwall and entertain Plymouth. They secured a brilliant victory on the New Cross ground by 4-1, and then wound up the season on May 1st by beating Plymouth 3-1. It was a great ending to a terrible season, and the club was again fortunately saved from extinction.

The match at the Den was probably one of the finest which the United have ever played, for they over-ran Millwall to such an extent that the score did not exaggerate their superiority. Knowing all it meant to the club, it was, perhaps, the tensest match I have ever witnessed and it was with a great sigh of relief that we left New Cross that evening. Bradshaw played at centre-forward that day. Practically the only asset the club possessed when the season closed was its membership of Division I of the Southern League and the right to the services of certain players when football was resumed – a very doubtful date to forecast amid the trials and setbacks of 1915. The Plymouth game finally rang down the curtain at the Roots Hall ground, which was destined during the war years to become a sandpit.

PART EIGHTEEN

After the Millwall match in April, 1915, I wrote: 'I journeyed to New Cross on Saturday somewhat in the frame of mind of a man who is about to attend the funeral of an old friend, but I returned buoyed up with new hopes that the calamity which had threatened for some weeks would be averted. The last obsequies of Southend United's hopes and aspirations were postponed, for the club accomplished a triumph the brilliancy of which was unexampled in its history.' The Southend team which saved the club that day was: Leahy; Marshall and Robson; Emery, Bassett and Steel; Wileman, Burton, Bradshaw, Burrill and Young.

During the following week came the news that Billy Sutherland, who had been called up with the Argyll and Sutherland Highlanders at the outset of the war, was the first ex-United player to make the Supreme Sacrifice. At home the United obtained 21 points, which was the same total as they reaped in the season 1913-14, but it was in their away performances that they showed the deficit of four points.

During 1913-14 they recorded three wins and five draws on foreign territory, making a total of 11 points, whereas in 1914-15 the away bag contained seven. Only one club, viz., Luton, furnished the Blues with four points, the United winning at Southend 1-0 and at Luton 4-3. Millwall, Croydon and Norwich were the trio of clubs which provided three points each. The Lions played a goal-less draw at Roots Hall.

The United journeyed to Norwich and effected a draw of one each, while the Canaries went under by four to one upon their visit to the seaside. When the United visited Norwich, the local Territorial unit, the 6th Essex Regiment, were stationed there and they attended the match in force and afforded the Blues so much vocal encouragement that it helped them to bring away a point. On Boxing Day a draw also took place at Croydon, and at home the United won by two to nil.

The following clubs furnished two points each: Southampton, 4-0; Bristol Rovers, 2-0; Cardiff, 2-1; Swindon, 2-1, and Plymouth, 3-1. Clubs providing one point each were: Crystal Palace (away), 1-1; Brighton, 2-2; Queen's Park Rangers, 1-1; Gillingham, 1-1; and Watford, 0-0, and these teams, of course, extracted points at the expense of Southend. Five clubs took all four points from Southend, viz., Reading, 2-0 and 3-0; West Ham, 1-0 and 3-1; Northampton, 1-0 and 2-1; Portsmouth, 1-0 and 2-0, and Exeter, 7-1 and 2-0. Two of the United's worst performances were when they allowed Gillingham to extract three points from them, and it is interesting to note the draw which they made at Southend was the only point the Kentish men obtained on the grounds of their opponents.

Compared with the results of the previous season, the United gained twelve points but lost sixteen. The gains were (Luton and Croydon being substituted for Merthyr and Coventry in 1913-14): Southampton, one point; Millwall, three; Norwich, two; Luton, three; Croydon, two, and Gillingham, one. The losses of points were: Watford, three; Reading, two; West Ham, three; Portsmouth, two; Exeter, three, Crystal Palace, one, and Plymouth, two.

With the following six clubs the distribution of the points was the same as in 1913-14 – Cardiff City, Northampton, Swindon, Brighton, Queen's Park Rangers and Bristol Rovers. One friendly contest was enjoyed during the season against West Ham, who kindly sent a team down in February to play a benefit match for the United, and this contest ended in a draw of one goal each, Bradshaw scoring for the homesters. This was the only game played outside League matches and cup-ties.

The United Reserves appeared in the South-Eastern League and they wound up the season in the middle of the table with 16 wins, 20 losses and four draws, 63 goals being scored for and 68 against. In addition, two matches with Brentford Reserves were deducted from the table owing to the Londoners' record being expunged through withdrawal from the competition. In these, the United Reserves obtained three points, drawing at Griffin Park and winning at Southend 7-2. The competition matches aroused little interest and were poorly patronized, and the fulfilment of the fixtures with long journeys proved a heavy drain on the finances of the club. The constant reshuffling of the team made their performances spasmodic and oftentimes poor, but they accomplished some excellent results, including wins at Tottenham, 4-1, Chelsea, 2-0, Luton and Watford, and draws at Croydon, Gillingham, Southampton and Woolwich.

Twelve matches were won in 1914-15 in the South-Eastern League at Roots Hall and eight visiting teams were successful, while away, four victories were registered, four draws and twelve defeats. This gave the club a total of 36 points, excluding the Brentford game, which was by no means a bad record, considering the somewhat mixed sides that had to be put on the field on occasions. In this competition the military in the town, which consisted of two battalions of the King's Royal Rifles and two battalions of the Rifle Brigade and the Border Regiment, rendered the club much valuable assistance. A competition was also held on the Roots Hall ground on Sundays during 1915, for which the proprietors of the *Southend Standard* gave medals.

In the Southern League competition the United called upon 24 players during the season, and the man who made the most appearances was George Marshall, who only missed one game after he came into the side in the fourth week in September, when Robson was injured at Northampton. Including the Swindon abandoned game, he made 35 appearances in the Southern League, and the next in order of merit were: A. Steel and A.W. Hamilton, 33 each; E. Emery, 32; A. Frost, 31; T. Lonsdale, 30; J. Young, 27; J. Burton and F. Burrill, 25 each; W. Mayo, 22; J. Neil, 21; H. Wileman, 19; M. Woodward, 16; Rodgerson and K. Bennett, 14 each; F. Robson and J. Bradshaw, 13 each; E. Leahy, 9; S. Bassett, 5; D. McWhirter, 4; Bombardier Plumb, 3; L.A. Louch, Eltringham and Rifleman Jackson, one each.

The following were the twelve players who took part in the three English Cup-ties: Lonsdale, 3; Robson, 1; Marshall, 3; Woodward, 2; Emery, Hamilton,

Steel, Mayo, Wileman, Frost, Bradshaw and Young, 3 each. No player took part in all the games and thus equalled the record of Emery in the previous season, when he did not miss one League or cup match in the eight months, while A. Wilson only missed one. The first team scored 45 Southern League goals (including the abandoned game against Swindon), three in the Football Association Cup, and one in a friendly game. Albert Frost again headed the list of goal scorers with 11 goals (10 Southern League and one English Cup), while F. Burrill was second with nine, Wileman coming third with six. Other scorers were: Burton, Rodgerson and Bradshaw, four each; Emery and Hamilton, three each; Bennett, two, and J. Young and Bombardier Plumb, one each, while one of the Luton backs turned the ball into his own net.

Including the two Brentford games, the goalscorers in the South-Eastern League were: Rodgerson, 12; Burrill and Burton, 10 each; Wileman, 7; Frost, 6; J.H. Bradshaw, 4; Axcell, Eltringham and Rifleman Jackson, three each; Woodward and Sergt. Wood, two each, and Bassett, J. Bradshaw, Spivey, R. Young and Bright, one each. Up to the time he met with his injury at Burnley, Lonsdale played brilliantly in goal. The two most consistent men in the United ranks were Marshall, who developed into one of the finest right-backs in the League, and Emery, who kept up his form in a wonderful manner.

The injury to Robson at Northampton was a serious blow to the club, for though he returned to the side late in the season, he never fully recovered his form. The half-back line was never up to the required standard, and the forwards were somewhat erratic. There were, on the whole, many failures and few successes in the United eleven of that season and the team hardly realized what was anticipated of it, though, of course, the depressing circumstances at the time had to be taken into account.

PART NINETEEN

At the ninth annual meeting in June, 1915, it was stated that, prior to the outbreak of hostilities, the year 1914-15 promised to be the most successful in the history of the club, but the directors regretted a loss of £1,293 18s. 4d. It was with the utmost difficulty that the management were able to complete the fixtures owing to the large decrease in the receipts, including the loss of the Christmas morning gate, caused by the postponement of the match owing to fog, and the increased expenses due to the suspension of cheap fares.

Of the four retiring directors, Messrs. O. Trigg, G.A. Weston, J.C. Ingram and T. Byford, only the first two offered themselves for re-election. The total deficit on the Company was then stated to be £2,827 8s. 9d. Professionalism was suspended until the end of the war. The London Combination arranged a tournament to carry on some football in the Metropolis from 1915 onwards, but the United's application for admittance was refused. In May, 1915, Mr. J. Bradshaw, former manager, joined up and in August left for France, and most of the other players joined the Colours.

On October 1st, 1915, the loyal old supporters once again thought they had seen the last of Southend United, for on that day the whole of the effects were sold up at Roots Hall. The story is best told in the report of the *Southend Telegraph* (now the *Southend and County Pictorial*) of October 2nd, which stated: 'Considerable surprise was caused in Southend on Thursday morning upon the publication of the *Southend Standard* containing the notice that, under distress for rent, Messrs. A. Prevost and Sons would sell by auction on Friday, at Roots Hall, Prittlewell, the whole of the stock-in-trade of the Southend United Football Club, Ltd.

The articles included ten iron turnstiles by Ellison and Co., goalposts, nets, scoring board, iron roller, wheelbarrow, drag, dibbing irons and sundry tools, 20 leather hand-bags, footballs, quantity of players' attire, iron bath, two gas geysers, portable heating stove and piping, sand screen, quantity of wooden grating, notice boards, stock of useful timber and sundry effects. That this brief announcement signified more than on the face of it was apparent, and enquiries made by the writer elicited the fact that on Monday evening the directors of the Southend United club decided upon voluntary liquidation of the Company.

Thus the somewhat chequered career of the Southend United Football Club, Ltd., is rapidly drawing to a close after a period of nine years. It will be recalled that at the last annual meeting of the Company it was reported the loss on last season's working was over £1,200, and the liabilities of the Company were nearly £3,000.

The exclusion of the United from the London Combination precluded any first-class football being played in the Borough this season, and, therefore, until the present week matters have been left in abeyance, and the announcement that the landlord had distrained for rent came as something in the nature of a bombshell to local football enthusiasts. As Coun. G. Radford, an ex-Chairman of the directors and always a loyal and warm supporter of the club, was known to be the landlord of the ground, the news caused all the more surprise, but Mr. Radford's reasons for the step he had taken are given below.

This was not the first occasion on which the Company has issued notices for voluntary liquidation, as some four years ago the usual statutory notices were given, but the situation was saved through certain gentlemen coming forward and finding the money. Throughout its career the club has been harassed with financial troubles, but various public appeals and the generosity of local supporters have averted a climax.

Now with football in the Borough lying practically dormant, there is no hope of saving the old club, and in a short space of time the Southend United Football Club, Ltd., will cease to exist. It does not, of course, necessarily mean that first-class football will be stopped, for the Southend United club still has its position in the Southern League, and before football restarts, with the permission of the Southern League and the Football Association, a new company can be formed to continue the club. All the players of the existing Company automatically are at the disposal of the Southern League, who will hold their transfers.

In view of the terrible crisis which the country is passing through, however, there is every hope that if a new club were started the League would not act harshly in this matter. The old Company does not owe a large sum to tradesmen, but the liabilities are chiefly for money advanced and wages due to players, and their late Secretary, Mr. J. Bradshaw, to whom the club in indebted to the extent of £50.'

On the Friday morning, October 1st, 1915, a representative of the *Southend Telegraph* saw Coun. Radford at his house in the Leigh Road and invited him to make a statement as to the reasons which had led him to levy distress on the Company. He said: 'I heard that the directors of the club were holding a meeting to go into liquidation, and I consulted my solicitor. I was advised that once the Company went into liquidation all the property passed to the liquidator and he would take possession and the things would be sold to pay the liquidation. As the club owed me a very large sum for rent and other things, I, therefore, had to protect myself and put a man in possession for rent. A notice was despatched to the directors stating that the things would be sold unless the rent was paid, but no reply was sent to the letter. I took the trouble to go to the Board meeting on Monday which the directors had called to consider going into liquidation, and I there opposed it as strongly as I could, as I considered liquidation was only a means of evading one's creditors and that it was unfair to try to do the players and others out of their money.

'I told the directors that I was quite willing to let the whole thing stop in abeyance until after the war and then see what turned up. I also had an interview with Mr. A.G. Hunt at Mr. T. Cooper's office and again offered to let the matter stay in abeyance, but the directors decided to go into voluntary liquidation, though they were not unanimous upon it. Therefore, I have been compelled to take the steps I have to protect myself. The directors by their action have forced my hand. The Company owes me £150 for rent, beside a large sum otherwise, and I shall be the greatest loser. The ground has been lying idle since last May, and I have not asked for a farthing rent. I was quite willing to let it stop in abeyance until football restarted.

'If creditors had pressed the club they could not have got an order in the County Court in view of the war and the fact that football was shut down. My policy has always been, 'Let's get the war over and see what can be done.' I took the step I did with very great regret, but I was legally advised to do so in order to protect myself. I shall probably be out of pocket over the sale after paying expenses.' In further conversation, Mr. Radford expressed the hope that it would not mean the end of first-class football in the town, but that a new company would be formed to carry on when the war was over. He said of course the grandstands, fencing, etc., were his property and would be available when football was restarted. 'It would be a thousand pities now that we are in Division I that football should die in the Borough,' added Mr. Radford.

Mr. E.J. Grant, the Vice-Chairman of the Club, who was present at the sale, told a *Southend Telegraph* representative that the directors thought that Mr. Radford had acted in an arbitrary way, and that no notification was sent to the directors of his intention to distrain for rent. The directors were surprised when they found a man in possession. He also denied that Mr. Radford ever suggested to them the matter should remain in abeyance. The directors called a meeting to consider the financial position last Monday, and it was only after they knew that the landlord had distrained for rent that they decided to go into voluntary liquidation. That decision, too, had to be approved by the shareholders and this had not been done as yet.

There was a crowd of about 100 people at Roots Hall to witness the obsequies of the Company at the auction sale on the Friday afternoon, including many people who had been prominently connected with the organization in the past, including Ald. John Francis, J.P., Councillors G. Radford, W.C. Illes and W.F. Scott, Messrs. R.A. Jones (late president), Oliver Trigg, E.J. Grant, A.G.H. Hunt and J.A. Faers and many others. The auctioneer was Mr. A.J.H. Prevost, himself a regular attendant at the matches and a son of a former Chairman of Directors.

Mr. Prevost, in opening the sale, said that, being a distress by the landlord, all the lots would be sold without reserve. He was sorry that was the end of the old Southend United Football Club, and he saw many faces present that day who were regular attendants at the matches in the past. He hoped their bids would be such that after the distraint had been paid there would be something left over for the club. Mr. Grant interrupted with a remark advising people not to bid. The sale opened with two galvanized pails, three enamelled basins, twelve tumblers and a wooden box, and these were knocked down to Mr. Swain for 3s., while an enamelled iron bath fetched 7s. Coun. Scott bought a copper geyser for 14s., and another fell to Mr. Finch for 16s. Two wooden benches and a folding table were knocked down to Mr. Scott for 2s., and then in quick succession Mr. Scott, after some brisk bidding, secured the following lots of football gear: Portable iron stove and piping, 16s.; box of lint bandages, brushes and few sundries, 2s.; four footballs and punchballs, 7s.; quantity of shin pads and gloves, 2s.; six pairs of football boots, 8s.; seven pairs of football boots, 6s.; 14 pairs of plimsolls and shoes and four pairs of old football boots, 4s.; 11 light blue jerseys, 4s.; 11 royal blue jerseys, 14s.; 11 royal blue jerseys, 20s.; three pairs of blue football knickers and a quantity of stockings, 5s.; ten pairs of football knickers, 5s.; five red Guernseys, 3s.; six pink and white shirts and green jersey, 2s.; six ditto and red jersey, 2s., five white jerseys, 12s.

There were some amusing asides, Coun. Scott stating that he had plenty of boys round his way to fit up with football things. 'You want a field to put them in,' retorted the auctioneer. 'Oh, I have got a field all right; now I will have a team of my own.' 'You will invite me to the opening?' queried the auctioneer. 'Yes, if you will provide the lunch,' answered Mr. Scott. When purchasing the knickers, Mr. Scott said he must have the suits complete, and, in buying the jerseys, he said he could set the whites against the reds. 'I wouldn't let anyone else have those good old shirts,' he exclaimed, in bidding for the royal blue jerseys. In offering the lint and bandages for sale, the 'auctioneer said those were in great demand at the present time. 'Not here, but at the Front,' answered the purchaser. 'But you're not at the Front, Scott,' said Mr. Prevost. 'I have sons who are,' retorted Coun. Scott.

A soldier named Hubbard bought twelve pairs of knickers for 5s., and Sergt. Abbott secured five red Guernseys for 3s., while Mr. Baker purchased 27 towels for 9s and ten pairs of football knickers for 3s. Sergt. Abbott secured two good footballs for 10s. A number of small Gladstone bags which players used were offered, and a soldier bought one for 4s., Mr. Gibbons one for 2s., Mr. Faers another for 5s., Sergt. Batchelor one for 6s., and Mr. J.C. Flaxman one for 5s., 'just,' he added, 'to have a relic of the old club.' Mr. Scott bought eight bags at prices ranging from 3s. to 6s., according to the state of repair they were in. Mr. Scott was also the successful bidder for the following fixtures, etc.: Two sets of Rugby football posts, 5s.; six lengths of timber, 9s.; two old seats with reversible backs, 2s.; wooden platform and few pieces of timber, 8s.; four corner flags and watering can, 2s.; eighteen lengths of wood grating (for standing on in the reserved enclosure), 9s.

Mr. J.C. Flaxman varied the monotony of Mr. Scott's voice, saying 'That's mine,' by purchasing two brooms, shovel, three crowbars, rammer, two pickaxes and a rake for 14s., and five lots of tarred felting for 9s.; but Mr. Scott was soon at it again and purchased under the hammer the following lots: Mowing machine, 4s.; large lawn mower, 8s.; oil stove, water can, two lawn mowers and scythe, 5s; thirteen glazed advertisement frames, 6s; fifty D.C. advertising boards, 9s; set cricket nets with stakes, etc., 5s.; iron roller, £1 10s.; grass harrow, 5s.; set of goal posts, fittings and nets, £1 7s. 6d.; old sand screen and quantity of timber, 18s. The other buyers included: Mr. Swain, quantity of timber, 9s; Mr. Cook, wheelbarrow, 10s.

When the telegraph board and numbers were offered by auction Mr. Scott enquired if he bought it, could he take the posts out of the ground? A member of the audience said he thought the board belonged to the *Evening News*. This Mr. Faers contradicted, and Mr. Radford said whoever bought the board would have his permission to take it out of the ground. It was later knocked down to Mr. Scott for £1. The sale of the turnstiles came last, and there was a spirited competition for these. A pair of rush preventative iron turnstiles, with partitions, were purchased by Mr. Scott for £4 5s., while Mr. J.W. McGuire bought two others at £2 apiece. The next four, however, went to Mr. Scott at the respective prices of £2, £2, £2 5s. and £2 5s, while two Norton's improved turnstiles, with indicators, also came in to the possession of the same buyer at £2 5s. each. This concluded the sale and the auctioneer thanked the audience for their attendance. The total proceeds of the sale were only £43 10s. 6d.

PART TWENTY

Nothing more was heard of the United's affairs until the annual meeting of the Company on Wednesday, May 2nd, 1917, when a deficit of £3,028 18s. 8d. was reported. The report of the directors presented to that meeting stated: 'As your club was not elected to the London Combination and it was not considered by your Directors to be prudent to attempt to carry on football in any other form during the war, your Company has remained inactive during the past year. The majority of the club's players have joined His Majesty's Forces or are engaged in work of national importance.

Owing to the prevailing conditions and the uncertainty as to the duration of the war, your directors have nothing of a definite character to report as to the future activities of your Company. Notwithstanding the difficulties which have to be faced, however, it is safe to assume that after the war the demand for first-class football in Southend will be as keen as ever, and your Directors are confident that, with the acquisition of some new directors and the enthusiastic support of the local public, it will be possible to place your Company on a sound basis, which will enable a football club to be run which will be worthy of the important town it represents. With the view of being prepared to commence football again by the time the war ends, it is the intention of your Directors to discuss and to decide as to what would appear to be the best plan to adopt to place your Company in a position to renew its activities.

Owing to the great difficulties which at present exist and the work involved, your Directors invite your support and assistance in this matter. In accordance with the Company's Articles of Association, the directors retiring by rotation are Messrs. Councillors G. Radford and H. Ward, neither of whom sought re-election. The Directors wish to place on record an expression of their deep regret of the death of Ald. A. Prevost, J.P., one of the founders and past Chairman of the club, who, up to the last game played at Roots Hall, was a regular and keen supporter. Also the deaths in action of Archie Wilson and Harry Owen, both of whom were, at different periods of the club's history, idols of the local supporters and who rendered yeoman service to the club.

The lease of Roots Hall has terminated and notice is hereby given that the Company's registered address is now: Blue Boar Hotel, Prittlewell, Southend-on-Sea. W.J. Kirby, Chairman.' E.E. ('Dits') Anderson and W. Sutherland, former United players, also fell during the war.

After the war, preparations were made for recommencing football in 1919-20, and the task was undertaken of reconstructing the Southend United club from the remnants of the old organization that remained. The Roots Hall ground was now unavailable, and, except that they retained their membership of the Southern League, Southend United had no assets, but a heavy millstone of debt. They had no ground on which to play, and the future was full of doubt and uncertainty. At the meeting of Southend Town Council on March 18th, 1919, Coun. John Mitchell proposed a resolution that the football pitch at Chalkwell Park should be granted gratuitously to the Southend United club and that they should be allowed to charge for admission to the ground. Coun. H. Ward seconded, and, after a brief discussion, Ald. A. Martin proposed, as an amendment, that the matter should be referred to the Entertainments and Parks Committee to make arrangements for a pitch to be allocated to the club at Chalkwell or Southchurch Parks. This course was adopted. It was, however, not necessary to call on the Corporation to allocate a pitch, as the Kursaal ground was ultimately obtained.

After many months of uncertainty and the encountering and surmounting of numerous difficulties, the *Southend Standard* was able to announce early in April, 1919, that football had been assured for the next season and that first-class football was saved for the town. After prolonged negotiations, Messrs. W.J. Kirby and E.J. Grant signed an agreement with the late Mr. C.J. Morehouse, managing director of the Kursaal, for the use of the Kursaal ground for the season 1919-20 at a rent of £200 per annum. The terms were cash down, and this the directors advanced.

The directors had hoped to return to the old ground at Roots Hall and secure an option on the adjoining land, but a portion had been cut up into allotments and it was found impossible to have it turfed in readiness for the next season. The Town Council were thanked for offering to provide a pitch at Chalkwell or Southchurch Parks. There was then no banking on the Kursaal ground and no grandstands except the old pavilion at the southern end, which was used as dressing rooms. It was, therefore, decided to call a public meeting to launch a scheme for erecting fencing, constructing banking and providing grandstand accommodation.

On May 20th, 1919, an enthusiastic meeting was held at the Kursaal to give Southend United a send-off and supplement the efforts of the directors to resuscitate the club and place it on a sound financial basis. The Mayor, Ald. F.W. Senier, J.P. (afterwards Sir Frederic Senier), presided and outlined the object of the meeting. Mr. W.J. Kirby, who explained the position for the club, suggested the game at that meeting was football and the teams engaged were 'Success' and 'Defeat.' Altogether, the club owed £1,789 10s., the largest creditor being one for £258. West Ham F.C. had promised to wipe out a sum due on a transfer fee. The sum of £468 was due to players of the club, but they were willing to take payments as funds allowed.

The Kursaal ground had to be fitted up, a grandstand and other accommodation provided, etc. The amount required to keep football in Southend was stated to be about £5,000. Addresses were delivered by Mr. G. Wagstaffe-Simmonds, a member of the Council of the Football Association and now a

Spurs director, and Mr. George F. Allison, later manager of the Arsenal Football Club and the well-known football broadcaster. On the motion of Coun. J. Mitchell, seconded by Coun. C. Neil, a resolution was passed pledging the meeting to co-operate with the directors in raising a capital sum of £5,000 to place the club on a sound financial basis.

On June 10th a further meeting was held at Clarence Hall, when the new manager (Mr. E. Liddell) was introduced. Major Sandercock, on behalf of the Finance Committee of Supporters, introduced a scheme for taking up shares in the club and it was announced that the total number of shillings raised towards the 100,000 shillings fund was 6,290, or a little more than £310. A further meeting of enthusiasts was convened at the Clarence Hall on July 11th, presided over by Major Sandercock, to make arrangements for the sale of 20,000 5s. shares. Mr. Wagstaffe-Simmonds was again the principal speaker, but the response to the appeals was disappointing.

PART TWENTY-ONE

On Saturday, August 9th, 1919, the opening took place of the United's new ground at the Kursaal, a reception being held on the field by the directors. The Mayor and Mayoress (Ald. F.W. and Mrs. Senier) were among those present. The playing pitch had by this time been fenced off and a terraced enclosure constructed for directors. It was stated that it was hoped to provide a small stand for use by October. The sum of £66 was taken up in shares that day, bringing the total to over £100, while the 100,000 shillings fund had reached a total of about 7,000.

To the regret of his many friends, Mr. Oliver Trigg, the Chairman of the Directors in their last season and one of the founders of the club, died in February, 1919, and his loss was severely felt when the work of reorganization started. In the reconstruction of the United club, however, there was cause for criticism, for two of its good friends, who had stuck to the old organization up to the last and ensured the club resuming its first-class status, were passed over. Mr. G. Radford, whose great services in 1914-15 enabled the club to conclude that season, was not invited to join the new Board, while though practically everyone else was reinstated in his pre-war position. Mr. J. Bradshaw, the former manager, was passed over when it came to that appointment, and Mr. E. Liddell, a former club centre-half, was selected. Mr. W.J. Kirby was elected Chairman of Directors, with Mr. E.J. Grant Vice-Chairman. Mr. Bradshaw subsequently was appointed manager of Swansea.

The conditions under which football was played in pre-war days and post-war years were entirely different. Gate money was double that of pre-war years, travelling expenses had increased 100 per cent., wages were much heavier owing to the decreased purchasing power of the £, and the Government took in Entertainment Tax nearly 25 per cent. of the receipts. The appeal for funds in Southend was somewhat disheartening, and the directors had to find money for the close season expenses, fitting up the ground and the erection of two small stands, but, thanks largely to the cup-ties, debts of over £1,200 were wiped out and the season finished with a balance in hand.

Most of the 1914-15 players available were re-signed, including E.H. Leahy, G. Marshall, E.W. Emery, M. Woodward, R.H. Young, F. Burrill, J. Young and H. Wileman. Among the new players obtained were Leonard Hill, a Leigh amateur, who subsequently signed professional forms for Queen's Park Rangers; Bob Reid, a full back from Burnley, who became captain; Percy Sands, formerly of the Arsenal; J. Bollington, an Army half-back; G.J. Nicholls, outside-right, late of Chelsea; J. Bellamy, formerly of Burnley and Fulham; D. Upex, Croydon Common; W. Bridgeman, outside-right, formerly of West Ham and Chelsea, and W. Lot Jones, the famous ex-Manchester City forward and Welsh International.

While staying in South Wales, Southend secured James H. Evans, a brilliant young full back, who rendered them great service and was subsequently capped three times for Wales. He and Lot Jones obtained Welsh international caps while assisting Southend. J.H. Evans first played for the United in a friendly match at Mid-Rhondda. G. Marshall, M. Woodward and F. Burrill were, before the end of the season, transferred at substantial figures to Wolverhampton Wanderers, who were Cup Finalists in the next season, and all three ex-United men appeared in the Final against the Spurs in 1921. Robson, a former United back, was transferred to Swansea before the season opened.

The first match at the Kursaal on August 30th against Portsmouth was lost 2-0, but the United succeeded on the following Monday, against Newport, by 3-0. Another home match was not won until they met Brentford, at the Kursaal, and they were victorious by 3-1. In this game Nicholls, the home outside-right, broke a leg. At this period Brentford were leading 1-0.

One of the United's most sensational victories that season was when they succeeded 1-0 at Fratton Park against Portsmouth, the ultimate champions, who had not previously lost at home. The other away successes were at Gillingham and Swansea. Among the teams they defeated at home were Plymouth Argyle (1-0), Luton (3-0), Millwall (1-0), Merthyr (2-1), Norwich (2-1) and Exeter (2-0), Finally, their record was: Won 13, lost 12 and drawn 17. Ten games were won at home, three lost and eight drawn, while away three were won, nine lost and nine drawn. The great percentage of drawn games will be noted. The team was not a great goal-scoring side, only registering 46 in 42 matches, with 48 against.

In the F.A. Cup of 1919-20 the United were only excused until the sixth qualifying round, and in that stage had to meet Watford at the Kursaal and won 1-0 a week before Christmas, 1919. Then in the first round proper, on January 10th, 1920, they were drawn at Southend against Sheffield United. The Southend ground at that stage was not in a fit condition to hold a large crowd and it had no banking, only a very small grandstand and little terracing.

Overtures were made for the tie to be played at Bramall Lane, Sheffield, but the Blades' directors would not agree to the Southend terms to transfer it there. So the tie looked like being played after all at the Kursaal.

However, on January 3rd, Southend startled the football world by winning at Portsmouth, with four reserves in the team, by 1-0. The ultimate champions had an unbeaten home record previously at Fratton Park, and on the following day Sheffield United accepted the United's terms for the match to be played at Bramall Lane. From a climatic point of view, it was a dreadful day on which the match was decided at Sheffield, for rain fell practically without cessation, and the United put up a plucky fight to lose 3-0. The Seasiders accepted a minimum of £750 as their share of the gate. The attendance was 39,700 and the receipts were £2,326, so, after the deduction of Entertainment Tax, both clubs pocketed about £800, and out of this sum the United paid nearly all the arrears of wages owing to players during the war season. Two friendlies were fulfilled during the season, viz., a draw at Tonypandy against Mid-Rhondda, and a home game against Gillingham, which was won 3-1.

PART TWENTY-TWO

To Marshall belonged the distinction of having played in every first team match in which the United participated in the 1919-20 season. He appeared in 42 League games, two F.A. Cup-ties and two friendlies, a total of 46 altogether. His partner, Bob Reid, was second with 40 League games, two Cup-ties and one friendly. The Southend skipper, H. Wileman, was third with 39 League appearances, two Cup-ties and one friendly.

In the Southern League the United utilized 23 players, and the League appearances were: Marshall 42, Reid 40, Wileman 39, J. Young 38, Jones 37, Burrill 32, Bollington 30, Leahy 26, Woodward 26, Evans 24, Nicholls 23, Upex 17, Allen 15, Emblem (a goalkeeper who earned great publicity by stopping five penalty kicks in succession) 13, Bridgeman 12, Sands 11, G. Walden 11, Emery 7, Frost 7, Bellamy 6, L. Hill 3, and Liddell and R.H. Young, one each. Leahy, Reid, Marshall, Wileman, Bollington, Evans, Burrill, Jones and J. Young played in each of the two Cup-ties, and Upex, Frost, Bellamy and Bridgeman in one.

Burrill was top goal-scorer in the League with 16 goals, while other successful marksmen were: Wileman 8, Lot Jones 6, Upex 5, Frost 4, Nicholls 2, and Bollington, J. Young, Bridgeman and Walden one each. J. Young obtained the goal in the Cup-tie against Watford. Though of moderate ability, the side were imbued with wonderful team spirit and pluck. They were never beaten and frequently pulled matches out of the fire that appeared to have been irrevocably lost.

Southend Reserves competed in the South-Eastern League, but were bottom of the table with 24 defeats, two wins and two draws. Upex and Schrier were top scorers with five goals each, while Oakley and Rogers got four each.

CHAPTER THREE

A Selection of Match Reports 1906-1920

Saturday, August 25th, 1906
Practice Match: 'A' TEAM 0. 'B' TEAM 4
Match report of the first game involving players of Southend United F.C.

Punctually at six o'clock, the time advertised for the kick-off, Referee J.T. Clark whistled the teams up. They were:–

'A' Team: Goal, Dobbin; backs, Perry (late South Weald) and Hagger; half backs, Bridge, Emery, and Ellis; forwards, Holden (late Portsmouth), Mitchell (late Derby County), Halse (late Wanstead), Watkins (late Millwall), and Jack (late Plymouth Argyle).

'B' Team: Goal, Cotton (late West Ham United); backs, Molyneux, captain (late Portsmouth), and Thomson (late Southend Athletic); halves, Freeman (late Grays United), T. Owen (late Southend Athletic), and Johnson (late Grays United); forwards, Butler, Axcell (late Grays United), 'Dark' (late Norwich City), Finn, and Bomb. Newland.

Mr. Trigg, the proprietor of the 'Blue Boar,' kicked off amid loud cheers, and considerable dash was put into the game. 'B' team proved themselves the stronger, and in the end scored four goals against 'A's' nil. Cotton made a fine goalkeeper, and some of his saves merited well deserved applause. He had some tricky shots to battle with, but he was equal to any of them.

Of the backs I need not say much. Thomson is well-known for his good defence and partnered by Molyneux, they made a fine pair. The latter player never missed a chance, and it is certain he never gave one. His protection of the goal mouth was grand, and we look forward to some exciting games with these two at back.

The play of the halves was a treat to watch. Tom Owen has not lost one particle of the life and go which he has always put into the game, whilst Johnson and Freeman make two excellent partners.

Of the forward quintet, 'they are a splendid line of attack.' During the whole of the game they kept well together, and, in the rush for goal, fairly baffled their opponents. Proof of this is in the fact that Finn and Newland managed to score a goal each – in fact, the latter scored two. 'Dark,' the dashing centre forward (who played under an assumed name and is a professional cricketer of some repute) notched a point.

It must not be thought that, because 'A' team did not score, their play was not up to the mark. Although they could not break the defence, they deserved to obtain at least one goal, and it was only the fine goalkeeping of Cotton that prevented this.

Goalkeeper Dobbin made some good saves, and the shots he did succumb to, he had not a chance with. Perry was an efficient back and was well partnered by Hagger. The halves were a good trio; Emery shining brightly.

The forward quintet played exceedingly well; Halse, the centre forward, playing a ripping game. Jack, the manager, on the outside left was smartly on the ball, and his play was much admired. Altogether the match was a very creditable start for the 'footer' season, and the gate was a very good one.

I understand that after the match, Newland, Emery, Cotgrove, Hagger, Finn, Ellis, Dobbin, and Butler were signed on. I am further told that the management were very much taken with the display of Newland, and that they also smiled graciously on Finn and Emery.

The team against Swindon Town will not be picked until Thursday night, but I hear it is likely to be the strongest available, and the local men are confident of doing themselves justice.

The attendance on Saturday (850) was very satisfactory, and I expect to see thousands present at the opening match.

Saturday, September 1st, 1906
Southern League, Second Division
SOUTHEND UNITED 0, SWINDON TOWN RESERVES 1
'the first competitive match'

Southend has seldom, if ever, seen such exciting football as was witnessed at Prittlewell on Saturday, when the United opened their Southern League programme with Swindon Town reserves as opponents.

The game was brimful of exciting incidents from beginning to end, interest not flagging one bit. Certainly Swindon won by 1-0, but this, in not the slightest degree gives an idea of the run of the game. Everybody was of the opinion that Swindon had good fortune to escape from a 3-1 defeat at the least. Everything seemed against Southend, and it was a marvel they did not score. It was not because shots were not well directed or easy, for they were both difficult and true.

Even the Swindon goalie, himself, admitted that his opponents were unfortunate; and he was entitled to express an opinion for it was he who saved Swindon right through. He was a marvel. Time after time he saved when 'goal' was on everybody's lips. It seemed impossible to penetrate that citadel while he was there, or while he was away on one occasion. How he saved the shots it is hard to describe, but he did and in a most wonderful fashion.

Southend started with bad luck from the commencement, and it followed them right through the innings. Halse was the most unfortunate one. He put in more shots than the rest of the side put together, and not many went astray, yet, no matter how difficult they were and how impossible they looked to save, the goalkeeper always reached them.

The locals played remarkably well and understand one another fairly of course, one could not expect to see them put forth their best, playing in such tremendous heat. It seemed absolutely cruel that the men should have to play on such a day. It was hot enough for cricket – and even uncomfortable sitting down watching. The sweltering players stuck fairly to the task in hand.

There was occasional weakness in the United's front rank. Holden, I understand, was in a position he is not used to – that is outside right – whilst Jack seemed to suffer from the heat at times. I can't see that the rest of the team can be improved upon, and, when the whole understand each other thoroughly, I am certain, and a prominent official of the Southern League who saw the game coincides with me, that it will take a rattling good team to beat the one which was put in the field against Swindon, providing they have ordinary luck.

Cotton only had about three goal kicks during the game, and the only difficult shot – the one which beat him – was a low trimmer which he could not get to. It was extraordinary to think that Swindon should have succeeded in this fashion, when Southend had been trying practically three quarters of the time without avail, Cotton had no chance to show his qualities, but the two backs were in fine fettle; kicking cleanly and with good judgment. The halves were a trio of hard and tricky workers and they had their opponents well in hand. It was a treat to see them at work, especially the A's late skipper. He played a rattling game.

Freeman has an action almost the same as Owen. Several times I mistook him for Harry. Johnson held his wing – a tricky one – splendidly, and seldom did they beat him. The forwards combined well and shot often, but they could do a little more of it. Halse was a little Jack in the box, though playing with an injured toe right through the game. Watkins is clever with his feet, but could shoot more often with advantage. Mitchell is a fine little player, who helps his centre splendidly. Holden is smart, but being on the wrong wing, no doubt handicapped him. Jack played a good game, but he, too, could get rid of the sphere quicker at times. Nevertheless, despite these criticisms, the team is one which, before the season has advanced very far, Southend will be proud of.

Swindon had to thank their goalie and backs for carrying off the game. The forwards appeared weak, with the exception of Coates in the centre, and Kidd at inside right. They were bottled up by the United halves, while, on the other hand, Swindon could not hold the opposing quintet in, and the main responsibility rested with the backs, who played nobly and well. They and the goalie understood each other thoroughly, and to that can be attributed a great deal of their success.

The game commenced briskly; the United getting down quickly by means of some clever passing. Swindon beat them back several times, but the United were fighting determinedly with the intention of scoring – an intention which, however, they were not allowed to carry out. A shot came across from Holden, the goalie fumbled, and Halse was smartly on the scene. He got the ball from him, dodged, but was then almost on the post. He tried to screw the ball round, but, to the home supporters' annoyance, it defied his efforts and insisted on going just outside the post.

This was Halse's first intimation that he was in for an unlucky time. He tried again a little later. When running right through, absolutely master over the movements of the leather, he seemed certain to score. Warman got back and Halse tricked him, and drove in a shot which Warman intercepted with his back. Time after time at this period of the game, the United, given only a particle of luck, should have scored, but Hemmings brought off saves which took away one's breath. Nobody but could admire his qualities, and he came in for rounds of applause.

Jack received the ball at close quarters with a good opening. He waited – minutes it seemed to some – before he did anything. He stood still for the approach of a player, but then neatly tricked him and shot; the goalie jumping and touching over the bar. The United were beaten back from the corner kick, but Jack got the sphere once more and transferred it to the centre, where Halse did not wait; shooting hard for the corner of the goal. Like a flash the goalie was at it, reaching across and pulling it down. Regaining his balance, he hooked it round and cleared. It was a fine piece of work.

Halse did not relish these reverses and tried again to penetrate. This time he made use of a fast ground shot, but Hemmings put that out of danger again. Johnson sent in a pretty dropping shot, which the goalie touched over the bar. The homesters returned again after a brief spell; the quintet working on business-like methods and making capable headway. Suddenly, Jack slung a pass to the centre, where Holden, close in, made a great blunder and shot high over the bar.

Despite the attempts of the visitors to relieve the pressure, they could not do so; Southend keeping them well in their own territory. A smart bit of combination was seen among the home forwards, but all at once it stopped and Halse raced away like a hare. He had seen this opportunity and taken it. He was nearly through, but several players had seen his move and were on him, a melee ensuing. Still he got in an effort; the custodian bringing off a brilliant save.

Swindon at last attacked, but it was of short duration, and not one which taxed the efforts of the Southend defence to any extent. Jerry stopped a nice shot close to goal, and sent the leather down to Jack who soon made tracks. He had only a back and the goalie in front, and when some distance from the citadel, passed across, but Jones, Swindon's right back who was playing a splendid game, got to it and cleared. Jack tried hard to score, and banged in a lightning shot, which, thanks to the goalie, Swindon did not see enter the net.

Play was confined to midfield for some time, till Southend ultimately secured the upper hand again and forced a corner. This was taken by Jack, and, from it, Owen got in a hard shot, which received similar treatment to all preceding efforts. Holden shot over again a little time after, then Halse made another desperate attempt. He was doing nearly all the shooting, and here he slammed in a fast low shot. 'Goal' some had on their lips, but the utterance was stifled by a groan, when, in miraculous fashion, Hemmings got his fist down to the ball and punched away; Watkins bowling the goalkeeper over.

Half-time score: 0-0.

The players retired from the field looking half-cooked.

With the sun in their faces, the homesters took charge again and beat down all opposition until the last rank was reached, when Warman stopped a pretty combined movement. Jack, very shortly after this, received from Freeman, and, tricking his opponents smartly on the way, made for goal. At close quarters he sent the leather across the front. Holden shot, and, although the players appealed for goal, the referee did not allow it; the goalie having saved in the nick of time. Jerry came into prominence now and stopped a rush finely. Kidd, a neat little player, whose dribbling was very smart, got through, and, by means of some clever movements, defeated several opponents, but he made a mistake when, with only one back to beat, he passed to a colleague, who was promptly pulled up for offside; Cotton saving the shot which was put in.

It was just after this that Swindon scored. They got down in a seemingly easy manner, and Coates romped through; banging in a stinging low shot which Cotton could not get to.

This awakened Southend, and from this time onward we saw practically a continual bombardment of the Swindon goal. Some of the incidents are impossible to describe, and one can little idea of what exciting times and hair breadth escapes there were. How the United failed to score is a miracle to me. Watkins had a fine opportunity to put his side on better terms, but it was a difficult one, and he shot behind.

Southend gave their supporters value for money; some pretty play being seen at this time. Freeman put across to Jack, who, after making the way a little easier, passed to Watkins. The latter raced towards goal, and sent in a stiff, low shot which passed just outside the post. Freeman was hurt at this period, but, on play being resumed, Southend got well down. They were unable to close quarters, and play dropped off a little until Halse made a brilliant run. He is a player who grasps opportunities as soon as they present themselves. He beat his opponents with some tricky footwork, and, passing the last back, Jones, shot hard. It was one of his favourite efforts with which he generally scores, low down by the post. Like a flash the goalie was at it again and saved on the ground. The United seemed to have new life, and the players worked together with a will.

There was no rest for Swindon, for they had all their work to keep themselves together. Holden, who had improved as the game proceeded, now sent a well-judged pass to Halse, who drove it towards goal, but the sphere was returned. There was a rush for the goal, and exciting incidents occurred all in a heap. The goal and the vicinity were crowded with players; one team with one object, the other with the reverse. How eager was the crowd, almost bursting with enthusiasm, thinking their favourites could do aught else but score. Jack got separated from the scrimmage and the ball came his way. He lifted it over the heads of the struggling players towards goal. 'Well, I'm blowed,' said one, as the sphere skidded along the crossbar into play again. Holden returned it, but the leather rebounded to Halse, who slammed in another hot shot, which just went behind.

It was an exciting few minutes. Another spell occurred almost directly after. A stiff shot came from the right wing. Hemmings saved finely, but rushed out after the ball to clear. He partially succeeded, but, whilst he was away, a ripping shot, which looked like going in under the crossbar, was sent from the centre. A fraction of a second would have done it, but Jones jumped up and headed away. Another shot was sent in, but caught the legs of a Swindon player.

Then Jack tried again, but this time Swindon breathed freely, for the ball rolled behind. The relief was very short, for Halse banged in again, but the ball rebounded off a player. Watkins received and put in a low effort. The goalie crouched and ran along to reach it. He succeeded in just tipping it round the post. After Southend had missed the upright again, by inches, the whistle went.

SOUTHEND UNITED: Cotton; Thomson and Molyneux (captain); Johnson, H. Owen, and Freeman; Holden, Mitchell, Halse, Watkins, and Jack.

SWINDON TOWN RESERVES: Hemmings; Warman and E. A. Jones; E. Jones, Oakden (captain), and Innes; Oakley, Reynolds, Coates, Kidd, and Saunders.

Saturday, December 29th, 1906
Southern League, Second Division
SOUTHEND UNITED 4, SALISBURY CITY 2

The United players have experienced many changes this holiday season as regards weather. On Saturday week they turned out at Wycombe on a hard frosty ground, on Monday at Millwall in damp weather and on a greasy ground, Tuesday morning was a fine, sunny and healthy one, and on Wednesday thick snow covered the playing pitch. On Saturday, when they met Salisbury City in the Southern League (Division II), a thaw had set in, but the ground which had been partially cleared of the snow was greasy and dangerous. Being a light team, however, the United did not take badly to the conditions.

Southend won the toss and got away directly. A pass was sent up to Halse and thus early in the game we saw him take the opportunity that presented itself. Sprinting away, he eluded Robbins. Stead ran out, but Halse easily beat him with a deft touch past. It seemed an easy goal, but it was not the goal that appealed to the spectator. It was the alertness which preceded it that told.

City replied gamely, their short passing being pretty to watch, but in front of goal they were weak. Owen kicked clear and the United made away. A well directed pass went out to Holden, who, after drawing the defence, centred accurately, but the ball was intercepted and cleared. Burns, the old Southampton player, who is in the Army now, obtained possession and dribbled smartly down, tricking a couple of opponents before he sent out to Parker. The latter centred, but Molyneux headed clear.

A fine run by Holden culminated in a well judged centre. Mitchell rushed up and, being tackled, put back to Johnson. In turn he transferred to Blott and the old Athletic player slung across. Axcell and Halse were ready to receive. Halse drove in, but Robbins intercepted the effort and Axcell replied off the rebound with a high shot, but Stead saved finely and threw the ball out to the wing.

A moment later Blott dropped in another centre and a hot grounder from Halse was cleverly gathered by the City goalie. The United were not to be frustrated in their designs and again came up to the attack; the halves following up well and picking up dropped passes neatly. Suddenly Halse was set going again, and deftly tricked Robbins before he sent in. It was a fast bouncing shot that hit the upright, and Stead, misjudging the distance, had thrown himself flat to save. As it was, the ball passed behind.

The visitors were clever at dribbling. By means of a combining run, Parker dropped in a high centre. It was nearly successful, Burns heading smartly in, but Cotton had 'all his eyes' open and coolly saved. The visiting right wing were being constantly fed, but Freeman and Molyneux were generally able to deal with that dangerous pair. Not long after the City attacked again and the ball travelled backwards and forwards from one wing to another in front of the goal mouth in bewildering fashion. It seemed that every moment a City man would dart up and pop the sphere through, until Jerry cleared with a sure kick. Blott was set going and in quick time was well down the field. Robbins caught him up, but Blott waited for him to pass and shot as the ball was trapped by his opponent. The effort went behind.

The visitors returned and Cotton saved a shot from the right, but in doing so was charged over in the goal mouth by Monk and Burns. A free kick for impeding relieved the pressure.

Holden gave a delightful run. Tricking three opponents in grand style, he drove in a fine left-footed shot, which skimmed along towards goal. Stead punched down as it passed, and Johnson received and sent back a ripping high shot, which sailed just over. Directly after Axcell sent in a warm effort. Halse, playing as well as ever, dodged away again. Touching past an opponent, he got to the ball and slammed in a good shot, which he saw saved. Mitchell followed directly after by putting by. Blott tried a high cross shot, which Stead, who was showing fine form in goal, fisted away. After one or two chances had been missed by the United, some interesting headwork occurred at close quarters to the City goal, the result of a well-placed kick by Molyneux. Mitchell put a stop to the display by tipping to Axcell and that smart little player slipped through and netted with a fast low shot.

Half-time: Southend 2, Salisbury, 0.

On the resumption, it was expected that, playing down the slope, Salisbury would give a good account of themselves. They went down directly; a correct pass finding its way out to Yates. Thomson, however, robbed him neatly, and Molyneux relieved pressure on the left.

Blott was seen suddenly to get possession and at rare pace dashed away. He beat Douley and Robbins smartly, and, dribbling close up, drove easily past Stead. The next moment, from another pretty run, Halse got past at short range. Five minutes of the second moiety had not gone when a hot shot well up by the crossbar was tipped over by the goalie and a corner accrued from it. Johnson headed in quickly. Stead caught the ball and to his dismay referee Aylott gave a goal for drawing over the line, although the goalie made an energetic appeal.

The United brought more pressure to bear and a spurt by Halse looked like reaping reward, but after brilliantly eluding a couple of players he lost. Dashing back after it, he set Holden going and the sprightly left-winger raced away and banged in a hot high shot. Stead saved with difficulty. The leather went out to Johnson, who drove back one of his specials. It was a flying kick, and the sphere whizzed just over the crossbar with hardly an inch to spare.

A sudden run by Burns made the home defence alert. He put the ball between Jerry and Molyneux, but the latter promptly stepped in front of him and raced for the ball, keeping his man off until Cotton rushed out and kicked clear. Axcell made a nice run and tricked Meston but shot by. Holden was centring well and the efforts were being dealt with capably. Halse hit the crossbar and Axcell followed a little later with a hot drive past.

Holden made another fast run. Away he went at rare pace, beating his opponents and, getting into good range, he shot hard. The ball shook the outside of the net. Owen set Halse to work and the nippy centre sent across to Holden, who dribbled strongly and shot along the ground. Stead gathered and cleared. He distinguished himself in dealing with a stinging effort by Axcell, after that player had executed a tricky movement. A foul against the United close in was dangerous, but Axcell intercepted the free kick and the ball rebounded towards the corner. Cotton raced out, but was promptly hustled by Burns. The latter tried to hook the sphere round, but it travelled behind.

The visitors made a united attack and all came up. Meston, the left back, decided to do a little forward work and rushed along. His presence was welcomed, and a pass was driven by him hard in along the floor to the far corner and Cotton was beaten. Directly after the home goalie made a clever clearance. He got smartly to a stiff shot, pulled it down, dodged several opponents, and then kicked out of touch with a host round him.

The United made away again and Mitchell tested Stead with a fast grounder, which he saved skilfully. Jerry next tried a long shot and the City custodian once again saved, this time with difficulty. Halse, set going by a judicious pass from Owen, dribbled scientifically past Robbins and finished up with a sharp stinging grounder. Stead gathered and punted away. Molyneux kicked up the field and Halse was seen at work again. He touched past Robbins and centred, but Mitchell missed the open goal.

The visitors made the last few moments of the game fairly lively and a clever run by the front rank saw a fast pass go to Burns, locally known as 'Jock,' who made no bones about the final effort and netted with a high rising drive. Result: Southend United 4, Salisbury City 2.

SOUTHEND UNITED: Cotton; Thomson and Molyneux (capt.); Johnson, Owen, and Freeman; Blott, Axcell, Halse, Watkins, and Holden.

SALISBURY CITY: Stead; Robbins and Meston; Douley, Metcalf, and Wentworth; Parker, Monk, Burns, Cavendish, and Yates.

Tuesday, January 1st, 1907
Friendly Match
SOUTHEND UNITED 2, MILLWALL 1

Although Millwall did not bring down the team advertised to meet the United, they travelled to Prittlewell with a strong combination; such players as Joyce, Aitken, Waterson, Comrie, Riley and Twigg who were in the side that was defeated by Reading on Saturday being included. They were trying a new man at centre forward, Smith by name, and a Scotchman of the robust type. He kept well in touch with both wings. Hunter and Dean who figured prominently in the Millwall attack against the biscuit team were both absent; their positions being filled by Millar and Milson. The home team was altered and Axcell took the place of Mitchell at inside right. The ground was extremely heavy and, as it was, the speed that was so frequently shown appeared marvellous.

The result 2-1 is likely to give a wrong impression. Millwall had numerous opportunities but their shooting, taking it right through, was decidedly poor. Despite that you must not suppose that Cotton was not kept at work suppose for he was much busier than Joyce, but has never been seen in better form at Prittlewell. Seldom has he been tried more, and talent which may have been lying dormant, was exercised to a great extent. He dealt coolly, yet smartly with the efforts that came his way and always chose the right moment to flurry an opponent.

The forwards played fine combination. Blott was the weak spot, but in Aitken he had an opponent made of stern and tough material. Axcell was the hero of the piece, but this was mainly through the attention paid to Halse. The Dockers, Comrie, Aitken and Co. failed to realise the fact that there was another who could ram home an attack almost as well as the little ex-Wanstead centre. The latter does his duty wonderfully well, and his name is prominent at present. That might have been the cause of the worrying tactics of the Dockers towards him. Suffice it to say he was given very little chance of doing anything great.

Axcell made up for this and sprung into a conspicuous position by bagging the brace of goals. Watkins, playing against his old love, gave a delightfully free game; his footwork and coolness in attack being brought out more than ever. Holden on the left revelled in the mud, and in company with 'Wattie' gave a clever display. These two players work well together. Holden, who has taken the position held by Axcell, plays a powerful game and hangs on to the ball where Axcell would get rid of it, but he has a delightful way of tricking an opponent and never gives up an attempt to get the ball until it is absolutely out of his reach. Axcell is like a terrier sometimes, but he has not that stubbornness – or it does not appear to be exhibited – of Holden's.

The halves were good, and very little could be chosen between them. Owen put in some clever work, whilst Johnson's vigorous tactics were successful. He is an untiring worker and compares favourably with his elder colleague, the good natured Freeman. The backs had difficult work, and the quick, fast and clever Dockers forwards found two sturdy fellows, capable of meeting them in a pitched fight. Joyce was as safe as a rock in goal. His arms closed round the ball as if it had fallen into a place specially prepared for it and his goal looked to be impregnable, and although he was beaten twice neither shots were efforts he had a chance of saving.

The backs were a fast pair, but in dealing with Axcell and Halse used somewhat questionable tactics, which the referee would have done well to notice. Waterson was very fast. Milson on the right was another clever player, whilst the other wing was well balanced by the play of Brown, who is a bewildering little dribbler. He has the idea of wing play and his centres are deadly. The success of the United lay in the fact that they were quick to snatch a chance as soon as it presented itself and rush away immediately, and the way Axcell took his opportunities was gratifying, Jimmy being warmly applauded. The forwards kept together well; the passing being well executed.

The home team started down the slope and after several exchanges the United suddenly made away; a pretty bout of passing taking place between Owen, Axcell and Blott on the right, but the latter tipped out of touch.

Millwall replied to this with a dash, passing being clever. Dean concluded the performance with a shot over, after steadying himself for the effort. Brown made a clever dribble past Owen and Thomson, but shot weakly at close range and Cotton saved.

Watkins suddenly gave Halse an opportunity and the centre darted away, passing Aitken quickly, then, to everybody's surprise – the whistle went. In reply to the crowd's query, 'offside' was given. Brown a tricky left winger with hair of Saxon colour, was making things hum on the left.

The United scored their first goal at this period. A dart by Halse saw the defence drawn and a slip through to Axcell was productive. He scuttled away and with Aitken in front of him, shot. The ball just skimmed the back's foot and Joyce, with his view obstructed, did not see the shot and made no attempt to save.

A moment later Axcell got another in, but Joyce put his arms round the ball like the hug of a bear. A couple of attacks were beaten out. Holden sent in a fine high cross shot, which Joyce judged exactly and punted away and a hot long drive from Watkins was met with terrific force by the same player.

Southend had their second success from Axcell. The sturdy little player got possession and made a clever run. Tricking several opponents, he went through on his own. Although the form of the famous goalie seemed to fill the goal, Axcell made no mistake, and shot low, to the right of him. Joyce threw himself flat, but the ball had gone by and Southend were two up.

Millwall were sore about this and attacked strongly, but, although a corner was forced, the leather was headed over. They were playing a fine forward game on the heavy ground; the passing being exact and well-timed and the dribbling of a high order. Thomson excelled himself in several breaking-up performances.

A grand piece of work by Brown nearly came off. He made away on the left at good speed and, being tackled by Thomson, banged hard across to the right. The referee got in the way and intercepted the effort and the sphere went back to Brown, who swung across again. The ball descended near the far upright and Dean tried to boot it in, but Molyneux, with a lightning spring, got the leather to his head and put to corner. Nothing came of this.

Holden got a pass from Halse and, tricking Riley, banged in a warm shot at the burly Joyce, but he dealt calmly with it. Play had been fairly even and, although the Millwall forwards were very smart and the halves capable, they could not score. The backs were a strong pair and the attention they paid to Halse proved they realised his worth. Passes innumerable were intercepted when they were intended for him. It was cat watching mouse and Halse found great difficulty in making use of opportunities.

Johnson stopped Brown splendidly, but Millwall were back and their front rank work dazzling. Fast low passes and clever footwork were the features, but they invariably finished up badly, or else Cotton distinguished himself with a smart save. Half-time: Southend 2, Millwall 0.

On the resumption we saw a fine rush away by Halse. He seemed to be waiting for just one chance, and directly it came he went like a hare. One of his opponents raced along beside him, and, apparently unseen by the referee, put his hand behind his shoulder in an attempt to throw him. Halse was thus put off the shot, and a little later a grand centre was punted at with a terrific effort by Halse, but he raised it and a shot by Axcell made Joyce throw himself full length to screw round the post.

The Dockers were now beginning to make things hum around the home goal and the ball bounced dangerously around. Several hot drives went by, but Cotton dealt safely with two long shots. A fast pass forward was made by Thomson, but the ball skidded like a flash past him. Twigg raced by, but Cotton came forward and kicked hard out of touch.

The Dockers were playing a bustling game now. The forwards were seen in a slight haze slipping on the greasy ground, dodging and dribbling, yet all the time keeping fine control over the slimy sphere.

A lightning movement by this rank nearly proved fruitful, for, getting right down, Millar had the goal practically at his mercy, but Cotton dashed across his goal and threw himself forward like an avalanche. Millar was forced to shoot and the ball rebounded off Cotton's foot back again to the sharpshooter and behind. Cotton's feet close together at such a range – not six inches – was an effectual barrier.

Raise was seen to make another dash away. He was abreast of Aitken in a flash and looked like passing him, when the artful Millwaller let Joyce do the work of banging back. Axcell got away with Halse and the latter left him in a good position. He drove hard, Joyce punched it down, and, picking up again, kicked to midfield.

A fascinating movement by Axcell, Halse and Watkins would only have wanted another six inches to touch the net. Axcell and Halse combined prettily, and Watkins, unattended, was left with a correct pass. He drove in hard; the leather going just by the upright. Blott shot by the next moment. Then Cotton's qualities as a goalie were again brought to the front, and he dealt capably with several stinging and dangerous efforts.

The result was certain now. Millwall could not get the two in the time that was left them, although they were making vigorous efforts to do so. They were playing the one back game, but Southend soon fell in with the conditions. Blott slung across a centre, and Watkins, dashing up without a man on him, went to meet the ball. We all expected a great shot, but Watkins just skimmed the ball sufficiently to put it behind the post.

A fine run by Holden, who, despite an appeal for offside, raced on, saw him get a fine shooting range. Joyce, upon whom the whole duty of saving devolved, crouched for the shot. Holden slammed in, Joyce fell to his knees and saved the fast drive that the left winger put in.

Directly after, Millwall went away with great spirit. Travelling strongly along, they worked within close range, and a hard shot from Twigg reached the net. Final score:– Southend 2, Millwall, 1.

Teams:

SOUTHEND: Cotton; Thomson and Molyneux; Johnson, Owen, and Freeman; Blott, Axcell, Halse, Watkins, and Holden.

MILLWALL: Joyce; Waterson and Aitken; Riley, Comrie, and Hughes; Milson, Millar, Smith, Twigg, and Brown.

Monday, April 22nd, 1907
South Eastern League, Second Division
Depot Battalion, Royal Engineers (Chatham) 0, Southend United 5

The United have only one more South Eastern League fixture, that with Tunbridge Wells, on Saturday. On Monday they made their position as champions of the South Eastern League secure by defeating the Depot Batt. Royal Engineers by their favourite score of 5-0: Halse scoring four (and his 88th) and Blott one. This was not a bad defeat upon this team, considering New Brompton, with a full eleven out, could only draw with them last week. Even should the United lose their remaining match with Tunbridge Wells, which is unlikely, they will still hold the title they have won by virtue of their goal average.

Admission prices for second eleven fixtures were: 4d. (ladies, soldiers in uniform and boys 2d.), 4d. extra for transfer to enclosure and stand.

Saturday, September 21st, 1907
F.A. Challenge Cup, Preliminary Round
Southend United 3, East Ham 0
Southend's first F.A. Cup-tie

On Saturday afternoon, the United met East Ham at Root's Hall, in the preliminary round of the English Cup. It was a hot afternoon, and it is doubtful whether the players would not have rather reposed in the 'shade of the old apple tree.' There were about 3,000 spectators present; the clubs being represented as follows:–

Southend: Cotton; Thomson and Molyneux; Emery, Owen and Axcell; Newland, Frost, Halse, Wilson and Jack.

East Ham: G.H. Hobart; W.A. Webbe and A.E. Taggart; S.D. Webbe, J. Parley and R. Martineau; A.E. Larder, B.J. Dover, W.S. Tyler, A.E. Scanes and S.E. Riley.

Referee, Mr. G.W. Walker, Luton.

Molyneux led his men on a few minutes before the advertised time of the kick-off, amid applause, followed a little later by East Ham in white jerseys, who also had a cordial reception. The coin was quickly in the air, and a cheer announced that the home skipper had beaten W.A. Webbe in the toss. Molyneux elected to defend the town goal, with the sun in his opponents' eyes. Play opened in midfield, until the United obtained a free. The United's captain placed well but W.A. Webbe headed away. Wilson centred across goal, which caused Hobart to run out. Frost dispossessed him, but put wide. A moment later, the custodian and the Grays man had a race for the leather, which cannoned off Wilson, going outside. Scanes worked nicely through, but the chance was lost by Tyler getting off-side. Jack fired in a good half volley, which hit the side net. Then Scanes caused Cotton to run out and field a long drive. Up to now the amateurs had been showing good form, with plenty of resource; some of their touches being neat.

Owen transferred to Jack, who in turn centred finely, the ball going out to Newland, who had a grand chance. He dallied too long, and Taggart covered an unprotected goal, and got his head in the way of the shot. Some long kicking from back to back was next witnessed, until Owen was fouled, and a free kick was taken by Molyneux, from which Newland hit the side of the meshes. Larder, for East Ham, made a nice sprint, finishing up with a commendable try, which earned cheers, and Jack performed a similar feat at the visitors' end. Southend's territory was then invaded, but Emery smartly robbed Scanes. Halse got Newland going, and the winger dropped beautifully into goal; but the custodian punched away. After Owen had been responsible for prettily tricking three opponents, East Ham got a bye. Then, after seventeen minutes play, the United cheered the hearts of their supporters by scoring a goal, to the accompaniment of loud cheers.

Frost passed the ball a long way in front for Halse to take. Hobart ran out and secured the leather, but Halse darted at him, upset him, and made him lose the sphere. Wilson secured it, and took pot aim at an open goal; the ball striking the right hand upright and going into the net. The cheers had scarcely died away, when two minutes later, Halse threaded his way through. He was tackled by W.A. Webbe and Taggart, but emerged from the struggle and touched the sphere past Hobart a second time. Two goals in two minutes, was following in the same footsteps as they served Tunbridge Wells Rangers. After this, the United forced two corners, but pressure was relieved by Newland putting over. Thomson was next conspicuous in breaking up two rushes by the visitors; the second time finishing up with a shot which just missed the post. The East Londoners were next prominent in some nice passing, which was nullified by Larder getting off-side. Returning to the attack, Scanes shot across the goal, but the home skipper intervened and kicked down the field.

Jack finished up a capital run by shooting just past the upright. S.D. Webbe smartly took the sphere off Wilson when in the act of taking aim. Some neat work between the home quintet was seen, and Jack missed the crossbar by a very narrow margin. A second later, Taggart intercepted Frost, only in the nick of time. For the Hammers, Riley beat Emery, and centred well, but Dover, who was up, did not accept the situation, and Axcell nipped in and relieved. Some fun was next seen as the visitors made a determined, but somewhat unwieldy, attack on the home citadel. Scanes had a good opportunity of getting through but dallied and in a general mix up, Emery emerged with the ball. Hobart was called upon to run out and clear, and this he did; at the same time receiving unceremonious attention from the home pivot.

Halse got in a fast left foot shot which Hobart successfully dealt with, and the ball, being sent back, he had to concede a corner from Jack. This was ballooned away by W.A. Webbe. Frost and Halse had pops at goal, with no further result. Then the game was temporarily stopped owing to Frost hurting his foot, but he soon resumed, although limping. The whistle then brought about a short cessation of hostilities with the score sheet: – Southend United, 2 East Ham, 0.

Upon the resumption, the sun was still shining brightly, now in the faces of the homesters. This did not deter them, however, and a free enabled Halse to all but get through. A brief incursion to the home territory followed, but Thomson was again the stumbling block. A spell of midfield play followed, until Jack again changed the venue. He centred in, Halse touched to Wilson, who quickly transferred back. The visitors appealed for off-side, but the Southender ran through, shooting into the far corner of the net, with Hobart standing helpless. Still on the aggressive, Jack, with a fine screw in, caused Hobart to handle, and Wilson, with a praiseworthy drive, grazed the upright. Off-side on the part of Scanes spoiled a break-away by the Londoners.

Halse judiciously fed Jack, and the 'Manager' dropped in a beautiful shot, which Hobart scrapped out from under the bar at the expense of a flag kick. Two further corners resulted, all accurately placed by Jack. The amateurs then had a turn, and Cotton fielded a long one. Halse gave Owen a chance, but the centre-half shot over. Some exciting scenes were next witnessed in the East Ham goal. Halse and Hobart had a run for the sphere, but the goalie just scraped away. The leather was returned, and at close quarters Wilson put into Hobart's hands. He saved at the expense of a corner, but Jack, on the alert again, drove in low and straight. The goalkeeper had a warm handful, and had to concede another corner. This was a signal for a hot bombardment of the visitors' goal for some minutes.

Jack again placed the flag kick right under the bar, and Halse shot into Hobart's hands. Newland got in a fine middle, from which the goalie saved from Wilson. Jack, who was 'hot' stuff and was in fine form, twice executed clever runs and finished up with fast low drives. On each occasion the defender of the citadel had to turn the sphere round the upright. Molyneux also had a shy at goal, and Hobart was called upon to fist away. Jack was next neatly pulled up by W.A. Webbe, which caused the ball to go to the other end. Tyler had an open goal, but he did not seem to know what to do with the ball, and kicked wildly; danger being thus averted. Newland raised the crowd's encomiums by a commendable sprint up the wing, and an equally good shot, which Hobart knocked down, and Parley relieved with an overhead kick.

A corner which fell the United's way was nicely taken, and in the ensuing melee, the ball was rushed the wrong side of the post. Larder careered away on the right, but, although he middled well, no one was up to meet it. Some nice combination was the next noticeable feature among the Blues' vanguard, which ended by Newland shooting in at lightning-like speed, the ball running along the crossbar and going over, nearly bringing about the downfall of an overzealous photographer, to the great amusement of the crowd. Frost was in a scoring position when Martineau took the ball from his toe. Jack again deserved to score with a fine drop into goal, but Hobart was there, and Wilson, paying over much attention to him, he was penalised for impeding. After Wilson had had another abortive attempt, the United had two more corners, both of which were fruitless.

From another capital middle by Jack, Frost just headed the wrong side of the post, and Southend's nimble pivot, taking a pass from Newland, narrowly missed adding to the total. A nice forward movement placed Frost with the ball and only the goalkeeper to beat, but he shot miles over the bar. In the last seconds, Halse received from Newland, but fired point blank at him, and the sphere rebounded off him. With nothing wanted but a gentle touch, Wilson, who was standing almost under the bar, shot over amid cries of 'Oh.' Nothing more of interest was done, and the final solo sounded.

Wednesday, December 18th, 1907
South Eastern League, First Division
CROYDON COMMON 7, SOUTHEND UNITED 1

Southend Standard report
Southend United came an awful cropper at Croydon on Wednesday, whence they journeyed with a weak team to play their return South Eastern engagement. The score was seven to one against the Blues; the Croydon men getting ample revenge for the two defeats which had been inflicted on the South Londoners previously this season. In September the United won at Croydon 3-0 in a Southern League match, and at Southend, 2-0 in a South Eastern fixture. Of late, Croydon have made great improvements in their ranks, and with the ground, which is an awful one, again against the United, the homesters, after leading 3-0 at the interval, put on four in the second moiety, whilst the seasiders could only reply once through Wilson.

Southend Telegraph report
After Wednesday's crushing defeat in the South Eastern League fixture at Croydon, the United have a hard struggle before them if they wish to reach the position they are aiming for the championship of the South Eastern League. The defeat of Wednesday is somewhat explained when it is understood that three of the goals were scored by the Blues' defence owing to misjudging a skidding ball. Two goals came from Emery's boot and one from Molyneux's – shots that Cotton could have saved, and a further point was added by Everest after he had fisted down unnoticed by the referee. Thomson was unable to play owing to an attack of muscular rheumatism. Emery and

Freeman did not play well together, Molyneux was hardly up to form, and Owen showed an inclination to dribble too much.

Wednesday, February 19th, 1908
United League
SOUTHEND UNITED 0, BRENTFORD 0

The game with Brentford, on Wednesday, was voted by those who saw it to have been one of the best contests seen at Roots Hall this season. The 'wasps' brought down their first Southern League team; the clubs being represented as follows:

SOUTHEND: Cotton; Thomson and Molyneux; Emery, Owen and Axcell; Harrod, Barrett, Little, Watkins, and Routs.

BRENTFORD: Williams; Watson and Clark; Jay, Hamilton and McAllister; Brown, Parsonage, Bowman, Corbett, and Underwood.

Despite the heavy going, the pace opened at a cracker; both ends being visited in quick succession. For Southend Harrod and Routs swung in centres with splendid accuracy, but the yellow and blacks' defence was in tip-top form. Little, Watkins, and Barrett all fired in hot shots, but Williams gave a fine display between the sticks. Both elevens showed good combination, and Underwood was exceedingly prominent for the visitors. He careered down the wing time after time, and Cotton again demonstrated what a capable goalkeeper he is by saving from Bowman and Corbett. The interval brought a welcome cessation of hostilities to the players.

The second half was equally well fought out, and despite valiant sorties on the two citadels, the defences came out of the ordeal with flying colours. For some time the United pressed, but Williams was ever on the alert. Harrod was a thorn in the side of the Brentford defenders, and he dropped in lovely centres time after time, while Routs was little behind him. About half way through the second moiety, Underwood nipped in a lovely centre, but Corbett, with only Cotton to beat, and standing about eight yards from goal, shot woefully wide. Thankful for this escape, the Blues retaliated, and a centre from Routs seemed likely to provide the much needed goal. Little received the ball within a few feet of him, but he somehow got the ball entangled between his feet, and only managed to get in a tame shot, which Williams easily saved. Towards the close, Brentford did more of the attacking, but the final solo arrived with the copy-book unblotted.

The Blues defence, as usual, was stronger than the attack, although at times the old war horse, Molyneux, was outpaced. What he lacked in this, however, he made up in judgment. Axcell signalled his re-appearance by a fine display, while Owen was in one of his most versatile moods, and Emery, although having a hot wing to hold, did his work very well. Harrod has quite justified the promise he already gave, and on Wednesday's form he seems to have filled the long-felt need of an outside right. Barrett was not in good form, being slow, while Little, in the centre, was extremely clever, but at times overdid it. He is not a really good shot, and at the close of Wednesday's game he was evidently fagged. Watkins was not seen to advantage, but the strain of so much play makes any delinquencies excusable. Routs again lent colour to the theory that that he is an outside left and not an outside right, and his centres and those of Harrod were quite a feature of the game.

Williams, in goal, is one of the best players in the South, while Watson and Clark are a reliable pair of backs; they are also very sturdy, being far too heavy for the Southend forwards. The halves were not a brilliant line; McAllister being the pick. Underwood was the most prominent forward, and his centres were always dangerous. He was, however, starved in the second half. Bowman I saw play for Aston Villa some six seasons ago, and after leaving the Claret and Blues, he went to Blackburn Rovers, leaving them for Brentford. He is a smart pivot; being quick with his head and feet, smart to perceive an opening, and a fairly good shot. Brown and Parsonage combined well together.

Easter Monday, April 20th, 1908
South Eastern League, First Division
SOUTHEND UNITED 3, WOOLWICH ARSENAL RESERVES 0

There was a crowd of over 4,000 at Roots Hall on Monday, on the occasion of the Arsenal Res. visit in the South Eastern League. It was a record attendance. The result, a win for the Blues by 3-0, showed the run of the play, taking the game throughout. 'Dits' Anderson, no doubt, attracted more than would otherwise have turned out, but he did not have much work to do, and was, therefore, unable to show his prowess. The teams were: –

SOUTHEND UNITED: Cotton; Thomson and Molyneux; Emery, Owen, and Freeman; Cotterill, Frost, King, Barrett, and Jack.

WOOLWICH ARSENAL RES.: Hopgood; Cross and Shaw; Bassett, Theobald, and Low; Anderson, Fuller, Elliott, Satterthwaite, and Rodger.

Molyneux lost the toss and had to kick down the slope against the wind. At the first run down Barrett tested Hopgood with a weak effort, and he saved. Arsenal then got away on the left, and Rodger slung in a nice centre to Elliott, who lost to Thomson. Barrett then made a fine dribble, and, taking the object past Bassett and Cross, forced a corner off the latter. There was some excitement from this, but Shaw cleared and the Reds came through; Rodger, however, meeting a pass heavily and Cotton kicked away.

The Reds were not long before they gave the Southend defence an anxious time, and with Thomson on the ground through collision with Rodgers, the inside men went prettily through until Elliott was left with an open goal, Harrod (not named in team line-up), however, was across like a flash, and with a hard kick sent to corner as Elliott was on the point of shooting. Quicker than it takes to write it down, the Blues were at the other end. A long kick ahead by King brought Hopgood out, and then there was a race between him, Frost, and Shaw. They all met at the same time. The custodian collided with Shaw and went down; the ball coming back to King. He drove back with his instep – wide.

The United tried another sortie, and with a well executed run they passed the intermediate line and Frost drove hard over the bar. There was very little difference between the teams, every line rivalling each other. Following upon a long pass forward, Satterthwaite and Elliott got away and were left with only Molyneux and Thomson in front. They made towards the latter, who, however, tackled finely and robbed him.

At the other end, King absolutely beat Hopgood with a fine drive at long range, but the ball hit the post and came out. Another well executed run saw Jack send across. Later the ball came out to Cotterill, who tapped back nicely, where King got his head to it. Hitting the post the ball rebounded onto the line and into the net. This came after twenty minutes play. Directly after Barrett drove a fine effort just past. Within five minutes, Barrett again missed by inches.

The Blues were now having the better of the game; the halves playing splendidly, whilst Molyneux and Co. were kicking and tackling with precision. Another advance due to a long kick by Molyneux drew Hopgood out again, with King racing for the leather. He got to it first and kicked out of touch. It was exactly half an hour after the commencement that the Blues' second point came. Owen gave a delightful exhibition of neat trickery and sent across to Cotterill, who centred at once, where Frost drove in. Hopgood should have saved, but, failing to do so, the leather entered the net, amidst another loud shout.

A corner conceded off Thomson culminated in some pressure being put upon the home goal, but a free relieved. Shaw was now defending grandly, and was rather more prominent than his partner. Owen was the shining light of the halves. He was getting through a tremendous amount of work, and he was seldom beaten; his tackling being really fine. Interval: – Southend, 2, Arsenal Res., 0.

The Arsenal re-arranged their forward line after the interval; Anderson taking his usual place in the centre and Elliott going outside right. Directly after the start Jack made three fast runs; all being dangerous. He slung in a couple of fine centres, the second being taken off King's foot by Cross and Barrett missed it as it came back. Another fine try by the Manager beat Hopgood as it flashed at an acute angle across the front, inches past the post. Thomson and Molyneux both robbed their respective wingers in turn, whilst the halves were doing their duty so capably that not a word of complaint can be made against them.

The men from Plumstead at last exerted themselves and a mistake occurred between Thomson and Cotton; the former keeping the man off for Cotton to take the ball, and the latter, evidently misinterpreting his designs, kicked weakly. Luckily there was plenty of screw on the ball, and it went back to corner. The kick proved exciting, but was cleared. After Barrett had driven in a hard shot that Cross felt as he headed away and saved a certain goal, the spectators were given an item that was not on the programme. A number of the crowd had gathered together on top of a shed and the sudden collapse of this caused the disappearance of many of them. There was a loud shout of merriment and the players stopped to watch the fun. Jack allowed himself to get offside whilst watching the scene, and that relieved the pressure that followed the accident. Directly after this, King was seen to dart past Theobald and race for the ball. Shaw took up the cudgels, but King gradually outpaced him. Rounding him, Shaw brought Cross with him, but these two failed to prevent the shot, and King had gone one more nearer his double figures.

The Reds now began to put more vigour into their efforts, and for a time had the better of the game. A hot shot from Fuller was saved by Cotton, but it dropped on the line, and he managed to clear at the second attempt. Rodger was next conspicuous, and, coming through, he was right under the bar, when Molyneux got his kick in and sent clear. Satterthwaite next shot behind with a fine opportunity.

Maidstone pressed, or rather the two men from that town did; King took up a pass, and, rounding Theobald, touched out to Cotterill, who was well up. These two went away together, and the run culminated in a capital centre that Shaw got to and put out of King's reach; Jack gaining a corner off Bassett from the rebound.

A pretty run, the left wing working like a machine, saw the Reds come down. Cotton caught the centre as Anderson was getting to it, and, rushing out, cleared.

At the other end, Barrett and King made good progress; the final tap from the former saw King turn and drive, Hopgood tipping over. Already, King was designated 'Halse' by the crowd, and he is certainly making a good second as regards shooting.

The Reds were back again, and Rodger, gaining possession on the left, lifted the object finely across; Cotton touching it off the post.

Play was getting fast again and journeys were frequent, but the defenders on both sides were equal to the occasions. Rodger kept trying some splendid shots, and Cotton had to concede another corner from that player. Following upon this, Cotton effected a clever clearance from a free kick, and then again Rodgers flashed into the picture taking a flying kick as a pass came across. Cotton saved grandly.

At the other end, Shaw was again worried, and Cotterill, putting him off the ball, left Frost to take it up, and that player, stopping it on the goal-line, centred finely, but Jack, after much hesitation, shot behind. Directly after Cotterill centred, but Barrett ballooned over the bar, and the final whistle came with the score: – Southend, 3. Arsenal Res. 0.

Tuesday, April 28th, 1908
Southern League, Second Division
WYCOMBE WANDERERS 1, SOUTHEND UNITED 4

There were still traces of the snow at picturesque High Wycombe on Tuesday, when the United paid their second visit to play their return fixture with the local Southern League club. The conditions were no better than on Saturday, when the snow was driving down, for there was a continual drizzle of rain and the ground was in a fearful condition. There were about twenty spectators when the game started; the result being a win for the Blues by 4-1.

Molyneux won the toss, and directly after the kick-off Jack and Watkins were busy; the former, receiving a touch from Watkins, sent a fine long shot from the touchline; Vickers punching away. Following this up, Cotterill got in a low drive from the other side, and Vickers again cleared.

For a moment or two there was a slight bombardment on the home goal, but, ultimately, this was ended by a long kick, and Wycombe were around the Blues goal; Cotton brilliantly saving a drive at close range from Pheby.

The going was extremely heavy – the pitter-patter was like so much music – and made work hard. Wycombe were playing the proper game under the circumstances, their forwards lying right on the Blues backs, thus harassing them, but Thomson and Molyneux kept their feet well upon the treacherous surface and kicked with wonderful precision.

Jack was responsible for the first miss. He received from Watkins and came right in past Toovey, but at close range shot wide.

The United then got away and a pretty attack was made. The ball was slung across to Frost, and that player, working an opening, slipped the ball through to King, who was soon past the defence. The custodian punched the shot away, and, later, Cotterill centred accurately; Watkins heading nicely towards the posts, but Vickers saved again.

Now the Blues began to settle down to the conditions, and Cotterill and Frost started a pretty game; the ex-Maidstone man sending in centres that always had an element of danger about them. Emery sent in a grand effort that dropped well in, and Vickers punched away again. King was putting in some pretty headwork, and twice he missed scoring by inches. Cotterill was working hard and well – dribbling smartly round his opponents time after time.

Wycombe, however, were often dangerous, and some half-back play by Tilbury and Roberts, who went to Stoke on trial recently, spoilt a good run. Langley, who was also with the Northern club, now made the pace on the right and drove a shot in that skimmed the crossbar.

At the other end, Watkins got in a couple of good efforts; the first, when he turned in a centre with his instep, was somewhat luckily saved.

The United were doing all the attacking, but the goal area in which they were working was in a very bad state, considerably worse than the top end, and the finish was poor.

Wycombe came up again at last, and, despite the stubborn defence of Molyneux and Thomson, they reached the eighteen yards area. Then the ball came across from Payne, and Harrod, going to tackle Langley, went down, and the winger was left with an open goal to shoot at, but his fast, low drive was splendidly saved by Cotton at full length.

After this, Jack was fed again, and went nicely down the wing with Watkins, and, receiving a final touch from him, sent back. King, as against the Arsenal, was put onside and netted with a high rising shot.

This was forty minutes after the start. Just before the interval Cotterill beat Buchanan and went on, but, when nearing the goal, was robbed by Toovey. Half-time: – Southend 1, Wycombe 0.

The United were the first away directly after the recommencement, and Jack, beating his half, slipped the ball through to Watkins, who, at an acute angle, drove for goal. Vickers failed to hold the fast effort and it slipped over his head, descending at the back of him. He turned and caught the object; running it up against the inside of the post. The ball touched the net, but the referee took no notice of the appeal, and a moment after gave King off-side when he received off an opponent at close range.

Although Wycombe were hard pressed, they were always ready for a burst, and their front line were speedy too.

They played a pretty combination game at times; Winters and Brown frequently being dangerous, but Thomson held them well in, with capable assistance from Emery.

The Blues second point was obtained ten minutes after the restart; Watkins running from just past the halfway line through the defence and shooting past Vickers, who had advanced to meet him.

Frost's was a fine goal five minutes after. He gained possession from Emery, and, dribbling in past Norman, he shot; the leather going like a rocket into the inside of the net and bouncing out again.

Directly after the locals made a well organised run; the left wing playing pretty football, but Pheby spoilt the run, which looked like materialising, by getting off-side. He netted, however.

In response, Jack, at the other end, drove in a terrific effort that beat Vickers and scraped the far-side post.

Ten minutes later, the United made another forward movement, and, following up a pass by Harrod, Watkins ran up and slipped the ball across, where Frost, touching past Buchanan, drove in under Vickers' uplifted leg. Cotterill was then prominent making a delightful run and beating player after player, finishing with a centre that was cleared. The ex-Maidstone winger made several smart recoveries upon the slippery ground.

Wycombe, at last, asserted themselves after a lengthy period of defence, and the forward line went away with a rush. Getting close in, they looked all right for a goal, and Roberts made it look still more an accomplished fact, for within twelve yards he made a great slash at the ball, and, on the instant Cotton's hands were up, and another brilliant save was effective.

Langley met it on the other side and drove hard across the front. A minute or two had passed, when Langley slung the ball across to the opponent's wing, where Payne, tackled by Emery, centred, and Pheby turned finely into the net. It was a good goal and well deserved. This acted as a stimulant upon the Wanderers, who now attacked with considerable energy, and there was some clean robust play.

The Blues steadily took the upper hand again and Frost was conspicuous; running through prettily and driving a shot against the goalie's legs. The rebound was met by Cotterill, who sent across, and King turned outside whilst off-side. The United were still attacking when the whistle went.

Saturday, October 17th, 1908
F.A. Challenge Cup, 2nd Qualifying Round
SOUTHEND UNITED 4, SHOEBURYNESS GARRISON 0

About five thousand spectators saw the game between Shoebury Garrison and Southend United, in the second round of the qualifying competition of the F.A. Cup, at Roots Hall on Saturday. Southend won by four-nil, a total they could have increased.

SOUTHEND UNITED: Cotton; Thomson and Molyneux, Emery, Owen and Blott; Birnie, Frost, Ronaldson, Wright and Jack.

SHOEBURY GARRISON: Salter; Chase and Kibbey; Johnson, Smith and Bradburn; Newland, Wake, Pritchard, Simnett and Parker.

The Garrison won the toss and kicked up the slope, Wake causing a false impression at the commencement of a real cup-tie game by at once slinging in a long shot. The United soon got to work, and Ronaldson gave Salter a warm shot to deal with, but the Garrison custodian was on the qui vive. Directly after he made a grand save from Jack while on the ground, and was quickly tackled by Frost and had to throw to corner. It was from this, five minutes after the start, that the Blues scored, Frost making the rigging bulge with a hard shot. The Soldiers played up pluckily and Wake sent Newland away with a fine pass, Jock centring splendidly. It was dangerous, and, with the line of forwards right up, Emery was lucky to clear off Thomson. Then the Blues settled down, and, served well by the halves, the front rank worried the visitors' backs, and Frost, who received from Ronaldson, gave Salter a warm shot to deal with, but the custodian again saved. Jack flashed past Johnson and drove in a stinger, but

Salter seemed to fill the goal, and he got to the shot and once more cleared. Simnett, by way of a change, tested Cotton with a beauty, and the Southend custodian had to punch over the bar. Simnett at this time was the best of the forwards, but Owen was playing splendidly at centre-half. Suddenly the United went down again, and Salter, when clearing, was charged by Frost, and a foul was awarded.

However, the Soldiers could not keep the professionals out for long, and Jack was soon sprinting towards goal again, and Ronaldson, trying to turn the centre, was brought to the ground. Newland was 'sent off' by Wake but Blott put a stop to his career and took the ball up, where it was ultimately transferred to Birnie, who zig-zagged down the wing and finally drove in a beautiful shot. Salter again sprang into the picture and saved grandly. But directly after he was beaten for the second time, Chase being penalised for bringing Ronaldson down in the area. Birnie took the kick and scored over Salter's head in the top of the net.

This success came after twenty minutes play. After this the United had matters practically their own way, and Jack and Wright performed prettily on the left, but Wright shot past. Then Birnie banged in a sharp centre, and Wright shot in under Salter's legs, but Chase nipped in and wildly kicked out when the ball was almost on the line. From a centre by Birnie, thirty minutes after the start, the trio of goals was completed, Jack tapping into the net. The Garrison made strong efforts to reply and gained a corner, but this was cleared, and the United returned, the pace being too hot for the Soldiers to stand. Kibbey and Chase were kicking finely now, and several times they were conspicuous in averting danger.

But they were not able to stop the opposing forwards every time. From a centre by Birnie, Ronaldson scored an off-side goal, but made up for it directly afterwards when he rushed forward and took the ball off Chase's toe and scored a fine goal. The Soldiers, taking advantage of the easing up of the home forwards, worked harder still, and Cotton had to jump across his goal and concede a corner from a high shot by Wake. From the scrimmage in front of goal, Wake injured his nose and had to be carried off, but nothing exciting occurred during his absence, and when he returned he got an ovation. His return acted as a tonic, and there was more bustle shown, but at the interval the score read: – Southend United 4, Garrison 0.

Upon the re-commencement it was seen Simnett had changed places with Pritchard, and it worked well. Ronaldson sent Birnie off with a long pass, but the winger's centre was cleared. Directly after Salter made a marvellous save from Wright, who drove in hard at close range but Salter's foot went out, and he turned the ball to corner. Some good work was put in by Frost and Birnie, but after an exciting tussle round the Soldiers' goal, the ball came out, and Newland was speeding down the wing the next moment. Molyneux failed to get in his kick and Newland centred finely, Thomson conceding a corner. The

United slackened considerably, and thus helped to make matters a bit more even, Johnson and Smith stopping Jack and Wright once or twice, and Kibbey also came round and robbed Jack when he had beaten Chase and Johnson. Simnett dribbled prettily, and then slammed in a capital shot which Cotton saved. Blott asserted himself, and, after beating Newland for the ball, raced up with it and centred, Frost failing to reach it.

Salter was still the shining artiste in the Soldiers' side and saved well from Jack and Frost in turn. Then the only good chance the Garrison had of scoring was missed by Wake, who kicked at the ball as if he wanted to get rid of it as quickly as possible. It went wide. The United might have increased the score, but Ronaldson and Blott tried to make amends by getting in a beauty. Directly after Wright narrowly missed scoring and Ronaldson tapped over Salter's head as he rushed out to clear. Chase, however, saved by rushing in and kicking over. Newland and Wake both tried shots before the close, but the Garrison had not been able to keep up the pace, and the Blues were making another attack, and Salter made his final save from Birnie as the whistle went. Southend 4, Garrison 0.

Saturday, November 21st, 1908
F. A. Challenge Cup 4th Qualifying Round
SOUTHEND UNITED 2, CROMER 0

The *Southend Standard* ran the following article on Cromer F.C.
The Cromer Football Club was formed in 1888 by a few football enthusiasts, of whom the President, Dr. H. C. Dent, was one. Coming to the year 1896, they joined the North Norfolk and Norwich League, and were winners on three occasions. In 1903 they joined the Norfolk and Suffolk League, and there are great hopes of them carrying off the championship this season, as up to the present they have not lost a match. Their record for the past three seasons, in the above league is 1905-06, third position; 1906-07, second position; and 1907-08, second position. The club have won the Cromer and Sheringham Charity Cup four times, played in the Norfolk Charity Competition several years, being finalists in 1904/05. They competed for the Norfolk Senior Cup, and in 1906/07 won the Lynn Hospital Cup. They are also holders of the 'Cromer' Lifeboat Cup.

This season Cromer have played nine matches, of which seven have been won, one drawn, and one lost, this being in the second round of the Amateur Cup Competition at Lowestoft, when Lowestoft won by the only goal of the match.

The goal average is 22 for 10 against. It will thus be seen that their record is such that any club might be proud of, and supposing their successes only to be local, the fact of them reaching the present stage of the English Cup competition is sufficient evidence that they are to be reckoned with.

On Saturday, at Roots Hall, Southend United and Cromer met to decide who would enter the final qualifying round of the English Cup competition. The fare provided did not prove much attraction, and the gate was only about 2,500.

The teams were represented as follows: –

SOUTHEND UNITED: Cotton; Axcell and Molyneux; Emery, Owen and Blott; Birnie, W. Peake, Ronaldson, Wright and Caldwell.

CROMER: T. Blogg; A.S. Cook and H. Bryant; A. Jenkinson, L. Syder and T. Randall; J. Palmer, J. Cutmore, H. Mann, C. Hurst and F. Griffin.

Referee: Mr. A.G. Arkell, London.

The spin of the coin was in favour of Molyneux and he decided to kick down the slope, with a slight breeze in the Norfolk men's favour. Cromer started in rather saucy fashion and Mann and Hurst led an attack only to be pulled up by Molyneux. Owen initiated a forward movement which resulted in the ball going to Ronaldson, who sent on to Wright. The inside-left whipped it back again, and Ronaldson shot well, but the leather passed across goal, just missing the far upright and going outside. Caldwell dropped in a judicious centre from which Wright tested Blogg with a terrific drive, but the custodian was equal to emergencies.

Later Wright looked like marking the score sheet, but Blogg scooped the sphere out, with Ronaldson paying him close attention. Birnie placed a corner admirably, from which Ronaldson secured and shot well, but the visitors' goalie again saved his citadel from downfall. Cutmore created somewhat of a diversion by racing away, but Cotton came out and punted up the field. After this Southend monopolised the play and were always hovering round the red and black's goal. Some clever footwork by Ronaldson and Wright saw the ball go out to Caldwell, who middled it accurately, but Peake headed wide. From a pass by Emery, Peake gave Ronaldson possession when well placed, but Bryant took the ball from him as he was getting through.

Cromer now carried play into the Southend territory and Cutmore fired a fast grounder at Cotton which he had little difficulty in dealing with. This acted as a tonic to the Blues and Birnie careered down the line and centred, and Wright seemed to be in a scoring position, but the ball was luckily intercepted by the back of one of the defenders. Peake snapped up a rebound off Cook's head a few yards from goal, but with only Blogg to beat he aimed wretchedly outside. Randall, to show that Cromer were not done with, gave Cotton a splendid shot to deal with right under the cross bar.

Birnie quickly changed the venue and shot finely but Blogg, by a superhuman effort, again saved his charge from downfall. Caldwell seized on the leather from the rebound and shot in, but Cook just saved as the ball was going through goal, at the expense of a corner. This resulted in Blogg again being called upon to clear his lines. The Blues forwards were now overdoing the passing game and the crowd were getting impatient for a goal. Peake sent the ball forward to Ronaldson and the pivot appeared to have the goal at his mercy, but drove the wrong side of the post.

Mann had a chance to get through for Cromer, but Axcell pulled him up at the expense of a corner. Palmer placed it well, but Cotton jumped up and fisted out. Birnie led another onslaught, but Blogg again intercepted his well placed centre and Caldwell seemed likely to open the scoring, but one of the backs managed to get the leather away.

Twenty-eight minutes had elapsed when Birnie gave Ronaldson a nice pass which the home centre took advantage of by beating Blogg with an oblique shot from short range. Scarcely had the ball been re-started when the Blues returned to the attack and Caldwell had a good try, but Blogg again frustrated his efforts. Soon after Ronaldson was manoeuvring the ball round, with no opponent near him, when he was suddenly seen to fall. He was carried off the field and it transpired he had twisted his ankle.

This left the Blues without a centre forward. Owen tried to dribble through, the ball eventually going to Caldwell, and Bryant miskicking, let in Peake, but Blogg managed to reach his shot and clear. Later Peake presented Wright with a clear opening, but he shot weakly outside, though it is only fair to say he was hampered by two opponents. Caldwell attempted to burst through and Bryant, in tackling him, got hurt and had to be carried off the field. The game was continued with ten men on either side and Wright centring, Peake got his cranium to the ball, only to divert it just wide. Half time arrived with Southend leading by the only goal.

On resuming, neither Ronaldson nor Bryant turned out, but the latter came on five minutes later. After Birnie had made a commendable effort to break down the opposition, Blott, with a great attempt, missed the bar by the barest fraction. A free to the visitors on the penalty line was of no avail, and a similar concession to the visitors saw Randall badly muddle the kick. From a head pass by Peake, Birnie forced a further flag-kick, which though well placed was fisted away by the agile visiting keeper. In quick succession also he got rid of shots from Caldwell and Peake, the last named being a splendid drive from close quarters.

Caldwell profited from a pretty transfer from Wright, and middled grandly, but Blogg again prevented a score. Owen crowned a fine bit of work by a well judged pass to Birnie, but the winger was pulled up for offside. Peake got the worst of a charge with the goalkeeper and momentarily was laid out. He was soon able to resume and later both he and Caldwell failed to take advantage of a fine centre from Birnie.

Later Birnie was a sinner in this respect for Blott gave him a chance in a thousand, but he missed it completely. Soon after this Blott got temporarily put hors de combat with a kick in the face, but he was soon fit again. Ten minutes from the close Caldwell screwed in a lovely shot off the line, and Peake put the Blues two up by heading into an unprotected net. Blott shaved the bar with a shot that deserved to score and several other efforts were rained in at Blogg, who, however, excelled in goal. In the last two minutes Southend forced four flag-kicks, and although the ball once hit the crossbar, no further score resulted and Southend ran out winners by two goals to nil.

AN ADVERTISEMENT ON THE FRONT PAGE OF THE
SOUTHEND STANDARD OF
THURSDAY, JANUARY 7TH, 1909 READ:

SOUTHEND UNITED F.C.
FOOTBALL ART SUPPLEMENTS.

WITH THE ISSUE OF 'IDEAS,' ON SALE
THURSDAY, A FINE SUPPLEMENT OF
SOUTHEND UNITED F.C.,

IN CLUB COLOURS, WILL BE GIVEN
AWAY FREE TO ALL READERS IN THE
SOUTH.

IT IS A PICTURE WELL WORTH FRAMING.
ON SALE EVERYWHERE.
PRICE 1D.

Wednesday, February 10th, 1909
United League (Southern Section)
SOUTHEND UNITED 4, BRENTFORD 3

Mud was flying in all directions at Root's Hall, on Wednesday afternoon, when Southend met Brentford in the United League. Earlier in the day it was anticipated the match would be postponed owing to the fall of snow overnight, but, as soon as it ceased falling, the work of clearing was commenced. There were between four and five hundred spectators present, and the ground was so slippery that good football was out of the question. The most noticeable feature of the game was Southend's rally. At one period – and in the second half, too – the Blues were losing three to one and then, as if some mysterious agency had been at work, they scored three more goals, and ran out winners; the scores being 4-3.

Southend had a mixed team in the field; Anderson being in the centre and Johnson at centre half, with Harrod as left half and Barrett outside right. Jack at outside left played a very good game; one goal coming from his foot and in another he took shares. Clark, at right back, was a distinct success. He kicked strongly, tackled well, and, considering the greasy state of the ball, cleared with judgment. Of the other players, it cannot be said that they did anything extraordinarily good, but the conditions were against them. The display given by Cotton – well, some of the onlookers could hardly believe that it was Cotton between the sticks, especially when two of the goals were scored. In the registering of the first goal, Brentford's inside left (Reid) lobbed the ball into the net. Cotton was at one end of the goal and the ball was placed the other. The custodian did not make an effort to save, whether he got stuck in the mud, or whether he thought the ball was going over, he only can say. The third goal of the match was almost as soft. Reid headed the ball on to the goal line, and it appeared to bounce over Cotton's hands. Brentford played a good game and of the two teams they took things more calmly, which was a wise course to adopt on such a ground.

The Blues won the toss and were the first to get anywhere dangerous. Frost shot into goal and McIver in clearing, allowed the ball to go over. The corner did not improve matters, as Jack, in an endeavour to score, shot over. The visitors made two successive visits to the home territory, which were relieved by Clark and Emery in turn. Then, following a little bit of midfield play, Hamilton, Brentford's outside right, put in a long cross shot which hit the crossbar. Molyneux kicked away and Jack ran down the wing and centred, but Anderson fell over the goalkeeper in his endeavour to score. Southend's invasion was not complete, for Jack again put in a centre; this time a corner resulting. The kick was taken and with a mighty boot, Clark landed the ball wide of the mark. The first goal of the match was scored by Brentford after a bout of passing by the forwards. Reid, as mentioned above, lobbed the ball into the net, with Cotton standing looking on.

This success appeared to liven the visitors up, likewise Southend, and in turn they each had a corner. Southend were fortunate to have their corner followed by two others in succession, and following out the old saying 'the third time pays for all,' Frost equalised. After the kick off the visitors came near to taking the lead again, but as Reid was about to shoot, Emery took the ball off his toe, and passing to Barrett, that player kicked over. In turn each side pressed but neither scored, and at the cross over honours were even.

Two minutes of the second moiety had hardly elapsed before Brentford took the lead; Reid heading the ball in. Southend then went for the visiting goal, and after the forwards had dallied about in front of the goalmouth, Johnson caused a fresh start by skying. On the right wing Harrod had a rare tussle and eventually a corner was forced, which ended with the visitors increasing their lead through McKenzie. It was here that Southend were two goals behind, and here also where they commenced in real earnest. Jack soon after reduced the lead through an individual effort, and then the group of spectators who invariably pitch their camp behind the visitors' goal commenced to shout and for a time one began to wonder whether Colney Hatch had sufficient accommodation. However, it was all for a good purpose, and a sort of stimulant to the Blues. Anderson swung the leather over to Jack and before the latter could centre a corner was given.

From the place kick, Wright made the scores level. The excitement and shouting were again intense, and both teams were doing their utmost to take the lead, Brentford being far from downhearted at the surprising 'bucking up' of the homesters. The winning goal came Southend's way; Frost scoring after Wright had had a shot at goal.

SOUTHEND: Cotton; Clark and Molyneux; Emery, Johnson and Harrod; Barrett, Frost, Anderson, Wright and Jack.

BRENTFORD: McIver; Ramsden and Ewing; Badger, Gordon and Hisbent; Hamilton, Land, McKenzie, Reid and Buxton.

Referee: Mr. F. Simpson, Camberwell.

Southend United's reserve side (or '2nd XI' as the club's handbook describes them) took over the club's fixtures in the United League for the 1909-10 season (in a division with Peterborough City, Hastings & St. Leonards United and New Brompton) – the first team concentrating on their Southern League engagements.

Monday, September 13th, 1909
Friendly Match
SOUTHEND UNITED 2, MANCHESTER UNITED 2

It was unfortunate that it rained nearly all day on Monday, when Southend United met Manchester United, the Cup holders, at Roots Hall, in a friendly encounter, which was part of the arrangement by which Blott was transferred to the Mancunians. Unfortunately, owing to an injury, Blott could not play, and his place was taken by Livingstone. The weather cleared about an hour before the kick-off, but the cold and damp prevented many from attending. About 2,500, however, braved the elements.

Both teams had a warm reception on taking the field. Those who did attend were rewarded by a brilliant exhibition of football. Bigden got hurt at Luton, and his place was again taken by Harrower, and Molyneux preferred to have a rest, which gave Murray, the young Partick Thistle back, a chance. At the request of Mr. Bentley, the directorate had forwarded complimentary passes to the band of the South Lancashire Regiment, at present performing on the Cliffs, in honour of the county to which they and the club belonged.

The teams were represented as follows: –

MANCHESTER UNITED: Moger; Stacey and Hayes; Duckworth, Roberts, and Downie; Livingstone, Halse, J. Turnbull, A. Turnbull, and Wall.

SOUTHEND UNITED: Cotton; Thomson and Murray; Emery, Owen, and Harrower; Brown, Frost, King, Wright, and Crews.

Referee, Mr. A.J. Kips, Willesden.

Owen, who captained Southend, lost the toss, and Southend kicked off up the gradient. Thomson and Owen were early called upon to pull up a rush by A. Turnbull. As if to show the Cup-holders were not to have it all their own way, King nearly broke through, but Roberts proved the stumbling block. Harrower placed the ball into goal, and King had a chance from an awkward angle, but clean missed his kick, while a moment later Downie very cleverly stopped the home pivot's intentions. Wall changed the venue and obtained an abortive corner, but back went the Blues, and Frost, tapping the ball on to Brown, the winger middled splendidly, but again Roberts got his cranium to it. Play was of the give and take order, and the Reds were quickly round Cotton again; the custodian deftly turning a warm handful past the post from Alec Turnbull. Wall took the resultant corner, and the ball came out to Duckworth, who drove it hard and straight out of Cotton's reach into the net from 25 yards range. Thus at the end of eight minutes Manchester were one up.

Emery was playing one of the games of his life, and was continually checking Wall and A. Turnbull, while the Southend front quintette were settling down to good football. One particularly clever piece of combination by the Blues vanguard saw King slip the leather to Wright, who made a grand attempt; the ball passing by the barest margin of the angle of the cross-bar. Southend next obtained a corner, which Brown place right under the bar, and Moger had to fist over to save from the persistent home forwards. In quick succession Frost missed a couple of openings; once having the misfortune to slip, while on another occasion Moger picked the ball right off his toe. After this the Blues were twice sent back on the score of off-side against King and Crews. The Manchester attack treated the spectators to a splendid exhibition of the short passing tactics, and this culminated in a terrific shot, which would probably have scored had not Murray charged it down. Southend tried to follow suit with long passing from wing to wing, but Crews nullified the movement by firing well outside the target.

A miskick by Thomson gave Halse his first opportunity, but the crowd had a chuckle when he clean missed the ball and it rolled over the line. Roberts tried to spring a surprise on the home defence and nearly succeeded with a magnificent shot from 40 yards out, which curled just the wrong side of the post, while the crowd roared their admiration. A judicious pass by Wright to Crews saw the left winger take the ball almost to the corner flag and centre perfectly across goal, where King received within a couple of yards of Moger. A goal seemed certain, but the home pivot did not put enough powder behind his shot, and Moger picked up the leather without seeming in the least perturbed. Back went the Blues, and Brown, supplying King with another well-judged centre, he headed just over the bar. J. Turnbull raced three-parts the length of the field, but could only shoot against the fence while travelling at top speed. Crews swung the ball in the vicinity of the Reds citadel again, but King again deflected the wrong side of the upright with his head though had he let the ball go on to Frost he might have scored. Frost next forced Hayes to concede a corner.

This was beautifully placed by Brown and Wright drove for the far corner of the net, but Hayes' head popped up and saved a certain goal. Emery fastened on the rebound, and with a fine effort missed the bar with very little to spare. A free for 'hands' saw Murray shoot into Moger's arms, and, later, Frost, by means of a clever single-handed effort, brought Moger to his knees, but he managed to get the ball away, while following this King almost converted another special centre from Brown.

It was a fine bit of play which led up to Southend's equaliser. Owen placed the ball to King, who smartly slipped it out to Crews. He raced for goal and whipped it in. King failed to reach it, but it went along to Frost, who, from close range, beat Moger all ends up. This came at the end of thirty minutes and was loudly cheered. Some amusement was caused by Halse being grassed by Owen. Just after Halse fouled the former and did not seem to appreciate it when the referee penalised him. Southend continued to have the better of the exchanges, and once when J. Turnbull did get within potting range of the home goal, Murray, who was creating a very favourable impression, neatly dispossessed him.

Not many moments afterwards Thomson cleverly repeated the feat when a goal looked imminent. Manchester began to infuse more dash into their play, and Wall placed the ball at the foot of 'Sandy' Turnbull, who had no difficulty in beating Cotton a second time. Turnbull was very much in evidence just at this period, and Thomson saved what looked like a serious situation right in the goalmouth. Halse made one of his spasmodic attempts to break through and flashed the leather across goal, but no one was up to take advantage of it and it passed outside. Southend carried play back to the Manchester territory, and Wright, with a swerving shot, narrowly missed the desired haven. Just on the interval 'Sandy' Turnbull broke away and a goal seemed certain. He shot hard and straight enough, but Cotton brought off a gallant save, and the interval was called with Manchester leading 2-1.

The teams turned straight round and re-commenced operations. The Blues, at the outset, took up the running, and Crews, centring, Brown caused Moger to handle. Away went the Manchester front rank in a line, and Wall placed the ball beautifully for J. Turnbull, but Emery again came to the rescue and placed into touch. Then the Southend goal had another marvellous escape from the Turnbulls. Livingstone centred the ball across to A. Turnbull who drove at Cotton with terrific speed. Cotton just managed to deflect the ball as the Turnbulls came rushing in. The ball appeared to be going into the net, with Cotton having no chance, but somehow he nipped round them, flicked the ball off Sandy Turnbull's head, and emerged with it amid a roar of approval.

After Brown and Frost had caused the defenders some uneasiness, Crews gave Moger a fast rising one to fist away. Brown was on the warpath again, and

King nearly turned one of his centres past Moger, but the custodian displayed great agility in getting at the ball.

Halse came into prominence when he wandered out on to the wing and squared the ball, but Wall, with a terrific lunge, sent it flying over the horizontal. Brown quickly transferred play, and with a fast travelling shot he appeared to be scoring, but the sphere found a safe resting place in Moger's arms, which appeared to reach all across the goal. Thomson smartly pulled up Wall, and Cotton had to leave his goal to stop J. Turnbull. Crews careered down the wing and placed prettily, but King was slow in taking advantage of it and it went begging. A free for 'hands' close in was placed by Harrower, and in an exciting scrimmage Moger dived down and took the leather from the toes of the home forwards.

Halse once shot right along the goal-line; the ball passing outside, while just afterwards A. Turnbull headed prettily to Halse, who had a pot shot at short range, but Cotton saved finely and managed to dispose of the ball. A brilliant piece of work by Brown saw him place the ball forward for King, who darted for goal at express speed. He appeared to have the goal at his mercy, but, to the chagrin of the spectators, he sent a trifle outside the far upright. Later, the centre-forward was given off-side within a few yards of goal.

Southend were pressing, and Crews offered Wright an opening which was not accepted. Snapping up a pass from Brown, King was right off for goal again, but the referee ruled he was offside. Wall travelled up the Manchester left and tipped the leather to Halse, who fired point blank at Cotton, the custodian only just saving and then at the second attempt. Southend had hard luck in not getting on equal terms, for King engineered a fine opening for Brown, who ran in a drove in a beauty. Quick as lightning, Moger's sinuous arms leapt up and tipped it over the bar. The corner-kick was admirably taken by Crews, and it appeared as if the goal must fall when Emery drove the ball back at great speed. It seemed to be going well out of Moger's reach, but the custodian literally flew across his goal and succeeded in turning the ball round the post. It was a marvellous save. Not to be denied, the Blues pegged away, and Brown, with a fine half volley, saw Moger tip over the horizontal.

The ensuing flagkick proved fruitless, but Crews secured and middled effectively to Wright, who headed on to Frost, standing close in, and the Southender crashed the ball into the rigging, thus equalising the scores twenty-three minutes after the resumption. Inspired by this success, Frost nearly broke down the defence again; Hayes having to concede a corner, which, however, Brown placed behind. Manchester tried hard to obtain the lead, but the Southend defence was sound; Murray being very sure in his kicking.

Once Halse got about ten yards out and all looked over bar shouting. He sent in one of his characteristic drives, which sped through the air like greased lightning, but Cotton held the ball, although the force of the shot knocked him down and he managed to throw the ball over the heads of two onrushing forwards for Murray to clear. Cotton deservedly had an ovation for this grand save.

Play was still of the ding-dong character, and Stacey only just intercepted a centre from Frost, while Emery earned a cheer for the smart way in which he put a full stop to J. Turnbull. Back went the Blues, and Wright missed a good opening when he allowed a capital middle from Brown to slip through his legs, while a second or two later Frost all but completed a trio of goals, just failing by the narrowest shave to turn to good account one of Crews' centres. A clever combined movement between King and Brown resulted in the pivot heading wide. Play ruled even up to the finish. Neither custodian was again seriously troubled, and the match ended in a draw of two goals each.

Southend played up to their old reputation, viz., the better the opposition the better they play, and I think that local supporters could hardly imagine that the clever team of Monday was the same ineffective side as succumbed to the Rangers. While everyone knows that at the outset Manchester took things fairly easily, they had all their work cut out to stave off the attacks of the Southenders in the second moiety, and but for Moger's able custodianship the Blues might easily have won. Three or four of Moger's saves were brilliant in the extreme, while two of Cotton's were of the same high calibre. Never have Southend played better football; their passing oftentimes being a treat to witness. Manchester were the cleverer team, and their understanding and combination were oftentimes nigh to perfection. They wove the ball in and out with geometrical precision, always keeping the sphere on the carpet. Their wing to wing play was also very fine.

The game all through reached a high standard of excellence, despite the heavy nature of the ground, and probably a more scientific exhibition has never been witnessed at Roots Hall. Certainly, Southend have never been seen to better advantage, and they fully justified Mr. Bentley's opinion of them that they are a very smart lot. In goal, Cotton displayed something of his old form and had no earthly chance with either of the shots that beat him. Thomson also gave of his best, and two mistakes were all that detracted from a capital display. Murray early found favour with the crowd, and after starting with two or three bad clearances, he settled down to playing a splendid game; his tackling, coolness, and judgment stamping him as a player of great ability. His place kicking and the lowness with which he kept the ball were also features of his play.

Whether Emery has aspirations of going to Manchester I don't know, but he certainly played one of the games of his life, and the international Wall has rarely been more closely watched and so often baulked. Owen was also in great form, and was always a thorn in the side of the Manchester attack. He has played behind Halse so many times that he knows his methods, with the result that on Monday little was seen of the ex-Southender, who did not over appreciate Owen's attentions. Harrower improved on his last game with the first team, and did very creditably. As a line, the Southend forwards were good. Brown was splendid on the outside right, and the way he centred the ball on the run was splendid. Frost has never played better, and it is pleasing to give him a word of encouragement. He was irresistible and had the satisfaction of bagging both goals. King was always energetic and fed his wings well, but his shooting might have had a little more sting. He struck one as being a trifle over-anxious. Wright was clever in his passing, though a little slow at times, and Crews, buoyed up by his Luton display, did really well and got in a number of useful centres.

The Manchester team were a fine all-round side. Moger was brilliant in goal, and the backs kicked and tackled like well-trained machines. Roberts was the outstanding personality in a line of three rattling halves, and J. Turnbull was the most conspicuous of a good line of forwards. Wall and A. Turnbull were the more brilliant wing, and really very little was seen of Halse, who had a warm reception from the crowd. We were all sorry that Blott could not turn out owing to an injury to his head at Tottenham, and join in wishing him a speedy recovery.

Thursday, May 5th, 1910
Friendly Match
UNION BERLIN 0, SOUTHEND UNITED 4

Writing on Thursday, at the close of the Berlin match, our Special Correspondent with the United Club on their German tour says the game that day was started before about 750 people; the small attendance being due to the wet weather. The teams were: –

BERLIN UNION: Eichelmann; Buchmann and Schwarzer; Potsch, Jurga and Steffen; Zeidler, Birlem, Weisener, Zeidler, and Piscara.

SOUTHEND UNITED: Toone; Murray and Thomson; Emery, Frost and Harrower; Parke, Sutherland, King, Harrod, and Anderson.

Referee: Herr Dutton.

Murray, who captained the side, won the toss, and after Weisener set the ball in motion, Southend took up the running. Hands against Buchmann gave Southend a penalty, and King, taking this, shot straight at Eichelmann. The goalie cleared, but King, following up, scored from the rebound and Southend were one up in the first minute of the game.

Southend, buoyed up with this success, were soon at it again, and Harrod forced a corner, though he sent the shot behind. The goalkick saw Zeidler in possession, and he made tracks to the opposite end, though he spoilt a good run by sending behind.

Midfield play ensued for a considerable time, but at length Harrod received on the line and made light of the Union's defence, smashing in a hard one at Eichelmann, which beat him and placed Southend two up.

This was, indeed, says the Standard correspondent, better than yesterday, for the Southenders were more together and played a much better game. Two goals in ten minutes was more like the thing and the Germans round the ropes seemed to enjoy our scoring.

We were having all the game and Sutherland, King and Harrod in turn missed easy chances. Eichelmann rose to the occasion and he saved his side repeatedly.

A foul against Frost took the play into the Southend quarters, but Murray cleared when things were looking dangerous. Parke got possession from him on the right and made ground, but his final effort went behind.

From the goalkick the Germans got away on the left, and Piscara centred. Weisener potted at Toone and gave him the first Berlin effort he had had to stop. This he did with ease and caused much amusement by the way in which he threw the ball nearly to the half way line.

Frost was doing good work in the halfback line, and from one of his passes, Sutherland nearly scored; the goalie saving on the line. A melee followed, and after the ball had been forced out about half-a-dozen times, Eichelmann cleared amid great excitement.

Harrower was now prominent, and, giving to King, some pretty passing was seen between the inside men; this ending in Eichelmann bringing off a wonderful save from Harrod.

A few minutes later, another penalty was awarded Southend for hands against Jurga; this time Frost tried his luck, but had the misfortune to see his shot go behind.

The interval was near at hand when King broke through and scored a third goal. Half-time: Southend, 3; Union, 0.

After the change Southend took up the running again and, putting on the pressure, Harrod and Sutherland missed easy chances. Emery became more prominent, though he had been doing his full share of the work at the time. He put in more good play that forced a corner, only to see Frost send behind the sticks.

Then our opponents had a spell and Toone was shortly afterwards called upon to save. The Germans tried their hardest and put forth every ounce of effort in them to score, but Murray, Thomson and Toone were as firm as the famous 'Gib' and prevented them opening an account on the Southend sheet.

Piscara and Zeidler showed splendid combination, but when it came to shooting they were all at sea. Several chances the home front line missed when a score seemed a dead certainty.

The pace moderated and give and take efforts were all we had till Harrower worked his way to within a dozen yards of goal. Here he took a 'wild' shot and the goal-keeper was not awakened.

Birlem was next away and he was down towards Toone when Thomson settled the account by dispossessing him of the ball and giving it to Frost.

Then on to Anderson went the leather, and 'Dits' got away well. He had extremely hard lines with a shot that just went over the bar, and King had the similar consolation from his colleagues just afterwards.

Our opponents had certainly been playing better this half, and it was a sad disappointment to their supporters to see Weisener miss an open goal after a good centre by Piscara.

King got possession in his own half from the goalkick and, racing at top speed, beat the backs. Thus he did the 'hat-trick' on the Germans and placed No. 4 to the Southend account. Nothing further happened and Southend won 4-0.

Wednesday, May 11th, 1910
Friendly Match
HOHENZOLLERN (HALLE) 1, SOUTHEND UNITED 3

Neue Sportwoche report (English translation)
The English professional team played their fourth match of their tour in Halle against Hohenzollern. In the history of local football this is the first time that Halle has played host within its walls to such a guest. Among the many spectators there were also many army officers to be seen. The game developed into an interesting struggle; one side, old, experienced campaigners equipped with all the technical subtleties; on the other side, a team endeavouring to combat the better eleven with energetic fast play. There was almost nothing to criticise about the team, except that one or two players appeared not properly versed in the art of shooting straight.

On the other hand, one could not but admire an exemplary display of combination play. It was a great pleasure to see the outstanding sureness the ball was stroked from man to man. Hohenzollern's team played brilliantly as ever when they find themselves faced with strong opposition. The team was infused with a fresh energetic spirit and gave the opposing defence a particularly tough time of it. The hero of the day was Kopp who played a fine game and was able to hold even the hardest shots; the forward line was somewhat weakened by the introduction of new team members. Gaebelein showed his brilliance again as did Zschenker to some extent.

England, with the wind in their backs, immediately took control with excellent play along the ground and were extremely dangerous in front of the opposing goal. With admirable sureness the Hohenzollern goalkeeper made save after save. After fifteen minutes of pressure the first ball rolled into the home team's goal. Although apparently unsettled at first, they soon rallied and dangerous situations developed in front of the English goal. A good cross from the left was unfortunately not exploited. Hohenzollern were obviously striving to show their best and succeeded until half-time to keep the result at 1-0 for England.

Now Hohenzollern had the wind in their favour and with their acknowledged customary skills, a very open game now developed. The English, with excellent steady, precise passing, developed a movement with sure man-to-man passing into the opposing penalty area and scored a second goal, to which Hohenzollern soon replied with a consolation goal from their inside-right. The game, already rich in interesting incidents, became more exciting and the English finally scored a third goal.

The game was characterised by fair play throughout, and for Hohenzollern as well as Halle football, the most satisfactory result is proof that German football has made a significant step towards the level of the English game. The referee Blüher (Leipziger F.C.) controlled the game in his usual thorough manner. The players were:

SOUTHEND UNITED: Toone; Murray, Molyneux (capt.); Harrod, Harwood, Harrower; Parke, Frost, King, Anderson, Wright.

HOHENZOLLERN: Kopp; Anger, Teller; Hechet, Troitzsch (capt.), Elsner; Zschenker, Rösler, Meyer, Mehling, Gaebelein.

Wednesday, September 28th, 1910
Southern Counties Charity Cup, 1st Round
SOUTHEND UNITED 1, CRYSTAL PALACE 1

Footballers had my sympathy on Wednesday, and certainly rushing about in the tropical weather we had should prove efficient training for this week. It was warm enough looking on, to say nothing of playing. Duty had to be done, however, and under the rays of a glaring sunshine Southend and the Crystal Palace had to fight at Roots Hall to decide who should enter the second round of the Southern Counties Charity Cup. Last season Brighton were the holders of the trophy, and Southend, after defeating New Brompton in the first round, lost by the odd goal in three at Park Royal to Queen's Park Rangers in the second stage of the competition. On this occasion the meeting proved abortive, for the teams will have to meet again on the slopes of Sydenham to decide who shall go into the second round. And it doesn't matter much who wins, and, to be candid, I daresay that either of the clubs would sooner have lost than had to meet again, for the competition is not a very important one.

The game ended in a draw of one goal each, and, frankly, Southend were not unlucky to live to fight another day. The Palace made several changes in the team that had lost their last three successive games against Bromley, Brentford and Norwich City, and the anxiety of the youngsters to keep their places was no doubt the cause why the Londoners put more energy and vim into their work, and seemed all out for a win, whereas the Southend men, with two or three exceptions, seemed a 'Devil-may-care' attitude, and impressed one with the fact that they were not at all obsessed with the importance of the encounter. It may be that after their defeat in the London Cup by Bromley that

Southend held the Palace too cheaply, but it was certainly a surprise to everyone when the visitors took the lead seven minutes after the start. Then Southend did not seem to make any serious effort at retaliation, and the Palace might easily have got more goals; in fact, they did get the ball into the net on two occasions, but each time there had been an obvious infringement of the rules. It was not until the second half that Southend really played at all, and then they were not long in equalising.

For a greater part of the match play dragged along in a slip-shod and apathetic manner, and it was chiefly the good display given by both sets of backs that relieved the game from mediocrity. It may be mentioned that Southend lost the first goal, and they kept up their reputation for inability to win after first having their defence penetrated. It is now over two years since they won after having the first point notched against them. Southend made one change in the team that so handsomely vanquished Northampton, but the experiment did not do much on the extreme right. The teams were as follows: –

SOUTHEND: Clark; Murray and Molyneux; Emery, Lavers and Craig; Sutherland, Frost, King, McKenna and Dunn.

CRYSTAL PALACE: Johnson; Collyer and Thompson; Spottiswood, Hatton and Hanger; Davies, Williams, Woodhouse, Lawrence and Myers.

The game opened very tamely, Southend playing down the slope in the first half. At the end of eight minutes Williams sprang a surprise on the Southend defence, for from long range he put in a fast grounder, which Clark had to throw himself at full length to save. Clark, however, failed to clear, and threw the leather at the feet of Woodhouse, who had the easiest task possible in putting it into the net. Soon afterwards, however, Clark saved well from Myers at close quarters, while at the other end Dunn twice got in lovely centres, but each time Johnson came out and punched up the field. The Palace goalkeeper was kept employed with efforts from Emery and King, but he proved equal to all demands. Davies made a fine sprint on the Palace right and wound up with a daisy cutter, which Clark had to divert round the upright for a corner. Resulting from a free kick, Johnson accomplished a brilliant save from Lavers. Williams next accepted a pass from Davies, but he was obviously offside, and the whistle sounded before he put the ball into the net, and the point was not allowed.

The next moment the Palace had broken through again, and this time Woodhouse beat Clark, but a foul had been committed on Murray, and no goal resulted. Before the interval, Johnson had a busy five minutes, but he kept his charge intact, and the refresher was called with the Palace ahead.

The teams had a longer breather than usual, and it was noticed when they came out again that both sides had discarded their heavy woollen jerseys and had substituted cotton shirts. Southend colours were now red and white, and as both sets of shirts were faded, it was with some difficulty that the colours could be distinguished. Resuming, Southend started as if they meant business, and Johnson had in the first minute to get away a promising shot from McKenna, which he did with a double-handed punch. Within two minutes, however, Southend were on level terms. Frost accepted a neat transfer from King, and was able to run in clear of the backs and beat Johnson, whom he had enticed out of goal, with a fast grounder into the far corner of the net. Soon after, when Johnson kicked against one of his own defenders and the ball rebounded, the Palace goal had a near escape, but Collyer saved the situation.

Southend were having the better of matters, and Sutherland, once had a clear field before him, but instead of going on his own he passed to King, who was somewhat hampered by the backs, and Johnson was easily able to negotiate his shot. At the other end Clark had all he could do to keep out a fine drive by Hatton, and from a pass from Sutherland, Frost missed by the proverbial inches. Myers once got in a beauty, but Clark caught his shot, and just before the end the Palace goal sustained a long siege. The referee sounded the final call with the scores standing at one each, but he evidently made a big mistake, for there were over five minutes to go, besides time which should have been allowed for stoppages. This was not the only mistake which Mr. A. Milton made, and several of his decisions, especially on the off-side rule, were, to say the least, peculiar. Spectators and players alike, however, were not sorry the game had fizzled out in this manner, for the spectators had seen enough, and the players must have had too much of a fatiguing encounter.

Long before the end men on both sides were obviously done up, and they were glad to kick the ball anywhere to gain a little respite. On such a day, and with no serious consequences at stake, it would be idle to attempt to criticise the men, and I don't intend to try. For Southend, Murray and Molyneux defended finely, and the former appears to be settling down to his last season's form. Lavers was the best of the three halves, for Emery and Craig were not up to form. Frost was the most conspicuous of the front line, for King did not seem disposed to exert himself, and the left wing never really settled down; Dunn having few chances. For the Palace, Collyer and Thompson, like their confreres in the Southend team, put up a splendid resistance at full-back, while Hanger was the best of the halves, and Williams and Davies the pick of the forwards. The fair-haired Williams was always in the picture, while Davies is a very speedy winger. Myers, who last season assisted Northfleet, has the making of a useful left winger.

Saturday, December 23rd, 1911
Southern League, Second Division
CHESHAM TOWN 0, SOUTHEND UNITED 9

This is Southend's record away League victory. Goalscorers were McNaught (3), Bradshaw (3), Wileman (2) and Parke. '... the Southend forwards must have hit the timber around the goal ten or a dozen times ...' reported the *Southend Standard.*

(Unfortunately, due to a fold in the page on the microfilm copy, the report cannot be reproduced.)

SEASON TICKET PRICES FOR THE 1911/12 SEASON
CENTRE RESERVED STAND 2/2/0 (£2.10), UNRESERVED 1/1/0 (£1.05)
LADIES 12/6 (£62½P) GROUND ONLY 12/6 (62½P)

Saturday, April 20th, 1912
Southern League, Second Division
SOUTHEND UNITED 4, TON PENTRE 0

Southend obtained substantial revenge for their defeat at Ton Pentre earlier in the season, by defeating the Welshmen by four goals to nil at Roots Hall on Saturday. The loss of any chance of promotion had robbed the game of any real interest and the attendance was very poor, only £37 being taken at the gates. There was an 'end-of-the-season' air about the whole of the play and so poor was the fare served up from a football point of view that it was impossible to manufacture any excitement. Ton Pentre are a force to be reckoned with upon their own mud-patch, but they have met with little success on foreign soil this season.

After the first five minutes of Saturday's game they were hopelessly outclassed, and it was only a question of how many goals Southend would win by. The fact that they had travelled up from Cardiff during the night; leaving the Welsh capital about 2a.m., did not add to the freshness of the side, and this incidentally is only another instance of the farce of the Second Division of the Southern League as at present constituted. While the men from Ystrad put up a very sound defence, their attack was so innocuous that it failed to cause the home side a moment's perturbation.

Wileman again led the Southend attack and performed his task well. He and Thomson have been Southend's most consistent players this season and Wileman has proved the one success of the forward line. He is well ahead of the Southend goalscorers and on Saturday again helped himself to a trio of cleverly obtained points. In fact, the play of the Southend forwards was above their average standard and their smart work was the one redeeming feature of an otherwise very poor game. It was one continuous struggle between the Ton Pentre defence and the Blues vanguard and on not more than two occasions during the whole game did the Glamorganshire men threaten danger.

The teams were represented as below, and under direction of Mr. F. Viveash: –

SOUTHEND: Nurthen; Thomson and Cairns; Layzell, Harwood and Arnold; McNaught, Wilson, Wileman, Bradshaw and Parke.

TON PENTRE: Percival; Jones and T. Williams; Davis, Martin and H. Tanner; Roberts, Hathaway, J. Williams, Curtis and Perkins.

The match requires very little description and there were few incidents worthy of record besides the actual scoring of the goals. The best shot during the opening fifteen minutes was delivered by Wileman, but Percival saved smartly. The first goal came three minutes later and was very well obtained. Bradshaw cleverly manoeuvred into position and while the Ton Pentre defence were in a quandary as to what was going to happen next, Wileman came along with a swift first timer and placed the ball into the net well out of Percival's reach. Within two minutes the Blues had obtained a second and this was traceable to a fine run and centre by McNaught, who placed the sphere so well that Bradshaw was promptly enabled to score with a judicious drive.

Southend continued to overplay their opponents, whose goal had some very narrow escapes and within a short space of time Wileman notched the third. It was like the previous one, the result of clever play by McNaught, who swung the ball across to Wileman, and he very deftly turned it into the net. Thus at the interval Southend held a three goals lead.

During the opening minutes of the second moiety Ton Pentre played slightly better, but they soon fell away again and it was once more all Southend. Fortunately for the Welshmen Southend found Percival in exceptionally fine form and but for his brilliant work in goal the score would have been easily doubled. He was completely beaten by a fine drive by Wileman slick into the corner of the net, but afterwards saved magnificently from McNaught twice, Wileman and Bradshaw.

Nurthen had little to do in the Southend goal, Thomson being able to dispose of most of the attempts they made to score, but Cairns was exceptionally weak in his kicking. Harwood was the best of the half-backs and played well, keeping the ball much lower than is his usual wont. Arnold and Layzell also kept their respective wings well in check. McNaught, who came into the team once more, displaced Chapman at outside right and gave one of the best exhibitions he has done this season. He put more energy into his work than usual and three of the goals were the result of his centres. Wilson was very unwell and really should not have played. He was, therefore, under a disadvantage, though he did useful service. Wileman is certainly the best centre forward Southend have had this season and in addition to his shooting powers, he fed his wings well. Bradshaw and Parke also got along well together on the left.

In addition to Percival's fine goalkeeping, Ton Pentre are also indebted to Jones and T. Williams, their two full backs, who put up a dour defence. The former, the old Everton player seems to have lost little of his cunning, and if slower than of yore he is still a very safe kick. Of the half-backs, all of whom had a gruelling time in the warm sun of an April afternoon, Martin was the most successful and tackled well. The forwards were, however, a very disjointed lot, and with the exception of occasional good work by Hathaway and Curtis, there was nothing in their play to commend itself.

Saturday, November 2nd, 1912
F. A. Challenge Cup, 2nd Qualifying Round
LEYTONSTONE 0, SOUTHEND UNITED 5

Southend Standard report

With consummate ease Southend United passed into the third of the qualifying round of the English Cup on Saturday, at the expense of Leytonstone, whom they defeated on their own ground by five goals to nil. Southend were first and their opponents nowhere. Had it not been for some unfortunate circumstances the United could easily have won by a dozen goals. Rarely has it been my lot to witness a game between senior teams, where both have pretensions to 'class' – for it must be remembered that Leytonstone compete in the Isthmian League with Ilford, the Caleys, Clapton, Dulwich Hamlet, etc. – in which one has shown such an overwhelming superiority as did Southend on Saturday. At a disadvantage all through, by reason of the smallness of the ground, which is little outside the minimum allowed, they completely mastered the amateurs.

When one considers the significance of the following facts, the disparity between the sides will be realised. Parke failed to turn up and take his place at outside left and Layzell, who was travelling as reserve and may be described as the utility man, was put in to partner Bradshaw. Without casting any reflection upon the ex-Prittlewell player, who is not a forward, it must be said the side was at considerable disadvantage.

The game had not been in progress long when Spencer was injured; his knee suffering as the result of a collision. He was unable afterwards to risk kicking with his left foot and did not participate in the game after the interval. Layzell went full back and Bradshaw was without a partner. A short time before the end Wileman was also hurt and had to be assisted off the field. Happily, none of the injuries were serious.

During the time when Southend had eleven men out they made rings round the home team. For the whole of the first 45 minutes Leytonstone only got out of their own territory about half-a-dozen times and then but for a very brief space. The initial ten seconds gave a criterion of what was to follow. Kicking off, Frost worked down the field and put the ball just outside the goal. Within five minutes, Southend were two goals up. Although they only scored twice more to the interval they played the Stripes to a standstill. Receiving good assistance from the half-backs the Southend forwards displayed perfect artistry. The right wing was the most prominent and it was a revelation to watch the adroitness of Wilson and Wileman upon so cramped a space. Bradshaw was in his best form, while Frost's dash filled in admirably.

It was only after the interval that Leytonstone got a look in and although they pressed Southend for some length and gave Kebbell several warm shots to negotiate, it cannot be said, looking as impartially as one could, that their efforts merited a goal. The absence of a player makes much difference to a side, which, added to that feeling of security in which Southend were, conduced to influence the visitors in not straining their energies to merely add goals. Leytonstone did look predominant, but they were very feeble when within the region of goal. They were knocked off the ball as an accomplished hand would bowl skittles over. In this respect, Thomson did the more damage; he was in brilliant form and got through a lot of work. His kicking was well judged and his anticipation particularly successful, but it was in his upsetting the opposing forwards that his play was most noticeable. Using his weight perfectly he time and again dispossessed an opponent in the easiest way possible, one or two being knocked half-a-dozen paces from him.

Perhaps an even more distinguished feature of the game than the obvious disparity of the teams was the conduct of the referee. He proved unable to exercise due control and restraint over the players. In the first half much spirit was displayed which might have been due to several causes, the early scoring by Southend, the fact that they employed robust, but perfectly legitimate methods, or the conduct of the crowd. Whenever a Southend player was unsuccessful a cry of derision went up from a section of the crowd.

To make things worse, McKee was nearly laid out, quite accidentally, but in the heat of a cup-tie a player is apt to put a different interpretation upon such accidents. Whatever the cause there was a lot of fouling – Southend not without a stain – that went unpenalised. The referee's ruling upon the off-side question – or lack of ruling – was decidedly conspicuous and had a detrimental effect upon the game. Not only was unfair kicking indulged in, but Mr. Riste allowed a considerable use of the hands. Once two of the United's players were literally held round the waist for fully ten seconds to prevent them getting the ball, yet a free kick was awarded Leytonstone.

Had the scores been more even and the prospects of the teams equal it would have been quite on the cards that much display of temper would have been shown. As it was, two of the players had a decidedly long 'Confab' upon the merit of each other's conduct, in which each appeared to give the other a solemn warning, and a Southend forward nearly had an altercation with one member of the crowd. It was pleasing to see a decided diminution of roughness in the second stage and the game concluded without any really untoward incident.

There was a large crowd present, nearly three thousand, and the takings approximated over seventy pounds. Thus Southend will not be much out having to play the match away. A large number of Southenders travelled with the team notwithstanding that they had to start at mid-day, which shows a gratifying amount of enthusiasm for the Club.

The game will not require a detailed amount of description. Thomson lost the toss, but there was little loss thereby and choice of ends mainly rested upon sentiment. Straight from the kick-off, before hardly a home player had touched the ball, Frost got in scoring position and put a fast drive just outside. After some pleasing combination on the part of Axcell and the left wing, Bradshaw sent the ball into the right hand side of the net from about twenty yards out. It was a fine goal. From the re-starting of the game, again Frost went down and narrowly missed for the second time. Breaking away, Markham ran along the touch line, but his effort went outside. A corner was awarded Southend and Layzell placed nicely. Bradshaw headed into goal and McKee just got to it. In less than five minutes Southend were two up, Frost converting a capital centre by Wilson. There was no more scoring for twenty-five minutes, but during that time Southend were constantly on the attack. They ran round their opponents with the utmost ease and McKee, despite his early upsetting, saved some first-rate shots.

The most praiseworthy effort on the part of Leytonstone was by Payne, who put in a beautifully placed dropping shot which Kebbell had some difficulty in clearing. The Southend right wingers were irresistible and a number of centres came from that source, although the smallness of the ground militated against their methods. A number of corners fell to Southend, but several of these were poorly placed by Layzell. Some, however, caused much perturbation in front of the home goal. The third and fourth goals came in as quick succession as the first. Bradshaw, quite twenty yards out, sent in a delightful shot which McKee made no effort to save. Then Frost followed within two or three minutes with one equally meritorious; which by its swiftness utterly deceived the keeper. It was an inspiring first half, portent of a complete rout of the amateur brigade.

Upon the resumption, Southend were minus Spencer, Layzell went full back, leaving only four forwards. Leytonstone were soon the aggressors, but without being dangerous. The same amount of energy was not being infused into the game, but on the other hand, the home side settled down to better football and showed some understanding and cohesion. Although much more in the picture than previously they could not shake the mastery of Southend. They put in several shots which gave Kebbell a chance of exhibiting his ability, and he cleared them with safety. At the other end, despite their handicap, the United forwards tried a number of times to increase their lead and there were some narrow misses; Frost and Bradshaw again being the marksmen. One shot from the centre-forward was only just tipped over the bar. Five minutes from time Wileman was hurt in a collision and retired. Almost immediately afterwards Bradshaw completed his hat-trick; catching a rebound from Frost he drove it into the net with great gusto. Thus the game ended.

The most satisfactory feature, from a Southend point of view, was the continued success of the rearranged forward line. True, they were playing against a much less accomplished set of players, but they put up sufficient opposition to give a fair test to the constitution. The Secretary-manager has shown of his very best form on the last couple of Saturdays and the three goals on Saturday were reminiscent of his scoring capabilities when he first joined the United. Frost's play adapts itself admirably to that of his colleagues. His dash is most valuable in combination with the work of the men on either side of him. Had Parke been present on Saturday it is quite likely the Blues' total of goals would have reached double figures.

Another improvement was the shooting of the centre-forward, while, generally, the opening out of the game and shooting with more frequency was responsible for the convincing display of the van. Another welcome appearance in the team was Jimmy Axcell. His play at left half was a great improvement upon any in that position this year. Almost unbeatable in defence, he gave the most valuable assistance to his forwards.

There was one weakness in the team and that was in respect of the pivot. Perhaps the failings of Moon were brought out more by the brilliance of the men on either side of him. Emery was able to do almost as he would with the men opposed to him. The Southend captain was in capital form at left back and Spencer kicked well when he was not lame. Kebbell did all that was required of him in goal. The Leytonstone custodian was the most prominent of his side. He certainly saved some fine shots and it was only his dogged display in the first half hour that was the salvation of his side. Duck and Jefferies stood the gruelling well, but the half-backs were hopelessly beaten. Of the forwards, the inside trio were the best; Pearce and Hardie trying hard to give their side a point.

SOUTHEND: Kebbell; Thomson, Spencer; Emery, Moon, Axcell; Wilson, Wileman, Frost, Bradshaw, Layzell.

LEYTONSTONE: W. McKee; F.J. Duck, P.W. Jefferies; J. Payne, C. Lee, S.F. Kennerley; H. Markham, W.E. Foss, G.D. Hardie, C.H. Pearce, J. Collar.

Referee: Mr. H.P. Riste, Surrey.

Leytonstone Express and Independent report

Played at Leytonstone, before close on 3,000 spectators. The visitors attacked immediately on the start and in two minutes Bradshaw had McKee beaten with a brilliant shot. Soon afterwards Frost scored a second, the ball hitting the post and going into the net. Southend continued to have the better of the exchanges and Bradshaw and Frost scored further goals before the interval, which arrived with Southend leading by 4-0.

On the restart, Southend played with ten men, Spencer having injured his leg, retiring from the game. Layzell, the outside left, took his place at left back. Leytonstone had more of the play during this half, and were unlucky not to score on one or two occasions. Wileman was carried off injured near the end of the game but Southend again got through, Bradshaw netting. Result:

Southend United 5, Leytonstone nil. Despite being beaten five times, McKee played brilliantly in the home goal.

LEYTONSTONE: W. McKee; F.J. Duck, P.W. Jefferies; J. Payne, C. Lee, S.F. Kennerley; H. Markham, W.F. Foss, G.D. Hardie, C.H. Pearce; J. Collar.

SOUTHEND UNITED: Kebbell; Thomson, Spencer; Emery, Moon, Axcell; Wilson, Wileman, Frost, Bradshaw, Layzell.

From 'FOOTBALL NOTES' in the *Leytonstone Express and Independent*
Leytonstone's important English Cup-tie v. Southend United on Saturday resulted in an unexpectedly heavy reverse, the score being 5-0 in favour of the Southern Leaguers.

One of the largest crowds seen on the ground for many years witnessed the game, and I consider all will agree that the score does not give Leytonstone the credit which is their due, for they were certainly not five goals inferior to Southend.

At the start of the game, Southend went off with a rush, and before five minutes had elapsed they were a goal to the good, although the point should have been disallowed, the player being some yards offside when he scored.

However, the chronicling of the fact will be but poor consolation to the Stones, seeing that the referee allowed the goal to stand, and it seemed to have an unsteadying influence on the homesters, who sustained another piece of misfortune just afterwards.

This came about by means of a shot which struck one upright, and, rebounding across the goal, entered the net out of McKee's reach.

Southend were thus two goals to the good after less than ten minutes play, and it seemed that the Stones were to have a very hard time.

However, they made great efforts to get a grip of the game, and some smart attacks were made on the Southend goal, and with a little steadiness in their efforts the lead against them should have been reduced.

Pearce on one occasion had an opening but Thomson came to the rescue of his side, and soon afterwards Foss looked like causing trouble from a pass by the left wing, but he failed to get proper control of the ball, and the danger was averted.

Soon afterwards, in the course of an attack on the Leytonstone goal, McKee was hurt, and although he soon resumed, the effects of the injury were apparent, and it was not long before Southend scored a third goal.

The visitors continued to have the better of the exchanges until half-time arrived, and scoring again crossed over with the substantial lead of four goals to none.

Against such a score the chances of Leytonstone seemed hopeless, but they started the second half in splendid style, and on many occasions the Southend defence was in difficulties and had to repeatedly send the ball out of play to relieve themselves from the persistency of the Leytonstone forwards.

During this half, Leytonstone proved themselves to be quite the equals of their conquerors and but for some smart clearances by Kebbell, they would have reduced the score against them.

The Southend goalie proved equal to all calls made upon him, and it would have been no disgrace to him had he failed to successfully deal with the efforts made by Hardie, Pearce, Foss and Markham, the latter of whom put across some dangerous centres.

However, success in the scoring line was denied to the Stones in spite of all their efforts, and with Southend scoring once more in the closing minutes, Leytonstone were defeated by five clear goals.

To my mind, the game was won and lost in the first ten minutes. The offside goal which opened the score, seemed to knock Leytonstone off their balance, and the lucky nature of the second goal proved their undoing.

From the effects of these reverses they certainly did not recover in the first half, although their display in the second portion certainly merits the warmest praise.

Southend laid the foundation for their success in the opening few minutes, and quite took Leytonstone by surprise with the persistency of their attack, and by not allowing the Stones to settle down to their game.

The result was a great disappointment to the followers of the Stones, who quite expected their favourites to give the professionals a very close game.

I, too, expected a much more favourable result, for on this season's form I considered Leytonstone stood more than an outside chance of taking part in the next round.

However, they did not produce their earlier promising form, and as a consequence sustained the heaviest reverse of the season. Still, the defeat was by no means a disgrace, and if its lessons are taken to heart will prove of ultimate good to the team.

The second half display was more in the nature of what we have come to expect from the Stones, and led the ardent followers of the club to conjecture what might have been had such form been seen in the opening portion.

Apart from the error which gave Southend their first goal, the referee did not show any marked ability in his control of the game. He did not have a difficult task, but even that he did not perform well.

Saturday, March 22nd, 1913
Southern Alliance
CARDIFF CITY 1, SOUTHEND UNITED 1

It is a curious fact that Southend are always seen to advantage on the Cardiff enclosure at Ninian Park and on Saturday they created a big surprise by effecting a draw of one goal each in the Southern Alliance competition. It was Southend's third visit there this season, each side having previously won one game, but not a great deal of importance was attaching to the encounter. The visitors only turned out five of the men who helped to win the points against Aberdare on the previous day. On the other hand, with the exception of their half-back line, Cardiff City had a full side out. Therefore, the performance was a very creditable one.

Rain had fallen in torrents all morning at Cardiff and the playing space resembled a drained off mill-pond, but the referee (Mr. Foster) pronounced it fit to play upon. After a little while the mud churned up into a quagmire, and soon the players were ankle deep in slush. Under the circumstances, it was small wonder that the football was humorous and of indifferent quality. There were not more than a thousand spectators present when the teams lined up, which was a big contrast to the previous day, when Cardiff thrashed Luton in the presence of over 20,000 people. However, those who did attend saw a fairly interesting and well-contested game, taking all the unfavourable conditions into consideration.

There was a great spice of originality amongst the Southend team, which did duty in the following order:- Kebbell; Wileman and Cairns; Stott, Moon and Layzell; Thomson, Wilson, Mason, Bradshaw and Parke. The spectacle of seeing Jerry Thomson on the wing with Wileman slamming away at full-back was not one of the least entertaining features of the game.

The Cardiff team was as follows: – Kneeshaw; Doncaster and Leah; G. Burton, Latham and McKechnie; Bennett, Clarke, Devlin, J. Burton and J. Evans. Southend were pressed in the opening few minutes, and the lower end into which Southend were kicking was practically submerged with water.

Play was of a very give and take order. The players did not seem over anxious to exert themselves to the full and when they did the ball somehow got into the water. Southend for a time quietly settled down into Cardiff quarters and Kneeshaw was several times called upon, one save of his from Bradshaw, who put in a long low drive, being clever. For Cardiff, Devlin missed a good opening after good work by J. Burton. The Southend defence were quite clever in keeping the Cardiff attacks at bay, Kebbell being responsible for some well-executed clearances. Southend were, however, more sustained in attack and Mason spoilt one good opportunity of drawing first blood by handling. At the other end, Kebbell made a grand save from J. Burton, and half-time was called with no score.

Almost immediately on the re-start, J. Burton scored for Cardiff with a magnificent drive which left Kebbell helpless. Just later Bradshaw took the ball through nicely and gave Parke a clean run in, but Kneeshaw saved his shot. He was, however, robbed by Mason and Bradshaw, and McKechnie, who had dropped back into goal, just managed to clear.

Towards the close a good combined movement by the Southend forwards saw Thomson centre, and Bradshaw running in equalised the scores for Southend. In the closing stages Southend came near winning, Kneeshaw making a fine save from Wilson. Nothing more was done and the game ended in a draw of one each.

For Southend, Wileman gave a surprisingly good exhibition at full back, while Stott was quite a success at right half. With a greasy ball, Kebbell kept goal magnificently. The forwards were somewhat handicapped by the heavy and muddy pitch, but at times their combination was good and Bradshaw and Thomson were the most conspicuous. Kneeshaw, in the Cardiff goal, experienced a good deal of luck, and of the full backs Doncaster seemed to revel in the mud. With the exception of Bennett, the Cardiff team had their best forwards out but they were well held by the experimental Southend defence which acquitted itself well. Many anticipated a runaway victory for Cardiff against such a 'scrap iron' eleven as that which represented the Blues, but they were agreeably surprised.

Wednesday, April 2nd, 1913
Southern Alliance
SOUTHEND UNITED 2, BRENTFORD 0

Brentford have succeeded at Roots Hall against Southend more frequently than any other club, and upon the occasion of their last three visits, prior to Wednesday, the Bees won on each occasion, including last season, when they administered the coup de grace to the Blues in the English Cup. On Wednesday, however, Southend reversed the usual order of things, for in a Southern Alliance fixture Brentford were deservedly beaten by two goals to nil. On the day's play Southend were quite the superior side, but there was a strong suspicion that neither eleven took the game very seriously and both had their thoughts more concentrated upon Southern League matters; Southend upon gaining promotion and Brentford upon saving themselves from relegation.

The turf was in excellent state, and the conditions were ideal for a good game. Some fairly creditable work was seen on either side, but the match, as a whole, lacked animation and energy, and the players, with few exceptions, went about their tasks in a lackadaisical manner. It might only have been a friendly for all the interest that was taken in the game and upon such a fine afternoon, it was a little disappointing to see a crowd only representing £24 present to witness the appearance of a First Division Southern League club. Those who were there were rather pleased with Southend's victory and also with the improved display of the local forwards, who, except in shooting, showed excellent form.

The game was gratifying, for it signalised the return to form of Wileman, who on Wednesday exhibited all his old-time dash, pertinacity and shooting power. He scored a capital goal, and he and Wilson made a fine wing. Curry also played well in the centre, although he met with a nasty accident in the first half through coming into contact with Rhodes' boot. Mason was, however, again a dead failure, his shooting being wretched, his passes ill-judged and his movements very slow. J.W. Batchellor, the Cliffe amateur, made a re-appearance in the Southend team at outside left, and did a lot of useful work, being more virile and thrustful than Parke.

Southend relied on the same half-back line that did so well at Ton Pentre, and Stott again proved himself a much better performer in the intermediate line than in the front rank. Moon gave a capital display and had the satisfaction of scoring his first goal for the Club, a fact upon which he was warmly congratulated by his colleagues. As usual, Thomson was safe and Spencer showed a welcome improvement on recent form. Kebbell was rested and Clarke was given an opportunity in goal, and though he made some good saves, his negociation of the leather was not as clean as that of Kebbell.

For the visitors, Price kept out at least half-a-dozen shots that deserved to score, and but for his good display between the sticks the score would have been considerably augmented. Rhodes seems to maintain his youth as well as ever, and though he was only called upon at the last minute, he was the best back on the field. Richards was the pick of the halves, and though Hendren and Morrison provided their inside forwards with plenty of openings, their work in front of goal was very weak. Towards the close, two or three of the Brentford players adopted rather questionable tactics.

One goal was scored in each half. During the first moiety Southend had the advantage of the slope and also enjoyed the bulk of the game. Brentford first got dangerous, but Purvey when close to goal shot feebly and Clarke easily saved. A pretty centre by Wilson saw Batchellor send in a fast straight drive, but Price happened to be in the right place and saved. Just later, Wileman missed a grand opportunity of giving Southend the lead, but after racing away on his own he put wide. It was a centre by Batchellor that led up to Southend's first goal at the end of twenty minutes play. Spratt miskicked the ball as it came across and Wileman dashing in gave Price no chance. Before the interval Mason had two glorious chances of improving Southend's position, but he shot very poorly.

The second half was more even than the first, and for a time Brentford tried hard to equalise. Once Clarke saved finely from Chapple, and on another occasion he had to fall at full length to save from Hendren. Southend, however, were soon on the aggressive again and Wilson squaring the leather well, the sphere came out to Moon, who completely beat Price with a fast shot from eighteen yards range. Wileman, with a pretty effort, came near making the total three, but the shot was a foot the wrong side of the post.

A beauty from Wilson also deserved to score, but Price managed to divert it round the post for a corner. In the concluding stages, Southend monopolised the play, but nothing more was done and Southend ran out winners by two to nil.

SOUTHEND: Clarke; Thomson and Spencer; Stott, Moon and Layzell; Wilson, Wileman, Curry, Mason and J.W. Batchellor.

BRENTFORD: Price; Rhodes and Spratt; Allright, Richards and Kennedy; Morrison, Chapple, Purvey, Smith and Hendren.

Referee: Mr. A.G. Askell.

SOUTHERN ALLIANCE
During the summer of 1913 the league rules were changed
(proposed by Portsmouth) to allow clubs to field 'the best available team.'
This resulted in very weak sides being fielded.
The league folded at the end of the season.

From the *Southend Standard* of 7th August, 1913
This year the United are making a new departure in the matter of
programme. It will be elegantly designed and will comprise 15 pages
in which will appear local notes, football gossip,
photographs of players and their careers, half-time scores, etc.
The production will be edited by Mr. G.A. Weston.

Saturday, January 10th, 1920
F.A. Challenge Cup, 1st Round
SOUTHEND UNITED 0, SHEFFIELD UNITED 3 (played at Bramall Lane)
Southend's last F.A. Cup-tie as a non-League club was against First Division Cup-holders Sheffield United

So far as Southend United is concerned Cup-tie excitement is over for another season. The club made their exit on the Sheffield United ground, on Saturday, by three goals to none, and, considering everything, I was not dissatisfied with the result. Having sold their right of ground no one could have expected the Blues to succeed, except by a fluke, for First League football is something above the Southern League standard, and the Blades have more than held their own in the higher division. The score did not represent the play, and the Blues had far more of the exchanges than a three goals margin would suggest. In fact, for a Cup-tie, it was a remarkably open game, and there were no long periods of attack by either side. The one noticeable attribute of the First Leaguers over Southend was the wonderful alacrity they displayed when on the ball, and the smartness with which they made ground.

In their general play they were little better in their footwork than the United, but it was their extra smartness on the ball and the lightning darts for goal which told their tale. Their play in this respect was an example to any inferior side, and I hope the United forwards will not soon forget the lessons learned. There was no going backward about Sheffield. The goal was their object, and they made straight for it. There was no needless ballooning in the air, and the leather went slick along the carpet to whomsoever it was intended. Still, for all their correct footwork, Sheffield are by no means a great side. At the Kursaal I think they would have fallen victims to Southend. They are not as good a side as Portsmouth, and judging by a display I saw Chelsea give against the Arsenal, they are a good way below the Pensioners. They have a one man forward line; and that one man is Fazackerly. He is a wonderful foot-baller; his command of the ball is superb, he is as elusive as an eel, and he is no sooner on the ball than he appears to fly for goal, while his shooting, all along the carpet, is never far off the mark.

All the Sheffield forwards play to Fazackerly, and it was probably due to the fact that the Southend defence did not policeman him sufficiently that they lost the match. Of fine physique, with long legs, he reminds one of Vivian Woodward at his very best, and England can have no better inside-left playing at the present time than Fazackerly. No wonder he is the idol of the Sheffield crowd, and a roar of approval goes up every time he receives the ball.

The cupholders are the possessors of a masterly defence. The understand-ing between their halves and full backs is very fine indeed, and I am forced to admit that the Southend forwards made little impression upon them, and they effectively smothered all attempts to break through. Only once did the Blues look like finding the net, and that was in the second half, when Burrill neg-lected a favourable opening. They organised many attacks on the Sheffield goal, but there was just that little bit of finish lacking which hall-marked the onslaughts of the Blades.

If the score had been two to nil, instead of three, it would have been a cor-rect indication of the game. The Southend goal had not to undergo anything like the bombardment or the long periods of attack that it did against Portsmouth. The homesters had the encouragement of an all-important goal in the first four minutes, when Fazackerly fairly caught the Southend defence napping before they had properly settled down to their game. This goal was cleverly worked for and obtained, but Southend would have made a much bet-ter fight of it had they been able to keep their charge intact for ten minutes.

The other two goals came as the result of free kicks. What they were for, perhaps, the referee knows, but I doubt whether anyone else in the ground did! The first was given close to the penalty area for a perfectly legitimate tackle by Reid. The Southend players felt very aggrieved at the decision, and they felt more sore when Fazackerly scored. The third goal was the result of a penalty, and a more ridiculous decision it would be hard to imagine. There was no imminent danger to the Southend goal at the time, but Leahy, in clearing, kicked the ball against Marshall. The leather struck the latter's hand, but it was purely accidental, and as the ball rebounded Leahy picked up and booted away. To the amazement of everyone, the referee signalled for a penalty. The Southend players protested, and in response to their repeated clamourings Mr. Gee consulted both linesmen, but in the end he adhered to his decision and gave a penalty. Milton took the kick, and Leahy stopped his first shot, but he failed to hold the leather, and Milton, following up the rebound, netted.

Considering the day the attendance was good. It was officially returned as 39,700, and receipts, £2,326. After deducting the entertainment tax and other expenses it is probable the net gate will be about £1,700, so that Southend's share should come to something over £800. This is probably about ten times the amount that would have been taken at the Kursaal on such a day, and, therefore, from a financial point of view Southend may be said to have done well out of the deal.

I am aware that the action of the directors in accepting the offer to go to Sheffield has caused resentment among some of their supporters, but I don't see how they could have done otherwise in the interests of the club. Looking at the financial straits in which they were placed they had no alternative but to accept the offer of the Yorkshire men. Mr. Nicholson, their secretary, told me had the day been fine the gate would probably have been over 50,000. It was a filthy day. The snow of Friday had made the playing pitch very heavy, and then when the rain came tumbling down at intervals on Saturday, the turf became much worse. It had been rolled before the game, and except for a little water in one goal, and one patch in the centre, it presented a billiard table appearance. Directly, however, players began to move about they went ankle deep in mud, and churned it up into a veritable quagmire.

Rain fell during practically the whole progress of the match, the ball became as heavy as lead, slippery and difficult to control. Despite this, football reached a high level. It was a pretty game to watch, and both teams exhibited excellent combination. The one criticism which could be levelled against the Southend defence was that the halves, at periods, seemed somewhat lost. They did not tackle with their usual success and confidence, and the Sheffield wingers were allowed a little too much latitude.

On the other hand, they fed their forwards well, and the combination of Southend was equal to anything they have shown previously this season. It was only when they came to close grips with the Blades' defence that they failed, but for all that Gough had quite a fair amount to do. On the whole it may be said of Southend that, although beaten, they were by no means disgraced, and judging by the comments of the Sheffield people leaving the ground, they had seen several inferior teams at Bramall Lane this season.

The wearers of the red and white stripes had been undergoing special training on the Derbyshire moors for the Cup-tie, and they took the field in the pink of condition. They were, however, without Utley, their captain, and Kitchen, their chief goalscorer, but they were fortunate in having very capable substitutes.

The match aroused wonderful interest in Sheffield, for it was the first Cup-tie there for five years, and local supporters were very anxious to see the Cupholders did not relinquish their grasp of their trophy. To most of them

Southend United were an unknown quantity, and the Blades did not make the mistake of under-estimating their opponents. The following note is an extract from the Sheffield United programme: – 'Southend United are worthy opponents to meet the Cupholders. They have the spirit to rise to a big occasion, and we shall see a stern struggle this afternoon.

Their fighting temperament is shown in their cup game with Watford, when they defeated a club that is in the running for the Southern League championship, and this spirit was further emphasised last Saturday, when they went to Portsmouth and humbled the Southern League leaders. Southend have experience and young ambitious blood blended in their team, the two elements to make a cup-fighting team.'

One could not help admiring the tenacity with which Southend stuck to their task. An early goal such as Sheffield obtained might have caused many sides to go to pieces. But not so the Blues. They kept pegging away, and trying to restore the balance, and it was not until three minutes before the interval that the second goal came.

Though it was generally accepted that this settled the issue the Seasiders never once wavered. As they had had the advantage of the wind in the first moiety, it was believed that the second forty-five would see Sheffield mostly on the attack. Instead, however, the visitors had quite their fair share of the game, and the Blades were only allowed to increase their score by means of a penalty. This speaks well for the solidarity of the defence.

Bramall Lane is a wonderful ground. It has stands on three sides of it, though those who occupy the stand on the cricket side of the enclosure are about 150 yards away from play, and must only get an indifferent view of it. It was the biggest crowd of people a Southend side has ever played before, and it was, looking down on the ground, a wonderful sight to see about 40,000 faces following with great interest and excitement the various phases of the game. They were a good sporting crowd however, and were not slow to recognise merit in the opposing side.

The Press box on the Bramall Lane ground is right at the top of the stand, all comfortably covered in, and it is a luxury to watch a match under such conditions compared with the arrangements at the Kursaal. It is, indeed, a bird's eye view. It will be noticed that both in attendance and receipts, the tie at Sheffield was the second largest of the round.

Not a little feeling crept into Saturday's game, and several players on both sides had to be spoken to by the referee. Mr. Gee's control of the game was not of the best, and some of his decisions were weak. In fact, the refereeing was the one blot on the game. Both the Football Association and the Leagues should revise their list of referees. The time has long gone by when some should be place on the retired list.

The Southend team travelled up to Sheffield on Friday night, accompanied by five directors and about twenty other enthusiasts, including some ladies.

They went to the Sheffield Hippodrome on Friday night to see 'The Splinters.' They had been quietly training at home all the week, and turned out as fit as fiddles. In fact, they finished the game much fresher than did the Blades.

Leahy had a good number of shots to deal with, and got through his task well. At the close the crowd accorded him quite an ovation. The majority of the shots which came to hand were not very difficult, but he showed good judgement in dealing with a large number of centres which dropped in close proximity of his bar. When Fazackerly obtained his second goal Leahy just got his hand to the sphere, but could not hold it, while he had bad luck with the penalty, after once parrying the shot.

Reid was hardly up to his best form. In the first half he was frequently beaten for pace in the mud, but in the second he improved greatly, and played with his old-time judgement. Marshall again showed brilliant form and good as were the Sheffield backs, they were not in front of Marshall. His kicking with a greasy and heavy ball was admirable, while he showed intelligent anticipation in breaking up the Sheffield combination.

The halves were not in their happiest vein. Wileman displayed rare determination, but was scarcely as successful in his tackling as his wont. Bollington did exceptionally well against three brainy forwards, but Evans scarcely held Fazackerly and Thompson. He was inclined to wander, with the result that Fazackerly had too much rope. In the last half-hour, however, Evans reached his top form and displayed far more confidence. Bridgeman, who was selected for the outside right position, was responsible for several good efforts and he and Burrill proved a capable wing, though the last named was not in the picture quite so much as usual.

Frost had few openings, but those he had he took full advantage of, and he swung the leather about well. Lot Jones was exceedingly clever and tried desperately to weave an opening for his colleagues. On many occasions he sent Young away with finely-judged passes, with the result that the left-winger was one of the most conspicuous men on the field.

Gough accounted for everything that came his way. Only once was he in difficulties and that was when he was bowled over in possession. Sturgess kicked with delightful ease and he and Milton exhibited a capital understanding, covering each other with great skill.

A tremendous worker was Beaumont at centre half and he proved of the utmost assistance to the men in front of him. Brelsford was an ideal wing half, while Pantling was ever in the train of the ball. Thompson was very fast off the mark and swung in many delightful centres from a variety of angles. The artistry of Fazackerly I have already referred to, and he was the brains of the front rank. Johnson demonstrated great dash but little else and he was hardly up to the calibre of the other men. Brayshaw was a sympathetic partner to Gillespie, who also showed by his well-timed centres that he knew where the goal lay.

The teams faced each other in the following order: –

SOUTHEND UNITED: Leahy; Reid and Marshall; Wileman, Bollington and Evans; Bridgeman, Burrill, Frost, Jones and Young.

SHEFFIELD UNITED: Gough; Sturgess and Milton; Brelsford, Beaumont and Pantling; Thompson, Fazackerly, Johnson, Brayshaw and Gillespie.

Referee, Mr. J. Gee, Manchester.

Wileman won the toss and elected to play towards the town goal. Leahy was early called upon in having to rush out and save from Gillespie. Fazackerly then secured about twenty yards out and, dribbling past four players, he scored a superb goal at the end of four minutes. The Southend backs were kicking with no great certainty at the outset.

The rain, which had so far only been drizzling, now came pelting down. Bridgeman initiated a Southend attack, but Sturgess dispossessed Frost. Back went Sheffield and Gillespie could only put the kick behind. Bridgeman was again the chief agent in a further sortie by the Blues, but the movement was spoiled by Lot Jones infringing the offside rule. Further trouble nearly befell Southend when a centre from Thompson got their defence in a tangle, but Leahy managed to pick up just as Brayshaw was full pelt for goal. Burrill was responsible for a smart effort which sent Bridgeman away and he forced a corner off Milton. This was booted away by Beaumont. Thompson centred for Brayshaw to head into the net, but he was yards offside and the whistle had previously gone for the infringement.

Burrill and Bridgeman went down the wing in fine style, but once more Southend were pulled up for offside. Jones gave to Young, who sent in a hot one, but Gough cleared smartly. At the other end Leahy had to race from his charge and boot away to prevent Fazackerly and Johnson getting through. Reid was hurt owing to coming into collision with another player's head and as a result he sustained a black eye but was able to resume. Leahy was called into action again to stop a beauty from Thompson. Fazackerly spelt danger when he again broke away past the Southend backs, but Leahy beat him in a race for the ball. A free kick to Southend was quickly nullified by offside, Frost being the transgressor. Gillespie caused Leahy to handle and the same player came into prominence again when he obtained a corner against Reid. He placed the kick perfectly and Fazackerly shot hard for the corner, but Leahy went to full-length to save.

On one or two occasions the Sheffield backs showed some difficulty in dealing with the greasy ball and a corner came Southend's way. This provided Young with a good opening but he lost a scoring chance with a shot sadly wide. Burrill had hard luck in not breaking through. Bollington saved an awkward situation following a corner. Three minutes from the 'refresher' Beaumont took a free twenty yards out and Fazackerly wheeled round and drove into the net. A third almost came in the next minute, for Johnson dashed forward and hit the crossbar. Before half-time Fazackerly obtained a corner, but it was fruitless and the interval arrived with the home club leading by two goals to nil.

Resuming, the homesters went down in good style, but offside sent them back again. The Southend had quite a turn and they were not outside the Sheffield territory for ten minutes, though Gough was not seriously challenged. A corner kick to Sheffield ended in Brelsford shooting wide. A free to the red and whites was charged down and in a scramble Johnson was hurt, but was able to continue on the field. Leahy did well to keep one out from Gillespie.

Young tested Gough with a rare teaser and before he could dispose of it he was bowled over by Frost, but he managed to clear his lines. Bridgeman next had a pot, but Gough proved his reliability again. Leahy earned cheers for a capital save from Johnson and then almost in the next minute he had to stop a beauty from Thompson. A free fell to Southend which was taken well by Wileman and this presented Burrill with an open goal, but he sent badly wide. After Leahy had dealt with a further dropping shot by Thompson. Gough negotiated two well-meant efforts from Jones and Young. In the closing stages Leahy was called upon two or three more occasions but he proved equal to all emergencies. Time was called, leaving Sheffield winners by three goals to nil.

CHAPTER FOUR

Southend United's Most Important Match?

The concluding match of the 1914-15 season was probably the most important in the club's history. Anything less than a victory would have seen Southend relegated to the Second Division for the 1919-20 season. This, almost certainly, would have seen Southend fail to gain membership of the new Third Division of the Football League at the end of that season.

Saturday, May 1st, 1915
Southern League, First Division
SOUTHEND UNITED 3, PLYMOUTH ARGYLE 1

On Saturday the curtain was finally rung down on the most chequered season in the history of football, and one that locally has been full of worries, disappointments, and failures. The application of the closure is a welcome relief to everyone who has had any connection with the game, but locally that relief is intensified by the fact that Southend United have retrieved what a fortnight ago looked like a hopeless position, and have made their place in Division I of the Southern League secure.

Now, whenever football is resumed, the United club will be able to restart where it left off – a first-class club. Many people probably hardly realised the vast importance of Saturday's game to the Southend club, for they were fighting not only for their position in Division I of the Southern League, but also for their existence as a club.

Had they lost and descended into Division II, it would probably have meant the end of the club, for when the game is resumed it would not have been easy to have formed a new club capable of fighting through Division II, with a prospect of promotion. Now, after the war, out of the ashes of the present club it is to be hoped that a new and flourishing organisation will mature.

Southend started the present season in brilliant style by defeating Southampton and Bristol; they have wound it up in equally dazzling fashion by victories over Millwall and Plymouth. The fame of that Millwall triumph will live for many a long day, but Plymouth was one of those sides that one expects Southend to defeat at home, for the Devonshire men have a poor away record. Still, the great issues hanging on the game made everyone view the contest with a little trepidation, especially as it was imperative to Southend in order to maintain their position that they should win.

Well, the United did win by three goals to one, and on the play they deserved to win by that score, and more. Five-sixths of the exchanges were conducted in the Plymouth territory, and after the scoring of the United's first goal by Emery, after eighteen minutes, the result rarely seemed to be in doubt. At one period in the second half, when the Pilgrims reduced Southend's two goal lead, the crowd had a bit of a shock, and there was a possibility of a draw, but this chance died away when Bradshaw scored the third.

For the United players the game was a trying one, and there was evidence at times that some of them were a trifle 'nervy.' They went out for victory from the first minute, and put plenty of dash into their play. While the Plymouth defence acquitted itself well, the forwards made little headway against the United defence, though at intervals they revealed flashes of very clever work. Safe in their position in the League the encounter was of little importance to them, but nevertheless they made Southend struggle hard to eke out their own salvation.

Like most clubs at the end of the season Plymouth were a trifle stale, for they have had to fight pretty hard in recent games to save their own bacon, and on Saturday they were not in one of their most effective humours, though admittedly they have been a very moderate side this season, and the fact of having so many old players in the team tells its tale when they are pitted against a young lot of men.

The contest, from a football point of view, was a very moderate one. One side had too much control of the leather for it to be really productive of a good game, but one had to admire the whole-hearted energy with which Southend set about their task, though there were times when their over-eagerness lost them openings. The Blues defence played very soundly throughout, and though the forwards did not show such fine form as they did at the Den, their display was quite the best they have given at home since the middle of February. They shot with more force and sting than has been their wont, and their play was rendered more effective by the way the football was swung about, and the introduction of understanding and method.

Had the team played like they did against Millwall and Plymouth they would not have been struggling to avoid relegation on Saturday. Southend have given their supporters many frights before, but this season they have had the closest shave imaginable. However, the splendid fight put up by the players in the last two games makes one ready to forgive many of the sins of the pest.

One of the features of the game was the brilliant work in the Plymouth goal of Craig. He played well in the first moiety, but in the second he made several saves bordering on the miraculous. Mr. Bob Jack tells me that he considers Craig is the best goalkeeper in the Southern League, and judging by his display on Saturday he has a career of great promise, for he has youth on his side. Southend certainly deserved a goal lead at the interval, though they were playing against wind and sun, and there was some discontent when Mr. Barton disallowed what looked like a good goal headed by Bradshaw. Contrary to general belief, however, the referee did not disallow the point on the ground of offside, but because he thought that Burrill had impeded Craig. The second half was nearly wholly contested in the Plymouth half, and shots were rained in at their goal, and it speaks well for Craig's prowess and agility that he was beaten but twice; Manager Bradshaw doing the trick each time.

Certainly the weather was not such as is conducive to good football and a lot of running about. It was a very hot afternoon – almost oppressive, and the ground was very hard and dry, clouds of dust being frequently raised in the scramble for the ball. On the concrete-like surface the leather frequently came up at very sharp angles and proved difficult to control.

It was mainly because the Blues adapted themselves much better to the conditions than their opponents and got the sphere more perfectly under control that they won. The attendance at the game showed that a large number of Southend people are still greatly interested in the club, and over 3,000 were present – quite the largest attendance for some months. While the crowd waxed quite enthusiastic at the home club's success it is safe to say that in no place will the news be more cordially welcomed than amongst the Southend lads who are fighting for their country at the front. All through the men in the trenches from Southend have taken a keen interest in the doings of the club, and have deplored the fact from time to time 'that the good old Blues are doing so badly.'

In goal, Leahy had almost a sinecure, and throughout the game he never had a difficult shot. He, however, appeared to be suffering from an attack of nerves, and the goal which Plymouth scored should have been stopped, as it was a very simple little header. Marshall played a faultless game, and Robson also kicked well and was responsible for some clever tackles. Next to Craig probably the man who stood out pre-eminently amongst his colleagues was Emery, who showed wonderful form. His tackling was irresistible, and he made several fine dribbles, one of which was deservedly rewarded by a goal. Emery has not played a better game this season. Bassett did not reproduce the good form he showed against Millwall, but put in some good service. Steel also did very well and fed his wing nicely.

While in no way wishing to adopt a position of 'I told you so,' the introduction of Bradshaw amongst the inside forwards has had much to do with the United's success in the last two games. For the last three seasons Bradshaw has had to come into the team – though not on the playing list – to pull the club out of a hole at the end of the season. This season it has again been the case. Untrained, he has played well, and there is little doubt that he is still the best inside man the United have. He has led the line well in the last two matches, and on Saturday crowned his performance by a couple of goals. Wileman again showed a considerable aptitude for the outside right position, and did some capital centring, while Burton played a cool and clever game. Burrill had very hard luck in not scoring on two or three occasions, but displayed some capital football. Young bustled into his work well, but would be more effective if he managed to get his centres in first time, instead of delaying a sufficient period to allow the opposing defence to get into position.

Little fault could be found with the Plymouth last line of defence, for in addition to Craig's goalkeeping, Atterbury and Butler defended well, though at times their kicking was not well directed. Atterbury and Butler have had a long association together, and as a pair they are probably the oldest playing for any club in England to-day. For seven years with short intervals here and there they have played uninterruptedly for Plymouth Argyle. An old fashioned favourite in 'Prince' Blott was operating at right-half for the Argyle, and he showed some of his old cleverness. Wilcox did a lot of good work in the centre, while Baker was not as energetic as usual. McCormick, whose right place is half-back, was not a success on the extreme wing, but Gallogley showed great trickiness and control of the ball. Burch was the most thrustful of the line, but little was seen of the left wing; so completely did Emery dominate them.

Under the direction of Mr. F.W. Barton the teams lined up as follows: –

SOUTHEND: Leahy; Marshall and Pvte. Robson; Emery, Bassett and Steel; Wileman, Barton, Bradshaw, Burrill and Young.

PLYMOUTH ARGYLE: Craig; Butler and Atterbury; Blott, Wilcox and Baker; McCormick, Gallogley, Burch, Forbes and Dixon.

Winning the toss the Argyle kicked down the slope, but the United immediately swarmed round the visitors' goal. Nice work by Burrill gave Bradshaw an opening, but as he was getting through Craig came out and smothered his shot. The Plymouth goalie was again called upon a moment later to save from Emery, while Burrill essayed a fine drive, which narrowly missed the bar. At the other end McCormick spoilt a couple of favourable opportunities by putting tamely outside.

Burch made a single-handed attempt to weave his way through, but was pulled in smart style by Robson. A corner to Southend was fruitless owing to Burrill getting into an offside position. Eighteen minutes from the start Bradshaw worked past Wilcox and gave to Burton, who was temporarily stopped, but Emery, following up, dribbled past two players and had Craig well beaten with a sharp oblique shot.

Back went Southend, and Wileman sent in a high one, which Craig only just kept out, and Bradshaw following up headed into the net. In the melee the referee adjudged that Burrill had impeded the Plymouth 'keeper, and the point was disallowed. At this point the Blues were having all the play, and in quick succession Craig had to twice clear from Bradshaw, who was adapting the right tactics in harassing the opposing backs. Dixon took the leather to the other end, but when matters looked dangerous Marshall nipped in and cleared. The Pilgrims obtained a corner, but Forbes headed wide. Just before the interval Burch got away and tested Leahy with a swift daisycutter, which he easily dealt with. At half-time Southend led by one goal to nil.

Upon the resumption, Burrill got clean away from a pass by Bradshaw, and sending in a sharp grounder, he appeared to have Craig beaten, when the goalkeeper made a lightning dive and whipped the ball out of the corner. Much disappointment was also caused when Bradshaw got clean away, but with only Craig to beat the goalie came out to meet him, and in a mix-up the Plymouth defenders saved the situation. Bassett next attempted to increase Southend's advantage, but his drive, following a corner, went less than a foot over the bar. Just later Bassett again came near scoring with an unexpected shot, but once again the Plymouth custodian parried his effort. The Blues were awarded a free about twenty yards out, and Wileman with a mighty drive seemed a certain scorer, but Craig brought off a wonderful clearance at the expense of a corner.

It was at this point simply Craig against the United forwards, and the 'keeper was again the hero of the situation in thwarting a well-directed one from Bassett. After sixty-five minutes the United supporters were made more comfortable, for Burton passed to Bradshaw, who, from twelve yards range, lifted the ball out of Craig's reach into the net. At first it looked as if the goalie had the sphere covered, but it swerved away from him as he jumped. Burrill looked a certain scorer a few moments later, but Craig earned loud cheers for a wonderful one-handed save.

With a quarter of an hour to go Plymouth reduced the lead. This was by means of a run by Gallogley, who placed the ball for McCormick to centre. This he did accurately, and Burch headed in. Leahy badly judged the flight of the ball, and though Marshall and Emery tried to prevent it going over the line they could not do so. The home supporters were not long kept in suspense, for Bradshaw ran through and scored the third amid much enthusiasm. Having restored the balance Southend enjoyed all the play until the close, Craig repeatedly distinguishing himself in goal. Thus Southend won by three goals to one.

CHAPTER FIVE

'Southend Standard' Football Memories

SOUTHEND UNITED REMINISCENCES 1920-21

PART TWENTY-TWO *(Continued from page 68)*

This season (1919-20) proved the end of the Southern League as a first-class competition, for at the annual meeting of the Football League, a Third Division was formed, and members of Division I of the Southern League were taken over as associate members of the League, to be known as the Southern Section. A Northern Section was formed twelve months later. The fact that Cardiff City were leaving the Southern League, as West Ham United had done in the previous season, had much to do with this decision. Meanwhile, there had been a change in the managership of Southend United, for Mr. Liddell was offered, and accepted, the position as manager of Queen's Park Rangers. He was succeeded by Mr. T. Mather (subsequently Secretary of Stoke and now of Newcastle United), who was previously assistant manager of Manchester City.

Among the new players whom Mr. Mather secured were: T. Capper, goal-keeper (Dundee), Barnes (Watford), W.A. Newton, full-back (Manchester City), J. Henderson, centre-half (Manchester City), C. Myers, inside-forward (Bradford City), J.A. Dorsett, outside-left (Manchester City) and T.A. Nuttall, inside-right (St. Mirren). Old players re-signed were Bob Reid and J. Evans (backs), Bollington and Wileman (half-backs), G.J. Nicholls and E. Allen (forwards). Several other amateurs were also obtained, while, as the position of centre-half caused the management some anxiety, they subsequently secured the transfer of Arthur Whalley, the Manchester United centre-half, who was probably the greatest pivot, general and skipper the United ever had.

It was felt that the formation of the Third Division opened out a new era, and provided an opportunity for Southend and the remainder of the old Southern League clubs to reach higher status. In the first season Crystal Palace proved to be the successful team to be promoted. In those days clubs met each other at home and away on successive Saturdays, and, as a result, many contests were far from pleasant.

Southend United started with a victory against Brighton, but then lost five of the next six fixtures, and eventually finished up with a position eighth from the bottom, with 14 successes, 22 losses and eight draws, goals for being 44 and against 59. At home they won 13, drew two and lost six, and away they were successful only once, six matches being drawn and 14 lost. They scored only 12 goals in the 21 away fixtures. In addition to Brighton, they won at the Kursaal against Grimsby 3-1, Watford 4-1, Queen's Park Rangers 1-0,

Portsmouth 2-1, Plymouth 2-1, Newport 2-1, Southampton 1-0, Reading 1-0, Gillingham 1-0, Bristol Rovers 1-0, Brentford 4-1, and Norwich City 3-1. Their single success away from home was against the champions, Crystal Palace 3-2, but the Palace obtained their revenge at the Kursaal in the last match of the season, winning 2-0.

After the contest at Selhurst against Crystal Palace, there was a demonstration against the United players and the referee (Mr. H. Curtis, now manager of Brentford), and the crowd invaded the pitch. As a result, the Palace ground was closed by the Football Association for a fortnight. Clubs who took four points from the Blues were: Swindon, Northampton, Merthyr, Swansea and Millwall, while Luton secured three. No club sacrificed four to Southend, but Plymouth, Newport and Brentford yielded three each.

Two outstandingly unpleasant games during that season were the meetings between Merthyr and Southend at the Kursaal and between Portsmouth and Southend at Fratton Park. In the first-mentioned game, on November 27th, 1920, scenes ended in Fairclough, the United centre-forward, being ordered from the field — a decision which Southend supporters deemed to be unwarranted — and there was an ugly demonstration at the close of the match against the referee and the visiting players, which subsequently drew a warning from the Football Association. Sergeant, a United amateur winger, broke a wrist in this match, so the United finished with ten men.

Then, at Portsmouth on November 13th, 1920, players apparently nursed grievances from the previous week and scenes most damaging to football were witnessed. I commented on these facts and deprecated the rough play, which I stated was injurious to the game and should be inquired into. The late Mr. C.E. Sutcliffe, until recently President of the Football League, who did not see the match, but who wrote an weekly article in a Portsmouth paper, severely criticised me for my remarks, but, when a Commission of the Football League enquired into the facts and severely cautioned both clubs as to their play in future, he apologized in the frankest terms.

PART TWENTY-THREE

This (1920-21) season was probably the United's most memorable one up to date in F.A. Cup-ties, for they reached the third round, after playing through from the sixth qualifying stage, and it was during this season that the unforgettable tie with Tottenham Hotspur was fought. The United first beat Hednesford Town 3-1 at Southend and in the first round proper had to meet Eccles United, whom they vanquished 5-1 at the Kursaal. Next they were drawn against Blackpool, also at Southend, and after an exciting encounter they beat the then Second Leaguers 1-0, Joe Dorsett scoring late in the second half. The then Mayor (the late Sir John Francis) gave the players a complimentary dinner at the Palace Hotel to celebrate the victory. Then in the third round on February 19th, the luck of the draw decided they should meet the

'Spurs at the Kursaal. Though the United ground had been equipped with a large grandstand, it was very deficient in banking and was not suited to holding a large crowd. Further accommodation was necessary, as it was expected there would be a considerable influx from North London.

The Southend supporters expressed a strong desire for the match to be played at the Kursaal and intimated that, sooner than the tie should be transferred to White Hart Lane, they would prefer a three shillings admittance fee. The directors ultimately decided that the match should be played at Southend and a three shillings admittance fee was decided upon, with 10s. 6d. and £1. 1s. tickets for the grandstand. Supporters of the club made the best use of the two intervening weeks to cart hundreds of loads of ballast to improve the bankings, and never did a club have a more enthusiastic if somewhat limited backing than the United. The directors spent £750 on trebling the terracing and accommodation. Despite the high charges, the attendance was 11,661, and the gate remains a record for the club to this day, viz. £2,963.

The match will ever remain a subject of controversy among older supporters of the Blues on account of several incidents that occurred. The late Joe Walters netted early what appeared to most to be a good goal for Southend, but the referee disallowed it. Walters ran in from behind the ball and was not in front of it. Then Nicholls scored for the United, but prior to the interval Cantrell equalized. Just before half-time was sounded the United were awarded a penalty kick, which Whalley was about to take, when the referee (Mr. N. Watson) moved the ball. Whalley moved it again, but the referee moved it once more and forbade Whalley to touch it again. Then, to the chagrin of the United supporters, Whalley shot wide. This incident had a marked effect on the morale of the United in the second half and the 'Spurs scored thrice through Banks, Bliss and Seed, to win 4-1.

The 'Spurs won the cup that year against the Wolves, whose eleven contained three ex-Southend players in Marshall, Woodward and Burrill. As the teams which played that afternoon are often a matter of argument, it is appropriate to give them: – Southend United: Capper; Newton and Evans (J.), Wileman, Whalley and Martin; Nicholls, Nuttall, Fairclough, Walters and Dorsett. Tottenham Hotspur: Jacques; Clay and M'Donald; Smith, Walters and Grimsdell; Banks, Seed, Cantrell, Bliss and Dimmock. In the Southend Charity Cup Final the United lost at home to the Arsenal, 4-0, The trophy was presented by the late Mr. E.T. Smith.

Before the end of the season, Fairclough was transferred to Bristol City and was out eight times for them, scoring five goals. The appearances of players in the Third Division were: T. Capper, 39; H. Wileman, 37; B. Martin, 36; T. Nuttall, 35; J. Dorsett, 34; J. Evans, 32; A. Whalley, 30; W. Newton, 29; R. Reid, 28; J. Henderson, 23; C. Myers, 22; E.J. Nicholls, 21; E. Allen, 4; H.A. Allen, 5; H. Baldwin, 7; E. Barnes, 1; J. Bollington, 1; H. Dickenson, 3; A. Ford, 7; R. Haynes, 1; J. Lawson, 6; E. Mather, 3; J. Mather (goal), 2; F. Sergeant, 2;

and T. Shaw and W.H. Lees, one each. In all games, Capper and Wileman made the most appearances, viz. 45 out of 49, and the next were Nuttall, 42; Martin, 40; Dorsett, 37; Evans, 36; Newton, 36; Whalley, 34; and Walters, 33. League goal-scorers were: Fairclough, 15; Nuttall, 9; Walters and Whalley, 5 each; Dorsett, 3; Myers, 2; Baldwin, E. Mather and Newton, one each. Hodson (Brentford) and Russell (Plymouth) accidentally sent the ball into their own net. During the season Wileman was granted a benefit, the third Southend player to receive one. Chiefly due to the proceeds from transfers, a profit was made on the season of £371.10s. No reserve team was run in the season 1920-21, Southend Corinthian occupying the Kursaal on alternate Saturdays, when they competed in the South Essex League.

CHAPTER SIX

A Selection of Match Reports 1920-1939

Monday, May 9th, 1921
Southend Charity Cup Final
SOUTHEND UNITED 0, ARSENAL 4

Southend United made an inglorious finish to an unsatisfactory season when they were beaten before their own spectators on Monday evening by the Arsenal, by four goals to nil. The result did not exaggerate the superiority of the wearers of the red shirts, for they won when and how they liked. They did not send a full First League team down, but the mixed eleven which they put in the field made Southend look very poor stuff indeed. If the Southend directors did not realise it before they must have had it painfully brought home to them with emphasis that without Whalley the team is mediocre, and that for the greater part of the second half of the season the centre-half has been, with some loyal assistance, carrying the side through. Whalley has been a splendid servant to the club, and his absence in the final match was to be regretted.

What must have been very apparent to the spectators was that in speed and dash the Arsenal were pre-eminently superior to the homesters, and they went through the cumbersome, clumsy and slow Southend defence at will. I wish that I could say something favourable about the display of the home team, but with the exception of a word of praise for the few players who never gave up trying, it is impossible. It was a shocking exhibition of lethargy and inefficiency. In such a contest too, it is reprehensible to see dirty tactics, and when, after a series of incidents which are only to be condemned, players came to blows and there was an ugly scene, it was about the limit for a charity game. In fairness to the Arsenal it must be confessed that the Southend players were largely to blame for what occurred, and the home spectators should have realised that instead of barracking the winners. I don't mind saying quite plainly that there were men on the field on Monday whom I am very pleased the directors do not intend to re-sign.

Local charities should benefit to a material sum as a result of the contest, and it was a happy thought on the part of Mr. Smith, one of the United directors, to present the Cup for the purpose. This year he also gave handsome gold medals, which the Arsenal players received. These should have been an incentive to the United players to have put a little more wholeheartedness into the play than they did, and it was a thousand pities that it should have been such a disappointing and unpleasant game, for the attendance was quite satisfactory, fully 5,000 people being present on a bright, pleasant evening. The Arsenal played football; the Blues did not. They were without method and under-standing, and indulged in wild and aimless kicking and passing. A breeze played tricks with the ball, but the Reds controlled it easily, and their quick, deft touches made rapid progress, while the Southend defence was outpaced throughout.

Mather, in the Southend goal, made some good saves, but was badly at sea many times and lacked anticipation and experience, while a dropping centre always had him guessing. Evans played well, but Reid was quickly done and beaten early in the game. Wileman alone played well among the halves, for Henderson was hopeless at centre-half, and Martin could not cope with the wing against him. Nuttall tried hard, but he was the only forward to do any-thing, and even he seemed to get disgusted before the end. Baldwin was dis-appointing and did not show his normal dash and fearlessness. Mather, except for an early effort, was never in the picture. Walters started well but the epi-demic seemed also to seize hold of him, and Newton played as if he didn't care.

On the other hand the Arsenal played wholeheartedly, and exhibited a fine defence. Dunn made some fine saves, though not appearing too confident in his clearing. Hutchens, the old Croydon Common back, was the best defend-er on the field and kicked with great power and good length, while Peart was little behind him. The halves were a level and effective trio. Rutherford rarely over-exerted himself, but when he did he displayed the master-mind and some of his efforts were delightfully clever. White was a splendid leader, with dash, speed and incisiveness, while Tonner on the left was clever and centred well.

The United played down the slope in the first half with the wind against them. Mather early made a good run, bearing out on to the right, and though he shot well, Dunn saved at the second attempt, gathering the ball in the cor-ner. Five minutes from the start, Tonner centred to White, who left Reid stand-ing still, and, breaking clean through, he scored a good goal. The Southend goalie cleared well from Pattison, following a corner, while Dunn scooped out a capital try from Nuttall. Walters then missed an open-goal, for after Dunn had left his charge to clear, the forward was given an empty net to shoot at, but he drove outside.

A mistake by J. Mather in failing to divert a centre from Tonner left Hopkins with an open goal, but he shot against the foot of the post and the ball re-bounced into play. It was nearly a bad a miss as that of Walters. Baldwin, with a fine centre, gave Walters another gilt-edged chance, but once more he missed. Rutherford dropped the ball in off the line with perfect accu-racy, and Tonner returning, White beat J. Mather, but just as the ball was going over the line Evans dashed in and saved what looked like a foregone conclu-sion. Walters made one commendable effort, but his shot passed just over, while J. Mather was somewhat fortunate to get a splendid attempt by White away at the second attempt. At half-time the Arsenal led by a goal to nil. E.

Mather was the first to come into prominence on resuming, and though he sent in a beauty from 18 yards range, Dunn managed to scrape it out of the corner.

The goalkeeper Mather earned cheers for a save at full length from Blyth. Rutherford centred beautifully and White headed through, but to the amazement of everyone the referee adjudged it offside. He was quite wrong, for the point was as legitimate as any that has been scored, for White was behind the ball. Nuttall made a great attempt to break through, and Baldwin nearly equalised; Dunn measuring his length on the ground to scrape it out of the corner. Rutherford raced away and placed so delightfully that White had no difficulty in scoring with a shot which left his foot like an arrow from a bow. Though Nuttall made one break through only to see Dunn save cleverly, Southend now gave up the ghost. In the last five minutes the Southend defence got into hopeless tangles and Blyth and Hopkins added soft points.

Teams: –

SOUTHEND: J. Mather; Reid and Evans; Wileman, Henderson and Martin; Baldwin, Nuttall, E. Mather, Walters and Newton.

ARSENAL: Dunn; Peart and Hutchens; Whittaker, Pattison and McKinnon; Rutherford, Blyth, White, Hopkins and Tonner.

Saturday, December 6th, 1924
Football League, Third Division (Southern Section)
SOUTHEND UNITED 6, BRENTFORD 1

Brentford are having a very unfortunate time and, notwithstanding all their changes and the acquisition of Alec Graham, the ex-Scottish International centre-half from the Arsenal, they were trounced at the Kursaal, on Saturday, by six goals to one. It was not surprising to find changes in a team that was beaten 5-3 by the amateurs of St. Albans the previous week, and it was evident from this game that if the 'Bees' are to make their way up the League ladder this season they will have to get busy soon. The United have played several better games this year, yet they were able to make the margin sufficiently large to indicate a decided superiority. O'Rawe was not able to play after his gruelling time at Reading and Dorey provided a substitute equal to the occasion. The outstanding feature, however, was the sudden development of a left wing such as the United have not had in previous matches. This was not so much due to the substitution of Wolfe for Macdonald at outside left as to the surprising incisiveness shown by Dobson, who established a personal record by scoring no fewer than four goals, McClelland claiming the other two. That for Brentford was headed by Rolph, the outside left, following a corner kick. Although the standard of football shown was not high by reason of the feeble opposition offered by the visitors, there was plenty to interest the crowd, who took an unusual delight in Dobson's achievement.

It is generally conceded that Harry Dobson can play good football in midfield, but is not a goal-getter. His work is generally that of leading up or starting an attack, and rarely is he seen to add the finishing touch. This year he seems to have kept his place in the team on his midfield work, though he has occasionally added a goal from the inside left position with his head. Yet those who did not see him play at Gillingham last season could not realise to the full his capabilities.

On a dry and worm-eaten pitch over in Kent he surprised many of his best friends by the way he came through with the ball and rounded off his efforts. In that game he was made to pay the penalty of a successful player who is not over robust. He received so much attention, after getting a couple of goals, that he had to be carried off the field, and it was a battered, bruised and sick man who went out to take his place, after the interval. That was one occasion when Dobson fully merited the confidence of his admirers. Saturday last was another and even more successful one.

The crowd that lined the Kursaal enclosure saw in a familiar figure a totally different player from the one to whom they were accustomed. This Dobson could come through with the ball, beat a couple of opponents by his dainty touches of toe and finish by a drive along the carpet, that left the eye-witnesses gasping. His cool nerve enabled him to shoot — with either foot be it remarked – where the goalkeeper was not, and when he failed to net the ball it was only the woodwork that beat him. Truly a transformation, a Dobson that was not recognised even by his best friends! Some people may be unkind enough to think that in this game Dobson surprised himself. I happen to know differently. In conversation with him a few weeks ago he showed the utmost self-confidence – a valuable asset, be it said, to player and critic alike. His parting words I well remember, 'I shall show them yet!' Naturally the determination he showed then comes back to mind on this occasion, and, personally, I am more than pleased that he has been as good as his word.

It is quite possible that there will be two opinions upon the success of Wolfe as an outside-left. The people near the little stand will not think as much of him as those on the other side perhaps, and if that happens to be the case the chief reason will be that the young Welshman played all his best football on one side of the ground. He had very few opportunities in the initial forty-five. Up to half-time, when he came more directly under the purview of the Kursaal side, he had done nothing of note and there can be small wonder if hasty judges had written his debut down as a failure. I am not inclined to take that view. He is a big, strong fellow, with a fair amount of speed, and his ability to work the ball is undoubted. Moreover, he has quite a full share of that attribute which is generally described by the simple word 'pluck.' There is not a trace of over-statement in those remarks, for in every game he has revealed those traits. Where he has disappointed hitherto has been in his tendency to try to do too much and to hang on to the ball until the best opening was lost.

That is a characteristic of many men who have good command of the ball, but when it is found it is usually in an inside position. By being put out on the wing Wolfe will be less likely to fall into that mistake, but at the same time it may be doubly fatal to him if he does. It must also be borne in mind that Wolfe's absence from the team has been prima fade, as the lawyers' say, due to an injury. I very much doubt whether he could have been kept out so long had it not been for that mishap.

It is true that he has had a run of two in the reserves of late, yet, to be perfectly fair to him, surely it would not be too much to say that his poor showing in the first half was chiefly due to his unaccustomed position and to the doubt as to the extent upon which he could rely upon his knee. When he warmed to his work in the second half the thrill of the play called him and in responding he grew more confident. If we judge him on his play after the interval we find a much better result and, speaking generally, I should think that if Wolfe makes up his mind to capture that place in the team he can easily do it, with benefit to himself and to the club. Where none are perfect, comparisons are odious and I will, therefore, leave the matter at that.

McClelland scored a goal in the first minute which certainly appeared to be offside. He put it into the net with his head from a forward pass by Edwards, and Mr. H.J. Weber, who was within a few yards of the spot and apparently in a very good position to judge, awarded the point. Unless he saw something which escaped the people in the stand, this initial mistake was a very bad one. An effort which followed a moment later was much more deserving of success. Broadbent misjudged the ball in the air and Johnson was quick to seize the opportunity and centre with the defence spread-eagled. McClelland did his best to reach the ball with a scythe-like sweep of his foot, but it evaded him and Edwards, who followed up smartly, made a great shot, which Gilbert did well to turn round the upright.

There was a gasp when the Brentford left broke away and H. Williams shot forward from a ground pass by Rolph, which he took in his stride. Donnelly touched the ball with his foot, and it was twisting in the direction of the goal when Hayes realised the change in direction and quickly pounced upon it. Then Dobson gave us a foretaste of what was to follow by snapping up a pass from McClelland on the edge of the penalty area, beating two opponents in a swerve to the right and then driving along the ground for the far post. Although he flung himself full length at the ball, Gilbert was beaten, but it struck the foot of the upright. Then, a quarter of an hour from the start, Hayes made the mistake of carrying the ball over the touchline in fielding a simple shot and the visitors were awarded a flag kick. This was well placed and with the ball turning away from him Hayes could only touch it with the tips of his fingers. Standing unmarked on the far side of the goal, the opposition having been centred upon H. Williams, Rolph met the ball with his head and sent it forward into the net.

With the scores level, the spectators saw the best the Brentford team were capable of producing. Taking a neat pass, Rolph made the situation look dangerous by a well-placed centre and Donnelly did well to clear the lines. This was followed by a pretty passing bout by Parker and Garnish, and the United backs had been beaten when the centre-forward grazed the bar with a hard drive. He was no more fortunate with his next attempt, for after a smart move on the left wing he tried a first time shot, which was well directed, but lacked sting, and Hayes was able to check-mate it.

The first chance of putting the Blues ahead fell to Bissett, who charged down an attempted clearance by Broadbent and found himself confronted by Gilbert only. The forward was in a fine position, slightly to the left of the goal, and it seemed odds on him scoring. As he shot Gilbert flung out arms and legs and his left boot happened to divert the ball, which went behind for a fruitless corner. In a match that produced seven goals this was one of the easiest chances of the day.

Then came Dobson's first. His tactics were similar to those which had so nearly brought him success earlier. He took a pass on the edge of the penalty area, beat each of the backs as they tackled him and concluded with a great shot well out of Gilbert's reach. Two minutes later Bissett whipped the ball out to Johnson somewhere near the half-way line. A foul was given against Cook, and from the kick McClelland headed to Dobson, who stood unmarked and scored his second, giving his side a lead of three goals to one at the interval.

Five minutes after the ball had again resumed its zig-zag journey a long kick from Donnelly set Wolfe in possession, and after winning a tussle with Cook near the line the winger centred along the ground and Dobson completed his hat-trick with a first-time shot. Still working, the inside left punched back to Edwards and the captain lobbed over to McClelland, who crashed a hard drive into the side net. Relief came when Parker and Clayson again combined in a good run, the latter shooting just out.

When Donnelly overdid things by dribbling too far, Parker obtained possession and, dashing through, shot over the crossbar as Sayles closed in upon him. For a time the exchanges were fairly even and then Bissett pushed a lovely pass forward for Johnson, who cut in at a great pace. The winger appeared to have an easy chance himself, but he preferred to touch the ball to McClelland, who easily deposited it at the back of the net. Then came a characteristic flash from Bissett, ending, however, with the only too frequent shot over the bar.

The Brentford opposition was being treated with little or no respect and when Wolfe took a good pass from Edwards and cleverly beat Cook, Gilbert had to fling himself full-length to save the shot at the foot of the upright. The probabilities are that it would have struck the woodwork, but the goalkeeper turned it round the post. Wolfe took the corner kick well and when Jewhurst and Dobson headed goalwards it looked as if once again the goalkeeper was going to be beaten, but Bissett used his hands instead of his head and the referee saw it. A few minutes later Wolfe was going through when an opponent handled just outside the area. The kick was placed over to McClelland, who headed on to the goal-line, where Dobson crowned a good day's work by adding the finishing touch. McClelland also had a try for his third by meeting a centre from Bissett and shaking the crossbar with his shot. The whistle went and it seemed that the referee had given him offside after the ball had come back from the bar, but that could hardly have been the case.

Brentford will have to find a few more men to back up Graham's efforts if they are ever to get away from the lowliest rung of the ladder. The forwards were not at all bad, but the wing halves and the backs were very weak, whilst Gilbert is not in that goalkeeping class which can save a forlorn hope. Graham himself was no great force and McClelland has played against several better men this season. 'Mac' was all through a powerful and efficient leader and was more than a match for the opposition, though it was chiefly centred upon him.

Dobson and Wolfe I have already dealt with and in the vanguard it only remains to be said that the right wing did not quite come up to expectations. Though it did provide McClelland with the second goal it could not be said that this flank was as persistent in attack as it has been against better players. Edwards was the best half-back, with Jewhurst starting slowly as usual and coming out on top at the finish. Dorey plugged along and was very useful in defence, but he has not yet learnt to give the ground pass to the wings. Sayles was boisterously effective and seemed to enjoy himself thoroughly. His kicking was of the type that invariably turned defence into attack. Donnelly was more than equal to the demands made upon him and Hayes had a comparatively light afternoon.

SOUTHEND UNITED: Hayes; Donnelly, Sayles; Jewhurst, Dorey, Edwards; Johnson, Bissett, McClelland, Dobson and Wolfe.

BRENTFORD: Gilbert; Cook, Broadbent; Walton, Graham, Johnstone; Clayson, Garnish, Parker, Williams (H.) and Rolph.

Referee: Mr. H.J. Weber, London.

Saturday, December 4th, 1926
Football League, Third Division (Southern Section)
SOUTHEND UNITED 5, CHARLTON ATHLETIC 0

A warm glow of confidence has filled the hearts of the Southend supporters following the defeat of Charlton by 5-0, on Saturday, and the game with Reading in the second round of the F.A. Cup is being awaited with every hope of a victorious issue. This feeling, based on the result of Saturday's match at the Kursaal, is all the stronger because it was the first time that the Blues have beaten the South Metropolitans. Now the record has been broken. Not only have the Blues beaten the one team that has for so long defied them, but they have given them the soundest trouncing of the season. Their worst defeat prior to Saturday was when the Reds lost by 4-1 to Bristol City. By the irony of fate, too, Charlton have been beaten this time by the score with which they defeated the Blues at the Valley at the end of last season. On the first half's play the team should do well.

In effect it might almost be said that there were two games between two different sets of teams at the Kursaal ground for this encounter. There was the dominant Southend of the first half against the struggling Athletic, with a weak intermediate line, and then in the second portion there was a United that was lacking in dash and precision of movement pitted against a still ineffective side of Londoners who could do little right. It was difficult to believe that it was the same United on the field after the change over.

On the resumption after the rest, it looked as though the Blues were going to content themselves with the lead they already had and were going to concentrate their energies on keeping the visitors at bay. This resting upon their laurels was disappointing to the spectators and took a lot of interest out of the game. Not until the closing stages did a goal come.

The first forty-five minutes flew by. The second three-quarters dragged. Even the score suggested the marked difference in the United's game. Against the conditions they played to win 4-0. In the second moiety they showed a slight superiority of 1-0. With such a good lead they could afford to ease up. The two wingers might have been more effective had they been faster on the ball, but, generally speaking, after the refresher the whole side was slower and not so incisive. They might had done much better had they cared to exert themselves, but they were rather lackadaisical.

In the first half the half-backs did great things by their swiftness and reliability. They worked more in unison than did the Reds' intermediate line. The latter was unable to hold the United vanguard. Sherlaw was well fed, and with reason, for he was the most dangerous of the Athletic's front line men. Cairns, like Hick, kept well up the field, but did not often become prominent. Tricker and Sherlaw made a good wing. Davies, as pivot, was unable to hold Hick. The Reds did not position themselves well, and, if there were any loose balls around, it was nearly always a Blue who found it.

The goals came from the usual source – Hick, Donovan and Smith – but the remaining forwards were closely associated with them. Hick had a good day and deserved his three goals, while Donovan, too, was as speedy and clever as ever. Smith's fault of waiting too much for the ball was again in evidence. The son of the old international might have got to a good many passes from both Beaumont and Donovan had he exerted himself a little more. He is inclined to wait until the ball is put right on to his foot. Passes went into touch on Saturday which should have been held. Donovan can be relied upon to place the ball to a colleague so that the latter can always get to it if he exercises determination. Robson made more attempts to get the ball, and some of his centres were well placed, but it was generally uncertain what would happen when he was given possession. It was upon Donovan, Hick and Surtees however, that the brunt of the foraging work fell. Donovan kept well back, as usual, and was the best forward on the field. Throwing himself whole-heartedly into the game, he again and again fed Hick and Smith. Once the ball was at his feet he rarely lost it to an opposing half. Hick was limping slightly with an injured knee in the second half, but even then he notched his third goal. Earlier in the game he was continually to the fore. Surtees was not so prominent as Donovan, but he accomplished a lot of useful work and he deserved a goal on at least two occasions. Robson and Surtees worked fairly well together, and, although they were unable to finish off their movements, their play was responsible for at least three of the goals.

Each of the United's goals were good ones. They were obtained by opportunities and none were gifts. Smith forced a corner and from his place kick the defenders conceded another. Robson took this and it culminated in Donovan getting his head to the ball, but Preedy stopped the effort. The Reds were unable to clear successfully and were by no means out of the wood. Play on the wing resulted in Robson getting his foot to the ball and dropping it in for Donovan to pounce upon it. Without a moment's hesitation he turned it between the two backs so that it rose beyond the reach of Preedy into the top of the net. Hick obtained the second goal in that fashion which is characteristic of him. Breaking away, he tapped out to Robson, who, in turn, kept the ball to himself a second or two, and at the opportune moment put across a fast centre. Hick was not too well placed, and the fact that Devine was bearing down on to him to force him away from goal towards the corner flag made things more difficult. Just when it looked as if he would lose possession, the leader of the Blues' attack twisted the ball in off the foot of Devine. The sphere turned and rolled into the far side of the net.

The goal which came next – then thirty-five minutes after the start – was a triumph of fine concerted work. A movement initiated by Jewhurst set Robson and Surtees on the move. Their progress was impeded by several visitors, but in spite of them they wove a way through and Donovan ran up to help. The inside left was surrounded by men in red jerseys and, being tackled, fell to the ground. He managed to square round however, and place the ball to Hick. It was a fine example of what determination and quick thinking can accomplish. Hick turned the leather into the net before Preedy had time to move, and then the Blues were three up. It did not look as if there would be another goal before the interval, but the home men were well away, carrying all before them, and they obtained one more. Two players shared the honour of it. They were Smith and Hick. Exciting times were frequent in the region of the visitor's goal, and a shot from Surtees had been saved with the ball almost rolling over the line. Anything might have happened when suddenly Hick drove for goal. The ball hit the underneath of the bar and dropped down to the ground. From the stand it looked as if it was over the line. Smith, however, followed up and slammed it into the back of the net to make sure.

The fifth goal came at the end of the second half. Smith had been trying to get in on the left, and a corner-kick came his way. The Athletic defenders cleared, but failed to put their own men in possession, with the consequence that the ball found its way to Robson. Taking it in, he swung it across the goal-mouth to Smith, who dropped it back to Hick, a few yards from goal. Instead of taking a first-timer, the centre-forward stopped the ball, looked to see where Preedy was standing and put the sphere well wide of him into the net.

SOUTHEND UNITED: Moore; French and Bell; Jewhurst, Purdy and Beaumont; Robson, Surtees, Hick, Donovan and Smith.

CHARLTON ATHLETIC: Preedy; Middleton and Devine; John, F. Davies and G.H. Armitage; Sherlaw, R.W. Tricker, Cairns, Rankin and Horton.

Referee: Mr. W.E. Russell, Swindon.

Easter Saturday, April 7th, 1928
Football League, Third Division (Southern Section)
SOUTHEND UNITED 7, QUEEN'S PARK RANGERS 0

Yes, the Blues won 7-0 and well the Rangers know it, for not only is that the heaviest defeat they have suffered this season, but it is the most substantial that has ever been registered by the Blues against them – or any other team for that matter – in first-class football. The score was once equalled – in 1910, when seven goals were run up against Millwall, but not since in first-class games, though in the second division of the Southern League they did eclipse this big scoring feat. The previous best victory of the Blues this season was against the Palace in September, when they defeated them 6-1. Saturday's loss was all the more bitter to the Rangers because only the previous afternoon they had a 'field day' at Newport, where they won 6-1.

From their point of view, it was a mean trick on the part of Fate to smile and smile practically with the same breath. If, however, their experience goes to show anything, it was that paper form is no true criterion, especially at holiday times. The prophets, for instance, were able to sit back with a complacent 'I-told-you-so' feeling after learning Friday's result, but while they were again right in their prognostications, there was not one who would have given Southend to run up the biggest score in the Football League for that day. Southend supporters, of course, were delighted and there was something to wax merry about at tea time after the match, for the score in no way exaggerated the Blues superiority. Two further goals, in fact, were disallowed on the grounds of offside and 'another' by Morris, who punched the ball into the net, served no more than to raise a ripple of laughter.

The Blues owed this success to the fact that they never let the Rangers settle down to consistent team work, although things were pretty even in the opening stages and it was not until they had obtained the first goal that they showed any promise of a good win. Exchanges in the first quarter of an hour were fast and the ball travelled quickly from end to end.

There was apparently a good team spirit amongst the Rangers and they executed some pretty movements. Having won the toss, they had the advantage of the wind in their favour and they kept the ball on the move. It was left to Sayer and Morris to carry out the first real raid into the visitor's territory. The half-backs were a bit shaky and Dixon seemed to be taking things too casually. With the backs to help them however, they did not let much pass and Jarvie had nothing to do beyond look on.

With the opening of the score by Hick fourteen minutes after the start, matters took on a different complexion and the Blues suddenly found their form. Thenceforth nothing went right for the visitors and they failed to stem the onslaughts of the Blues, who all but ran them off their feet. Rounce – the Tilbury man – and Lofthouse, on the left wing, with the help of Turner, tried to 'pull the fat out of the fire,' but their efforts to mix the metaphors were 'nipped in the bud' by the Southend defenders, who took a hold of the game.

The Rangers' passes were snapped up every time. Their forwards were practically 'starved' and had nothing to do but sympathise with the backs in their distress. Gilhooley was not up to the standard that had been anticipated and Frew could have shown him several points. It was not that the Rangers cracked up – they were sufficiently lucky to keep the Blues on the alert all the time. It was the first goal that set the seal to their fate, putting the Blues in the winning frame of mind. After that there seemed but little else to do but sit back and count.

The only forward not to score was Sayer. He certainly had one gilt-edged chance in the first half, but put high over. Yet if anyone deserved to have a finger in the pie, he did, for he was again responsible for a big percentage of the movements which led to net-finding shots. Hick had a good day, playing instead of Baron, who was declared too unwell to turn out, and he scored three good goals. Baron saw the doctor when he arrived back from Brighton and was ordered to bed. As stated, Hick opened the scoring just about a quarter of an hour from the start. It was a good goal and a trifle unexpected. Morris squared the ball across to the front of the goal and neither of the backs was able to intercept it. Hick fell in line, so to speak, with the leather and it was running past the goalmouth towards the opposite wing when Hick wheeled round and, with his left foot, cleverly placed it out of Cunningham's reach into the right-hand corner of the net.

Then the fun started and within another six minutes the Blues were three up. Clenshaw having come more into the limelight, the left-wing had been attacking and a corner was conceded. The Southender took the kick and the ball swerved well out. Dixon was up and, getting his head to the ball, nodded cleanly by Cunningham. Morris put on the third point with a glorious drive from over thirty yards range. Cunningham had run out and executed a double-fisted punch and the leather fell at the feet of Morris who coolly lifted it into the back of the empty net. Then Cunningham had a respite and when the teams changed over the Blues were still only three goals in front.

They dominated the game however, and the visitors were restricted to their own half, rarely getting away. Yet the second half was twenty minutes old before the spectators had what they had been waiting for – namely, the fourth goal. Morris had been very persistent, and, following a duel with Cunningham, whom he baulked from clearing, the ball went out to Dixon. The right half decided to play a lone hand and set out for goal, although he had the whole of the defence to contend with. His ball control was deceptively clever and he broke through the half-back line. Instead of passing, however, as the two backs had anticipated, to the left wing, where Donovan was possibly in a scoring position, he pushed it forward to Hick, for the Southend leader to register his second goal. A few minutes later Donovan sped through on his own and – bang! – that was the fifth. Number six was not far behind and Hick was again the marksman, having run through after receiving the ball from Sayer.

With that the majority of the spectators were content, but those who left the ground missed one of the most unexpected goals ever seen at the Kursaal, but the delighted roar that greeted it told them they had missed something. Clenshaw delivered the knock-out two minutes from the end with a powerful kick from the wing. No one doubted for a moment that Cunningham would not be able to save it and the players of both sides retired from his vicinity as the ball began to drop down towards him. Suddenly it was noticed that he was in difficulties and undecided what to do. The ball, instead of dropping into his arms or else on to the top of the net, did neither. It flew down just under the bar and bounced behind Cunningham in the net. It was one of the type of shots which so often hit the bar and spectators say, 'Another two inches lower and it would have been in.' Well, Clenshaw's shot had that two inches and the supporters' joy was unbounded.

Yet, in spite of their success, the forwards, though good, gave the impression that they were not at their best. They owed their goals to the fact that their shots were well directed enough to find the mark. Cunningham had a bad day, for he had few good saves to make and nearly every well-directed shot found the net. The Southend half-backs were the heroes of the day, because of the way in which they kept the men in front plied with passes of all kinds. Frew had a capital day, his tackling being timely and accurate, but he was not a whit better than his two colleagues. He kept well up the field and favoured the inside forwards with plenty of opportunities. Both Sayer and Donovan constituted themselves as the spoon-feeders of their colleagues, with the result that the visiting defenders were always kept busy. Andrews looked after Clenshaw better and Dixon, in company with Sayer and Morris, again played the triangle game to perfection. The backs were sound, but Jarvis had no opportunity to show whether he was on form or not. He received the ball exactly four times from off opponents' feet, but French obliged him with one or two kicks in the second half, when he began to get stiff.

Rosier's bold and confident tackling sapped the sting of the visitor's attacks on the occasions when Goddard got lively, but the Rangers' leader was not much in the picture. The understanding between the backs and halves was too good for the Londoners, in spite of their desperate attempts to rally. Neil, by the way, nearly scored for the Blues once when he put the ball back to his goal-keeper in the closing stages. Individually and collectively, however, the Rangers did not impress as being as good as the Blues. There was not much comparison between the wingers, Clenshaw being easily the best of the two left-footed men and Morris was smarter than Coward. The general superiority of the Blues is, in fact, not exaggerated by the score.

SOUTHEND UNITED: Jarvis; French and Rosier; Dixon, Frew and Andrews; Morris, Sayer, Hick, Donovan and Clenshaw.

QUEEN'S PARK RANGERS: Cunningham; Pierce and Young; Neil, Gilhooley and Turner; Coward, J.C. Burns, Goddard, Rounce and Lofthouse.

Referee: Mr. F.W. Reeve, Devonport.

Thursday, September 17th, 1931
Football League, Third Division (Southern Section)
THAMES 1, SOUTHEND UNITED 3

In an amazing match at West Ham Stadium, on Thursday, Southend United defeated Thames 3-1. Amazing is the only word which adequately describes the game, for its features combined to make it one of the most outstanding for many seasons. First there was a penalty kick awarded to the United that had to be taken twice, and, after missing with his first effort, French netted with the second. Then the last twenty minutes were fought out in light that made it practically impossible to follow the flight of the ball, and the only indication of the run of the play were the movements of twenty pairs of white knickers – the rest being almost invisible in the bad light – and finally there was a last minute goal that scarcely anyone saw plainly. All I could discern from the Press box was the sudden jerk of Crompton's leg, the white-jerseyed upflung arms of McDonough, the Thames 'keeper, and then the rest of the United team rushing to shake hands with the winger.

Several hundreds of United supporters journeyed to the ground by coach and rail, and they witnessed a contest that will linger long in the memory. They watched their team produce football of an exceedingly high standard, and, what is more important, the revelation of a team spirit that brooked no opposition. They saw Crompton in a series of dazzling runs, finishing up with well-delivered shots and centres that only superb keeping by McDonough could check, and they saw Shankly leading a thrustful attack with great skill and dash.

At the Kursaal the team must be sensitive to the criticism – often unfair – that they receive from the supporters, but away from all this they are a really different side, and it is their whole-heartedness and purpose that have brought them full points in each of the three away fixtures to date. On Thursday they were brilliant at times with their quick passing movements that found the home defence spreadeagled, and they deserved to have crossed over with a more substantial lead than the only goal scored, the spot-kick by French. The initial ten minutes of the second half were the real test, for Thames deservedly equalized and the game reached a pitch where the United might easily have cracked. Sterling work by the defence, however, turned the tide and, after Shankly had put the visitors ahead, the Thames side fell into the fatal error of falling back on the defensive too much. This was quickly turned to advantage by the United half-backs, who plied their forwards, especially Crompton, who was the best forward on the field, with passes, and the final score should have been at least 5-1 instead of 3-1.

The first half goal came in the twenty-third minute, when Crompton was cutting in towards goal, and was brought down by a tackle from behind from Woosnam. The spot-kick was taken by French and there was a terrific roar when it was seen that the ball had flashed outside the left-hand upright. Another and louder roar followed when the referee again pointed to the spot, ordering the kick to be re-taken because a Thames player has crossed the line before French had shot. The back made no mistake with his second effort, the ball hitting the back of the net, high up, with terrific force. Five minutes after the restart Thames equalized through McCarthy. Mann had got a centre from the right and, as Moore caught it, he was hustled by Lennox and the ball shot up out of his hands into the air, for McCarthy to head into an untenanted goal.

During the next five minutes it was touch and go, but the United half-backs and full backs refused to lose their grip on the game, and in the fourteenth minute of the second moiety Crompton got in a high centre that Shankly converted in fine style, meeting the ball about two feet from the ground with his instep. Barnett missed two very easy chances before the end, the one being from point blank range, when he could have walked the ball into the net, and then came Crompton's 'unseen' goal just before the final whistle. McDonough ran out to meet his shot and got his hands to the ball as it was going over his head, but failed to hold it. At least this is how it was described to me after the match, for it was not possible to see the ball from the grandstand.

The light was poor at the start of the match, and got so bad that it was a wonder the referee allowed it to proceed and finish. In Southend, I am told, it was pitch dark at 7.25 and supporters at home never dreamt there could be a conclusion.

The key to the United's success to date has been the excellent defence, in which the members of the intermediate line have been prominent for the way they have refused to get 'rattled.' This is not in any sense belittling to the backs, far from it, for they have proved their capabilities, and on Thursday they seldom faltered. Robinson played finely and kicked with excellent direction. Moore's keeping was as usual, which means that it was of a tip-top order, but it really rested with the toiling half-back line to lay the foundations of victory. They kept the ball on the carpet and pushed it up the field with just the necessary force and direction to be of use, whilst all three excelled with deadly tackling.

I thought that Dixon crowded into the centre a little too much in the first half, and this left French to face the elusive Dimmock. At first the United back was left guessing, but gradually he anticipated the ex-Spurs player's tricks and in the end Dimmock had little chance to become dangerous. Still, Dixon can be forgiven for any small fault, as the rest of his play was that of a captain, courageous and confident, whilst Wilson's energetic tackling and passing, allied to Donovan's heading and deft footwork, did the trick. The Thames line broke down time and again against the rock-like barrier, and their most dangerous efforts were nearly always individualistic rather than combined. Dimmock was the best of the line, and Lennox was a foraging leader, who tried desperately hard. Bailey, the old United forward, put in one or two clever touches, but neither McCarthy nor he was able to combine properly with Lennox.

Last, but not least, the United attack. The work of Crompton and Pike always caught the eye. The winger was a constant source of trouble to Thames, evading their watching and slamming in shots and centres with frequency and accuracy. He erred now and then in trying to shoot too hard, and this meant loss of accuracy, but generally his efforts were such that a goal seemed quite likely every time he got away. He was given a good start by the right kind of passes from his partner, Pike, also from Shankly and Wilson.

Pike revealed greater willingness to go into a tackle and was a rare schemer. Shankly threw off the cloak of hesitancy and slowness that seems to enshroud him at Southend and appeared as a dashing leader who used his wings with great discretion and never seemed at a loss in a tight corner. Some of his work was clever – clever enough, too, to draw words of admiration from Mr. Charles Buchan, the old English international, who sat next to me. There was one piece in particular that should have resulted in a goal had Barnett not been so weak in shooting. Shankly forced his way through a crowd of players and shaped as if to shoot into the left-hand side of the net. Instead, he deftly slipped the ball across to Barnett, who was unmarked and close in, only to see the winger boot it wildly over the bar. On another occasion a centre from Crompton was missed by everyone in the middle and the ball went to Barnett, again unmarked. He delayed so long with his shot that McDonough was able to position and block the opening.

Jones only put in one good shot, but he paved the way for many more by forcing for his colleagues the openings, and the inside trio worked together in better fashion than hitherto this season. Against such an incisive attack, in which the Blues vanguard kept the ball low, the Thames defence did well, especially Spence. At Southend McDonough saved Thames from a heavy defeat, and on Thursday he was chiefly responsible for the score only being 3-1. There was nothing flashy about his work, although it was thoroughly effective. Both backs showed signs of flustering when pressed hard, and I think the Club could do no better than to bring in their player-manager, Donnelly, the ex-United back, who is a defender of the right type. The game started at 5.54p.m. instead of 6 o'clock owing to the bad light, and the teams changed straight over at the end of the first half. Southend supporters left the ground quite satisfied with their visit and content with the knowledge that, if the United reproduce such form in each away game, the list of victories must increase rapidly. Congratulations to Southend on a magnificent display! May it be repeated at Northampton.

The teams were: –

THAMES: McDonough; Graham and Smith; Woosnam, Spence and Riddock; Mann, Bailey, Lennox, McCarthy and Dimmock.

SOUTHEND UNITED: Moore; French and Robinson; Dixon, Wilson and Donovan; Barnett, Jones, Shankly, Pike and Crompton.

Referee, Mr. S.F. Rous (later Sir Stanley Rous)

Saturday, December 10th, 1932
F.A. Challenge Cup, 2nd Round
SOUTHEND UNITED 4, SCARBOROUGH 1

The *Southend Standard* ran the following article on Scarborough F.C.

The Scarborough club has a long and honoured history. As an amateur organisation they were formed in 1879-80, and are original members of the Northern Football League. Since embracing professionalism (1925-26), they have had a fine record. In the following season they entered the Midland League and finished second. In the next year they dropped to seventh place, but in 1929-30, the jubilee year of the club, they celebrated it by securing the championship. In 1930-31 they reached the third round proper of the F.A. Cup, losing to Grimsby 3-1 at Scarborough. Saturday will help to supply the answer as to how far they will progress in 1932-33. Their loss at Lincoln, on Saturday, rather spoilt a good record, for until that day they had never failed to score fewer than two goals in an away match, and six of their last seven away games had been won.

The Midland League lost its sole remaining representative in the F.A. Cup, on Saturday, when Scarborough made their eagerly awaited visit to the Kursaal and enabled the United to secure entry into the third round – when all the First and Second Division clubs participate – by four goals to one. Whilst the victory was more or less anticipated, interest in the game was heightened by the fact that it represented a duel between the more vigorous, open methods found amongst the Northern Clubs and the more scientific tactics of the South. As I indicated in my comments on the Scarborough Club last week, much depended on whether Southend would be bustled off their game. Well, as the 7,813 spectators who paid for admission will have appreciated, the United, after showing an indication of playing Scarborough at their own game, settled down to their own type of play, with the result that the half-time lead of 2-1 was increased by two more points, although they represented only about half of what should have been added.

The quick attacking movements of the visitors in the first half, when they were playing with their backs to a strong breeze, generally failed against a steady defence, and the Blues, like a runner that lets an opponent make the pace and then goes ahead at the finish, came into their own in the latter forty-five with a series of fast attacks that emphasized the good and bad points of the Scarborough team. Although not of a particularly high standard of football, the game was brimful of interest and incident, and it was a pity the cold wind kept the gate down to the 8,000 mark. The receipts, by the way, were £502. 8s. 6d.

Scarborough's go-ahead methods at the outset of the contest gave the United defence plenty to think about, for their first-time passing kept the ball swinging from wing to wing. In Cup-tie football an early goal is a tremendous asset, and I think every United supporter present must have been a wee bit apprehensive if those opening moments, when the Scarborough forwards, led by Clayson, the ex-Torquay United player surged into the United goal area. The slightest wavering on the part of the United defence, especially the backs, might easily have altered the whole complexion of the game, but they came out of the ordeal with flying colours. Burkinshaw, the Boro captain, ended this 'testing-stage' with a. fine first-time shot that Whitelaw did well to tip on to the bar. He cleared from the rebound and the United retaliated with an attack that gave them the opening goal of the match.

Against a half-back line which was obviously used to covering forwards whose methods were similar to those of their own, the United made ground through the trickery of Jones. He eluded sliding tackles with ease and he delighted the crowd with a run that ended in a square centre from near the line after he had drawn the defence out of position. Morfitt was about eight yards out, and, although his first attempt to convert the pass was weak and rose up to reach the bar, he made certain of a goal when it rebounded to his feet and he shot into the net. It was really the individual work of Jones that brought this success in the third minute, and the victory also might be traced more to individual efforts than to general team work. Yet it should be understood that the United's combination was greatly superior to that of their visitors.

The movement that brought Scarborough the equalizer two minutes later was that type of attack where the ball is pushed right down the field and the forwards converge on it. It is not of the usual run of kick-and-push football, because this is deliberately done to get the opposing defence on the run and so enable the forwards to burst through.

That is exactly what happened against the United. Following a corner, poor positioning amongst the home defenders led to Randle jumping in to head a ball that Robinson was waiting for, and, before the defensive lines could be reformed, the ball had gone to Wraith, Scarborough's inside-left and leading goalscorer, who sent in a first-time shot. It was an effort worthy of a goal and yet it was sheer bad luck for the United that the ball did enter the net. The shot beat Whitelaw all the way, and, when he flung himself outward from the goal to push the ball away, he missed and it sailed over his head to hit the under-side of the crossbar. From here the ball rebounded outward, but struck Whitelaw on the back, the goalkeeper not having had time to turn round, and from there it rebounded again, this time into the net.

One could easily tell where the 120-odd Scarborough supporters were located by their great shout of glee. Whilst this success served to gladden the visitors, it also served to stiffen the determination of the homesters not to be so caught a second time. One could almost sense the feeling of the United defence when they lined up a minute or so later to check Burkinshaw's open-ing when he went to take a free-kick just outside the penalty area. There was a solid line of players for him to negotiate, and his attempt to crash the ball through was foiled by Randle, who tried to head the ball away and caught it in the face, being thus knocked out. He recovered soon but obviously felt the effects of the blow for some time.

Whereas Scarborough failed with their free-kick, the United succeeded with the one awarded them in the seventeenth minute. Dixon took it and dropped the ball over to the left-hand side of the Woodgrange Drive goal. Severn badly misjudged the bounce of the ball and it fell in front of Robson, who knocked it forward with his knee and then shot into the far side of the net. As Jones was successful with his subtle runs, it was only to be expected that Lewis quickly fell into his habit of trying to walk the ball in. It was fatal in his case, for the quick tackling of the Scarborough halves robbed him near-ly every time, when a flick of the foot would have found a colleague unmarked. The United's success, from the goals point of view, rested, as I have indicated, on individual efforts, for, apart from the fact that the honour of the first goal largely belonged to Jones, the rest were all the result of the work of Robson and Morfitt. Using the passes from the half-backs, Robson had matters pretty much his own way against Weightman and Severn, and he gave Morfitt just the type of centres that the leader could get his head to.

Yet, despite the repeated efforts of the homesters, it was not until half an hour of the second half had elapsed that Morfitt beat Langford with a head-er and scored the goal that really put the issue beyond doubt. At that time, Scarborough were already showing signs of going to pieces, and it was not surprising to see Morfitt again head in soon afterwards. The third goal was obtained from a centre by Barnett and the fourth from one by Robson. Had the finishing of the United been at all in keeping with the approach work – but, then, that is an old story this season.

It must be irritating for the defence to strive as they do and keep their end up whilst the forwards fritter away their chances. If Morfitt has no luck with his headers it is not much use looking to the inside forwards to shoot goals. Undoubtedly, Jones was the cleverest footballer on Saturday, but, after all, cleverness can be one thing and goal-shooting another. Morfitt provides the flash in the line and, whilst that is needed, I would like to see Shankly brought in as leader and Morfitt take one of the inside berths. Shankly, in my opinion, is the better leader of the two, and, with Morfitt's headwork, the pair should be able to get goals.

One could not blame Whitelaw for the goal against him, but he made one mistake in the second half that would have resulted in another goal had it not been for a smart piece of work by Dixon. The goalkeeper dived out to punch clear a free-kick taken by Weightman, but he missed and the ball was going towards the net when Dixon ran into the goalmouth and cleared. Apart from one or two misunderstandings with Handle, who played as if suffering from the effects of his being hit in the face, the backs kept their lines clear without undue exertion once the 'edge' had been worn off the Scarborough attack. Robinson and Donovan had the most work to do, for against them was the more aggressive of the visiting wings.

One phase of Donovan's play that was particularly good was the way he killed the ball and had it under immediate control. Dixon had a fairly easy time on the right, for Halford, the 17-years-old winger, was practically starved throughout and Wraith had not the forethought to see that his passes to Clayson would always be intercepted owing to the fact that Randle followed him like a shadow and one, or both, of the backs were generally close at hand. Barnett played a quiet but useful game, his chief fault being his inability to lift and place his corner-kicks to advantage. Jones thoroughly enjoyed himself, but the opposition was not clever enough to see through his tricks as others have done and, consequently, they failed to run on his inside and so force his passes to the wing.

Despite his knocks, Morfitt was a great trier, and one could overlook his bad wing passing when thinking of the fine way he got his head to the ball. He never gave up and, with a little luck, would have had another two points. Lewis will not fit in well in the line until he learns the right moment to part with the ball. Robson did well and showed that he has recovered some of his shooting powers, and Langford had all he could do to hold several of his shots. The tall goalkeeper handled the ball very confidently and did not seem worried by the fact that his covering backs, Severn and Williams were not always to be relied upon. Of the two young wing halves, Weightman was the best, whilst

Burkinshaw worked exceedingly hard in the centre. He looked done up at the end and, no doubt, trying to keep up with Morfitt had something to do with this. The chief thing one can say about Clayson is that he tried hard with the poor support offered him. Both Wraith and Swan sent him too many bad passes and the failure to use the left wing made the attack lop-sided. Swan was a very clever, scheming forward.

The teams were: –

SOUTHEND UNITED: Whitelaw; Hatfield and Robinson; Dixon, Randle and Donovan; Barnett, Jones, Morfitt, Lewis and Robson.

SCARBOROUGH: Langford; Severn and Williams; Weightman, Burkinshaw and Bartley; Jenkinson, Swan, Clayson, Wraith and Halford.

Referee: Mr. G. W. Ward, Nottingham.

Saturday, November 25th, 1933
F.A. Challenge Cup, 1st Round
LONDON PAPER MILLS (DARTFORD) 0, SOUTHEND UNITED 1

The *Southend Standard* ran the following article on London Paper Mills F.C. London Paper Mills continued in winning vein last Saturday winning at Bexley Heath 5-2. They have some well-known old professionals in the team, including Vango, the ex-Queen's Park Rangers centre-half. To date in the Kent League they have won four games and lost one, and, in addition to the F.A. Cup successes, when they vanquished Ryde Sports 4-2 in the final qualifying round, they have overcome Swanley Athletic in the Kent Senior Cup 3-2. The London Paper Mills Sports Club was founded in 1924 and won the Dartford League in the second year of its formation. They then entered the South London Alliance, Division 1, and lost the championship by a fraction of a goal in the first season, but were winners of the competition in the following year.

The club next entered the London Business Houses League (Premier Division), and, after winning the championship in their first season of membership, they failed to hold it in the second by one point. They also triumphed in the London Business Houses Senior Cup two years in succession and the Albert E. Reed Inter-Mills League for three years in succession. They have also proved to be the club to create the record of being winners of the Miller Hospital Cup for three years in succession. As the United Reserves will also be away from home at Millwall, no doubt large numbers of Southend followers will make the journey to Dartford, where the Paper Mills ground is at the Brent.

By the narrowest of margins Southend United scraped through their F.A. Cup-tie with the works team of the London Paper Mills at Dartford, on Saturday, by 1-0. The feature of the tie was the poor display put up by the professionals as against the wonderful wholeheartedness of the Mills side. On its face value, the fixture should have meant an easy win for Southend, but, such had been their performances in previous weeks that many nursed an uneasy feeling that the amateurs with everything to win and nothing to lose, might turn the tables – shades of Walsall and the Arsenal last season! As it was, Southend played sufficiently well to win the game, but few bouquets could be handed out to them.

True, the smallness of the ground and its uneven surface upset them to a considerable extent, but, taking all things into consideration, it must be record-ed that their performance and 1-0 victory were a very drab affair. One quite expected them to take some time to settle down, yet, as the minutes passed and the play, if anything, deteriorated, the crowd waxed sarcastic and their com-ments were directed chiefly to the forwards, whose passing was very bad. Over-kicking by the half-backs did not help matters and the one redeeming feature was the steadying influence of Dixon, whose introduction into the team for that purpose was certainly a move in the right direction to help weld the eleven together. One of the chief failings of the other men was that they can play well individually, but they lack that knack of making their colleagues play up to them. Dixon's field direction and encouragement on Saturday were responsible for the better efforts at constructive play in the second half, and it was good work on his part that led to the only goal of the match.

He opened a movement that ended in Stoker, the right winger, getting in a centre that dropped in the centre of the field and near the edge of the penal-ty area. Fryar, who had been very patchy in his play, breasted the ball down and shot coolly out of the reach of Covington, the Mills seventeen-years-old reserve goalkeeper, who was deputizing for Collum, who had broken a collar-bone in the previous round against Ryde Sports. It was a good goal and the best movement of the match, with the exception of one effort by the home-sters in the opening half. Incidentally it was Stoker's most accurate piece of work, for both McMahon and he were poor.

The United forwards – and some of the defenders, in addition – appeared to be labouring under a superiority complex at the outset and tried to be too clever. The Mills defenders retaliated with fast tackling that upset their oppo-nents, and the game developed itself into much hefty kicking between the hacks. The over-eagerness of the Mills players to get rid of the ball at once was an error in the opposite direction and it was not until the second half, when the United struck the happy medium and were more careful in consequence, that their movements began to look like an attempt at combination and not a chance affair.

The steady kicking of Worthey and Bateman and the influence of Dixon communicated themselves to the forwards until another fault began to appear. This was a tendency for each attacker to put the onus on a colleague of shoot-ing, and a number of scoring chances were wasted in this way. Why more long shots of the type tried by Fryar were not delivered it was hard to say, for

Covington, despite his fine display, lacked height and reach to cover any fast efforts aimed at the top corners.

Whitelaw was never seriously troubled, although he had a dozen goal-kicks before Covington touched the ball. The Southend backs ably supported the spoiling efforts of the intermediate men, who were inclined at times to hold the ball too long, and they were fairly safe in dealing with the long upfield kicks with which Charnley, the ex-Wolverhampton player, and his two wing halves tried to set their attack going. Worthey was steadier and he was more accurate in placing the ball than Bateman, although both gave nothing away and covered each other better than in previous games. Randle was constantly preventing C. Hills, the home leader, from getting the ball, and Dixon and Robertson did most of the attack initiating, with the former much to the fore.

Of the forwards, I have already commented on the weakness of both wings, and it was an open question as to who was the least effective. Stevens roamed far too much towards both wings, but I believe he thought that the only sure way of getting the ball was to fetch it himself. Apart from the poor support he received, he was well covered by Charnley, who played a real captain's game in urging his young colleagues on to greater efforts. Lane had a bad first half and Fryar was not much better, but there was a definite improvement in their work in their second. Lane also figured as the only forward with any ideas of shooting. One of his efforts in the first half beat Covington all the way, but the spin carried it over the bar. As in the previous week, I formed the impression that Lane is happier at inside-left. The Dartford supporters who remembered Barnett at school there were very disappointed that he was not playing – just as Collum, who is his brother-in-law, regretted he could not turn out.

The Mills first struggle against a Football League side was all to their credit, although I feel that, had the match been played at the Kursaal, they would have been just as much at sea on a full-sized pitch as were the Blues on one under the maximum. Once the initial period of settling down was overcome, they tackled their work with enthusiasm and several played themselves practically to a standstill. Young Arben, for instance, looked leg weary before the end, but he never gave up trying and, similarly, Hammond, the other wing-half, was particularly energetic.

Covington stood his test exceedingly well and the combination of experience and youth for backs went a long way to keeping the score down. The experience was supplied by Vango, last season with Queen's Park Rangers, and the youth by Walker. Vango and Charnley are the only two players with any experience of League football in the side, and, apart from these and Thomas, the remainder are all youngsters who have worked in the Mill since soon after leaving school.

The outstanding Mills forward was easily Quarton, the dark-headed inside-right. He strove hard both to open the attack and also score himself and, if he did take too much on himself at times, he could be forgiven. Quarton, who has distinguished himself as a sprinter and jumper (I believe he holds a 220 yards title), has attracted the attention of a number of League clubs, as has his partner, Paine. The latter was the best winger and, when Thomas was injured, proved his versatility by crossing over to the left and playing equally as well there. Whatever ability C. Hills may possess as a leader, he had no opportunity of displaying it on Saturday, for Randle was shadowing him all the time.

The Mills Club officials agreed to lose financially in order to stage the match before their own supporters, and I was sorry the trouble they took to 'put their house in order' was not justified. For instance, the posts and railing round the pitch were all pulled up and set back in order that two more rows of seating could be put round. There was room for 1,000 on these seats, and the price fixed was 1s. per head. From the stand I saw about a couple of dozen only using them. The stand itself holds 250 and there were several empty seats. The two terraces at the back of the north goal were estimated to hold 600 and I doubt if there were half that number there.

Of the crowd of 2, 110 (a £136 'gate,' with £99 net receipts), there was a fair sprinkling of Southenders, who must have wondered several times if the energetic homesters might not suddenly break away and score. They must have also wondered if the trip had been worthwhile. Looking at my notes on the game, I found only four items on the first half. The first recorded Stevens missing a possible opening through kicking the ball too far ahead when trying to work into the goalmouth, the second was of the fine movement made by the homesters, to which I have already referred; the third indicated an opening made by Fryar, ending in Covington punching away McMahon's centre and Stoker shooting wide; and the fourth recalled a miskick by Bateman that let Paine through. Luckily for the United, Worthey took in the situation at a glance and moved up, so that the Mills inside-forwards were all off-side when the ball was squared. Fryar's goal was obtained after ten minutes of the second half had passed, and it was soon after that when Thomas twisted his knee and went on the wing.

Apart from the goal, I suppose the most notable item in the second half was when Stevens, receiving in an unmarked position, failed to see Walker on the goal line and shot so that the back cleared. It was a grand opportunity and the centre-forward could have practically walked the ball through. One's sympathies were with the Mills, for they fought hard to overcome the experience of their opponents – experience that peeped out in many ways, such as anticipating the bounce of the ball, etc., and they never gave up trying until the final whistle. They were not discredited in their defeat, whereas the United received credit only in the fact that they won through to the second round. Incidentally, it was their first victory for five weeks. Teams: –

LONDON PAPER MILLS: A. Covington; A.J. Vango, W. Walker; G. Arben, S. Charnley, J. Hammond; G. Paine, J. Quarton, C. Hills, L. Thomas, J. Hills.

SOUTHEND UNITED: Whitelaw; Worthey, Bateman; Dixon, Randle, Robertson; Stoker, Lane, Stevens, A. Fryar, McMahon.

Referee: Mr. T.S. Hewlett.

Saturday, September 5th, 1936
Football League, Third Division (Southern Section)
SOUTHEND UNITED 9, NEWPORT COUNTY 2

Southend's new attack – introduced because of the disappointing form of the vanguard relied upon for the opening two matches – celebrated its appearance, on Saturday, at the Stadium, by trouncing a weak Newport side to the tune of nine goals to two, after leading 4-1 at the interval. Only Bolan retained his position in the forward line and Goddard led the quintet, with Dickinson and Oswald forming the left wing and Lane at inside right. Early last season, against Crystal Palace, at the Stadium, the United experienced one of those afternoons when everything 'came off' for them, and so it again proved on Saturday.

The run of the game went dead against Newport and Southend simply could not help scoring. It almost appeared like adding insult to injury that they should be leading 8-2 and then have a penalty awarded them. This allowed Everest, the former Cardiff City captain and full-back, to show, for the second successive game, what an artiste he is with the spot-kick. Two steps, an almost lazy leg action, and the ball sped like a bullet into the left-hand corner of the net, just skimming the grass. Newport's much vaunted defence, with the exception of curly-headed Hall, the left-half, crumpled so completely that one could not really say that the new United attack had a severe testing. Every member of the line found the net and some of the goals were obtained so easily as to be almost in the category of 'gifts.' The scorers were Goddard (three), Lane (two), Dickinson, Bolan, Oswald and Everest.

The team was naturally anxious to retrieve some of its lost prestige of the previous Wednesday against Watford and one could sense from the start that they were out to fulfil this ideal. At the outset it was also quickly plain that the Newport defence, particularly the backs and goalkeeper, were decidedly shaky, lacking understanding and speed. Small wonder then that goals came at regular intervals.

The first was in the ninth minute and was of rather a scrambling nature. Oswald put Dickinson through on the left wing, and the ex-Rotherham forward cut in, but passed weakly along the ground. Goddard was up with the play and retrieved the leather and Lane, who spent most of his time cruising around as a second inside-left flicked it over the goal-keeper's head. It was going into the net when Bolan made doubly sure of it. Many credited Goddard with the goal, but actually it was Bolan who netted, taking the ball just before it crossed the line. Southend's attack was not too convincing in front of goal, but gradually open play brought a series of good positional movements, and in the nineteenth minute a very neat piece of work between Bolan and Lane enabled Goddard to tap the ball into the net just as Bowles was diving for it. Bolan and Lane played to each other with a precision that left Kelso helpless, and Lane squared the ball for Goddard to net. The ball, incidentally, was first secured by Bolan from a weak goal kick by Bowles. Why the goalkeeper did not hand over the duty of taking goal kicks to either of the backs, I could not understand, for his kicks were short and generally went to a United forward. At the other end, Nelson or Everest demonstrated how a goal kick could be dropped well over the half-way line.

The third United success was the outcome of another weak kick was Bowles. Lane secured the ball, ran forward and sent in a fine shot that the goal-keeper deflected with his foot, and Goddard, well up as usual, accepted the invitation and tapped it past him. There was no spectacular slamming of the ball, but a leisurely neat, placed kick that a cool-headed leader knows how to use. Oswald, who had been finishing rather disappointingly, made amends in the thirty-sixth minute by 'walking' his way past opposition along the touch line, and passing to Lane, who easily netted. Southend kept up the pressure, and, with the half-backs lending a helping hand, it was not altogether surprising to see Newport's attack get through at last. They had tried hard against a steady defence, and just before half-time they found a loophole when the United rearguard was well up the field. Lowry, the inside-right, worked over to the left, and a low ground shot beat MacKenzie.

Ruthlessly attacking from the start of the second half, Southend quickly increased their lead for, after three minutes, Bolan went through, following a pass by Lane, and he turned the ball in for Goddard to reproduce his 'flick' shot. Bowles got a hand to the ball, but could not stop it going past him. Five minutes later Newport's attack broke away and a high centre from Crisp fell just inside the goal area. Hickman, with his back practically to the goal, head-ed the ball and it passed into the net high up and brushed the post at the same time.

The end of a quarter of an hour's play saw the United do something which they do not often do, viz. score from a corner kick. Oswald sent over the flag-kick, and, when the ball fell in a ruck of players, Dickinson got his head to it and netted his first goal for the Blues. A fine piece of ball work by Oswald saw Lane receive the final pass and bring the score up to 7-2, whilst the left winger completed the scoring by the forward line when Goddard sent him through clear of the defence in the thirtieth minute. After Bolan had netted an offside goal, Dickinson was brought down in the penalty area and Everest added the ninth from the spot.

With weak opposition and the ball always running kindly for them, it was only natural that the Southend team were able to play well. Goddard's leader-ship was definitely an important factor in the attack, and he was always ready for the ball when the goal area was reached. Dickinson paved the way for several of the United's successes and he quickly struck up a useful understanding with Oswald.

The latter, who lost his place last season to Willshaw, demonstrated that he still has the better ball control, although some of his centres were badly placed. It was just the type of game to suit Lane. Bolan was always dangerous on the right, although he had to face Newport's best defender. I thought Hall as good a player as there was on the field, although Deacon and Carr were responsible for useful service to their forwards.

Turner and the backs, Nelson and Everest, gave the Newport forwards little chance of concentrating upon the goal. Crisp and Lowry tried hard on the visitor's left wing, with Hall giving excellent backing, but the other forwards could not get going.

The United's score of nine goals, apart from being the highest in all Divisions of the Football League on Saturday, was the highest they had achieved in League matches since they joined Division I of the Southern League in 1908.

Their previous best had been three 7-0 victories against Queen's Park Rangers, Millwall and Crystal Palace. In November, 1934 they won 10-1 at home against Golders Green in the F.A. Cup. Saturday's result put the crowd of over 7,300 in high humour, and it is not often that one hears the home supporters chanting, 'One, two, three.'

The rain which fell up to the time of the kick-off probably kept hundreds of spectators away, but those who were there certainly had something about which to talk. The rain took some of the 'iron' out of the turf and control was difficult at times. Teams: –

SOUTHEND UNITED: MacKenzie; Nelson and Everest; Deacon, Turner and Carr; Bolan, Lane, Goddard, Dickinson and Oswald.

NEWPORT COUNTY: Bowles; Williams and Kelso; Edwards, Webb and Hall; Appleby, Hickman, Owen, Lowry and Crisp.

Referee: Capt. G. Hamilton-Jones, Woolwich.

Wednesday, April 21st, 1937
John Moss Challenge Cup, (the 'Hospital Cup')
SOUTHEND UNITED 4, WEST HAM UNITED 2

Fielding the same team that defeated Aston Villa at Villa Park 2-0 on Saturday, West Ham expected to avenge last year's defeat and this season annex the coveted Moss Challenge Cup in the annual encounter at the Southend Stadium, against Southend United, on Wednesday, but the United retained the magnificent 100-guineas trophy by a margin of 4-2. In a first half of rather dull football, the Blues obtained the only goal, Firth cleverly heading into the net a centre from Willshaw in the fifth minute.

The second half contained all the thrills and five goals, and, although West Ham pressed heavily on several occasions, they could not penetrate a stubborn defence more than twice. West Ham played in fits and starts – as if tired one minute and then going all out the next – and had it not been for two great saves by Bryan, the home custodian, they might easily have equalized.

One save was from a penalty-kick awarded for hands in the twenty-fifth minute of the second half, and taken by Goulden. He sent the ball hard for the right-hand corner, but Bryan, with wonderful anticipation, hurled himself sideways and punched the ball clear with his left fist. He made an almost identical clearance from Morton, who had equalized for West Ham quickly following the re-start, later in the struggle. Willshaw scored the second United goal with a great drive from the edge of the penalty area, and Firth added a third with a spinning hook shot.

The fourth was claimed by Willshaw, who was able to get in close to goal after tricking Bicknell. Near to the end, a fine shot from Morton hit the bar, and Small had no difficulty in netting from the rebound. Bryan was outstanding in the United defence for his judgment of the ball and anticipation. Excellent work was also forthcoming from the wing half-backs, Spelman and Carr, whilst in the attack Firth was always thrustful, and Harris put over some neat centres from the right wing.

Martin, who had been on the sick list, returned to lead the attack against his old colleagues, but Walker (R.) gave him few chances of getting through. Kirkaldie, the former United winger, who was one of the scorers against Aston Villa, found the going difficult against Robinson, and Morton, was the chief danger in the line in spite of the efforts of Brook to hold him in check. It was just as well, too, that Turner or the backs were able to prevent Small and his colleagues from converting several excellent centres. The defence, with Walker (R.) outstanding in holding the centre of the field, was apt to take matters too lightly at times, and this led to two of the United points.

At the conclusion, the cup was presented to Turner, the United captain, by Mr. Henry Channon, M.P. for Southend, who watched the match in company with the Mayor (Ald. W. Miles), directors and officials of both clubs and the United Supporters' Club who had undertaken all the arrangements for the game.

Two-thirds of the proceeds go to the Southend General Hospital through the Sportsmen's Appeal Fund, and one-third to West Ham Hospital. Each player also received a fountain-pen.

The teams were: –

SOUTHEND UNITED: Bryan; Brook and Robinson; Spelman, Turner and Carr; Harris, Firth, Martin, Oswald and Willshaw.

WEST HAM: Weare; Bicknell and Walker (C.); Fenton (E.), Walker (R.) and Cockroft; Kirkaldie, Green, Small, Goulden and Morton.

Referee, Mr. A.V. Boorer, Upminster.

Saturday, January 7th, 1939
F.A. Challenge Cup, 3rd Round
CHESTERFIELD 1, SOUTHEND UNITED 1
abandoned after seventy-five minutes (fog)

After the countryside had been in the grip of snow and ice for several days, considerable doubts existed until Friday night as to whether or not the Chesterfield ground would be fit for the following day's third round Cup-tie with Southend United, but in the end it was another and totally unexpected adverse weather element, fog, that brought about the abandonment of the game fifteen minutes from the end, when the scores were level, each side having scored a goal.

The terrible conditions underfoot were bad enough, but the thick fog which enveloped the town and district an hour before the kick-off was something that could not be overcome. Actually, the match was little short of farcical, and no one would have been surprised had the referee ordered a postponement on account of the state of the ground alone, long before the arrival of the fog. Pools of water like miniature lakes lay over a pitch that was waterlogged on top, following the rapid thaw that started during the night, but which was still frozen hard an inch or two below the surface. Where the grass was showing it quickly churned up like a bog, and accurate football was almost an impossibility.

However, the game would have been finished had it not been for the fog, and it seemed unfair to the visitors that, at a period when they had not only fought back to level terms after a half-time deficit, but had definitely gained the upper hand, they should not have at least had the consolation of a replay on their own ground. To give some idea of the denseness of the fog, let me say that both goals were scored by half-backs with shots that the goalkeepers did not see until it was too late.

From my position in the Chesterfield Press-box, I saw Spedding, the home reserve right-half, volley a loose ball into the direction of the United goalmouth. At that time, twenty minutes after the start, there could just be discerned a shadowy figure that we knew was MacKenzie, and when the ball, rising into the fog, was lost from view, I watched him, because it was evident from the direction of the kick, that it would land somewhere near him. MacKenzie, as he told me in the dressing room later, was startled to see the ball dropping down over his head, and although he flung up his hands it fell into the net.

The United's equalizer, scored by Hague, who was selected as the centre-half, from a free-kick just outside the penalty area, I could not see. This was in the sixty-first minute, and the Chesterfield goal at the time was quite invisible from the Press-box. The most I could see was a very dim line of players as the Chesterfield defenders lined up to try to cover the goal. I saw Hague place the ball on a little island in the midst of a big pool of water, take a short run and lob it over their heads – then came a great shout and the sight of Hague jumping up and down – He had scored! United players materialising from all sides confirmed that. Not having seen what happened – one could not even see the goal or the Chesterfield goalkeeper – I asked Hague for his version later on.

'I knew there was little hope of trying a hard, low shot, so I tried a lob for the right-hand corner, toeing the ball fairly high over the heads of the defenders,' he said. 'The goalkeeper realised his danger too late, and although he jumped and got the fingertips of his left hand to the ball, he could not stop it going into the net.' So that was that – both custodians beaten by shots which they could not see throughout the flight of the ball, and which under normal conditions they might have saved.

I thought that at the time of the abandonment the fog was no thicker than it had been in the first half, when it had been impossible to distinguish who was who at the far side of the field and the spectators could be heard but not seen. The United players thought so too, for they protested to the referee that having gone so far, he should finish the game, for they held that the visibility at that time was no worse than it had been previously. I sought the view of the referee, and he stated that the fog was so bad that he and the linesmen could not keep each other in sight, and he was unable to see when infringements were signalled. Just previous to the abandonment, one linesman reported to the referee that he had been 'flagging' in vain.

The referee was on the ground at 11a.m. and watched the work carried out right up to the kick-off to try to minimise the underfoot conditions. Unemployed men scattered several tons of sand over the worst pools, and a light mechanical roller was used to try to 'squeeze' the pitch, so that the water could be swept off amongst the piles of snow around the touch-line. At noon on Friday the men had been engaged in clearing several inches of snow from the pitch and setting out coke braziers to try to thaw the ground, which was then frozen solid. Twenty-four hours later they were trying to soak up some of the water from a pitch that was just like a sheet of saturated sponge! And then, as if Nature was playing a determined hand against the affairs of men, came the fog to score the victory.

It was impossible to see enough of the players to offer any criticisms, but I can say that whenever they came within view – recognition distance, rather – the Southend side, all of whom wore knee bandages, appeared to be giving more than they got, and I feel confident, from the manner in which the attack was constantly in the Chesterfield area, that Southend would certainly not have lost in the second half.

Indeed, it appeared that the United were unlucky not to be leading when they left the field, because a left-footed drive by Bolan, who had just returned to the field after attention for a hurt ankle (we saw the ball start on its journey, but that was all) nearly beat the home goalkeeper. It was a sudden chorus from the 'invisible choir' behind the goal that told people in other parts of the ground that there had been a narrow escape. As far as could be ascertained by dint of much eyestrain and occasional front-of-stand glimpses of the players, the United were most dangerous down the right wing, and the experiment of playing Bushby in the middle, vice Trainer, was justified.

Bushby, who was quick enough to beat Seagrave, made two good attempts to burst through. Once he was dead unlucky in over-running a ball that stopped short in a pool of water after he had rounded the Chesterfield centre-half. In the first half it was the United's left flank that was nearer the grandstand, and we saw some fine defensive play by Jackson, who returned to the half-back position and assisted Robinson in checking the Lyon-Hughes wing, which was the most dangerous section of the Chesterfield attack.

Hague, selected because of the heavy going, was seen to make some excellent tackles and relieve pressure with his head. He had some exciting duels with Milligan, the home leader, and generally appeared to come off best. Quick changes of the play on the right indicated that Milne and Harris must have made many timely clearances. The Chesterfield backs, Milburn and Kidd, were a definite stumbling block to the United in the first half, but in the second half they tired, as did Seagrave, the centre-half.

The two sets of players might well be called plucky warriors to fight as they did, for it was frequently a case of 'every man for himself.' If they fell over or were charged down, it meant a bath in mud and water, and it was frequently noticed that after a player had kicked the ball others in the vicinity had to wipe the mud splashes from their eyes.

When play went to one end of the field the goalkeeper at the other end was left in a sort of 'splendid isolation' and was quite unable to see what his colleagues were doing. Both custodians, as a result, were kept on tenterhooks in case there should suddenly emerge out of the fog players who wore the opposing colours.

The United, by the way, played in red, because Chesterfield wear blue and white stripes, but even the bright red could not be distinguished on the far side of the field. I could pick out the United players more quickly than I could those of the home side simply because the Blues wore white shorts, and they showed up better than the black ones of Chesterfield.

One way and another, the 'affair' was most unsatisfactory, particularly so when taking into consideration that fact that the United shaped like the winning side in the second half. They had the Chesterfield defence constantly in trouble and seemed to be better able to face the prevailing conditions. Incidentally, a former United manager that I saw at the ground, Mr. Ned Liddell, who afterwards was chief scout for West Ham and then manager of Luton, was full of praise for his old team. Those who know 'Ned' will remember that enthusiasm is not his strong point, and one of the first things he said to me was that Southend had got Chesterfield on the run.

The United players were bitterly disappointed, and so were their supporters who travelled up from Southend. These latter numbered between 70 and 80 (as compared with 600 who went up from Yeovil to cheer their side to a draw against Sheffield Wednesday), and amongst them were 30 members of the unemployed, whose fares had been paid for by Mr. I. Dinkernor and whose admittance fees were found by the United.

On Friday, knowing the snow and ice with which Chesterfield had to contend, the United directors tried to effect an insurance against the game not taking place, being desirous of covering the fares of the unemployed so that they could see a replay, but no company would accept the premium. The United, who took both centre-halves, Jones and Hague, stayed the night at Sheffield, where Mr. C.N. Newitt, the Club Chairman, was the recipient of a letter from the Reading F.C. (against whom the Blues lost 3-0 the previous week), wishing them the best of luck.

It being impossible to see the spectators on the far side of the field, I had no idea as to how many were present until the official returns were made, showing that 8, 149 paid, with receipts of £540. As the usual Chesterfield gate is about 13,000, and they expected more for the game, it will be seen how the ill-luck that dogged the United over the matter of the Christmas holiday games continued.

The teams were: –

CHESTERFIELD: Middleton; Milburn and Kidd; Spedding, Seagrave and Weightman; Hughes, Lyon, Milligan, Lowe and Sullivan.

SOUTHEND UNITED: MacKenzie; Milne and Robinson; Harris, Hague and Jackson; Smirk, Bolan, Bushby, Bell and Muncie.

Referee: R.S.M. F.C. Green, Birmingham.

CHAPTER SEVEN

The Football League Third Division

SOUTHERN SECTION CUP 1933-34 to 1938-39

Thursday, February 22nd, 1934
Second Round
COVENTRY CITY 3, SOUTHEND UNITED 1

Southend United included Barrow in their team which journeyed to Coventry, on Thursday, in the Southern Section Cup, but other changes which were made were not successful and the United lost by 3-1. Alterations made by Coventry proved more beneficial, but they hardly enjoyed the superiority that the score suggested. Frith opened the score for Coventry after 37 minutes, and Lauderdale added a second before the interval. Barnett reduced the arrears, but the City retaliated with a goal by Bacon. Coventry's half-back line dominated the game and were able to hold the Southend wingers, of whom Barrow gave a promising display. The teams were: –

COVENTRY CITY: Pearson; Brown and Wilmot; Barker, Mason and Boileau; Bacon, Lauderdale, Bourton, Frith and Richards.

SOUTHEND UNITED: Moore; Worthey and Robinson; Morfitt, Wilson (J.) and Smith; Barnett, Jones, Stevens, Lane and Barrow.

Referee: Mr. E.R. Westwood, Walsall.

Wednesday, September 19th, 1934
First Round
SOUTHEND UNITED 1, BRIGHTON & HOVE ALBION 1

There is generally a calm before a storm and this saying could well be adapted to describe the match at the Southend Stadium, on Wednesday evening, between the United and Brighton in the first round of the Southern Section Cup. The first half and opening part of the second portion provided a lull before the storm that followed. There was an electrifying minute during which each side scored a goal and then fast and furious play followed amidst applause that rolled like thunder under the stand roofs. It was not good football, but of the spectacular kind that the crowd like to watch. It did not produce any more goals and the match ended in a draw of one goal each, which was a fair reflex of the exchanges. Brighton were the more resourceful side, but Southend had the balance of the attack and delivered most shots. There was a slight improvement in their team work and the re-inclusion in the attack of Oswald infused some much needed life into the movements, whilst Smith's re-appearance at left-half strengthened the intermediate line. A total of 4,442 spectators paid

£265 7s. 6d. for admission. Under the rules of the competition, the clubs had to turn out full-strength sides.

Robertson was tried at left-back, but performed little better than Robinson, whom he displaced. It was hoped that Mackay, the newcomer from Plymouth Argyle, would be at right half, but, owing to delay in obtaining his signature, he did not turn out and a trial was given to Todd. He worked hard and promised well, but showed obvious lack of experience, especially in his positional play. Oswald appeared at inside-left as partner to Clark and was easily the brightest forward on the field. In the first half he had more shots at goal -and good attempts at that – than all the rest of both sets of forwards together, but the hardest worker on the field was Jones (E.) at inside-right. He was unlucky with some of his efforts, but, apart from the individual movements, it was obvious that it will not do to have two such clever players as Oswald and he hanging so far back when attacks are being launched. It threw the remainder of the line out of its stride and, as Johnson was unable to control the ball or distribute it effectively, there was little wonder that the Brighton backs, King and Jones, had matters much their own way, quite apart from the steadiness at centre-half of Mooney.

Jones, the Brighton back, may be a veteran – he served in the Great War and was wounded at Ypres, so that dates him – but he was too good for Lane, and his bald head was always bobbing up to take passes meant for the winger. At right back, King – over 6ft. 3in. – towered above Oswald and Clark and he also had little difficulty in dominating that side of the field when the ball was high up.

To a man Brighton had Southend beaten when it came to heading, but they also found the United defence offering a sturdy resistance which, if not exactly pretty, was effective. Stevenson put in some useful work and Wilson was as good as Mooney, and that meant that both centre-forwards were more or less out of the picture. The best defender on view was Walker, who has been with Brighton since leaving Walsall in 1929. He was fast and accurate and Jones and he always had the measure of Lane and Jones (E.), despite the continuous efforts of the latter. The respective attacks were rarely impressive, although the visitors set the pace. Farrell and Thompson, the best Brighton wing, were not quite as good as the Oswald and Clark combination, but the United pair were well checked by King.

There were few incidents in the opening half beyond Oswald's shots at goal and, although the United attacked strenuously, the finishing was bad through lack of positional play, and it was left to Brighton to secure – and miss – the best scoring chance. This was from a free-kick by Smith, after Wilson had fouled Brown. Walker, running up on the left for the pass, missed his shot when he would have probably caught Whitelaw unsighted. The posts and bar were all hit by shots from the United in the second half, but, from a typical Brighton raid – that is, with the ball being headed from man to man – the visitors opened the scoring. The leather was sent back to Mooney and, from 25 yards range, he shot low for the right-hand corner. Whitelaw was confused by a missed kick at the ball by Robertson and the result was that both allowed it to pass and it entered the net.

Then came the lightning-like reply. From the kick-off, Johnson raced through and turned the ball towards Lane. It struck Walker's hands and a penalty was awarded, although it appeared quite an unintentional case of handling. Lane took the spot kick and scored, despite a desperate effort by Thomson in goal. After that both teams went at it 'hammer and tongs,' without avail. The teams were: –

SOUTHEND UNITED: Whitelaw; Stevenson and Robertson; Todd, Wilson (J.), and Smith; Lane, Jones (E.), Johnson, Oswald and Clark.

BRIGHTON: Thomson; King and Jones; Darling, Mooney and Walker; Thompson, Farrell, Brown, Smith and Payne.

Referee: Mr. W. J. Lewington.

Wednesday, September 26th, 1934
First Round Re-play
BRIGHTON & HOVE ALBION 3, SOUTHEND UNITED 1

Southend United's interest in the Southern Section Cup ceased on Wednesday, when they visited Brighton in the re-played first round tie. At one period of the game however, it appeared that the side might advance further, but an easing up of the whole team enabled Brighton to increase their score to 3-1 and so win a scrambling game, in which neither side could claim credit for any really bright football. A first half of dull and depressing exchanges was devoid of interest, except for a goal by each team and two amazing escapes by the visitors. The brightest patch came in the opening quarter of an hour of the second moiety, when Southend did most of the attacking, but seldom got past the steady Brighton backs.

After that, the homesters had matters more or less their own way and secured a victory because they took their chances. Both teams made considerable changes from the elevens that met at the Stadium and the United introduced Tom Wilson and Kelly as backs, with Todd taking the place at right-half of the injured Mackay, and Morfitt displacing Smith on the left. Clark was dropped and the left wing was formed by Cheesmur and Oswald.

There were scarcely any good movements from either side and the ball was kicked up and down the field in a manner that suggested that the players had as little interest in the fixture as the general public, for there were only about 2,000 present. Of two poor teams, Brighton were slightly superior because of the quicker way they moved to the ball. They made their play faster than that of the United and should have doubled their score. Several times the United defenders kicked out from the goalmouth when Whitelaw was beaten, and the post and bar were also struck. Brown and Johnson scored for their respective teams in the first half. There was not an outstanding player on either side, but it was one of the least prominent – Egan, of Brighton -who obtained one of the goals.

The scores were level after twenty minutes of the second half had elapsed, when Egan drove the leather through a ruck of players into the net. The brightest spot of the whole game was the United's point and Johnson's hook that beat Thomson was a real gem – no goalkeeper could have saved it. The United were one down after twenty-five minutes, Brown having netted, and Southend had a turn of attacking. The sphere was passed and re-passed across the penalty area in a way that suggested the attack would probably peter out, when Johnson converted a centre from Lane in fine style. Egan's shot made the score 2-1 and the United were 'fading' rapidly, when a long wing centre was sent in by Jepson. Whitelaw caught the ball above his head, but failed to hold it and it dropped over his shoulders into the goal.

Apart from this lapse, Whitelaw was safe, but he was not so cool and con-fident in his handling as Thomson. Brighton had a great advantage in their backs, for, as happened at Southend, King and Jones were reliable without being brilliant, and they appeared to do more work with their heads than with their feet. Kelly, the United left-back, was nervous and often his haste to rec-tify mistakes led him into deeper blunders.

Tom Wilson worked hard to try and cover his colleagues and twice he saved goals, once kicking over the bar when Whitelaw was on the ground and Brown looked certain to score. Wilson is as good as any of the backs Southend possess and I should like to see him persevered with. His namesake had a rare duel with Brown, and the old West Ham player was just as much out of the game as was Johnson owing to the marking of Mooney. I have seen both cen-tre-halves, however, play better games.

Credit must go to Morfitt for his hard work at left-half, and it was not his fault that the dangerous Brighton raids developed down his wing. It was a match where the United could have done well with a bustling and clever half-back like Mackay, for although Todd gave of his best, it was not quite good enough. The homesters were better served by their trio, although their versa-tile Walker was not included. There was little to choose between the two sets of forwards, except that Brighton were quicker on the ball owing to the fact they moved into position with a better sense of anticipation than did the United.

There was an inclination to overdo the number of passes by the visitors when they were converging on goal and King and Jones had only to keep posi-tion to be sure of getting the ball sooner or later. It was hoped there would be some bright exchanges from Cheesmur and Oswald, but they were never more than ordinary, although I still feel that they are the best left wing the United possess. Neither centre-forward was allowed to do much and all four in-sides were below par. Brighton had more of the attacking to their credit, because their stronger wing, Jepson and Farrell, found the weakness opposite them and took advantage of it. Practically every movement that got the United defence in trouble – and the goals – developed from their-efforts. Somehow the match lacked the atmosphere of a cup-tie. The teams were: –

BRIGHTON: Thomson; King and Jones; Darling, Mooney and Barber; Jepson, Farrell, Brown, Egan and Wilson.

SOUTHEND UNITED: Whitelaw; Wilson (T.) and Kelly; Todd, Wilson (J.) and Morfitt; Lane, Jones (E.), Johnson, Cheesmur and Oswald.

Referee: Mr. W.J. Lewington.

Wednesday, October 2nd, 1935
First Round
SOUTHEND UNITED 3, NEWPORT COUNTY 0

Newport claimed that they were unlucky to lose 7-1 to Brighton on Saturday, but no one could say they were again out of fortune to be defeated 3-0 by the United at the Stadium, on Wednesday, in the first round of the Southern Section Cup. The Blues opened the game in such half-hearted fashion that the Newport attack was constantly bearing down on MacKenzie's goal. Poor shooting and a sterling defence by Turner thwarted them, with the result that the custodian had little to worry about in the way of direct shots. Turner, ably assisted by Robinson, held the fort until the United put a little more spirit into their play, and at the interval the home side led 2-0.

This was scarcely deserved, but was a reward for the superior finish of the home attack. Stevens, a constant thorn in the side of the Newport defence, headed the first goal from a centre by Oswald, and the centre-forward made the opening from which Lane netted the second.

This point was lucky in a way, for Lane missed Stevens' centre and the ball hit Kelso and rebounded to the feet of the inside-left. Southend played far better football after the resumption, and Newport gradually wilted against the onslaughts launched in quick succession. Oswald was the star of the line, twinkling in and out of the opposition and dropping accurate centres into the goalmouth. Had Lane been at all on form he should have converted several of these, but all his dash and energy led to nothing. Firth schemed well, but Deacon made too many mistakes. He did, however, get across to the centre from which Frith headed the third goal, the ball striking the underside of the crossbar and rebounding over the line.

Had Newport been a good team, they might have forced a draw in the closing stages, for haphazard kicking by several of the Blues' defenders enabled them to get a good grip of the play. MacKenzie had to be alert several times, and Turner, Robinson and Kelly put up a bold front. Carr dropped back to lend a hand and managed to stop with his body a shot from Parle that would otherwise have found the net, for MacKenzie was on the ground. Kelly, who came into the side in order that Nelson could be rested, put plenty of enthusiasm into his work and was very prominent in the second half.

There was not, however, much degree of understanding between the defenders, and the loose positional work would have been fatal had the opposition been stronger. Throughout the methods were slip-shod and there were few redeeming features. Newport were best served by McKay (inside-right) and Burgess (left-half), who almost looked like twins on the field so much were they alike. Briggs made many excellent saves, but the team generally was very mediocre, especially the forwards when getting near to shooting distance. They probably missed Green, who was injured at Brighton and is claimed to be their best forward. The clubs of the Third Division have little use for the Southern Cup competition, and one sensed this on Wednesday that this spirit had communicated itself to the teams. Gate receipts were £210. The teams were: –

SOUTHEND UNITED: MacKenzie; Robinson and Kelly; Spelman, Turner and Carr; Deacon, Firth, Stevens, Lane and Oswald.

NEWPORT: Briggs; Jenkins and Kelso; Davies, Craven and Burgess; Appleby, McKay, Smith, Parle and Thomas.

Referee: Mr. A.J. Jewell.

Monday, November 11th, 1935
Quarter-final
CRYSTAL PALACE 3, SOUTHEND UNITED 2

Southend United's interest in the Southern Section Cup ceased on Monday, when their third round match at Selhurst Park ended in a 3-2 defeat by the Crystal Palace – and a defeat, too, which, I think I am right in saying, will not worry the management unduly, for the competition finds little favour amongst the clubs. Judging by the half-hearted play by the Glaziers in the first half, it did not appear as if they were anxious to proceed further, but after a goal-less half both sides put more life into their play and the five goals were registered in the second forty-five. The Palace opened with the aid of a penalty awarded against Carr, who brought Turner down. Rooke's shot looked to me to be within MacKenzie's reach, but he failed to fling up his hands sufficiently quickly. Three minutes later Oswald put a centre to the far side of the goal and Deacon headed it back, for Lane to help it into the net.

A partial clearance by MacKenzie led to Hanson putting the Palace ahead again, and Rooke made the score 3-1 by heading through a corner taken by Turner. Lane reduced the arrears when he converted a pass from Stevens, who played on the right wing. The ball was going to Morfitt, who led the attack, but, just as he drew his foot to shoot, the eager Lane got in first. With the last kick of the game Morfitt should have equalised, but sent the ball the wrong side of a post.

It was refreshing to see the enthusiasm Morfitt brought into the attack, and it was not all his fault the United did not get more goals. Stevens' pass that led to Lane's second goal was the only good thing he did. Deacon, playing at inside-right, was good and bad in patches, and in the second half received a kick over the left eye which afterwards had to be stitched. Lane was the cleverest forward and deserved his success. Carr played well at left-half, and Nelson kicked strongly. Purdon was the pick of the Palace halves for the way he kept Morfitt away from goal, and both backs played soundly. Rooke did not impress as the Palace leader, and the versatile Turner was as good a forward as there was on view. The teams were: –

Crystal Palace: Stanbury; Thorpe and Waterfield; Wilde, Purdon and Smith; Turner, Birtly, Rooke, Waldron and Hanson.

Southend United: MacKenzie; Nelson and Robinson; Spelman, Turner and Carr; Stevens, Deacon, Morfitt, Lane and Oswald.

Referee: Mr. A.J. Jewell.

Wednesday, October 28th, 1936
Second Round
Southend United 0, Clapton Orient 2

Southend United's exit from the Southern Section League Cup on Wednesday was a poor performance. Entertaining Clapton Orient in the second round – after receiving a bye in the first – the Londoners gained a 2-0 victory. Although Southend pressed for long periods in both halves, one could not but help gain the impression that the homesters had little heart in the game. There methods were slap dash. The shooting was very erratic and there appeared at times a complete lack of understanding both in defence and attack. In the view of the lack of interest in Southern Section Cup-ties, the attendance of 2,068 (£132. 10s. 6d.) could be considered satisfactory, but the crowd must have left the ground feeling that their afternoon had been wasted from the spectacular point of view.

Clapton Orient, with the exception of Fisher, at centre-forward, were at full strength, whereas the United had five reserves, but that did not make any excuse for the ragged football. The United should have won the game, although there was no gainsaying the fact that the Orient were deserving of their victory, for they at least did take their chances. The United had the opportunities, including a penalty that was missed, of netting half a dozen, but Lane and Firth, in particular, seemed to be out of form.

Fisher scored the only first half goal from close range after chasing a long up-field punt. Just after the restart of the game a foul on the centre spot saw Turner drop the ball just in front of the Orient goal. Hillam ran out and collided with Affleck, his centre-half, and the ball rebounded off them and was dropped under the bar, when Hearty punched it clear. Everest took the spot-kick and fired wide of the goal. After thirty-five minutes, Miles, the tiny Orient left winger, took advantage of the fact that the United defenders were all up helping the attack to break through. The backs could not catch him and, from his resulting centre, Fisher easily netted. Teams: –

SOUTHEND UNITED: MacKenzie; Robinson and Everest; Spelman, Turner and Jackson; Oswald, Firth, Goddard, Lane and Bird.

CLAPTON ORIENT: Hillam; Hearty and Herod; Taylor, Affleck and Heineman; McCombe, Fletcher, Fisher, Smith and Miles.

Referee: Mr. S.L. Clark, Southgate, N.14.

Wednesday, September 22nd, 1937
First Round
SOUTHEND UNITED 1, EXETER CITY 2

Ever since the Third Division Section Challenge Cup competitions were inaugurated, the clubs in both Southern and Northern Sections have shown a great lack of interest. Gate receipts, which are pooled, have dwindled each season, indicating the absence of public support, but the powers that be have so far failed to heed the signs and the competitions continue. Southend last season offered little resistance to Clapton Orient at the Stadium, and the Londoners went into the next round, and, on Wednesday, Exeter progressed in similar fashion by 2-1.

After nearly forty-five minutes of scrappy, uneventful play, in which neither team looked like scoring, Bell put Southend ahead from close range. In the second half Exeter, who throughout were better together as a team, equalised through Bowl, their centre-forward, and towards the close he netted again to give the Devon side the victory. On their form Southend did not deserve anything else but defeat, although from the point of view of scoring chances, they should have been the victors.

The game was never really interesting, and on both sides there was a tendency to go at half speed, and most of the cardinal points of the game were neglected. The passing was bad, the shooting was poor, the team-work weak, and the positioning of the players, with the exception of the backs, left much to be desired. The backs were Nelson and Robinson, neither of whom gave much away, whilst MacKenzie behind them zealously guarded his charge and was scarcely to be blamed for the shots that passed him.

The United's half-back line consisted of Deacon, Hague and Wright, and they have played far better. Deacon was the pick, and it was mistakes in the centre of this section of the defence that had a lot to do with the defeat. The United were led by Dickinson, who did very little beyond a backward header in the second half that nearly caught the Exeter goalkeeper unawares. Neither Harris nor Bell were as effective as they should have been, particularly in front of goal, whilst young McAdam, playing in place of Bolan on the right wing, had a bad first half for his debut with the first eleven, but improved in the second. Lane was the best of a poor line, which seldom worked in unison, and Southend's football could rightly be described as apathetic. There was a crowd of 2,680 present, and from their comments it was obvious that they regarded the game in a farcical light. Southend are not likely to grieve over their dismissal. Wednesday's teams were: –

SOUTHEND UNITED: MacKenzie; Nelson and Robinson; Deacon, Hague and Wright; McAdam, Harris, Dickinson, Bell and Lane.

EXETER: Tierney; Brown and Clarke; Kavanagh, Davies and Angus; Miles, Bussey, Bowl, Ebdon and Liddle.

Referee: Mr. L. Brown, Barnes.

Wednesday, September 28th, 1938
First Round
NORTHAMPTON TOWN 1, SOUTHEND UNITED 1

Lack of interest in the Southern Section Cup Competition appeared to be evident at Northampton on Wednesday, where only a few hundred spectators saw Southend United and Northampton Town draw 1-1 in the first round of the tournament. Although the players did not lack energy, the game seldom reached more than a moderate standard, and there were too many mistakes in finishing for either side to be regarded as a good team. Northampton were a little more polished in midfield. On the other hand, the Southend forwards gave Gormlie at least as much trouble as came the way of Hankey at the other end.

For Southend, Robinson played well at full-back and Hague did a lot of work at centre-half, whilst of the forwards Trainer and Hall were perhaps the best in a line that was, as a whole, uncertain. Northampton had a fine goalkeeper in Gormlie and an accurate back in Gunn. Their strength, however, was at wing half-back, where both McCullough and Postlethwaite played admirably. There was something missing in the encounter, which suggested that neither side treated it as seriously as they would have done a League match. Too much time was wasted in elaborate passing, and the tackling occasionally lacked the skill that one expected.

Eighteen minutes from the start, McCullough finished up a neat piece of work with a capital cross shot, and, although Milne made a splendid attempt to kick the ball away from under the bar, it was no surprise that a goal was allowed. Just an hour of the game had gone before Southend equalised through Smirk, who cut in to hit a loose ball out of Gormlie's reach.

NORTHAMPTON TOWN: Gormlie; Gunn and Russell; McCullough, Thayne and Postlethwaite; Cuff, Allen, Hewitt, McCartney and Rodger.

SOUTHEND UNITED: Hankey; Milne and Robinson; Harris, Hague and Bushby; Smirk, Davis, Trainer, Hall and Muncie.

Wednesday, October 5th, 1938
First Round Re-play
SOUTHEND UNITED 2, NORTHAMPTON TOWN 3

Extra time was necessary in the Southern Section Cup first round replay at the Stadium, on Wednesday, between the United and Northampton. The first meeting of the clubs on the previous Wednesday ended in a draw of 1-1, and at full time on Wednesday the score was 2-2. In the first half of the extra time, Northampton were able to net an easy goal, and that concluded the scoring in a poor and scrambling match, at which barely a thousand people attended. Southend were a goal down at half-time, and Northampton added their second – both goals were scored by Allen, the centre-forward – before Davis, the Southend inside-right, replied twice in the space of two minutes. Allen netted the winning goal after Hague, in making a back-pass to Hillam, sent the ball wide and left the opposing centre-forward with an easy opportunity, which he accepted.

On the first half play, Northampton were the better balanced side, their players using the ball more accurately than did the United on a rain-soaked and greasy pitch. Both sides missed excellent scoring chances – Southend were mostly at fault in this – and the first goal was not obtained until a minute before the interval. Southend should have won the match in the second forty-five minutes, but their good approach work ended whenever they were within shooting distance. Milne was the outstanding defender, and the forwards all suffered from a desire the keep the ball too close. Smirk and Davis put in the best touches, but there was not sufficient understanding in the attack to carry it to success when close to goal. Northampton were best served by their winger Hunel, who made the first two goals possible, and Allen, who took his chances.

The teams were: –

SOUTHEND UNITED: Hillam; Milne and Robinson; Harris, Hague and Bushby; Smirk, Davis, Trainer, Hall and Muncie.

NORTHAMPTON: Gormlie; Platt and Russell; Bosse, Dickinson and Postlethwaite; Hunel, Blunt, Allen, Lauderdale and Rodger.

Referee, Mr. H.C. Williams.

CHAPTER EIGHT

The Abandoned 1939-40 Season

Saturday, August 12th, 1939
Public Practice Match
BLUES 4, REDS 2

With the exception of Fairchild, a full-back, formerly with the Arsenal, who was being rested following a slight injury sustained while training, all Southend United's new players were on view at the Stadium on Saturday, when a long-awaited event for local football patrons – the Blues' first public trial match – took place. It was ironical that this curtain-raiser to the League football campaign for the season 1939-40 should be held on one of the finest days of this very disappointing summer, especially after the autumn weather the district has been experiencing of late. Despite this and the numerous counter-attractions in the Borough, including the County Cricket Festival at Southchurch Park, the Carnival Queen Matinee at the Gaumont Cinema and the final stages of the Women's Bowling Tournament, a crowd of about 2,000 gathered to give the new players a welcome. Supporters must have been well pleased with what they saw, for the match produced some very bright play and two of the new men at least appeared certain, if Saturday's game is any criterion, of securing their positions in the first eleven. Undoubtedly the best display was given by Jack Ormandy, formerly of Bury, and it seems that at long last the United have found someone to solve their left wing problem. Ormandy showed fine speed and ball control and scored two splendid goals – both the result of real opportunism. There was some fine sparkling play on his wing in the first half, when Shallcross, at inside-left, combined cleverly with him and made some splendid passes. After the interval, Shallcross, who was suffering from stitch rather badly, dropped out of the game and was replaced by Walton, but the latter failed to emulate the success of his predecessor.

Another newcomer, Black, who it will be recalled played some fine games for Plymouth Argyle, does not seem to have lost any of his guile, and he was one of the best half-backs on the field. A strong tackier, who seldom wastes the ball, he should greatly add to the strength of the Blues' defence. Johnston, who formerly played for Limerick and came to Southend with a high reputation, was a great trier in the opening half and made many fine efforts to break through and score. His attempts at distribution were creditable. In the later stages, however, he lost his earlier dash, and Martin, who was at centre-forward on the opposing side, attracted more attention. Johnston will doubtless prove a good capture – his first half display revealed that he is a player of considerable ability – but he will probably not displace Martin in the United's attack at the start of the season, for the versatile Martin is still a very dangerous raider. Sibley, who played for Barking, the Athenian League side last season, saw too little of the ball for anyone to fairly assess his value, but he, nevertheless, made some neat movements and showed a good turn of speed.

Coyde, Newcastle, another left winger, was also given few chances to prove his worth, and Tucker, formerly with the Wolves, gave a disappointing display in his first outing at the Stadium. He nearly always went the wrong way to tackle the wily Ormandy, and was altogether given a worrying afternoon. The other new player was Roper, who also comes from Barking, and he took Hillam's place in goal after half-time. He was only beaten once, with almost the last kick of the game, and by a shot which gave him no chance. I liked the way he shaped to make a save and throughout he dealt with all shots with confidence and ability. Although naturally enough chief interest centred on the players who had been signed on since the close of last season, many supporters were anxious to see how their favourites of last campaign would shape.

Many eyes were focussed on young Smirk, the right winger who came to Southend last year and quickly earned for himself the reputation of being one of the best wingers in the Third Division – a distinction he well deserved on his earlier games with the Blues. Then it will be remembered Smirk lost his brilliance and for many matches one looked in vain for the winger to get back to his old form. In fairness to Smirk, it must be pointed out that he was not in the best of health for some time.

Towards the end of the season, however, he again played some fine games, and it was encouraging to see him take a prominent part in Saturday's practice match, and we hope it will be an omen for a successful season. Smirk might well have stolen some of Ormandy's thunder, but for the brilliance of Trainer, who was at left-back on the opposing side. The Blues' former centre-forward should prove himself a full-back of class, and his fearlessness on the field and strong kicking made him a problem indeed for any attacker. Although the veteran Dave Robinson can by no means be left out of the running, Trainer should get the left-back position.

On Saturday, Trainer did not give Smirk an inch of room and sometimes he beat the winger for possession by speed – a feat in itself. Milne had a good match and will doubtless be retained at right-back, as also will Hague (centre-half) and Harris (right-half), who were two of Southend's most consistent players last season. The experience of Bell and Bolan should enable them to keep their places – at the start at least – though Shallcross and H. Scaife are going to give the management a deal of thought before they decide on the inside positions.

Neither Jackson nor Downey appear likely to be preferred to Black, though Leighton, who is one of the Blues' most versatile players, is also one of the most skilful men on the books and there are few who use the ball better. Hankey, when he returns from his ten weeks Reservist training, should be the first team goalkeeper, and in the meantime he has two very able deputies in Hillam and Roper. As usual in these practice matches the Reds were opposed to Blues, and there were three changes – all in the Blues eleven – at half-time. The Blues, incidentally, were successful by four goals to two. In the early stages the Reds were the more impressive side, and Bolan gave them the lead after fourteen minutes. Black instigated the movement, and from his pass Sibley transferred to Bolan, who turned the ball well out of Hillam's reach with a clever shot. Smirk was dangerous a moment later, but when an equalizer seemed likely Jones worried him into shooting wide. Within six minutes, however, Ormandy brought the ball in from the wing and cleverly beat Hankey with a right-footed shot which found a billet in the near corner of the net.

The Blues improved after this, and Scaife, Shallcross and Ormandy were prominent in subsequent raids. Johnson also gave the Reds defence some anxious moments, and once Hankey only just stopped his shot on the goal-line. Shallcross and Ormandy made a fine partnership, and the tussles between Trainer and Smirk provided some entertaining football. When the Reds attacked Martin and Bolan were most prominent. After the interval, Roper displaced Hillam, Downey (for Jackson) and Walton (for Shallcross). Five minutes after the resumption, Scaife scored a good goal from close range to give the Blues the lead, and soon afterwards Ormandy, receiving from Harris, made it three. This was the best goal of the afternoon and was a real pile-driver, which Hankey never saw until the ball was in the net. Walton obtained the Blues fourth goal, and with almost the last kick of the game Martin scored from a free-kick on the edge of the penalty area, awarded for a foul on him-self by Hague. The numbering of the players is going to prove a popular innovation, judging by the remarks I heard when leaving the Stadium, and it will undoubtedly enable spectators to follow the players better. The official attendance on Saturday was about 2,000, of whom 1,510 paid £40. 6s. 3d. at the turnstiles. Teams were (names in parentheses are players who came in after the interval, and former teams): –

BLUES: Hillam (Roper, Barking); Milne, Robinson; Harris, Hague, Jackson (Downey); Smirk, H. Scaife, Johnston (Limerick), Shallcross (Walton) Ormandy (Bury).

REDS: Hankey; Tucker (Wolves); Trainer; Leighton; Jones, Black (Plymouth); Sibley (Barking), Bolan, Martin, Bell, Coyde (Newcastle).

Referee: E.T. Drake.

Wednesday, August 16th, 1939
Sportsmen's Appeal Fund
SOUTHEND UNITED 2, COLCHESTER UNITED 2

If every League match during the approaching season contains the same excellent qualities as those that were witnessed in Wednesday evening's charity match at the Stadium between the United and Colchester, then the Blues are sure to obtain all the support for which they have been appealing. There were four goals – two scored by each side – some excellent team work, sparkling individual touches and a commendable keenness that quite outweighed the occasional ragged edges.

Colchester fielded a team in which were many players who have made their names in League football, and midway through the second half they led 2-1 on their merits. Southend United staged a fighting finish, and, with play totally different from that which one might expect in a friendly pre-season game, drew level. Light, the ex-West Bromwich Albion goalkeeper, frustrated their continued efforts to win, and the match finished on a note that thoroughly pleased the crowd of 1,753. They paid £101. 7s. 6d., and this will be divided between the Southend General Hospital and the Colchester Hospital.

Once again the deadly wing play and accurate shooting and centring of Ormandy, the former Bury winger, were pleasing features, and, with the thoughtful distribution of Black, secured from Plymouth, behind him, the left wing was easily the most progressive and dangerous. Ormandy, although on the small side, showed little fear, and the duels between Birch, the former Fulham back, and he were well worth watching.

Black's general field work and placing of the ball stamped him as a player of class, and I was glad to see the manner in which he made his colleagues run into position for the ball. True, he was a trifle slow at times and one or two of his passes went astray, but, generally speaking, his exhibition had that polished touch one might expect of him. His footballing ability, if combined with the necessary pace for League football, should make a great difference to the United defence, and the left flank should show a marked improvement in the coming season to that of last year.

A good many spectators left the ground convinced that Sibley, the young player from Barking, will develop into a smart player, and if his progress in the future bears out his present promise, the United will have made a real discovery. His shots were well on the mark, and it was a quick header on his part that enabled Martin to race through and slip the ball past the advancing goalkeeper for the only first-half goal. Credit, however, must also be accorded Black for his part in that success. He drew an opponent out of position and cleverly beat his man before giving Sibley the ball with one of those raking cross-field passes that catch the defence in two minds. The other three United forwards, Bolan, Martin and Bell, did not show up to the same advantage, although each made some excellent scoring attempts. Martin early on found Leslie, the Colchester recruit from Guildford, a strong and quick tackier, and seldom was he able to beat him. Bell, with Black and Ormandy as his immediate colleagues, will probably give better performances, whilst Bolan did not seem himself without Smirk as his wing partner, although this was no reflection on Sibley.

Of the United defenders other than Black some fine work was revealed by Hillam in goal, and Milne did well to hold Astill, the old Wolves winger, as he did. Harris was one of the hardest workers, but his transfers to his forwards were mixed, some being excellent and the others poor. Often he spoilt a fine piece of retrieving by placing the ball nearer a Colchester player than to his own man.

Hague made few errors, but what he did make were dangerous, and it was an absence of efficient covering tactics between himself and the backs, Milne and Trainer, that led to both Colchester goals. When they were scored the backs were spread-eagled and Hague beaten. This poor positional play must be remedied or else the United will be giving away more goals than they will score. The benefit of Black's cool play may be a help in the right direction in this respect if the other defenders can copy his style.

The United had an interest last year in Pritchard, the fair-headed ex-Newport player, who was inside-right in the first half and leader in the second. He scored both Colchester goals, being quick to accept the openings left by the United backs. Martin's first-half goal was in the twenty-fifth minute, and Pritchard obtained his pair in the fifty-second and fifty-fourth minutes of the game. Apart from those, he made other dangerous raids, and once Hillam had to effect a brilliant save to stop him heading through. Cheyne the ex-Chelsea player, was the schemer of the attack, and Pritchard, the thrusters, with Astill making some useful contributions on the left. Birch and Light took the defensive honours, although Leslie made an excellent job of subduing Martin. The United leader seized a chance to equalize for the Blues by jumping up over Bolan's shoulder in the sixtieth minute to head into the net a centre from Ormandy. He had hard luck also in not winning the game with a header that Light knocked up on to the bar for a brilliant save. The teams were: –

SOUTHEND UNITED: Hillam; Milne and Trainer; Harris, Hague and Black; Sibley, Bolan, Martin, Bell and Ormandy.

COLCHESTER: Light; Birch and Worton; Morris, Leslie and Wallis; Murray, Pritchard, Law, Cheyne and Astill.

Saturday, August 19th, 1939
Football League Jubilee Benevolent Fund
SOUTHEND UNITED 1, CLAPTON ORIENT 1

Some disappointment was felt that only three thousand people turned up at the Stadium on Saturday to see the Blues play their first match of the season against a side from the same Division. It was the best opportunity yet for supporters to see the team in action. Probably the gloriously fine afternoon was responsible, however, and, despite the many other attractive matches played last week-end for the Football League Jubilee Benevolent Fund, they did not make the same strong appeal as a year ago, when half a million people paid

£22,000 to watch the games. In comparison, 350,000 people saw Saturday's Jubilee matches. It is difficult, however, to be football-minded in the weather the district has been experiencing of late, and the conditions are very trying for the players. Present form, therefore, should not be judged too critically.

For the second time in four days, supporters of Southend United had an opportunity of seeing their favourite competitive football team when Clapton Orient were the visitors to the Stadium on Saturday. A contest of fluctuating fortunes ended in a draw of one goal each, which was a fair result on the general run of the play, though the Orient, with more scoring chances, could have won. It was the first occasion this season that local football patrons had seen the United opposed to a team of their own Division, and many, doubtless, attended in the hope of being able to assess the possibilities of the Blues.

They were not too disappointed in what they saw, for, although Southend had many shortcomings on Saturday and allowed their opponents to dominate the exchanges after they had themselves appeared to have gained the upper hand, it must be realized that the players were obviously taking no undue chances on a hard ground and in a friendly encounter, and the cohesion that was lacking was only to be expected at this early stage of the campaign.

Frankly, I was a little disappointed at the Blues display after the great promise of the public trial a week earlier, but it is easy to criticize when twenty-two footballers are rushing about for ninety minutes in weather such as was experienced last week-end. This heat-wave Soccer, with the thermometer jumping up into the eighties, cannot, and should not in fairness to those taking part, be viewed too seriously, and I marvelled that such a fast pace was maintained throughout this match under the existing conditions. It was in these circumstances, therefore, quite a good match, and there was plenty of entertaining football by both sides to keep interest alive until the last kick.

It is impossible at this stage to accurately predict the chances of the Southend Club, and only after the first few League matches have been fought will anyone be able to assess the true value of the team. With the added strength of the defence by the inclusion of Black and the two other notable captures of Ormandy, from Bury, and that very promising young player, Sibley, late of Barking, the Athenian League Club, there is every reason to be optimistic and even begin to wonder to ourselves whether or not this is going to be Southend United's year for promotion, at last.

Last year, it will be recalled, the United entertained Clapton Orient in a similar match, and on that occasion the Blues were successful by the solitary goal scored. The return game should have been played at the Osborne Road enclosure, Leyton, but, on account of the many other attractions in London on Saturday, it was decided to once again stage it at Southend. The attendance of 3,340 people, who paid £194. 8s., was considerably below last year's similar gate, when £280 was taken at the turnstiles. The United did not have their full team in the field as Milne, who has had to go on the sick list with a swollen instep, and Smirk, who had a slightly pulled calf muscle, were both rested. Tucker, formerly with the Wolves, was at right-back, and the youthful Sibley appeared on the right wing. There were six newcomers in the Orient side, and they were Ellis (the custodian), Bungay (a full back), McNeil (the centre-half) and Gore, McFadyen and Willshaw (forwards). The last-named is, of course, the former Southend left winger, whose departure from Ashton Gate, Bristol, created rather a surprise, for he was a regular first team player.

The United opened promisingly, and it was against the run of play when the visitors went into the lead through a goal scored by Gore, their right winger. McFadyen caught the home defence unawares with a cleverly placed pass through the middle, and before a tackle could be made Gore had slipped the ball well out of Hillam's reach to score an excellent point.

This success was after twenty-five minutes play, but within two minutes the Blues were on equal terms again, when Johnston rounded off one of the best moves of the afternoon with a picture goal. Tucker and Harris were the instigators, and after the Southend right-half had passed to Sibley, the winger made a perfect centre and Johnston did the rest. It was movements such as this which must have made the crowd forget the less inspiring football that was shown.

There were plenty of brainy examples in the middle of the field, but promising attacks too often petered out through weak finishing. Clapton Orient had a splendid defence, and the Southend forwards, well marked throughout, were seldom allowed to appear dangerous in front of goal. The 'O's' are a big side this year, and if they can reproduce their second half form in their subsequent League matches they should enjoy one of their best seasons of late. They made some storming attacks in the closing stages, and only the brilliance of Hillam in the United goal kept their lively forwards at bay. Hillam gave an outstanding performance between the sticks, and it is some time since better goalkeeping has been seen at the Stadium.

In one hectic onslaught by the Clapton forwards he showed very clever anticipation to throw himself at full length to keep out an effort by Gore. Whilst most spectators fully expected the winger to have a shot, Hillam anticipated he would instead square the ball to an inside colleague, and a very dangerous situation was thus saved. United Supporters must have been surprised at the spirited display of Willshaw on the Orient left wing, and he certainly showed less hesitancy when going into a tackle. He was also responsible for two of the fiercest drives of the day, and the force of one almost carried the United goalkeeper over the line.

McFadyen, the visitor's inside-right, was another dangerous raider, and Gore also gave an impressive display. Williams, the centre-forward, though a rare trier, was not so much in the picture. Hague saw to that. Trainer was by far the steadier of the Southend backs, and he was a great stopper. There was, however, a lack of understanding among the Blues defence on occasions, and their citadel had some narrow escapes as a result. Tucker has yet to gain more experience in covering up, and all too frequently he gave his opponents too much room in which to work. Hague had an anxious time, and under the circumstances did very well, and his distribution of the ball showed a marked improvement. Black, who has, incidentally, been elected Captain of the Club, was one of the most accomplished players on the field, and he wasted few balls. The same could not be said of Harris, who was never at his best, though no one worked harder.

The forwards were good individually, but their combined efforts gave the Orient defence little trouble. Johnston, always on the look-out for an opening, was well held by McNeil after the early prominence of the Blues leader, and the many attempts that were made to find the centre-forward down the middle hardly ever reached their objective.

Both the wingers revealed plenty of speed and good ball control, and in the opening forty-five minutes particularly Sibley made some grand centres. He is a great trier, who should quickly develop into one of the most promising players on the Club's books. Unfortunately, he saw little of the ball after the interval when most of the United's attacks, few though they were, came from the left wing. Although the Bell-Ormandy partnership did not produce the clever football that was seen when Shallcross was at inside to the former Bury player in the trial match, there was, nevertheless, some capital movements on the wing. Ormandy, already a favourite with the crowd, is one of the best captures Manager David Jack has made if his early form is any criterion. With the experience and ability of Black behind them, this wing has the possibilities of becoming one of the best in the Section.

Neither Bell nor Bolan was very impressive on Saturday's showing, though both sometimes caught the eye with a clever move. Bolan was, however, suffering from an injured arm. There was too much indecision, however, in front of goal, and if the Blues are to become a real attacking force this season the forwards must learn to shoot more quickly and more often. Once Bolan and Johnston passed back to each other in front of goal when a first-time shot by either would probably have found the back of the Orient net. Undoubtedly, the splendid performance of McNeil, the visitor's pivot, had a considerable effect on the efforts of the Blues forwards, while he was given good support by both the backs, Bungay and Rumbold, though the latter had an annoying tendency to kick into touch on every possible occasion when the United's left wing threatened danger.

Southend produced their brightest play in the first forty-five minutes, and two fine efforts by Johnston, with a header, and Bell deserved better fate. Bell's shot was kicked away by Bungay from off the goal line when a goal seemed inevitable. During another Southend onslaught Bolan was unfortunate to see his shot crash against the cross-bar. The Orient, though seldom in the ascendancy during this period, gave the home defence, who were inclined to get flurried when under pressure, some anxious moments. There was a very dull period in the first twenty minutes that followed the interval, but when Clapton Orient began to apply pressure the spectators were treated to the most thrilling incidents of the match. Williams, a persistent leader, McFadyen and Willshaw were prominent in these raids, but Hillam was their equal every time, and at this stage he alone stood between Southend and defeat. The teams were: –

SOUTHEND UNITED: Hillam; Tucker and Trainer; Harris, Hague and Black; Sibley, Bolan, Johnston, Bell and Ormandy.

CLAPTON ORIENT: Ellis; Rumbold and Bungay; Taylor, McNeil and Black; Gore, McFadyen, Williams, Crawford and Willshaw.

Referee: Mr. F.S.C. Riggs.

Saturday, August 19th, 1939
Football League Jubilee Benevolent Fund
CLAPTON ORIENT RESERVES 4, SOUTHEND UNITED RESERVES 0

For their Jubilee Benevolent Fund match with Clapton Orient Reserves at the Osborne Road Ground, Leyton on Saturday, Southend United Reserves took the opportunity of trying some of the promising young players on the Club's books. Although the Junior Blues were beaten by 4-0, the final result was not by any means a fair reflection of the play. For the greater part of the game Southend enjoyed an equal share of the exchanges, but the home forwards showed better finishing.

During the game Walton and Shallcross changed positions on the left wing, and Scaife was moved from the left inside position to outside-right. An interested spectator was Mr. David Jack, the United manager, who was watching the Junior Blues centre-forward, Vincent McGrane, an 18-years-old lad from a Liverpool club, who was on trial. Although playing very well on occasions, the newcomer was rather overweighted and had few chances to be really dangerous. McGrane has now returned to his home town, but Manager Jack informed me this week that he intended to have another look at the youngster next season. Coyde, first at outside-right and later as an inside forward, was outstanding in the Southend attack, while another player to give a good account of himself was Fairchild, the former Arsenal full-back.

Roper, the ex-Barking custodian, made some wonderful saves in the second half. Robinson, playing at left-back, was not at his best, however, and Jones did not rise to the occasion. There was little to choose between the teams in mid-field, but there will have to be some tightening up in the defence. Leighton showed a number of fine touches, as usual, and if only he could rectify faulty retrieving and covering up he would, without a doubt, be one of the best men Southend possesses. The Orient scored two goals in each half, and the slackness of the Blues defence down the middle made the winners task easier.

SOUTHEND UNITED RESERVES fielded the following side: Roper; Fairchild and Robinson; Leighton, Jones and Jackson; Coyde, H. Scaife, V. McGrane, Shallcross and Walton.

Saturday, August 26th, 1939
Football League, Third Division (Southern Section)
SOUTHEND UNITED 3, WALSALL 2

Southend United opened their League programme at the Stadium on Saturday with a fine victory over Walsall by three goals to two. It was a satisfactory start in many ways, for not only did the United gain the maximum points, but their football suggested that they are going to be a hard side to beat on their ground this season. Nevertheless, a tightening-up of the defence is still needed, for there were some anxious moments, due to poor covering, when Walsall attacked. For the most part, however, it was an entertaining contest, and a fast pace was maintained by both sides throughout, despite the blazing sunshine.

Many spectators, in view of Walsall's lowly position in the table in recent years, were, no doubt, surprised to see the Midlands side reveal such dash. But Walsall, strengthened by their latest captures, the chief of whom is Dai Richards, who captained Wales when they defeated England last season, played some delightful football on occasions, and a clever set of forwards always seemed likely to save the game by their great persistency. The Blues deserved their success, but there was very little to choose between the teams, and the visitors were better served at half-back.

Had the United's middle line emulated the play of the rest of the team Southend would doubtless have gained a more convincing victory, for the attack was in great form, with the new wingers, Ormandy, from Bury, and Sibley, from Barking, as schemers-in-chief. Hague was not as much at fault as the wing halves, for he had all his work cut out to look after Alsop, a rare opportunist, whose bustling methods were sufficient to put any centre-half off his usual game. As a stopper, Hague did some invaluable work – and it was no easy task against the clever Walsall attack – but his clearances were erratic and he was too often content merely to boot the ball up-field and clear his lines rather than place the ball to better advantage.

I was very disappointed at Black's display, though it must be said he would suddenly catch the eye with a brilliant piece of dribbling or with one of those accurate passes to the feet of a colleague. He appeared worried by the wiles of Hancocks, the Walsall right winger, who had a great match, and was too busy chasing the elusive winger to give his own forwards much assistance. Harris was also well below his normal form, and he was given little rest by Bulger and Talbot, who formed a fine left-wing partnership for Walsall. It was all the more commendable that Ormandy and Sibley should do so well under those circumstances, but they received admirable assistance from their inside forwards,

Bell and Smirk. I was particularly impressed with the latter's performance at inside-right, and he made some glorious openings for the 19-years-old ex-Barking winger.

Last campaign, it will be recalled, Smirk, then playing at outside-right, frequently 'switched' with Bolan and proved a dangerous raider from the inside position. No less prominent was the work carried out by Bell and Ormandy on the opposite wing, and Bell opened the game in his best style. Ormandy again revealed some delightful touches, and he deserved special credit for his display when one considered that he had in opposition the International Richards, and a particularly fine and hefty full-back in Beeson. This did not worry Ormandy, however, who hardly put a foot wrong from start to finish. Ably led by Martin, who, though less prominent than the other four, was, nevertheless, a fine opportunist, this Southend attack was one of the best seen at the Stadium for some time past and augers well for a successful season for the Club.

Another pleasing feature from the United's point of view was the promising game played by Fairchild, the former Arsenal player, who came into the side at the last minute in place of Milne, who was also on the injured list. This young player, who did so well for the Reserves at Leyton the previous week, showed promise of developing into a useful defender with more experience. He has a fine kick, and his tackling and positioning were good, but there were times when he could not cope with the wiles of his opponents. Robinson, as usual, was a tireless worker and never gave up trying. To complete this Southend United side on its first League outing this season, Hillam, in goal, made many fine saves and stood no chance with the two shots that did find their way past him into the net.

Southend United were actually seen to best advantage in the first half, for in the period that followed the interval Walsall were on top. The first five minutes of the game probably provided the most exciting incidents, when both goals in turn experienced amazing escapes. After Hillam had made a clever interception to beat Alsop for a centre from Bulger, at the other end Beeson had to give away a corner to stop Ormandy. Then Black brought Talbot down a foot outside the penalty area, and Richards shot into the side netting.

The game was nine minutes old when the United secured the lead. Fairchild took a free-kick from the half-way line, the ball touched Thayne's head on its way out to Ormandy and the winger, holding off the efforts of Beeson, crashed the ball into the far corner of the net with a great shot.

The Blues delighted their supporters with their brilliance at this stage, and within six minutes the Walsall citadel fell a second time, when Bell headed past Strong from Ormandy's well-place corner-kick. It was a beautifully placed header, which gave the custodian no chance, although he flung himself at full-length in an unsuccessful effort to prevent a goal. Despite these early shocks, however, Walsall rallied splendidly and Hillam brought off the best save of the match to keep out a shot from Bulger; then Hague kicked away from off the goal-line.

It was no more than they deserved when, after 25 minutes, Walsall reduced the deficit, Alsop scoring from close in after good work by Bulger. Southend enjoyed the better of the remaining play before half-time, but there was no further scoring. Four minutes after the resumption the Blues struck again, when Thayne had back luck to deflect Sibley's shot past his own goalkeeper. Six minutes afterwards Talbot, the Walsall inside-left, started a beautiful move-ment which led to the visitors scoring a second goal. After 'selling the dummy' to Harris, he made a deal of ground before transferring to Bulger, who beat Hillam for the ball and sent the leather crashing into the net.

It was bad luck that a few minutes after this, Beeson, the Midlands club's right-back, should injure himself in a collision with Martin. He was off the field for five minutes to receive attention, and resumed on the right wing. Richards went to full-back, Walton to right-half and Hancocks moved to inside-right.

Curiously enough, the changes did not seem to affect the Walsall team in any way, for Beeson, after he had rested his injured leg, gave the Southend defence some anxious moments and blossomed into a dangerous raider. Indeed, during this period Walsall seemed very likely to draw level, and with a little better luck in front of goal an equalizer would undoubtedly have come. Once, after Bulger had hit an upright, Hillam and Alsop finished in the net together. The United should have been awarded a penalty, however, when Strong, running out to save his charge, appeared to foul Sibley. Both sides made determined efforts to score again before the close, and the final whistle came with the Blues back in the ascendancy.

Walsall, incidentally, lost at the Stadium for the fourth consecutive time, but the Midland team will not be easy to overcome on their own pitch this season and will probably give more fancied teams in the Division some shocks before the campaign is much older. In Beeson, Richards and Thayne they have three fine defenders, and Strong is a goalkeeper of the highest class. He made some great saves on Saturday, especially from Ormandy and Bell. Alsop will give opposing defences some worrying moments, while Bulger and Hancocks are lively wingers who should prove equally dangerous.

I also liked the play of Talbot, an inside forward who has adopted a game similar in many ways to Alex James and, more recently, Bryn Jones. For the most part he hangs back amongst the halves, then he will seize on a loose ball, beat his man and open out the opponents defence with a long cross-pass. There is little doubt that the 6,500 spectators (5,570 paid for admission at the turnstiles) thoroughly enjoyed the first League match of the new season at the Stadium, and if all the subsequent games provide local patrons with such entertaining fare they will have little to grumble at – especially if the United continue in winning vein – and, with a tightening-up of defensive weaknesses, there is no reason why they should not do so. With Black and Harris back to their best form, the Southend forwards, strengthened by Ormandy and now Sibley, will take some holding. The first hurdle has been successfully negotiated, and now we look forward to seeing the Blues make a great bid for championship honours this year. An attendance of over 6,000 was quite a good beginning, especially considering the international situation, but there is still plenty of spare room at the Stadium, and there is nothing like good vocal support to spur a team on to greater efforts.

The teams were: –

SOUTHEND UNITED: Hillam; Fairchild and Robinson; Harris, Hague and Black; Sibley, Smirk, Martin, Bell and Ormandy.

WALSALL: Strong; Beeson and Male; Richards, Thayne and Godfrey; Hancocks, Walton, Alsop, Talbot and Bulger.

Referee: Mr. H.C. Williams, Fulham.

Saturday, August 26th, 1939
Football Combination
BOURNEMOUTH & BOSCOMBE ATHLETIC RESERVES 2,
SOUTHEND UNITED RESERVES 4

Southend United Reserves began their Football Combination programme at Bournemouth on Saturday, when they defeated Bournemouth and Boscombe Reserves by 4-2. Although the home side scored first through their inside-left, McCann, after only ten minutes play, the Junior Blues were generally on top, playing splendid football. An equalizer came when Davis, receiving the ball from Leighton, went through on his own to score. Downey, who played with rare opportunism, had a good chance to give Southend the lead a moment after, but he hurried his shot and sent wide.

Although the United were for the most part in the ascendancy, Bournemouth persevered, but Roper, backed up by a sound defence, was equal to the occasion. Soon after the interval, Walton broke away on the left, centred accurately, and Downey beat the goalkeeper with a brilliant header. This was the best goal of the match. Five minutes later Southend struck again, when Downey, coming from apparently an off-side position, went through unchallenged to score. The home players appealed against the point, but their protests were of no avail.

Midway through the second half, Bournemouth decreased the lead, Langley being the marksman. The Hampshire side never appeared likely to save the game, however, and Southend, maintaining their grip, scored again before the close through Shallcross. In the later stages, the United did as they wished with their opponents and were unlucky not to further increase their lead. Roper kept a good goal for Southend, and Trainer was the better of the full-backs, always having the measure of the Bournemouth right wing, which seldom threatened danger. Tucker gave admirable support, though a little weak in tackling on occasions, while Jones, at centre-half, showed a marked improvement.

The opposing centre-forward, as a result, had a poor game. Leighton made some clever openings for his wing, but the outstanding personality in the Southend side, and indeed on the field, was Jackson, who was in great form at left-half. Coyde played very direct football and formed a dangerous wing with Davis, who, incidentally, was the best forward. Downey was a great trier, and led the attack well. His first goal was a 'picture.' Shallcross played a brainy game, while Walton revealed his best form. The McCann-McDougal left wing for Bournemouth gave the Southend defence most trouble, and Wilkinson, Cook and Wilson also did well for the homesters. The teams were: –

SOUTHEND UNITED RESERVES: Roper; Tucker and Trainer; Leighton, Jones and Jackson; Coyde, Davis, Downey, Shallcross and Walton.

BOURNEMOUTH RESERVES: Stone; Millar and Wilkinson; Cook, Wilson and Woodward; Smart, Tagg, Langley, McCann and McDougal.

Wednesday, August 30th, 1939
Football Combination
SOUTHEND UNITED RESERVES 2, CHELSEA RESERVES 1

A penalty goal midway through the second half gave Southend United Reserves both points against Chelsea Reserves, whom they beat by 2-1 in a Football Combination match at the Stadium on Wednesday. The victory was well deserved, however, and the Junior Blues did extremely well to overcome the powerful side Chelsea had fielded. There were many familiar names in the visitors eleven, but this did not worry Southend, who played splendid football throughout. The forwards especially were in scintillating form and the Chelsea goal had some anxious moments. The defence was a little uncertain in the early stages, but later they, too, played with great determination, and a Chelsea attack which had hitherto looked a dangerous combination was kept very quiet.

The Junior Blues made three positional changes from the team which did duty at Bournemouth. Singleton returned to centre-forward, Downey dropped back to left-half and Jackson moved across to right-half in place of Leighton, who was injured in Saturday's match. Chelsea fielded a very strong eleven, which included such well-known players as Jackson, O'Hare, Buchanan, Payne and Mills.

Southend attacked for the greater portion of the opening half, and on the run of the play deserved to be ahead at the half-way stage. The Chelsea attack showed some delightful movements, however, and Payne and Buchanan formed the most dangerous wing partnership in the game during this period. Buchanan especially had some brilliant touches, and he gave Trainer a most worrying time, though the Southend full-back improved after the interval.

Mills was also a great opportunist and he gave Jones little peace. The Southend wing halves were in good form and Tucker was the coolest defender on the field. The home defence showed a marked improvement in the second half, Jones getting the measure of the tall Chelsea leader, while the Payne-Buchanan wing faded out.

The Chelsea defence, Griffiths excepted, never inspired much confidence when under pressure, and a lively Southend attack worked the ball exceptionally well, some fine movements resulting. Southend were a goal up within five minutes of the start, when Singleton, securing from Walton, drove the ball to the right of Jackson with a splendidly placed shot. The goalkeeper made a great effort to save, but the ball just escaped his grasp. The Junior Blues continued to do most of the attacking, but Chelsea threatened danger when they raided down their right wing.

The visitors were hardly worth the equalizer, however, which came after twenty-six minutes, Payne scoring from a loose ball following a scrimmage. The Southend defence was at fault here, and hesitation, aided by poor covering, made Payne's way to goal easier. Southend should have taken the lead again before the interval, for the Chelsea backs were erratic, and Vaux, who persisted in kicking into touch on every possible occasion, aroused the crowd's indignation.

Despite this though, the best scoring chance of the half was presented to Smale, the Chelsea left winger, following great work by Buchanan and Payne. He had an open goal, but sent the leather yards wide of the mark.
Southend's ascendancy was even more marked after the change-over, and they fully deserved to score again, which they did after 65 minutes. Walton, after receiving from Singleton, was going through on his own when he was brought down unfairly and, from the penalty spot, Davis crashed the ball into the back of the net with a great drive.

The subsequent play, though becoming a little over-keen on occasions, provided many thrills and both goals had narrow escapes. For a time Jackson, in the Chelsea goal, was the hardest worked player on the field, and his citadel had a charmed life. Coyde, Singleton and Davis were on the mark, and Walton, who had a splendid game, made some clever passes. For most of the match Walton played at inside-left, Shallcross going on the wing early in the first half, following an injury. Singleton revealed some very neat touches, Coyde was a speedy winger, and Davis and Walton made the openings.

Chelsea had a fine opportunity to equalize three minutes from the end, but Buchanan, standing only a few yards out and with no-one near him, shot outside. It was a near thing for the home team, but Chelsea would have been lucky to have saved a point, for Southend had played the better football and enjoyed by far the greater portion of the exchanges. The play of the whole side was indeed worthy of high praise, and victory, even on their own ground, against a team of so many 'stars,' was no mean achievement.

SOUTHEND UNITED RESERVES: Roper; Tucker and Trainer; Jackson, Jones and Downey; Coyde, Davis, Singleton, Shallcross and Walton.

CHELSEA RESERVES: Jackson; O'Hare and Vaux; Mayes, Griffiths and Alexander; Buchanan, Payne, Mills, Foss and Smale.

Referee: Mr. W. Copp.

Thursday, August 31st, 1939
Football League, Third Division (Southern Section)
CLAPTON ORIENT 0, SOUTHEND UNITED 0

A game of fluctuating fortunes, in which defences were generally on top, saw Southend United play a goal-less draw with Clapton Orient at the Osborne Road enclosure, Leyton, on Thursday evening. The football, though fast and keenly fought throughout, never reached great heights. The Orient are a big, bustling side this year – a good Cup-fighting eleven unless I am mistaken – but their vigorous attacks, dangerous though they often were, did not rattle the Southend defence, which was at its best. The United, in fact, did very well to gain a point away to Clapton Orient, where in past seasons they have not been too successful.

The Orient were undoubtedly the better side after the interval, but in the opening forty-five minutes the United did most of the attacking, and throughout, despite the home side's later superiority, they played the more scientific football. The Orient showed some neat touches down the right wing, but for the most part they lacked the cleverness of the Southend players. This was particularly noticeable before the interval, when the Blues made some smart interpassing movements and found their men much better than did their opponents.

Indeed, the United began so well that they appeared likely to run away with the match. It was curious that an injury to Taylor, the homester's right-half, should coincide with an Orient recovery, for from that point onwards they showed renewed enthusiasm and put Southend right off their game. Their vigorous methods were not copy-book football by any means, but by swinging the ball about well and following up keenly Clapton made a series of dangerous attacks.

The Blues, as a consequence, lost their earlier balance, and an overworked defence was seldom able to give their own forwards many openings. Most of the Orient's attacks broke down near goal, however, for Hague and Hillam, both in great form, were masters of the situation. The other defenders, of whom Harris was outstanding, were particularly prominent in the second half and rendered admirable assistance.

The Southend attack, after promising so much at the start, faded out altogether later on, although Martin and Smirk were always dangerous when they got the ball. The Orient had to resort to offside tactics to keep out the Blues leader, and one or two promising raids broke down as a result. Sibley made some smart runs in the opening half, but he did little of note after the interval. Ormandy and Bell, though not so much in the picture as they were in the Walsall encounter, nevertheless played their part well in the period of ascendancy, though Ormandy never really got going.

The Orient defence was erratic when hard-pressed, but later, following a spell of relief, it improved considerably. It is strange how the fortunes of a game often change so quickly, for Southend, at one time a very predominant side, were later pegged back to such an extent that the Orient completely took over the mastery before the end. With a little more luck in front of goal, Southend might well have had a winning lead at the half-way stage.

The game took its remarkable turn after the interval, when the Orient, revealing much better form, gave the United's defence little peace, and it was as well that Hague and his colleagues were in their best form. There was, however, a lack of cohesion and finish. The Southend centre-half was a great stopper, and his clever interceptions frequently caused a halt to the Orient's efforts to force their way through.

The coolness of Fairchild – no one kicked a better length than the ex-Arsenal full-back – the unflinching spirit of Robinson and another fine display of goalkeeping by Hillam contributed largely towards the United being able to stave off defeat. They should, however, have won the game in the first half. Black was quite the most polished half-back on the field, and he did invaluable work. No one rendered better assistance to the defence when the Orient were pressing, while he made glorious openings earlier on. Harris, too, showed a marked improvement on his form of the previous Saturday, and he used the ball to much better advantage. So much did he improve as the game progressed that in the closing period he was the best half-back on the field. As usual, he played himself almost to a standstill.

At times the Orient attack was somewhat handicapped owing to an injury just before the interval to Taylor, their right-half, who was a passenger at outside-left throughout the second moiety. Hann, the inside-right, dropped back to the right-half position. It was surprising, therefore, that the homesters should do so well during that period, but Williams, McFadyen and Gore, who were in splendid form, more than compensated for this, while Willshaw was much more in the limelight playing at inside-left than he had been on the wing. McNeil was the Orient's best defender.

One of the most interested spectators among the 6,000 people present at the game was Mr. George Allison, the Arsenal manager. Sibley, the Southend right winger, certainly appears booked for a promising future in the game. Though the majority of the home supporters probably came away thinking the Orient unlucky not to have won both points, the Blues, to my mind, well deserved to draw, firstly, for their supremacy in the earlier stages, and, secondly, for the great work put in by the defence when things began to look very black for Southend. Few and far between though the United's onslaughts were during this spell, they were still often dangerous when the pressure was relieved, and once Martin was only just wide of the mark with a stinging drive. Unfortunately, two minutes before the final whistle Fairchild, the Southend right-back, twisted his back in attempting a clearance and had to be carried to the touch-line. It is hoped, however, that the injury is not serious.

The closeness of this encounter made the exchanges particularly keen in the closing stages, and the game was stopped more than once for other players to receive treatment. It was not a great contest; there was an absence of finish about both attacks, and as a spectacle it did not rank high. The result shows a gain of a point on last year's match. The teams were:–

CLAPTON ORIENT: Ellis; Rumbold and Bungay; Taylor, McNeil and Black; Gore, McFadyen, Williams, Hann and Willshaw.

SOUTHEND UNITED: Hillam; Fairchild and Robinson; Harris, Hague and Black; Sibley, Smirk, Martin, Bell and Ormandy.

Referee: Mr. P. Stevens (Luton).

Saturday, September 2nd, 1939
Football League, Third Division (Southern Section)
READING 1, SOUTHEND UNITED 0

Southend United had poor luck in their match against Reading at Elm Park on Saturday, which they lost by the solitary goal. For eighty minutes the Blues had more than their share of the exchanges, and following a series of dangerous raids it only seemed a matter of time before their efforts would secure a goal. Then, with only nine minutes left for play, Reading retaliated and three corners were forced in quick succession. Hillam, in the Southend goal, had made two glorious saves just previously, but from the third corner kick the ball went out to Dougall following a scrimmage in the goalmouth. The home right-half tried a shot, which Hillam, though unsighted, got his hands to, but before he could get the ball clear Maurice Edelston, the Amateur International, dashed up to force it into the net.

The United's bad luck did not end at this, for within five minutes, after persistent raids on the Reading citadel, Black, from a free-kick, deceived the goalkeeper with his shot to score what appeared to be a grand goal. To the dismay of the Southend players, however, the referee disallowed the point, and those in the Press box understood the official had ruled that Martin, who was on the spot to force the ball through if necessary, had either been guilty of obstruction or had fouled the custodian, though the centre-forward did not appear to have committed either of the offences. After the match, I enquired of Mr. P. S.V. Reed, the referee, why he had disallowed Southend's goal, and he replied, 'I gave Martin offside.' This did not appear to have been so, as Wilson, the Reading right-back, was standing on the goal-line.

A moment after this incident the Blues deserved a penalty when a Reading defender clearly obstructed Ormandy inside the prescribed area. Once again, however, the referee decided against the appeal. The team deserved special credit for their great efforts in the remaining minutes to save a point which they so richly deserved, but Reading gained one of their luckiest victories. The Southend players gave a particularly creditable exhibition, especially when one considered for a moment the tiring journey they had experienced from London.

There was little difficulty in either getting to London from Southend or making progress to Paddington Station, but there scenes were presented which will forever live in my memory. The station was a mass of parents and children all evacuating from the capital to safer places, but despite the multitude of people, not once did I see any congestion, signs of panic, or even outward sorrow. They just lined the platforms with their cases and necessary belongings, awaiting the arrival of the next train to take them to the various reception areas down the line. At lunch the Southend party met the Bristol Rovers team, up to play Crystal Palace.

They had apparently reached London comfortably. Although the Southend team missed the train they intended to catch, owing to the great crowds, they arrived at Reading at three o'clock, fifteen minutes before the kick-off, and with the assistance of a kindly policeman, who stopped an already crowded trolley bus to get the players to the ground, and a lightning changing act, the game started dead on time. The majority of the Southend team had had to stand in crowded corridors on the journey down, however, and it was a tribute to their stamina and determination to give of their best that they played such good football.

I was disappointed at the display of the Biscuitmen, particularly when it is realized that the same side, with one exception, had defeated the strong Crystal Palace eleven by 5-0 on the previous Wednesday. The inability of Young, their usual left halfback, to be able to appear owing to a leg injury undoubtedly affected them, for Edwards, who deputized, was quite out of his class, and his mistakes put the other home defenders out of their stride.

Fullwood, who enjoyed a good game at left-back for Reading, covered up well under the circumstances, but Sibley and Smirk, the United's best forwards, were a constant danger, and it was as well the home goalkeeper was in form. Holmes, their centre-half, was never impressive, and Martin, had he been quicker on the ball, might well have won the game for Southend long before the deciding goal was scored. Twice in the opening half, when a defender made a pass back to the custodian, Martin nearly intercepted, but for the most part he lacked his usual bustle, and Holmes was consequently made to look better than he actually was. Bell was also below his best, though no one worked harder, and Ormandy could never get going. True, the outside-left had no easy task against the burly Joe Wilson, the former Southend centre-half, who was later converted into a full back when he went to Brentford. Wilson, who is still a fine stopper, made some hefty clearances and was quite the best full back of the game. His tactics seemed to unsettle the ex-Bury winger, and as a result few dangerous moves came from the Southend left wing. There were some sparkling movements down the right, however, and Smirk, though I still consider him better on the wing, again made some very clever runs, and he was Southend's deadliest marksman.

Sibley improves with every game, and it was written of him in the Reading programme: 'How London clubs missed him is a mystery. Destined for highest honours in the game.' This reflects credit on Manager David Jack for his latest capture, and is a good omen for the future of the Club. The ex-Barking winger gave further indication of the talent he possesses and was always causing trouble to the home defenders.

The three outstanding players in the Southend defence were Hague, Harris and Hillam, the latter again keeping a brilliant goal until that unlucky incident for which he could in no way be blamed. Hague was always McPhee's master and the Blues' pivot made very few mistakes. His quick tackling and interceptions frequently brought relief when the home forwards were dangerous. Harris, too, made good use of the ball and had some brilliant periods. He gave Smallwood, the Reading left winger, a bad game, though Edelston, who was the homesters outstanding forward, was always dangerous when he had the ball, and the old Brentford player, now in the colours of his father's club (Mr. J. Edelston is Reading's manager) made some glorious moves which might well have produced a goal if it had not been for the clever recovery of the Southend defenders.

Edelston was seen to best advantage in the first half, for later he saw little of the ball and, like his colleagues, he also developed the fault of ragged passing. Chitty, on the Reading right wing, was the more prominent of the home forwards at this stage, and it was from this quarter that the most danger came after the interval. The Reading forwards, however, relied too much on short passing, which got them nowhere against a quick-tackling defence. Their strange ineffectiveness as compared with the brilliant form displayed against the Palace was increased by the poor support given by their half-backs, who had all their work cut out to keep Southend's nippy attack at bay.

As neither Milne nor Fairchild, who was injured in the last minute of the Clapton Orient game, were fit, Tucker, who came to Southend this season from Wolverhampton Wanderers, was at right-back, and he did extremely well. On occasions his keenness to get the ball away led to miskicking, but he compensated for these slips with some timely clearances when the home forwards threatened to break through. Robinson, though not quite at his best, nevertheless defended stubbornly and conceded little.

The Southend skipper, Tommy Black, had also played better football, but, although some of his passing lacked its usual accuracy and astuteness, as usual he was a great worker and he was the instigator of many of Southend's most dangerous moves. As a stylist he had no better on the field, and his footwork on occasions was a delight to watch and was only equalled as a spectacle by the brilliant touches of Edelston and Smirk.

With more effective finishing, the United would have been at least a goal up at the interval, and early on in the second half Sibley shot against the crossbar following Ormandy's corner kick. The play had been keen and interesting to watch in the earlier stages, but for a long spell in the second moiety the game developed into kick and scramble of the worst type, which must have nearly sent the spectators to sleep.

Nearly all the excitement of this half and indeed the best football of the encounter was crowded into the last quarter of an hour, and the crowd doubtless forgot the previous shortcomings as a result. The Blues, who had appeared to have at last got really on top and were doing everything but score, were pegged back by a determined Reading defence. There followed the three corners, when Hillam 'brought the house down' with brilliant goalkeeping; then came Reading's goal, scored as it was against the run of the preceding play.

This was the last we saw of the home attack, for from that period until the close Southend redoubled their efforts to regain lost ground. Once Martin was going through on his own, but he stumbled on his way to goal and a fine opportunity for an equalizer was lost. Then there was the incident of the disallowed goal and, finally, the foul on Ormandy, but despite subsequent pressure the home goal somehow remained intact, and the whistle eventually brought relief. The Blues seem doomed for bad luck at Reading, for last season two defensive errors and a disputed goal cost them the points. Saturday's attendance was about 8,500, of whom 7,595 paid for admission at the turnstiles. The teams were: –

READING: Gale; Wilson and Fullwood; Dougall, Holmes and Edwards; Chitty, Taylor, McPhee, M. Edelston and Smallwood.

SOUTHEND UNITED: Hillam; Tucker and Robinson; Harris, Hague and Black; Sibley, Smirk, Martin, Bell and Ormandy.

Saturday, September 2nd, 1939
Football Combination
SOUTHEND UNITED RESERVES 1, SOUTHAMPTON RESERVES 2

Although from other clubs came the reports of diminished crowds owing to the imminence of war, an average number of Southend United supporters turned out to cheer on the Junior Blues, very conscious of the fact that it might be the last professional match played in Southend for some time. There was a gate of about 2,250. Circumstances being conductive to a certain unwanted latitude and tolerance on the part of the supporters, the Southend team's fatal lack of balance and finishing power which enabled Southampton to win a somewhat dull game by the odd goal in three, passed without the comment it might in normal circumstances have received. There were a few signs of impatience at times, but generally the atmosphere was one of straining for glimpses of football to store in the memory against that long, empty sportless era which most of us then regarded as inevitable.

It is a pity then that what later proved to be Southend's valedictory match for the time being at the Stadium should have proved so singularly lacking in entertainment and distracting qualities. The fault lay not so much with the players as with the selectors of the team, who were forced to make some last-minute adjustments that proved singularly uninspired, and completely destroyed the balance and thrust.

No one could cavil at Jackson taking Tucker's place at right back, but to take Davis from the front line and place him in the half-back line was a move completely lacking in foresight, as Davis proved in the last minute of the match, when he forcefully assumed his characteristic attacker's dash and scored one of the best goals of the match.

There was an audible sigh of disappointment from the crowd when the final whistle sounded a little later, for it was obvious that Davis's decision to throw defensive tactics overboard had provided the solution to the right wing problem. H. Scaife, who occupied Davis's usual place at inside right, was a brake on possible movements on the right, for the most part lying too far back and invariably ignoring the speedy Coyde and pushing the ball far out to the left, where Walton, and later Shallcross, found Webber and Williams effective dampers to spectacular wing rushes.

Coyde, on the right wing, might have nullified the efforts of Smith and Noyce, had Scaife partnered him properly, but he was never certain of support and being disinclined to touch it inside where it might be completely wasted he fought a losing battle with the Southampton defenders. Singleton, in the centre, showed a useful turn of speed, but his shooting was not particularly brilliant, although Brophy at centre-half was almost twice his size and not easy to work round. Shallcross played fairly well in the opening exchanges, but half way through the first half he exchanged places with Walton on the wing, an arrangement which did not prove effective, mainly because Walton's shooting was sadly inaccurate.

At the outset some fine play by Bradley suggested that Southend might have great difficulty in subduing the Southampton winger, but the standard of his play deteriorated as the game wore on, and McGibbons, centre-forward, was the man who caused the Southend defence, and Jones in particular, most anxiety. As tall and as heavy as the Southend centre-half is, his runs down the centre many times found Jones a trifle slow and uncertain, and Trainer was responsible for the bulk of the work, although Jackson, when he reminded himself that he was not in the intermediate trio, stemmed quite a number of flank movements. Apart from the two shots which resulted in Southampton's goals, Roper was called upon but seldom, and the crowd had little opportunity to judge his prowess. Both goal-producing shots were difficult, and perhaps he anticipated the second one just a shade too late. Downey, playing at left-half, displayed more energy than his colleagues and was responsible for much of the left-wing liveliness.

Early on Southampton displayed a better combination than Southend, their passing being surer and more constructive, and it was after five minutes play that Bradley was sent away down the left wing to fire in a perfect shot from 30 yards range, which found the corner of the net well out of Roper's reach. Southend dominated the subsequent play for long periods, but player after player missed chances and half-time saw Southampton easily retaining their one-goal lead.

The second half still saw Southend striving without avail to draw level, and about a quarter of an hour from the conclusion, McGibbons and Bates ran through, overcame Jones' challenge on the right, and the former was able to slant the ball into the net to give Southampton their second point, Roper anticipating its direction but acting too slowly to touch it out. It was a minute from the end when Davis ran through brilliantly and put the ball into the far corner of the net to give Southend their only goal. The teams were: –

SOUTHEND UNITED RESERVES: Roper; Jackson and Trainer; Davis, Jones and Downey; Coyde, H. Scaife, Singleton, Shallcross and Walton.

SOUTHAMPTON RESERVES: Stainsbridge; Williams and Noyce; Webber, Brophy and Smith; Dean, Bates, McGibbons, Cocker and Bradley.

CHAPTER NINE

A Selection of Match Reports 1939-1946

Saturday, March 16th, 1940
Football League, South Division (Group 'D')
SOUTHEND UNITED 8, BRIGHTON & HOVE ALBION 2

Saturday's fixture against Brighton at the Stadium on Saturday, when the United achieved their best win of the season by trouncing the Sussex seaside team by 8-2, was convincing proof that one of Southend's major and urgent needs is a good centre-forward, capable of inspiring the other forwards and developing the latent possibilities of the team. Ludford, obtained on loan for the afternoon from Tottenham Hotspur, proved just the player for the job, and he had his reward, for he registered no fewer than four of the eight Southend goals, and achieved a hat-trick in the second half, when he obtained three goals.

The management of the United have been very conscious of the need for a centre-forward from the start of the season, but in the last few weeks, with war-time exigencies emphasizing the lack of striking power, the need for a good leader has been keenly felt. I think the climax came during the Orient match, when the Southend forwards were obviously more polished and clever than their opponents, and yet lacked the dash and penetrative ability to secure the goals. It should be remembered that four of the players who have been turning out regularly in the United forward line are wingers, and it is hardly surprising that it has been found impossible to make a centre-forward out of any of them. Bolan persevered in that position for some weeks, but, obviously, he was wasted there, as was proved later when he was given a less restricted position.

Thus it came about that, although it is strictly against the policy of the club to borrow players and deprive the regulars of their Saturday afternoon earnings, it was felt that unless an attempt was made to change the playing fortunes of the team despondency and the resultant lack of confidence would pluck the heart out of the team altogether. The choice of Ludford to lead the attack was a most satisfactory one, for the 'Spurs centre-forward, although not in the spectacular category, certainly did much to inspire his colleagues, and play converged naturally to the centre, where Ludford was always ready to seize an opportunity of breaking through or working an opening for his colleagues. He made mistakes, but so did some of the others, and if every scoring attempt had come off Southend would have been wallowing in goals.

I have never doubted the capabilities of Sibley, Smirk and Ormandy, and on Saturday they were at their best. Ormandy and Sibley treated the crowd to some splendid wing play, and once the former made a single-handed dash down the centre at so fast a pace that if the ball had been directed another foot to the right it would have skimmed in past the upright and been easily the best goal of the season. Smirk, although seldom having necessity to come to the front, was extremely successful in partnering Ormandy, and although he found Risdon and Marriott well versed in the stopping art his liveliness generally nullified their efforts. Bolan, as inside partner to Sibley on the other wing, was also a hard worker, and his play developed a welcome crispness in the second half. Southend were comfortably in the lead when he was injured about a quarter of an hour from the end and had to leave the ground.

There was an all-Southend intermediate line. Leighton, on the right, played an energetic game, and, besides keeping the forwards well supplied, he was called upon more than once to go to the assistance of McColgan, of Queen's Park Rangers, who was in Milne's place at right-back. Jones, at centre-half, made a number of mistakes, for the Brighton forwards were quickly off the mark, and Southend by no means dominated the play territorially.

On one or two occasions it was a speedy dash goalwards by Walton that averted Brighton goals. McColgan was the least impressive of the three borrowed players, and Milne could give him many marks. He gave an unfortunate impression of indifference in the first quarter of an hour which his subsequently improved play did not entirely erase. Chalkley, of West Ham, brought in to rest Robinson, was much steadier. His tackling was neat and effortless, and his placing was extremely helpful at times. Hankey, back in goal, showed fine anticipation and dealt confidently with a number of difficult shots, his position being nothing like the sinecure the score suggested.

It was the first time Southend's borrowing policy has paid, for it will be remembered that most of the attempts to fill in gaps with outside players earlier in the season, when the United were running two teams, resulted in poorly balanced and ineffective elevens. With Ludford in the forefront, the United's dangers in the preliminary round of the Football League Cup would be considerably reduced.

At first it appeared that even with outside help Southend would be unable to overcome that fatal inability to finish off promising movements, and on one occasion it even seemed that Ludford had been infected, for he turned the ball tamely back when he had a clear, short run to the goal, with only the custodian to beat. After a quarter of an hour Southend began to employ more direct attacking methods, and, following a free-kick for handling, near the right touchline, Leighton dropped the ball across to Sibley, who headed across the goalmouth for Bolan to nod the ball down into the net.

Southend's defensive weakness on the right gave Bott, the Brighton left winger, many opportunities of putting the inside men through, and it was his centre, after half an hour, that enabled Wilson to beat the advancing Hankey and then transfer for Davie to score the equalizer. Straight from the restart, however, Southend took the lead again in brilliant and unequivocal style, for, after a short wing run, Ormandy centred to Bolan, who short-passed to Sibley, for the latter to put it straight past Mee into the net. Five minutes later Mee, after being bombarded by Ludford and Sibley, failed to get to a hard drive from Ormandy.

It was a bad mistake on McColgan's part that let Davie, the Brighton centre-forward through to score his second goal, but just on half-time Walton was fouled in the penalty area after a tussle with Marriott, the Brighton right-back, and although Mee saved from the spot-kick, taken by Chalkley, Ludford made no mistake when he promptly returned the ball. Ludford scored the first three goals of the second half.

The first came when he headed through from a corner, the second when Mee had partially saved from Bolan and Ludford bundled it into the net with his body, and the third when, after a solo run from the half-way line, he bested Martin and then shot from long range; Mee, who came out, deflected the ball with his foot into the net. The last goal was scored by Smirk, following a centre from Ormandy. The gate receipts were £98; 1,839 paying for admission. The teams were: –

SOUTHEND UNITED: Hankey; McColgan and Chalkley; Leighton, Jones and Walton; Sibley, Bolan, Ludford, Smirk and Ormandy.

BRIGHTON: Mee; Marriott and Martin; Risdon, Stevens and Darling; Evans, Wilson, Davie, Stephens and Bott.

Referee: Mr. G.T. Gould.

FROM THE *Southend Standard* OF 15TH AUGUST, 1940

Several references to Southend United's arrangements with Chelmsford were made at the annual meeting of the Chelmsford City Club, on Friday, when a loss of £766. 13s. 2d on the past season was reported. Mr. F.C. Thomas presided.

The Chairman referred to the adverse weather encountered, and said about £600 was spent on additions and improvements to the ground. He added: 'We made very strenuous efforts to be admitted to the Football League for the duration of the war. While at one time we had slight hopes, these faded out, and in the end there was nothing for us to do but to suspend operations for the time being. Southend United approached us with a view to using our ground for the coming season.

We readily accepted, knowing that the arrangement will provide first-class football for our loyal and large body of enthusiastic supporters. Although it is Southend United, Mr. Harry Warren, our manager, will be the manager, and many of our players will appear in the Southend colours. So, really, it will be Southend and Chelmsford, and we shall see some fine football.' He moved the adoption of the report and balance sheet.

Coun. F.C. Langton (Vice-Chairman of the Directors), seconding, said that during the close season they spent something like £700 to £800 on summer wages, but that proved to be pretty well abortive. Also, over £600 was spent on ground improvements. It was no earthly good arranging friendly matches with junior clubs for the coming season, for nothing but the best would satisfy Chelmsford. Reluctantly, they decided that there was nothing to do but to rest on their laurels for the time being.

Then Southend approached them, terms had been arranged, and an agreement would be signed covering the whole of the expenses, so it was possible that a small margin might go into the coffers of the City Club. 'It will not be Southend playing; it will be Southend and Chelmsford United. We shall rely upon our wonderful crowd of supporters to come to our matches in full force. There is no town in this country, in proportion to its size, that can show such enthusiastic football support as Chelmsford.

That is evinced by the fact that £500 in shares was taken out during the trying times of last year. The time must come when we shall get proper recognition from the League. We shall surely find ourselves in the Football League. We have a future, and it behoves us to stick to the club. We have made ourselves famous in all parts of the country, and despite the black-out and attendant difficulties, we shall come out on top.'

Mr. Harry Warren addressed the meeting on Club prospects, and especially thanked the Supporters' Club for its wonderful help. He had, he said, been greatly honoured by being appointed manager of Chelmsford and Southend – a responsible position which he much appreciated. It would appear that there would be about four or five Southend players, and that the remainder would be City players, of whom Rickett, Turton, Parry (O.), Parry (W.), Sliman, Jones (L.), Jones (F.), Wright, McLuckie and Burley were available.

The teams which would visit Chelmsford would be: Arsenal, Portsmouth, West Ham United, Tottenham Hotspur, Watford, Clapton Orient and Norwich City. There were four matches still to be arranged. Whatever profit was made would benefit Chelmsford as much as Southend, and the arrangement should be a great success.

Saturday, November 2nd, 1940
Football League, South Regional Division
SOUTHEND UNITED 3, WEST HAM UNITED 1

Any ideas that West Ham might have harboured of securing another easy victory at the expense of Southend United, whom they visited at Chelmsford on Saturday, were upset and, instead of consolidating their 11-0 success of the previous week, they were well beaten by 3-1. It was rather difficult to reconcile the display of the United on Saturday with that of the previous week. I said of that match that the chief difference between the sides in the first half, when territorial progress was about equal, was that West Ham scored practically every time they went down the field. With almost an identical attack for the return game, they did nothing of the kind. Smarting no doubt, over their heaviest defeat on record, the Blues went off the mark in great style and it only needed an opening goal to make a great difference in their form. That goal, scored in the first half by Burley, was the turning point of the game, for it gave the home club just that touch of confidence and elation that they had previously lacked. The United were two up at the interval, and, although the Hammers reduced the deficit and, for a period, looked like equalizing, the United recovered well and made the issue safe. Incidentally, as Brighton lost 5-1 at Aldershot and Swansea went down 4-1 at Bristol against the City, the United climbed from the bottom of the Regional ladder three rungs up.

I was interested to see how the present United team would fare on a heavier ground – I say the present team, for it contains only three or four of last term's players each Saturday – and was most agreeably surprised. Saturday's exhibition, it is true, may prove to be just one of those days when everything went right and each player pulls his weight, but, at all events, it was the Blues best exhibition of the season.

Despite the uncertain foothold, there were bouts of accurate passing and combination which even West Ham, one of the best teams in the competition, could not surpass. Jones (F.), who has been out of form as the United leader, produced one of his characteristic touches to score the second goal and was definitely more confident in his actions, although still a long way below his old self. The weight of Turton and Sliman in the defence came into its own. Both these big-built players found the going well suited to their styles, and Sliman has seldom played a better game. Try as he did, Foreman had a lean afternoon against his watchful opponent. The introduction at right-half of Leighton was a happy choice. With the play slowed to his liking, Leighton made his presence felt by some beautifully judged passes and his service to the front line should have been turned to greater use.

Gunner Fuller had to fill the role of left fullback, as Calland could not get leave from his unit, and he made quite a good job of the unaccustomed position. His excellent headwork several times relieved awkward situations, and on one occasion he saved a goal when Rickett was well beaten. In the attack, Bell and Burley were the more progressive wing, chiefly because they kept better position than Fieldus and Jones (L.), who too frequently closed in on the centre. There were far too many attempts to carry the ball through with close passing – a fatal error on such a pitch. Parry was a great worker at left-half, although his use of the ball lacked the accurate placing that was shown by Leighton.

The Macauley-Foreman-Goulden trio who did so much damage against the Blues at Boleyn Castle must have felt strangely restrained. One reason was they were not given so much room in which to move and another was the fact that they were met with a totally different spirit. They were crowded off the ball, and Sliman was a tower of strength against the spear-head.

The wingers were unable to make any spectacular runs and the half-backs seldom got the ball to them clear of opponents. A certain amount of feeling crept into the exchanges as the United, encouraged by the fact that the run of the play was with them, swept impetuously towards goal and nearly rushed the Hammers defence off its feet. Chalkley, who the previous week had helped the United, did not find the task of marking Burley at all easy, while Barrett was not able to turn so quickly as he had done in the former match.

The opening goal resulted from a centre by Jones (L.), after a neat piece of combination with Fieldus and Leighton. As Conway went for the ball, Jones (F.) partially foiled him with his head and it dropped for Burley to shoot home. Jones (F.), in registering the second goal, deserved his success, for Barrett had already shouldered him off the ball and only his superior speed enabled him to recover and beat the advancing goalkeeper. Foxall reduced the deficit after Rickett had pushed out a shot from Chapman, and for a while in the second half it looked as if the West Ham machine was going into top gear and would run smoothly on. However, the defence of the United proved too stiff an uphill task and Burley settled matters with a lightning header. Fieldus sent across a corner-kick that Savage, trying to head away, could only just touch. The ball skidded across the goalmouth and Burley raced in to head past Conway. A few more exhibitions of Saturday's enthusiastic play, with its blending of combination and individual efforts, and the United will rise rapidly away from the bottom section of the table. It was a great pity, however, that only a few hundred were present to witness a game which had quite a taste of pre-war vintage and, at times, a distinct cup-tie flavour. Teams: –

SOUTHEND UNITED: Rickett; Turton and Gunner C. Fuller; Leighton, Sliman and Parry; Fieldus, Jones (L.), Jones (F.), Bell and Burley.

WEST HAM: Conway; Chalkley and Savage; Fenton, Barrett and Lewis; Chapman, Macaulay, Foreman, Goulden and Foxall.

Saturday, January 25th, 1941
Football League, South Division
SOUTHEND UNITED 2, BRIGHTON & HOVE ALBION 0

Southend United's first victory in the new Football League South was gained on Saturday, at Chelmsford, at the expense of Brighton, who this season have proved the Aunt Sally of the Southern football clubs. They did not win a single game in the Regional competition, and on Saturday went down 2-0 simply because they revealed no finishing abilities. From a territorial standpoint the visitors might have drawn, particularly in the second half, when they threw the United back on to the defence, but the shots were for the most part wide of the goal. Of the many corner-kicks which they forced, not one could be turned to account. Both the United's goals were obtained in the first half, the opening point being secured by Burley, the left winger, and the second by Jones (F.), the leader, whose shooting efforts during the game were the best he has shown this season. The Blues were awarded a penalty in the second half for a foul on Jones (F.), but Calland, who has previously been so deadly from the spot, drove wide.

I was very interested in the form displayed on the Brighton left wing by C. Harman. He beat Parry with ease and revealed a good control of the ball. I asked Manager Charlie Webb where he came from and he said Harman was a 16-years-old local boy, who had sought a game. As Brighton have high hopes for post-war football when they move to their new ground at the Brighton Stadium, Harman may be expected to figure prominently.

Brighton also had the best player on view in Martin, the cool and resourceful left-back, who, but for the war, would have gone to Brentford for a big cheque. Apart from Westby at centre-half and Darling as the 'general' of the line, the other players did not back up sufficiently to accept their chances. Davenport, who has played for Torquay, was a great trier, but his shooting was very poor. However, there were some efforts which caused Rickett to give of his best, and one fine save by him was when he tipped an oblique shot from Davenport past the far post.

Southend did not play at all smoothly owing to lack of balance. Parry seemed most unhappy as right-back, while the work of the right flank was patchy – perhaps the interceptions of Martin had more effect than was apparent. Sliman made a few mistakes as pivot, but twice a snap judgment on his part proved wrong and might have led to trouble. Fuller's appearance suggested that he must have found pleasure in covering himself with mud as well as glory. Leighton's game was, as usual, sedate and oft-times neat and classical, but it lacked speed. Wright was another player whose ballwork was better than his speed and combination as a unit of the attack. There were several good bouts of passing between Bell and Burley, but the former never seemed able to get the ball to his liking for a shot. Teams: –

SOUTHEND UNITED: Rickett; Parry and Calland; C. Fuller, Sliman and Leighton; Jones (L.), Wright, Jones (F.), Bell and Burley.

BRIGHTON: Mee; McNaughton and Martin; Risden, Westby and G. Hickman; C. Chase, Darling, Davenport, Isaac and C. Harman.

Referee: Mr. A.T. Ford, Ilford.

Saturday, February 1st, 1941
Football League, South Division
SOUTHEND UNITED 6, SOUTHAMPTON 4

Exciting play was witnessed in Southend United's home game with Southampton at Chelmsford, on Saturday, and the ball was seldom long in midfield. From end-to-end the play swept in a series of hectic rushes, which resulted in thrilling goalmouth scrambles, and ten goals were scored. Of these the United claimed six, the last two being obtained after Rickett, their goal-keeper, had been carried from the field, following a kick on the body.

The contest was ideal from the spectators point of view, because of the almost continuous excitement. Southampton opened the scoring, and then led 2-0, their young and fast forward line beating the slower-moving United defence in fine style. Then the Blues began to fight back, a clever goal from a free-kick paving the way. At half-time they were on level terms, and then they added two more. After Rickett was hurt, Fieldus donned his jersey and the United could not hold the visitors, who began to pile on pressure. They reduced the home lead to 4-3, but then the United staged an attack that ended in a goal. Southampton returned and the score was again reduced to a goal lead – 5-4. It looked long odds on the visitors equalizing, but the tired homesters put up a splendid rally in the last stages and scored again to win 6-4. There were about 600 spectators present.

Manager Tom Parker's team contained several players in their teens, and they set a fast and lively pace at the outset, which well deserved its reward. Mee, son of a former well-known player, notched the first point, and then Hyam scored an unusual goal. Southend had repelled an attack, and Rickett, running to the edge of the penalty area, punted the ball up the field. Hyam was only just over the half-way line, and he took a first-time shot that, aided by the wind, sailed past Rickett and entered the net as he was trying to recover his position.

The United's first goal rightly won the applause of the crowd, and drew an appreciative comment from Manager Parker sitting beside me. The Blues were awarded a free-kick just outside the penalty area, and Southampton's defence lined up to face the ball. Leighton took the shot, but he made no attempt to score. He carefully slipped it to the right of the lined-up players, and Jones (L.), running in, shot home behind them. Burley, who had previously missed a sit-ter, rounded off a clever lobbed pass by McLuckie, to make the scores level. Bell and Jones (F.) added the first two second half points, and then came Rickett's injury, on his own goal-line. Stroud beat the new goalkeeper to make it 4-3, and then the energetic Fuller got in the Southampton goalkeeper's way trying to head a high ball, and it fell on a defender and rebounded into the net. Stroud took advantage of a defensive error to again beat Fieldus, but Fuller crowned a great afternoon's play by heading a fine goal following a corner taken by Jones (L.).

Fuller played his best game of the season, and was indefatigable through-out. He makes far better use of the ball than he did last season, and frequent-ly drew a man before sending his winger away. The wing pair, Jones (L.) and Leighton, also fitted into the scheme admirably and were definitely more dan-gerous than their colleagues on the left wing, Bell and Burley, the latter being below his usual good form. Jones (F.) made several excellent attempts, but Ellerington did not give him much rope.

Southend were weakest in the back division, but this was made up by the strength of the half-back line. Rickett was sent to hospital for observation after being attended to by the Club Medical Officer, Dr. A.G. Bewes.

Southampton, who have to play all their matches away from home, have some excellent material on which to build. Noss, sixteen years of age, did exceedingly well at right-half, while Barry and Mee were also prominent on the left. Southend were able to pull round after their early deficit because they had the balance of experience. Sliman, McLuckie and Leighton all putting out telling passes and opening the game accurately. Considering their second half handicap, the Blues put up a fine finish, and their victory was fully deserved. Teams: –

SOUTHEND UNITED: Rickett; Parry and Fieldus; C. Fuller, Sliman and McLuckie; Jones (L.), Leighton, Jones (F.), Bell and Burley.

SOUTHAMPTON: White; Roles and Pickering; Noss, Ellerington and Barry; Hassell, Hyam, Hooper, Stroud and Mee.

Referee: Mr. Dunning, Galleywood.

Saturday, March 1st, 1941
Football League (War) Cup, Second Round, First Leg
SOUTHEND UNITED 2, WEST HAM UNITED 1

The sprinkling of West Ham supporters who were among the crowd at Chelmsford, on Saturday, were very disappointed at their team's display against Southend United in their first 'leg' of the League War Cup second round tie. Anticipations of an easy away victory faded and the rather patronising remarks shouted in my ear in the early stages turned, during progress of the game, to excuses. There was some validity for these, as the United's 2-1 victory was achieved against a side playing ten men for three-parts of the game. Although the Blues did extremely well against the War Cup holders and leaders of the Regional Competition, the margin in their favour will probably not be sufficient to help them through the second leg next Saturday at West Ham. There is, however, hope that they may survive. Had Southend accepted all their chances, the prospect would have been a bright one, for they could easily have won by 4-1 or 5-1.

As it was, three excellent opportunities were missed in the first half, when neither side scored and the homesters had the advantage of a fairly stiff wind. However, against a team including many well-known players, the Blues gave an excellent display. While their footballing standard did not approach that of West Ham, especially when it came to passing accurately along the ground, their eagerness and will to win were too much for their opponents, who evidently started with a false estimate of the quality of the opposition.

West Ham, in my view, sowed the seeds of their own defeat by their rather casual approach to the game. The Blues' enthusiasm did not allow them to pull the match round, and then the loss of Green, the right half-back, with a damaged knee, proved an additional handicap.

Southend established a 2-0 lead through Burley and Wright, while Foxall, moving from the wing into the centre, obtained the Hammers goal. Incidentally, that point would not have been scored had Rickett not dashed out of goal and been beaten by a lob. It was a case of quick decision – and Rickett decided the wrong way.

Still, no goalkeeper is infallible, and both Rickett and Medhurst handled with confidence several awkward shots. Medhurst was beaten first by a rather curious shot by Burley. Jones (F.) worked out to the left and let go with a great drive which the West Ham keeper tipped on to the bar. A corner resulted, and Jones (L.) dropped this well into the goalmouth. A scramble ended with the ball swinging out to Jones (L.) again and he lobbed it back. Burley was moving forward and the ball fell partly behind him. He reached back and hooked it with his right foot. It ricocheted forward and upwards into the net. Medhurst evidently thought the ball was going to pass behind the winger. Wright scored a very neat goal for the second, after some thoughtful midfield work by McLuckie.

With a crowd of over 3,000, plenty of vocal support, and some bright and exciting play, the match was a typical cup-tie. One noticeable point about the individual performances was the persistence of some of the clever men in hanging on to the ball too long. It was fatal against hard and fast tackling, and West Ham did not begin to show their worth until they swung the ball about more quickly. Careful marking was a keynote of the United's success, and McLuckie was well to the fore as a kind of 'forward centre-half,' who linked the defence and the attack. He was constantly finding a gap in midfield, a sort of 'no-man's-land,' and securing possession.

West Ham, although missing the forward work of Goulden, were represented by a team much stronger than that of Southend, but, as is often the case in cup-ties, a side which has everything to gain upsets their opponents by the whole-heartedness of their play. The visitors had Hobbis, the Charlton forward, and Foxall on their wings, and the clever Macaulay inside, but not one of the trio could strike his best form – perhaps I should say was not given the opportunity to get into his stride. Persistence in trying to weave a way through the defence simply ended in trouble.

Much of the ineffectiveness of West Ham's attack was due to the tactics of the United half-backs – three men playing three distinct roles. Sliman was a dominant third back, who held Foreman well in check and received excellent support from Parry and Calland. On Sliman's right, C. Fuller threw himself into the fray with all his usual enthusiasm, working at top pressure to defend and also attack whenever the chance occurred. The left-half, McLuckie, developed the role of mid-field 'general,' and it was amazing the number of times the ball seemed to go straight to him – a tribute to his anticipation. In the forward line, Jones (L.) and Leighton were more aggressive as a pair than Burley and Wright, but the left wing, in obtaining the goals, did its share in achieving victory.

Medhurst played well in the West Ham goal – and the fact that he did so speaks for the thrust developed by the homesters. West Ham's weakest section was the full-backs, Bicknell and Chalkley (the latter helped Southend last season), who could not hold the United wingers. Big Jim Barrett may have lost his turn of speed, but Jones (F.) found it exceedingly difficult to get past him.

The Hammers also owed much to their defence, but it was obviously handicapped by the absence of Green. Corbett was a great trier on the left, and Foxall had to keep dropping back to help until he changed places with Foreman in the second half. Small and Foreman were the greatest disappointments. It is curious that West Ham's only defeat in the Regional Competition was at Chelmsford. However, on Saturday, at West Ham, they have to gain victory by two clear goals, and it will be a wonderful effort on the part of Southend if they can pull through. Teams: –

SOUTHEND UNITED: Rickett; Parry and Calland; C. Fuller, Sliman and McLuckie; Jones (L.), Leighton, Jones (F.), Wright and Burley.

WEST HAM: Medhurst; Bicknell and Chalkley; Green, Barrett and Corbett; Foxall, Small, Foreman, Macaulay and Hobbis.

Saturday, April 5th, 1941
Football League, South Division
BRIGHTON & HOVE ALBION 2, SOUTHEND UNITED 2

Southend United exploited the fact that Brighton and Hove Albion lacked the necessary cohesion and fast-moving attacks in the match at Hove on Saturday and were able to draw 2-2. The game was one of the best seen at Hove this season. Southend, who were without Calland, McLuckie and Walsh, had the better of the opening exchanges, and Jones (F.) was particularly prominent. His good work was soon rewarded when he put his side ahead after Rickett had made many fine saves. This was a prelude to an Albion attack, and for a while Rickett was extremely hard pressed. After many brilliant clearances, a shot from Balmer beat him. Jones (L.) hit an upright.

A few minutes after the restart, the Albion notched their second goal through Balmer, and for a period it was all Albion. Only Rickett and the homes side's none-too-good finishing restrained the forwards. From a breakaway, Jones (F.) was again prominent and his very fine pass to Wright saw the inside-left glide through the home defence and beat the approaching Mee. Southend definitely owed their draw to Rickett, who was a man inspired between the sticks, and Jones, who scored the first goal and 'made' the second.

Hollingworth, a former Newcastle and Barrow back, and Parry stopped many Albion rushes. Teams: –

SOUTHEND UNITED: Rickett; Hollingworth and Parry; C. Fuller, Sliman and Leighton; Jones (L.), Fieldus, Jones (F.), Wright and Burley.

BRIGHTON AND HOVE ALBION: Mee; Risdon and Darling; Chase, Wilson (F.) and McInnes; Eastham, Wilson (J.), Davie, Balmer and Parvin.

Referee: Mr. A.H. Parvin.

Easter Saturday, April 12th, 1941
Football League, South Division
SOUTHEND UNITED 3, PORTSMOUTH 1

Before what was easily the best home crowd of the season, on Saturday, the Southend team gave a great exhibition of second-half rallying power by turning a first half deficit of 1-0 into a 3-1 victory over their Portsmouth visitors. It was forty-five minutes of thrills that amply made up for any lack of footballing brilliancy, and the strong Pompey side had to play second string to an eleven who refused to be subdued by superior skill. The turning point of the game was when the United attack was altered for the second period, Jones (F.) taking over the leadership from Walsh.

Up to then, Walsh had been beaten time after time by the tall and quick-moving Rowe, but the Portsmouth centre-half was unable to cope with the methods of Jones. Rowe eventually got at loggerheads with his opponent, and ended by having his name taken by the referee. He lost his grip on the centre-forward, and Jones was able to score the equalizer.

Then, from a mighty free-kick in his own half by Calland, who made a welcome return to the left full-back position for Southend, Jones was able to head on to the bar, and Burley ran in to put the homesters ahead. Shortly afterwards, Walsh, who was much more forceful when he went inside-left, kicked the ball from the goalkeeper's hands after he had made a full-length save, and again Burley nipped in and netted.

The first forty-five minutes gave little indication of the complete change that was to come over the game. Portsmouth, more accurate in their use of the ball, and definitely quicker in moving to it, had the better of the exchanges. The inability of Walsh to get away from Rowe had a great effect on the movements of the home attack, and none of the other forwards appeared to be able to settle down against their fast-moving and deadly tackling opponents.

It was a case of the Blues always struggling to catch up, and not quite succeeding. Actually, they were lucky to change over with only the single goal deficit. Apart from speed, the visitors also had the advantage of the wind, and they should have made their lead more substantial, but only Gardner was well on the mark. He scored their goal and came near with two other great drives. As they have done in other matches this season, Southend went all out in the second half, and once Rowe lost his hold on the centre of the field, it was only a question of time before the equalizer was scored. Jones' contribution to the victory was his best of the season, and Walsh showed far greater powers of penetration as an inside forward than he did as leader. Although the other members of the vanguard all pulled their weight in the second half rally, I did not think any of them were as effective as they have been in former matches. Jones (L.) and Burley did not produce the clever runs through that one is used to witnessing, and Wright's distribution was very patchy.

The defence, which looked like getting rattled once or twice, held out well against Portsmouth when they had the run of the ball, but there was one noticeable feature during both moieties of the game – that was the gap left in the middle of the field; there was no link as there should have been, and perhaps this was due to the absence of McLuckie, who generally takes up that role. However, these criticisms do not detract from the fact that the team as a whole put up a great fight and thoroughly deserved their success.

Portsmouth, with seven of their team who won the F.A. Cup, no doubt thought that they would win, but once Rowe fell away from his fine form, it was the beginning of the end. Walker could hardly be criticised for the goals against him, and he showed how a custodian can set his own team in action by throwing the ball to his wingers. I saw him do so in the Cup final against the Wolves, running to the edge of the penalty area and then throwing it accurately to an unmarked colleague.

Morgan and Rochford were steady until the United crowded on the pressure and the home half-backs joined the forwards in sweeping aside Rowe and his wing defenders. The crowd of 2,500 (£105), went away well satisfied with their entertainment, all the more so because the homesters had pulled the game round in such heartening fashion. Teams: –

SOUTHEND UNITED: Rickett; C. Fuller and Calland; Leighton, Sliman and Parry; Jones (F.), Jones (L.), Walsh, Wright and Burley.

PORTSMOUTH: Walker; Morgan and Rochford; Flewin, Rowe and Summerbee; Emery, Guthrie, Anderson, Gardner and Parker.

Referee: Mr. A.T. Ford, Ilford.

Easter Monday, April 14th, 1941
Football League, South Division
PORTSMOUTH 1, SOUTHEND UNITED 2

The Blues, in winning the return match at Portsmouth, on Easter Monday, achieved their first League South away victory of the season, and administered the initial defeat at Fratton Park on Pompey. The final score of 2-1 was a true representation of the balance of play. Portsmouth had previously won all six of their League South home matches, and it was expected that they would keep their record intact against the Blues, but once again Southend fought back in fine fashion, and in the closing stages piled on tremendous pressure, scoring the winning goal from a penalty in the last three minutes. It was due to Rickett, in the visitors' goal, that Portsmouth failed to take the lead when they had the assistance of the wind in the first half.

The United went ahead midway through the second portion. Ward, a Sheffield Wednesday player, who has also helped Portsmouth, scoring from ten yards range, after Burley had done the initial work on the right wing. Pompey equalized through Black, their inside-left, who dribbled from the halfway line to score from three yards range. In the closing minutes, Southend went all out for the decider, and Burley looked like scoring when he was brought down in the penalty area. Wright secured the winning goal from the spot. All the Southend team played well, Rickett especially receiving an ovation from the 2,600 spectators.

TEAM: Rickett; Fuller and Parry; Jones (L.), Sliman and Leighton; Jones, E. (W.B.A.), Fieldus, Ward (Sheffield Wednesday), Wright and Burley.

Saturday, May 17th, 1941
Football League, South Regional Division
CRYSTAL PALACE 7, SOUTHEND UNITED 0

Rickett, Southend United's goal-keeper in the match at Crystal Palace on Saturday, figured in a scene which ended in his walking off the field and refusing to obey the referee's order to return. The United, who eventually lost 7-0, opened in excellent style and, but for indifferent finishing, might have established a lead during the opening twenty minutes. Then McLuckie, during a tackle, fell heavily and twisted a knee. He had to be carried off the field and did not return. Southend were disorganized and the Palace scored three goals, all of which were hotly disputed by the visitors because of offside in two instances, while in the third it was claimed that the ball hit the crossbar and did not cross the line.

The climax came when Collins, the Palace right half, netted a fourth from what appeared to be clearly an off-side position. Rickett protested to the referee, and when the latter refused to consult the linesmen, the goalkeeper walked to the dressing room. The referee followed and, as Rickett refused to return, asked for his jersey. This the official took back, and Fieldus, who had been playing centre-forward, went in goal. Meanwhile, the game was held up for ten minutes. Thus the United finished the game with only nine men, and the Palace, by scoring three more goals, boosted their average sufficiently to claim the leadership of the South Regional League. Scorers for the Palace were Gillespie and Robson (two each), Blackman, Collins and Smith.

The United team was: Rickett; Parry and Calland; Jones (L.), Sliman and McLuckie; Smirk, Wright, Fieldus, Burley and Jones (E.). The match was watched by 2,500 spectators.

Wednesday, September 12th, 1945
Football League, Third Division (Southern Section) (North of Thames Region)
SOUTHEND UNITED 7, NOTTS. COUNTY 3

Southend United gained their first victory this season on Wednesday when they beat Notts. County, the best team they have met so far, by 7-3. When the visitors led 2-0 after 36 minutes play, 5,000 spectators at the Stadium thought it was all up with the United, but they fought back to level the scores at 2-2 by the interval. Changing straight round, another 60 seconds saw them in arrears, three more minutes and they were on terms again and then after 20 minutes of the second-half they took the lead for the first time, and after that they never looked back, although, it must be admitted, the County had the misfortune to lose their left-winger through an injury.

Before Morrad went off mid-way through the second-half, Major Buckley's eleven home-produced youngsters had played a brilliant game, and they well deserved the lead they held early on. It was the United's grim determination which gained them applause, and although Leighton's play left a lot to be desired, I gave him full marks for this match, for he paved the way for two goals which Southend badly needed to prevent them going right to pieces.

Pye gave the visitors the lead after 16 minutes and Beresford, left with an open goal, added the second when only nine minutes remained before the breather. Then Jackson, Gardiner and Walton had a scramble in the goalmouth, and after the ball had rebounded from an upright, Walton tapped it over. Up to then, Leighton had had been run off his feet, but he never gave in. Then, with a masterly touch, he sent the ball over Parker's head, leaving Gardiner with only the goalkeeper to beat, which he did with a smasher.

Southend supporters were roaring with delight – until Pye made it 3-2. Back came Leighton with a similar move again, and this time Jackson (H.) equalised. Thereafter it was a procession, and goals came in this order: Gardiner, Walton, Jackson (H.) and Jones (L.).

To score seven goals in gaining their first full points was going some, and now they have tasted victory, I expect to see the United repeat it. The turning point was the never-say-die spirit, either as a team or individually. There was no throwing up the sponge when beaten for the ball, despite the fact that when the County were at their best they took some stopping.

Seven goals should be enough to satisfy any supporter, but the United could have made it more. Faults I detected were a disinclination to centre straight away and before the defence could get into position; too much clever ball work by Jackson (H.), who often tried to beat half the team himself, and a failure to mark the second ring of men at a throw in. The ball was up in the air a good deal too, although, as stated, I admit it was in the net seven times.

Smith, of Port Vale, and Harvey (Hoffmann Athletic) strengthened the United defence, although at times they were spreadeagled by the first-time passing of the opposition. The forwards, all guests with the exception of Walton, had a field day, and if anybody else wants to pick holes in their play, I refuse to do so on this occasion.

SOUTHEND UNITED: Reid; Smith and Harvey; Leighton, Jones (C.) and Jackson (R.G.); Jones (L.), Marshall, Gardiner, Jackson (H.) and Walton.

NOTTS. COUNTY: Wiseman; Southwell and Allen; Elmer, Parker and Stancer; Beresford, McPherson, Strain, Pye and Morrad.

Referee: Mr. W.E. Wood, Bedford.

Saturday, November 17th, 1945
F.A. Challenge Cup, 1st Round, 1st Leg
WATFORD 1, SOUTHEND UNITED 1

Southend United's prospects of entering the next round of the F.A. Cup are distinctly bright after their draw of 1-1, at Watford, on Saturday. Up to the semi-finals, the matches are played on home and away basis, so when Watford visit the Stadium next Saturday, the United require only to win to put them in the next round. Should another draw result, extra time will be played until a decision is reached, and, in order to allow time for an extra half-hour, the kick-off has been fixed by the F.A. to 2.15 p.m.

It cannot be gainsaid that Watford should have won on their own ground by a substantial margin, but that does not mean that Southend were lucky to share the goals. It was Conway alone who saved the Blues from suffering what might have been a humiliating reverse. Time and again Watford were left with only the United goalkeeper to beat, but just as often Conway brought off something remarkable.

The circumstances of how Conway is eligible to play for Southend in the F.A. Cup have already been explained. Watford were decidedly sceptical, and after special enquiries, must now be very disappointed indeed that his appearance was quite legitimate. Conway even earned applause from the Watford crowd, and that is a high tribute, considering the disappointment they must have felt when the goals were missed.

The only goal the home side scored was registered twenty minutes after the start, prior to which Southend had done most of the attacking. Drinkwater, who played for Golders Green in a Cup-tie against Southend some years ago, placed a corner-kick accurately, and as Conway came out to gather the ball, he was shut in by Lewis and Beckett, allowing Davies to head the ball into the net. It was surprising that the referee allowed the point to stand, because Conway was definitely obstructed, but the United players accepted the decision and there was no gesticulating crowd round the official. Nor did they object a few minutes later when Smirk was brought down when he had only the goalkeeper to beat, but on the run of the play in the first half, Watford were deserving of the interval lead.

Southend shuffled the forwards for the second half, Dudley going to out-side-right, and Smirk to inside-left, but it remained for Watford to set the pace. The few spectators from Southend had little to enthuse over until near the end, when Dudley went up the right wing. He beat Harris, and was cutting in for goal unmarked, when the referee stopped play for an infringement on the winger. It seemed to be penalising the United by stopping Dudley and Watford made what appeared to be a solid line in front of their goal. Jones told me afterwards that actually Smirk was left with a few feet of space, and Leighton saw this when he took the free-kick. He sent the ball accurately over to Smirk, who made no mistake with a header. A few seconds later the final whistle sounded, and, leaving the Press box, I heard a Watford director remark, 'There goes Watford out of the Cup.' It would be unwise to take next Saturday's result for granted, but there seems no reason why the United should not gain the verdict.

The forward line was a big experiment, with the introduction of three play-ers, all of whom have come straight from junior football, and it must have been an ordeal for two of them to make their first senior appearance in a cup match. There were, in fact, indications of stage fright, but there were also flashes of clever football, and distinct promise for the future. Dudley was the most outstanding, although inclined to try to beat all the opposition on his own. With more experience he will know the exact moment to get rid of the ball, and when he does he will be a valuable asset.

Thompson, the youngest of three footballing brothers at Leigh, has just returned home after a long spell in a prison camp. Although he looks a hefty youth, he told me he had not yet regained his full strength, and when he is on form, he will take some stopping. Peters had an off-day, and was a long way below the form he has shown in the reserve side. The other forwards were Gardiner and Smirk. The centre-forward was crowded out by a heavy defence, and it was not until the second half, when he changed positions, that Smirk was in the picture. The attendance was 5,808 and the receipts £440.

WATFORD: Bland; O'Brien and Harris; Gillespie, Shaw and Gray; Jones, Davies, Lewis, Beckett and Drinkwater.

SOUTHEND UNITED: Conway; Jackson and J. Harvey; Leighton, Jones and Walton; Smirk, C. Thompson, J. Gardiner, Dudley and Peters.

Referee: Mr. W. Vine, Osterley Park.

Saturday, November 24th, 1945
F.A. Challenge Cup, 1st Round, 2nd Leg
SOUTHEND UNITED 0, WATFORD 3 *(Watford win 4-1 on aggregate score)*

Southend United made an inglorious exit from the F.A. Cup on Saturday, when they lost at home to Watford in the return game by 3-0. The visitors were by far the superior team and although the United had the chances to have scored enough goals to have given them the victory, such a result would have been decidedly against the run of the play.

After the draw at Vicarage Road, the United started off in impressive fashion, but they fell away after twice failing, when it seemed harder not to score than to get the ball into the net, and then a penalty incident, which will be talked of at the Stadium for a long time, finally put paid to their efforts. The game was only ten minutes old when O'Brien headed out a shot from a few yards by Walton and then Mee saved when it seemed impossible from Smirk. The ball certainly did not run kindly for the United and gradually this initial dash faded out and it was in the 27th minute that Drinkwater passed to Lewis, who finished up in the net with the ball after a melee. About ten minutes later, Lewis put Watford further in front, when the Southend centre-half placed the ball almost to his feet.

Then came the penalty incident which had the most unsettling effect on the United, although in the circumstances the referee was right in his decision. Dudley took a corner kick and someone must have handled, for the referee pointed to the spot. Smirk placed the ball for the kick and the players lined up in the usual fashion. Smirk ran in to shoot, but a split second before his boot met the ball, a Watford defender evidently committed some sort of infringement and the referee blew his whistle. Simultaneously the ball crashed into the net just under the crossbar. Having virtually stopped play just before the kick was taken, the referee had no choice but to abide by his decision, and order the kick to be retaken, with what seemed the inevitable result – Smirk sent wide.

After that it was Watford's game and a poor clearance by Humphreys halfway through the second half allowed Gray to smash in a shot from 30 yards range, which tore a hole in the back of the net.

The United had to change the team which drew at Watford, and because they were not successful there was a lot of dissatisfaction. Actually, no single person can be blamed for the defeat, but the half-back line was not up to requirements. Watford were the better team and the United were forced into submission. There was no connection between the United defence and the forwards, no schemer in the attack and no one able to organise the backs against the Watford onslaughts.

The visitors were a hefty side, but their best man was the experienced, yet diminutive forward, Drinkwater, who almost toyed with Humphreys at times. Gray, although somewhat bustling against the small Southend forwards, played a fine constructive game and contributed largely to Watford's success. The idea of playing Smirk at inside left was to get him away from Gray, but Smirk did not shine and in the second half he went back on the wing, Dudley to the centre, and Gardiner onto the left wing, Walton becoming an inside forward. The switch certainly put life into the vanguard but by this time Watford had them mastered. The 'gate' was the largest this season and 8,000 people paid £650.

SOUTHEND UNITED: Conway; Humphreys and J. Harvey; Jackson, Jones (C.) and Leighton; Dudley, E. Hockey, J. Gardiner, Smirk and Walton.

WATFORD: Mee; O'Brien and Jones; Gillespie, Shaw and Gray; B. Jezzard, Beckett, Lewis, Davies and Drinkwater.

F.A. CHALLENGE CUP

In a strange coincidence, Southend's first opponents in the F.A. Challenge Cup after both World War I and World War II were Watford.
In 1919-20, in the first Cup-tie played at the new Kursaal ground, United won 1-0 in the sixth qualifying round. In 1945-46 Watford won 4-1 in the only season that saw ties played over two legs (1-1 away, 0-3 at home).

Good Friday, April 19th, 1946
London Combination
SOUTHEND UNITED 0, CRYSTAL PALACE 0

A goal-less draw, the second at the Stadium within three days, was the result of the London Combination match on Good Friday, when a record crowd for the Reserves watched the meeting of Southend United Reserves and Crystal Palace Reserves. Southend, trying out a new player and some old ones in new positions, had to fight hard to hold the speedy Palace forwards and the switching of Ormandy from his usual position of outside left to outside right did not improve matters. Purvis, the newcomer, played well at inside-right, but tried to cover too great an area and his nimbleness, which had been evident at the start, flagged considerably towards the interval. Playing in his first game for two years, Purvis is a discovery of Smirk, with whom he played in Germany. He was also a prisoner-of-war for some years in Singapore.

The Palace were hampered when late in the game, Stubbs, at centre-half, left the field with a damaged wrist. Although the Palace were on top, the home team were never forced into submission, but relied on sudden attacks by solitary players rather than the teamwork used by their opponents.

SOUTHEND UNITED RESERVES: Davis; Humphries and O'Brien; Savage, Woodward and Phypers; Ormandy, Purvis, Gardiner, Jenkins and Peters.

Saturday, April 20th, 1946
Friendly
SOUTHEND UNITED RESERVES 3, PORTSMOUTH RESERVES 0

A 3-0 win was the result of a thrill-packed match on Saturday when a Portsmouth team visited the Stadium in a friendly game with Southend United Reserves. With many changes in the side, the outlook for the United was poor, particularly when, on comparing the two teams man for man, the Portsmouth team towered over the home players.

The play was fast, and although at no time was it an exhibition football, there was never a dull moment. Peters scored before the interval, when he nodded the ball over Butler's head into the net.

Gardiner scored the other two, following the interval. Valiant attempts were made by Butler to save them, but it was evident that he was not being sufficiently covered by his full-backs.

SOUTHEND UNITED RESERVES: Davis; Fairchild and O'Brien; Savage, Illingworth and Armeson; Taylor, Linton, Gardiner, Jenkins and Peters.

Wednesday, May 1st, 1946
Benefit match for Wilfred Armory
FOLKESTONE TOWN 1, SOUTHEND UNITED 4

Folkestone, Hythe and District Herald report
The match on the Cheriton Road ground on Wednesday evening between Folkestone and Southend United was attended by a big crowd, and with the weather propitious and a keen and attractive struggle in the offing, there was nothing to mar the success of Wilfred Armory's well deserved benefit match. Although Southend, spurred by a goal in the first minute, won by 4-1, the spectators must have left the ground with no regrets, for the match they had witnessed was a most enjoyable one in every respect.

Southend had three grand forwards in Wainwright, Sibley and Bennett, to whose swift movements their side owed much of their success.

Folkestone was strengthened by several guest players, of whom Slater and Tivendale were the most prominent. Law was a 100 per cent trier, but did not have too good a match, thanks to the watchdog methods of Alexander. His goal towards the end was deserved, for he had many tries to find the net.

Folkestone had no need to reproach themselves upon their defeat. It was a good sound team, but Southend had the all-important extra touch of class.

Wilfred Armory had a great reception when he walked across the ground accompanied by Mr. Harry Warren, the Southend manager, and other friends. All efforts to get him to the 'mike' failed, and it was left to Mr. R. Muddle, Chairman of the Folkestone Club, to speak a few words during the interval.

'I cannot get Wilfred to come here,' Mr. Muddle said, 'so I must say thank-you a lot, everyone, for coming here to-night. It is greatly appreciated by Wilfred and by the Club.'

Folkestone kicked off against the sun, and were a goal down within a minute. Smirke raced through and pushed the ball forward to Wainwright, who shot. Hammond reached the ball, but fumbled it, and the visiting centre had an easy chance to net.

Law, profiting from a miskick, went away, but was forced to shoot from an impossible angle, and it was left to Jenkins, a half-back, to cause Davis to make his first save. Law forced a corner, from which Southend got on the move again, and Smirke headed against an upright. Two shots were cleared from almost the line before the attack was repelled.

Folkestone were having a fair share of the play, but the visitors were the more dangerous side, and after 25 minutes Wainwright headed through from Sibley's centre. Play continued fast and interesting, and after Law had fired a fierce shot narrowly over the bar Thompson, at the other end, emulated his colleague's feat by heading against the woodwork.

Within a minute of the resumption Wainwright was the third forward to hit the woodwork. Give and take play ensued, Folkestone being by no means over-played, but Wainwright completed his 'hat trick' by heading through from a free kick.

Law scored his consolation goal ten minutes from the end, following neat combination, but just before time Thompson restored his side's three goals advantage.

FOLKESTONE: Hammond; Warman, Stanniforth; Wilson, Henderson, Jenkins; Woodcock, Campbell, Law, Slater and Tivendale.

SOUTHEND UNITED: Davis; Humphreys, Bell; Montgomery, Alexander, Attwood; Sibley, Smirke, Wainwright, Thompson and Bennett.

Referee: Mr. A.E. Leckie.

CHAPTER TEN

The Football League Third Division

SOUTHERN SECTION CUP: 1945-46 QUALIFYING COMPETITION

Saturday, January 12th, 1946
SOUTHEND UNITED 4, NORTHAMPTON TOWN 3

In a game lacking many of the finer points of football, but abounding in thrills, Southend United secured revenge for two previous defeats this season, when they beat Northampton 4-3 at the Stadium before 6,000 spectators on Saturday. After establishing a two goals lead in the first eight minutes, the United allowed the visitors to get on terms, and eventually take the lead, but two goals in the last ten minutes gave the United a well-deserved victory, and their first brace of points in the Third Division North Section cup. Once again, it was pleasing to see the never-say-die spirit in the Southend ranks.

Owing to injuries and the departure of Macklin with his unit, Peters had to be played on the right wing. Had he been able to kick with his right foot, the United would have doubled their score, for he frequently lost possession in trying to get into a position to centre with his left foot. Nevertheless, he maintained the previous promise shown, and scored the first goal after six minutes play, when Scott, the visitors custodian, allowed the ball to cannon off his chest into the net, although Whitchurch, who again played a remarkable game, added the second two minutes later, when he dribbled through on his own and beat the goalkeeper with a shot lobbed over Smalley's head. Before the interval, Morrall had scored for the visitors from what seemed an offside position, and then, five minutes after half-time, Smalley equalised from a penalty for a foul on Wilson.

The crowd did not agree with some of the referee's decisions, and Smalley received some adverse comments for the way he stopped Whitchurch. Cautions on Jackson and Wilson quietened things down a bit, and it sobered up both the United and their supporters when Morrall gave Northampton the lead ten minutes from the end. In a storming finish, Dudley dribbled through to equalise, and a few seconds before the final whistle, Gilberg put Southend in front once more. Southend were at times a little weak under pressure, but they played as a team, and meant business all the way through. Bennett (Leicester), playing in the place so well filled by Goodyear, now claimed by Luton, had a good match, and stood up well to the buffetings of the heavy opposition. Northampton did not impress; if this was the side for which Millwall offered five figures for five players – I heard £25,000 mentioned in the Cobblers' dressing room – then Southend could obtain the same amount, if not more, for two or three players.

SOUTHEND UNITED: Conway; Milne and Bell; Bennett, Jackson and Walton; Peters, Gilberg, Dudley, Gibson and Whitchurch.

NORTHAMPTON: Scott; Smalley and Barren; Blunt, Skelton and Lowery; Roberts, Hughes, Morrall, Wilson and Fowler.

Saturday, January 19th, 1946
NORTHAMPTON TOWN 0, SOUTHEND UNITED 1

Southend deserved their 'double' over Northampton, which was gained by a single goal victory on Saturday. Playing under treacherous conditions, a greasy surface on a bone-hard ground, they adopted more suitable methods than the home team. Northampton had more of the game, but played into their opponents hands by keeping the ball in the air, which gave the defenders time to intercept. They also relied too much on individual attacks.

Southend showed better combination and their system of long, low passes proved more effective on the tricky ground. They had some luck, though. The only goal came from a long shot by Richards, which Scott allowed to pass over his head. Another time, in a goalmouth scramble, the Cobblers appeared to have the ball over the line before it was kicked out, but the referee refused to award a goal. Bell made a splendid save when he headed out Hughes' drive with Conway out of position. He dived right across the goalmouth to achieve this. On the other hand, Southend should have scored a second near the end, when Gilberg shot yards wide from a penalty awarded for a foul on himself. Southend had other chances of scoring, but could not hit the target, although Smirk and Dudley went close.

Apart from the situations created by numerous miskicks, play was not very exciting and it was regarded as the poorest game seen at the County Ground this season. The players could not be blamed, though, for refusing to risk the serious injuries which might have resulted from a more vigorous display. Southend were well served by Jackson, who held up Morrall, the home leader, and Humphreys, who tackled strongly at right-back. Bell and Conway also shone. All the forwards were enterprising, although they impressed more as a line than individually. Teams:

NORTHAMPTON: Scott; Smalley and Barren; Bosse, Dennison and Lowery; Roberts, Hughes, Morrall, Wilson and Fowler.

SOUTHEND: Conway; Humphreys and Bell; Montgomery, Jackson and Walton; Smirk, Gilberg, Dudley, Richards and Pierson.

Saturday, January 26th, 1946
SOUTHEND UNITED 2, IPSWICH TOWN 1

Southend United gained a well-deserved, although somewhat fortunate victory by 2-1 over Ipswich at the Stadium on Saturday, to maintain their hundred per cent. record in the Third Division South (Northern Section) Cup Competition. The visitors failed to convert a penalty ten minutes from the end, and thus lost a chance of taking a point when they were definitely the inferior team. About 7,000 witnessed the contest.

It was not a match in which the football reached great heights, but there was always plenty of excitement, and the United might have had two or three more goals with a little better luck. Smirk once dribbled half the length of the field, only to see his shot hit the far upright and bounce back; the right winger also missed by inches after he had run in to meet a pass from Pierson, and Dudley had a shot from point-blank range parried. Ipswich, too, were often dangerous, and Conway stopped one shot when a goal seemed certain.

Gilberg opened the scoring after eleven minutes, and two minutes from the interval, Little equalised following a corner. Sam Bell gave Southend the lead after twelve minutes of the second half had elapsed, following a corner taken by Pierson.

It was pleasing to see Goodyear playing again, possible because Luton had no match, but the honours of this game went to Montgomery, who, although a half-back, played at full back owing to injuries to Milne and Humphreys. 'Monty,' as he was inevitably called, was rarely beaten whether the ball was in the air or on the ground, and he was always judicious when parting with it. As Hull are not playing this season owing to ground difficulties, he should be readily available to the United, and should be an asset as a half-back. Sam Bell, the pre-war forward, made a reappearance, and, although he scored a goal, he was not up to the standard necessary nowadays. Pierson, the ex-schoolboy winger, who was on West Ham's ground staff before the war, turned out at outside left, but he had too few passes to judge his worth.

Ipswich were well represented in defence and at centre-half; McLuckie's generalship was apparent, but at times some of the younger United forwards made rings round him.

In the return match next Saturday, the United will do well to earn a point. On Boxing Day they lost at Ipswich 3-1.

SOUTHEND UNITED: Conway; Montgomery and Sid Bell; Goodyear, Jackson and Walton; Smirk, Gilberg, Dudley, Sam Bell and J. Pierson.

IPSWICH: Saphin; Southam (W.B.A.) and Parry; Bell, O'Mahony and McLuckie; Trenter, Little, Price, Gillespie (Palace) and Perrett.

Saturday, February 2nd, 1946
IPSWICH TOWN 2, SOUTHEND UNITED 1

Southend lost their 100 per cent. League III South Cup record and leadership of the North Section, on Saturday at Ipswich, where the homesters won somewhat fortunately 2-1. Despite the heavy rains of the week, the ground, one of the finest in the country, was in excellent condition, but a shower half an hour before the start made the ball greasy, and on top of this, a strong wind was blowing from corner to corner, and to make matters worse was gusty, while eddies were caused by the stands and covered accommodation and the gaps between them.

An indication of the wind's pranks is given by the fact that in the second half alone, two defences which had shown the previous week that they were strong defenders and sure, hard kickers, conceded no fewer than 18 corners, the first ten coming at the rate at more than one every two minutes. While Ipswich claimed a 2-1 proportion of the flag kicks, actually those for the United carried the more danger by reason of the visitors height advantage, but there were many thrills in both goalmouths in each half as swerving balls came from the flag into the crowded area.

Only one corner kick, however, was converted, and that by Day, who staggered backwards to get his head to a ball that was passing beyond the far post and give Ipswich the winning goal in the sixty-third minute.

Outstanding work by McLuckie and Perrett, the wing halves, gave the home side the balance of play, but the United defence stood up well to pressure and launched disconcerting counter-attacks, particularly `through Pierson and Smirk, the latter making a solo run half the length of the field to score the equaliser three minutes from the interval.

Ipswich had opened the scoring in the seventh minute, when Day was checked by Jackson and the ball curled away for Little, who was following up, to drive past Conway. The goalkeeper came through with high honours, some of his saves being instinctively brilliant, while on others his judgement was remarkably sound. He made one slip early on when he dropped the ball when challenged by Day, but Jackson promptly sat on it till the referee gave relief. Teams: –

IPSWICH: Burns; Bell and Parry; Perrett, O'Mahony and McLuckie; Trenter, Little, Day, Gillespie and Edwards.

SOUTHEND UNITED: Conway; Humphreys and Bell; Montgomery, Jackson and Walton; Smirk, Marshall, Dudley, Gilberg and Pierson.

Saturday, February 16th, 1946
QUEEN'S PARK RANGERS 4, SOUTHEND UNITED 0

Southend United gave an extremely poor and disappointing display at Shepherd's Bush on Saturday, when they lost 4-0 to Queen's Park Rangers. Not once during the whole game did the United put in a shot which even looked like scoring, whereas the Rangers were only prevented from running into double figures by a brilliant display by Conway.

Owing to the illness of Dudley, Southend included C. Richards, an amateur from Coalville, Leicestershire, at centre-forward, but it was impossible to judge his worth. In the first place, the ball was seldom in his vicinity, and when it was,

Roy Hollis, sitting over the ball, is United's all-time top scorer with 260 in all competitions. This photo is dated November 1955, shortly after the return to Roots Hall

Harry Threadgold did not like playing under floodlights

Gary Poole

Right-back Gary Poole was signed by Barry Fry from Plymouth for what was then a Southend record fee of £400,000

Ronnie Whelan (left) and Chris Powell (right), past and future international players

Southend United 0, Manchester City 1

January 28th, 1955

Manchester City's hero goalkeeper Bert Trautman dives into a sea of mud to rescue the ball from the feet of Southend forwards. United players battling for the ball are left-winger John McGuigan and leader Roy Hollis with Kevin Baron (right) and Crichton Lockhart standing by in case the ball breaks to them. City right-back Bill Leivers covers the goal-line.

Hard to believe but there was a time when Southend United looked set to move to Basildon

Football facts and figures
could once be found in
packs of chewing gum

Brett Angell's goals were one of the main reasons for Southend's two consecutive promotions in the early 1990s

Southend keeper Paul Sansome gathers the ball under pressure during the 1994-95 season

Jimmy Lawler was an ever-present in Southend's 1951-52 team

A Roots Hall match programme from the late 1950s, showing its spartan facilities

Soon after moving to the Stadium, United's programme was still promoting the Kursaal

TONIGHT'S TEAMS

Southend United XI		Japan International XI
M. CAWSTON	1	MITSUHISA TAGUCHI
M. STEAD	2	KAZUMI TSUBOTA
S. COLLINS	3	KIYOTAKA MATSUI
P. CLARK	4	HISASHI KATO
S. YATES	5	TETSUO SUGAMATA
R. POUNTNEY	6	AKIHIRO NISHIMURA
A. OWERS	7	SHINJI TANAKA
G. PENNYFATHER	8	TAKESHI KOSHIDA
G. SHEPHERD	9	SATOSHI TSUNAMI
S. PHILLIPS	10	YUTAKA IKEUCHI
D. GREAVES	11	HIDEKI MAEDA
W. MAY	12	KOJI TANAKA
J. KEELEY	13	TAKESHI OKADA
M. ANGUS	14	NOBUTOSHI KANEDA
G. SKIVINGTON	15	YAHIRO KAZAMA
	16	TOSHIO MATSUURA
	17	MASAFUMI YOKOYAMA
	18	KAZUSHI KIMURA
	19	HIROMI HARA
	20	KOICHI HASHIRATANI

FRIENDLY MATCH OFFICIALS
Referee: DAVE AXCELL (Barling Magna)
Linesmen: P. J. BRENNAN (Benfleet) red flag   M. PEARSON (Shoebury) yellow flag

Roots Hall hosted this 'international' with Japan as a pre-season game on 12 August 1983. Japan beat Peter Morris's team 1-0. Southend played in all red, Japan in blue

This Southend United team photograph was printed as a postcard.
The ball has been painted 'S.U.F.C. 1924-5'

A young Andy Edwards puffs out his cheeks as he tries to block

Centre-half Jimmy Stirling played for
Southend from 1950 to 1960

Southend's players about to set off for Manchester City in the Littlewoods Cup second leg in October 1986. Southend lost 1-2. The Maine Road crowd was under 10,000

The match programme from Southend's Professional Floodlit Challenge Cup-tie against Coventry. Roots Hall staged these evening cup-ties on Mondays

Dennis Thompson played in the early 1950s, mostly at outside-left, but on occasions in every other forward position

Four Southend players hunt the ball (from left):
Steve Tilson, Andy Sussex, Mick Bodley, Chris Powell

Irishman Pat Scully was an integral
part of Southend's promotion team
under Dave Webb

Southend won 4-0 and Peter
Silvester scored all four goals.
But United were still relegated

Ernie Shepherd nearly became the first ever manager to win promotion for Southend United. Sadly his teams finished sixth, sixth, and seventh in the late 1960s

SOUTHEND F.C. — 1956-57

BACK ROW *(l. to r.)* **Jim Duthie: Jim Sterling: Arthur Williamson: Harry Threadgold:**
Dennis Howe: Jim Lawler
FRONT ROW *(l. to r.)* **Gordon Barker: Ron Tulloch: Roy Hollis: Jim Thomson:**
Alex Duchart

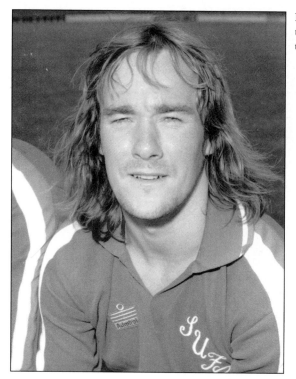

Pint-sized Dave Cunningham turned out for four seasons in the mid-1970s

This unusual montage postcard was issued in 1991 to celebrate back-to-back promotions

Official Programme 1/-
United v. Weymouth
F.A. Cup 1st Round. Kick-Off 3.00 p.m. Saturday, 21st November, 1970.

Southend won this FA Cup-tie 7-0, despite wearing Chelsea's traditional strip of royal blue shirts and shorts, with white socks

In the late 1980s police search supporters entering the North Bank for alcohol

The quality is poor, but Joe Jacques featured on this series of Sun Soccer Stamps

Tommy Capper was United's goalkeeper at the start of the Football League era in 1920

Mike Lapper goes in hard, watched by Mark Hone,
Keith Dublin and Phil Gridelet (1995-96)

You could never call him a club-
hopper. Goalkeeper Paul Sansome
played 156 League games for
Millwall before playing 308 for
Southend United

Harry Baldwin was in Southend
United's team that entered the
Football League in 1920

Darryl Flahavan makes a flying save, with Tony Richards (No 25) looking on

32 Facts & Views From

Stephen Tilson

1. NAME: Stephen Tilson
2. BIRTHDAY: 27th July 1966
3. BORN AT: Wickford
4. WEIGHT: 12st 3lbs
5. HEIGHT: 5' 11"
6. WENT TO SCHOOL AT: Bromfords
7. FAMILY: Girlfriend - Zena
8. LIVES AT: Wickford
9. PETS: 2 dogs
10. FAV. FOOD: Steak
11. WORST FOOD: Foreign Foods
12. FAV. DRINK: Blackcurrant & Lemonade
13. BEST TV SHOWS: Only Fools & Horses
14. WORST TV SHOWS: Mr. Bean
15. BEST MUSIC: Soul
16. WORST MUSIC: Heavy Metal
17. BEST RADIO STATION: Essex Radio
18. FAVOURITE D.J.:   Steve Wright
19. CAR: Escort Cabriolet - smashed up the rear
20. AFTERSHAVE: Eternity
21. BEST FILM: Ghost
22. BEST ACTOR: Patrick Swayze
23. BEST ACTRESS: Demi Moore
24. MOST FAMOUS PERSON MET: Jimmy Greaves
25. PLAYER MOST ADMIRED: John Barnes
26. MOST DIFFICULT OPPONENT: Paul Gascoigne
27. WORST INJURY: Hernia Operation
28. PREVIOUS CLUBS: Bowers, Basildon, Witham
29. PLAYING POSITION: Left-Midfield
30. BEST GOAL: Home to Grimsby 1990
31. MOST MEMORABLE MATCH: Promotion v Brentford even though we lost
32. BIGGEST INFLUENCE ON CAREER: Dad and Danny Greaves

Steve Tilson, interviewed as a player. How would he answer these questions now?

Walter Jennings took over in goal from Tommy Capper at the start of the 1922-23 season

Younger supporters may never have seen the colossal South Terrace, which was just about full only once, for the FA Cup visit of Liverpool in January 1979

Pat Laverty was an inside-forward during the 1960-61 season

Roots Hall as it used to be. A 2-2 night game with Wrexham in February 1983. The deserted South Bank tells the story. The crowd was just 2,512

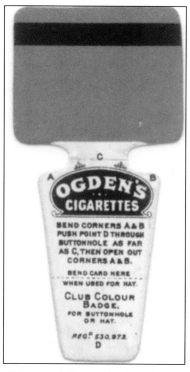

This unusual cigarette 'peg' was intended to be folded and inserted into a buttonhole or hat

Outside-left George Davies in an unusual strip of neck without laces and 'V' hoops down the front of the shirt. He played in the early 1920s

Albert Wakefield was a prolific goalscorer from 1949 to 1953

Southend United line up before the start of the 1976-77 season, having just been relegated

Left-half Blakey Martin was a near-regular in Southend United's first two seasons in the Football League

Dave Regis launches himself above the defence at Roots Hall (1995-96)

Keith Roe, compiler of *The Southend United Chronicles*, gets his copy of Peter Mason and Dave Goody's excellent official history, signed by Phil Gridelet and Graham Bressington

Right-winger Robert Firth joined Southend United in 1922, but stayed only one season

Alan Little was a regular in United's midfield in the mid-1970s. He returned to manage the club briefly in 1999-2000

Mounted police try to clear the Roots Hall pitch as Southend beat Derby County 4-3 in the final match of the 1993-94 season

John Cornwell in pursuit, with young Spencer Prior (left) before he transferred to Norwich

On 1 January 1938, while Southend's first team were crashing 1-7 at Bournemouth, the reserves played host to Luton in the London Combination

Tony Bentley played for Southend United from 1961 to 1971, initially as a right-winger but then as right-back

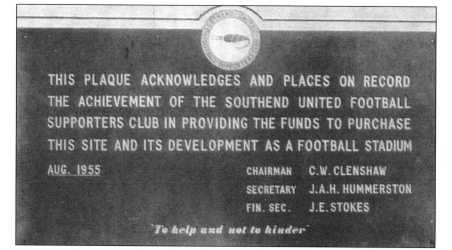

THIS PLAQUE ACKNOWLEDGES AND PLACES ON RECORD THE ACHIEVEMENT OF THE SOUTHEND UNITED FOOTBALL SUPPORTERS CLUB IN PROVIDING THE FUNDS TO PURCHASE THIS SITE AND ITS DEVELOPMENT AS A FOOTBALL STADIUM

AUG. 1955

CHAIRMAN   C.W. CLENSHAW
SECRETARY   J.A.H. HUMMERSTON
FIN. SEC.   J.E. STOKES

'To help and not to hinder'

Trevor Roberts was one of Southend's finest goalkeepers. After transferring to Cambridge United in 1970 he contracted cancer of the lung and then the brain. He is pictured here, smiling but gaunt, in the Abbey Stadium dressing room as a combined Cambridge/Southend United team played West Ham in a testimonial for him. A month later, in June 1972, he was dead, aged 30

Andy Thomson heads for goal at Roots Hall during the 1995-96 season

Southend skipper Mike Marsh drives forward, with Paul Byrne in support

This might not look too eye-catching, but this image is not on paper but on glorious silk

Southend United and Union Jacks do not often go together.
Here, fans are off to Europe in the Anglo-Italian Cup

Peter Butler starred in Southend
United's midfield before joining West
Ham in the Premiership

Skippers Keith Jones (Southend) and Trevor Peake (Luton) before the kick off at
Kenilworth Road in 1994-95. The game ended 2-2

Police and stewards deal with an intruder during the home FA Cup-tie with Millwall in
January 1993. Stan Collymore scored Southend's winning goal

he had to contend with Ridyard, a clever and experienced half-back. Only once was Richards in the game and that was when he gave Smirk a perfect pass for a brilliant run by the winger, finished up by a wild shot at goal. But for that one move, one would have been justified in thinking that Southend were trying full-backs and goalkeepers as forwards. The inside men could not get the ball, try as they would, and the wingers seemed only half-hearted in their efforts to get it.

Three of the Rangers goals, through Mallett and Stock (2) came in the first half, and the fourth was twenty minutes from the end by Heath.

QUEEN'S PARK RANGERS: Allen; Reay and Jefferson; Daniels, Ridyard and Chapman; Swinfen, Mallett, Stock, Heath and Pattison.

SOUTHEND UNITED: Conway; Fairchild and Bell; Montgomery, Jackson and Walton; Smirk, Gilberg, C. Richards, Marshall and Ormandy.

Saturday, February 23rd, 1946
SOUTHEND UNITED 1, NORWICH CITY 0

The one bright spot in Southend United's performance when they defeated Norwich by the only goal at the Stadium, on Saturday, was the display of Harris, the pre-war half-back, who has been assisting Northampton. He gave an outstanding performance in an otherwise mediocre match, and the 5,000 spectators were not only glad to see him back, but hoped he has come to stay. The high wind, playing tricks as it blew round the ends of the stands, mitigated against clever play, and the ground was sticky in places, but, making due allowance for all the difficulties, it was a very poor match.

The inclusion of Gibson and Thompson in the forward line was looked forward to with great interest, and, although Gibson turned out to be the best forward on the field, the attack as a whole was not strengthened. Walton, on the left wing, was right off form, and Thompson usually came off second best in his tussles with the opposition. The consequence was that neither Smirk nor Dudley saw a great deal of the ball, and when it was in the centre, it was too awkwardly placed for the leader to do anything with.

Montgomery, as well as Harris, played a sound game in the middle line, but had rather too much to do with a shaky forward line as well as an overworked defence.

Jackson played a courageous game as pivot, but it cannot be denied that the centre is not his best position, and it would be interesting to see the effect of a change in places between himself and Montgomery, although probably the latter lacks the experience for such a responsible position.

Humphreys and Bell both had the same failing, getting rid of the ball anywhere. It was noticeable that Norwich, as did Queen's Park Rangers the week before, used a short kick so long as they found one of their own players, and with the same tactics Southend would have been a more dangerous side.

Conway played his usual brilliant game. It seems every week that one has to write, 'But for Conway —' and the same applies to Saturday's match.

Norwich were well served in defence, although it was a mistake by Taylor which led to the goal which gave Southend both points. Seven minutes after the interval, Taylor misjudged a pass upfield, and Gibson got the ball out to Smirk, the winger centred accurately, and Gibson fired into the net. It was a well deserved goal, although Norwich had failed from better positions.

Reilly was a strong centre-half, and Jones and Plunkett put in some good centres, which should have been turned to account. On the whole, Norwich gave the better display and hardly deserved to forfeit both points.

SOUTHEND UNITED: Conway; Humphreys and Bell; Harris, Jackson and Montgomery; Smirk, Thompson, Dudley, Gibson and Walton.

NORWICH CITY: Hall; Reid and Taylor; Flack, Reilly and Proctor; Plunkett, Church, Johnson, Chapman and Jones.

Saturday, March 2nd, 1946
NORWICH CITY 0, SOUTHEND UNITED 1

Winning by the only goal of the match for the second week in succession, Southend United completed a fine double over Norwich City on Saturday, and wiped out the dual success which the Canaries scored at their expense last October.

The weather was miserable and the 4,017 spectators who saw the Canaries beaten by a hard battling United were enthusiasts. It was one of the worst days for football that could be imagined.

For the second week running Southend had to face the wind in the first half and this time they also had to contend with fast driven masses of snow and sleet. Again, however, their defenders stood up to the trying conditions with sustained determination, and the shield they set up in front of Conway was so strong that the City forwards, although they had by far the most of the play territorially, seldom looked like scoring.

Conway handled what came his way with his usual confidence and in front of him Humphreys played a sterling match, tackling the kicking so cleanly that it could be said that he did not put a foot wrong. Southend included four of their amateurs, and each of them had a share in the victory of the side. At left back J. Harvey, if not so sure as Humphreys, still enjoyed a good game. The half-backs as a line, were very sound, with Montgomery and Jackson always doing a sound job.

It stood to the credit of the defence as a whole that they maintained such a stout front all through the first half, when the sleet was driving in their faces and the turf in front of their goal was badly cut up. In spite of these difficulties the United rear-guard kept their feet and their heads, and the City, but they all broke down and units. (sic)

Of the teams as a whole it could be written down as a day when defences were superior to attacks, and United were certainly more impressive when defending than when they were in the City half. Two-thirds of the advances were put in by the City, but they all broke down and Conway did not deal with more than three or four really good shots.

On the other hand, Hall in the City goal had punched over two fierce shots, one from Pierson and one from Gibson, before Southend scored what was destined to be the solitary goal of the game, 12 minutes after the kick-off. Southend were awarded a free kick 40 yards out, and Jackson placed the ball at the foot of Gardiner who was in an inside-right position just outside the City penalty 'box.' Steadying himself, Gardiner lifted across a well-placed centre and Cyril Thompson was rightly positioned to use his head and turn the ball into the net, well wide of Hall.

For a quarter of an hour before the interval and for twenty minutes afterwards the United forwards did not enjoy much of the attacking, but the crowd were given more anxious moments by the menace of the visitors in quick breaks-away. Southend were stronger on the right than the left and Gardiner, who was heavily shaken up in a collision shortly before the end and spent some time on the touch-line, was about their best forward. Each of the others did useful work at times in Southend raids. Though on the balance of play the City did not deserve to lose, the United were to be complimented on making good use of their early scoring opportunity and then hanging on to their advantage so dourly.

NORWICH CITY: Hall; Reid and Taylor; Flack, Reilly and Proctor; Plunkett, Church, D. Pickwick, Chapman and Jones.

SOUTHEND UNITED: Conway; Humphreys and J. Harvey; Montgomery, Jackson and Walton; J. Gardiner, Gibson, Dudley, C. Thompson and J. Pierson.

Saturday, March 9th, 1946
SOUTHEND UNITED 2, WALSALL 2

Holding a lead of 2-0 mid-way through the second half, Southend United fell away unaccountably, and were eventually forced to share four goals with Walsall at the Stadium on Saturday. Thus they lost the opportunity of taking the leadership of the Third Division South, North Section, Cup Competition. Walsall remain at the top, with one more point than the United, who have a match in hand.

Saturday's display was not outstanding, considering that the contestants were fighting for first place in the league, and for three-parts of the game, Walsall were completely subdued, without the United showing anything brilliant. It was in the last 25 minutes that the visitors began playing anything like football, and their open movements had the tired out United bewildered. It was disappointing to the six thousand spectators to see Southend concede two goals after having the game in their pocket and galling that the man responsible was 42-years-old Alsop, who was still galloping about when the younger United players had shot their bolt.

Cyril Thompson, former captain of Southend schoolboys team, marked his debut as a professional, for the United by scoring the first goal, five minutes before the interval, with a powerful shot from 20 yards range. Thompson showed much better form all round and should prove a valuable asset with further experience. He almost had a second goal a few seconds later when Lewis took the ball off his toe in daring fashion.

The second goal came eight minutes after the interval. At one minute the ball was dangerously near the home goal. Jackson cleared to Montgomery; the wing half placed perfectly for Smirk to gather in his stride, and almost before the visiting forwards had had time to turn round, Smirk had flashed the ball into the net off the far upright. It was a brilliant goal. It looked short odds on a runaway victory for Southend but then for some unaccountable reason they fell on the defensive. Walsall switched their forwards round and veteran Alsop went to centre-forward, Hancocks to the left wing and Kelly to outside-right. From the middle of the field, Alsop brought all his generalship to bear and the visitors used long swinging passes. Hancocks scored for them after a round of passing mid-way through the second half, and then five minutes from the end, Alsop equalised.

The division of the spoils was a fair reward for Walsall for their persistency, but their general display belied their position and it will be surprising if they are at the top when the deciding games are played between the two sections. Hancocks, reported to be under the surveillance of Arsenal was by far their best winger. Southend played well enough, but there was something lacking – that indescribable unison which Tommy Dixon infused into the team in 1931-32. It will be remembered that when Dixon was injured, the rest of the team went to pieces and could do nothing until he returned. That is how they played on Saturday.

SOUTHEND UNITED: Conway; Humphreys and J. Harvey; Montgomery, Jackson and Walton; Smirk, Gibson, Dudley, Thompson and Bennett.

WALSALL: Lewis: Methley and Shelton; Crutchley, Foulkes and Newman; Hancocks, Millard, Kelly, Talbot and Alsop.

Saturday, March 16th, 1946
WALSALL 2, SOUTHEND UNITED 0

Southend United's defeat at Walsall certainly did not destroy their chance of qualifying for the semi-final of the Third South (North) Cup. They are still only three points behind the leaders with a match in hand. Their outlook, however, would have been much more promising if they had made better use of their chances during the first half at Fellows Park on Saturday.

Taking the game as a whole, Walsall deserved both points. Undoubtedly they did more attacking than the United. Mostly, however, it was haphazard in character, and its lack of plan and purpose, apart from the important part played in it by Hancocks, enabled the Southend defence to deal with it effectively, even without Conway being often seriously tested.

Fewer though they were, the movements of the United forwards, especially before the interval, were more constructively carried out, and there were several occasions when the Walsall half-backs were outmanoeuvred and the full-backs were in difficulties.

Unfortunately for Southend, they had no opportunist in the line to snap up the openings which were created. Once Dudley could hardly have failed to score if he had gathered a pass from Bennett more promptly, and amongst other escapes for Walsall, the ball was luckily scrambled off the line after Lewis had been drawn out of goal. The opportunities were there, and if the United forwards had been capable of a bit more 'punch' into their finishing, Walsall might at the least have found themselves faced with the task of making a recovery such as they effected at the Stadium a week previously.

As it was, the Midlanders had the second half, with the slope in their favour, in which to fulfil their own hopes and the expectations of the crowd of 8,000.

That they succeeded was due almost entirely to the cleverness of Hancocks, who carried on in this match where he had left off as 'the best player on the field,' to quote one of the critics, as the outside-left for the Army against the R.A.F. at Stamford Bridge a few days previously.

Whereas Jackson kept a tight grip on Wilshaw, a 'guest' centre-forward from Wolverhampton Wanderers, and Humphreys and Montgomery held their own against Talbot and Alsop, the 'Stanley Matthews' feinting and footwork of Hancocks were often too much for Walton and Bell to cope with, and the contribution of the Walsall outside-right proved to be the decisive factor. Immediately after the resumption he swung over a centre from which Alsop scored, and about twenty minutes from the end he left Conway helpless with a splendid shot from near the edge of the penalty area.

Except that Dudley and Harris were only foiled by a daring dive by Lewis a few minutes after Walsall's first goal, and that the goalkeeper later had to move quickly to get to a shot by Thompson, not so much was seen of the Southend forwards in the second half, but once or twice Smirk used his speed to outpace Shelton.

Teams: –

WALSALL: Lewis; Methley and Shelton; Crutchley, Foulkes and Newman; Hancocks, Mullard, Wilshaw, Talbot and Alsop.

SOUTHEND UNITED: Conway; Humphreys and Bell; Montgomery, Jackson and Walton; Smirk, Harris, Dudley, Thompson and Bennett.

Referee: Mr. R.C. Greenwood (London).

Saturday, March 23rd, 1946
SOUTHEND UNITED 2, CLAPTON ORIENT 1

Southend United maintained their somewhat slight interest in the Third Division South, north section cup, when they defeated Clapton Orient by 2-1 at the Stadium on Saturday.

As Southend have an outstanding match with the Rangers, this might well prove decisive. It has not yet been arranged, but is most likely to be on a Wednesday evening either just before or just after Easter. The Rangers have a crowded programme to fulfil, which might give Southend an advantage, but Walsall, the danger club so far as the United are concerned, have a somewhat easier schedule. Nevertheless, the Blues can be depended upon to put up a fighting finish in their endeavour to gain honours so soon after their resumption.

In the match against Clapton Orient, Southend well deserved their victory, but were lucky to get both points, for it was not until a matter of seconds from the end that Montgomery got the winning goal. On the other hand, it was unlucky for Southend that the Orient were awarded a penalty from which they secured their only goal and which for such a long time looked as if it would give them a division of the spoils.

Throughout the first half the Blues showed a marked superiority, but failed unaccountably in front of goal. Dudley fired over the top from an unmarked position, and Smirk chose to dribble instead of shooting after Gibson had placed a sitter for him. These were but two of the chances the Blues had. Smirk was unlucky on more than one occasion, and even Montgomery made some praiseworthy attempts. There was no doubt as to the better team, but there was not the thrust in the centre, and when the Blues took the field after the interval, it was not surprising that there had been a forward shuffle, Thompson going to centre-forward, Bennett to inside-left and Dudley to the left wing.

Within a few seconds of the restart, Southend had taken the lead. Smirk dribbled down the wing and flashed across a centre to Thompson. The leader tried to get the ball under control, but it cannoned off his foot into the net for a well deserved but surprising goal. Fifteen minutes later, the Orient were awarded a penalty, when Baynham fell over Milne's foot. If it were an offence at all, it was quite a yard outside the penalty area, but the referee stuck to his decision to award a spot kick and Parr converted almost leisurely.

Thereafter, the Orient were never outside their own half, and it was amazing that Southend could not score. Then, when a draw seemed inevitable, two corners followed in quick succession, Montgomery headed into the net from a crowd of players, a fine reward for a splendid display.

Clapton Orient were not an outstanding side and Southend played well enough to inspire confidence for the return match next Saturday at Leyton.

Smirk played one of his best games, and it was pleasing to see Jackson and Walton on the top of their form. Dudley was somewhat unfortunate with his actual shooting; but showed a fine sense of positional play, and only wants one or two goals to restore his confidence. He is gaining experience with every match and should yet live up to his early promise. Conway, Milne and Bell all played a sound game. The attendance was 6,390 and the receipts £681, of which £274 goes in tax.

SOUTHEND UNITED: Conway; Milne and Bell; Montgomery, Jackson and Walton; Smirk, Gibson, Dudley, Thompson and Bennett.

CLAPTON ORIENT: Lewis; Clarke and Ferrier; Froom, Bartlett and Liddle; Merritt, H. Parr, Howshall, Pullen and Baynham.

Referee: Mr. G. Johnson, Surrey.

Saturday, March 30th, 1946
CLAPTON ORIENT 0, SOUTHEND UNITED 3

Southend United accomplished the best performance achieved on the Leyton ground this season when they defeated Clapton Orient by 3-0 on Saturday. Queen's Park Rangers and Mansfield are the only other teams to have won there this season, and in each case the score was 2-0. The United's victory was no fluke. For long periods, as they did at the Stadium the previous week, they monopolised the play, and the only times Conway was tested were two or three times when Baynham sent in some corner kicks accurately.

During the week the Orient had signed on Lewis from West Bromwich Albion and Baynham from Brentford, and played as guests Barnard, for whom the Arsenal paid Colchester and West Ham a total of £750 a few weeks ago, and Jobling, of Charlton. But all the king's horses couldn't stop Southend, and an attendance of 10,000, a record for this season, saw the Orient overwhelmed. It was an ill-fated day for the home side, because the club has received such a large amount of publicity following the appointment of Mr. Charles Hewitt as Manager, and the return as President of Mr. H. Garland Wells, who allowed the redemption of a large number of debentures in an effort to get the club on a sound basis.

The only change Southend made was the inclusion of Humphreys for Milne. It was the first time this season that it had been possible to field a team with such little alteration and the players responded by playing like a machine. Every man put his best into the game, but if anyone deserved mention it was Smirk, who took a prominent part in every goal. The first he scored himself after 18 minutes, from a corner by Bennett. The left-winger place the ball accurately and after several players had headed, Smirk, who had roamed over to the left of the goal, nodded the ball past Lewis. Fifteen minutes after the interval, a free kick well out was placed by Walton to Smirk, whose shot Lewis punched to the feet of Thompson, who added the second. The last goal, 20 minutes from the end, came from a typical run by the winger. He left the defence standing and gave a perfect centre to Dudley, who headed in from short range.

On their display on Saturday, Southend had probably the best half-back line in the Southern section, with Jackson a tower of strength and completely subduing the much boosted opposing centre-forward. Thompson is improving considerably in his ball control and Gibson dispelled doubts as to his stamina by finishing on a gruelling day as freshly as he started. Dudley showed a return to form and justified all the confidence place in him. Southend still have an interest in the league cup. On the same form they should win at Brighton next Saturday, and they will get my vote to peg Queen's Park Rangers down.

SOUTHEND UNITED: Conway; Humphreys and Bell; Montgomery, Jackson and Walton; Smirk, Gibson, Dudley, Thompson and Bennett.

CLAPTON ORIENT: Lewis; Clark and Parley; Jobling, Bartlett and Liddle; Carter, Parr, Barnard, Pullen and Baynham.

Saturday, April 6th, 1946
BRIGHTON AND HOVE ALBION 2, SOUTHEND UNITED 2

Another fine performance by Southend United, when they drew 2-2 at Brighton on Saturday, gives them an excellent chance to participate in the League Cup semi-finals. They are now third in the Northern section, with 16 points.

The United have the best opportunity of all three contestants of improving their position, and if they play as they have done in their last two games, they might easily take eight points from the four remaining encounters, three of which are at home. All the best football at Brighton came from Southend, and although the Albion missed one or two chances, their first goal was decidedly fortunate, and, but for Conway being hemmed in, they would never have scored it. The ball came over from a corner, and was swerving away from goal. Conway was prevented from getting to it by two Brighton players, and although he jumped, he could not quite reach the ball to prevent Davie heading in.

That goal was fifteen minutes after the start, and both prior to it, and after, Southend had stormed their opponents' citadel, and it was no surprise when Thompson got the ball into the net from a corner accurately placed by Smirk, four minutes after Brighton had taken the lead.

The Albion again went ahead midway through the second half, when Whent broke through and gave Moore an opportunity to head a perfect goal, but the best move of the match was when Southend equalised. Dudley gained possession near the half-way line, and after a short dribble, he sent forward to Thompson, who resisted all efforts to bustle him off, and he ran on to beat Baldwin with a beautiful shot.

For three parts of the game, Southend were attacking, using the ball skilfully, and generally outplaying their opponents. Their display was more creditable, for whereas Brighton had out a team composed of nine pre-war players, and all regular participants, it was only the first time the United had been able to field the same eleven for two consecutive weeks.

The Blues played really first-class football which drew the admiration of the 5,000 crowd, and before half-time the spectators were cheering on Dudley in preference to their own men. Thompson and Smirk were in brilliant form again, and the defence, while not faultless, endeavoured to make the ball do the work, and also covered up their goal.

Incidentally, I walked along Brighton and Hove front before the match and was struck by the absence of the visitors.

SOUTHEND UNITED: Conway; Humphreys and Bell; Montgomery, Jackson and Walton; Smirk, Gibson, Dudley, Thompson and Bennett.

BRIGHTON: Baldwin; Green and Marriott; Darling, Risdon and J. Whent; Moore, Wilson, Davie, Philbin and Stephens.

Referee: Mr. H.C. Williams.

Saturday, April 13th, 1946
SOUTHEND UNITED 1, BRIGHTON AND HOVE ALBION 1

The United's performance against Brighton was a bitter disappointment to nearly 7,000 spectators, a record attendance this season for the Stadium, for with so much at stake, it was anticipated they would at least put up a stern fight. Instead, it was a most uninspiring display, and not until the last 15 minutes was there sufficient excitement to raise a cheer. After Thompson had headed a goal from a corner-kick by Smirk, exactly seventeen minutes from the end, Southend piled on the pressure, but it was Brighton who scored, Stephens having an easy chance after a defensive mistake. With almost the last kick of the game the United put the ball in the net, but Thompson and Dudley were ruled offside. There was some excuse for the Blues; Humphreys, suffering from boils, was unable to play and it was decided to give O'Brien, just signed on as a professional, a chance. He was, however, completely overcome by the occasion and the defence had a gruelling time, Jackson performing nobly, but this handicap did not excuse the lack of thrust in the forward line. The ball was seldom sent to the middle from the wings, and time and again passes went straight to the feet of opponents.

The hot day and brilliant sunshine might have had a good deal to do with the poor display, and the less said about it the better.

SOUTHEND: Conway; O'Brien and Bell; Montgomery, Jackson and Walton; Smirk, Gibson, Dudley, Thompson and Bennett.

BRIGHTON: Baldwin; Green and Marriott; Darling, Trainor and J. Whent; Hillman, Wilson, Davie, D. Broomfield and Stephens.

Wednesday, April 17th, 1946
SOUTHEND UNITED 0, QUEEN'S PARK RANGERS 0

Southend United's game with Queen's Park Rangers, at the Stadium, on Wednesday evening, provided top-of-the-table football, with no goals, the Rangers thus gaining the vital point, to put them at the head of the Division III (South) table on goal average.

It must have been one of the fastest games played at the Stadium for some time, both teams hurtling the ball up and down the field, to bring minute-by-minute thrills. Only once did the pace look like running down, in spite of a heavy and slippery ball. Southend, on balance, probably had most chances, and certainly had the best one of the match when Referee Plinston, after consulting the linesman, awarded a penalty for handling in a melee, and Thompson dug into the turf and wasted the chance with the tamest penalty possible, the ball not only hugging the ground, but running wide.

Southend made several changes in their team, dropping Dudley from centre-forward and bringing Montgomery into that position from left half. From one match, in which the football was too headlong for any infighting in front of goals, it was difficult to judge the experiment. He did not impress much in the first half, but in the second he let the ball do the work and swung out some useful passes to the wings. In a different game, his ability to shoot hard, might have proved highly effective, but few players can make much impression on Allen, in the Rangers goal, who was always so sure and safe in his handling that he never looked flustered, even in the tightest situation. After seeing Allen, it is not difficult to understand why the Rangers have only had nine goals scored against them in the competition.

Smirk had his fill of football on Wednesday. He played in an Army Area final at Colchester in the afternoon, and was rushed by car to Southend for the evening fixture. Although overshadowed by the experienced left-back Swinfen, in the first half, he certainly had his measure in the second and threatened danger time and again from the right.

Southend were also well-served by two Chelmsford guests, Jones (L.), at right-half, and Burley on the left wing. Walton, at left-half opened well, but was outshone by the energetic Jackson in the centre, who broke up many promising Rangers' movements.

For the Rangers, Leary on the right wing was always menacing, but McEwan thrust boldly through the centre to test Conway several times. The light was poor towards the end, and the greyhound track lights were switched on to help the spectators, about 7,600 of them, home. Teams:

SOUTHEND UNITED: Conway; Milne and Bell; Jones (L.), Jackson and Walton; Smirk, Gibson, Montgomery, Thompson and Burley.

QUEEN'S PARK RANGERS: Allen; Rose and Swinfen; Daniels, Ridyard and Farrow; Leary, Mallett, McEwan, Hatton and Pattison.

Saturday, April 20th, 1946
PORT VALE 2, SOUTHEND UNITED 1

Monday, April 22nd, 1946
SOUTHEND UNITED 1, PORT VALE 1

Southend United have concluded their first season after closing down for the greater part of the war in a far more satisfactory position than one would have hoped in the circumstances and considerably better than deemed possible at the practice matches last August.

In the League Cup competition they have finished fourth, rather disappointing when so recently they appeared to have a chance of being second. Queen's Park Rangers and Walsall, however, came up at the end with a storming finish, whereas the United gained only four points from their last five matches.

At Hanley, on Saturday, Southend were decidedly unfortunate to lose 2-1, for they were easily the better side, and had what the Vale players themselves agreed was a perfect goal disallowed. In addition, the Potters' winning point was scored from an apparently offside position, which situation the home side again agreed was correct. Jackson obtained Southend's goal from a penalty, Cheadle and Bellis being the home side's marksmen.

At the Stadium, on Monday, Southend should have scored half-a-dozen goals, but, instead, had to be satisfied with a draw of 1-1. The visitors got their goal in the first half, in one of their few raids; Bell passed back to Conway when tackled by Pointon, unaware that Bellis was on his blind side, and the winger had no difficulty in beating Conway. For the remainder of the game the United dominated the play, but it was not until twenty minutes from the end that Thompson scored the equaliser from a pass by Woodward. In the closing stages half the Southend team was hobbling about the field injured. A record 'gate' for the season, just short of 8,000, saw the match.

The excellent support which the United have received has ensured a financial success of this season, so that everything is favourable for the next campaign, when it is probable normal competitions will prevail.

For the second part of the season Southend have managed with only two guests, chief being Montgomery (Hull City). An outstanding half-back, no greater tribute can be made to him than the fact that the directors are leaving no stone unturned to secure him as a regular player. Bennett (Spurs) has usually done duty on the left wing, and has given excellent service.

In having four ex-prisoners of war in their team – Jackson, Smirk, Bell and Thompson – the United have probably a unique record in the Football League.

CHAPTER ELEVEN

A Selection of Match Reports 1946-1966

Saturday, October 12th, 1946
Football League, Third Division, (Southern Section)
SOUTHEND UNITED 2, SWINDON TOWN 0

Southend United played football of a championship standard to beat Swindon by 2-0 before a crowd of 10,000 at the Stadium on Saturday, and, as a result, they move up to fourth position in the table, only two points behind Cardiff, who displace Queen's Park Rangers from the leadership. Had not Dudley sustained an ankle injury in the second half, the United would probably have had a larger margin, for the scoring chances were there, but the home leader had not the speed to get to the ball before his opponents. Swindon proved by far the best team Southend have met since they resumed after the war, and it was highly satisfactory to see the Blues excel in a duel with a really clever side.

No one could have wished to see better football than the first-half exchanges, and the visitors deserved just as many goals as Southend, but after the change-over, while the United retained all their speed and skill, Swindon fell away and in the end, the Blues were unlucky that their superiority did not amount to more goals than the two registered before the interval.

On this form, Southend have a definite chance of the championship, and the position has become interesting since Bristol Rovers, no match for the Blues on their own ground, defeated the Rangers at Shepherd's Bush on Saturday, by 2-0 and deserved it. Cardiff hold the lead by virtue of having played one more match than the other teams at the top of the table, and they look dangerous, because they appear to have the reserve side as well. The Welshman are the next visitors at the Stadium, and if the fine weather holds until then, a rare tussle is in store. In the meantime, Southend visit Bournemouth, where they have no easy task.

As already stated, Swindon are the best team Southend have yet met this season, and the first half was equal to any First Division game. The play swept from end to end in breathless fashion, not by means of kick and rush methods, but by clever football manoeuvres. Lucas, Welsh International, was the mainspring of the visitors, but he had an equal, even a peer, in Harris, who sent forward some of the best passes any attack could wish to receive. Jackson and Montgomery completed a half-back line, which played as well as any seen this season. The reason they were so sound is no doubt due to the reliable men behind them, for they had nothing to worry about in defence. Linton has become a really reliable defender and if Frank Walton is persevered with, the United should have a pair of backs the equal of any in the Third Division.

The forwards, unlike those of Swindon, played as a line, and swept the ball about from wing to wing in a manner which worried the visiting defence. They played with a purpose and understanding which did everyone credit. Whenever a half-back moved up into the attack, so someone fell back to cover the defence, and spectators had the excitement of seeing Harris shooting at goal, and Montgomery heading goalwards from corner kicks. Thompson was a real live wire, and Sibley played his best game yet.

Swindon were the equal of Southend in the first half, but they made the mistake of relying too much on Lucas, who, having played for Wales, was naturally kept under close observation by the Blues. He was, however, a tricky player, and usually beat his man, but was not allowed to get far, because of the backing-up process adopted by the United. When Stephens, the visiting centre-forward, started the clever stuff, Swindon just about signed their doom, for, as a result, they had hardly a real shot at goal. The passes came in from Jones and Williams, but they were not turned to account. As is usual with Swindon, they had a robust defence, but not quite good enough to hold the smart United forwards.

Southend's first goal came after thirty-five minutes, and was the result of Dudley's persistence.- He fought hard to retrieve a ball on the goal-line, and centred to Thompson, who banged home a smasher. The second was two minutes before the interval, when Smirk centred after working with Sibley, enabling Dudley to beat Boulton. The greater part of the second half exchanges were fought in the Swindon half, but the United could not add to their lead. Swindon had one fine chance when Hankey was lured out of goal, but with the target at his mercy, Stephens fired wildly over the cross-bar.

All told, it was a brilliant match, which more than satisfied the spectators. Teams: –

SOUTHEND UNITED: Hankey; Linton and Walton (F.); Harris, Jackson and Montgomery; Sibley, Smirk, Dudley, Thompson and Lane.

SWINDON: Boulton; Young and Trim; Cousins, Bingham and Lloyd; Jones, Lucas, Stephens, Painter and Williams.

Referee: Mr. P. Stevens, Luton.

Saturday, December 14th, 1946
F.A. Challenge Cup, 2nd Round
BARNET 2, SOUTHEND UNITED 9

Southend United triumphed over deplorable conditions at Barnet, on Saturday, to win their Second Round F.A. Cup-tie by the second highest score they have ever recorded in the competition – 9-2. Barnet, holders of the F.A. Amateur Cup, were at no stage of the game any match for the Blues, and, had the ground been in better condition, it is probable that it would have assisted Southend to run well into double figures, rather than have shown the amateurs in a better light. The score was the highest aggregate of the day among the leading clubs of the country.

As it was, the home goal posts saved at least half-a-dozen additional goals for Southend, while the frequency with which the ball stuck in the mud allowed the defence to clear, when in normal circumstances they would have been spreadeagled. Southend got all their goals through brilliant combination, and in a style which drew forth admiration from the Barnet supporters.

Unfortunately, all the United efforts did not receive the same approbation, and Sheard, who was brought in at centre-half because Jackson had pulled a muscle, was subjected to considerable barracking. Several free-kicks were given against him, and, whilst they were mostly for infringements which could be classed as cup-tie exuberance, there were two cases of obstruction which were needless. Such tactics were the more unfortunate because otherwise the game was conducted in the most sporting spirit, and the trainers were on the field only twice. Reilly, the home left-winger, had to leave the field midway through the second half, when he injured a leg. Both he and Linton went to kick the ball at the same time, and the Barnet player sustained a nasty jar, which prevented him taking any further part, but it was during his absence that the home side secured their second goal.

Barnet took their defeat like true sportsmen, and wished Southend well in the competition. With their defeat, the last of the amateur sides went out of the tournament.

The crowd of 8,065 just failed to beat the ground record established last season when Queen's Park Rangers beat the Athenian leaguers 6-2. Had it not been for the early morning fog, the gate would doubtless have been much larger. At one time, mist began to blow over the ground and it looked doubtful that the game would be finished, but it cleared up before the end of the match, and at no time was it difficult to follow the game owing to fog. The liberal coating of mud, however, made it hard for strangers to recognize the players, and before the end one or two participants rolled up their shorts like children at the seaside, to prevent the mud from flapping on their legs.

Quite half of the spectators came from Southend, many by coach, but a large proportion by private cars, and one Southend enthusiast went up early in the morning to sell blue and white favours. The United went by coach and arrived without mishap, although at one time, in the vicinity of Romford, there were apprehensions when the fog began to thicken. Barnet received them well, and dispensed hospitality which would have done credit to many league clubs. The ground is well appointed for an amateur side, but the pitch, known locally as the mud heap, lived well up to its name, and the conditions could not have been worse had the game been played on the Southend foreshore.

Despite such circumstances, the United played dazzling football. They won the toss and chose the advantage of the slope — a move which pleased the home supporters, because Barnet prefer to have the help of the incline in the second half. While such a policy might pay against amateur opponents, it was fatal against a well-trained professional team, although, as it turned out, the pitch made no noticeable difference to the Blues.

On the other hand, Barnet might have got an early goal and they had the slope, which could have made a deal of difference to the ultimate result. Within the first two minutes Southend had taken three corner kicks, and it was obvious at that stage there would be a glut of goals, and that it would be Southend scoring them.

The exchanges were just seven minutes old when Lane opened the account. His shot first hit the crossbar and bounced out to Smirk, who returned it to Lane for the opening goal. A minute later Thompson scored the second from Smirk's centre. For a short spell Barnet were inspired, and they got their first goal when Kelleher dribbled through, drew Sheard, and passed to the unmarked Phipps, who made no mistake. In the 35th minute Smirk eluded the defence and passed to Lane for a third goal, the left winger got another from Sibley's pass in the 38th minute, and, just before half-time, Sibley headed in from a corner kick by Lane. At the interval, the United led 5-1.

Two minutes after the changeover, Bennett scored after Thompson had hit the cross-bar. A minute later, Smirk sent in one of his swerving wing shots, which Bunker attempted to clear, but the ball skidded into his own net, and in the twelfth minute of the second half Sibley registered the eighth from Thompson, after Lane had weaved his way through. It was soon after this that Reilly left the field, but Barnet were not deterred and Phipps was left with an open goal to score their second. Seven minutes from the end, Bennett completed the tally. Scorers were Lane (3), Sibley (2), Bennett (2), Thompson and Bunker (own goal).

Smirk, it will be seen, does not figure in the list of scorers, but actually he deserved credit for about half of the goals, and he made enough openings for several more. He played a really inspired game, and served the ball up to his colleagues on a plate. I heard him described as international standard, and there was little doubt that he was.

On a day when Southend played remarkable football, Smirk stood head and shoulders above the rest. Lane, Sibley and Bennett also did extremely well, and considering that Thompson had to work up and down the field ankle-deep in ooze he gave one of his best performances. The wing-halves, Harris and Montgomery, were right on the top of their form, and were rarely beaten for possession. Sheard, on the other hand, was not at all reliable, for while he got the ball away at times when it seemed impossible, there were occasions when he blundered badly. With the United doing so much attacking, he had a lot of ground to cover, and the speedy Barnet forwards often found him out of position. Linton, Walton and Hankey had more work than the score suggested, and all did everything that could be expected. The backs were particularly outstanding.

Barnet had a really clever forward line, and while Leek did well at centre-half, there was a defensive weakness which Southend were quick to find, but any defence in the country would have had a gruelling time against Southend on Saturday. Powell positioned himself well for some of Smirk's centres, but he had little chance with the shots that beat him. Finch and Reilly were fast on the wings, and Kelleher endeavoured to get the front line going, but in all departments Barnet were out-classed. The game only served to show the wide difference there is between amateur and professional football. Teams: –

BARNET: H. Powell; E. Bunker and E. Hawkins; J.G. Gerrans, T. Leek and F. Pymm; L.C. Finch, D. Kelleher, R.W. Phipps, A.P. Hawkes and P. Reilly.

SOUTHEND UNITED: Hankey; Linton and Walton (F.); Harris, Sheard and Montgomery; Sibley, Smirk, Thompson, Bennett and Lane.

Referee: Mr. E.V. Pitt.

Thursday, April 15th, 1948
Benefit Match for Frank Walton
SOUTHEND UNITED 0, MIDDLESBROUGH 3

Against Middlesbrough in an almost too-friendly friendly, United were beaten easily three goals to nil on Thursday. A large crowd turned up for this benefit game for Frank Walton and saw a grand exhibition of football, at least from Middlesbrough, if not from the Blues.

David Jack's boys took things very easily, piled on three goals with all the ease in the world, tried vainly to give the Blues a start, but the United were just not having any. They put the ball over the bar, behind, at the side, in fact, any-where but the goal itself.

Fans watching Middlesbrough – in particular Mannion and Fenton, the England forwards – saw more good passes in this one match than they have for the rest of the season.

It was a delight to watch the smooth precision-like movements of the First Division team, and Walker's goal – a real snorter from the wing – was one straight from the book.

LIGHTNING STRIKE ON 19TH APRIL, 1948

When lightning struck down eight of the players in the Army football match at Aldershot on Monday, Mr. Nevil Hewitt, G.C., and Mr. Harry Warren, Chairman and Manager of Southend United, were watching the game.

Playing in the match was French, the Blues half-back, who was captaining the 121st Training Regiment. French was throwing in the ball when the light-ning struck. Speaking to Mr. Warren later, he said: 'I had the ball in my hand; suddenly there was a flash and I felt my arm and hands go dead. That's all I can remember.' Mr. Warren, continuing the story, 'The flash dazzled us, and then I saw French crumple up in a heap on the ground. Eight more players were in a similar position. For a few seconds we were all too stunned to do anything. I thought the referee was dead, but he recovered later on.' This is probably the last time French will play for an Army side.

He is expecting to be demobilized within a few weeks, and will be making regular appearances with the Blues next season.

Saturday, April 2nd, 1949
Football League, Third Division (Southern Section)
SWANSEA TOWN 2, SOUTHEND UNITED 2

This was the only point Swansea dropped at home all season and the only time they conceded more than one goal.

The soccer world had a few shocks over the week-end. Manchester went out of the F.A. Cup – and lowly Southend made rings round Swansea on their own mud patch and brought home a very valuable point.

Had it not been for centre-forward Richards, United might have brought home two points, for he scored the equalising goal for the Welsh club a few seconds from time.

It was a subdued Swansea crowd which left the Vetch Field; their hopes had been well and truly dowsed, not only by the torrential rain, but by the poor display of their side, leading the promotion race. For the majority of the game United played football worthy of the leading position in the League.

This, incidentally, was the first home match this season where Swansea had been forced to share the points.

Supporters, bearing in mind the pitiful performance given by Blues at the Stadium, would not have recognised the thrustful United forwards, who, with their extremely dangerous raids, riddled the Swansea defence time after time. Butler was at the top of his form and gave the experienced Keane a very gruelling day. McAlinden, playing the best game of his United career, was always on hand to start the attacking moves and his combination and understanding with Lawler was well worth watching.

Grant was very vigorous at centre-forward, and his Swansea policeman (Newell), had a busy day keeping him under control.

The Blues wing half-backs had a good day, French, in particular, for his first goal, which would have set United supporters well alight had they seen it. Excitement topped boiling point in the first two minutes, when the referee awarded a penalty against Southend for an infringement by Jack Pritchard, who was brought in at the last minute for Lindsay, not fully recovered from his injury.

Paul took the shot and Nash managed to tip it on to the bar for a grand save. Other forwards followed up as the shot came out again, but the United defence regained control and cleared their lines. Both sides were finding it difficult to keep the heavy rain-soaked ball under control, but Blues kept their passes short and adapted themselves better. After ten minutes United went ahead. McAlinden and Butler again went through and Butler sent over a pass inside the penalty area. French, coming into practically the centre-forward position, drove into the corner of the net.

The Swansea crowd began to clamour for goals and the Welshmen instituted a series of attacks with vigorous football. Thornhill was injured and received constant attention from Wilf Copping, and then Nash was booted on the spine. Later he had to receive further attention after a heavy kick on the leg.

Swansea obtained the equaliser when Paul put in a shot from 35 yards, which was headed out by a defender to Richards, whose first-time shot entered the top corner of the goal.

Full time had been reached at this stage, but the referee, Mr. B.M. Griffiths (Newport), was allowing extra time for that taken by trainers' frequent attentions to the injured.

Two minutes of extra time had ticked by when Grant scored the Blues' second goal. For once during the game the Blues had all five forwards and two wing halves plugging away in front of goal.

Grant got his foot to the ball and his shot hit the inside of the post, rebounded to the other side of the goal, struck the inside post again and rebounded into goal.

Swansea, however, mounted a full-scale attack, which resulted in a free-kick being awarded against the Blues. The shot went into the goal area. Paddy Nash was prevented from gathering the ball by his severe spinal injury and the Swansea forwards bundled the ball into the net as well as most of the defenders, to gain the equalising goal.

After the game the Swansea directors congratulated the Southend side, saying they were the best side to visit their ground this year.

Wednesday, April 19th, 1950
Essex Professional Cup Final
SOUTHEND UNITED 2, LEYTON ORIENT 1
(played at West Ham United F.C.)

Southend United won the Essex County Football Association Professional Cup by beating Leyton Orient 2-1 in the final at West Ham on Wednesday. After a goal-less first half, both sides got into their stride and thrills were fast and furious.

After 55 minutes play, Wakefield opened the score for United with a brilliant run through after receiving from Stubbs, netting with a great drive.

Leyton Orient, however, soon got level through a disputed penalty for hands. Walton netted (1-1).

Southend pressed hard and chances were missed by Stubbs and Clough. In the 80th minute United gained the winning goal, when Wakefield, following attractive work by Jones and Wallbanks, drove hard into the net (2-1).

Leyton Orient went all out to save the game in the closing stages, and forced two corners, but United's goal remained intact. Both Davies and Paddy Nash were injured, and there is doubt if they will be fit for Saturday's game with Northampton.

SOUTHEND UNITED line-up was: Nash; Lindsay and Walton; Wallbanks, Sheard and French; Jones, Davies, Wakefield, Stubbs and Clough.

The trophy was presented to Frank Walton, who skippered the side in the absence of Jimmy McAlinden, by Sir Herbert Dunnico, J.P., President of Essex Football Association. As a memento of the occasion, each player received a pair of crested gold cuff-links instead of the usual medals.

Tuesday, April 10th, 1951
Football League, Third Division (Southern Section)
SOUTHEND UNITED 3, NOTTINGHAM FOREST 2

What a week it has been for United fans! They had hardly recovered from the great struggle by a 10-men United side against Norwich – where the Canaries scraped home with a 2-0 victory – when Notts Forest, leaders of the Third Division (South) and hot favourites for promotion, arrived at the Stadium on Tuesday.

There, before a crowd exceeding 12,000, Blues, playing wonderful football, won a thrill-packed game by 3-2.

It was the Blues forward line, back to its normal composition, with Grant as leader, Stubbs at inside-left and skipper Jimmy McAlinden at inside-right, which bore the promotion look.

They were yards faster on the ball, and always dangerous, with Joe Sibley lobbing the ball into the Notts goal area with deadly accuracy.

Blues piled up a useful lead with Grant scoring after six minutes. Stubbs passed to Grant, the Notts centre-half miskicked and the centre-forward, darting through, lobbed the ball into the net. Blues continued to exert heavy pressure, but then the Notts forwards came into the game, but goal-scoring Ardron rarely wriggled free of Jimmy Stirling's grip.

Notts piled on terrific pressure, but United's defence was solid. Just before half-time French increased their lead.

Blues broke away through Sibley, who centred; Stubbs tapped the ball to Jack French, who crashed it into the net without hesitation.

The second half opened quietly, with end to end play, but the last 15 minutes were loaded with thrills. After thirty minutes Loughran handled in the penalty area and Gager scored from the spot-kick. This set the Notts forwards alight and two minutes later the unfortunate Loughran made another bloomer which resulted in Scott netting the equaliser.

With thirty seconds to go, a draw looked certain. Blues forced a corner, and the crowd were on tip-toe with expectancy.

Tippett's corner skimmed along the cross-bar and Thomas fisted it clear. Blues were rightly awarded a penalty and a hush settled over the ground as Anderson went up to take the kick, and he crashed the ball into the net.

With this victory, Blues moved up to fourth place in the table on Wednesday morning.

Thursday, May 14th, 1953
Friendly Match
R.C. LENS 3, SOUTHEND UNITED 4

Southend United started their tour of the Continent with a brilliant 4-3 win over R. C. Lens, but unfortunately their Paris fixture was postponed and will not be played until later.

United have been afforded a warm reception and before the start of their game each member of the side was presented with a miner's lamp, for coal-mining is the industry of the area. This ceremony was followed by the release of hundreds of pigeons.

Blues new players featured in the line-up. In goal was Jimmy Brown (on loan from Hearts), and the backs were Bill Pavitt (ex-Fulham) and Duggins. Half-backs were Whitehead (on loan from Hearts), Stirling and Bridge. The forwards line-up was Sibley, McAlinden, Grant, Bainbridge and Lowder.

Sibley scored Blues first goal, and followed this with another great goal, following a cut in from the wing.

Blues had a 2-0 lead at half-time then Sibley hit the post with a great shot, and Lowder slammed in the return.

Bainbridge scored the fourth 20 minutes from time, but the game was not over. Lens fought hard – they were on a £20 bonus for a win – and scored three quick goals making the score 4-3 with five minutes to go. The game finished at a cracking pace, and the crowd was in a frenzy, but Blues gained the day.

Wednesday, May 6th, 1953
Essex Professional Cup Final
SOUTHEND UNITED 4, LEYTON ORIENT 1

By beating Leyton Orient 4-1 at the Stadium on Wednesday night, Southend United became the first team to win the Essex Professional Cup on two occasions. They were the first holders in 1949-50, when, ironically, they again defeated Leyton Orient in the final.

This game was grand entertainment and a large crowd watched the Blues gain the verdict. United were without Loughran and McAlinden, Anderson was at right-back, and Thompson inside-right. Centre-half Jimmy Stirling took over the captaincy of the side.

O'Neil scored after 15 minutes, heading in from a Sibley corner, and Facey equalised for Orient after 35 minutes. In the second half United took control. Thompson was brought down in the area and Burns netted from the spot.

After 65 minutes United went further ahead when O'Neil netted from a Bainbridge flag-kick. Finally the goal of the match was scored by Sibley crashing in a drive on the run.

Although Orient fielded their full League side, the renowned centre-forward, Pacey, was hardly seen, being kept well under control by Stirling. After the game Sir Herbert Dunnico, LL.D., J.P., presented the trophy to Jimmy Stirling.

Saturday, August 21st, 1954
Football League, Third Division (Southern Section)
SOUTHEND UNITED 4, SHREWSBURY TOWN 1

Over 14,000 spectators saw Southend United make a wonderful start to the new season by soundly defeating Shrewsbury 4-1 at the Stadium on Saturday. It was certainly a grand tonic to the supporters, management and the players.

The two 'new boys' showed up in an excellent light, although Bill Anderson, the ex-Hibs inside forward, failed to score after his glut of goals in the trial game. In fact, at times he was a trifle slow on the ball.

His colleagues, particularly in the second half, presented him with many, many chances to score, but he allowed them to slip by.

However, Blues' new signing from Liverpool, Kevin Baron, contributed two grand goals which delighted the fans. Roy Hollis and Ken Bainbridge gained the remaining two goals.

It was altogether a satisfactory match, which set the fans purring and, of course, the more enthusiastic and optimistic of them were talking about Blues being in the promotion race.

Certainly the display was heartening. The goals were shared among the line, and with all due respect to Jimmy McAlinden, it was nice to see Blues' new schemer-in-chief so much among the goals.

Although Bainbridge scored, he is capable of a better display than he gave on Saturday. Blues' half-back line was superb. Duthie in particular worked exceptionally hard. He is deceptive and showed a considerable turn of speed on his many raids into the Shrewsbury goal area. Stirling was an effective centre-half, while Burns completed a grand trio.

For the first 15 minutes of this game it looked as if Shrewsbury would be more than a match for United. Their men moved quickly into position and sent in shots from all angles. Beynon moved on to a loose ball, and the United goal was in danger as he broke through. Fortunately Stirling was on hand and he tackled Beynon and cleared. After this tackle the right-half had to receive attention from the trainer and resumed with his ankle well plastered.

At this stage the efforts of the United forwards were too individual and they failed to a concerted combine effectively. Sibley and Bainbridge both went near, but it was Shrewsbury who went ahead.

Beynon and O'Donnell were the instigators of the move and sent the ball through to Hudson. The centre flicked it through to Price, who burst through on the left and netted from close range. (0-1.)

This reverse did the Blues a power of good. They started to work as a team and Baron equalised a minute later. It was a wonderful effort by the inside forward. He beat three defenders and flashed the ball low into the net. (1-1.)

On level terms Blues set about taking control of the game. After 22 minutes they went ahead. Baron had a shot saved by his former Liverpool colleague Crossley. The ball rebounded to Bainbridge who netted with a first time shot from a narrow angle. (2-1.)

Two minutes later Southend went further ahead. Hollis burst through the middle at a speed which left Candlin standing, and netted with a drive which flashed past the advancing goalkeeper. (3-1.)

Although there was no further score until a minute from full-time, there was no doubt who were the masters. During the second half Anderson had many chances, but he seemed a trifle slow moving to the ball.

Both wings were constantly in action and with Baron and Hollis providing a two-headed attack the visiting defence was kept at full stretch.

A corner a minute from time led to the Blues' fourth and final goal. Bainbridge sent over the kick, Anderson headed against the bar and Baron made no mistake when the ball rebounded. (4-1.) Teams:

UNITED: Threadgold; Pavitt and Anderson; Duthie, Stirling and Burns; Sibley, W. Anderson, Hollis, Baron and Bainbridge.

SHREWSBURY: Crossley; Bannister and Dodd; Beynon, Candlin and Maloney; Price, O'Donnell, Hudson, McCue and Loughmane.

Monday, May 20th, 1957
Friendly Match
CARLSBAD DYNAMO 2, SOUTHEND UNITED 2

Ten minutes from time Southend held a commanding 2-0 lead yet the Czech team drew level with two goals inside two minutes. The match played on Monday week, an extra one added to the Blues' schedule, was played in cup-tie spirit, Blues switched Smith for D'Arcy on the right wing in the second half.

Blues opened strongly and McCrory was prominent. He once beat three men in a row and sent in a scorching drive. Baron 'netted', but was ruled offside, and D'Arcy shot past the post after the Dynamo goalkeeper dropped a hot shot in a goalmouth scramble.

The Czech crowd showed some anger when the referee whistled the Carlsbad inside left offside as he put the ball into the Blues net.

Blues took up the running again and Costello was only just wide of the post with a shot. The referee waved away Blues' claim for a penalty when Costello was brought down by the goalkeeper as he was about to score.

A neat move gave Blues the lead after 67 minutes. Duthie placed a free-kick at McGuigan's feet and the winger centred for McCrory to score.

Five minutes later McGuigan weaved his way brilliantly down the wing, beating three men on the way and put a perfect pass to Baron who put Blues 2-0 ahead.

With only eight minutes remaining for play the Dynamo right-half placed a free-kick for the centre-forward to beat Threadgold from close in to reduce the Blues lead and a minute later the scores were level when, after a harmless looking movement, the outside right put the ball into the net.

Stirling was a tower of strength at centre-half and with Duthie was outstanding in defence. Southend United team: –

Threadgold; Howe, Anderson; Duthie, Stirling, Duffy; D'Arcy (Smith second half), McCrory, Costello, Baron and McGuigan.

Saturday, May 25th, 1957
Friendly Match
BUDJOVICE 0, SOUTHEND UNITED 4

The Blues registered a fine win on Saturday to end their tour of Czechoslovakia. Lou Costello, Blues new centre-forward, scored his first goals for the Blues – two of them. McCrory got the other two. Blues might have been ahead in the first minute when Baron sent Costello through, but his shot skimmed over the crossbar.

McGuigan was knocked spinning in the penalty area, but Blues' appeals for a penalty were turned down and in the next minute Baron was sent down though again no penalty resulted.

At 33 minutes Smith put in a centre from the right and Costello scored from close in. Budjovice sent in two substitutes for the second half. Early in this half Baron twice shaved the upright with goalworthy shots. After 60 minutes Williamson placed a free-kick to Costello who made a chance for McCrory and he scored.

At 70 minutes a passing movement between Costello and McCrory set up another chance and McCrory put Blues 3-0 ahead.

Duthie squared a ball back off the dead ball line and Costello should have scored, but a minute later, the 85th, Costello nodded in a corner kick from McGuigan to complete the scoring.

SOUTHEND UNITED: Threadgold; Williamson, Anderson; Duthie, Stirling, Howe; Smith, McCrory, Costello, Baron, McGuigan.

Tuesday, May 28th, 1957
Friendly Match
SPARTA ROTTERDAM 0, SOUTHEND UNITED 0

For their final match of the summer tour Blues kept their score sheet blank against the Dutch Football League champions, who fielded a side containing four full internationals. The Sparta centre-half has over thirty caps for Holland.

The side is coached by a Southend man, Dennis Nevil, and not so long ago held Leeds United (John Charles and all) to a 4-4 draw.

Blues showed signs of strain and tiredness after their long journey. They left Prague by train early on Monday morning and travelled through Nuremburg and Cologne, arriving in Rotterdam at mid-day on Tuesday...some 28 hours travelling. At 7.15p.m., after only a brief rest, Blues had to take on this strong Dutch side. In all the circumstances they did well to draw.

Again Stirling was outstanding in defence. The forwards did not grab the few chances that came their way; had they done so a win would not have been against the run of play.

SOUTHEND UNITED: Threadgold; Williamson, Anderson; Duthie, Stirling, Duffy; Smith, McCrory, Costello, Baron, McGuigan.

Wednesday, October 16th, 1957
Friendly Match
SOUTHEND UNITED 5, SPARTA ROTTERDAM 2

It took 90 minutes of non-stop burlesque for Southend to show these Dutch boys – three times champions of the Netherlands top division since the war; anything West Ham could do, Blues could equal.

Rain all yesterday (Wednesday) morning made the pitch a swamp. Players slithered and slid along a surface which resembled one great green oozing bath sponge more than a soccer pitch.

The ball played tricks which brought laughter and tears, sometimes skidding, heartlessly breaking up promising moves, sometimes plopping to a halt with the same result.

As if to demonstrate just how bad it really was, Ronson charged out in a cloud of spray to save from van Ede, capped three times for Holland, after two minutes.

Sam McCrory travelled five yards on his back after he was fouled by de Koning and then as Costello scrambled about with Schilders (the 20-years-old Dutch 'B' capped giant for whom Sparta paid £10,000) on the wing McCrory ran to the middle. Over came the ball. Beyer almost created a tidal wave as he surged out and McCrory jabbed it down for Crossan to send a shot skimming into the net after 22 minutes.

For the second half Blues made three changes, Roy Hollis taking over from Lou Costello as centre-forward, Costello relieving right-half Duthie, and Gordon Barker coming in for Crossan on the right wing.

Sparta also made alterations. Verhoeven giving way to Verbeek at right-half and Daniels taking the inside-right berth from van de Gijp, who moved to centre-forward.

Ronson was soon in action with a 'guilty' save on the goalline. Referee Alf Bond ran over to linesman Len Forge before deciding 'no goal.'

The game warmed up as Sam McCrory placed a perfect pass to Baron, who made it 2-0. A minute later McCrory had a shot charged down but when given a second chance, he scored.

Anderson and Stirling sandwiched inside-left Bosselar and the 21-years-old Dutchman, with 13 full caps behind him, made no mistake with his spot kick. Hollis rose to head in a McGuigan corner for Blues' fourth and then Baron was brought down by de Koning. The crowd called for Anderson to take the spot kick and he scored. Stirling brought a grand save from Ronson when he attempted a pass back which caught the goalkeeper unawares and finally, with three minutes left, Ronson hurried forward to gather a ball, overslid and kept on sliding. He could only sit and watch as Daniels put in the last word for Sparta with their second goal.

SOUTHEND: Ronson; Williamson, Anderson; Duthie (Costello), Stirling, Smith; Crossan (Barker), McCrory, Costello (Hollis), Baron, McGuigan.

SPARTA: Beyer; Hendricks, van de Lee; Verhoeven, Schilder, de Koning; van Linster, van de Gijp, van Ede, Bosselar, de Vries.

Saturday, January 18th, 1958
Football League, Third Division (Southern Section)
SOUTHEND UNITED 0, BRIGHTON & HOVE ALBION 2

'What we have we hold' was the Brighton motto at Roots Hall on Saturday, where smash and grab tactics paid dividends for the league leaders and sent Blues reeling into the lower half of the table once again. Someone somewhere must have a plan that can upset a side playing ten men in the penalty area solidly on defence. Whoever he is he's certainly not to be found in the United team, for there was no method or plan about their efforts to snatch a deserved equaliser.

Deserved only because they had so much of the game. The efforts to score were not so brilliant, especially by the front line men, and 'hit it and hope' seemed to be Blues only line of approach to the problem set by Brighton.

Brighton boss, Billy Lane, gambled in his team selection by dropping the club's leading scorer, Peter Harburn, and giving a League debut to 20-years-old centre forward Aubrey Thorne. Southend dropped Baron and re-called McCrory, while Barker came in for the injured McGuigan.

Thorne had a great debut, scoring after 17 minutes, having shown how dangerous he was likely to be with a snap shot on the turn after only two minutes. Barker's appearance on Blues left wing was not a success. Veteran Brighton full-back Des Tennant soon discovered that Barker seldom used his left foot for centres and this made the defender's job much easier.

New boy Duggie Price did not show the Roots Hall fans half the pace and fire he turned on for his debut at Colchester the previous week. There was, just once or twice, a hint of his speed, but his shooting ability and power he kept hidden. The fans would have been pleased to see how hard he can hit a ball, especially at that crucial moment just five minutes after Brighton had scored when Hollis cut a pass back and Price, running in, scooped a gentle shot straight at Gill.

Brighton snatched the lead after 17 minutes. United, all up in attack, were caught by a long clearance by Bates and Thorne raced down the middle to beat Threadgold as he advanced.

From that moment on almost nothing was seen of the Brighton forwards as far as orthodox approach work was concerned. They were too busy most of the time backing up overworked defensive colleagues in the Brighton goalmouth.

Yet for all their pressure Blues seldom looked like scoring and Brighton always looked dangerous in sudden and devastating breaks.

There was, for instance, the 10 minute spell just before half-time when Blues forced five corners in a row. Blues looked set for an equaliser and even Jim Stirling came up to try and force the ball home. Yet in the twinkling of an eye a Brighton boot had swung the ball way down field and the eager Thorne was chasing in for a second goal.

Threadgold, diving, blocked the ball which ran out to Gordon. Again it was Thorne who rose to nod Gordon's centre goalwards and Threadgold almost brought the house down with a wonderful leaping twisting dive to his right to snatch the ball down.

The second half parade of Blues defenders shunting forward to blast drives at, through and around a veritable forest of striped Brighton shirts became almost monotonous.

Brighton relieved the situation a couple of times. Once Anderson kicked a Sexton shot off the line, then Gordon broke away to fire across an open goal and, of course, Frankie Howard scored a second goal for Brighton with three minutes left to play.

The best of Southend's bids for a goal were chased off the line by Brighton defenders when Gill had been beaten. Ellis twice headed away scoring headers from Hollis, and Whitfield blocked a Duffy drive. Williamson, Anderson and Duffy put in some of the best shots of the match, but it too often looked as though the best Blues could hope for was an 'own-goal' from a sliced clearance or a mistimed header by a Brighton defender.

The goal that finally sealed the match was yet another break from defence to attack by Brighton. A quick through ball by Wilson sent in Sexton with a good chance. Threadgold managed to block the shot, but Howard, completely unhurried, steered the ball into the net off the far post.

SOUTHEND UNITED: Threadgold; Williamson, Anderson; Duffy, Stirling, Smith; Crossan, McCrory, Hollis, Price, Barker.

BRIGHTON: Gill; Tennant, Ellis; Bates, Whitfield, Wilson; Gordon, Sexton, Thorne, Foreman, Howard.

Referee, R.G. Warnke (Coventry); attendance, 10,631, paid £1,206 (11,665).

Saturday, October 24th, 1959
Football League, Third Division
SOUTHEND UNITED 7, TRANMERE ROVERS 1

This was United's biggest win at Roots Hall, but the goals came so easily that there was little excitement. And the opposition, particularly in defence, was so weak it was impossible to say if United had improved much on previous performances. But apart from the goals, which were a sight for sore eyes, the match was a treat to watch after the previous Monday's floodlight Cup debacle. Even after the ball had passed goalkeeper George Payne for the seventh time, Tranmere still tried to play football – completely clean football.

This Tranmere team was only a shadow of the side who took two points away from Roots Hall last season and then held Southend to a draw in the return match. It was pathetic at times to watch the way Southend ambled through a powerless, panic-stricken defence to give George Payne a nightmare. Roy Hollis, playing his first League game since September 14th, netted two of the seven goals which were shared by four of the five Southend forwards.

And despite a few cries of 'Granddad,' 34-years-old Roy is still a lot more effective leading the attack than either Lou Costello or Brian Houghton. Fast little Welshman, Duggie Price, had another wonderful game at inside-left, and gave United the lead with a beautifully taken goal.

It came in the ninth minute, after Hollis and young Bobby Kellard had come close to netting. Right-half Willie Morrison crashed in a McCrory pass first time and Payne could only push the ball away as he dived.

Price beat right-back Harold Bell, and his low shot curled inside the posts from a fantastic angle. Hollis made the second ten minutes later. He raced past centre-half Ralph Millington and squared the ball when only three yards out. It passed Price, but right-winger Alex Stenhouse was there to hammer it home. Payne did well to cover a Hollis shot soon afterwards as the Southend centre-forward ran on to another opportunist pass from skipper Sam McCrory.

In the 27th minute Price flicked the ball over Bell's head, moved round the right-back and headed over the line, it seemed. But Millington hooked the ball out and referee T.W. Dawes (Norwich) waved play on. Then Morrison was breaking through, his shot caught Payne out of position but was deflected wide by left-half Wilf Charlton, the only member of the Tranmere rearguard to have a good game. Three minutes from the break schemer McCrory hit his first. Hollis leapt to head down a Kellard corner and the skipper's side-footed shot swerved past Payne.

Tranmere played determinedly for just a few minutes after the re-start, and hit bad luck straight away. A centre from left-winger Ken McDevitt was headed against the bar by inside-right Keith Williams, and right-winger Ken Finney dived forward to head the rebound over the line, but the goal was disallowed for no apparent reason.

After 54 minutes Hollis headed number four. He jumped to head a Price centre, and Payne could only help the ball into the net as it flew towards the top corner. Tranmere claimed their consolation four minutes later. Left-half Wilf Charlton was standing just inside the penalty area when he headed a centre from Finney – and it was a winner all the way.

Williams came close to grabbing a second after 61 minutes but Threadgold flicked the winger's header over the bar. Then Williamson's boot stopped a shot from McDonnell, who was standing unmarked. McCrory added Southend's fifth when John Duffy stabbed a Stenhouse pass into the Tranmere goalmouth. The United skipper drove the ball over the line from five yards.

Price made it 6-1 10 minutes later. His shot flew off McDevitt and just inside a post as Payne moved the wrong way. A minute later Kellard nearly made the scoring line complete. But his shot was half stopped by Payne, and it needed Roy Hollis to slide the ball over the line for number seven.

SOUTHEND UNITED: Threadgold; Williamson, Anderson; Morrison, Watson, Duffy; Stenhouse, McCrory, Hollis, Price, Kellard.

TRANMERE ROVERS: Payne; Bell, Frith; Farrell, Millington, Charlton; Finney, Williams, Rowley, McDonnell, McDevitt.

Monday, October 26th, 1959
Southern Professional Floodlight Challenge Cup, 2nd Round, Re-play
COVENTRY CITY 4, SOUTHEND UNITED 0

Any hopes that a glamour club would visit Roots Hall in the third round of the Southern Floodlight Cup virtually disappeared a minute after the kick-off at Coventry on Monday night. Both sides fielded sadly understrength teams through injuries, and Coventry proved it was they who had the superior reserve strength. Only four of the team that thrashed Tranmere 7-1 last Saturday were in the Southend line-up.

In an after-the-game comment downcast manager Eddie Perry said: 'Of course I fielded the strongest side at my disposal; that is a rule of the competition. I wanted to see a club like the Arsenal at Southend in the next round, but that won't happen now.'

Coventry turned on the fireworks from the first whistle, and 6,813 spectators watched the shape of things to come when centre-forward Satchwell
blazed the ball inches over the bar.

Three minutes later, a creaking defence cracked. Right-winger Boxley slung
across a dangerous inswinging corner that Daley slammed home on the volley,
and from then on the men from the South were never in with a chance.

With the stopwatch showing eight minutes Coventry were two up when
right-half Nicholas caught the defence flat-footed to score his first goal for his
club since leaving Chelsea in January, 1958 – a lob over the advancing Tennant.
Reg Ryan, the Coventry skipper, was another ex-First Division man to give a
display as bright as the Coventry floodlights.

Mainly through his precision passes, Coventry had the ball in the net eight
times – four being judged offside.

The one-way traffic towards the Southend goal in the first half-hour was
jolted to a stop when Houghton raced up the field into the 18 yards box.
Goalkeeper Lightening swept his legs from under him, but any chance of the
score sheet taking on a respectable appearance vanished when Stenhouse
cracked the penalty against an upright and out of play.

Straight from the goal-kick, in four movements, Coventry's Simcoe had the
ball in the net for goal number three – and number four at 30 minutes came
from another Simcoe 12 yards volley. Only Costello and McCrory matched the
Midlanders in skill – but nobody should base the outcome of Saturday's match
on the same field on this performance.

The return of match-fit men should strengthen a Southend side whose display was too bad to be true.

COVENTRY: Lightening; Kirk, Austin; Nicholas, Ballard, Farmer; Boxley,
Simcoe, Satchwell, Ryan, Daley.

SOUTHEND: Tennant; Whale, Anderson; Costello, Walker, Smith;
Stenhouse, McCrory, Williamson, Stubbs and Houghton,

Monday, April 30th, 1962
Eastern Counties League
SOUTHEND UNITED 3, HARWICH & PARKESTON 3

Southend United Manager Ted Fenton introduced five young amateurs into
his Eastern Counties League side against Harwich and Parkeston at Roots Hall
on Monday, and for the first time this season used the League as it should be
used, as a starting ground for young players. Although the game itself was not
all that inspiring, the youngsters – especially inside-right Pat Donovan and
goalkeeper Terry O'Reilly – did reasonably well.

Frankie Banks started off at outside-right, but in the second half he
switched with W. Scarbrow to right-half, and showed himself as a real terrier
in defence and attack.

United took a 30 minute lead, when Williamson got the ball out to Pat Kerrins, who scored with a dipping shot. Four minutes later Southend increased their lead when Spenney beat the Harwich goalkeeper in a race for the ball, and lobbed an easy goal. Just before half-time R. Stevens reduced the arrears for Harwich, crashing the ball into the net from a left-wing corner.

Twelve minutes after the break Harwich left-half A. Eaton came steaming through the middle, and, with the Southend defence retreating, he sent in an unstoppable shot from the edge of the area. Southend gradually got back into the game and Pat Kerrins slammed home a great goal in the 70th minute to regain the lead.

Harwich left-winger M. Nicoll missed three 'sitters' before ex-Southend amateur Peter Palmer grabbed a well-deserved equaliser for Harwich five minutes from time. Teams: –

SOUTHEND: T. O'Reilly; Shiels, Duncan; W. Scarbrow, Costello, Williamson; F. Banks, P. Donovan, R. Spenney, McKinney, Kerrins.

HARWICH: E. Jones; C. Saunders, J. Smiles; D. Bacon, D. Candy, A. Eaton; D. Powell, P. Palmer, R. Stevens, R. Ryan, M. Nicoll.

Tuesday, May 1st, 1962
Essex Professional Cup Final
SOUTHEND UNITED 2, COLCHESTER UNITED 0

Southend United won the Essex Professional Cup for the fifth time on Tuesday, when they outplayed near neighbours Colchester in a tough, exciting struggle. The result was in doubt until 10 minutes from the end when, with Southend hanging on grimly to a 1-0 lead, Colchester were awarded a left-wing corner. As quick as lightning, United outside-right Billy Wall intercepted Peter Wright's flag kick, swept the ball upfield to Ken Jones, lurking in the open space, and he ran through to score and make the game safe for the Blues.

Justice was done, and Southend skipper Peter Watson was handed the handsome trophy by the Essex County Association Chairman (Mr. John W. Bowers) amid jubilation by success-starved United fans.

Colchester, who have won promotion from Division IV this term, were given a lesson in the art of fast, direct football and can thank their reserve goalkeeper George Ramage for not conceding at least five goals. Fielding four second-string players, Colchester were rationed to a mere two chances in front of goal, and their 40 goal inside-left, Bobby Hunt, was completely subdued by Southend's converted winger Tony Bentley.

The entire Southend defence was on top form, and the two reserves – goalkeeper Peter Goy and left-half Lou Costello – could not be faulted. All five Southend forwards worked as a unit, and the left-wing pair, John McKinven and Bobby Kellard, switched continuously to give Colchester's over-worked defence a real headache.

McKinven has not played better all season, and proved to his critics that he is still the best ball-playing inside-forward on the books. Centre-forward Ray Brand was slow, but combined well with Ken Jones in midfield to produce some wide open spaces in the Colchester defence.

Southend were worthy winners, and manager Ted Fenton must have taken great personal pride in this victory – his brother Benny manages Colchester! After 12 minutes of all-out attacking on the Colchester goal Southend took the lead, when McKinven picked the ball up on the half-way line and pushed a glorious pass to Kellard, moving into the inside-left position.

Bobby raced across field, holding off a tackle from Colchester's right-back, Richie Griffiths, and fired in a low shot, which did not rise more than six inches off the ground, into the corner of the net. Southend kept up the pressure, and from an Anderson free kick on the half-way line Fryatt moved up to nod the ball down. The ball ran loose, but Ramage hurled himself at Brand's feet to make a good save.

After 33 minutes Ramage excelled himself again when he threw himself down to stop a Brand header from Kellard's well-placed corner. Five minutes from half-time Kellard raced through the middle and sent Ramage scrambling across the face of the goal with a power drive from the edge of the area.

Jones went close with a good shot after the break, and in the 56th minute Ramage made two splendid saves from a Brand header and a low Jones drive.

Colchester's inside-right, Sammy McLeod, produced his side's best shot of the match 15 minutes from time, when he hit a right-wing corner on the volley only for Goy to save at the foot of a post.

Then with Colchester launching an all-out effort, came that match-winning Jones goal, and the final whistle went with schoolboys invading the pitch anxious to pat the eleven Southend stars on the back. Teams: –

SOUTHEND: Goy; Fryatt, Anderson; Bentley, Watson, Costello; Wall, Jones, Brand, McKinven, Kellard.

COLCHESTER: Ramage; Griffiths, Fowler; Rumney, Forbes, Brown; Foster, McLeod, Coleman, Hunt, R., Wright.

Sunday, May 26th, 1963
Friendly Match
CORK HIBERNIAN 1, SOUTHEND UNITED 2

The Blues got off to a fine start on their Irish tour, when they won their first game on Sunday. They beat Cork Hibernian 2-1, with goals from Ken Jones and John McKinven.

But the tour has had its disappointments for the Blues. Their namesakes, Southend United, for some unknown reason called off their fixture at Waterford, scheduled for Tuesday, and so reduced it to a rather unprofitable two-match trip.

The United party has had to wait from Monday until today (Thursday) for their other game, against Shamrock Rovers in Dublin.

Saturday, January 11th, 1964
Football League Third Division
QUEEN'S PARK RANGERS 4, SOUTHEND UNITED 5

Southend United Manager Ted Fenton may at last have come up with a front line permutation to save the Blues from relegation this season despite the fact that Saturday's goal glut at Loftus Road was mainly due to defensive errors.

Even allowing for their rearguard blunders, Rangers would have won this game against any other Southend attack fielded in recent weeks. Instead, they were bowled over, as I was, by five forwards who spared themselves nothing and who, for sheer tenacity, earned themselves what I hope proves their biggest morale-lifting victory this season.

And no matter how much defences were to blame, it needed tenacity to take both points from a team fiery enough to strike four times on their home ground. For the first time in what seems an age, I can say Manager Fenton's treble-chance pay-off lay in his inside trio of Smith, Conway and Beesley.

Right-winger Derek Woodley, in devastating form, set the match to the fire, and, for once, all responded and kept it raging to the end. The winger opened the scoring with the type of shot for which he had been long forgotten, and he went on to 'make' another goal, but after this start the inside-forwards took over, making and taking their chances in a way that was a sight for my sore eyes.

Leader Jim Conway with just one goal to his name in 10 games, put the Blues in front after Rangers equalised for the one and only time, and four minutes from the end he juggled in a picture goal with all the cocky confidence in the world.

Throughout the game, Conway and Smith worked well together, and although Smith was said to have got his place only because the ground would not have suited Ken Jones, he looks like keeping it. The inside-right also crowned a great game by grabbing an opportunist fourth goal. Mike Beesley, ousting Benny Friel at inside-left, did not score, but certainly earned his recall. Accurate, intelligent passing and fine positioning marked his performance, and when he was not adding weight to the attack he was plugging the defence.

Left-winger John McKinven, the creator of so many missed chances this season, laid on Conway's first goal, but had an otherwise unusually quiet game, which reflected credit on 19 years-old full-back Brian Taylor, who, with the irrepressible Mike Keen, was the only solid Rangers defender. But to see Southend succeed with McKinven blotted out also said a lot for this new forward line. Terry Bradbury made a fighting comeback, and Peter Watson was indispensable, despite twice being foxed by Stuart Leary late in the game.

Brian Rhodes saw the ball pass him four times, but he deputised magnificently for the injured Peter Goy. He always picked up cleanly and was not lacking in courage during some frenzied spells in the Blues' goalmouth.

So, after months of experimenting, Ted Fenton has produced one 90-minute showing of a potentially dangerous forward-line. Whether this form lasts remains to be seen, but certainly Rangers will remember this bright display by the Blues – a big difference to that at Roots Hall in September when Rangers won 3-1.

The difference was noticeable before the 14th minute, when Woodley laid the trail for United's first away win since August 31st. The winger was unmarked 25 yards out as Smith and Conway brought the ball through, and his searing drive, after Smith slipped the ball across, left young Peter Springett rooted to his goal-line as it hit the net. Woodley almost got a second in the same way soon after but this time Springett plucked the ball from under the bar.

Rangers levelled for the only time in the 27th minute when Lou Costello, hesitating, was robbed by Leary. He slipped the ball quickly inside to the fast-moving Bedford, who went on unchallenged to beat Rhodes.

Southend's spirit never flagged, and three minutes later they were in front to stay. Woodley crossed one to the far post, and as Springett and Taylor tried to shield it and let it run over for a goal kick, McKinven poked the ball from between them into an empty goalmouth, where Conway was waiting to push it over the line.

Rangers were completely off balance now, and it was more than emphasised after another two minutes lapse. Woodley drove Costello's short free kick hard and low across the goalmouth. Springett dived out and missed it completely, and amazed left-back Pat Brady sliced the ball into his own net.

Seventeen-year-old Greek right-winger Seth Vafiadis reduced the Blues' 3-1 interval lead in the 56th as the game developed into a battle royal. Rhodes did well to smother a Bedford shot, but the ball spun loose and the winger fired into an open net. The game flared up just before this, when Rangers thought the referee had ignored a Costello foul, and, as Woodley raced away with the ball he was up-ended and injured.

During this spell of openly-shown tempers, things were not improved when, moments after Vafiadis scored, frantic appeals for a penalty were turned down following a heavy tackle on Rangers' new signing George McLeod.

A minute after this – the 58th – Bradbury floated a free kick into the Rangers goalmouth, and Smith hooked it on the volley into the roof of the net to make it 2-4. Rangers made another penalty appeal when Tony Bentley broke up an attack and brought the ball away but again it was turned down.

Eleven minutes from time, Rangers once more reduced the Blues' two-goal lead when a McLeod centre was swerving wide and Watson let it go, but Leary racing in behind him, headed the ball like a bullet into the top of the net.

Conway made certain Blues would collect both points with the goal of the match in the 86th minute.

Smith gave him the pass, and the burly centre-forward nodded the ball over Springett's head and side-stepped Malcolm before slipping it into the net.

Goal-hungry supporters had had their fill, but in the last minute Stuart Leary beat Watson and let loose a 15-yard rising shot which Rhodes could only help into the net. Teams: –

QUEEN'S PARK RANGERS: Springett; Taylor, Brady (P.); Malcolm, Brady (R.), Keen; Vafiadis, Bedford, Leary, Graham, McLeod.

SOUTHEND UNITED: Rhodes; Costello, King; Bentley, Watson, Bradbury; Woodley, Smith, Conway, Beesley, McKinven.

Saturday, August 8th, 1964
Charity match
SOUTHEND UNITED 4, IPSWICH TOWN 2

There were few new faces to be seen in Southend United's pre-season window display at Roots Hall on Saturday, but the old ones were still good value for money as they licked the fallen idols of East Anglia, Second Division Ipswich Town.

The Blues' polished, at times classic, play was identical to that of the same time last year. Now, as then, it ponders the same question – can they sustain this stylish rhythm throughout the hurly-burly of the League programme?

They failed last season, as United teams over four decades have failed, but I hope, for the sake of club and supporters, that this time they can finally lose that much maligned record of being the only team never to have left the Third Division – and I mean by promotion, not relegation.

It would be a tonic, too, for people like myself who write about the possibility of success, which the Roots Hall crowds crave and pray for, and then weekly print how that possibility grows smaller.

With all the inaccurate crystal ball gazing of the past, it would be a foolish man who would predict Southend's fate in the next nine months.

Mid-way through the season, it should need no insight to know exactly which way the Blues are headed, and whether rising or sliding, that will be the time to comment on the club's efforts.

At this stage, one can only recall Manager Ted Fenton's statement that he is confident of his players, and that his words were certainly borne out by Saturday's display.

Of the three new signings making their first Roots Hall display, goalkeeper Ian McKechnie was undoubtedly the best of them, and his tremendous drop kicks, if well placed, could be a surprise source of danger during the season. Young Scottish trialist Jim McDonald, who played at inside-left in the first half, was out of touch through the pace of the game as much as anything else, and although left-wing partner Howe had a better time, he was completely overshadowed by his second-half replacement, young apprentice Derek Ewing. Because of his inexperience, Ewing's performance stands out from the rest. He played with tenacious confidence and ability, brilliantly laid on a goal for Ray Smith, and looked more like the natural understudy for John McKinven than Howe. The other top-class performance came from transfer seeking right-back Lou Costello, wing-halves Tony Bentley and Terry Bradbury, and Derek Woodley on the right-wing. These four especially found all the holes in a ragged Ipswich defensive net, and Woodley, in particularly fiery mood, made left-back Mick McNiel look worth nowhere near the £15,000 the Suffolk club recently splashed out for him.

Taken all round, the game left Ipswich manager Jack Milburn with seemingly far more problems than Ted Fenton. Saturday's result was a reversal of a 26-years-old scoreline, for when Ipswich came up from the Southern League in 1938, Southend provided their first opposition, and they won 4-2.

At Roots Hall, Ipswich opened the scoring through their best combination of inside-right Danny Hegan and centre-forward Gerry Baker. In the sixth minute, soon after hitting a post, Hegan pulled a ball back for Baker to blaze home from the edge of the 'box.' But it was a short-lived lead.

Six minutes later United captain Tony Bentley proved the benefit of shooting at every opportunity when he picked up a loose ball in midfield and smashed a 30-yard drive past goalkeeper Roy Bailey.

After another two-minute lapse, Ipswich centre-half Jack Bolton, racing back to beat off a challenge from Bobby Gilfillan and Jim Conway, hooked the ball into his own net to put the Blues in front.

Southend came close to going further ahead several times before the 35th minute, when McDonald picked up a Howe pass. He hammered it across the goal, Bailey pushed it out, but straight to Conway, who was quick to nod it back over the goal-keeper's head.

In the second half, with Smith coming in at inside-right, Mike Beesley at inside-left and Gilfillan switching to centre-forward, Southend had a more powerful inside trio, but less accuracy in their finishing.

It was the enthusiasm of young Ewing which brought them their final goal in the 51st minute. He beat off two tackles and managed to pull the ball back at the last moment for Ray Smith, who headed it home on the run.

Ipswich left-winger Frank Brogan made the score look respectable nine minutes later when he held off Peter Watson and slipped the ball slowly past the advancing McKechnie. Teams –

UNITED: McKechnie; Costello, King; Bentley, Watson, Bradbury; Woodley, Gilfillan (Smith), Conway (Gilfillan), McDonald (Beesley), Howe (Ewing).

IPSWICH: Bailey (Thorburn); Davin (Carberry), McNiel; Baxter, Bolton, Dougan; Blackwood, Hegan (Colrain), Baker, Colrain (Leadbetter), Brogan.

Attendance: 3,060.

Saturday, November 7th, 1964
Football League, Third Division
SOUTHEND UNITED 6, COLCHESTER UNITED 3

These goals so earnestly sought away from home came again in a flood at
Roots Hall on Saturday to send neighbouring Colchester nose-diving still further into obscurity.

In the Blues last home game three weeks ago Bristol Rovers, who took over
the League leadership on Saturday, went crashing to the same tune, and, if
there was any consolation for crumbling Colchester, that was it.

Colchester, like Bristol, took a quick lead – in the fifth minute – but were
then tortured, tormented and finally mockingly tantalised into clumsy defeat,
until, for 10 minutes near the end, they gallantly mustered what remained of
their pride to score twice more through forwards who were effective enough
when given the chance. And they had very few chances after trying to put out
the Blues fire with that early goal inspired by their man-of-the-match, inside-
right Arthur Longbottom.

But undoubtedly the man of the match was once again Southend's
Malcolm Slater. A miserable-looking left-back John Fowler, noted for his
crunching tackles, never came close to stopping the right-winger, who was
constantly prompted, for ever nudged on, by the clean, cool-thinking distribution of inside partner Andy Smillie.

On the opposite flank lay the goalscorers, inside-left Bobby Gilfillan, who
slammed in four with a calm anticipation which I hope will stay with him, and
winger John McKinven, who, like Slater and Fowler, toyed with the experienced Duncan Forbes, and at times 'lost' him altogether, twice to hit the
remaining goals.

The Southend defence rarely had its work cut out and coasted so leisurely
through this local derby that full-backs John Neal and Lou Costello were able
to lay on three of Gilfillan's goals, but were caught napping by Colchester's
surprising, late come-back.

Two youngsters one could only sympathise with were the visitors' 18-year-
old goalkeeper Alan Buck, and 21-year-old centre-half Michael Loughton,
making his League debut, who remained competent and commendably cool
under pressure, which caused a few others, more experienced, to lose their
heads.

Only in the opening couple of minutes was young Loughton unsure of
himself, and a back-header from Ray Smith which went inches wide was the
closest Southend's leader was to come to scoring.

It was immediately following this that Colchester rushed into a surprise
lead. Longbottom switched the ball to recalled right-winger Barry Aitchison, it
came loose in the penalty area as he tried to walk through three Southend
defenders, and leader Pat Connolly drove it in from 15 yards.

When Southend equalised after 10 minutes Colchester wilted like a punctured balloon. Andy Smillie slipped a Slater corner across the goalmouth to McKinven, and the winger hit the ball perfectly first time.

The Blues were in front to stay four minutes later. Neal swept upfield and sent across a probing centre which young Buck could only push out as it swerved, and Bobby Gilfillan slammed the ball back past him for the first of his four goals, which included a hat-trick.

McKinven was in the middle to blast home a Ray Smith centre from short range soon afterwards, and from trailing, Southend had zipped in three in six minutes to take over completely.

In the 25th minute skipper Tony Bentley headed a Slater centre narrowly over the top, and two minutes later another full-blooded Gilfillan shot from McKinven's corner was kicked off the line by Forbes.

Colchester started to recover slightly from the lightning reversal of fortunes after half an hour, and when left-back John Docherty put Longbottom through, Southend goalkeeper Ian McKechnie had his first piece of real action in diving at the inside-forward's feet to rob him just inside the penalty area.

But Slater came agonisingly close four minutes later with a left-footed drive after bursting round Fowler, and in the 37th minute he set one up for Smillie, whose shot was turned round a post.

McKechnie punched away a Connolly lob two minutes after this, and did well to cover Docherty's crushing follow-up volley.

Colchester were sent recoiling again after these odd flashes of retaliation by another Gilfillan goal on the stroke of half-time. Yet another Slater centre came across, and Southend's inside-left rose high above out-classed right-half Derek Trevis to nod the ball into the top of the net.

Young Buck went down brilliantly to get in the way of a lightning, low shot from McKinven in the 53rd minute, and Forbes quickly turned the ball round the corner.

The respite lasted only another two minutes before Gilfillan was there again, Neal once more raced upfield on to a McKinven pass, Loughton failed to head away his centre, and Gilfillan calmly breasted the ball down before blasting it past the unhappy Buck.

It was only now, 5-1 down, that Colchester started to play with a vengeance. McKechnie pushed a Garry Salisbury shot round a post and two minutes later dropped another drive from the inside-left, but there was nobody to take advantage of it.

A 20-yard Trevis free-kick in the 65th minute cannoned off McKechnie's chest out to Aitchison, but the winger screwed his shot inches wide.

Colchester's hardest worker, Longbottom, got the first of the late goals their pluck deserved when, in the 71st minute, he fastened expertly on to a Connolly pass and blazed the ball past McKechnie from just inside the penalty area.

Their third goal in the 77th minute this time came from Connolly, who pounced and bundled the ball into the net when McKechnie let Longbottom's centre slip.

But just one minute later Southend planted the seal very firmly on this game that Colchester desperately wanted, and needed, to win, when Gilfillan dashed in to volley a Lou Costello free-kick into the roof of the net. Teams :-

SOUTHEND UNITED: McKechnie; Costello, Neal; Bentley, Watson, Bradbury; Slater, Smillie, Smith, Gilfillan, McKinven.

COLCHESTER UNITED: Buck; Forbes, Fowler; Trevis, Loughton, Docherty; Aitchison, Longbottom, Connolly, Salisbury, Grice.

CHAPTER TWELVE

Brighton and Hove Albion F.C.

Although Northampton Town have scored more goals (19) in any two matches against the United (1-11 in 1909-10 and 0-8 in 1923-24), Brighton and Hove Albion remain the only club to have twice scored nine goals against the Blues in a League match.

Saturday, April 6th, 1912
South Eastern League, First Division
BRIGHTON & HOVE ALBION RESERVES 9, SOUTHEND UNITED 0

On Saturday Southend had to send a team to Brighton to play Brighton and Hove Albion Reserves in the return South Eastern League match. As the first eleven did not get back to Paddington until too late to catch any connection to Brighton, a very mixed eleven had to do duty, as the following list of players will show:- Chinnery; Layzell and Harrod; R. Chapman, J. Cooper and Cane; J. Goose, S. Shrier, Holman, V. Walters and W.W.T. Whistler. For sixty minutes of the game Southend did well. Chinnery played a magnificent game in goal, and received quite an ovation at the interval, which arrived with Brighton a goal up.

In the second half Cane got injured and had to be carried off, and it was after this that the Southend collapse set in. Brighton had to obtain eight goals to complete their century for the season in the South Eastern League and they went for all they were worth. There was a crowd of about five thousand present and when the home side completed the century there was a scene of great enthusiasm. The final score was Brighton, 9; Southend, 0.

Saturday, November 27th, 1965
Football League, Third Division
BRIGHTON & HOVE ALBION 9, SOUTHEND UNITED 1

There must have been many moments of sadness in the long playing history of Southend United. But few, if any, could have been sadder than this sorry display on the Goldstone Road Ground on Saturday. It was murder.

This must surely have been the ultimate in United's 90 minutes of shame and humiliation. And let me say straight away – this was NO parody of justice in the score-line. Brighton COULD have had another two or three goals quite easily and STILL been good value for a win by a higher margin.

It is a problem where to start after such a shocking exhibition! It would be so easy to blame young Ray White in goal; but, while he was at fault on more than one occasion, he received as much cover and protection from those in front of him as a parasol would give in a gale-force wind and thunderstorm combined.

The defence was as full of holes as a string vest and was pierced just as easily. Up front the forwards were little, if any, better, being so ineffective that the game was 32 minutes old before they saw the white of the Brighton goalposts. Just HOW ineffective they were can be seen from a recital of their so-called scoring efforts. That 32nd minute was a weak and wide shot from Malcolm Slater and was the ONLY approach to the home goal in the first 45 minutes.

Five minutes after the interval Derek Woodley (brought in at centre-forward) centred across the face of the goal with not another forward in sight, and in the 56th minute young Chris Barnard had the best United shot brilliantly saved.

Mel Slack, one of the very few Blues players NOT made to look silly, was rewarded for his efforts in the 72nd minute, when he took a pass inside from the right, took three or four steps then unleashed an unstoppable shot from nigh on 30 yards that was in the net before the 'keeper could move. But by then Brighton were six in front.

Then two good attempts from John McKinven in the 84th minute, the first being saved with difficulty and the second turned over the bar for a corner. And that was Southend United, that was!

But for the rest of the game it was Brighton all the way. They were superior in every department and hammered home that superiority at every opportunity once they got their noses in front and found that they were meeting with only token opposition.

Not one of the home side had a bad game (they were not allowed to), but their strength and solidarity could be seen in all departments.

Eire international right-back Jimmy Magill, signed from Arsenal earlier this season, was a tower of confidence to the rest of the defence. Right-half Derek Leek, having his first game since being signed from Northampton, was at the back of most attacking moves, and much-travelled Charlie Livesey was a continual threat at centre-forward.

But, then, United were so poor that ANYBODY would have been a threat against them on this display.

Brighton had obviously set their target long before the 11,124 spectators started their chant of 'We want 10; we want 10.' And yet most of their nine goals were more the result of shocking defensive tactics and errors than as a result of their own contrivance.

All their goals came in three bouts of three. They got the first three in a 14-minute spell in the first half, their second three in a four-minute burst after an hour's play and their final three in a hectic last five minutes.

The seventh minute started the scoring spree, when Magill whipped a long ball into the goalmouth. It was headed out, but then three United defenders stood flatfooted as Jimmy Collins belted it home from six yards. Eight minutes later outside-left Goodchild took an inswinging corner which White turned into his own net as he was challenged by a couple of forwards.

Another six minutes and right-winger Gould half-volleyed a left-wing cross from the edge of the box with never a challenge being offered.

The 59th minute set off the second bout of fireworks when inside-left Smith cracked one in from close range after two shots had been cleared off the line.

Two minutes later he went through for another with the United defence in one of their many tangles and another two minutes saw Goodchild hit a cross-shot past White as the 'keeper came out to narrow the angle.

Then came Slack's goal and five minutes later skipper Terry Bradbury was carried off after a tackle, and Bobby King substituted in the forward-line with Andy Smillie dropping back to wing-half.

But United's humiliation was not yet complete! There was still that nightmare last five minutes to face. It was the Brighton left-back, Baxter, who lobbed a long centre for Livesey to climb and head down into the net in the 85th minute.

Three minutes later Smith got his third goal with a piledriver from 25 yards and Livesey ended the unhappy saga in the last minute, when he ran on to a through-pass from Collins to slip the ball past White.

There was just not any more time left to give the home supporters their request for 'We want ten.' But United had been counted out long before the final whistle granted them reprieve in the solitude of their dressing-room.
Teams: –

BRIGHTON: Powney; Magill and Baxter; Leek, Gall and Turner; Gould, Collins, Livesey, Smith and Goodchild.

SOUTHEND: White; Bentley and Neal; Slack, May and Bradbury (King); Slater, Barnard, Woodley, Smillie and McKinven.

CHAPTER THIRTEEN

A Selection of Match Reports 1966-2003

Friday, March 29th, 1968
Football League, Fourth Division
SOUTHEND UNITED 7, WORKINGTON 0

Statisticians were in their element at Roots Hall on Friday night as 13,970 fervent fans roared on United in a footballing fiesta which brought them four goals in the first half and three in the second without reply to register their biggest League victory since the war. It all happened after the shakiest start I have seen Blues forced to endure during most of this season, and, believe it or not, there were many among the crowd who became Oliver Twistish in repeatedly asking for more.

With no records at our elbows in the Press box, memory failed to recall any League victory by so wide a margin as this, certainly not in the post-war era. The nearest one could get to a similar goal feat was United's 9-2 win at Barnet in an F.A. Cup-tie shortly after the war.

But this United performance and goal margin could not have come at a better time. The win consolidated their second place in the Fourth Division table and the margin took them to third highest home scorers to give their goal average the boost it so badly needed.

And, although I had forecast a big win on this occasion, I began to have my doubts in those early stages as Workington started off like a house on fire.

Graham Birks had to concede a first-minute corner as he kicked a Holliday centre off Greig's toe in front of goal. Holliday, who created most of the opening trouble, then shot high over following a good run; Kirkman mishit his shot from another Holliday pass and Birks gave away another corner in attempting a pass back to Trevor Roberts.

It looked even worse when John McKinven, having recovered from a belt in the ribs, lobbed wide of the posts with goalkeeper Ower stranded on his own penalty spot after his defence had been caught out appealing for off-side and McKinven and Andy Smillie were left clear on their own.

But the Workington reprieve was only temporary as United went into a 17th-minute lead. Smillie sent Billy Best away on the right wing and then galloped on into the middle to be right on the spot when the cross came over to side-foot it into the net.

Then came 12 minutes of prop and cop before United really took the bit between their teeth and asserted their authority with a spell of three goals in six minutes. New boy Eddie Clayton, making his home debut, had the crowd on their feet as sheer persistency and personal ability brought United's second goal. He ploughed his way through on the right, twice recovering balls from tackles he might well have succumbed to, before angling his drive just inside the far post.

Best got the next one four minutes later, just after Mel Slack had powered one over the top. Clayton pushed a useful-looking ball through the middle and Best latched on to it to shoot first time and Ower could only help the ball into the net. Two minutes later, McKinven made up for his earlier miss when he smashed in a short-range effort after Smillie had headed down to him a Birks free-kick.

Workington's best player at this stage was Tinnion, brought on as substitute for the injured Butler, just as United opened their scoring account. United could easily have had another couple before the half-time whistle from referee R.V. Spittle (Caister-on-Sea), as Slack had a good effort saved and Smillie a slide-rule lob tipped over the bar.

Workington's best attempt was just before the interval, when Trevor Roberts pushed a shot from Tinnion round the post for a corner.

Flushed with the half-time scoreline, it was an anticipatory crowd who eagerly awaited the second half. And they were not disappointed. A minute after the game restarted, McKinven waltzed his way past two defenders on the left before powering an unstoppable shot into the far corner of the net.

Eddie May headed wide from a McKinven centre shortly afterwards and then surprised even himself in the 53rd minute by heading in United's sixth from a Birks free-kick to take the Blues to their highest score of the season and celebrate his own 100th League appearance.

With just over half-an-hour to go the natives became restless as McKinven shot just past the far post after another brilliant run and Mike Beesley nodded one in which skimmed the bar after Smillie had pin-pointed the cross.

But starved for most of the season of a goal-glut, the Oliver Twisties were far from happy with the interim between May's sixth goal and the last by Clayton two minutes from the end to complete the scoring. Best rolled the ball back to the edge of the penalty area and Clayton made no bones about banging it into the back of the net.

A brief summary would show that Clayton soon made himself a firm favourite with the crowd and his two goals merely finalised a capital all-round display. His mere presence, and the effect it had on the other players, will for ever remain merely a matter of opinion. But I, for one, am certain that his being there has lifted everyone's performance by a lot more than a little.

Of course, there were faults, some of which stood out like a sore thumb and have done for most of the season. But it would be carping criticism to try to take anyone to task after such a convincing win.

I can sympathise with both sides of the fence in this case. First with the great crowd which rallied round United in such splendid fashion until the going became too easy. And, let's face it, Blues will meet few defences as weak as this one was. The fans soon appreciated this situation and began howling for blood as soon as the scoring rate slumped, much in the manner of cricketing crowds. The score might have been into double figures and would still not have been too complimentary to United's superiority. But, after all, seven isn't a bad score to have beneath your belts when you come off the field at the final whistle. The situation must have been equally as embarrassing for the players. They at last showed the killer instinct by their approach to the game and the way they rattled up the goals.

SOUTHEND: Roberts; Bentley and Birks; McMillan, May and Slack; Chisnall, Best, Smillie, Clayton and McKinven. Sub. Stevenson.

WORKINGTON: Ower; Tugman and Butler (Tinnion); Kirkman, Flynn and Geidmintis; Greig, McLean, Spencer, Griffin and Holliday.

Tuesday, August 13th, 1968
Football League Cup, 1st Round
BOURNEMOUTH & BOSCOMBE ATHLETIC 1, SOUTHEND UNITED 6

Southend United turned in a magnificent display to thrash Bournemouth 6-1 at Dean Court on Tuesday evening in the First Round of the Football League Cup.

It was their biggest away victory since 1957-58 when they beat Exeter 5-0 in Division III (South). United were three up at the break with goals from McKinven, Chisnall and Kurila, Best and Clayton netted in the second half before Bournemouth got a consolation, but Blues got a sixth before the close through Clayton to clinch an easy passage into the second round.

With both teams opting for a 4-3-3 formation this First Round of the Football League Cup at Dean Court on Tuesday soon developed into a stalemate. The tactics of each team were so similar that early on it looked as though a definite result would be a coincidence.

The United defence was compact in the early stages and Lawrie Leslie was called upon only to deal with long-distance efforts. Billy Best and Andy Smillie were prominent when Blues went over to attack.

It was United who grabbed the all-important opening goal after 14 minutes. Tony Bentley and Phil Chisnall covered 50 yards in the build up before Smillie's centre from the right was scooped into the net by John McKinven.

Once in the lead, United took control and netted twice more without reply before the game was 30 minutes old. Chisnall increased the lead after 22 minutes when he netted from the edge of the area.

Graham Birks sent Smillie through on the left and the ensuing centre had goalkeeper Jones coming out in an attempt to clear. But he only managed to slice the ball to Chisnall who was left facing an empty net.

John Kurila made it three after 29 minutes when he headed in from a McKinven corner.

Blues had overran a demoralised defence while still managing to retain a seven-man rear line of their own when Bournemouth broke. Keeper Leslie had to make only one really great effort in the first half.

Adams replaced East in the Bournemouth line-up for the second half. But it was United who went further ahead after 52 minutes. Eddie Clayton started the move from the half-way line with a great cross-field pass which split the home defence. Smillie was left clear on the right and his centre cleared a lone defender for Best to head accurately past Jones.

Blues went nap right on the hour from the third of three successive Smillie left-wing corners in a minute. Kurila had worried the defence as they all landed at the near post and, from the third, the ball ran loose to Clayton, who shot high into the net from six yards.

Two minutes after the third goal Mike Beesley came on to replace McKinven, who had been injured earlier. Completely in command, United paid for their over-confidence when Bournemouth reduced the arrears after 80 minutes. A quick ball through the middle had three defenders leaving it to each other as Hold dashed between them to score.

Clayton completed the scoring five minutes from the end. After an interchange of passes with Best he calmly walked round Jones before shooting into the empty net. United's only defensive lapse was excusable in such a magnificent display. This was one of the best combined United efforts for many years. Congratulations to Manager Ernie Shepherd and his 'system' and the team for the way they played it but, when it all boiled down, it simply meant that every man pulled his weight and gave a little extra.

BOURNEMOUTH: Jones; Miller, J. White, Stocks and Naylor; Bumstead, K. White and Pound; East, Hold and Peters. Sub. Adams.

SOUTHEND: Leslie; Bentley, Birks, McMillan and Stone; Kurila, Clayton and Best; Smillie, Chisnall and McKinven. Sub. Beesley.

Saturday, November 16th, 1968
F.A. Challenge Cup, 1st Round
SOUTHEND UNITED 9, KING'S LYNN 0

The Slaughter of the innocents! That, to use a trite expression and with due respect to the opposition, just about sums up United's first round F.A. Cup victory at Roots Hall on Saturday, which took them beyond this stage for the first time for three seasons.

Four goals in the first half and five in the second, without any response from the visitors, tells its own story. In fact, so great was Blues' superiority it was only a galaxy of goals that would have served to satisfy the bulk of United fans in the crowd of 9,983, the fourth largest 'gate' of the 40 ties.

These Southern Leaguers were not a bad side; they could play much worse and still win the Championship. They might have scored in their first attack in the first minute and, despite United going ahead two minutes after the start, were still in with a chance and fighting back boldly until another two United goals between the 26th and 29th minutes really knocked the stuffing out of them.

Then an own goal six minutes before half-time to put Blues four in front settled the issue and the second half was merely a formality of how many United would win by.

To anyone connected with United and their promotion hopes, there is a danger of falling between two schools of thought if the scoreline is to be the only consideration.

On the one hand, such a massive victory could lead to the self-assurance of complacency that they are the best team in the country – or, at least in the division. The other point of view is that the opposition was so poor that anything less than nine would have been unthinkable.

I prefer to take the middle view. As former United favourite Reg Davies, now their player-manager, remarked after the game: 'We could have played defensively and lost by two or three goals; we played our normal attacking game and lost by nine. But at least we hope the crowd had an entertaining game to watch and got their moneysworth.' And nine goals against ANY opposition is not bad going. They still have to be chiselled out and banged in.

The most gratifying part of the result from my point of view was not the final score, but the way it was achieved. United started by paying the visitors the compliment of going all out from the first to the final whistle and never underestimating them.

Not many League sides in this round would have stood up to a United in this form. They were tight at the back (despite a few, tiny cracks which appeared occasionally), masterly in midfield and penetrating up front.

And without detracting from the performances of any of the other players, it was the professionalism and application of Eddie Clayton and Phil Chisnall which really stamped its mark on the game.

United 'officially,' as far as one could see, opted for their normal 4-2-4 line up. But with Chisnall taking over from the Cup-tied Dave Chambers, it eventually turned out to be a 4-2-1-3, with Chisnall the odd man out (or in) coming from the back with telling effect after his midfield perambulations.

Clayton and Chisnall are much of a muchness in football style and ability. It was their distribution which prompted most of United's attacks. If Chisnall could ever turn his advantage of years over Clayton into yards of thought and action then he would not be worried about gaining a regular place in United's team – he would be back in the First Division.

Between them, these two, for me, form the complete professional footballer! And they have the advantage of being able to make the others play, too. The game, itself, needs little description, apart from the goals. Lynn kicked off and forced an immediate corner from a position which could have opened their account. And, apart from Malcolm Lindsay heading over from a Davies free-kick after 22 minutes, this was just about their sum attacking total of chances in the first 15 minutes.

They were even more out of it after the interval, when their two wing-halves David Brooks and skipper Micky Wright (making his 418th consecutive appearance for them) continued to attack – leaving big gaps in the middle – and had one or two long-range efforts which were well off target. The rest of the game was United's. United's goal time-table tells the story.

Two minutes: Chisnall intercepted a bad Lynn pass, pushed a beautiful square ball for Gary Moore to run on to and hammer in from the edge of the box past goalkeeper Norman Coe.

26 minutes: Another Chisnall interception, a low cross from the left and Billy Best cracked it home from about four yards after his first effort had rebounded from the goalkeeper.

29 minutes: Clayton beat three men in a crossfield run before pinpointing a through ball to the left for Chisnall to hit it past Coe from a narrow angle.

39 minutes: Chico Hamilton slung over a long centre from the right and Lynn right-back Tony Haskins, trying to head behind for a corner, only managed to steer it past his own 'keeper.

62 minutes: After Southend had forced three corners, Best had headed into Coe's arms and Moore had had a 'goal' disallowed for hands, Best was on the spot to flick in a Hamilton pass after Chisnall had started the move.

72 minutes: Best again on the spot to nudge the ball in from Hamilton after he had started the move himself.

80 minutes: Moore used his weight to bundle the ball in after John Kurila had headed on a Hamilton corner.

81 minutes: A mishit clearance went straight to Chisnall on the edge of the penalty area and his shot hardly left the ground as it found its way inside a post.

89 minutes: Tony Bentley made another of his many overlapping runs on the right, remembered his schooling as a winger and pinpointed his centre for Moore to outjump a set of defenders and nod neatly into the net.

Take into account the disallowed 'goals' of Moore and Chisnall (this looked a good 'un in the first half), the times efforts hit the 'keeper (who could not be blamed for those which beat him) and Lynn can have no regrets for the margin of their defeat.

Congratulations to the entire United team for an all-out display which should do wonders for the moral of themselves and their supporters, and, after Clayton and Chisnall, particularly to Moore on his three-goal Cup debut for United.

All those who have been hollering for a big 'un for years are now going to say 'I told you so,' and, I must say, he is proving them right up to now. And praise, too, for Billy Best, now beginning to buzz at his busiest, for his three goals.

SOUTHEND: Roberts, Bentley, Birks, McMillan, Beesley, Kurila, Clayton, Best, Moore, Chisnall and Hamilton. Sub. Baber.

KING'S LYNN: Coe, Haskins, Mullet, Brooks, Porter, Wright, Savino, Davies, Lindsay, Jenkins and Clarke. Sub. Hawksby.

Referee: Mr. J.H. Yates (Redditch).

Saturday, April 5th, 1969
Football League Fourth Division
SOUTHEND UNITED 0, GRIMSBY TOWN 1

United for promotion? This optimistic slogan must have produced the biggest horse-laugh of the Easter holidays for the 9,750 spectators who witnessed this sorry spectacle at Roots Hall on Saturday. I can honestly say, with little fear of contradiction, that this was one of the worst displays from a Southend side that it has ever been my misfortune to have to sit through.

And to make matters worse Grimsby had little to offer, seemed resigned to having to apply for re-election and were not very interested in the proceedings. Yet they still managed to take both points for the first time after seven visits to Roots Hall.

At three o'clock, United's promotion hopes, if not very bright, were at least fair to middling. An hour-and-a-half later, after a puerile and putrid display had reached rock bottom, there was little, if anything, to be said in their favour.

It was unfortunate for Blues that goalkeeper Trevor Roberts and skipper Eddie Clayton were both unfit. But Lawrie Leslie and Sammy McMillan should have been more than capable and experienced deputies. Phil Chisnall and John Baber were introduced into the forward line and Micky Beesley named as substitute. But once Baber had an early knock it was only a question of time before he was withdrawn permanently and Beesley took over after 38 minutes.

Add to United's troubles the fact that Graham Birks asked to be and was duly sent off by referee R.A. Paine (Hounslow) after 67 minutes and that should probably supply sufficient excuses for United's defeat. But even taking all these incidents into account, they should still have finished up with a big winning margin. The number of scoring chances they missed could only have been equalled by those which went adrift in the last home game against Scunthorpe.

Grimsby had only one near-miss in the first half, when Birks headed a Keith Jobling header from a Stuart Brace corner off the line. But the rest of the half belonged almost entirely to United. Chisnall set one chance up on a plate for former Mariners' centre-forward, Gary Moore, who for the first time in many games, was too slow to accept it. And this was the start of United's tale of woe!

A Moore header from a Birks centre was just wide; Baber hit goalkeeper John Macey after a Billy Best pass had left him clear, Best, himself, headed a

Chisnall centre just over the bar and then a minute later shot wide from in front of an open goal.

Grimsby had three tentative attempts before Beesley replaced Baber and then Best, three times in four minutes before the interval, was off target. First he headed over another centre from Chisnall, then he tapped a centre from Chico Hamilton into Macey's hands before left-footing well wide after being put clean through.

And, of course, the inevitable had to happen in the second half, with Grimsby bringing on Gordon Walker for Mike Hickman.

Moore was just wide from the restart and a Best header from Hamilton hit Macey and bounced out before Birks got his marching orders. He was involved with Town's Stuart Brace, retaliated when provoked, and was the one to be seen and sent off.

But even with ten men, United were still a better side when it came to the arts and crafts. Brace had his name taken, Dave Worthington cleared a header off the line, and Leslie saved well from Brace before the latter scored the winning goal. The tall, gangling Walker, pushed a long ball into an open space, Leslie came out, and Brace slotted the ball into the net from way out despite the unavailing attempts of John Kurila to overtake it.

And that was just about that! Beesley had a goal disallowed after belting in following a corner after the referee had consulted a linesman and United had another 'goal' disallowed with little objection. Teams:

SOUTHEND: Leslie, Lindsey, Birks, Bentley, McMillan, Kurila, Chisnall, Best, Moore, Hamilton and Baber (Beesley).

GRIMSBY: Macey, Worthington, Duncliffe, Campbell, Jobling, Ross, Brace, Davidson, Hickman (Walker), Boylen, Cockburn.

Monday, May 4th, 1970
Friendly Match
SOUTHEND UNITED 0, FIORENTINA 1

Beaten they may have been. But at least Blues signed off the season with a glimmer of hope for the future against globe-trotting AC Fiorentina. It must be remembered that the lira-laden Italian club won their own domestic championship last year, and less than a couple of months ago still had an interest in the European Cup before bowing out to the might of Celtic. Admittedly they were without two of their stars – they are winging their way to Mexico – but they still possessed players who have campaigned with some success throughout the Continent.

Among them was Amarildo, the former Milan forward who helped guide Brazil to their World Cup triumph eight years ago. So, as far as Southend are concerned, there was no disgrace in defeat. Indeed, they have every reason to be satisfied with their performance. Roared on by an 8,679 crowd, the biggest at Roots Hall for many months, they turned in a display which helped one forget the miseries of a disappointing season. Certainly in terms of entertainment the match had more value for money than most of their League encounters.

And it was good to see that United took the field without an inferiority complex. They may have lacked the finesse of their opponents, but they more than made up for it with sheer endeavour.

As expected, Fiorentina brought with them the defensive wall which is part and parcel of the Italian game. Whenever they lost possession, they threw up a shield of seven men around their goal, but that is not to say they were purely defensive.

Far from it. It was not just a case of contain and counter. Whenever the opportunity presented itself they moved forward with grace and efficiency, and Lloyd had to be constantly on the alert, particularly from the powerful shooting of left winger Luciano Chiarugi. He was a constant source of trouble to the United rearguard and together with Mariani on the opposite flank often had Blues' defence at full stretch.

The big difference between the sides lay in speed of thought and limb. The Italians always had the extra yard of pace on the ball and in a split second knew what to do when in possession.

In contrast, United were that little too deliberate and did not have the knack of playing the ball on to a man while in full flight. Something at which the Italians, by their speedy and thrustful excursions, were very proficient.

Despite the agile brain of the swarthy Amarildo, United more than held their own in midfield. Chisnall, who in recent weeks has played a prominent part in Blues' successful fight in staving off re-election, was always on hand to keep prompting his forwards, while Moore could often be found deep denying Fiorentina control.

And when Blues were really on the move forward, it was refreshing to see full-backs Lindsey and Simpson coming through to add strength on the flanks. Indeed, it was the tactic which caused most consternation in the Italians' ranks, and more than once they were reduced to panic as the ball floated across the face of the goal. But thanks to Salvatore Esposito, Bernardo Rogora and Bandoni they held firm when pressure was at its fiercest.

At the back for Blues, young Barnett did a fine job in containing the experienced Mario Maraschi, while Beesley turned in one of his best displays. He was always in the thick of things, breaking up dangerous Italian raids with first time tackling and pushing the ball forward to set his own side in motion.

The goal which gave Fiorentina their victory came midway through the opening half and was an object lesson in timing and simplicity. Amarildo gained the ball in midfield and then bided his time before delivering an inch-perfect pass to Mariani, streaking down towards goal. Then the right winger shook off a couple of tackles before slamming the ball out of the reach of Lloyd into the far corner of the net.

United strove valiantly to get back on terms and Best, twice, and Moore saw efforts scream narrowly wide of the woodwork.

After the interval, Roy Pack substituted for David Chambers and Lindsey was thrown up into attack. And the move nearly brought the desired result twenty minutes from the end. Chisnall, after getting himself out of trouble near the corner flag, played the ball back and there was Lindsey sending in a thundering shot which whistled a fraction over the bar from 18 yards.

Pack, incidentally, gave a competent show in the back four. Given a free by Oxford United, manager Arthur Rowley used the match to size him up before deciding whether to take him on to the Roots Hall staff.

And Pack obliged by giving a calm, efficient performance which could see him signing on the dotted line. But so did all the players.

SOUTHEND UNITED: Lloyd, Lindsey, Simpson, Chisnall, Barnett, Beesley, Hunt (Taylor), Best, Garner, Moore, Chambers (Pack).

FIORENTINA: Bandoni, Rogora, Longini, Esposito, Carpenetti, Marinelli, Mariani, Rizzo, Maraschi, Amarildo, Chiarugi.

Tuesday, September 1st, 1970
Friendly Match
SOUTHEND UNITED YOUTH 6, NORRKOPING YOUTH 0

Although Norrkoping held out for 20 minutes they fell away badly and by half-time were 3-0 in arrears, Spud Taylor notching two.

In the second half United showed some very nice touches and the Swedes became desperate and some of the tackling was late. Excellent movements brought three more goals. Complete scorers were Taylor (3), Vickery, Prior and M. O'Conner.

Saturday, November 21st, 1970
F.A. Challenge Cup, 1st Round
SOUTHEND UNITED 7, WEYMOUTH 0

With ruthless ease and power, Southend United demonstrated the vast advantages of full-time training in this first round F. A. Cup massacre of Weymouth at Roots Hall on Saturday. The visitors, a collection of part-timers, were completely over-whelmed by opponents sharper in both mind and body.

What hopes the Southern Leaguers may have entertained of providing one of the shocks of the day, were cruelly shattered almost before they had time to sample the Southend air.

It took only two minutes for Blues to hammer home the first of seven nails into the Weymouth coffin. Bill Garner flicked the ball in following a break by Phil Chisnall down the right wing, and from that moment onwards the match was as good as over.

For all Weymouth's pluck and courage, they never remotely threatened to upset the balance of power. United were yards sharper on the ball, created immense space for themselves as a result of their more intelligent reading of the game, and for once, the combination of these two factors led to a glut of goals for the fans to cheer. It was the explosive finishing which must have pleased manager Arthur Rowley most.

I know they were expected to win with plenty to spare. But their superiority in this match was hardly greater than in the recent clash against Crewe – and we all know what happened then.

Top of the shots, of course, was Bill Garner. It was he who cracked in United's three first-half goals and as an added bonus, he produced a brilliant diving header to record his fourth after the break. Two goals by Best and a vicious Lewis volley which brought the crowd to its feet, completed Weymouth's destruction and the lesson on how to finish. Also on United's credit side was their killer instinct, or, if you like, true professionalism.

Even when they were seven goals up, they showed no mercy as they sought for richer reward. They still continued to chase and challenge for every ball, qualities which should see them make welcome strides up the League ladder. The visitors' plan of campaign was ruined by that opening goal. They came with the emphasis on defence, relying solely on the efforts of Gary Townend and Trevor Allen up front.

When Garner struck, the damage was done. They had neither the skill or the men to switch their tactics effectively as Blues went on to emphasise that there is a sizeable gulf between Fourth Division and Southern League standards. This is a fact that United have rammed home in this competition before. Two years ago, they hit a total of 19 goals in the matches against Brentwood and King's Lynn. Chisnall and Keith Lindsey played a prominent part in bringing about Weymouth's downfall, dictating the pattern of events as they liked. They were the complete master in midfield and Garner, Best and company carried on the good work up front.

Their deft touches and swift interchanging of positions left Weymouth's defenders demoralised. Occasionally they did gain respite in isolated breakaways, but apart from a couple of efforts by Allen, Brian Lloyd was never troubled. It goes without saying that Blues will not always find it so easy.

Neither will opposing defences if this game has served to whet the appetite of Southend's strikers!

SOUTHEND: Lloyd, Bentley, Simpson, Lindsey, Beesley, Smith, Chisnall, Best, Garner, Moore (Chambers), Lewis.

WEYMOUTH: Clarke, Barry, Glover, Rounsevell, Hobson, Bumstead, McCarthy, Kearns, Allen, Townend, Bennett.

SCORERS: Garner (2 mins, 19 mins, 32 mins, 74 mins), Best (47 mins, 60 mins), Lewis (57 mins).

Attendance 7,206.

Monday, November 23rd, 1970
Eastern Professional Floodlight League
SOUTHEND UNITED 5, BOSTON UNITED 2

Boston United, bubbling with confidence following their F.A. Cup giantkilling act over Southport, were brought down to earth by Southend United at Roots Hall last night. The man who really sent them toppling in the Eastern Professional Floodlight Competition was Peter Taylor – even though he was only on the pitch for 45 minutes. Teenager Taylor joined the battle when Billy Best was pulled off at the interval with a slight ankle injury. And he grasped his chance with both hands or, to be more precise, both feet. Midway through the half Taylor, fed by Dave Chambers, powered in a superb ground shot from 18 yards and a couple of minutes from the end scored with an even better one. From fully 25 yards, he unleashed a glorious drive which arrowed its way into the roof of the net before goalkeeper White could move.

Young Taylor has earned himself something of a reputation for his dynamic shooting – and this match served to emphasise why. A couple of further efforts were only narrowly off target while in addition, he displayed many neat touches of distribution. Mick Beesley, too, must have been pleased with his night's work following his switch into attack. He used his height to full advantage to nod home in each half.

United's nap hand was completed by fullback Keith Lindsey, his 30th minute swerving drive opening the scoring. The three goal margin by which Blues triumphed was a fair reflection of their superiority. The Lincolnshire club were repeatedly forced back by the more fluent and effective policy of their opponents. Blues moved the ball about with much more purpose and speed and such was their dominance, Alex Smith and Lindsey were often to be seen in attacking forays. Boston did break through twice to net through Froggatt and Smith (penalty) but by then Southend were well in control.

The only black spot for Blues was the booking of Dave Barnett following a tackle on the visiting centre forward. A harsh decision when compared with some of the treatment handed out by Boston.

SOUTHEND: Bowley, Smith, Lindsey, Barnett, Fallon, Simpson, Cowan, Martin-Chambers, Best (Taylor), Beesley, Lewis.

BOSTON UNITED: White, Creaser, Keeble, Smith, Gibson, Jobling, Good, McLean, Froggatt, Weaver, Howells.

Monday, January 25th, 1971
Eastern Professional Floodlight League
SOUTHEND UNITED 2, CAMBRIDGE UNITED 1

Bill Garner, fighting back to match fitness, gave his self-confidence a tremendous fillip when he powered home a great header just four minutes from time to settle this Eastern Professional Floodlight Competition game at Roots Hall last night.

Up til then big Bill had been having an indifferent night, but he moved onto Keith Lindsey's free kick with determination and gave former United favourite Trevor Roberts no chance from 12 yards.

The goal brought pleasure to the 493 fans and justice to the Blues, who had outplayed Cambridge for much of the game and yet saw themselves in danger of losing the credit from an 83rd minute equaliser.

Both sides got bogged down in the mid-field mud, but Southend, quicker on the ball, looked the better side.

The visitors were their own worst enemy as they wasted a great deal of effort trying to go down the middle past uncompromising Mick Beesley and Dave Barnett when they had a potential match winner in right winger Peter Leggett. Cambridge had four serious shots at goal, three from Leggett crosses. It was the third which Bob Howe turned into the net for the equaliser, giving trialist goalkeeper John Roberts no chance.

Talking of Roberts, playing his first game for United since arriving from Bradford City, there is not much one can say on this performance, he had so little to do. He made one good save in the first half, going down to a strong shot from Ray Peachey, and what little distribution he did was efficient and quick. An already tried and tested League performer, he was never under any pressure.

For Cambridge, both ex-Blues Mel Slack and Roberts performed with credit, although Slack had his name taken in the second half for a late tackle on Keith Lindsey.

Southend looked like scoring in the early stages when Kevin Fallon worried Roberts four times in the first 15 minutes, once getting the ball past him only to see it strike the base of the post.

United's opening goal came in the 62nd minute when a Fallon header was partially cleared, but blasted back across the goal by Bernie Lewis for Dave Barnett to slam it home.

SOUTHEND UNITED: Roberts, Lindsey, Harmston, Lumsden, Barnett, Beesley, Lewis, Fallon, Garner, Chisnall, Taylor. Sub., Cowan.

CAMBRIDGE UNITED: Roberts, Thompson, Grant, Walker, Eades, Harvey, Leggett, Slack, Howe, Peachey, Harris. Sub., Cassidy.

Saturday, May 1st, 1971
Football League, Fourth Division
NORTHAMPTON TOWN 0, SOUTHEND UNITED 2

These two points cleared Southend from the ignominy of having to apply for re-election. But more important, they enabled the players to regain the self-respect and confidence which augers well for next season.

Wednesday's 0-0 home draw with Exeter was forgotten as soon as Blues took the field at the County Ground. They played like masters from the start, even though they had an early shock when Keith Lindsey was carried off with an ankle injury after 13 minutes and Spud Taylor replaced him five minutes later. Billy Best, buzzing against his former club, took over in the back four and helped United survive 'til the interval. Best and Bernie Lewis had missed good early chances but their tactics mainly were to contain rather than overwhelm the opposition.

Alex Smith was outstanding during this pressure. He can rarely have played a better game all season, and stretching across the line in excellent support were Geoff Barker, skipper Joe Jacques and, of course, Best.

A half-time think-in dropped Dave Elliott into the back four and left Best free once again in midfield. And this made all the difference. Goalkeeper John Roberts was in serious difficulties only once in the second period when he parried a Fairbrother shot towards his net in the 76th minute and Smith was forced to head over his own bar.

But by then United were in front, Gary Moore picking up a loose ball 25 yards out and blasting a shot well out of stand-in keeper Hill's reach. Best drew Hill off his line to set up a second goal for Taylor.

NORTHAMPTON: Hill, Neal, Heslop, Clarke, Townsend, Oman, McGleish, Gould, Buchanan, Fairbrother, Hawkins.

SOUTHEND: Roberts, Lindsey (Taylor), Smith, Elliott, Barker, Jacques, Johnson, Best, Moore, Hunt, Lewis.

SCORERS: Moore (58 min), Taylor (84 min). Attendance: 3,713.

Friday, July 30th, 1971
Friendly Match
TULA METALLIST 2, SOUTHEND UNITED 1

Southend United lost the second match of their Russian tour, but again played with enough enterprise and skill on Friday to have won. Blues forwards missed many chances and had Billy Best managed to send home a bouncing ball in the last minute they would have drawn.

Bill Garner had earlier missed three good chances. However, United's build-up was often good with Johnson and Taylor outstanding and new boy Ternent having another good game before a crowd of more than 20,000.

Manager Arthur Rowley made three changes from the side beaten in Kalinin. Garner, Taylor and Barnett replaced Duck, Lewis and Piekalnietis.
Southend again opened uncertainly and were a goal down in 12 minutes through Mishustin. For much of the first half Blues were on the defensive and Jacques stood out in a cool and dogged rearguard.

Then on the half hour Johnson sent home the rebound from a Garner shot to equalise. Blues now came into the game more and another attempt by

Garner was tipped over for a corner. Two minutes after half-time, the Russians took the lead again through a surprise dropping shot by full-back Mastrukov. Blues fought their way back into the game and built up many promising attacks only to fail in front of goal. The game ended with two successive United corners and that opportunity from which Best might so easily have scored.

Team: Roberts, Lindsey, Smith, Elliott, Barnett, Jacques, Johnson, Best, Garner, Ternent, Taylor.

Wednesday, May 17th, 1972
Mid-week League Cup Final
Southend United 8, Millwall 1

Saving their most scintillating form for this last competitive game of the season at Roots Hall last night, United made certain of retaining the Mid-Week League Cup as they romped their way through a goal spree in the final.

But it wasn't only the margin of victory which was impressive. Even more impressive was the way it was achieved. Never a devotee of formation football last night went a long way to converting me. Blues played a 4-3-3 line up and for once used the system as it was intended.

They were sound at the back, with John Piekalnietis and David Hogg outstanding but splendidly backed by Steve Dyer and Peter Woods. They also had a power house engine room in midfield where Alex Smith, Dave Barnett and Spud Taylor reigned supreme.

And once the ball was played out quickly, the front three, backed strongly from behind, tore the Millwall defence apart. Young Bobby Bennett was far from outshone by his seniors Terry Johnson and George Duck, the latter replaced by Gary Jenkins midway through the second half. Goalkeeper John Roberts was rarely called into action, but was confident in all he did until beaten by Steve Brown, who scored Millwall's consolation goal three minutes from the end. But by then, Blues were already eight in front, five of them coming in the first half. All the goals came from splendid build-ups.

The scorers were Johnson (3), Taylor (2), Duck (2) and Barnett.

On this display there are quite a few Third and Fourth Division clubs who would like to turn out this Blues side every week.

Southend: Roberts, Hogg, Woods, Smith, Piekalnietis, Dyer, Johnson, Barnett, Duck (Jenkins), Bennett, Taylor.

Monday, November 6th, 1972
Friendly Match
Southend United 1, Zenit Leningrad 1

Southend youngster Bobby Bennett grabbed last night's unique opportunity to lay the foundations for his first team future.

Bennett, 20, whose skills have been confined to reserve football since his impressive debut against Chelsea in the League Cup two months ago, used this Roots Hall friendly to remind manager Arthur Rowley of his talents.

And if he didn't actually overrun the Russian First Division side single-handed, the power and promise of his performance was unquestionably the most exciting feature of the match.

Rowley may wish to continue his policy of covering up a player who started last season as a Staines Town amateur. But he must have it in the back of the mind that the youngster could grow into a replacement for £100,000 Bill Garner. And some of the fans who saw last night's match would already claim that the Southend manager is being over protective by keeping Bennett out of the League side. Certainly Southend's first team strikers are already looking over their shoulders at the massive frame of the youngster.

None more so than the luckless Gary Moore for whom home matches are now becoming something of an ordeal. He suffered the now customary barracking from a section of the fans from the moment he replaced Peter Taylor at the interval. Moore responded with a header which almost brought Southend's winner and then just failed to latch on to a Bennett header across his path.

Bennett headed Blues in front in the 27th minute, picking his spot after Best had nodded back Ternent's cross. The Russians came back with some moves which fulfilled their manager's pledge that they were here to play attacking football.

Khromtchenkov missed one great chance, but made amends four minutes from half time when he put Zintchenko through for the equaliser.

Robin Wainwright, guesting for Southend from Second Division Luton, showed some promising touches in the first half. But he tailed off a bit in the second half.

SOUTHEND: Bellotti, Booth, Ternent, Elliott, Albeson, Harrison, Johnson, Best, Bennett, Wainwright, Taylor (Moore).

ZENIT: Pronin, Deremov, Lokhov, Golubev, Zagumennykh, Sadyrin, Nokolajev, Vjun (Bviavin), Trembach (Kokh), Zintchenko, Khromtchenkov (Ivanov).

Tuesday, January 16th, 1973
Friendly Match
SOUTHEND UNITED 3, VOLENDAM 0

This clash at Roots Hall last night served its purpose of giving Blues some much needed match practice after a 10-day break from competitive combat. But the quality of the Dutch was such that it failed to test their skill or resources. The difference in class was as wide as the distance between the two countries and Southend can have little excuse for not winning by a far greater margin.

That they didn't was due to their inability to produce any real accuracy in the box. Time and again, Blues sliced through Volendam's hesitant defence only to blaze the ball wide.

Manager Arthur Rowley can hardly have learned much from his experiment of playing Terry Johnson in midfield. The Dutch lacked players of sufficient stature in this department to seriously challenge Johnson's ability and it is obvious the United chief will have to put his theory to the test again.

Peter Taylor, despite missing the game's best chance when he shot wildly over from five yards, emerged as United's brightest star. He played a part in all three goals, the first after only seven minutes when he drew the goalkeeper to leave Dave Elliott with the simplest of tasks to slip the ball into the empty net. Twenty-one minutes later, a cross from the right enabled Chris Guthrie to launch himself for a magnificent diving header to score the second.

At this point I expected the Volendam floodgates to open. But the goals never materialised. And the fans had to wait nearly another hour before Tommy Horsfall, substituted for Gary Moore, grabbed a third goal from close range.

Volendam, who lost 'keeper Straaten with a shoulder injury late in the game, reserved the best of their three goalscoring attempts until the final minute. Then Mol gave Don Mackay his only anxious moment with a rasping drive which just skimmed the bar.

SOUTHEND: Mackay, Booth, Smith, Elliott, Albeson, Moody, Johnson T., Best, Guthrie (K. Johnson), Moore (Horsfall), Taylor.

VOLENDAM: Hoogland (Straaten), Boer, Braan, Schilder, Jan Jonk, Buls, Braam (Bond), Jac Jonk (Mol), Kwakman, Ferreira, Kok.

Saturday, November 3rd, 1973
Football League, Third Division
SOUTHEND UNITED 5, HUDDERSFIELD 2

Manager Arthur Rowley's insistence that Southend United can climb into the promotion race by Christmas gained the support of the fans as Huddersfield were humbled 5-2 at Roots Hall on Saturday. With Stuart Brace in the role of chief executioner, Blues subjected the Yorkshiremen to a blitz they will not forget for a long time.

The home striker powered in a hat-trick and, together with his colleagues, was accorded a standing ovation at the final whistle.

Yet it would be wrong to suggest that in terms of pure soccer, this was Southend's best performance of the season. The truth is that they have played better – the two games against Southport spring readily to mind – without just reward.

This is a significant factor which should not be allowed to go unnoticed. If they can crack five when below their best, think what can happen when they click into top gear – especially if the opposing defence proves as benevolent as Huddersfield's.

For, while acknowledging the Yorkshiremen had class players in Alan Gowling and Phil Summerill in attack, their rearguard was too bad to be true. It was amazing the amount of room Brace was allowed. No-one seemed remotely interested in picking him up, with the result that he was usually left free to hare down on the visiting goal. Chris Guthrie, who had a hand in four of the goals, also took full advantage of a defence that played either too square or too forward and United always looked menacing when in possession.

Huddersfield's glaring problems at the back tended to reduce United's failings at the back to minor deficiencies. But that was not the case, both the visitors goals were gifted through hesitancy or slack marking.

At least a couple of defenders were slow to make a challenge on Summerill as he fastened on to a throw-in to lay on the first of Gowling's two goals. Then they failed to spot the former Manchester United player darting through the middle as he hit an equaliser just on half-time.

Between and after these setbacks, however, United superbly demonstrated their skills up front. With Denis Booth and Dave Elliott quick to supplement the spearhead, Town were given a really tough time although it was not until the 32nd minute that their defence was prised open for the first time.

Goalkeeper Terry Poole could only palm out a Guthrie header and Brace pounced to equalise Gowling's second minute effort by slamming the ball into the roof of the net.

Three minutes later, full-back Geoff Hutt bundled Guthrie off the ball and Brian Albeson strode up to put away the penalty. The second half was 10 minutes old when Elliott restored Southend's lead, finding the net from 20 yards after the ball had run loose from a corner.

Booth, Terry Johnson and Guthrie linked up for Brace to make it four before the same player completed a great hat-trick ten minutes from time, bringing his tally to six goals in four matches.

GOALS: Southend (Brace 32, 68 and 80 mins.), Albeson (pen. 35 mins.), Elliott (55 mins.) Huddersfield: Gowling (2 and 44 mins.). Attendance: 7,035.

Friday, August 9th, 1974
Friendly Match
SOUTHEND UNITED 7, BONNER SPORT CLUB 0

Southend United's seven-goal avalanche at Roots Hall on Friday night left manager Arthur Rowley smiling and highly satisfied.

Before they went into action against Bonner, the West German outfit, the Blues boss declared: 'I am looking for more than victory tonight. I want the lads to really hit the goals trail to give them that extra degree of confidence with which to start the league programme.'

The United squad duly obliged by scoring some spectacular goals to keep Rowley and the sparse 1,686 fans happy.

Admittedly the West Germans were so inferior that they were unable to present the home side with a stern test. But that does not detract from some fine finishing on United's part. Creating chances is one thing, accepting them is another. And they certainly snapped up their chances with a simplicity that was missing in several of their league matches last season.

While Blues would no doubt have wished for a tougher test, the game served to show that David Cunningham is ready to make a serious bid for a first team place. He ran intelligently from deep positions, sprayed the ball about accurately and got on the list of marksmen with a fine solo effort shortly before the end.

Chris Guthrie, too, rattled in a couple of good goals and had another spectacular effort disallowed because one of his colleagues was offside.

The German attack was so short of pace and attacking ideas that new signing Bob Worthington and the rest of the defenders were unable to show their defensive qualities.

Apart from one snap shot in the first half, Southend goalkeeper Malcolm Webster was just a spectator. Not so Phoyu, his opposite number. The German 'keeper was constantly in action but it was not until the 20th minute that he was beaten. Then Dave Elliott began the spree with a penalty following a foul on Stuart Brace. Guthrie grabbed both his goals in the first half, then Neil Townsend moved up to fire in a header in the 65th minute.

By now the visitors were completely demoralised and Steve Lamb, who came on for Brace, netted a fifth. This was followed by Cunningham's effort in the 80th minute and in the last seconds Terry Johnson completed the rout when he was left with a free header.

SOUTHEND: Webster, Dyer, Worthington, Elliott, Townsend, Moody, Brace (Lamb), Ford (Johnson), Guthrie, Cunningham, Love (Coulson).

Saturday, December 28th, 1974
Essex Senior League
SOUTHEND UNITED 'A' v COGGESHALL TOWN

Postponed, due to 'Southend United forgetting about the match!'

Tuesday, February 17th, 1976
Football League, Third Division
SOUTHEND UNITED 4, BRIGHTON & HOVE ALBION 0

As manager Arthur Rowley predicted, Brighton last night fell victims to a vicious backlash when Southend United got the cup defeat at Derby out of their system.

But even he confessed surprise by the manner in which promotion-chasing Brighton were demolished by a four-goal spectacular from Peter Silvester.

As soon as the match started, it was evident the visitors had come to Roots Hall looking for a draw. They played a sweeper behind the back four and very often had four players stretched across midfield. 'I couldn't really understand their tactics at all,' said a smiling Blues boss afterwards.

'It's all very well adopting a cautious attitude, but they took it to the extreme. Even when they fell a goal behind, they made no attempt to alter their tactics and come out and attack us. I appreciate they had three forwards out through injury but that's hardly an excuse. They have one of the biggest playing staffs in the Third Division so I imagine they're not short of strikers. Still, I'm not complaining. I only wish other teams would play that way against us!'

For 32 minutes, Brighton's defensive web managed to hold firm against a succession of attacks. But once Silvester broke the deadlock, Blues never looked in danger of having their winning bonus snatched away from them.

For most of the match, United goalkeeper Malcolm Webster was reduced to a lonely figure watching the action at the other end. He was called upon to make one save in the 90 minutes and would probably have drifted off to sleep had he not been employed by the occasional back pass!

What a different story it was for Brighton's Peter Grummitt. From the moment he had to dive full-length in the fifth minute to turn aside a drive from Terry Nicholl, he was constantly in action.

And while he pulled off a string of fine saves, he also needed quite a bit of luck on his side to stem off an avalanche of goals. On at least half a dozen occasions, he was left stranded as shots were either hit or deflected the wrong side of the woodwork.

With Silvester having such a great night, it is easy to overlook the part played by other members of the side. But one must not forget the work of his partner, Stuart Parker, always running to pull defenders out of position or the influence of midfield.

Here, Alan Little and Terry Nicholl provided the power, while Ken Foggo underlined his class and experience in the way he laid on the final goal. Collecting the ball in midfield he kept possession until Silvester moved back from an offside position.

Then, with a carefully measured chip over the defence, he sent Silvester racing clear to hit a low drive past the despairing Grummitt.

Blues' first-half goal followed a. short corner between Ron Pountney and Nicholl who floated the ball over to the far post. Tony Hadley's header came back from underneath the bar and Silvester chested it over the line.

Three minutes after the break, Pountney beat two defenders on the right to lay on a header and no sooner had the cheers died down when Silvester had grabbed his hat-trick.

Graham Winstanley tried to head back to his 'keeper but the pass was too short and the Blues striker nipped in to intercept and score.

Then came Silvester's fourth to give United their biggest victory of the season and lift them two more places clear of the relegation zone.

Brighton's assistant manager Brian Daykin said today: 'Silvester did his job well. He took good advantage of some bad defensive play. We played the same team at Bury and got a point. But against Southend we didn't play well defensively in the second half.'

Friday, December 9th, 1977
Football League, Fourth Division
SOUTHEND UNITED 4, NEWPORT COUNTY 2

Southend United have at last broken the home barrier which had threatened to suffocate their promotion surge.

So believes John Lattimer after watching his side pull off one of the greatest recoveries in their history as they stormed to a 4-2 victory over Newport County, on Friday night.

And, judging by the incredible scenes of jubilation at the end when hundreds of fans invaded the pitch to swamp their heroes, there is no-one prepared to argue with him. In a breathtaking final five minutes, Blues scored three times to haul themselves to a triumph which seemed a million miles away when they trailed 2-0 – with just over quarter-of-an-hour remaining.

It was an effort which left Lattimer, in charge of the team while manager Dave Smith lay in hospital recovering from a nose operation, as drained emotionally as his players were physically. He looked pale and weary at the end but, with the aid of a reviving tot, recovered to pay tribute to his band of fighters. 'They did me and the club proud,' he said. 'But more important, they won a great battle with themselves. While the lads have been playing some great stuff away, they had only won four at Roots Hall and were getting a little worried the way visiting clubs kept nicking points. I don't think they've got anything to worry about now. This was the ideal tonic to sweep aside any lingering doubts over their ability to turn it on at home.'

But Lattimer is the first to admit that he shared those doubts when Tony Byrne pounced five minutes after the break to add to Brian Clark's 44th minute effort. 'When we found ourselves a goal down at the interval I wasn't all that concerned,' he recalled.

'We had been creating chances and thought we could still win if we remained patient and kept getting enough crosses over. But I was a little worried when Newport's second went in. It's asking a lot for a side to come from two behind – it doesn't happen very often.

'In the end, however, everything came right. I just can't praise the lads enough or the fans who gave them such great support.'

While United's emphasis on keeping it cool and simple stood them in good stead, Lattimer believes their trump card was one of stamina. 'We were as strong at the end as at the start,' he declared.

And County boss Colin Addison was in no mood to dispute that. 'We collapsed like a deck of cards,' was his dejected comment. 'Had the game gone on another five minutes, I feel pretty sure Southend would have scored another couple.' The acrobatics of Gary Plumley to keep out efforts from Micky Laverick and Tony Hadley plus bad misses by Gerry Fell and Hadley combined to frustrate Blues in the opening half-hour. But they also had their moments of great relief, notably when Steve Yates appeared to handle in the penalty area and again when the woodwork came to their rescue. On both occasions Ray Guscott was the deprived striker, but he was left unconcerned by his misfortune as Newport coasted into a 2-0 lead after 50 minutes.

Possessing greater venom up front and more direct in their approach, Newport appeared set at this point to leap-frog above Blues in the table.

How wrong can you be? As the visitors wilted, Hadley enjoying probably his most impressive game, inspired Blues into frenzied action. With Micky Laverick lending powerful support, Newport found themselves being pushed further and further back and it came as no real surprise when Hadley reduced the arrears as he rose to head in a free-kick from his midfield partner.

It was a success which spurred Blues into ever-greater effort, but it seemed they were destined to fight a losing battle as unmarked Alan Foggon drove wide of an upright with seven minutes to go. Then it all happened. With five minutes remaining, Frank Banks moved up on the right to provide the cross from which Derrick Parker headed an equaliser and, 60 seconds later, another surge by Hadley helped Blues into the lead for the first time.

This time Fell was on the end of his cross, launching himself into a spectacular dive to head past a shattered Plumley.

And, while they were still rejoicing in the stand and terraces, Fell struck again two minutes from time when he latched on to an Alan Moody pass to race upfield and crack in an unforgettable drive on an unforgettable night.

SCORERS: Southend, Hadley (75), Parker (85), Fell (87 and 88); Newport, Clark (45), Byrne (50).

ATTENDANCE: 5,840

TEAM: Rafter, Moody, Banks, Laverick, Townsend, Yates, Morris, Foggon, Parker, Fell, Hadley. Sub.: Pountney.

Monday, March 10th, 1980
Friendly Match
SOUTHEND UNITED 2, HVIDOVRE 0

Teenager Garry Nelson was given a glimpse last night of how Southend United boss Dave Smith sees his first-team future.

With Derek Spence away on Irish international training duty, Smith gave Nelson a free-striking role in the friendly clash with Danish First Division outfit Hvidovre ... and he came up trumps.

Nelson didn't get his name on the scoresheet in the 2-0 victory, but did enough to impress Smith that he could become a similar type of player to England ace Tony Woodcock.

Smith said after the game: 'I'm not talking stupid when I speak of Nelson in the same breath as Woodcock – he could develop along those lines. Circumstances have forced us to play him as a flank-midfield player this season – and that won't do him any harm at all, it all adds to the youngster's experience. But he has the skill, speed and guts to do a free striking job and that's how I see his future.' And that move would suit Nelson down to the ground. He told me:

'I'm just happy to be in the team irrespective of where I play. But I must confess I enjoyed playing in that position last night and once I get a little bit stronger I'm sure I can slot in there. I love getting goals and obviously stand more chance of scoring if I'm operating in or around the penalty area.'

It was Nelson and his partner Keith Mercer who always proved a difficult handful for the Danes. And 18-year old Nelson came so close to getting one of those goals he loves so much in a magic second-half moment. He pulled down a long ball on the edge of the box, turned sweetly leaving a defender off balance and only a great save by giant 'keeper Curlei Nielsen kept out his low shot.

Nielsen was certainly kept busy in a game in which Southend always held more menace than Hvidovre. Only some fierce clinical tackling by the Danish outfit kept Southend down to two goals and made them realise that this was something more than just a friendly run-out.

Hvidovre are in this country on a week's training exercise to warm up for their new season and they were in no mood to simply stroll about.

And Southend, to their credit, were prepared to complete on equal terms to earn a victory which must bolster their confidence for the tough battles ahead. Blues can take heart from the fact that they beat a side containing two full internationals, including the Danish skipper Sten Ziegler, and half a dozen under-21 stars.

And a sports writer over from Denmark covering the mini-tour reckons the League they play in is equal to our middle-of-the-road Second Division teams. Apart from Nelson and Mercer up front, there was a lot to appreciate in Southend's play and the opening goal after half an hour rounded off one of the neatest moves seen at Roots Hall for many a long day.

Jeff Hull, another impressive youngster who stuck at his job manfully despite some pretty intimidating tackles, set things moving with a raking pass out to Ron Pountney on the left.

Pountney sped clear and sent in a perfect cross which Mercer met to squeeze his header between the diving Nielsen and his near post.

A picture goal which was just about what Blues deserved after twice seeing Nielsen thwart them with super saves from Mercer and a ferocious Micky Stead free-kick.

Mind you Mervyn Cawston at the other end wasn't allowed to have an evening off and earned his money with a tremendous save to keep out a 25-yard rocket from Ted Gapinski.

In fact Hvidovre only caused problems with those speculative long-range efforts although they showed an intelligent use of open space and in Henrik Jensen had the best midfielder on view.

Southend kept plugging away after the break and finally got the reward their pressure deserved eight minutes from time after a rare boob from Nielsen. Steve Yates curled in a corner from the right which Nielsen completely missed, leaving Pountney with the simple job of heading into an unguarded net.

SOUTHEND: Cawston, Dudley, Yates, Stead, Hadley, Cusack, Gray, Pountney, Spence, Mercer, Hull. Subs: Keeley, Tuohy and Walker.

HVIDOVRE: Nielsen, Christensen, Ziegler, J.K. Petersen (Vang), Hansen, Jensen, Kirk, Lindahl, Gapinski, Rasmussen, J. Petersen.

Friday, August 29th, 1980
Football League, Fourth Division
NORTHAMPTON TOWN 0, SOUTHEND UNITED 0
(Abandoned after 45 minutes – floodlight failure)

Angry Southend United fans besieged the Northampton Town offices after Friday night's game was abandoned amid a storm of controversy. Referee Derek Lloyd called a halt to the goalless Fourth Division clash at half-time after one set of floodlight pylons went out.

But Blues fans and players were bitter about the decision which robbed them of a chance of staying top of the table.

Supporters had to be escorted out of the offices when then went to complain after being told there would be no entrance money refunded. One fan told me: 'It's disgusting. I've travelled all this way up from Southend and, with petrol and admission money, I reckon it has cost me at least £10 to watch 45 minutes soccer. I feel the Northampton club are to blame and should have least give us our money back.'

And Southend players, too, felt the game should have been allowed to continue or at least the referee should have consulted them before abandoning the match. Defender Alan Moody said: 'We were quite happy to carry on. Obviously, the conditions were not ideal but we felt we were managing to play without too much trouble. Anyway, we had defended the end where the light was worse and hadn't been in too much trouble. We were gradually getting on top and, with the wind and slope in our favour in the second-half, we would have won with ease. I wonder what the ref would have done had they been leading 2-0 at half-time!'

Skipper Micky Stead spoke for most of the team when he said: 'I felt the referee should have asked the people with most to lose – the players and managers – before calling the game off. 'We were confident we would beat them – we got stronger the longer the game went on.'

Blues boss Dave Smith admitted to being 'disappointed' when the game was stopped. 'I think Northampton were happier about the ref s decision than we were,' he added.

The referee had stopped the game for nine minutes towards the end of the half to see if the lights could be repaired. But agreed to try again when the club's electrician Brian Edwards said he wasn't prepared to risk a fire by trying to repair the blown fuse. He switched one of his linesmen to the darker side of the ground but came off at the interval, signalling the match was at an end. Lloyd told me later: 'We have used our common sense – one of the players could have got badly injured out there. Anyway, I couldn't see my linesman properly and he couldn't see across the pitch. We gave it a try but it was no use. This is the first time in nearly 25 years as a referee that anything like this had happened to me.'

I personally had sympathy with fans and players because I had no trouble at all following the play from the press box right at the back of the stand.

Both teams had got through the first half without any bother and conditions were certainly not going to get any worse.

It was ironic that this was the last time the 20 year-old lights were going to be used by Northampton – a new set are due to be installed within the next two weeks.

Blues struggled a bit early on never really getting to grips the Cobblers in midfield, but were gradually becoming masters of the engine room and created the most danger towards the end of the 45 minutes.

Terry Gray forced the first real save of the match from goalkeeper Andy Poole when he pounced on a Derek Spence flick but saw his shot charged down for a corner. Spence was always a threat to the Northampton defence while Keith Mercer gave him solid support.

Blues looked tight and secure at the back with Moody and Dave Cusack giving absolutely nothing away.

Saturday, October 11th, 1980
Football League, Fourth Division
HALIFAX TOWN 1, SOUTHEND UNITED 5

Dave Cusack collected a double bonus as Southend United roared to a devastating 5-1 victory at Halifax on Saturday to grab the Fourth Division leadership.

For as well as collecting a rare goal, the towering central defender picked up a £10 wager from former West Ham striker Brian Dear. The bet was struck after Blues had gone nap against Port Vale way back in August.

'Brian then said we wouldn't get five goals in a match again this season,' said the United acting skipper, 'I told him he was talking rubbish but he wouldn't listen. So we struck the bet and now I'm going along to collect my winnings. It's the easiest money I've made,' added Cusack with a twinkle in his eye.

The only thing that marred Cusack's delight in scoring only the fourth League goal of his career was that his father Ted missed it. Although he travelled the 40-odd miles from his home to watch the game, he was still making his way from the visitors' lounge when Cusack struck Blues' third goal four minutes after the break.

'I don't think hell forgive me for that,' said dad. 'He's really given me some stick over it. But there's always another day and I'll just have to make sure I watch the whole 90 minutes in future in case he scores again.'

Cusack junior, however, was in forgiving mood after Halifax had been totally destroyed by him and his team-mates. The boss' message before the start was that we had to really compete against the Halifaxes of this world if we are to keep in the promotion hunt. And that's exactly what we did,' he said.

'The great thing was that we never eased up at all. Mind you, I'm a bit sick about us conceding a late goal but it was still a great performance by the lads.' No-one can dispute that. Blues oozed class and confidence as they ran the Yorkshiremen dizzy with a display which could easily have brought them more goals.

The midfield quartet quickly established a stranglehold Halifax never looked like breaking as they set up a tidal wave of attacks. And with the home defenders sluggish both physically and mentally, it soon became a question of not whether Blues would win – but how big their margin of victory would be. The game was 20 minutes old when Southend began their surge with a goal of stealth and simplicity.

Phil Dudley fed Keith Mercer on the right and he sped forward to lay on a square pass which left the unmarked Derek Spence with the easy task of beating goalkeeper John Kilner with a low shot from 10 yards. Five minutes later, the visitors were celebrating a second goal, this time Alan Moody nodded the ball over the line after a thunderous drive from Tony Hadley had cannoned off the underside of the bar.

Any lingering hopes Halifax may have entertained of making a game of it disappeared when Cusack moved up to get his name on the scoresheet. As the home defence failed to get a head to Anton Otulakowski's corner, the ball dropped to the defender on the left edge of the box and, given time and space, he moved a couple of paces forward before drilling in a fierce, low shot.

That was the beginning of the end as far as Halifax were concerned. Before then, they had been slow and uncertain at the back. Afterwards, even greater holes appeared as they pushed more men forward in an attempt to create some impression on Blues defence.

They rarely looked like succeeding. The back four swallowed up everything in the air and were unyielding on the deck.

The result was that they quickly snuffed out Halifax raids and launched their own with long, searching passes.

One of the best examples was provided by Cusack 20 minutes from the end. For it was his carefully measured ball down the left flank which sent Spence racing along the line. And when the cross came over, Terry Gray headed in at the far post.

Within two minutes, livewire Gray capped a fine performance with a carbon-copy second, this time Otulakowski and Ron Pountney setting up the move which again left Kilner plucking the ball out of the net. A muddle in the Blues defence did allow Halifax a consolation goal from Tommy O'Neil two minutes from time, but it hardly spared them from embarrassment.

Blues manager Dave Smith beamed his delight at the end. 'It was a marvellous show,' he said. As for Halifax boss George Kirby? Well, according to former Blues player Kevin Johnson, who came on as second-half substitute – 'He went crackers.'

HALIFAX: Kilner, Nattress, Burton, Evans, Harris, Hendrie, Firth, Allatt, Graham, O'Neil, McIlwraith, (Johnson).

SOUTHEND UNITED: Cawston, Dudley, Yates, Hadley, Moody, Cusack, Gray, Pountney, Spence, Mercer, Otulakowski (Nelson).

Friday, March 13th, 1981
Football League, Fourth Division
SOUTHEND UNITED 5 HALIFAX TOWN 1

The champagne will flow after Southend United's next home game against Crewe in just under a fortnight's time.

That's the firm belief of manager Dave Smith after watching his side pulverise Halifax 5-1 at Roots Hall on Friday night to take another huge step towards Division Three. 'The champers can now be put on ice,' beamed a delighted Smith following the weekend trouncing of the Tykes. We should pick up at least a point at Scunthorpe next Sunday and that would probably leave us needing to beat Crewe to clinch promotion. In our present mood, I can't see us failing.'

Smith's confident note was echoed by his players. 'There's no way we'll slip up now,' declared skipper Micky Stead.

Dave Cusack was even more adamant. 'Not only will we win promotion, but we'll go up as champions,' boomed the lanky central defender. 'We've been at the top for most of the season and we are not going to be knocked off our perch now.'

Cusack's prediction received a great boost some 24 hours later when it became known that nearest rivals Lincoln had suffered a defeat at York which leaves them five points adrift of the Blues with only a game in hand.

But on their current form, Southend hardly need outside help in their drive for the championship. Halifax will testify to that after falling victims to some of the most clinical and explosive finishing seen at Roots Hall for a long time. Alan Moody's first half volley would have won any Goal of the Month award while Ron Pountney's effort after the interval was nearly as spectacular.

Yet an evening which ended in Southend setting a new club record of 26 League victories in a season, hardly captured the imagination of home fans early on.

In fact, it was a case of Blues in Blunderland during the first half-hour as they repeatedly gifted the ball to their opponents. As a result, they spent a fair amount of time scurrying about trying to regain possession in their own half.

Only occasionally in the initial stages did Blues string enough passes together to penetrate deep into the visitors' half. And even then, there was a marked reluctance to go wide and attempt to get behind the Yorkshire club's defence.

When it suddenly dawned on them that this was the best way to stretch Halifax, Southend were soon to go in front. Anton Otulakowski proved to be the pioneer, clipping over a left wing cross which was unaccountably punched clear by Billy Ayre as he went up with Derek Spence.

Referee Clive White had no hesitation in pointing to the penalty spot and Cusack struck home a fierce rising shot that was to transform the pattern of the game.

No sooner had the cheers died away than Moody struck a 32nd minute goal which he described as 'the best of my career.' Again it stemmed from Otulakowski. His teasing cross was only partially cleared, and as the ball dropped on the edge of the box, Moody met it on the volley to bend a screaming shot into the top right-hand corner of the net.

From that moment onwards, the result of the match was never in doubt – only the final margin of victory – as Blues set about underlining the gulf separating the two sides in the table. Tony Hadley, Pountney and Otulakowski poured through from midfield while Stead marked his return after suspension with a performance which emphasised his qualities as both defender and raider.

With Cusack and Moody also advancing at every opportunity, it all added up to a searching test for the Halifax defence – and one they never looked like overcoming. The mystery was that the visitors managed to survive until the 63rd minute before conceding a third goal, a glancing header from Spence to finish off a Pountney centre and signal his 20th success of the season.

That sparked off a glorious spell of Blues-soccer which was soon to bring further rewards.

A move started in their own half by Stead and Hadley was carried on by Spence down the right. The Irishman then hit a low pass into the box where Pountney slipped inside his challenger before unleashing a thunderous drive into the roof of the net. Two minutes later, in the 74th minute, Terry Gray got his name on the score-sheet as he swooped to convert a Pountney cross.

John Kilner, the visiting 'keeper, must have wondered what he had done to deserve to be on the end of such explosive shooting. Yet it was only his brilliance which prevented Keith Mercer and Hadley adding to Blues' tally.

Southend, however, were no doubt satisfied with their nap hand, but it was obvious Mervyn Cawston was not at all happy by the manner in which they gave Halifax their consolation goal four minutes from time.

Moody was the culprit, his sloppy square pass being seized upon by the hard-working Tommy Graham who raced forward to beat the Blues 'keeper with a rasping drive.

That was the first goal Cawston had conceded at Roots Hall this year and he showed his annoyance by throwing down his gloves before going to retrieve the ball. Still, the thought of that bubbly next week should help him forgive and forget.

SOUTHEND UNITED: Cawston, Stead, Yates, Hadley, Moody, Cusack, Gray, Pountney, Spence, Mercer, Otulakowski. Sub: Nelson.

HALIFAX: Kilner, Ward, Burton, Harris, Ayre, Hendrie, Firth, Graham, Chambers, Nattress, McIlwraith. Sub: Bullock.

Monday, October 31st, 1983
Football League, Third Division
SOUTHEND UNITED 6, BRENTFORD 0

A half-hour pep talk conducted in the privacy of manager Peter Morris' office set Southend United up for a scorching 6-0 victory against Brentford at Roots Hall last night.

It was given to young midfield players Glenn Pennyfather and Brian Ferguson, and they each responded with a two-goal performance which far surpassed the Blues chiefs expectations.

'I felt they were probably lacking a little bit of confidence, and I called them in to reassure them they were in the side on merit,' revealed Morris. I told them to get forward a bit more in support of the front men and really express themselves – and they did just that. Both lads have the talent to become very good players indeed and last night's display should serve to give them that extra belief in their ability.'

That last remark should also apply to the whole side. Following three defeats in their four previous matches, Blues' battering of Brentford can only have boosted confidence for a testing month ahead which includes away games at promotion-chasing Newport and Sheffield United.

Ironically, the early part of the evening promised to be another one of frustration for Southend.

For over half an hour all their efforts to break through came to nought as a stream of shots were either delivered or deflected wide of the woodwork. But once Ferguson was brilliantly put through by the impressive Steve Phillips to chip the ball over the goalkeeper in the 38th minute, the result was never in doubt.

Blues simply overwhelmed Brentford with the vision and venom of their attacks so much so that Brentford must have been somewhat relieved to escape an even more humiliating defeat.

The energy and drive of Ferguson and Pennyfather dovetailed perfectly with the more subtle touches of Billy Kellock and Phillips, and it came as no surprise that Brentford were finally buried beneath an avalanche of goals.

Probably more surprising was that striker Roy McDonough, as in the 6-1 thrashing of Scunthorpe a month earlier, failed to get his name on the score-sheet. But this was one occasion when he had no need to reproach himself. He had a telling hand in three of the goals and his wholehearted running repeatedly hustled the visitors into a succession of errors.

Certainly neither Francis Joseph or Keith Cassells were able to set the same type of problems at the other end against a defence superbly held together by Chris Turner and Alan Moody. They won virtually everything in the air, while their crisp tackling and acute positional sense ensured that goalkeeper Gerry Peyton had a relatively untroubled night.

Ferguson's opening thrust was quickly added to by Pennyfather, who, a couple of minutes before the break, stole down the middle to find the net with a header from Micky Stead's cross.

Any hopes Brentford may have entertained of staging a revival in the second half were quickly shattered five minutes after the break. It was then that Kellock and McDonough linked up superbly to feed Phillips to their right and the in-form striker drove low and hard from just inside the box to record his ninth goal in 11 games.

As the Brentford defenders became even more demoralised, Blues tightened their grip with a fourth goal in the 63rd minute. Again McDonough engineered it. Winning possession from Tony Spencer on the halfway line, he raced to the edge of the penalty area before checking and laying the ball back to Pennyfather. And the youngster, electing to chip rather than blast his shot, was rewarded with probably the best goal of his career to date.

Ten minutes from time Blues won their twelfth corner, and from it Greig Shepherd rose to meet Steve Collins' accurate kick and power in a point-blank header. No sooner had the cheers died down then home fans were celebrating another success. This time the Brentford defence could only partially clear a Kellock free-kick and Ferguson pounced to leave goalkeeper Trevor Swinburne helpless and shoot Blues to their biggest win of the season.

SOUTHEND UNITED: Peyton, Stead, Collins, Ferguson, Moody, Turner, Phillips, Kellock, McDonough, Shepherd, Pennyfather. Sub.: Pountney.

BRENTFORD: Swinburne, Rowe, Spencer, Salmann, Whitehead, Booker (Mahoney 58 mins), Kamara, Joseph, Cassells, Bullivant, Roberts.

Tuesday, December 16th, 1986
Football League Associate Members' Cup, Group stage
SOUTHEND UNITED 5, CAMBRIDGE UNITED 4

Even an amazing recovery which brought them four goals in the last 16 minutes failed to save Southend United's players from the wrath of manager Dave Webb at Roots Hall last night. 'At times we were diabolical,' was his reaction as he looked back on the 5-4 victory over Cambridge which booked a place in the knock-out stages of the Freight Rover Trophy.

'I daren't repeat what I said to a few of the lads. Let's say I felt it was time to kick a few up the backside – and I did just that. Anyone would think we are a Christmas club the way we are currently giving goals away. Earlier in the season defenders would attack the ball and there would be two or three players dropping off ready to snuff out the danger. Now that's just not happening. We just stand in a line and look likely to concede a goal every time the opposition attacks. And that's something that has to be put right quickly if we are not to ruin what we have achieved in the opening months of the season.'

It wasn't only Blues' defenders who incurred the anger of Webb as he cut loose in the dressing-room for half an hour or so after the match. 'The rest of the lads also came in for a bit of stick,' he admitted. 'Football is supposed to be a team game – and we hardly ever gave that impression. Okay, we came from behind to score five goals, but there wasn't one of them that was well worked and could be put down to our own creative talents. We were just lucky to find Cambridge as sloppy as us. It's time we started winning on our own merits and not on the mistakes of others.'

Considering Blues twice recovered from a two-goal deficit – and also missed a penalty during a dramatic finale – one could be forgiven for believing Webb is a very hard man to please. But in truth, Southend's efforts were at times pathetic against a team which included just four first team regulars. The oceans of space they gave away and their failure to mount an effective challenge in critical areas smacked of an outfit hell-bent on self-destruction.

One player to emerge with any credit at all was Roy McDonough – and he was only on the field for 18 minutes after arriving as substitute for the injured Dean Neal. He may lack finesse, but at least supplied the fight and aggression which sparked off Southend's dramatic revival.

McDonough's willingness to get in where it hurts and compete for every ball completely unnerved Cambridge – and must surely have earned him a place in the starting line-up at Wolves on Saturday.

As Blues struggled to get their act together, the menacing Mark Schiavi set up goals for Lindsay Smith and Aiden Dodson in the 24th and 28th minutes.

Dave Martin quickly pulled one back following a free kick, but within another couple of minutes Blues were to emphasise the pantomime season was really with us by leaving Colin Littlejohns in acres of space to restore the visitors two goal lead. And that's the way things stood until McDonough was thrust into action in the 72nd minute. Within 10 minutes Blues stormed ahead through Pennyfather, twice, and Martin Ling to give the meagre 945 spectators something to cheer about. As the drama continued, Richard Cadette squandered a penalty, McDonough scored number five and Littlejohns struck in the closing seconds as Cambridge again exposed their rival's defensive limitations.

Then came Webb's salvo.

SOUTHEND: Stannard, Roberts, Johnson, O'Shea, Martin, Hall, Clark, Pennyfather, Cadette, Neal (McDonough 72 mins), Ling.

CAMBRIDGE: Casey, Measham, A. Kimble, Bowman, Smith, Dodson (Conway 69 mins), Littlejohns, Tong, Rigby (Futtes 71 mins), Schiavi, D. Kimble.

Saturday, September 9th, 1989
Football League, Division Four
ALDERSHOT 0, SOUTHEND UNITED 5

Transfer-listed Gary Bennett stole the show as he and Southend United continued their rip-roaring start to the season on Saturday with the 5-0 thrashing of Aldershot. It was Bennett who pointed the way to victory with his fourth goal of the campaign before he went on to completely demoralise fullback Ian Phillips as he ran riot down the right wing.

But Blues manager Dave Webb did a neat body swerve when asked if he was about to take the striker off the list. 'All my players are on the list – at a price,' he countered tongue-in-cheek. But more realistically he added: 'On the evidence of this latest performance there's no way I would want any of the players to leave.' Bennett, meanwhile, is just happy to be part of the first team set-up and banging in a few goals which have helped Blues launch the season with an unbeaten League and Cup run of six matches.

'It's not up to me to ask to come off the list – I never requested to be put there in the first place,' he said. 'As far as I'm concerned it's up to the boss to have words with me about the future. Naturally I am delighted the way things have worked out for me in the opening weeks, particularly as I didn't expect to figure much in the first team squad after being made available for transfer. But give the boss his due. He said before the start of the season that everyone would be judged on merit and given a fair crack of the whip if they delivered the goods in pre-season friendlies.

'Thankfully I grabbed a couple of goals against Grays followed by five against Basildon. They filled me with the type of confidence which was missing last season and now I'm really enjoying my football again. But I know I have to keep performing well to hold on to my place. Getting into the team is one thing but staying there is another, particularly with the competition for places so fierce. All I can do is give it my best shots.'

On the evidence of the weekend Bennett will certainly take some shifting. But as well as he played, he'll be the first to admit that Aldershot's annihilation was the result of superb teamwork.

In short, Blues were streets ahead in every department as they overwhelmed their opponents through being so much quicker in mind and body. That Aldershot were reduced to nervous wrecks was clearly illustrated by the fact they were panicked into conceding two own goals, the second of which would have won any 'Goal of the Month' award had it been at the other end. Colin Smith was credited with that when, after going up with Mario Walsh, he left goalkeeper David Coles helpless with a powerful header from Jason Cook's corner.

Walsh, in fact, had a hand in all five goals, his first contribution coming in the 12th minute when he touched on a long throw-in from Paul Roberts to provide Bennett with the chance to rifle home from 10 yards. Six minutes later, Kevan Brown could only divert the ball into his own net as he tried to cut out a Walsh pass meant for Martin Ling – and it soon became obvious Blues were in no mood to surrender a two goal advantage as they did on the same ground last season. With Peter Butler and Cook dominating midfield, Aldershot hardly got within striking distance of Southend's goal, and when they did they were usually tackled out of it before lining up a shot.

The mystery was that Blues, after a series of near misses, had to wait until the 63rd minute before consolidating their lead, Walsh and Spencer Prior combining down the right for David Crown to apply the finishing touch. Soon afterwards, Walsh slipped a short ball to his right for Crown to smash in his seventh goal of the season and then came Smiths' blunder right on time to complete the rout.

ALDERSHOT: Coles, Brown (Claridge 64 min), Phillips, Coyne, Smith, Wignall (Burvill 47 min), Williams, Puckett, Banton, Henry, Stewart.

SOUTHEND UNITED: Sansome, Dixon, Roberts, Martin, Prior, Ling, Cook, Butler, Crown, Walsh, Bennett. Subs (not used): Brush and McDonough.

Attendance: 2,255.

Saturday, January 27th, 1990
Football League, Fourth Division
SOUTHEND UNITED 5 ALDERSHOT 0

David Crown, the match ball safely tucked under his arm, could not disguise his delight at hitting back at his critics following Southend United's 5-0 thrashing of Aldershot on Saturday.

'There were a few people at my throat when I wasn't finding the net,' he said recalling a nine-match spell either side of Christmas when he failed to score. That barren period also included a three-match absence because of a torn hamstring, but final proof that he has made a full recovery came at Roots Hall at the weekend as Blues boosted their promotion challenge.

'Even when the ball wasn't going into the net I didn't think I was playing too badly,' said Crown. 'The trouble is that some people are quick to condemn a striker as having a bad game if he fails to score. I've learned to accept that there are spells when things do not work out in front of goal. A few weeks ago the woodwork was keeping shots out and no-one was more gutted than me. Now, thank goodness, I'm finding the net again and I'm a so-called hero. Nothing gives me greater satisfaction than scoring and hopefully there are a few more to come, particularly if we play as well as a team, as we did in this match. At the end of the day it was down to the rest of the lads that I'm walking off with the match ball after scoring my first hat-trick for Southend.'

At the risk of earning Crown's wrath for being over-critical, he should have had even more goals to celebrate. On two other occasions he was faced with only the goalkeeper to beat, only to drive wide and then hit David Coles.

But his failure to accept that second chance brought no complaints from Martin Ling. For when the ball broke loose the winger pounced to lash in his second goal of the game with all the venom of a player still incensed at having been relegated to the subs bench for the three previous games.

The sheer pace and aggressive running of Crown and Ling subjected the Aldershot defenders to the type of afternoon that will haunt them for weeks ahead, especially Steve Wignall. He looked every one of his 35 years as he struggled to keep Crown in check.

Aldershot also found themselves overrun and outfought in midfield where the greater subtlety of Steve Tilson dovetailed admirably with the unquenchable fire of Peter Butler and Dave Martin.

Only when they had completed their nap hand did Southend become sloppy and allow their opponents a sniff at goal. But even when they were awarded a 69th minute penalty they failed to score. Paul Sansome saw to that when he dived to his right to deny Paul Coombs and bring off his third spotkick save of the campaign.

Considering Paul Roberts' tackle on Coombs looked fair in the first place, justice was seen to be done when Sansome guessed correctly to ensure Blues emerged with a repeat of the 5-0 victory they collected at Aldershot in September.

It was Ling who drove Blues in front in the 12th minute, applying the finishing touch from close range when Crown pulled the ball back from the right. Then it was Crown's turn as, in the space of 16 minutes, he collected the third hat-trick of his career – the others being against Halifax and Crewe while at Cambridge.

The first two, in the 35th and 43rd minutes, were gifted by blundering Aldershot defenders. Kevan Brown could only look on in horror as Crown fastened on to his intended back pass before lifting the ball into the net, and then the striker robbed Wignall on the edge of the box to deal out further punishment. Six minutes after the break came the hat-trick, thanks to the type of pass which will not be bettered all season. It came from Guy Butters whose trusty left foot delivered the ball all of 50 yards to leave Crown racing clear to hammer in his 19th goal of the season.

SOUTHEND UNITED: Sansome, Dixon, Roberts, Martin, Butters, Brush, Tilson, Butler, Crown, McDonough, Ling. Subs (not used): Clark, Bennett. Attendance: 2,821.

Tuesday, February 26th, 1991
Football League Associate Members' Cup, Second Round
SOUTHEND UNITED 7, TORQUAY UNITED 0

Andy Ansah's first hat-trick at senior level took Southend United a step nearer Wembley as they crushed Torquay 7-0 in a sensational second-half performance at Roots Hall last night. And, after starring in his side's Leyland-DAF Cup success in the Southern Area quarter-finals, the 21-year-old forward is hoping for an extended run as an out and out striker.

'I prefer to play down the middle where I can feed off one of the big fellows,' said the man who has played most of his games on the right wing since joining Blues from Brentford last season.

Ansah underlined his preference with a goal during Saturday's victory at Fulham and rammed home the message in style last night after manager David Webb had sprung something of a major shock by relegating leading marksman Brett Angell to the substitute's bench.

Yet a goal feast had seemed a million miles away as the interval arrived with both sides seeking to break the deadlock following an opening 45 minutes of sheer boredom.

So what was the message that Webb imparted in the dressing-room which brought about a remarkable transformation that was to bury Torquay beneath an avalanche of goals?

'The gaffer told us to start playing the ball into feet instead of hitting it long and high,' revealed Ansah. 'He stressed we could then make things happen rather than hope that they would. And he was proved absolutely right. Once we got to grips with the game there was only ever going to be one result, although I never expected we would finish up scoring seven.'

That took Southend's total in the competition this season to a stunning 23 in four matches – they knocked in 10 against Aldershot in the first round – and set up a home semi-final next Tuesday against the winners of tomorrow night's duel between Hereford and Brentford.

The midfield trio of Dave Martin, Steve Tilson and Peter Butler spent most of the first-half looking skywards as the game passed them by. But once Blues started to use their brains and feet, the tie took on a totally different complexion.

Torquay's dominance in the air gave way to uncertainty and slowness as they were made to fight a ground battle which ultimately heaped utter embarrassment on Dave Smith, the former Blues boss now in charge of the Devon club. The visiting dressing-room remained out of bounds for some considerable time after the final whistle before Smith emerged attempting to put on a smiling, brave face.

He did not seek to offer excuses nor sing the praises of the victors. Asked to explain what went wrong after the break he would only say 'They scored more goals than us.'

He was probably too shell-shocked to say much else after his forces suffered the type of rout currently being inflicted on Saddam Hussein's troops. A stunning dipping volley from 25 yards by Andy Edwards, an impressive figure in the heart of defence, opened the floodgates 10 minutes after the break.

After that a calculator was needed to keep track of the goals. A Martin penalty, awarded somewhat harshly when Adam Locke was challenged by Peter Whiston, quickly followed before Ansah's speed off the mark brought him goals in the 69th and 70th minutes.

A Tilson corner in the 72nd minute saw Martin rise to head Blues' fifth before Paul Clark's superb ball to the right flank enabled Locke to race forward and provide the cross which left substitute Angell with the task of supplying the finishing touch. Torquay's night of humiliation was then completed as Chris Powell, Tilson and Angell set up Ansah's hat-trick to take Blues closer to their Wembley dream.

SOUTHEND: Sansome, Austin, Powell, Martin, Edwards, Tilson, Clark, Butler, Ansah, Benjamin (Angell 71 mins), Locke. Sub (not used): Cornwell.

TORQUAY: Howell, P. Holmes, Uzzell, Whiston, Elliott, Musker (Saunders 62 mins), Smith, M. Holmes (Myers 62 mins), Tynan, Edwards, Loram.

Attendance: 2,273.

Saturday, May 4th 1991
Football League, Third Division
BURY 0, SOUTHEND UNITED 1

Master of suspense Alfred Hitchcock could not have scripted a more dramatic scenario to Southend United's history-making promotion clincher to Division Two on Saturday. The Blues, down to 10 men from just before half-time and facing an awkward swirling wind after the break, faced a mammoth job simply to survive against a Bury side desperate for victory to boost their hopes of a play-off spot.

But the harsh sending-off of Irish Under-21 international Pat Scully only served to pump even more energy and determination into his team-mates.

They grew in strength and stature the longer the game went on. And when Ian Benjamin twisted to ram in an Andy Ansah cross eight minutes from time, for the only goal of the match, the three points were deservedly in the locker amid delirious scenes from the hordes of travelling fans.

The club, as famous for its see-saw act between Divisions Three and Four as is the town of Southend for its Pier, was in the Second Division at last after 85 years of trying. Few could begrudge United their moment of glory. They had overcome seemingly impossible odds when referee Paul Vane from the West Midlands dismissed Scully for a challenge on winger David Lee which was certainly hard but did not deserve more than a yellow card.

'I was absolutely devastated when the ref brought out the red card, but the lads didn't let it affect them and if anything got better and stronger in the second half,' said the Irishman signed for £100,000 from Arsenal just before the transfer deadline in March. I just prayed that my sending-off would not wreck all that the players have fought for this season – I would never have been able to forgive myself if it had.'

Scully was the first to race on the pitch and hug his team-mates when the final whistle went to spark off celebrations which went on for at least half-an-hour before the 1,500 Blues supporters were finally persuaded to leave the ground and make the long journey home.

There were heroes in every department. David Martin dropped back alongside mighty skipper Paul Clark to fill Scully's defensive boots and performed magnificently, while behind them 'keeper Paul Sansome made two vital saves within a minute – first fisting a dipping 30-yarder from Liam Robinson against the crossbar after 75 minutes and then turning a header from Peter Valentine over the top from the resulting corner.

Little midfielder Peter Butler, back at the club which rejected him after a mere 11 games in 1986-87, showed Bury just what they missed with 90 minutes of non-stop tackling and drive which left me exhausted just watching. And the two men left up front, Andy Ansah and Brett Angell, ran themselves into the ground chasing every ball and not allowing the home side a second's respite. But in the end it was Benjamin, who at 29 has played for eight clubs before bringing his talents to Roots Hall last season, who stole the glory on an afternoon when, with so much at stake for both teams, chances were always going to be at a premium.

Nerves and the occasion seemed to take over once the whites of the goalposts came into sight. Other than the golden goal moment the best Southend efforts came from Ansah, who had one second half shot smothered and two before the break which were sliced just the wrong side of the woodwork, while Angell was inches away from converting a 39th minute cross from Christian Hyslop.

After celebrating out on the pitch and in the dressing room, Benjamin, described by boss David Webb as 'the best signing I've ever made,' emerged to tell me, 'It's great for me personally to have scored the goal to create history for Southend United – a real dream come true – but the other lads deserve tremendous credit for what they did.

'We all felt the ref over-reacted on Pat's sending off, he seemed to be swayed by the crowd, but it only succeeded in making us even more determined. We said at half-time that we had to pull together and make sure we didn't lose our shape, discipline or pattern and it worked a treat.

'I always felt we could nick it and when Andy's cross fell to my feet I just turned and hit it – I knew it was a goal from the moment the ball left my boot. 'It was wonderful for our fans who were absolutely brilliant and helped keep us going when we faced a real uphill battle. They never stopped shouting and urging us on and we responded in the best way possible.

'The young lads in the team were superb and showed that the club has a tremendous future. They can certainly do well in a higher grade of football – even an 'old man' like me is looking forward to helping to play a vital role in Division Two!'

And Webb, the manager with the Midas touch who has guided Southend to promotion in successive seasons, took it all in his stride at the end. He shut himself away in the dressing room as his players took all the accolades out on the pitch.

I went to tell him the fans were calling for him, but he was already soaking in the bath, a deserved glass of whisky in his hands. 'Let the lads who have done the job enjoy their moment of glory – I'll celebrate with the supporters once we have clinched the championship,' he said.

And the most successful manager ever at Southend refused to blow his own trumpet, preferring to heap praise on the young team he has built on a shoestring budget in an era of huge spending elsewhere.

'I was pleased for Benjamin that he scored the all-important goal because he typifies what I am trying to develop here – 100 per cent professional players,' added Webb.

'Benji gives so much and yet asks for so little – he is the best player I have ever worked with – and to think we got him on a free transfer! But we had a magnificent bunch of players out there today who did the club proud – they had a mountain to climb and scaled the peak.

'This was our little Everest and now we must look to our home games against Leyton Orient on Tuesday evening and Brentford on Saturday to finish the season in style and take the title which we will have earned.

'We have been on top or thereabouts for nearly the whole season – up there to be shot at. There have been one or two little dodgy spells but these players have proved so resilient, bouncing back and proving people who have written them off or doubted their credentials wrong time and time again.

'I feel so pleased for them and everyone at Roots Hall from the tea lady to the hardiest fanatic on the North Bank – Southend United has arrived at last and let's all savour and enjoy it.'

And when the team flew back into Southend Airport on their chartered aircraft, there were hundreds waiting to acclaim them and for the first time Webb allowed his usual stiff upper lip to quiver.

Met also by his wife Michelle and young son Daniel, he unashamedly brushed a tear or two from his eye – and I suspect a few people in the town who had waited years for this big moment also wept a bit themselves too.

As chairman Vic Jobson, who has masterminded Blues' rise from the ashes of crippling debt and despair, said: 'It's at times like this that you remember people who have given their all for this club over the years and are not here today to see this historic moment – people like past player, director and chairman Frank Walton, who sadly died, and like the father whose son wrote to me last week. 'The son, a Blues fan, told me his dad, who recently passed away aged 92. had always dreamed of seeing United in the Second Division.

'Let's just say I hope they are up there somewhere looking down and enjoying this as much as we are.' And so say all of us.

Wednesday, January 1st, 1992
Football League, Second Division
SOUTHEND UNITED 4, NEWCASTLE UNITED 0

Southend United blasted their way into the New Year yesterday with a crushing 4-0 win over much troubled Newcastle – their biggest victory so far in what is turning out to be a simply amazing season.

And yet in all honestly this was far from Blues' most convincing display although few in the bumper 9,458 crowd were complaining. Newcastle possibly enjoyed the lion's share of possession but unlike Southend couldn't find the all-important finish although it must be admitted they did not enjoy the best of fortune as they did on their last visit to Roots Hall – winning 5-1 in May 1960.

This time they had no-one with the explosive power and appetite of top marksman Brett Angell whose knock-out double act took his tally this term to 18 – but an incredible 44 goals in 81 first-team games since arriving for a bargain £100,000 from Stockport. And for hit-man Angell the difference between the two teams boiled down to one thing – confidence.

'We're really buzzing at the moment and making the most of our chances while they are struggling near the bottom of the table with nothing going right,' was his apt after match summing up. I felt we kept their back-four under intense pressure and pounced when the cracks inevitably appeared while they knocked the ball about well but had nothing to offer in the vital last third of the pitch.'

And on being told of his tremendous strike record since joining Blues, Angell said modestly: 'You know I don't worry about things like that. I'm just glad to keep doing the job I was brought here to do. It's a team game and the other lads deserve as much credit as me for laying on the chances.

'I had about the same number of goals this time last season and hopefully I'll continue to bang them in like today ... who knows what I'll end up with.'

But his manager David Webb was more glowing in his praise of the big front-man whose game has improved immeasurably since coming to Roots Hall. 'Brett just gets better and better,' purred the Blues chief. 'He has worked very hard at improving various parts of his game and is now beginning to reap the rewards. He is lethal round the box and in fact underlined why we got the points today. Perhaps we didn't play as well as I would have liked but our finishing was superb while they huffed and puffed a lot but lacked that vital thrust in front of goal.'

Very true. The corner count of eight for Newcastle and just one for Southend perhaps reflected the possession the visitors enjoyed but when it came to shots on target Blues produced 14 to Newcastle's paltry four!

In fairness the Geordies hit the woodwork on two occasions while fullback Chris Powell twice headed off the line in 60 amazing second-half seconds but they rarely threatened to produce the necessary venom while in contrast Southend looked likely to score everytime they poured forward.

Blues got off to the perfect start with a goal after just two minutes when Angell dispossessed Alan Thompson before hitting a shot which deflected off Kevin Scott to leave 'keeper Tommy Wright stranded.

Ian Benjamin, who showed some superb touches, was unlucky with a 14th minute volley before Paul Sansome was stung into action, turning Steve Watson's stinging shot round a post. Benjamin had another shot well saved before Steve Howey bundled the ball against a post after the tireless Gavin Peacock created the half-chance.

But Southend produced another killer blow in first-half injury time when Keith Jones scored his first League goal since arriving for a record £175.000 from Brentford just over two months ago – drilling in a great low shot from the edge of the area.

Andy Ansah wriggled his way through straight from me restart and drove weakly at Wright but made up for that miss after 56 minutes when he rose superbly to head in a chip from Jones following a flowing move down the right. To their credit the Newcastle babes refused to die and Sansome did well to thwart substitute Andy Hunt before Lee Clark smacked another shot against the inside of a post.

Then came Powell's two clearances before Angell wrapped it all up when he fastened onto Matt Appleby's poor back pass before coolly rounding Wright and tucking the ball into the net to put Southend in tremendous heart for Saturday's tough F.A. Cup trip to mighty Everton.

For a few short hours Blues stood proudly at the top of the table, but after the afternoon results they are in third place behind Blackburn and Ipswich.

SOUTHEND: Sansome, Austin, Powell, Jones (sub 62 minutes Butler), Scully, Prior, Ansah, Cornwell, Tilson, Benjamin, Angell. Sub (not used): Locke.

NEWCASTLE: Wright, Watson, Bodin, Thompson, Scott, Appleby, Clark, Peacock, Kelly (sub 45 minutes Hunt), Howey, Makel. Sub (not used): Bradshaw.

Wednesday, September 1st, 1993
Football League, First Division
WEST BROMWICH ALBION 2, SOUTHEND UNITED 2

Top soccer bosses Howard Kendall of Everton and Southampton's Ian Branfoot watched goalpoacher Brett Angell take his seemingly inevitable move to the Premiership a step closer with both goals in Southend United's dramatic 2-2 draw at West Brom last night.

And the delighted 25 year-old transfer seeker, who took his tally to five in the last three games, told me afterwards: 'Perhaps that's given one or two people a little nudge and persuaded them to give me a chance. I feel my game is gradually sharpening up – I made a poor start to the season and couldn't complain when the manager dropped me – it gave me the kick up the backside that I needed. My goals weren't spectacular tonight – it was a case of being in the right place at the right time. But this game is all about taking your chances and I'm hoping I am making a few people sit up and take notice.'

But Angell was the first to acknowledge that the way manager Barry Fry has got the team playing is bound to create lots of goal chances. 'We are certainly a lively side,' he said. 'The gaffer encourages us to knock the ball around and get it into the box from dangerous areas – I can only finish off what the midfield and wingers create. We were not happy with the goals we conceded tonight but proved that we have the right spirit and attitude by coming back from two goals down to earn a point and keep our unbeaten League run going.' Indeed it was that never-say-die battling approach which produced a point which Blues certainly deserved but, until a dramatic last minute strike, looked as if they were doomed not to get.

There were only seconds left when Southend mounted yet another swift attack on the battered West Brom defence. Chris Powell, substitute Paul Harding and little Derek Payne combined to free winger Ricky Otto and when his low cross came in there was Angell to bundle the ball over the line.

It was a decisive goal which silenced the screams of 14,000 Midland soccer fanatics who had earlier been left howling in frustration after Angell had pulled a goal back in the 64th minute – his instinctive back heel creeping into the corner of the net after Payne had driven in Harding's long throw.

This was a night when Blues needed to dredge up all their courage and resources as their back four showed alarming frailties at times, and were only saved by the agility of Paul Sansome and coolness of Powell who seems to grow in stature with every game.

West Brom scythed through the middle of Southend's defence almost at will at the start of each half – Kevin Donovan, Bob Taylor and Andy Hunt were all left completely in the clear in the first four minutes but 'keeper Sansome and poor finishing ensured survival.

But Blues weathered the storm and began to exert pressure on an equally vulnerable home defence but Angell failed to get a positive touch to another Otto cross and was then denied by a great one-handed save from Tony Lange when his header looked destined for the back of the net.

The lively Otto went full length to head home a Jason Lee cross on the half-hour but the 'goal' was ruled out by a linesman who decided he was off-side although, from my vantage point, he seemed to come from behind a defender. Adam Locke sent a fierce 25 yarder inches wide and then Angell volleyed into the side netting after Lee created the half chance.

The second-half started the same as the first with Sansome spreading himself to save from Hunt and then making the stop of the night to turn a header from ex-West Ham man Gary Strodder over the bar. But he was left help-less when West Brom's Taylor took advantage of slack marking to score twice in the 52nd and 57th minutes to put the home side on the way to what looked three certain points.

Fry immediately pulled off Locke and Graham Bressington for Jonathan Hunt and on-loan Paul Harding and reshuffled his line-up to spark off that late revival which left him relieved and delighted.

'We showed tremendous character and spirit to come back in what was a very intimidating atmosphere,' said Fry. 'You can never write us off because we are the type of side that will always create chances and, with Angell on that form, have the ability to finish them off – I hope Brett stays … but I'm begin-ning to doubt we'll be able to hang on to him.' Teams:

WEST BROM: Lange, Fereday, Lilwall, Bradley, Raven, Strodder, Hunt, Ham-ilton, Taylor, O'Regan, Donovan. Subs (not used) Ampadu, Burgess and Naylor.

SOUTHEND: Sansome, Locke (sub 58 minutes Hunt), Powell, Sussex, Edwards, Bressington (sub 58 minutes Harding), Ansah, Payne, Lee, Otto, Angell. Goalkeeper sub not used Royce.

Attendance: 14,482.

Saturday, October 1st, 1994
Football League, First Division
SUNDERLAND 0, SOUTHEND UNITED 1

History-making Southend United's defence, severely criticised for leaking nine goals in their previous two away games, performed heroics to seal a great win at Sunderland on Saturday.

Blues became the first side ever to win four successive matches at the Roker Park stronghold but they had to withstand an Alamo-type second-half siege. And nobody did better to help keep Southend's second clean sheet of the season than new duo Mark Hone and Keith Dublin.

Hone showed supreme coolness under pressure while Dublin was a real giant – never wilting in the heat of battle. 'A result like this may shock other teams but not us – we've got much more belief and confidence and feel we can match anybody at the moment,' hero Dublin told me. The whole team worked so hard for this victory. Sure we were under pressure at times, you can't expect to come to a place like this and get an easy ride, but everyone played their part. Dave Regis and Roger Willis have come in and given us more all-round power and we don't look like collapsing as we did a few weeks ago.'

And Hone is delighted that his £25,000 move from non-League Welling United is already reaping such rich rewards. Our dressing room is really bubbling now – a big difference to earlier in the season – and if we can keep putting in this sort of effort then there's no reason why we can't continue to climb up the table,' he said.

Indeed every blue shirt worked until they dropped – defending superbly from front to back. Dave Regis and Andy Thomson chased all over the pitch closing down defenders in possession, the midfield snapped and snarled for 90 minutes while the back-four reigned supreme – the few things they missed were tidied up by back-to-form 'keeper Paul Sansome.

Sansome made two crucial saves after the break when he blocked an effort from strongman Don Goodman with his legs and then kept out a fierce shot from Craig Russell.

Mind you Blues themselves couldn't be ignored at the other end – a great saving tackle by Kevin Ball denied Thomson while the ever threatening Ricky Otto burst through eight minutes from time but sent his shot agonisingly wide of the far post.

But in the end victory was earned via a slick 16th minute move – Roger Willis heading a Sunderland corner out to Otto who sprinted away and fed the hard grafting Phil Gridelet. A neat ball inside put Thomson free and the clinical assassin just doesn't miss those one-to-one chances with the 'keeper.

It was substitute goalie Alec Chamberlain's first touch after coming on for Tony Norman who suffered a nasty bang in the face when trying to claim a right-wing corner after only eight minutes. Boss Peter Taylor was obviously delighted with his brave fighters – 'We worked hard as a team and I couldn't ask for more,' was his after-match reaction. Our two new signings Willis and Regis have made us stronger as a team and we fancy our chances more now when it comes to a battle. But I think Hone was brilliant – the best player on the park … absolutely superb! Three wins on the trot has given the whole place a huge lift but we've got to keep the ball rolling at Barnsley next weekend.' Teams:

SUNDERLAND: Norman (sub 8 mins Chamberlain), Kubicki, Ord, Ball, Melville, Smith, Martin Gray (sub 72 mins Rodgerson), Goodman, P. Gray, Owers, Russell. Sub (not used): Michael Gray.

SOUTHEND: Sansome, Hone, Powell, Gridelet, Edwards, Dublin, Willis, Whelan, Regis, Otto, Thomson. Subs (not used): Tilson, Forrester, Royce.

Attendance: 15,520.

Saturday, December 10th, 1994
Football League, First Division
MIDDLESBROUGH 1, SOUTHEND UNITED 2

Phil Gridelet turned on a superb match-winning display to rock his soccer hero Bryan Robson in a huge First Division upset on Saturday. Robson's Middlesbrough were red hot favourites to march further ahead at the top against a Southend United side who had only won once on their travels this season.

But midfield strongman Gridelet and his Blues pals had other ideas as they turned on a tremendous team display to claim a victory which lifted them to ninth in the table and within touching distance of the battle for a play-off place. Southend soaked up tremendous pressure at times but boss Peter Taylor's decision to play with Graham Bressington as sweeper proved a master stroke as they held Boro's twin strike force of John Hendrie and Paul Wilkinson in a vice like grip.

But it was Gridelet's power and sheer determination which turned the tide in Southend's favour – making one and scoring his first ever League goal. And afterwards the 27 year old hero admitted it was the sight of Robson in the opposition dug-out which helped light his fire. 'Bryan has always been my idol and to score a goal and turn in a performance like that in front of him was a real dream come true,' Gridelet told me afterwards.

But this wasn't just about me today – all the lads worked so hard ... we proved we're not the easy touch a lot of people said we were after those heavy defeats at Wolves and Port Vale.'

On his spectacular 66th minute goal – winning the ball in midfield and driving through to rifle a shot into the top corner of the net from fully 30 yards – Gridelet said: 'The manager has been having a go at me for not getting on the scoresheet and hopefully that strike will give me the confidence to shoot more often. We proved today we can take on the best and beat them – we may be a small club but we've got good players with big ambition.'

Taylor was obviously delighted saying: 'The work-rate of the players was tremendous – everyone played their part in what was a terrific allround performance to be proud of. Bressington did brilliantly at the back but it would be hard to pick any individuals out as everybody played their part – without doubt our best away display of the season.'

Middlesbrough assistant boss Viv Anderson's after-match comment that 'Southend came for a point and nicked three' had more than a hint of sour grapes about it as his men were rarely given a clear sight of goal while Blues always threatened to catch them on the break.

With the strong wind at their backs, Middlesbrough drove forward in the first-half but Paul Sansome turned a stinging shot from Alan Moore over the bar after just 12 minutes and both Nigel Pearson and Wilkinson headed wide of the target when well placed.

Andy Thomson had a shot tipped over the bar but most of the 16,843 crowd were silenced two minutes before the break when Gridelet hit a great cross in for Julian Hails, making his full first-team debut after signing on non-contract from Fulham, to control and hook into the roof of the net.

It was reward for some neat play from Hails, who stepped in for the injured Roger Willis, and when Gridelet blasted that second goal Boro looked out for the count.

But John Hendrie's well taken goal 12 minutes from the end set up a nail-biting finish. Sansome made a great save with his legs as Southend were forced to defend grimly but held firm to claim their second win in the North-east – their only previous away success coming at Sunderland. Teams:

MIDDLESBROUGH: Miller, Morris, Whyte, Vickers, Pearson, Mustoe, Cox, Todd (sub 76 minutes Moreno, sub 80 minutes Blackmore), Wilkinson, Hendrie, Moore. Goalkeeper sub not used Roberts.

SOUTHEND: Sansome, Hone, Powell, Gridelet, Edwards, Dublin, Bressington, Whelan, Jones, Hails, Thomson. Subs (not used): Tilson, Sussex and goalkeeper Royce.

Tuesday, December 27th, 1994
Football League, First Division
SOUTHEND UNITED 2, WEST BROMWICH ALBION 1

Southend United's human dynamo Phil Gridelet doesn't score many goals but they don't come much better than yesterday's matchwinner – only the second he's notched in the League in his career.

Groans of disappointment from the fans when Gridelet somehow screwed the ball over a gaping goal from six yards out, were turned to jubilant celebrations just 60 seconds later when he sent a stunning effort from fully 25 yards screaming into the top corner of the net.

That 57th minute golden strike put the icing on what was a gritty fightback by Blues who had 'keeper Paul Sansome to thank for still being in the game after a nightmare first 20 minutes.

Sansome was beaten after only four minutes by Lee Ashcroft's sweet low shot from the edge of the area but then turned on the heroics to keep out efforts from Andy Hunt, Ashcroft and Darren Bradley.

Slowly but surely Southend pulled themselves together and came to terms with a difficult, muddy surface. Gridelet gave warning of what was to come with a great dipping volley which Stuart Naylor tipped over the bar as Ronnie Whelan began to stamp his influence on the proceedings.

And once the equaliser went in seven minutes before half-time – Kieran O'Regan judged to have turned a low cross from the impressive Julian Hails, touched on by Gridelet, into his own net – West Brom were always forced to play second fiddle.

Even some amazing decisions by Portsmouth ref Mike Pierce – described by Albion boss Alan Buckley as 'some of the most incredible I've ever seen' – failed to take the shine off what was gripping Christmas fayre.

And the first thing that man-of-the-match Gridelet did afterwards was to share his bottle of champagne with his ten other team-mates because as he said 'this result wasn't just about my goal – we showed tremendous character and spirit to battle our way back.'

Of his earlier miss Gridelet said: 'I don't like scoring easy goals! But having muffed that one I made up my mind that the next time I got in shooting range I'd have a go and luckily it came off.

'It was a similar strike to my first ever League goal scored at Middlesbrough last month, and I'm also glad to have rewarded the manager's faith in me as he keeps encouraging my forward runs.'

Taylor, too, was full of praise for his goal hero saying: 'After that bad miss there are not many players who would have had the bottle a minute later to try a shot like that – it speaks volumes for Phil's character.'

Watched by a best of the season 6,856 crowd, but still the second worst home Christmas gate since 1913, Blues stormed back after that dreadful opening spell and also with the memory of a sad collapse the previous day at Charlton still in their minds.

They took the game to Albion and with a little more steadiness should really have won by a much bigger margin – Andy Thomson, Roger Willis and Andy Ansah all guilty of snatching at chances which came their way.

Skipper Chris Powell was also desperately unlucky with a 73rd minute curling shot which beat the 'keeper all ends up only to come back off the inside of a post. Although Gridelet deservedly took most of the after-match accolades my personal star award went to newcomer Hails who showed some neat control and touches on the treacherous, divot strewn pitch.

Hails was desperately unlucky to be booked by Pierce who strangely judged that his 80th minute plunge into the box under a heavy challenge from a desperate defender was a con trick.

As Albion's angry boss Buckley said: 'I thought that was a definite penalty and we should have had one too in the last seconds – how the referee could turn them down was beyond me and to book the Southend man was adding insult to injury.'

But he had no complaints about the red card shown to his striker Bob Taylor five minutes from time for a second bookable offence – 'it was a stupid thing to do and he deserved what he got,' said Buckley.

SOUTHEND: Sansome, Hone, Powell, Gridelet, Edwards, Dublin, Hails, Whelan, Willis, Ansah, Thomson. Subs (not used): Iorfa, Tilson and goalkeeper Royce.

WEST BROM: Naylor, O'Regan (sub 75 minutes Smith), Lilwall, Bradley (sub 56 minutes Parsley), Mardon, Edwards, Donovan, Ashcroft, Taylor, Hunt, Hamilton. Goalkeeper sub not used: Germaine.

Saturday, December 2nd, 1995
Football League, First Division
SOUTHEND UNITED 3, BIRMINGHAM CITY 1

Southend United produced the victory over Barry Fry's Birmingham which their fans had been praying for – turning on the style and putting on their most impressive show of the season.

High-flying Brum were not just brought down to earth but brought to their knees by a Blues outfit which displayed skill, passion and an appetite the visitors just couldn't match. In fact Birmingham were a shade lucky to get off so lightly as rampant Southend hit the woodwork twice, missed one great chance and were only inches away from converting crosses on two occasions.

They had no-one to match dynamic front duo Dave Regis and Paul Byrne while central defensive tough guys Mike Lapper and Mick Bodley coped superbly with the gangling menace of Kevin Francis and scruffy goalgrabber Steve Claridge who had to be told by referee Richard Poulain of Huddersfield to literally pull his socks up!

And this was a match when midfield powerhouse Phil Gridelet, who promised supporters a game to remember, regained much of his missing box-to-box energy while Mike Marsh sprayed the ball around to great effect.

But it would perhaps be unfair to pick out individuals after a thrilling team display which could prove the springboard for a dramatic push into the play-off zone.

Birmingham played early on with the confidence you would expect from a side boasting just one defeat from their last 18 games, but Blues slowly but surely got a grip and took command.

Regis, set up by Byrne, blasted a great chance over the bar after 14 minutes while at the other end Francis had a shot deflected over the top before Claridge stunned most in a best of the season 7,770 crowd with a 29th minute opener.

Francis broke away on the right and Simon Royce, with a rare but fatal rush of blood to the head, opted to try a suicidal tackle which ended with the ball ballooning up for Claridge to hook into the empty net.

But then two goals in a sizzling two minute spell just before the break turned the game on its head.

First, Bodley thundered in a tremendous header off the underside of the bar from Byrne's free-kick and then Regis pounced to tap in after Ian Bennett fumbled an awkward bouncing shot from star man Byrne.

Those crucial strikes must have made the half-time cuppa taste sweet in the Southend dressing room and they came out looking determined to grab the all important third goal. Julian Hails saw a header turned against a post by Bennett and Gary Jones somehow sliced the rebound wide from six yards and then Bennett sprang to his left to keep out a Regis header.

But this was a match when Southend were not to be denied and Byrne's first League goal after 71 minutes settled any lingering doubts – collecting a crossfield ball from Regis before cutting inside two defenders and drilling in a low shot into the far corner of the net. The goal knocked the stuffing out of Birmingham who were forced to hang on grimly.

Birmingham staged a late push to salvage something from the afternoon but Blues held firm with Royce's safe handling and the determination of the men in front of him making sure they didn't throw them any crumbs.

SOUTHEND (4-4-2 formation): Royce, Dublin, Lapper, Bodley, Powell, Byrne, Marsh, Gridelet, Hails, Regis, Jones. Subs (not used): Thomson, Tilson, Read.

BIRMINGHAM: Bennett, Forsyth, Frain, Castle (sub 18 minutes Donowa), Edwards, Daish, Hunt (sub 56 minutes Poole), Claridge, Francis, Preece (sub 56 minutes Charlery), Hill.

Referee: R. Poulain (Huddersfield). Attendance: 7,770.

Saturday, April 13th, 1996
Football League, First Division
CRYSTAL PALACE 2, SOUTHEND UNITED 0

Sadly understrength Southend United were easily pushed aside as Crystal Palace boosted their promotion bid with a comfortable afternoon's work on Saturday. The side Blues put out faced a task akin to trying to climb Everest in carpet slippers and slithered to a predictable defeat.

Palace went into the clash boasting just one defeat in 12 games while injury-ravaged Southend had won only once in the previous eight and the difference in confidence shone through like a beacon.

I can hardly remember a 90 minutes like this when Blues failed to get one shot on target, while the home side's superior power and strength meant a busy time for boss Ronnie Whelan's reshaped back-line.

He experimented with three men in the heart of defence and Julian Hails and Steve Tilson as attacking wing-backs. The fact that it succeeded up to a point could be measured by all of the better performances coming from this department.

Mark McNally was superbly disciplined while 'keeper Simon Royce also had a sound game – having no chance with the goals which beat him and also saving a late penalty.

The midfield found it hard to spark off a makeshift frontline which was totally over-powered – Keith Dublin and Roger Willis hardly getting a kick or able to make any headway at all. Mike Marsh and Paul Byrne did their best but unhappily their attempts to find a way through found no cutting edge at the end.

Palace quickly stamped their authority on the action and went ahead after just seven minutes – Dave Hopkins finding Dougie Freedman who controlled an awkward bouncing ball to hold off Mick Bodley and rifle a shot low into the far corner of the net. Dublin volleyed over from the edge of the area after 14 minutes and then Phil Gridelet was desperately unlucky with a rasping shot from 18 yards which scraped the crossbar. But it was Palace who still called most of the shots with Carl Veart sending one header wide of a gaping goal and another crashing against the woodwork.

Southend looked determined to try and salvage something at the start of the second-half but Tilson's control let him down when put in the clear by Marsh, and a free-kick from Byrne in a dangerous position was hit with too much pace and Roget headed behind.

Gridelet powered through but, with three players screaming for the ball to his right, decided to find Marsh to his left and the cross was easily dealt with by Nigel Martyn.

Most in the 15,672 crowd were soon celebrating as Palace virtually wrapped the game up after 59 minutes when a shot from Simon Rodger was touched into the net by a woefully unmarked Freeman.

Roget hobbled off 17 minutes from the end and his replacement Mark Hone was harshly judged to have brought down Bruce Dyer in the closing stages but Royce denied Freedman his hat-trick with a fine full length save.

Unhappily the poor game was matched by the officials – referee Richard Poulain of Huddersfield was hardly ever up with the action while the bizarre flagging from one of the linesmen had to be seen to be believed – they had a nightmare!

Saturday, September 7th, 1996
Football League, First Division
SOUTHEND UNITED 5, BOLTON WANDERERS 2

Southend United regained some Essex pride when they demolished Lancashire big-guns Bolton to emphatically chalk-up their first win of the season. While the county's cricketers were being humiliated by Lancs, in the NatWest Trophy Blues lorded it up with a stunning victory which completely turned the formbook upside down.

Few pundits could see Bolton doing anything but extend their unbeaten start to the season but Ronnie Whelan's battlers had other ideas. They chased and harried the table-toppers right from the start, knocking them out of their stride and but for two great goal-line clearances from full-back Steve McAnespie the final score might have been even more convincing.

Mind you Southend's vulnerable back-line was left grateful that Nathan Blake left his shooting boots in the dressing room as he missed two golden chances at vital stages of the game – a minute after the kick-off and again just after half-time when the score was still 2-2.

But let's not dwell on too many negative aspects as this was a thrilling performance from the home side with some truly superb goals which should pump some much-needed confidence into those blue shirts. For once Southend refused to let their heads drop even when Bolton twice came from behind in the opening period courtesy of two soft goals.

Skipper Mike Marsh led his troops in great style – tackling like a tiger and imposing his silky skills on the game right from the start. He was run close for man-of-the-match honours by Steve Tilson who seems to revel in his new wing-back role – taming Bolton's speed merchant David Lee and also getting forward himself to send in dangerous crosses and shots.

Andy Harris also showed a maturity beyond his 19 years to prop up a defence which creaked at times while behind him Paul Sansome, in the side on merit after Simon Royce was fit again following a back injury, never put a foot or hand wrong.

But it was up front that Southend were most impressive with both Jeroen Boere and Paul Williams running themselves into the ground as they not only closed people down but also proved a real handful for Bolton's hard pressed defence.

Williams, on a month's contract after being released by Crystal Palace and only in the side because of Andy Rammell's Achilles injury, provided the pace and craft while Boere had the brawn and strength. Together they formed a lethal combination which could yet blossom and force boss Ronnie Whelan to rethink his priorities when it comes to bringing in new faces.

Blues recovered from a shaky start to set the ball rolling on this goal feast when Boere hooked in after Keith Dublin headed on Julian Hails' 5th minute corner.

John Nielsen and Williams both tested the Bolton 'keeper before the visitors levelled with a real sickening goal – Alan Thompson's mishit shot falling perfectly for Blake to stab home after 23 minutes. But just two minutes later came the goal of the match, and possibly the season. Williams had a shot blocked and when the ball came out to Nielsen the Dane unleashed a tremendous volley into the top corner of the net from fully 25 yards.

Mark McNally tried an effort from similar range but Keith Branagan tipped the ball over the bar but it was Bolton who equalised after 31 minutes when

McAnespie threaded the ball through for John McGinlay to slip into the net past the despairing boot of McNally.

Paul Sansome saved well from Blake and Marsh chipped a cheeky free-kick agonisingly wide before a pulsating first-half came to a close. But the action was just as fast and furious after the restart – Williams and Boere went close and Blake headed a great chance wide at the other end before McAnespie rescued his side with two great clearances off the line to deny Phil Gridelet and Boere.

But Southend were in no mood to be denied with Boere picking the ball up on the right, cutting inside and beating two defenders before slotting a low 65th minute shot into the net corner. Four minutes later Dublin, who looked much happier in the heart of defence, hit a long ball for Williams to beat the offside trap and coolly send a neat swerving shot past Branagan. Blues rubbed salt in Bolton's gaping wounds 10 minutes from the end when sub Andy Todd sent Nielsen crashing to the ground under a crude challenge and Marsh capped a superb individual performance by slotting the penalty.

SOUTHEND (in 3-2-3-2 formation): Sansome: McNally, Harris, Dublin; Hails, Tilson; Gridelet, Marsh, Nielsen; Boere, Williams. Subs (not used) Byrne, Roget and Lapper.

BOLTON: Branagan, McAnespie (sub 73 minutes Bergsson), Phillips, Frandsen, Taggart, Fairclough, Johansen (sub 73 minutes Todd), Lee (sub 75 minutes Taylor), Blake, McGinlay, Thompson.

Referee: M.J. Brandwood (Lichfield, Staffs.). Attendance: 4,475

Saturday, October 28th, 2000
Football League, Third Division
MANSFIELD TOWN 1, SOUTHEND UNITED 1

It was a tale of two penalties at Mansfield Town on Saturday as Southend United battled bravely against the elements to earn a Third Division draw. The Seasiders fell behind to an early opportunist strike from Stags hitman Chris Greenacre, before levelling things up soon after from the penalty spot, with Blues top-scorer Martin Carruthers doing the honours.

However, Mansfield were awarded a penalty of their own three minutes short of the half-time interval, but Greenacre was denied the chance to double his tally as Southend keeper Andy Woodman smothered the front-runner's effort. And the stalemate couldn't be broken during the second period as both sides fought against torrential rain and blasting winds, which at one stage bent the Field Mill corner flags in half, as well as each other.

Indeed, if it was not for the sponge like Mansfield pitch, which took the brunt of the punishing weather, then this game may not have finished at all.

However, it did and Southend, who remain sixth in the league table, extended their unbeaten run to a magnificent 12 matches, even though

Mansfield probably just edged out the Shrimpers in terms of possession and chances.

Last season, Blues would have collapsed under similar pressure, but this Southend side is made of sterner stuff. The Stags always looked lively flying forward and they cruelly exposed Seasiders full-back Martin Booty's failure to defend his ground, concentrating the majority of their attacking efforts down his flank. Mansfield's left-winger Wayne Corden continually left Booty behind as he darted forward and fired numerous threatening centres into the Southend penalty box.

But luckily for the Shrimpers the remainder of their four-man rearguard, skipper Phil Whelan, fellow centre-half Leo Roget and left-back Damon Searle were on top of their game and managed to cover for their colleague, snuffing out Mansfield's animated frontmen at every opportunity. And in central midfield, Blues had another superb performer in Mark Tinkler – who sadly looks set to join Hartlepool United today.

The former Leeds United player was tenacious in the tackle, strong in the air and able to pick out his passes accurately despite the storms overhead. Tinkler proved at the weekend that he is a class act and if he is heading for pastures new then Blues manager David Webb will have to move quickly to sign a replacement who can fill the massive void his departure will leave behind. However, the Shrimpers chief's latest addition to his squad, diminutive forward Ben Abbey, looked useful after making his debut as a substitute. The pacey 22-year-old, who made a free transfer move from Oxford United on Friday, used the ball intelligently and almost snatched a late winner after replacing Trevor Fitzpatrick, who struggled to make an impression.

And finally, Southend's brilliant fans need a mention after they easily filled the away section of Mansfield's ground, which officially holds 550 supporters, but made the noise of thousands as they inspired their team to steal another precious point. Mansfield Town hitman Chris Greenacre gave Southend United an early wake-up call at Field Mill on Saturday.

The Shrimpers had just started to get to grips with their hosts, playing in front of the Stags haunting empty main stand which is still under construction.

But the Blues had the stuffing knocked out of them after seven minutes when Mansfield's wily left-winger Wayne Corden made the most of a missed tackle by Southend right-back Martyn Booty, before catching his fellow defenders Phil Whelan and Damon Searle cold with a diagonal ball.

And former Manchester City forward Greenacre was quick to capitalise on the confusion as he picked up the loose ball and floated a well placed 20-yard effort over the head of Seasiders keeper Andy Woodman as he got caught in no-man's land rushing off his line.

The reaction of Southend's players was to get stuck straight back in to their hosts as they battled against the howling winds and torrential rain which battered every side of the Stags' half-built stadium.

And Shrimpers midfielder David Lee triggered the first of a number of events which would lead to Blues' equaliser. Lee cut out a weak pass from Mansfield defender Bobby Hassell 25 yards from goal and lashed in a well struck shot, which deflected off Jon Fortune and flew over the bar.

Lee then took the resulting left-wing corner, whipping the ball in under the Mansfield crossbar, leaving home custodian Bobby Mimms to punch away frantically.

However, the rebound fell to Leo Roget on the left-hand edge of the Stags penalty area, where the Southend defender was bundled over clumsily by Greenacre, handing the Seasiders a spot-kick.

Shrimpers forward Martin Carruthers stepped up to face Mimms, despite missing Blues' only other penalty at Torquay United earlier in the season. And it was the right decision, as the striker planted a low shot into the left-hand corner of the Mansfield net, sending Mimms the wrong way in the process, to register his sixth goal of the current campaign after 16 minutes. Two minutes later, Southend's central midfielder Mark Tinkler hit a 20-yard drive well wide of the goal, before home forward Danny Bacon's left-wing cross found team-mate Darrell Clarke inside Blues' box, but Woodman gathered his deflected ten-yard effort.

Carruthers then teed up Shrimpers midfielder Kevin Maher for a long-range drive which missed the target and Seasiders frontman Trevor Fitzpatrick found Mimms' hands with a feeble attempt. Lee then ballooned a 25-yard free-kick into orbit, following a foul on Tinkler by Mansfield centre-half Fortune.

Stags playmaker Mark Blake replied by hitting an attempt over Woodman's goal and Greenacre did well to get in front of Roget and meet Mansfield full-back Dave Jervis' left-wing cross, but he failed to hit the target.

After 37 minutes, Mimms got down well to turn away an awkward skidding Tinkler effort. And Forbes went close with a first-time drive after another wind assisted flag-kick from Lee was only half-cleared.

But Mansfield should have taken the lead three minutes before the interval when they were awarded a highly dubious penalty. Bacon backed into Roget at the far post and threw himself to the floor after Booty had failed to cut out Lee Williams' right-wing centre and referee Alan Kaye fell for the home striker's con-trick.

But justice prevailed as Woodman smothered Greenacre's spot-kick, although the marksman was left cursing his luck as he got to the rebound first with his head, but the ball hit the foot of the right post.

After the break the weather grew even worse and Mansfield started better. Fortune broke into the box following a slip from Tinkler, but could only find a well positioned Woodman with his shot after 52 minutes. And four minutes later, the Southend goalie foiled Mansfield again as Greenacre pulled the ball back for Clarke from the left, but Woodman stood firm at his near post and blocked the midfielder's point-blank crack at goal.

Mansfield continued to drive forward with Hassell going close from long range just after the hour, before Lee blocked another shot from the same player after 71 minutes.

Maher was denied by Mimms after striking a near-perfect volley from the edge of the box and his midfield partner Tinkler shot wide after steaming forward in the 83rd minute. And with the game fizzling out, Southend new-boy Ben Abbey nearly grabbed a late winner. Booty did well to win the ball and curl a pass to Abbey on the left-flank, giving the striker the chance to head for goal and let fly with a 20-yarder, which Mimms clutched at the second attempt.

MANSFIELD: Mimms, Robinson, Fortune, Jervis, Hassell, Corden, Blake, Clarke, Williams, Greenacre, Bacon (Boulding). Subs not used: Asher, Andrews, Disley and Pilkington.

SOUTHEND: Woodman, Booty, Searle, Roget, Whelan, Tinkler, Maher, Forbes, Lee, Fitzpatrick (Abbey 62), Carruthers. Subs not used: Johnson McSweeney, Hunter and Flahavan.

Attendance: 2,200.

CHAPTER FOURTEEN

Double Figures 1906-1990

Saturday, September 15th, 1906
Southern League, Second Division
SOUTHEND UNITED 12, (Halse 5, Newland 3, Mitchell 2, Freeman, Axcell)
ROYAL ENGINEERS (ALDERSHOT) 0

After the creditable result obtained at Tunbridge Wells on the previous Saturday, it was not surprising to find that the Southern League fixture with the Royal Engineers attracted almost 2,000 spectators to Roots Hall on Saturday. The United had two alterations in the side which has so far represented the Club; Holden and Secretary Jack standing down and thus admitting of the introduction of Bomb. Newland at outside right and the promising Leigh youth, Axcell, on the other wing. Prior to the game starting, the home team (who were rigged out in their Club colours, the new Royal blue jerseys, etc.) sat for a photograph, but prompt to the advertised kick-off time Molyneux was again favoured with the toss of the coin.

Kicking off up hill, the Engineers opened up with a pretty movement on the right wing, but a return by Owen set the home forwards at work, and Halse, breaking through, missed with a right foot shot by inches only. The visitors made a little headway on the left, but thus early the game promised to lean one way; and the Blue-jerseyed forwards seemed to be always on the ball, careless finishing alone delaying the commencement of the scoring.

For ten minutes the play hung around the Engineers' citadel, and then Newland was applauded for a neat piece of work, nipping in smartly to the middle of the goal and driving from six yards hard in; the goalkeeper gathering the quick shot cleverly and clearing. The effort deserved a score, and the soldier had thus soon found favour with the crowd.

Pressure was still maintained, but the home shooting, though frequent, was generally a little off the billet and what was well directed brought out the good points in goal of Roberts. Watkins was to blame with a bad miss from five yards out, skying the ball over after a delightfully executed movement, in which all the home attackers participated. Axcell's first centre was noteworthy, and in a proper businesslike style, he took a pass from Freeman first time and winged it across goal but Roberts removed the danger with a splendid heave. Still hovering around the custodian Mitchell raised hope with a shot which the goalie just reached and tipped over the bar, and again added to his laurels by thumping away Newland's well-taken corner.

Halse then secured from a huge return by Molyneux, and, breaking sharply past the opposing halves and backs, he had a clear run through, but the ball bounced awkwardly against his knee and the glorious chance was unluckily spoilt. However, next minute the desired opportunity came his way, and, receiving after a clever bout of passing between Owen, Watkins and Mitchell, the lively centre opened the scoring. The Engineers' efforts to make headway were easily stopped by Owen and his confreres in the middle line, and seldom did the visitors cross midfield.

Watkins got on the move after good tackling by Freeman and Owen, and, working into position he slipped through a pass all along the floor to Halse, and, after twenty minutes play, the United stood two goals up; Halse steadying up and crashing a fast rising shot past Roberts.

A show how the game was going. Thirty minutes passed before Cotton had the chance of a kick, and then a bit of slack work between Johnson and Thomson let Dadswell away, and he came near scoring with a splendid effort which rattled the side net. The crowd rather enjoyed the Engineers' breakaway and encouraged the visitors on, but they could not rally another attack, and operations were resumed at the other end by Newland, who, well backed up by Johnson and Mitchell, put in a series of commendable runs which invariably finished with accurate centres.

Axcell also was pleasing by his unselfish work on the left wing, never hesitating to cross quickly and square. Good work by Watkins and Halse left a clear field to Newland, but Referee McQue unhesitatingly whistled him up offside. Freeman essayed a shot which skimmed the bar and followed up later with some strong tackling which cleared the way for Watkins. A correct pass left Axcell with a chance to show his merit, and the wing man slipped neatly past Smith and, squared a low centre, to which Halse galloped up at top speed and netted; the goalkeeper not having an earthly chance.

The Engineers now realised they were helpless against their more clever and better trained opponents, and set themselves to play on defence, the inside forwards falling back to assist, but, notwithstanding that, the homesters found no difficulty in indulging in a show of the more scientific points of Soccer, the forwards combining perfectly and at times bewildered the outclassed soldiers by their prowess in dribbling and what is known as the 'tick-tack' game. The home halves also could not resist a little exhibition work, and Owen especially was shining in attack, because he could get nothing to do hardly in the way of defensive work. He manoeuvred a good opening for Mitchell, and the inside right did not fail to seize the chance running close up to Roberts, and deftly touching in No. 4 with the outside of his right foot.

Little time elapsed before Freeman took a pot shot, which annexed a fifth goal for the United, and spectators began to shout out for the half dozen, but, to relieve the monotony, the Engineers managed to transfer play to the top end, and reckless tactics by the home defence nearly let down Cotton's charge. A fair bully ensued round the home goal, and Cotton had to look lively in saving two creditable drives from the from the centre forward, Pearson, and outside left, but eventually the ball slithered outside and Cotton was exercised with his second free kick, which sent Newland off on the right, and he cleverly worked past his opposing half and back at a rare pace, but again Roberts baulked the way with another smart clearance; the interval arriving shortly after with the score standing five-nil in favour of the home team.

The game resumed, and in a trice the home forwards were peppering Roberts, who saved again and again. Badly supported as he was by his backs, the goalie was giving a magnificent show, but the persistent banging was bound to get home, and Mitchell had no mercy in adding No. 6 with a sharp first time shot well out of the goalie's reach, and, after a spell of give and take work about midfield, in which Owen and Molyneux shone, the centre half fed the centre, and Halse, running through the backs with the greatest ease, drove home No. 7 and the fourth off his own boot.

Very little time elapsed before the clever centre, receiving from Watkins, added another to the total. Spectators got greedy and called out for double figures, and the Engineers' backs and half-backs were floundering about in desperate efforts to stem the tide, but the homesters simply toyed with them, and in generous mood did not press home many promising movements overdoing the fancy game, but the scoring had not yet finished. Watkins was on the point of netting when tripped badly inside the fatal area, and a penalty was awarded, but the team captain, Molyneux, did not distinguish himself in the taking of the same; the shot being typically 'full back' and clearing the crossbar by a yard or two.

To renewed shouts of 'More goals,' Halse walked the ball into the net, but the referee would not hallmark it; the little centre being penalised off-side.

A sudden burst away by the visitors' right wing found Freeman a little work to do and in a rough and tumble struggle with his opponents, the home half fell onto his wrist and a minute or two's grace was given him to recover. Nothing remarkable happened in the next few minutes, but, for the first time in the game, a corner kick was awarded the visitors and well placed by Dadswell, but the effort went for nothing; Thomson booting the ball to midfield. To make matters worse for the unfortunate R.E.'s, Barnes, the right half, was laid out; receiving a hard driven ball against the wind. He did not pull round quickly, and was removed to the dressing rooms for medical attention. Dr. Hopkins kindly stepped from the stand and gave his valued services. With Barnes unable to resume, the now well beaten Engineers were completely at sea, and seldom were the United backs called on.

Cotton, who was never enquired for, may as well have kept Barnes company in the dressing room. Owen, Johnson, and Freeman were keeping the visiting forwards completely under control and plying the home vanguard with pass after pass. Newland and Axcell were galloping away at every chance, and the inside men were doing tolling work, which was all nullified, however, by the extraordinary defence of Roberts. Time and again he cleared when the show looked all over and the home crowd heartily applauded as he turned shot after shot away, but the home forwards were insatiable, and Newland well deserved the ninth goal; Owen setting him off and Newland, who has rare speed, left McDonald standing, and swinging into the centre, he pulverised Roberts with an unstoppable shot. The place kick only served for Johnson to get hold and again presented Newland with another opening, and that player obliged by again sprinting clean away and repeating his former performance. This time, however, the run was finished in a more elaborate manner, as Roberts, having left his goal to meet the oncoming forward, the Garrison man dodged him about 18 yards out and then coolly walked No. 10 into the open goal.

It is useless to report further on the later stages of the game, which continued around the visitors' citadel, but Axcell deserves mention for a neat effort which credited him with goal No. 11; the goalkeeper being well beaten by a low left foot drive from the nimble winger. Newland completed the picture by striding away much in the style of his previous successful runs and annexing his third for the day. The Engineers retired with the remarkable score against them of 12 goals to nil.

The visiting custodian was heartily cheered by the crowd as he left the field, and undoubtedly his extraordinary display had saved his side from what might have been a more sensational defeat.

No need to refer to Cotton – he had an idle time. Thomson and Molyneux did their little bit in easy style. I believe George did not take great pains over the penalty; it looked a sympathetic miss.

Owen took the honours in a fine half-back line, working hard right through and his placing to the forwards was especially correct. He kept the ball low and disposed of his passes to the best advantage. Johnson and freeman played a 'heady' game, and overpowered the opposing forwards, who were anything but tip-toppers. Halse, in virtue of his harvest of five goals, deserves all thanks, and, no mistake about it there are very few to equal him in the alert way he snaps up and drives home all kinds of centres, and what I like is his readiness to seize his opportunities and dart through on his own. It is a paying game for a centre forward.

Newland was in glorious form, and gained his three goals by three first-rate single-handed efforts he made backs of the backs when he strode away, and he invariably sends across a lofty accurate centre which spells danger. His services should be utilised by the Club whenever obtainable. Watkins put in a lot of serviceable work and he does not mind roughing it a bit. He appears to take a lot of buffeting intended for Halse, and undoubtedly nurses the centre well. Thus a lot of his most valuable work passes unnoticed. I like his shooting too, although on Saturday last no luck attended it. In conjunction with Axcell, a very capable left wing was made up, and, the ex-Leigh player must be commended for his excellent debut. The management need have no hesitation in again introducing Axcell. He plays a paying game and knows just when to part with his centres, which, on Saturday, were driven across goal with deliberate certainty and correct direction. Mitchell put in telling work too, but it struck me-he did not enter into the game with the same gusto that distinguished the other forwards. Perhaps he felt a bit of sympathy for his moderate opponents. The two goals he got were classy – the one a fast drive and the other a tricky touch past.

Outside of Roberts, it would be hopeless to look for any merit in the visiting team. Outclassed at every phase of the game, the only word of favour I can give is that they never gave up, and they tried manfully against their overpowering masters. The brunt of the work, as can readily be seen, fell to Roberts, and he will never play a better game. If he saved one he must have cleared what looked like twenty further certainties, and, after his magnificent defence, deserves all sympathy that he had to pick twelve out of the net. The harvest of goals will stand a substantial asset in the United's goal columns, and we hope to hear from Portsmouth, where the team has an important Southern League match on Saturday, that the forwards have maintained their rapacity and success. Probably Holden and Jack may be played at Portsmouth, as they both know the ground well; Holden, as is known, having completed three seasons on the Portsmouth staff.

The teams were: –

SOUTHEND UNITED: Cotton; Thomson and Molyneux; Johnson, Owen and Freeman; Bomb. Newland, Mitchell, Halse, Watkins, and Axcell.

ROYAL ENGINEERS: Roberts; McDonald and Smith; Hamilton, Black and Barnes; Dadswell, Wibrow, Pearson, Cambrey, and Gallagher.

Saturday, December 15th, 1906
South Eastern League, Second Division
SOUTHEND UNITED 13 (Axcell 5, Frost 4, Blott 2, Holden, Watkins)
CHESHAM GENERALS 0

Not only was Saturday's game a tale of a victory, but a tale of record goal scoring by the United, who, beside beating their previous highest score, passed the total of one hundred goals for the season. Halse, Mitchell and Freeman dropped out of the home team and their places were taken by Axcell, Frost and Barclay, of Wanstead. The visitors were a young lot of amateurs, but several played up to professional form.

Molyneux, won the toss and defended the West Street end. Southend directly took the upper hand and, before three minutes had elapsed, Holden scored with a hot shot. This was the beginning of a terrific onslaught in which the United's greed got beyond control. In the next minute Blott got possession and launched the ball towards goal. Webb collared, but could not clear before Blott was up upon him and had netted. Very few minutes were allowed to go by – ten minutes from the start – when Axcell considered it was time to have a finger in the pie and drove in a shot, which was too hot for Webb to hold.

Cotton then had his first kick, but easily punted away. Frost and Barclay were prominent in the next movements, and soon after Owen shot past with a good effort.

It was seen the Generals were not such an experienced team as the United. Their two wings were dangerous when they got away, but it was seldom they did so. Passes out by the centre were too soft and nearly always intercepted by the home team.

So deadly were the United, and they were playing so well together, that they again forced their opponents to act strictly on the defensive. They were unable to stand the pressure that was brought to bear upon them and again, with the hands of the watch giving the time that had elapsed at fifteen minutes, Axcell received and made no mistake; his boot sending the ball like a rocket into the net for the fourth time in all.

A magnificent run by Holden, in which he beat his opponents cleverly opened the eyes of the visitors. He had hard luck in shooting inches past. Barclay sent Frost going and the latter, dribbling nicely round an opponent, shot over the bar from an awkward position. Molyneux was not content with the work he was doing at back, and came up and made a fine long drive, which the goalie diverted. After Johnson had hit the net post with a hot shot, Webb had to deal with efforts from all the forwards.

It was only Southend in the picture. The occasional plucky efforts by the visitors were easily stopped by the defence, who kept Cotton quite out in the cold; Thomson, especially, was kicking strongly and his tackling was safe. The home forwards gave a smart exhibition in front of goal. Watkins tipped in to Axcell, who made a hard drive, but Webb smartly saved. Half-time:

Southend 4, Chesham, 0.

Southend attacked directly after the interval; Watkins putting a fine shot along the crossbar from the goal line. The visitors made a clever run on the right; Moreton and Green showing up prettily against Molyneux, ultimately beating him. Green centred accurately, but Richardson was pulled up for off-side, although he tested Cotton with a terrific shot at close range, which the Southend custodian saved remarkably well.

A well-judged centre by Frost was headed over the post. A pass out to Blott by Axcell saw the old Athletic player get away with a clear field. He centred squarely, but Webb, jumping up, fisted away. After Watkins had put in a stinging effort, skimming the crossbar, we saw Frost go away finely. Outwitting Mayo, the left back, with pretty footwork, he slammed in a shot all along the floor, which Webb could not get down to in time.

Southend did not stop. They went down like a pack of hounds, but kept good formation. Blott centred and Watkins headed past. Another goal came Southend's way when Axcell went down in brilliant manner. His work was charming to watch. He lost to the back, but recovered and, screwing round, netted with a hook shot; the ball hitting the top of the rigging. This was the half a dozen and the crowd began to cry for more and they were satisfied. They were longing to see the hundred reached and the team were all trying to make the record up to that. Each strove to score the goal that would make that total. Frost was set going by the halves and tipped into Axcell. The latter shot, the goalie ran out to clear and booted away, with Frost in close attendance and Axcell sent back just as Webb got in and he saved awkwardly, but could not deal with the subsequent effort which Axcell, following closely up, drove in hard.

And so the score grew and goals came from Blott, Axcell, Frost (thrice), his second making up the century, and Watkins; the United thus coming out winners by the margin of 13-0. Teams: –

SOUTHEND UNITED: Cotton; Molyneux (capt.) and Thomson; A. Barclay, Owen and Johnson; Holden, Watkins, Axcell, A. Frost and S.P. Blott.

CHESHAM GENERALS: Webb; Mayo and Spicer; Reynolds, D'Wight and Lacey; White, Maunder, Richardson, Moreton and Green.

Referee: Mr. T.W. Handford, Kensal Rise.

Thursday, December 30th, 1909
Southern League, First Division
NORTHAMPTON 11 (Lewis 4, Walden 3, Freeman 2, Walker, Owen, own goal)
SOUTHEND UNITED 1 (Sutherland)

Thursday was a black day for Southend football, and the magnitude of the United's defeat at Northampton will not be readily forgotten. I can well imagine local supporters asking in indignant terms what on earth they were up to, but if the truth must be told, it may at once be said that while the Northampton forwards were in the deadliest humour that it was possible for an attacking force to be in, the Southend backs and half-backs were leg-weary, apathetic, and uncertain. Molyneux was given a rest and this gave a trial to Cairns, who had won golden opinions with the reserves. Bigden was given another chance at left half, and Wright came in vice Sugden at inside left.

After their heavy holiday programme it was expected that Northampton would be a trifle stale, but the extreme contrary proved the case, and any hopes that Southend had of success were very rudely dispelled before the interval.

The Blues gave a trial to Toone in goal, who did so well against the junior Sotons on Monday and despite the fact that he was beaten eleven times, I venture to think that the Southend directors have found a really first-class goalkeeper. Each goal which Northampton scored was obtained with an unstoppable shot from so close a range as twelve to nine yards, while Toone's custodianship in the early stages was brilliant and stamped him as a really fine goalkeeper. Directors and players were extremely sorry that he should have had such an inauspicious introduction to Southern League football, but not one iota of the blame of the heaviness of the defeat could be laid at his door. Of massive build he possesses all the natural advantages of a goalkeeper and he can throw and fist a ball a marvellous distance.

The County Ground, which is in the midst of alterations and extensions, was in a very muddy and heavy state for the encounter, a fact that militated against Southend at the start. There was a large holiday crowd present when the teams turned out, a crowd in a mid-week match that must have made Southenders green with envy. Football has become extremely popular in the Boot town and there were fully 10,000 persons to watch the Cobblers set up another home record. Three times before the Claret and Whites have scored ten goals to nil at home, but never before have they got eleven, and never before have twelve goals been obtained in one match there. Owen, who captained the visitors, lost the toss and the teams lined up in the following order:

NORTHAMPTON: Thorp; Brittain and Lloyd Davies; Manning, F. Dunkley, and McDiarmid; Whittaker, Walker, Walden, Lewis and Freeman.

SOUTHEND: P.E.S. Toone; Murray and Cairns; Emery, Owen and Bigden; Brown, Sutherland, King, Wright and Crews.

Referee: Mr. J.W. Heath, Birmingham.

Playing up the slope, Southend were first to become dangerous and Brown worked an opening for Sutherland only for him to be ruled offside. Then the Blues' citadel had a narrow escape, for a brilliant piece of work by Freeman saw Whittaker and Walker have an open goal, but the latter drove outside. The Bootmen continued to press and Freeman next gave Lewis a golden opportunity, but though he got clean past the backs he fired a few inches outside. Brown was very conspicuous on the Southend right, and after forcing an abortive corner, he provided King with a scoring chance, only for the pivot to be wrongly given offside. Toone distinguished himself twice in rapid succession in saving grand long volleys from the foot of Brittain. The Blues had another look in and a pretty effort by Brown saw Sutherland dart in and give Thorp a hot shot which he saved well.

Toone was soon again busy in the defence of the Southend fortress and he dealt in cool style with a terrific drive from Lewis and later kept out a well directed shot from Whittaker. Brown led a Southend onslaught which King pounced on and drove in hard, but Thorp, amid loud cheers, saved finely by diving and rescuing the sphere from the far corner of the posts. The Cobblers then dashed away, and Lewis was responsible for a magnificent low drive which Toone saved in great style.

Southend's misfortune then commenced at the end of twenty minutes, when Freeman careered away and let fly with a lightning drive. Toone was shaping well to save it, when Owen, in attempting to deflect it's course, drove it with great force into his own net. The Blues retaliated smartly and King, with a first-timer, narrowly missed equalising. Then from a corner the home goal had a very near squeak.

The Northampton quintette went away in a line again, and Toone came out and took the leather from Walden's toe. The second goal to the Cobblers came at the end of half an hour's play and was due to a miskick by Murray, who let drive at one of Freeman's centres, clean missed it, and allowed Lewis and Walker to walk the ball into the net; the latter putting on the final touch. The last ten minutes of the first half then produced three more points. It was extremely poor and weak play by Cairns and Murray that allowed Lewis to out-wit them both and manoeuvre to within a yard or so of goal to add a third. Another beautiful middle by Freeman found Cairns at fault again, and he let in Walden to score the fourth.

The fifth point was a fine piece of individual play by Freeman, who waltzed round Murray, left him standing, and with a terrific cross shot had Toone again beaten. Thus the last four goals had been absolutely given away by the backs, who had little support from the halves, and Northants crossed over with a lead of five goals to nil.

Resuming, Northampton went away with a characteristic burst, and after Toone had saved capitally from Walden, Southend had all the play for the next five minutes, in which Crews was the most prominent player in the picture. Thrice in as many minutes he tested the home custodian, but each time his shots were disposed of. But the Cobblers were out for goals and six minutes from the re-start, Freeman made up the half dozen. Manning, by good judge-ment, slung the ball to Walker, and thence it travelled along the whole front rank to the outside left, who dashed in and scored with a similar shot to the fifth.

While this movement was going on, some of the Southend defenders were falling over themselves in hopeless confusion. The Blues' forwards, especially King and Brown, tried desperately hard to get through, and after Thorp had saved well from Crews, King just failed to convert a delightful centre by Brown.

At this point Lewis scored his sixtieth goal of the season and the seventh of the match. The Northants demon goal-getter snapped up a perfect centre from Whittaker and again found the rigging with a rasper which Toone prob-ably never saw. At this point Owen had to leave the field owing to a severe injury, and King dropped to centre half and Brown came in centre forward. Handicapped in this way, Southend were largely confined to their own half, especially as the homesters were playing brilliant and correct football. Freeman, who was constantly keeping his inside men plied with perfect mid-dles, gave Walden an opening to score an eighth from six yards range, but just after this the home goal had a narrow squeak from a shot by Wright, follow-ing good work by Brown, but Thorp saved magnificently at the expense of a fruitless corner.

Walden worked an opening for Lewis to add a ninth with an electrifying drive, and hardly had the game been re-started when Lewis again ran round the disorganised and tired Southend defence and completed the double figures amid an outburst of cheering.

A free kick against Manning led up to Southend's solitary point for Brown securing, worked an admirable chance for Sutherland, which the ex-soldier speedily accepted by lifting the sphere into the far corner of the net. This seemed as if it would complete the scoring, but in the last second of the game Freeman, who had been playing magnificently, gave Walden a brainy pass, and the little centre forward at the second attempt put it well out of Toone's reach. Thus the game ended with Northampton winners by the phenomenal score of eleven goals to one.

There was not the slightest doubt that it was the Northampton men's day out, and though everything came off for them, they deserved every goal for the splendid understanding, combination and deadly marksmanship of their forwards. It was the sort of day when they would probably have beaten any team in England by a substantial margin and it was only the very palpable weakness of the Southend defence which intensified the total. The passing of the forwards was delightful, while the geometrical precision with which they wove the sphere in and out was very fascinating, added to this they had two extremely fast and clever wingers who romped away from the Southend halves every time, and no fewer than seven of their goals were traceable to Freeman, who was par excellence.

With the exception of Exeter I have seen every Southern League club this season, but none have approached the high all round standard of the Northampton side as they appeared on Thursday. They are a better team than they were last season, and the fact that they are not again heading the Southern League table is due to the improved quality of the teams all round. It is hard to distinguish and single out players for a special mention in such a side, but though Bonthron was absent at right back, Brittain was a fine substitute and was, if anything, more conspicuous than Lloyd Davies, who captained the side. The amateur, Fred Dunkley, who deputised McCartney at centre half, played a rare bustling and yet scientific game, while McDiarmid, who last year was performing on the wing, has developed into a brilliant and brainy half back. Manning was also in capital fettle.

The forwards, as a line, were well nigh perfect, and, despite the heaviness of the ball, swung it about with unfailing accuracy; bad passes being exceptions rather than the rule. Another thing which they are to be complimented upon was their magnificent shooting. After the first twenty minutes they took every scoring chance, and on each occasion the sphere was always placed with great adroitness out of the goalkeeper's reach. In fact, Toone never got near one of the scoring shots, while most of them found the meshes at the velocity of a cannon ball. As already stated, Freeman was a great instrument in the victory, and was brilliance itself, while Lewis was the star artist of the inside men, manipulating the sphere with great subtlety, while his marksmanship was always on the spot.

Despite his short stature, Walden proved a most capable understudy for Lessons; being very tricky and feeding his wings well. Walker and Whittaker, though he did not share in the spoils like the others, were a very speedy and useful pair.

As mentioned earlier in these notes, Toone could not be blamed for a single goal, but, on the other hand, he displayed form which satisfied the directors that were present and also his fellow players that he is no mean custodian, and more will sure to be heard of him in the future. The presence of Molyneux was sadly missed. Murray and Cairns seemed to have no plan of campaign for dealing with the incisive attacks of their opponents. In fact, the nippy Midlanders soon got them into a hopeless tangle, from which they never extricated themselves. Murray has never been so out-engineered, and time after time Lewis and Freeman galloped past him without any apparent effort. Cairns did several smart things, but was generally not reliable. This must be said in fairness to the backs, that the halves in front of them rendered them very little assistance, except Owen, until he got hurt and when he retired the debacle was completed.

Emery evidently cannot stand the strain of three matches in five days, and this usually speedy and thrustful half back was wholly ineffective. Remembering Emery's general consistency, this lapse may be looked over, but it was, nevertheless, a fact that hardly once during the whole ninety minutes was he any match for Lewis and Freeman.

Emery's off colour, of course, meant a big drawback for Southend, especially as Bigden, the other wing half, was too slow to adequately cope with Walker and Whittaker. Owen did fairly well until he got injured and received a terrible gash in his leg, which will keep him out of the team for some weeks. It was an unfortunate slip when he put through his own goal, and it was a peculiar coincidence that in the corresponding match last year, when Northampton won 2-1, he did the same thing from a corner. Owen retired after the seventh goal had been registered.

Owing to the fact that they received little assistance from the intermediate line, the Southend forwards were under a cloud, and suffered from a lack of opportunities.

They did, however, make some capital efforts, and though Northants did the bulk of the pressing in the first moiety, the second forty-five was not so one-sided as the score of six to one would signify. Norman Brown was by far the most conspicuous of the attackers, and tried desperately hard, and it was due to his play that Sutherland was enabled to score.

When Owen got hurt, King, who had been doing creditable work at centre forward, dropped back to centre-half, and lent useful assistance here, and

Brown then changed over into the centre with Sutherland at outside right. With the exception of scoring, Sutherland did little, while the efforts of Wright and Crews were spasmodic; the winger putting in all his best work in the first half hour of the second half.

Saturday, November 24th 1934
F.A. *Challenge Cup, 1st Round*
SOUTHEND UNITED 10 (Johnson 5, Cheesmur 2, Lane, Deacon, Carr, penalty)
GOLDERS GREEN 1 (Drinkwater)

The *Southend Standard* ran the following article on Golders Green F.C.
Although Southend United have in a large measure been responsible for their own lack of success in their League encounters, it must be admitted that they have not had the best of luck this season, but in the F. A. Cup Fortune's smile has been turned their way at last.

First, because they have, in the first round proper, the advantage of being drawn to play on their own ground and, secondly, because their opponents are an amateur side who should not be likely to cause them any great trouble in reaching the second round.

Golders Green, the Athenian League side, formerly known as the Hampstead F.C., will provide the opposition on Saturday by virtue of their success in their replayed tie last week with Ilford. Golders Green commenced to play under this title last season, when they won the Middlesex Senior Cup, and this term they are in the top flight of the Athenian League. They have won five out of nine games, and lost four, scoring 23 times, against 14. Last Saturday they visited Barking and were defeated 2-1. The Club is led by F.P. Evans, an Amateur International, and there are several County representatives amongst the players.

After holding their own for the first twenty minutes, Golders Green gradually lost their grip of the game at the Stadium on Saturday, when they met the United in the first round proper of the F. A. Cup and they crossed over 3-0 down.

The second half was just one long 'fade-out,' and, although careless defensive play enabled them to score one goal, the Blues went on to reach double figures. Of their ten goals, Johnson claimed five, Cheesmur, the centre-forward, scored twice, and Deacon, Carr and Lane obtained one each. Even the most optimistic of the large crowd of North Londoners present did not expect the Green to win, but they did believe the Athenian League team would give the homesters a good game.

They did – until the fast pace had proved too great a strain on their stores of energy, and after that the players were often left floundering by the superior footwork and ball-placing of the professionals. As I expected, the second half saw the visitors struggling pluckily, but they were leg-weary and the Blues did just as they liked. The feature of the game, so far as the United were concerned, was the good work between Cheesmur and Johnson. Between them they rent gaps in the opposing defence with a regularity that was almost monotonous, and the latter indulged in shooting practice with frequent success. However, more of that anon. First some general observations.

Whilst Golders Green were not the attraction that, say Ilford, whom they beat in the previous round, would have been, and the kick-off was advanced to 2.15 p.m., the visitors will receive a cheque for over £200 as their share of the 'gate.' Just over 8,500 paid for admission, the receipts totalling £531, and I don't think I am giving away a secret when I say that the sum that the Green receive will be a real godsend.

The special trains from Cricklewood and Hampstead Heath were well supported, and there was a steady stream of spectators until ten minutes after the kick-off. Before the game and during the interval the crowd was entertained by selections by the well-balanced band of boys from the Nazareth Home and a collection was taken for the Mayor's Distress Fund. A crowd loves to see goals, and, no doubt, they left the Stadium in great spirits, for some of the points notched by the Blues were really fine efforts.

The majority of Johnson's 'bag' and the two points by Cheesmur were excellent examples of good shooting, and it made one sigh to think of the disinclination to do it in the League matches. I was glad to hear the warm reception given to the Green and to any bits of clever play by their team. There were some cries against Kelly when he collided with and hurt Breagan, but it was a pure accident. Breagan received a knee injury and was limping in the second half until a few minutes from time, when he had to leave the field.

The game had a sensational opening, the United sweeping down and a centre from Oswald being handled close to goal by Bucci. Lane, who was making his re-appearance with the first team since his injury in September, and who has generally proved so deadly with the spot-kick, took the shot and sent the ball just to the right of Godding, the Green goal-keeper. There was not a lot of power behind the drive, and Godding stuck out his right foot and cleared. Encouraged by this escape from early disaster, the visitors stormed to the other end, and matters did not look any too rosy for the United when Moore was brought into action several times through lack of understanding by the defence. Both the Green wings were prominent, and, with neither of the backs particularly safe, it was touch and go.

Happily, the home side came out of the ordeal before any damage was done, and, in the twenty-fourth minute, the scoring was opened. It was a goal worth seeing too. An accurate pass from Carr sped straight to Cheesmur, who had his back to goal. The leader deftly flicked it sideways between the backs, and Johnson slipped through to net with a beautiful shot. Within two minutes Deacon, who had been prominent with several unsuccessful shots and headers, pushed the ball forward to Cheesmur. This time the backs moved to cover Johnson, and the centre forward swerved between them and beat Godding with another fine effort. Just before half-time Deacon was at length rewarded, this time heading through a centre from Lane.

At the interval, reflection on the play gave the Green quite a fair share of points, for they had spiritedly tried to upset the Blues. Drinkwater, the outside-left, had several times beaten Morfitt with ease, and, on the other side, Breagan gave Kelly a trying time. In the centre, Freddy Evans, the English amateur international, attempted to make use of one of their centres, but Wilson was always there, and the two wing half-backs, Mackay and Carr, helped to deaden the Green's efforts through the centre. Carr was the best of the trio, being particularly accurate with some of his ground passing and always being noticeable with his headwork.

During the first half Oswald and Deacon came into prominence, materially backed by Carr. Oswald is, I believe, gradually regaining his proper form, and we shall probably see some excellent work from that wing trio in the future – if they are kept together. From the visitors' side, honours went unquestionably to Godding. Admittedly he had plenty to do once the United 'snapped out' of their indecision, but his work showed that the Arsenal were not far wrong in giving him a run with their Combination team. One save in particular stood out in my mind. Johnson fired in a fierce shot through a ruck of players. Godding dived across the goalmouth a shade too quick and the ball looked like passing in over his waist as he was falling. With great presence of mind, he punched upward with the right fist and sent the ball high over the bar.

Richardson and his youthful colleague, Boston, defended stoutly, but were often out-manoeuvred. Boston received a severe cut over the right eye in a collision with Deacon, but resumed after treatment at the side of the field and played quite well considering the shaking he received. Broadis, marking Cheesmur, could find no way of anticipating just where the leader would flick the passes he received – more than 60 per cent of Cheesmur's distribution was made by deliberate sliced kicks and ankle flicks – and in their co-operation I believe Cheesmur and Johnson may prove a factor that will go a long way to lifting the Blues from the bottom of the table. If Johnson could always be on the mark as he was on Saturday, Cheesmur may well concentrate on the Dean role of keeping his back to the goal and heading or flicking the ball in front of the inside men. It paid on Saturday, and it would pay against any other team if cultivated. What happened in the second half?

The rest of the United attack were quick to realise that Cheesmur was a match winner and effaced themselves to the extent of becoming willing sources of passes. The leader twisted and turned them to the best advantage with excellent ball control, and Johnson waited nearby for the pass he knew would be coming. Whilst congratulations go to Johnson for his success, they must go also to Cheesmur for his clever leadership and to the rest of the players as a whole for realising the type of game that had to be played.

The second half was something in the nature of a 'procession,' with Golders Green making one or two isolated visits to the United territory. A rather mild foul by Richardson on Johnson saw the United awarded another penalty kick soon after the game had re-started. Carr was called up for this, and, although he scored, the shot was a poor one and Godding nearly saved it.

The fifth goal was rather unusual in that Lane could not help scoring it! A beautiful corner kick by Oswald dropped over Godding's fist and 'ran down' Lane's legs and off his foot into the net. He simply stood still and the ball did the rest. After this the 'cracking' in the visiting defence that had been visible in one or two parts became general, and it became obvious that it was simply a question as to how many the United could pile on. Godding made his first mistake of the match when he dropped the ball for Johnson to net No. 6. Then Cheesmur delighted the spectators by trapping the leather in such a manner that it ran up his body and then heading it over an advancing back so that Johnson could take it in his stride. Result, No. 7.

Then Johnson repaid his leader for services rendered by a neat through pass that Cheesmur converted with a beautiful shot. The United defence had moved well up field during the pressure, and careless positioning let Drinkwater in to score the Green's solitary point with a capital cross drive. An attempted back-kick to Godding enabled Johnson to nip in and score the ninth point, and shortly afterwards he rounded off the good work with the tenth. Here Oswald centred and Cheesmur 'sold the dummy' to Broadis by letting the ball go through his legs to Johnson.

So much for the goals. Where a team fades out as the Green did on Saturday the victors are apt to look a better side than they really are, and I think that was the case on Saturday. Moore was safe enough, but Morfitt did not have such a good match.

Kelly did pretty well against his opposing wing and recovered better. Carr was the best of the half-backs, neither Wilson nor Mackay playing up to standard. Lane does not seem to have suffered much as a result of his injury, but is not yet back on his best form. Of course, one could not really expect an amateur side to stand the pace so well as a highly trained professional team, and thereon hangs much of Saturday's tale. One thing about the match – it gave the supporters something else to talk about than the previous displays. Drinkwater was outstanding in the visitors' attack.

The teams were: —

Southend United: Moore; Morfitt and Kelly; Mackay, Wilson (J.) and Carr; Lane, Johnson, Cheesmur, Deacon and Oswald.

Golders Green: A.C. Godding; W.G. Boston, W.J. Richardson; R. White, A. Broadis, G. Bucci; A.J. Breagan, T.E. Edwards, P.P. Evans, C. Drinkwater.

Referee: Mr. L. Brown.

Saturday, October 26th, 1940
Football League, South Regional Division
WEST HAM 11 (Foreman 4, Foxall 3, Barrett, Fenton, Goulden, Macauley)
SOUTHEND UNITED 0

I wonder what the old supporters of the Blues thought when they saw or heard Saturday's result from Boleyn Castle. The Hammers were eight up at half-time, and finished winners by 11-0! It was a debacle. It was a curious game, for in the first half, strange though it may seem from the score, the visitors had just as large a share of the play as did West Ham. The sole difference was that practically every time West Ham went down field, they found the net. When Southend attacked they pressed to the goalmouth and then failed to finish off their onslaughts.

In one way and another the Blues' struggle for existence has been beset by ill-luck and misfortune. Forced to leave the Stadium, they have found the greatest difficulty in carrying on, despite sacrifices by the players and management. Even greater blows have been the inability to field the elevens desired. Something has happened each week to necessitate last minute changes, and these have generally had an adverse effect. It has been disheartening work for directors, management and players, but I know all have done their best to keep things going. The moral of all this preamble is for my readers not to be too condemnatory when hearing of the weekly results. Actually, Saturday's defeat was the heaviest in their history, the previous worst being 11-1 at Northampton in December, 1909.

With Fuller, Calland and Sliman not available at the last minute on Saturday, Southend had to do some hasty borrowing. Chalkley, down to play for West Ham, put on a blue jersey, and thus returned temporarily to the club he assisted so often last season. He played at right full-back, and Phybus (Tottenham) was luckily at the ground and he turned out as left-back. Turton, normally the right full-back, went to centre-half, and Jones (L.), usually on the wing, appeared at right-half. Edwards, who was on the Ipswich books, was at centre-forward; and Jones (F.), who has been playing there, went on the right wing.

Through a defence that played hard, but which, owing to its strangeness, lacked understanding and cohesion, the West Ham forwards, ably led by Foreman and the polished Macaulay, cut like a knife through a cheese. Southend made quite as many raids, but what a difference when it came to the final efforts! Turton did his best, but was generally standing on the wrong side of Foreman, and Edwards had no such luck in getting away from Dick Walker. The West Ham line, with Goulden and Macaulay constantly drawing the uncertain visitors defence out of position, had two well-balanced wings, while behind Barrett, despite his weight, was an extra forward, as well as a source of constructive passes. Southend's enthusiasm gave them scoring opportunities, but the only player on the side to really come out of the game with credit was Burley, on the left wing.

Of the Hammers solid and workmanlike side, best play was forthcoming in the attack from the inside trio. Foreman, who opened the scoring, got four of the eleven. Barrett headed the second, Foxall drove in the third from an acute angle. Fenton, the right-half, headed the next. Foreman raced through and flicked in No. 5, and scored again after a goal by Foxall, while Goulden completed the first half tally. Macaulay obtained a well-deserved point to open the second half, in which the other successful marksmen were Foxall and Foreman. Teams: –

WEST HAM: Conway; Savage and Walker (C.); Fenton, Walker (R.) and Barrett; Small, Macaulay, Foreman, Goulden and Foxall.

SOUTHEND UNITED: Rickett; Chalkley and Phybus; Jones (L.), Turton and Walton; Jones (F.), Parry, Edwards, Bell and Burley.

Saturday, December 7th, 1968
F.A. Challenge Cup, 2nd Round
SOUTHEND UNITED 10 (Best 5, Moore 4, McMillan)
BRENTWOOD TOWN 1 (Stratton)

I can only say that this overwhelming victory in the second round of the F.A. Cup at Roots Hall on Saturday before 13, 107 spectators was the massacre of the minnows.

After being 3-1 up at half-time Blues added seven more without reply in the second half, the last 45 minutes being, with due respect to the opposition, 'by kind permission of Southend United.' And, if not exactly over-shadowed, Gary Moore's four headed goals in United's first five was outdone by Billy Best heading the next three and then increasing his personal total to five, the last four in the final six minutes of the game.

As a competitive match, the game lasted exactly four minutes: for the opening 60 seconds it took United to go one goal in front and for the three minutes between Brentwood equalising and Blues going ahead again. From then on it was one-way traffic – all towards the Brentwood goal.

Second in the First Division of the Southern League, with promotion to the Premier Division as their main objective, these part-timers, in their own sphere, must be a force to be reckoned with. But, to put it bluntly, among the big boys of League football they were completely out of their class.

But, as they expected to go out in this round -with a share of a big 'gate' as their reward – and, as United also expected to win easily, both clubs must have been highly delighted.

The one thing that was proved was that dedicated professionalism will always – or almost always – be too strong for anything less. And, although United's final winning margin was achieved by a late goal burst, it was always a question of by just how many they would win by once they went in front for the second time.

Apart from a table of the goals, there is very little that one can say about the game. United's defence was more than adequate against opposition that provided attacking ploys more by coincidence than design. But the little they had to do they did well and with the minimum of effort. Skipper Sammy McMillan and Mike Beesley had a comfortable afternoon, despite the latter having what must have been a rather painful bump on his rump when he fell from a great height in the first half.

Tony Bentley and Graham Birks simply proved what was missing at Colchester eight days earlier when not only did they tighten up the back four, but also supplied overlapping sorties to add to the efficiency of the attack.

United's three front runners proved to be more than enough. Gary Moore's height alone scares the pants off opposing defences; but he also has the footballing ability to go with it, works like mad and brings the rest of his forwards into the game. His four goals were no more than he deserved and near misses might easily have doubled his total.

Billy Best buzzed to more effect than he has done in any other game this season. In my book he was having a splendid game even BEFORE his goal spree of netting the last five, four of them in the final six minutes. This was the coincidental pay-off as a bonus for effort and endeavour, and was richly deserved.

Chico Hamilton had another of those games when everything seemed to go right at the wrong time or wrong at the right time. He ran into a lot of trouble in midfield when he was the player in charge, yet still managed to have more than a willing hand in five of United's goals. He is so graced with natural talent that he must surely learn the hard way and in 12 month's time I am certain that he will be twice the player he is today.

I have deliberately left the middle powerhouse of United until the last. They could have been playing as a mid-field trio, but once again we had John Kurila and Eddie Clayton as centre-duetists with Phil Chisnall as the wandering minstrel. But, as it turned out, Kurila wandered with good effect between back and front, while Chisnall did his stint going forward from mid-field.

Moore and Best brought their aggregate of goals up to 15 of the 19 United have scored in their two Cup rounds to date, after getting three apiece in the last round against King's Lynn.

But Saturday's goals posed an interesting question. The United fans who, for years, have been crying out for a big'un in the middle must have been laughing their heads off and patting themselves on the back when Moore, in impeccable style, headed in four of Blues' first five goals. And, as Moore stands six feet and more than a bit, their acclamation was fully justified – until Best joined the goalscorers.

Standing at least seven or eight inches shorter than Moore, Best came along to also head in the next three goals which, I would say, leaves the honours even or, at least, proves that if you are good enough then lack of inches is no serious disadvantage.

Apart from the goals, the rest of the game is quickly summed up. Hamilton had goalkeeper Billy Dunbar making a second grab at a whizbanger in the seventh minute; outside-left David Hyde was back on his own goal-line to clear a Kurila header in the 30th minute; Reg Stratton miscued to Trevor Roberts in the 37th minute; Roberts saved from Mike Maynard in the 40th Clayton hit the angle of post and bar in the 55th and had Dunbar stretching again in the 62nd McMillan cleared off the line when Eddie Dilsworth beat a stretched defence in the 70th and Best and Hamilton both went close, but not close enough.

The goal chart sums up the rest of the 90 minutes: –

One minute: Clayton held the ball on the left until he forced Birks into position for a clear run and the full-back's centre was judged to perfection by Moore at the far post as he headed past Dunbar.

Seventeen minutes: A tragic moment for United as Kurila passed back to Roberts with nothing to spare and Stratton moved in to force the ball in for an equaliser.

Twenty minutes: A repeat of United's first goal as Moore rose elegantly to head in Hamilton's centre from the left.

Thirty-five minutes: McMillan intercepted in mid-field, ran on before passing to Best and was carried forward by his own impetus to be on the spot to slot home when Best sent over the return pass.

Fifty-two minutes: Another brilliant Moore header as his reflexes acted superbly to a quick one-two by Best and a Hamilton centre to flash the ball into the net.

Sixty-three minutes: The same formula as the previous goal as Moore nodded in a Hamilton centre.

Seventy-one minutes: The first of Best's five as he headed in direct from a Hamilton right-wing corner.

Eighty-four minutes: Another Best header into the net, and again from Hamilton's cross, this time from the left.

Eighty-seven minutes: Moore headed on a Birks centre and Best was there to nod it in.

Eighty-eight minutes: A bit of argy-bargy in the Brentwood goalmouth and Best made no bones of hammering the ball into the back of the net.

Eighty-nine minutes: Double figures came up on the board when McMillan slideruled a pass through the middle and Best clipped the ball around Dunbar to complete the scoring. Teams: –

SOUTHEND: Roberts, Bentley, Birks, McMillan, Beesley, Kurila, Clayton, Chisnall, Moore, Best and Hamilton. Sub: Baber.

BRENTWOOD: Dunbar, Jones, Butterfield, Maynard, Loughton, Stevenson, Foster, Mansfield (Bumpstead), Stratton, Dilsworth, Hyde.

Referee: Mr. J.K. Taylor (Wolverhampton).

Tuesday, November 6th, 1990
Football League Associate Members' Cup (Sponsored as Leyland-DAF Cup)
Preliminary Round (Group stage)
SOUTHEND UNITED 10 (Angell 4, Benjamin 2, Tilson 2, Prior, Ansah)
ALDERSHOT 1 (Banton)

Southend United's destroyer in chief Brett Angell savoured last night's 10-1 thrashing of poor Aldershot in the Leyland Daf Cup – but immediately looked forward to Saturday's far more vital home game against Fulham.

'The lads were simply magnificent tonight but we are all professional enough to know that we must keep our feet firmly on the ground and not get carried away by this result – the Fulham game is one we must focus all our attention on. Results like this are great for the morale but we must not let it sidetrack us from our sole objective and that's promotion from Division 3.'

Angell cracked in a first-half hat-trick – the third of his professional career – and then rubbed salt in the wound with a superb fourth to take his tally for the season to twelve.

Boss David Webb was another who refused to get carried away by the club's biggest ever win against League opposition – the previous highest victory in the Blues history was also 10-1 against non-League Golders Green in the F. A. Cup way back in the '30's.

'What can you say about a display like that. You can use all the superlatives you like and it won't mirror the achievement of our players,' he said. 'I want them to celebrate tonight's win because results like this only come once in a lifetime.

But I can assure you it will be business as usual when they report back for training on Thursday and start preparing for the Fulham game – there won't be time for a 'heads in the clouds' attitude – I'll see to that!'

Shattered 'Shots manager Len Walker still looked shellshocked an hour after the dust had settled on what he freely described as 'the most embarrassing night of my football life. I don't think I ever got beaten by double figures when I played in the Cubs,' he said.

'We were second best in every department. Southend simply outcompeted and outplayed us – it's no use looking for excuses. We were destroyed and ripped apart by a superb team.'

The only pity was that a paltry 1,281 crowd was there to witness history being made – surely Saturday's game will produce a bumper gate –. if it doesn't then there's something wrong somewhere with the football followers of South East Essex.

While Angell was obviously the individual star of the night all the other ten players joined in a thrilling team performance – even goalkeeper Paul Sansome made a couple of memorable saves when the men in front of him lost concentration for a split second.

If you are being churlish then perhaps the only disappointment was that Blues did not manage to keep a cleansheet although Dale Banton's 83rd minute strike must have been precious little consolation to a side which had been battered from the very first minute.

Southend, who know what it's like to be the victims of a hammering having suffered an 8-0 humiliation at Crystal Palace in the Rumbelows Cup last month, showed no mercy.

John Cornwell, who along with energy man Peter Butler had a storming game in the middle of the park, blazed over the bar after only three minutes but the few hardy fans did not have to wait much longer before starting their champagne night.

Steve Tilson, who as well as scoring twice also had a hand in four of the other goals, crossed from the left for the tireless Ian Benjamin to spark off the massacre with a neat close range strike after six minutes.

14 minutes – little wing wizard Andy Ansah cut in from the right and crossed for Tilson to score with a looping header.

25 minutes – Tilson's corner was flicked on by Cornwell at the near post and Angell chested the ball down before volleying into the net.

32 minutes – Angell chased a long ball down-field and rounded stranded 'keeper Jon Sheffield before planting the ball home.

41 minutes – Angell completed a great first-half hat-trick by climbing high to head into the corner of the net after Benjamin and Ansah had combined to set up the chance.

55 minutes – Spencer Prior, before the match the only outfield player in the team not to have scored this season, outjumped the defence to head a fine goal from another inch perfect Tilson centre.

68 minutes – Tilson's corner was met by Benjamin whose effort was hooked off the line only to fall for Ansah to rifle the goal of the night into the roof of the net.

74 minutes – Butler played a great ball in for Angell to swivel and chip another memorable goal from just inside the box.

78 minutes – Ansah's persistence won the ball and when his shot came back off the bar Benjamin reacted quickest to stab into an empty goal.

80 minutes – Benjamin was again fast onto a through ball and evaded Sheffield before turning the ball into Tilson's path and his right foot did the rest. That made it 10-0 but with seven minutes left substitute Dale Banton wriggled free and hit a sweet shot low into the corner after the home defence for once went to sleep.

But that should not detract from what was for my money the best performance by the back-four this term. Peter Cawley and Prior shut tight on anything Aldershot tried to throw at them while the young full-backs Dean Austin and Chris Powell supported the front men superbly but did not shirk their defensive responsibilities when called on. Teams:–

SOUTHEND UNITED: Sansome, Austin, Powell, Cornwell, Prior, Tilson, Cawley, Butler, Ansah, Benjamin, Angell. Subs (not used): Locke, Edwards.

ALDERSHOT: Sheffield, Brown, Cooper, Randell, Wignall (sub 25 mins Banton), Flower, Whitlock, Puckett, Williams, Henry, Stewart. Sub (not used): Burvill.

CHAPTER FIFTEEN

Into Europe 1993-1995

Tuesday, October 12th, 1993
Anglo-Italian Cup, International Round, Group 'B'
FIORENTINA 3, SOUTHEND UNITED 0

Arrivederci! That was the message from Italian aces Fiorentina as they simply outclassed Southend United and cruised to a 3-0 Anglo-Italian Cup win last night. Blues could not have had a tougher baptism in competitive European action against the fallen giants of Italy – Fiorentina having been relegated to Serie B for the first time in 54 years but currently topping the table and looking certs for an immediate return to the top flight.

The passing and movement of the home players wasn't just from a different country it was, at times, on a different planet. And the way they supported the man in possession is something Southend could at least learn from.

Fiorentina looked like a well oiled machine – a silky smooth Mercedes compared to a hard working Ford Fiesta. But as overworked defender Graham Bressington said afterwards their squad did cost £64 million to put together compared to Southend's mixture of basement bargains.

'We didn't honestly expect to come here and play them off the park – they've got superb quality players in every position,' he told me. 'But it would not be fair to knock our lads. We never threw in the towel, kept plugging away and might have scored a couple ourselves.'

Indeed I would never accuse any side Barry Fry sends out of not sticking bravely to their job, although it must have been like chasing shadows at times, but I always had the feeling that Fiorentina could have stepped into a higher gear should it have been necessary.

The players, fresh from a 4-1 win over near neighbours Pisa on Sunday, seemed content to do just enough, but that would have been too much for most Premiership clubs let alone a First Division outfit. Fry himself admitted as much when he said: They were a different class – easily the best side I've had to face for a long time.

'Had it not been against my team, then I'm sure I would have enjoyed the high quality of football they produced, but it was agonising to see us on the rack like that. The worrying thing about us at the moment is that we don't look like scoring. We had the odd half chance tonight but to be honest hardly troubled their 'keeper.

'But has been a great experience for my young team and I would hope they will go away, think about it, and learn a useful lesson. If they do then we could yet benefit from this defeat.'

Southend's 200 plus fans who went into the superb stadium in Florence by chanting 'You're not famous anymore' as they took the field, but they quickly rammed those taunts back down their throats as they turned on some magical stuff and took the lead after only eight minutes.

Argentinian star Gabriel Batistuta showed a stunning turn of pace to fasten onto Zeronelli's neat through ball, cut past the Blues defence with frightening ease before firing low into the far corner of the net. Banchelli somehow drove against Paul Sansome's legs as he was again left completely in the clear before Southend enjoyed a mini purple patch – Brett Angell getting the ball in the net only to be ruled offside, Chris Powell driving straight at the 'keeper who then did well to pluck a dangerous cross from Ricky Otto off the head of the inrushing Keith Jones.

But it all proved to be something of a false dawn as Fiorentina made it 2-0 six minutes into the second half with another almost embarrassingly easy goal – Orlando hitting a great 30 yard ball for Tosto to cross and the lethal Batistuta was there for a simple finish.

Fry pulled off Gary Poole and Angell to bring on Jonathan Hunt and Jason Lee but that did nothing to end the torture as Sansome made a great save to deny Dell'Oglio. When Fiorentina started to rest on their laurels a bit substitute goalie Mareggini did well to rush out and kick clear from Otto and then clutch a Tommy Mooney effort after a corner was headed back by David Howell.

But it was almost inevitable that Sansome, who was, along with skipper Jones and Powell, the pick of the Southend side, would be left picking the ball out of the net again when another tremendous move ended with Orlando tapping in from close range.

And so that was it for Blues who flew home immediately after the game bloodied but having retained some pride. It's my bet that Fiorentina will win the Anglo-Italian Cup with consummate ease and I think it's fair to say that the other sides Southend will face in the competition are unlikely to prove quite so formidable.

While I love the way the Italians play the game -more even than their ice cream and beautiful women – I do wish they would cut out the dramatic histrionics almost every time they are tackled. It's hard to take them writhing around one minute as if both legs are broken and then setting up another brilliant move the next – but apart from that little niggle they were a joy to watch.

Teams:–

FIORENTINA: Scalabrelli (sub. 40 minutes Mareggini), Faccenda, Tosto, Zironelli, Bruno, D'Anna (sub. 45 minutes Pioli), Dell'Oglio, Amerini, Batistuta, Orlando, Banchelli. Subs (not used): Luppi, Di Sole, Flachi.

SOUTHEND UNITED: Sansome, Poole (sub. 68 minutes Hunt), Powell, Jones, Howell, Bressington, Gridelet, Payne, Mooney, Otto (sub. 68 minutes Lee). Subs (not used): Royce, Edwards, Scully.

Tuesday, November 9th, 1993
Anglo-Italian Cup, International Round, Group 'B'
COSENZA 1, SOUTHEND UNITED 2

Southend United produced one of their best performances of the season on a stormy night in Southern Italy to win a game which saw the best and very worst of Italian football.

Brett Angell's last minute strike saw the Blues secure two vital points in a 2-1 win at Cosenza which had manager Barry Fry pleading with fans to roar his team to Wembley. But a brilliant team display capped by Angell's two goals was overshadowed by the thuggish antics of Cosenza, who tried every trick in the book to rock the Blues.

The game started in whirlwind fashion and the Italians showed great skill and flair as they put the Blues' defence under pressure from the off. The Blues fans thought the team were one down inside seven minutes but a close range effort by Lemme was ruled offside.

Ricky Otto broke free on the left but his cross was smothered by keeper Zunico on the quarter hour. And three minutes later Negri made a theatrical dive under a challenge from Graham Bressington but his penalty pleas were waved away by referee Roger Milford. Southend came closest to taking the lead on 26 minutes when a curled cross from Jonathan Hunt went just inches from a flying Angell, after he outwitted the Cosenza defence.

The hosts then put Southend under the cosh but after 39 minutes the Blues scored their first after Otto hassled on the left and the loose ball was gleefully collected by Angell who strode into the box to lift it over the advancing keeper. The goal stunned the 2,000 crowd – only 441 paid, the rest were complimentaries – but within three minutes of the restart Cosenza levelled the scores. Fabricio Fabris picked up the ball 30 yards out and from 25 yards unleashed a shot which sizzled by Sansome and into the roof of the net.

Then it all went sour. The Italians swapped their skill with the ball for skill with the fist, elbow, boot and play acting. Referee Roger Milford left the field with a pulled thigh muscle shortly before halftime and substitute ref B. Priest of Birmingham was left with plenty to do as the hosts tried to get Ricky Otto sent off.

The entire Cosenza team went for the winger after Sconziano fell – as if hit with a brick – as Otto ran away from him. Fry then took Otto off and young Phil Gridelet, who had been injured half a minute before by a high kick which left him with stud marks down the length of his back.

Substitutes Jason Lee and David Howell had been on the pitch less than a minute when Lee was elbowed in the face by Napolitano with the ball 50 yards away.

But as the Italians continued their dirty tricks the Blues rose in stature and as the game entered the final ten minutes they pushed forward.

Angell, Lee and Howell went close but they left the best until last. In the 89th minute Hunt picked up the ball out on the right and his pinpoint cross was met by Brett Angell whose header hit the back of the net before Zunico could raise a gloved hand.

The team trooped off with Barry Fry saying he was delighted with the way they played. He said: 'It was a brilliant display in the worst of conditions. 'I would not have been happy with the draw and I think we deserved all the points. The players handled themselves well and I told them at half time we could beat this team if we played good football. I took Ricky Otto off because they were trying to get him sent off. The number two had done his job and rattled Ricky and I thought he was in danger of getting himself sent off. I now want the fans at home to turn out next week and for our other game to roar us into the semi final stage and onto Wembley. This is our chance to get to Wembley this season but we need the fans to play their part.'

Two goal Angell said: 'I am delighted to have got the goals but this was a great team performance and I think we deserved to win.'

Blues start their home challenge against Pescara on Tuesday.

COSENZA: Zunico, Sconziano, Compagno (Matrone 76 mins), Napoli, Napolitano, Rubino, Fabris, Caramel, Negri, Maiellaro (Fiore 70 mins), Lemme.

SOUTHEND: Sansome, Gridelet (Howell 55 mins), Powell, K. Jones, Edwards, Bressington, Hunt, Payne, G. Jones, Otto (Lee 55 mins), Angell.

Attendance 2,000.

Bookings: Maiellaro 55 mins, Lee 71 mins.

Tuesday, November 16th, 1993
Anglo-Italian Cup, International Round, Group 'B'
SOUTHEND UNITED 1, PESCARA 3

Southend United boss Barry Fry blasted his players for 'lacking the stomach for a fight and bottling it' as his Wembley dream turned into a nightmare after they crashed 3-1 to Pescara, in last night's Anglo-Italian Cup clash at Roots Hall. It was thoroughbreds against cart horses with the Italians so swift and deadly on the break and Blues in comparison laboured and simply unable to string a couple of decent passes together.

And when Southend did get in sight of goal the finishing was abysmal although in fairness 'keeper Marco Savorani, who collected the man-of-the-match award, looked virtually unbeatable. From the 2nd minute when Gary Jones got through on a one-to-one and the goalie somehow got his leg in the way of a goalbound effort he didn't look back – in fact the whole Italian side just grew in stature.

The Blues defence caved in as Pescara romped into a 2-0 lead inside the first 19 minutes and never looked like surrendering it. It all left Fry bitterly disappointed as he emerged from the dressing room to tell me: 'We had a great chance to go top of our group tonight and put ourselves in pole position to qualify for the Wembley Final – it's going to be a mammoth task to do it now.

'I appealed in the *Echo* for the people of Southend to come out and back us and I thought they responded magnificently – 3,603 for a game in this competition is superb – but the players let them down badly.

'Front men like Ricky Otto and Brett Angell, who you expect to go out and win matches for you, were hopeless, and I can't remember Keith Jones getting a kick – we were pathetic. Pescara were a different class – one minute they had eight or nine back in defence and the next there were four or six streaming forward in attack – they gave us a football lesson.'

It's the Jekyll and Hyde performances from his men which must be most worrying for Fry -commitment and passion at Cosenza and against Luton on Saturday was replaced by amateur defending and feeble finishing last night.

For me only two Southend men escaped criticism – full-back Chris Powell who played a stormer despite suffering from 'flu and little Derek Payne never gave up the midfield battle. But as Fry said the front men were powder puff and allowed themselves to be totally dominated by an Italian outfit which, with the season only 11 games old, is already on its third manager!

As Payne said Southend were also very naive tactically – allowing themselves to be sucked in and hit on the counter attack. 'Hopefully we will learn from this and be better prepared when we face our next make-or-break game in the competition against Padova in December,' he said.

'Had we taken our early chances it might have been a different story but we didn't and they made us pay for it – I've rarely known our players so quiet after a game – the boss rightly gave us an ear bashing and we must repair the damage at Sunderland on Saturday.'

Blues were caught cold by two decisive breaks by Pescara – speedy winger Frederic Massara twice leaving men in his wake to set up simple goals for Guiseppe Compagno and John Sivebaek in that disastrous opening 19 minutes. But Southend had their chances. After Jones' early blunder, Angell somehow failed to force the ball over the line from a few yards out and Savorani did well to tip Jonathan Hunt's ambitious overhead kick to safety.

But you always had the feeling that the well oiled Pescara machine could cause more damage to Southend and that's precisely what happened eight minutes into the second half – left-back Antonio Nobile haring away from the half-way line to send a shot whistling through a stranded Paul Sansome.

Angell missed another good chance and then Savorani tipped a rising shot from Gary Jones over the bar before substitute Jason Lee provided a glimmer of hope after 68 minutes – forcing the ball in at the far post after Otto's first decent run and cross of the night.

But Pescara, with a 100 per cent record in the competition, stayed in cool command although Angell summed up Southend's dismal night by heading over the bar from inside the six yard box with only eight minutes left on the clock. Southend's hopes of emerging top English club in their Group were boosted with defeats for West Brom and Stoke – although Portsmouth did emerge victorious. Teams:–

SOUTHEND UNITED: Sansome, Poole, Powell, K. Jones, Edwards (sub. Howell 29 minutes), Bressington, Hunt (sub. Lee 56 minutes), Payne, G. Jones, Otto, Angell. Subs (not used): Gridelet, Mooney and Royce.

PESCARA: Savorani, Alfieri, Nobile, Sivebaek, Dicara, Loseto, Iulis, Ceredi (sub. Palladini 51 minutes), Compagno, Ferretti (sub. Toro 80 minutes), Massara. Subs (not used): Martinelli, Marco, Terrenzi.

Wednesday, December 22nd, 1993
Anglo-Italian Cup, International Round, Group 'B'
SOUTHEND UNITED 5, PADOVA 2

Southend United well and truly exorcised the ghost of former boss Barry Fry last night after crushing Padova 5-2 and roaring into the semi-final of the Anglo-Italian Cup. And super sub Gary Jones, who transformed the game when he came on in the second-half for Tommy Mooney, summed up the pleasure the players felt at earning new manager Peter Taylor his first win since Fry's controversial departure to Birmingham City.

'There's been a big upheaval here in the last couple of weeks but we are professionals and must forget Barry – he's gone but Southend is still alive and kicking,' he told me. 'Peter Taylor has his own way of doing things -I'm sure he will do well here and prove a big success – this result was our Christmas present to him. Tonight's result is just the tonic the boss and the lads needed and it's important that we build on it in the League – starting against Charlton on Monday.'

Taylor couldn't disguise his delight at breaking his duck since taking over the Roots Hall hotseat less than two weeks ago. The players showed their true colours tonight and it was great to see those superb goals go in – and there could and should have been even more,' he said.

'I am a very proud man and the fans were terrific – they knew what my first win as manager of this club meant to me and I couldn't be happier.' Blues looked to have paid the penalty for some woeful first-half finishing when they went in 1-0 down at the break – Giordano's 18th minute goal giving Padova an undeserved edge. Big Jason Lee had somehow missed two great chances from inside the six yard box while Mooney sliced another golden opportunity well wide. But Gary Jones entered the scene to torment the Italian defence with some darting runs into the channels which simply ripped them apart. He teed up an equaliser for Lee after 50 minutes and then Andy Edwards headed in a cross from the hard grafting Derek Payne 12 minutes later.

Even a lucky Padova equaliser when Cuicchi's 75th minute free-kick deflected off the wall and squirmed into the corner of the net failed to extinguish Southend's fire, and they were back in front before you could say Barry Fry.

Jones raced through to fire home and then he set up Ricky Otto for a cool finish after 78 minutes. And in the dying seconds Jones capped a memorable night by again beating the Italians desperate offside trap by getting free and slotting the ball past the 'keeper with arrogant ease.

'I thoroughly enjoyed myself tonight and will obviously be disappointed if I'm not in the starting line-up against Charlton,' said hero Jones. I couldn't do much more than score two and make two but it's up to the manager – the big thing is that Southend United are back – there is definitely life under Peter Taylor!'

A word of praise for the 1,518 hardy souls who braved a cold and miserable night and helped send Blues into a two-legged semi-final against Notts. County with a place at Wembley the glittering prize. Teams:–

SOUTHEND UNITED: Sansome, Poole, Powell, K. Jones, Edwards, Bodley, Hunt, Payne, Mooney (sub. G. Jones 45 minutes), Otto, Lee. Subs (not used): Bressington, Gridelet, Tilson and Royce.

PADOVA: Bianco, Cuicchi, Tentoni, Ruffini, Rosa, Ottoni (sub. 36 minutes Gabrieli), Giordano (sub. 70 minutes Longhi), Cavezzi, Galderisi, Coppola, Maniero. Subs (not used): Bonaiuti, Nunziata, Pellizzaro.

Tuesday, September 5th, 1995
Anglo-Italian Cup, International Round, Group 'B'
SOUTHEND UNITED 0, BRESCIA 0

Chris Powell was left bemused and shattered last night after being sent off for the first time in his career as Southend United were held to a goalless draw by Brescia in one of the most amazing games ever seen at Roots Hall.

Referee Marcello Cardona let so many tackles go unpunished in the Anglo-Italian clash that the almost inevitable happened – the game boiled over 12 minutes from the end and left Powell the victim along with Brescia's Stefano Bonometti. Blues sub Dominic Iorfa was felled by yet another crude challenge and suddenly it all erupted – players kicking and punching each other amid chaotic and ugly scenes. The ref raced at least 40 yards from the action but once things died down appeared from nowhere to flourish red cards in dramatic fashion.

'I couldn't believe the ref picked me out – I wasn't involved at all and can only assume it was a case of mistaken identity,' Powell told me afterwards.

'It looks as if he had to justify doing something and just picked on a player from each side at random. I feel sick because I had hoped to go through my career without ever getting sent off – to go like this is very distressing.'

Luckily Powell won't be punished by missing any League games as he just gets a two match ban in the Anglo-Italian competition.

Southend player/boss Ronnie Whelan was equally at a loss to explain the action of the referee who also sent Salvatore Giunta off six minutes later for upending Phil Gridelet.

But one thing which Whelan admitted was worrying him is his side's lack of goals – this was the third blank in the last four games and he must be hoping top striker Andy Thomson recovers from his badly bruised thigh in time for Saturday's trip to Sunderland.

'It's something we've got to work on in training,' he said. 'But tonight was never going to be a goal feast – the Italians make it difficult and are experts at closing the game down and there were not a great deal of clear cut openings.'

Indeed Andy Ansah possibly came the closest to breaking the deadlock with a couple of shots which giant 'keeper Nello Cusin held under the bar and also hit the woodwork with a first-half effort.

Paul Byrne and Jones both had efforts saved by Cusin's legs while at the other end Simon Royce held on to a couple of free-kicks and Maurizio Neri muffed two good openings late on.

Southend's most expensive ever capture Mike Marsh slotted in well and looks as if he will prove worth the £500,000 – spraying the ball around intelligently.

SOUTHEND UNITED: Royce, Dublin, Bodley, Lapper (sub. 59 minutes Hone), Powell, Byrne, Marsh (sub. 79 minutes Tilson), Gridelet, Hayes (sub. 68 minutes Iorfa), Jones, Ansah. Subs (not used): Sansome, Hails.

BRESCIA: Cusin, Costi, Savino, Mezzanotti, Luzardi, Bonometti, Neri, Volpi, Lunini (sub. 59 minutes Campolonghi), Giunta, Ambrosetti.
Subs (not used): Disarno, Lambertini, A. Filippini, E. Filippini.

Attendance: 2,849.

Wednesday, October 11th, 1995
Anglo-Italian Cup, International Round, Group 'B'
REGGIANA 1, SOUTHEND UNITED 1

Blues, who had lost their two previous matches without scoring a goal, followed up their goalless home draw against Brescia last month with another vital point yesterday.

Reggiana pressed hard early on and 'keeper Simon Royce had to make two sparkling saves either side of half-time.

The Italians took the lead through Palombo after 53 minutes but Southend battled back and struck with an equaliser 16 minutes later – a shot from Julian Hails being helped over the line by Steve Tilson.

It was Blues who pushed forward looking for the winner in the last 20 minutes but Reggiana held firm.

More than 100 fans made the trip by jet with the team and helped swell a dismal crowd of under 800.

Wednesday, November 8th, 1995
Anglo-Italian Cup, International Round, Group 'B'
SALERNITANA 2, SOUTHEND UNITED 1

Southend United will have to win their final Anglo/Italian Cup tie at home to Foggia next month to stand any chance of qualifying for the English semi-final. That was made clear after Blues battled bravely but went down 2-1 in Salernitana last night, Dave Regis scoring for the Blues.

Ipswich definitely clinched their semi spot with a 1-0 win over Foggia but the second place is still wide open between Southend, Stoke City and West Brom and will go down to that final match on December 13.

Wednesday, December 13th, 1995
Anglo-Italian Cup, International Round, Group 'B'
SOUTHEND UNITED 1, FOGGIA 2

A series of crazy refereeing decisions left Southend United angry and frustrated as they were dumped out of the Anglo/Italian Cup by Foggia at Roots Hall last night.

It was a mystery why eccentric ref Luigi Deprisco from Napoli didn't give 'keeper Botticella more than a yellow card when he felled Julian Hails as he raced through on goal after 19 minutes. Mike Marsh converted the spot kick for his first goal for Blues since arriving for a record £500,000 from Galatasaray three months ago.

But all the talk afterwards unhappily concentrated more on Deprisco's abysmal handling of the match rather than the football itself. Player/boss Ronnie Whelan said: 'You don't like to see people sent off but the goalie brought Hails down and the rules are clear – he had to go.

'I saw Ludek Miklosko banished for a far less cynical foul than this one in West Ham's match at Everton on Monday but it was not a very good display by the referee or linesmen tonight – we were unhappy with a number of their decisions.'

And full-back Chris Powell also blasted the officials saying: 'The goalie had earlier sent Phil Gridelet flying and we only got a corner and then he pulled Hails down when he had a certain goalscoring chance – how he stayed on the pitch I'll never know.

'We're upset at ending our recent good run but we didn't really want the distraction of this Cup – the League is our priority and we feel we've got a great chance of forcing our way into the play-offs.'

The referee refused to comment on the incident before hurrying off to join the Foggia players for a meal at a local Italian restaurant.

And the game got off to a bad start with Foggia getting lost on their way to Southend and forcing the kick-off to be delayed for half-an-hour.

As if to add insult to injury guess what gift the Italians gave Southend as a memento of the game ... a clock!

Blues started brightly and could easily have been 2-0 up inside the first 17 minutes – Phil Gridelet and Roger Willis both having efforts cleared off the line by desperate defender Parisi.

Then came the controversial penalty incident to put Southend deservedly in front and Willis, still looking in need of match sharpness following his long injury lay-off, wasted a great chance just before the break when he failed to force the ball home from close range.

The Italians woke up after half-time and Mick Bodley was forced to put in a storming defensive display to keep them out. But even he was helpless to stop Zanchetta bundling his way through to equalise on the hour and then Sano somehow squeezed the ball in from a narrow angle three minutes from the end.

Whelan rang the changes and Dominic Iorfa came on to test the Foggia back-line with his pace. Unhappily his final ball left a lot to be desired, but anyway Deprisco's constant whistling and some incredible offside decisions ensured this was not to be Southend's night.

Attendance: 2,570

SOUTHEND: (4-4-2 formation): Royce; Dublin, Lapper, Bodley, Powell (sub. 65 minutes Hone); Byrne, Marsh, Gridelet, Hails; Thomson (sub. 65 minutes Iorfa), Willis (sub. 80 minutes Regis). Subs (not used): Tilson and Sansome.

FOGGIA: Botticella, Gasparini, Anastasi (sub. 88 minutes Bari), Sciacca, Parisi, Bianchini, Marazzina, Sano, Kolivanov, Zanchetta (sub. 60 minutes Consagra), Corcia (sub. 45 minutes Giacobbo).

Referee: Luigi Deprisco (Napoli).

CHAPTER SIXTEEN

Semi-finals 1912-2005

Monday, April 22nd, 1912
Southern Counties Charity Cup, Semi-final
READING 0, SOUTHEND UNITED 1
(played at White Hart Lane, Tottenham Hotspur F.C.)

The Southern Counties Charity Cup has probably brought out the abilities of the Southend team more than any competition this season, and the eleven have shown such good form in this competition, which, if it had only been reproduced in their League matches, must have resulted in promotion. It is a feather in their caps to have reached the final of the tournament, a feat previously without parallel by a Second Division club, and to do this they have had to remove from their path three First Division Southern League Clubs. They are now pitted against a fourth, viz., Coventry City.

In the opening match of the season they defeated New Brompton, at Gillingham, by the decisive score of three to nil; in the second round they gained their first victory over Queen's Park Rangers by five goals to four, after Griffiths, their then goalkeeper, presented the Londoners with at least three goals, and on Monday, on the Tottenham Hotspur ground in White Hart Lane, they vanquished Reading in the semi-final by a goal to nothing. Reading had previously given the coup de grace to Swindon, last year's winners, and also Brighton, the finalists of the previous season with the Railwaymen and the holders of the cup in 1909-10. Therefore, the performance was no mean one, especially remembering the Biscuitmen's reputation as a cup-fighting team which they earned this season.

Reading had conquered such a fine side as Aston Villa in the English Cup, after making a draw at the Lower Grounds, and in the third round they only lost to Manchester United after a drawn game. Therefore, as the Reading side only differed with two exceptions from that which made history in the Cup, Southend's performance was a very creditable one. The absentees in the Berkshire team were Caldwell, their goalkeeper, who last week was transferred to Everton, and W.G. Bailey, their amateur inside right, but otherwise they were at full strength. Southend played the same side that defeated Ton Pentre; Murray and Emery not having recovered from their injuries. Therefore, it may be said that both sides started quits as far as strength was concerned.

Though, perhaps, not productive of a game of really good class football, the match on Monday was interesting and there were periods when each side displayed very creditable combination. The Biscuitmen, however, did not strike one as being a great side and there was no doubt that the victory went to the better team on the day's play. The Seasiders were smarter on the ball, more accurate in their kicking, displayed a better understanding and were more organised in their attacks than Reading. It was a typical cup-tie and neither side gave anything away, though the earlier impression left on my mind was that the First Leaguers were inclined to hold their less fortunate brethren a little too cheaply. This fault, however, soon became apparent to them and they quickly found that their opposition was as much as they could cope with.

In either half the Royal Blues did the bulk of the defensive work, and while the occasions on which the Westerners got dangerous could be counted on the fingers of one hand, Southend were constantly harassing their defence and a little more steadiness in front of goal would have resulted in a more pronounced win. Reading rather tried to over do the fancy work and this proved unprofitable against the Southend half-backs, who, for once, adapted themselves to the needs of the moment and played cup-tie football. There was plenty of good honest charging, and the game throughout was conducted in a good sporting spirit. With one exception every man on the Southend side acquitted himself well, and they were immensely pleased with their triumph.

It was unfortunate that the game had to be played at the tail end of the season, because only about a thousand spectators assembled. The match was originally fixed to take place in February, on the Monday before Reading had to play Manchester United, but here again Southend's proverbial hard luck asserted itself, for the Biscuitmen absolutely refused to play and the match had to be postponed.

Southend claimed the game, but the Committee dismissed this claim and ordered the match to take place on Monday. At the date when the game should have been played Reading would have had a great drawing capacity as the conquerors of Aston Villa, but the sporting world, in common with other popular fancies, has a short memory and the fame of Reading has now been almost forgotten. Consequently, Monday's gate only realised £27, and as Southend only get a third after deducting expenses, they will barely cover their travelling expenses. If the game had been played in February they would probably have got £40 out of the deal.

It was announced that H.M. Lamoine, the Clapton goalkeeper, would be between the sticks for the United, but, unfortunately, he got injured on Saturday and could not turn out, and Nurthen again held the fort. Among the interested spectators of the match was our old friend and manager Mr. Bob Jack, who still has a warm corner in his heart for the Club he managed in the early days and who had been staying at Southend over the week-end, after Plymouth's match with Watford. It was a pleasure to renew old acquaintances and one could not help congratulating Mr. Jack on the success of his club in the Southern League and wishing them championship honours. Mr. Jack told me that had Plymouth not gone through the first month of the season without a victory, they would have won the League easily.

Under the direction of Mr. A.W. McQue, who last season refereed the English Cup final, the teams lined up as follows:–

READING: H. Stevens; Smith and Bartholomew; Smart, Hanney, and Bradley; Lee, Gadsby, Foster, Andrews, and Greer.

SOUTHEND: Nurthen; Thomson and Cairns; Layzell, Harwood, and Arnold; McNaught, Wilson, Wileman, Bradshaw, and Parke.

Thomson won the toss for Southend and played with the advantage of a slight breeze and with the sun in his opponents' faces. The ground was as dry as a bone and often flew up in clouds of dust as the players scampered along. As a consequence, the ball was very lively and took a great deal of controlling, while the brilliant sunshine often proved disconcerting to the players. Play opened very quietly and the only incident worthy of record during the initial ten minutes was a hot shot from Foster, which Nurthen saved brilliantly at full length and just got the ball away as Andrews came dashing up. The Blues retaliated and McNaught came close with a shot that struck the outside of the meshes. It seemed certain that a lovely drive from Bradshaw would find the billet, but suddenly Bartholomew's head bobbed up and diverted its course.

Southend pressed strongly, and following a corner to them the Reading goal experienced a perilously near escape. Reading gained a similar concession at the other end, but Bradshaw cleared an ugly shot from Greer. The hopes of Southend were raised when they obtained a penalty after half-an-hour's play. Hanney deliberately punched down a centre from Wilson and Mr. McQue had no hesitation in awarding a penalty. Wileman was entrusted with the kick, but to the chagrin of the crowd – who all seemed friendly disposed towards Southend – he shivered the crossbar with a terrific shot and as the ball rebounded into play, Parke put outside.

The Berkshire men were encouraged by this escape and attacked strongly and once Foster netted, but the referee had previously blown for offside; the Reading centre being yards on the wrong side of the Southend backs. Southend were quickly on the aggressive again and Smith, the right back, nearly put through his own goal in attempting to clear a centre from McNaught, but fortunately for them the leather went for a corner, which was abortive. At half time there was a blank score sheet and it seemed on the run of the play that the spoils would go to the side that could score.

The only goal of the match was notched in the opening four minutes of the second moiety. It was a very prettily obtained and well worked for point. The chief credit of the goal belongs to Bradshaw, who had wandered over to the right wing and, neatly beating Bartholomew, he screwed the ball into the goalmouth, right off the line. Parke was in waiting, and applying his cranium to the sphere, he completely beat Stephens. Soon after this the Blues came near obtaining a second, for Parke met a centre from McNaught and missed the bar by the barest margin. Following a corner to Southend, Greer raced away and made a superb effort to equalise, but his shot scraped the top of the bar.

For some time after this Southend were top dogs and Stephens saved well from a capital oblique shot from the toe of Bradshaw, while at the other end Nurthen had to exert himself to parry a hot one from Foster. Again Southend took up the whip hand and McNaught caused Stephens a lot of trouble with a sharp shot, and he managed to save, though surrounded by three Southend forwards. In the closing stages the Blues strove their upmost to maintain their lead and acted on the defensive. They held the Reading attack well and except on one occasion, when they obtained a free just outside the penalty area, they never looked like scoring. Southend thus deservedly ran out winners by a goal to love.

Nurthen saved well on two or three occasions and he deserves every credit for the one in the early stages of the game. Thomson was in magnificent form and Cairns, though kicking rather poorly on several occasions, put in a lot of sound defensive work. Layzell played probably the best game he has ever done in the Southend colours, and deserves a special word of praise, while Harwood and Arnold were both in great form. McNaught was the only man on the side who failed to play well. Wilson did his best and Wileman seemed more settled in his duties as a centre and passed well to his wings. Bradshaw played a nice game and Parke was as good as any forward on the field.

For Reading, Stephens had much more work to do than his confrere in the Southend goal and did it well. In fact, had Caldwell been there he could not have saved the goal. The kicking of the Reading backs, however, was very faulty and had it not been for the great assistance they received from their halves, especially Hanney, they would have crumbled up badly. Hanney is a great centre-half, while Smart is little behind him as a half-back, and Bradley also did well. Of the forwards, who did not strike one as being a very dangerous quintet; Foster and Greer were the most prominent.

The final tie has been provisionally fixed for the Fulham ground on Monday next, Southend's opponents being Coventry City, who defeated Plymouth Argyle, at Plymouth, in the other semi-final, by three goals to two.

Wednesday, January 26th, 1994
Anglo-Italian Cup, Semi-final, First leg
SOUTHEND UNITED 1, NOTTS. COUNTY 0

Keeper Simon Royce was the hero in last night's controversial Anglo-Italian Cup semi-final 1st leg which hinged on two penalty decisions – one which was given and one which wasn't.

The Southend United goalie threw himself to his left to keep out Gary Lund's 39th minute spot kick, after Gary Poole was harshly judged by ref Ron

Groves from Weston-super-Mare to have handled, to ensure a narrow 1-0 win.

But Notts. County looked lucky to escape when Phil Turner's more blatant handball went unpunished midway through the second-half. 'If the incident in our box was a penalty then I can't see how the referee ignored that one at the other end of the pitch,' said Royce afterwards. Obviously I was delighted to save their effort -Lund struck it well but I went the right way and got my forearm to the ball. With away goals counting double in this competition that save could prove very important at the end of the day.'

Phil Gridelet was another key Blues man – netting his first goal for the club when he bundled the ball in at the far post after Andy Edwards flicked on Jonathan Hunt's 5th minute corner. And he reckoned afterwards it could set Southend up for a dream Wembley Final when they go to County for the second leg on February 8.

'We could have won by more goals but they will have to come out more at home and you've always got to fancy us on the break,' said Gridelet. 'But this was an important win for us – the lads were really down after our run of five defeats on the trot but the atmosphere in the dressing room is bubbling again – that result could be the turning point in our season. We kept our shape and were far more disciplined tonight – I can't remember County having a chance apart from that diabolical penalty.'

Indeed but for several superb saves by County 'keeper Steve Cherry Blues could be halfway down Wembley Way right now. He made a great stop to keep Jason Lee's powerful 61st minute header out and also denied Hunt, the energetic Derek Payne and lively Ricky Otto late on. But will one goal be enough to see Southend to that big day at Wembley?

'If we go up there with the same professional attitude that we showed tonight then I don't see why we shouldn't come out winning the tie,' said boss Peter Taylor. 'The lads showed a lot of character after recent bad results and were only denied a more convincing win by some great goalkeeping and an amazing penalty decision which went against us. We have won tonight without producing our best attacking form, and I'm confident we have enough forward power to come through in the second leg which will be far more open than tonight.' As Taylor said the result was probably more important than the performance but at least battling Southend, who have given some terrible goals away in recent weeks, look tighter and more solid.

Payne and Gridelet worked so hard in the middle of the park closing people down while the defence hardly gave County, who arrived boasting a run of four wins from the last five outings, a look in. Up front Gary Jones showed some great touches, Lee's height and power always posed a threat and Otto's pace and trickery had the visitor's running around in circles at times.

The big mystery to me is how West Ham, so desperate for central defenders, could let giant Colin Foster join County on loan. I lost count of the vital headers, tackles and important interceptions he made – Hammers could certainly do with his imposing presence right now. Teams:–

SOUTHEND: Royce, Poole, Powell, Gridelet, Edwards, Bodley, Hunt, Payne, Jones (sub. 76 minutes Mooney), Otto, Lee. Subs, (not used): Bressington, Sussex, Locke and Oliver.

NOTTS. COUNTY: Cherry, Johnson, Sherlock, Palmer, Foster, Turner, Devlin, Draper, Lund, Agana, Legg. Subs, (not used): McSwegan, Murphy, Simpson and Catlin.

Attendance: 3,706.

Wednesday, February 16th, 1994
Anglo-Italian Cup, Semi-final, Second leg
NOTTS. COUNTY 1, SOUTHEND UNITED 0
(aggregate score 1-1; Notts. County win 4-3 on kicks from the penalty mark)

Southend United's Wembley dream died in the cruellest way possible last night – losing in a dramatic penalty shoot-out.

The Anglo-Italian Cup semi-final at Notts. County was left hanging in the balance 1-1 on aggregate after extra time which left the spot kick lottery to decide who faced Brescia on soccer's greatest stage next month. But in the end the nailbiting tension proved too much for skipper Gary Poole and Graham Bressington who failed to find the net leaving County 4-3 winners.

Andy Sussex, Tommy Mooney and Jonathan Hunt made no mistakes while Paul Sansome saved from Meindert Dijkstra but unhappily Phil Turner, Gary Lund, Gary McSwegan and Mark Draper all coolly slotted their efforts.

It all left Southend players devastated – sinking to the ground in tears and disbelief at the end as County went on a lap of honour.

Blues bitterly disappointed boss Peter Taylor summed it all up afterwards when he told me: 'To decide a Wembley final on penalties is hard. It's a terrible way for any team to go out but no-one yet has come up with an adequate alternative.

'Both teams worked hard and, together with some superb supporters, were a credit to their clubs. It was a tight game and unfortunately we didn't hit the target from the chances we created. There are plenty of tears in the dressing room because we all thought it was going to be our year and we went into the game in a very positive frame of mind.'

On the Bressington penalty miss – he blazed his shot high and wide of the target – Taylor said: 'If I was a gambling man I would have put my mortgage on Graham sticking his away, but perhaps he was too confident and took his eye off the ball at the last second because he said he didn't connect with it right. Perhaps in hindsight Poole should not have taken the first one. He was upset that the spot kicks were taken at the opposite end to our supporters and was not in the right frame of mind.'

Taylor refused to condemn wing star Ricky Otto, so often the hero for Blues this season, for a bad miss in the first-half of extra-time – somehow heading a Gary Jones cross over the bar when it looked easier to score.

'Obviously it's very frustrating when something like that happens,' said the Blues chief. 'If Ricky hits the target and the 'keeper saves it then there's nothing you can do but to put the ball over from that position is hard to take.'

And in truth that was the story of the night for Southend – too often players either snatched at chances or tried to break the back of the net instead of being clinical. County always carried that little bit more threat with little Derek Payne heading one effort off the line and Sansome being forced to make several desperate stops, while Steve Cherry at the other end was rarely given an uncomfortable moment.

There was a sense of inevitability about County's goal after 69 minutes which wiped out Blues slender 1-0 lead from the 1st leg – the most dangerous striker on view Paul Devlin going past two defenders before firing low into the corner of the net. Up until then a mixture of good fortune and stout defending from Sansome, Bressington and Andy Edwards had held the more eager home side at bay.

Phil Gridelet and Derek Payne battled manfully in the middle of the park while Jason Lee was the pick of the front men although most of his hard graft was done outside the box – he, too, lacking that vital cutting edge in front of goal. Hunt and Otto looked to have the potential to cause problems down the flanks but too often took the wrong option – shooting when they should cross and putting the ball into the box when perhaps a shot was the better alternative. But as I say Southend certainly could not be faulted for effort, it's simply that the early season goal menace has deserted them – this current team cries out for the cold assassin's head of 'old' strikers like David Crown and Steve Phillips. Teams:–

NOTTS. COUNTY: Cherry, Palmer, Dijkstra, Turner, Foster, Johnson (sub. 96 minutes Sherlock), Devlin, Draper, Lund, Legg, McSwegan. Subs, (not used): Matthews, Catlin, Simpson and Wilson.

SOUTHEND UNITED: Sansome, Poole, Powell, Gridelet, Edwards, Bressington, Hunt, Payne (sub. 81 minutes Sussex), Jones, Otto, Lee (sub. 81 minutes Mooney). Subs, (not used): Tilson, Bodley and Royce.

Attendance: 5,485.

Tuesday, March 13th, 2001
Football League Trophy, Semi-final, First leg, Sponsored as Football League LDV Vans Trophy Southern Area Final
SOUTHEND UNITED 1, BRENTFORD 2

Roots Hall visitors Brentford stole a slender, but crucial lead during last night's exciting LDV Vans Trophy southern final first leg match against Southend

United. And the Second Division side's unlikely hero was right wing-back Michael Dobson, who grabbed two precious second-half strikes either side of a headed goal from Shrimpers skipper Phil Whelan.

Blues now face a tough, but not impossible task, during next Tuesday's second leg at Griffin Park, when they will attempt to keep their dreams of a first major cup final alive by overturning the one goal deficit. David Webb's Third Division battlers may have their work cut out for them, but if they get a slice of luck in front of goal they will have a great chance of reaching Cardiff's Millennium stadium in April.

There was not much to choose between the Blues and the Bees at Roots Hall, despite the 20 places separating the two sides on the league ladder before kick-off. Webb made five changes to the team which had slipped to a second consecutive defeat in disastrous style, 3-0 at home to Blackpool, at the weekend. And the transformation was there for all to see. The side had more balance and played with a fluency not enjoyed over the past few games.

Although, for all of their possession Southend were still frustrated in the final third of the field, which made Webb's decision to rest striker Mark Rawle from his squad puzzling. However, the biggest influence on Blues' much improved performance was midfielder Kevin Maher's return from a two-match suspension.

Maher has been sorely missed, leaving Southend resembling an out of tune orchestra in need of urgent guidance from their conductor. But he returned to the stage front against Brentford, putting in a composed 90 minutes, which ticked right at the heart of the Seasiders' most positive moments.

Martyn Booty was also reinstated after finishing a one-game ban and the right-back played like a man possessed, getting stuck into challenges and making good progress down the flank. Russell Williamson made the most of a rare chance to shine on the left-wing and Michael Black was employed on the other channel. And Webb's final change was to hand a rare start, although his second of this competition, to veteran central defender Rob Newman and the 37-year-old never let anybody down. In the best traditions of cup football, this important tie kicked off at a lightning quick pace – a tempo which both sides managed to tirelessly maintain for most of the game.

Brentford carved out the first chance of the match, with striker Lloyd Owusu meeting a near post right-wing cross from Paul Gibbs, but heading well wide of the Southend goal after two minutes. And Blues frontman David Lee did exactly the same from Black's centre almost straight away at the other end. Owusu should have opened the scoring after nine minutes when he broke clear of the Southend defence, but he screwed amateurishly high and wide from just inside the box.

Two minutes later, Lee registered the first real shot on target as he turned in a flash 25-yards out and hammered a low drive into Bees goalkeeper Olafur Gottskalksson's hands.

As the action continued to switch from end to end at the blink of an eye, Brentford midfielder Martin Rowlands steered a weak header into Blues custodian Darryl Flahavan's gloves. And Black played a smart one-two with Southend forward Ben Abbey on the right-hand side of the Brentford box, before curling a shot across the face of the Londoners' goalmouth.

Blues were starting to hold a firm grip on the territorial stakes at this stage and Abbey went close with an attempt to lob Gottskalksson from 45-yards, after Lee had pressurised the Icelandic international into a poor clearance.

Brentford defender David Theobald then did well to block a shot from a rampant Booty, before Abbey picked up the loose ball and scooped just over the bar.

Theobald thwarted Southend again on 28 minutes, this time hooking Williamson's shot off the goal-line, after the diminutive midfielder had cut out Barren Powell's header back to Gottskalksson. And Blues left-back Damon Searle smashed a free-kick through the Brentford wall, but straight at the keeper. Brentford were now hanging on desperately and Powell, who was a colossus at the back for the visitors, nicked Booty's pin-point cross off the head of Lee, as the forward hurled himself goalward.

Williamson finished the half by cutting in smartly from the left-flank and unleashing a 25-yard drive which was comfortable for Gottskalksson.

And after the restart, Williamson was denied a certain goal by Dobson, who somehow managed to beat the midfielder to Booty's wicked right-wing cross and head clear. But Southend's concerted pressure meant nothing after 56 minutes as Brentford snatched the lead in controversial circumstances. The referee awarded a free-kick on the half-way line to the visitors when he should have opted for a drop-ball, after Blues midfielder Leon Johnson and his opposite number Paul Evans innocently clashed heads.

Brentford defender Gavin Mahon launched a long pass into the heart of the Southend penalty box, leaving Dobson to bend an unstoppable 18-yard shot inside the right-hand post at the second attempt as the Seasiders failed to clear their lines.

However, justice prevailed as Blues equalised 60 seconds later through a set play of their own. Black guided a left-wing free-kick to the back post for Whelan to beat Theobald and claim his second goal of the season as he headed past Gottskalksson from a couple of yards out.

But Dobson, who started out in football as a striker, had the last word as he claimed what would prove to be the winner in the 64th minute. Powell headed a viciously whipped right-wing cross from Evans back into the path of the fullback, whose 15-yard volley struck the inside of the left post and beat Flahavan, despite Searle's best efforts on the goal-line.

Full of confidence, Brentford stepped up a gear and could have claimed further goals when Whelan blocked Owusu, before midfielder Ivar Ingimarsson drilled wide.

Owusu then headed another good chance over the Southend crossbar, before midfield team-mate Evans struck a fierce 25-yard free-kick past the right post.

With 77 minutes played, Abbey tried his luck from a similar distance, but his shot lacked the power to trouble Gottskalksson. And Webb made his last throw of the dice ten minutes from time, bringing on two substitutes, hitman Martin Carruthers and midfielder Stuart Thurgood.

Carruthers made an immediate impact, flicking a header on to Abbey, who dragged the ball past Theobald with his first touch to create an opening for himself, but hardly troubled Gottskalksson with a terrible shot.

And in the very last minute, Blues came within a whisker of a dramatic late, late equaliser. Thurgood won the ball on the edge of the Brentford box, allowing Maher to send over a right-wing centre, which Carruthers stretched to agonisingly glance inches over the visitors' bar.

UNITED (in 4-4-2 formation): Flahavan; Booty, Searle, Williamson, Newman; Whelan, Maher, Johnson (sub. Thurgood 80 minutes), Black; Abbey, Lee (sub. Carruthers 81 minutes). Subs, (not used): McSweeney, Bramble and Porter.

BRENTFORD: Gottskalksson, Powell, Ingimarsson, Evans, Mahon, Owusu, Partridge (McCammon), Rowlands, Dobson, Gibbs (Lovett), Theobald. Subs, (not used): Smith, Williams and Charles.

Attendance: 5,055.

Tuesday, March 20th, 2001
Football League Trophy, Semi-final, Second leg, Sponsored as Football League LDV Vans Trophy, Southern Area Final
BRENTFORD 2, SOUTHEND UNITED 1
(Brentford win 4-2 on aggregate score)

Southend United's bid to make the first major cup final of their history ended in a brave defeat during last night's LDV Vans Trophy southern final second leg at Brentford. Blues travelled to Griffin Park knowing they had to overturn a one-goal deficit against the Second Division Bees, following their first leg 2-1 Roots Hall reverse.

And the Shrimpers put on a both passionate and gutsy display as they tried to fight back and clinch a place in the grand final at Cardiff's Millennium Stadium next month. But yet again, lady luck cruelly turned her back on the Third Division Shrimpers, whose superhuman efforts were acknowledged by a standing ovation from 1,000 proud travelling fans at the final whistle.

Blues have now gone 95 long years without making it to a major cup final, but their current crop of players did everything within their power to end such a miserable record at Brentford. Although starting as the underdogs, this was Southend's best chance of breaking their jinx, since their Anglo-Italian cup anguish against Notts. County in 1994.

On that occasion, Blues suffered the heartbreak of bowing out in a penalty shoot-out lottery at Meadow Lane, which robbed them of a trip to the hallowed turf of Wembley.

But this loss was just as painful for the Seasiders' success-starved supporters. Blues started off in determined mood against Brentford, who were made to battle every inch of the way for their triumph. But midfielder Ivar Ingimarsson got the Bees buzzing with an early goal, which gave the hosts a 3-1 advantage on aggregate and seemingly one boot in Cardiff. But Southend showed tremendous character to bounce straight back with, ironically, Welshman Damon Searle grabbing his first goal for the Shrimpers before half-time.

And the Seasiders stepped up another gear after the break as they took the game to Brentford in their own backyard. But Blues' frustrating inability to make their chances count haunted them yet again as they were denied an all important second goal on a number of occasions, with striker Martin Carruthers the biggest culprit, missing a six-yard sitter.

And after surviving Southend's bombardment of their goal, Brentford inevitably broke away and scored with their first attack as frontman Lloyd Owusu finally crushed the Shrimpers' cup dream. There was also the added spice of Blues boss David Webb making his first return to Griffin Park since he sold the club four years ago.

The Shrimpers chief was given a police escort to the dugout as the Brentford fans hurled angry abuse at the man they claim made a mint on his way through the exit door. And the irate home supporters were stirred up even more after eight minutes as their defender Darren Powell and Blues hitman Carruthers sent each other crashing into the advertising boards which earned them both bookings.

Brentford prised open the first opportunity of the game three minutes later, when striker Scott Partridge angled a drive past the right post under pressure from Southend skipper Phil Whelan. But the Bees got it right on 13 minutes, punishing a far from attentive Shrimpers defence at a set-play.

Whelan was penalised for a tangle with Partridge on the right flank, allowing Brentford captain Paul Evans to whip over a quickly taken free-kick, which Ingimarsson prodded past Blues goalkeeper Darryl Flahavan from ten yards. Partridge nearly found Owusu with a low cross a few minutes later, after latching on to David Lee's lazy pass. And Southend winger Scott Forbes took Whelan's long pass down the left channel and warmed Bees goalie Olafur Gottskalksson's gloves from 15 yards. Dead-ball specialist Evans then curled a free-kick past the right post, before Searle showed his opposite number how it should be done at the other end of the pitch on 26 minutes.

Carruthers was sent sprawling on the right-hand edge of the Brentford box, allowing Searle to smash a fierce 20-yard equaliser, which hit Bees defender David Theobald and crashed into the top left-hand corner of the net.

Within 60 seconds, Blues hitman Tes Bramble latched on to a poor goal-kick from Gottskalksson, shrugged off Theobald and tried to find Carruthers with a low right-wing centre, which Powell cleared.

And Icelandic Ingimarsson was given a free jump by Southend midfielder Leon Johnson on 34 minutes, but he could only steer another Evans set-play straight at Flahavan. Bees midfielder Martin Rowlands then burst through the centre of the park and outpaced Shrimpers defender Rob Newman, before lashing a shot into the right side netting. And Evans finished the half by drilling two long range efforts past the left Southend upright.

But Blues grew in confidence after the break and upped the tempo, with central midfielders Kevin Maher and Johnson exerting more influence, which put Brentford on the back-foot almost straight away.

Nine minutes into the restart, Lee cut in from the right-wing and hit a skidding 20-yard shot, which Gottskalksson could only parry. Forbes looked favourite to reach the rebound and seemed to have a good shout for a penalty when he was bundled over by home defender Michael Dobson, who followed through and injured his own keeper.

Gottskalksson was forced to leave the pitch with concussion, handing a home debut to rookie youngster Paul Smith, who would enjoy a performance to remember. On the hour, Newman ghosted in at the far post to meet Lee's left-wing corner, only to be denied by Theobald's legs. But Brentford could have got their noses back in front almost straight away when Owusu's clever flick put Evans in a point blank shoot-out with Flahavan, but the Shrimpers custodian saved with his legs.

And this let off boosted Southend. After 69 minutes, Bramble smartly turned Theobald and found Lee on the right flank, whose centre across the face of the Brentford goal was narrowly missed by Carruthers' lunging legs at the far post. Smith then made catching Maher's 20 yard snap-shot look simple, before somehow clawing Forbes' cracking drive across goal away from the inside of his left post.

From the resulting right-wing Lee corner, Newman's close range half-volley was kicked off the goal-line by Rowlands. And during the finale of a frantic two-minute attacking spell for Blues, Lee found his range from the right wing again.

He picked out an unmarked Carruthers, who could only blast the ball straight at Smith from six yards when he should have levelled the tie, before Whelan's follow-up was blocked on the line by Powell.

And with a golden opportunity missed, Brentford took the first chance which came their way on 79 minutes, destroying the Seasiders' last hopes of a trophy miracle.

Wing-back Paul Gibbs made a surging run down the left flank and found Owusu, who took advantage of a rare moment of disarray in Blues' defence to turn and plant a 15-yard drive past Flahavan.

And with the clock ticking away, Brentford were reduced to ten men, when Powell was sent off for his second yellow card after clattering Forbes. But no tackle, no matter how hard, could have shattered Blues' heroes as much as the final whistle, which left them empty-handed when they were worthy of so much more!

UNITED (in 4-4-2 formation): Flahavan; Booty, Searle, Forbes (sub. 89 minutes Williamson), Newman; Whelan, Maher, Johnson, Lee; Carruthers (sub. 85 minutes Abbey), Bramble. Subs, (not used): Thurgood, McSweeney and Porter.

BRENTFORD: Gottskalksson (Smith), Powell, Ingimarsson, Evans, Mahon, Owusu (McCammon), Partridge (Lovett), Rowlands, Dobson, Gibbs, Theobald. Subs, (not used): Folan and Williams.

Attendance: 6,579.

Tuesday, February 10th, 2004
Football League Trophy, Semi-final, First leg, Sponsored as Football League LDV Vans Trophy, Southern Area Final
COLCHESTER UNITED 2, SOUTHEND UNITED 3

Southend United secured another unexpected victory over local rivals Colchester last night as goals from Leon Constantine, Drewe Broughton and fit-again forward Tes Bramble handed the struggling Shrimpers a well-deserved 3-2 triumph at Layer Road.

But, despite enduring a shaky start to an exciting evening of action – which saw the Seasiders concede the game's opening goal after just seven minutes – Steve Tilson's side should have been celebrating a more convincing triumph against the U's in the southern final of the LDV Vans Trophy.

Blues bossed the majority of an eagerly-anticipated match and, at 3-1 up, looked set to record a resounding score-line to virtually cement a final slot in Cardiff against either Second Division Blackpool or Sheffield Wednesday. But a harsh red card brandished to Shrimpers striker Drewe Broughton and a well-taken header from the home side's Wayne Andrews soon stopped that and provided a grandstand finale for the near-capacity crowd.

With Mark Warren marshalling the Seasiders back four on his return to his former side though and, with captain Kevin Maher pulling the strings in the centre of the park, the Roots Hall side stood firm to hang on to their narrow and often nervy advantage.

And that was no more than the Shrimpers deserved, having looked far sharper and more skilful than their Essex rivals for large parts of a topsy-turvy encounter which had both sets of supporters on the edge of their seats.

As in the previous rounds of the competition against both Luton Town and QPR, Blues again converted a high percentage of their chances facing opposition from a higher division, with Leon Constantine striking home his 13th goal of the season in delightful fashion.

Drewe Broughton also continued his recent revival by heading a close-range effort past Simon Brown, who was later left red-faced as a tame Tes Bramble shot somehow squirmed through his grasp and trickled over the goal-line.

As a result, the Shrimpers have edged even closer to the Millennium Stadium, but there is still everything for both sides to play for.

Another nail-biting 90 minutes full of twists and turns for the Roots Hall faithful seems to be on the cards for the return leg next Tuesday. But if the standard of last night's showing can be repeated and possibly improved next time around, Blues could soon be lifting the spirits of their success-starved supporters.

Colchester started the brighter of the two sides, with Blues full back Jamie Stuart clearing a dangerous Scott McGleish cross to safety at the back post in the seventh minute of the match.

But, from the resulting Karl Duguid corner, the U's opened the scoring as centre back Alan White rolled the ball into the path of the on-rushing Thomas Pinault, who duly half-volleyed home his first goal since August into the top left hand corner of the net from 14 yards.

But the shell-shocked Shrimpers soon hit back with skipper Kevin Maher firing a deflected 25-yard drive wide of the right post and fellow midfielder Mark Gower dragging another long-range shot past the opposite post having intercepted a poor pass from Pinault.

Having survived the scares, Rowan Vine then just failed to convert a curling cross from Scott McGleish in the 16th minute, but just 60 seconds later the Blues were back level following some fine forward play from Tes Bramble. The former Cambridge City striker held off the attentions of the on-loan Liam Chilvers to deliver a fine cross-field ball to Leon Constantine, who fired home a delightful first time shot into the bottom left hand corner of Simon Brown's goal from 18 yards.

The shaky U's shot stopper then just beat fit-again midfielder Lewis Hunt to a well-struck Mark Gower centre and, following a neatly-constructed counter attack from the home side, Jamie Stuart did well to divert Scott McGleish's shot away from the Shrimpers net at the other end of the field.

Vine then headed Chilvers' flick, from a Joe Keith corner, straight at Darryl Flahavan from seven yards, before the Blues replied with Leon Cort forcing Brown into action with another aerial effort from a fine Gower cross.

Bramble then fired a fierce half volley just past the U's right post in the 40th minute and, moments later, the Shrimpers took the lead as Drewe Broughton headed home from five yards after Cort's header, from a Mark Gower corner, had bounced back off the left post.

Vine then came close to levelling proceedings on the stroke of half time – dragging a 10-yard shot agonisingly wide of the Southend goal. But immediately after the interval Blues' Broughton just failed to reach Leon Constantine's chipped right-wing cross after the Shrimpers top scorer had jinked his way around Paul Tierney.

Duncan Jupp then bravely cleared a dangerous Kem Izzet centre from inside his own six-yard box and, with 68 minutes on the clock, Steve Tilson's side extended their advantage as Tes Bramble chested down a quickly-taken Kevin Maher free-kick to fire home a trickling, low, left-foot shot which somehow squirmed under the body of an embarrassed Brown.

Colchester captain Duguid then forced Darryl Flahavan to tip an accurate 25-yard free kick around the right post, while Leon Constantine soon hit a wayward long-range effort over the cross bar in a quick Blues break forward.

But the Shrimpers were then controversially reduced to 10 men as Drewe Broughton picked up his second yellow card of the evening for kicking the ball away.

And, just seconds after the striker's dismissal, U's substitute Wayne Andrews leapt high to nod McGleish's header, from another Keith corner, past Flahavan from close range.

But, despite their numerical disadvantage, the Shrimpers stood firm to secure a well-deserved win, as home full back Sam Stockley struck a 25-yard shot inches off target in the closing action of an eventful and evenly contested encounter.

Steve Tilson was delighted last night after his Southend United side took a big step towards their first major cup final. The care-taker boss was thrilled to win the first leg of the southern area LDV Vans final with Essex rivals Colchester – and thought the win could have been more convincing than 3-2.

'We worked our socks off for 90 minutes and played some really good football at times – we thoroughly deserved our win,' said the 37-year-old.

'Between them the lads covered every blade of grass on the pitch, but I'm a little disappointed that there was only one goal between the teams.

'At 3-1 up I thought we could have put them out of sight and got another couple of goals to make things easier for the second game next Tuesday. Drewe got sent off even though he didn't make a bad tackle in the whole game.

'The first booking was for an elbow apparently, but for the second one Drewe's saying he had his back to the linesman and he couldn't hear the whistle, so it's disappointing for us.

'It was a sending off for nothing really and it put us under pressure because we were in such a good position. We were looking comfortable, but even though they scored soon after Drewe was dismissed, we dug in with 10 men and that's a credit to the lads.'

SOUTHEND UNITED: Flahavan; Jupp; Cort; Warren; Stuart; Constantine (Clark); Maher; Hunt (Wilson); Gower; Broughton; Bramble (Pettefer). Subs, (not used): Emberson; McSweeney.

Att: 5,401

Tuesday, February 17th, 2004
Football League Trophy, Semi-final, Second leg, Sponsored as Football League LDV Vans Trophy, Southern Area Final
Southend United 1, Colchester United 1
(Southend United win 4-3 on aggregate score)

Southend United secured an exciting 4-3 aggregate victory over local rivals Colchester last night in a thrilling tussle at a packed Roots Hall in the southern final of the LDV Vans Trophy.

The Shrimpers more than matched their Second Division opponents during a well-deserved 1-1 draw and will now face either Blackpool or Sheffield Wednesday in the club's first ever cup final at the magical Millennium Stadium on March 21. But Blues were made to work hard for their fourth successive league and cup win as the U's began brightly and, as in the first leg at Layer Road, Phil Parkinson's men hit home an early goal as Kem Izzet converted a low left-foot shot past Darryl Flahavan.

The strike seemed to spark the Shrimpers into life however as the lowly Third Division side began to continually carve open the Colchester back four – with skipper Kevin Maher again pulling the strings at the heart of the Southend midfield.

As a result, both Drewe Broughton and Tes Bramble came close to bringing the Blues back level and, with the half-time whistle imminent, Broughton slammed what proved to be the tie's decisive goal past a helpless Simon Brown from seven yards. The former Kidderminster Harriers forward has now scored five goals in his last four LDV Vans Trophy games and is beginning to impress on a consistent basis after enduring a tough baptism to life with the Blues.

Broughton, who was sent off during the first leg last Tuesday, also won a number of headers against a battered Colchester back four and produced yet another committed performance for a Southend side that suddenly seems to have a spring in their step once again. It was not just Broughton who impressed against the U's though as determined defender Mark Warren was colossal at the centre of the Blues back four – making a number of crucial challenges to deny his former side.

But Warren's effort and impressive endeavour was shown by all the Shrimpers players during an unforgettable night of action at Roots Hall. The passionate display also brought smiles to the club's long-suffering fans who were forced to endure a seemingly never ending amount of injury time as the U's pressed to take the game into extra time.

Thankfully the Shrimpers rearguard stood firm to emerge victorious from the eagerly-anticipated 'Battle of Essex' to set up a memorable March weekend in Wales. The visitors began brightly against the Blues and broke the deadlock in the opening action of the evening – following a neatly-constructed counterattack down the left flank.

On-rushing U's midfielder Kem Izzet swapped passes with striker Scott McGleish to fire home a low, left-foot shot which squirmed past Darryl Flahavan to trickle into the bottom left-hand corner of the net.

The third-minute strike cancelled out the Shrimpers one-goal lead from the opening leg but Blues soon hit back with only a well-timed, last ditch challenge from Liam Chilvers stopping Drewe Broughton racing clean through on goal.

Seasiders skipper Kevin Maher then dragged a low, long-range effort wide of the target, while Darryl Flahavan soon palmed away a deep and dangerous Karl Duguid cross at the other end of the field.

Broughton then saw his 14-yard shot deflected to safety by full back Sam Stockley before the former Kidderminster Harriers forward wasted a golden opportunity to bring Blues back level – heading a Mark Gower free kick wide of the right post from just six yards.

Tes Bramble then also came close to levelling proceedings as he forced Simon Brown into action with a close-range volley from a fine Kevin Maher pass. But, having survived the scares, Phil Parkinson's men then broke forward as McGleish sent a diving header wide of the left post after Flahavan had failed to deal with a long Greg Halford throw in. With both sides continuing to create chances, Broughton then slammed a 12-yard shot against Colchester's left post having neatly turned Chilvers.

And, just seconds later, the U's Craig Fagan somehow side tapped Halford's excellent curling cross wide of the right upright from close range.

In reply, Bramble then sent in a fizzing half-volley flying just inches over the North Bank net before Thomas Pinault fired a low, 25-yard shot straight into the grateful gloves of Darryl Flahavan. Moments later and, in the 40th minute of the match, Colchester winger Joseph Keith lobbed a tame 10-yard effort over the Shrimpers goal after a volleyed pass from Karl Duguid had split open the home side's rearguard.

Two minutes later, it was Blues' turn to hold their heads in their hands as Broughton was denied by the legs of Brown in a one-on-one situation, with Bramble's volleyed effort from the resulting rebound somehow being scrambled off the U's goal-line by Alan White.

But the Shrimpers were not to be denied and, on the stroke of half time, they finally got back on level terms as Leon Court flicked on Duncan Jupp's right-wing cross to enable Broughton to slam home an emphatic seven-yard shot past the exposed Colchester custodian.

After the interval, Bramble fired an angled drive straight at Brown and, in the 61st minute, Mark Gower sent a long-range shot flying wide of the left post.

The visitors soon began to work their way back into the game with the speedy Fagan drilling an inviting effort across the face of the Shrimpers six-yard box and Leon Cort heading away a well-struck Duguid free kick in the 71st minute.

With play soon switching back to the opposite end of the pitch however, Broughton then headed Tes Bramble's right wing centre over the South Stand net, and, seconds later, Bramble scuffed a seven-yard shot into the gloves of Brown when he should have done better.

The Shrimpers striker then saw Brown tip his scorching 25-yard shot around the right post before Thomas Pinault sent a rising half-volley over the Southend goal from 18 yards in the closing action of an entertaining and ultimately rewarding encounter for the success-starved Roots Hall faithful.

Shrimpers caretaker chief Steve Tilson was smiling at the final whistle despite enduring an agonising encounter against their spirited Second Division opponents.

'That was the longest 90 minutes of my life,' admitted Tilson. 'They scored early on but we showed great character to get back in it and created some great chances in the first half. The second half was a very long 45 minutes though. We soaked up a lot of pressure but they never really looked like hurting us and we had chances too. Tes missed a great opportunity from about seven yards and their keeper made a couple of good saves. We thoroughly deserved to win and all the lads are shattered – they gave it everything and that's what we expect.'

Tilson added he was delighted to have secured his fourth successive victory and could not wait for the final in Wales.

'It's great – I never got to a final as a player and maybe now I might have to pick myself,' joked the 37-year-old.

'I'll tap Ron up for a few bob to try and get the lads some suits and it will be a great day for everyone connected with the club. I've been to the Millennium Stadium and it's a hell of a place – it's unbelievable – and it will be fantastic for us going there.'

SOUTHEND UNITED: Flahavan; Jupp; Warren; Cort; Stuart; Constantine; Maher; Hunt; Gower (Pettefer); Broughton; Bramble. Subs, (not used): Robinson; Wilson; Clark; McSweeney.

Att: 9,603

Tuesday, February 15th, 2005
Football League Trophy, Semi-final, First leg, Sponsored as Football League LDV Vans Trophy, Southern Area Final
BRISTOL ROVERS 1, SOUTHEND UNITED 2

The pre-match talk from the Bristol Rovers camp concentrated on a contagious flu bug which had swept through the Memorial Stadium side's first team squad.

But at the final whistle last night, it was The Gas boss Ian Atkins who was as sick as a parrot as his side – which amazingly started with just one lone striker – deservedly suffered a 2-1 reverse against the Shrimpers.

Goals from Lawrie Dudfield and Mark Gower handed Southend a first leg triumph in the LDV Vans Trophy southern area final as the Essex outfit edged even closer to another appearance at the Millennium Stadium.

And it was no more than a battling display from Blues warranted as they began the encounter brightly. After just seven minutes Dudfield failed to connect properly with a fine Lewis Hunt cross but, only seconds later, the same duo combined for the game's opening goal.

Gower fed the ball into Hunt's path and he delivered another dangerous centre for Dudfield to head high into the top right hand corner of the net from seven yards. The former Northampton Town forward then saw another aerial effort – from Gower's left-wing cross – scrambled to safety by Craig Hinton before Steve Elliott bravely blocked a well-struck shot from Adam Barrett.

The Shrimpers' early domination soon forced the hosts to tinker with their tactics and, after only 25 minutes, Atkins introduced tall targetman Richard Walker into the action to enable a switch to a 4-4-2 system. That immediately sparked the Pirates and their frustrated fans into life with Craig Disley dragging a 20-yard shot wide of the right post.

Then, with 30 minutes on the clock, the home side wasted an even better opportunity to draw back level as referee Richard Beeby harshly pointed to the penalty spot after adjudging Barrett to have fouled Disley. The decision again angered the aggrieved Southend defenders but, as the protests died down, striker Junior Agogo stepped forward to slam the subsequent spot kick against the underside of the cross bar.

Having survived the scare, the Seasiders' Tes Bramble – who was making his first start since New Year's Day – then lashed a long-range effort off target, while at the other end Darryl Flahavan gathered an awkward Agogo effort at the second attempt.

In reply, a low left foot shot from Gower was then tipped around the post by former Shrimpers loanee Ryan Clarke and, immediately after the interval, the Bristol-born shot-stopper easily collected a 12-yard effort from Mark Bentley. Flahavan soon repeated Clarke's heroics by tipping a vicious free kick from Steve Elliott around the left post.

But, the ex-Blackpool defender was not to be denied and, from the resulting Ryan Williams corner, in the 56th minute, he headed a low seven-yard effort into the bottom right-hand corner of the net. The shell-shocked Shrimpers then replied with Prior nodding a dangerous Kevin Maher corner across the face of goal and Bentley heading Hunt's right wing cross straight at Clarke.

That short period of pressure was rewarded as Blues regained the lead in magnificent fashion after 67 minutes. Gower cut in off the left flank to fire a superb, swerving 25-yard shot into the net via the underside of the cross bar and right post.

A last-ditch Robbie Ryan challenge then stopped Dudfield registering another effort on target but Rovers replied with James Hunt sending a scorching long-range shot inches past the right post.

With both teams continuing to carve out chances, Barrett – facing his former side – headed a Maher corner over the Bristol goal from close range before Walker nodded a 12-yard effort on to the top of the Blues' cross bar Shrimpers sub Wayne Gray also went close with a header which flew just wide from a Maher corner and, deep into added on time, Rovers' Ryan stabbed an instinctive seven-yard shot off target following a poor punch from Flahavan.

BRISTOL ROVERS: Clarke, Lescott, Hinton, Elliott, Ryan, Disley, Campbell, Hunt, Trollope (Walker), Williams, Agogo. Subs not used: Forrester, Anderson, Haldane, Shakes.

SOUTHEND UNITED: Flahavan, Hunt, Prior, Barrett, Wilson, Pettefer, Maher, Bentley, Gower (Nicolau), Dudfield, Bramble (Gray). Subs not used: Holloway, Eastwood & Jupp.

Referee: Richard Beeby (Northampton)

Attendance: 7, 110

Tuesday, March 8th, 2005
Football League Trophy, Semi-final, Second leg, Sponsored as Football League LDV Vans Trophy, Southern Area Final
SOUTHEND UNITED 2, BRISTOL ROVERS 2
(Southend United win 4-3 on aggregate score)

Southend United ground out a nervy 2-2 draw with a battling Bristol Rovers side last night to set up a return to the Millennium Stadium in the LDV Vans Trophy. Twelve months on from losing to Blackpool in the club's first ever competitive cup final, Steve Tilson's revamped and rejuvenated Shrimpers will be heading back to Wales for another as they face Wrexham.

Clinical, close range strikes from forwards Wayne Gray and Freddy Eastwood ensured a 4-3 aggregate win and that April clash with the Dragons as the deadly duo caused Rovers a whole host of problems all evening. As a result, after just four minutes, visiting keeper Kevin Miller rushed off his goal-line to block Gray's prodded effort with his legs and, just seconds later, Eastwood sent a long range strike off target.

Having survived the early scares, the Pirates soon hit back with James Hunt striking the top of the South Stand crossbar from 25 yards and Aaron Lescott firing a similar shot straight at Darryl Flahavan.

With play immediately switching back to the other end of the field, Eastwood then struck a superb 25-yard shot inches past the left post before Mark Gower cut in off the left flank to fire a curling effort over the cross-bar.

But, with 30 minutes on the clock, the home side broke the deadlock and extended their overall advantage, as Miller failed to hold a long range strike from Eastwood to enable a determined Gray to gratefully slide home the resulting rebound into the bottom right hand corner of the net from close range.

In reply, Junior Agogo then nodded Craig Hinton's right wing cross over Flahavan's goal and, in the 44th minute, Rovers were back level as substitute Ryan Williams, who had earlier replaced the injured Paul Trollope, dispossessed Spencer prior on the left flank.

The former Hull City winger then delivered a fine cross which Agogo turned into the path of Richard Walker to head home from six yards for his seventh goal of the season. The well-taken effort was the first the Shrimpers had conceded on their own soil this year but, just seconds later, they almost let in another as Agogo nodded over.

After the interval, Blues again began to threaten and, in the 59th minute, the impressive Eastwood volleyed Carl Pettefer's inviting centre against the crossbar.

Prior, attempting to atone for his earlier error, then headed Gower's left wing corner over the cross bar and, after 61 minutes, the Seasiders finally regained the lead as Gray charged down an attempted defensive clearance from Christian Edwards. The ex-Wimbledon forward then raced down the left wing to unselfishly tee up the unmarked Eastwood with a well-placed pass, which the youngster agonisingly debated over before eventually cutting inside and unleashing a deflected right foot shot into the bottom right hand corner of the net.

Rovers boss Ian Atkins responded by introducing Ricky Shakes into the action and switching to an attacking 4-3-3 formation in pursuit of much-needed goals. And, in the 73rd minute, the change in system was rewarded as the Memorial Stadium outfit again equalised in stunning fashion as Agogo slammed a speculative left foot volley from 25 yards into the roof of the North Bank net to stun the Shrimpers faithful.

The tie was now closely poised with the visitors needing just one more effort to take the game to extra time.

But in the last few minutes it was Southend who came closest to scoring as Mark Bentley headed another Gower corner wide from six yards before referee Phil Crossley finally blew the final whistle to spark wild celebrations from the Seasiders.

SOUTHEND UNITED: Flahavan, Jupp, Prior, Barrett, Wilson, Pettefer, Maher, Bentley, Gower (Nicolau 90), Gray (Dudfield 83), Eastwood. Subs not used: Holloway, Bramble & Kightly.

BRISTOL ROVERS: Miller, Lescott, Ryan, Edwards (Shakes 63), Elliott, Hunt, Anderson, Hinton, Walker, Agogo, Trollope (Williams 40). Subs not used: Clarke, Forrester, Haldane.

Referee: Phil Crossley (Kent)

Attendance: 8, 145

Sunday, May 15th, 2005
Football League Two Promotion Play-offs, Semi-final, First leg
NORTHAMPTON TOWN 0, SOUTHEND UNITED 0

Southend United dug deep to grind out a determined 0-0 draw at Northampton Town yesterday in an even and keenly contested play-off semi-final clash at a noisy Sixfields Stadium.

The spirited Shrimpers produced a solid showing and came close to claiming a narrow triumph in a largely uneventful encounter as substitute midfielder Luke Guttridge wasted a golden chance in the closing stages. At the other end of the field however, the in-form Darryl Flahavan did well to deny Andy Kirk in the dying minutes to leave the tie delicately poised ahead of next weekend's second leg.

The Seasiders – who for the first time this season assembled in a huddle before kick-off – started strongly with Mark Gower sending a deflected fifth minute free kick wide of the right post. Moments later, Tes Bramble – who was making his first Southend start since February – headed Carl Pettefer's deep cross straight at Lee Harper before the home side began to work their way into the game.

As a result, Scott McGleish, a summer transfer target for the Shrimpers, soon woefully miskicked the ball from close range and, in the ninth minute, Cobblers captain Chris Willmott headed Charley Hearn's left wing corner over the crossbar. McGleish then fired a low 12-yard shot into the grateful gloves of Flahavan, but the effort sparked Blues back into life with Freddy Eastwood shooting wide of the target from 25 yards after a barnstorming burst forward from Adam Barrett. In the move of the match, Mark Bentley then headed a 41st minute effort at Harper from 12 yards following a neatly constructed counter-attack involving both Eastwood and Mark Gower. But, just seconds later, it was the home side's turn to almost open the scoring as a screaming 30-yard volley from Lee Williamson on the stroke of half-time was impressively palmed away by a diving Flahavan.

After the break and, with Lawrie Dudfield on for the injured Tes Bramble, Southend created the half's opening chances with Bentley heading a Gower corner off target and Barrett firing wide of the left post from 20 yards. Shrimpers skipper Maher then sent a long range, half-volley wide of the left post but, in the 69th minute, the hosts should have broken the deadlock as McGleish headed Hearn's left wing centre over Flahavan's goal from just six yards. Fellow forward Andy Kirk then saw his goal-bound 10-yard shot brilliantly blocked by a well-positioned Duncan Jupp and, having survived the scare, the Seasiders then wasted their best chance of the afternoon.

With 78 minutes on the clock, Eastwood superbly worked his way around Luke Chambers to deliver a pin-point left wing cross into the path of the on-rushing Luke Guttridge.

But, despite being just six yards from goal, the former Cambridge United midfielder – who turned Northampton down in favour of a switch to Southend – headed wide of the right post when a goal seemed inevitable.

Dudfield then struck a 20-yard shot straight at Harper and, in the 90th minute, Colin Calderwood's men almost netted a dramatic last gasp winner as Kirk raced onto a fine Hearn ball forward.

The ex-Boston United front-runner burst into the left hand side of the Blues penalty box and unleashed a fine left foot shot which seemed destined for the opposite corner of the net until Flahavan sprung across his goal to superbly push the effort away for a corner.

That ensured a deserved draw for the promotion pushing Shrimpers who now face another do-or-die decider this weekend.

SOUTHEND UNITED: Flahavan, Jupp, Prior, Barrett, Wilson, Pettefer, Maher, Bentley, Gower (Guttridge 60), Bramble (Dudfield 46), Eastwood (Gray 87). Subs. not used: Griemink & Edwards.

NORTHAMPTON TOWN: Harper, Chambers, Willmott, Murray, Kirk, Low (Sabin 73), McGleish, Rowson, Hearn, Williamson (Smith 58), Togwell. Subs. not used: Bunn, Hunt & Richards.

Referee: Lee Mason (Lancashire). Attendance: 6,601.

Saturday, May 21st, 2005
Football League Two Promotion Play-offs, Semi-final, Second leg
SOUTHEND UNITED 1, NORTHAMPTON TOWN 0
(Southend United win 1-0 on aggregate score)

A competitive do or die cup tie, played in an electric atmosphere, which was eventually settled by a calmly taken spot kick. But forget Patrick Vieira, Arsenal and the F.A. Cup, this was Southend United and the League Two play-offs as a packed Roots Hall went wild as Freddy Eastwood's 49th minute penalty secured a 1-0 victory over Northampton Town to keep alive the club's chances of promotion.

Steve Tilson's side now face Lincoln City in another winner takes all encounter at the Millennium Stadium following this tight, tense but ultimately triumphant clash with the Cobblers. And that is despite Northampton starting the stronger of the two sides as Charley Hearn struck a third minute shot, from 20 yards, straight at Darryl Flahavan.

Seconds later, Andy Kirk also fired a long-range drive into the grateful gloves of the Seasiders shot stopper but the ambitious effort sparked the home side into life as they also began to work their way into the game.

As a result, the recalled Nicky Nicolau sent a well struck shot from 25 yards wide of the left post in the 13th minute before Eastwood dragged an angled drive across the face of goal after collecting a fantastic through ball from Kevin Maher.

Eastwood then turned provider as his intelligent pass found the on-rushing Adam Barrett whose low left wing cross rolled invitingly into the path of Mark Bentley.

But the midfielder's shot was deflected by Fred Murray and impressively pushed around the right upright by a diving Lee Harper. Having survived the scare, the visitors soon hit back with Andy Kirk shooting just wide of the target while under immense pressure from a sliding Che Wilson. And on the stroke of half time the former Boston United forward was at it again as his 14 yard effort zipped past the right post.

After the interval however, it was the hosts who began to dominate proceedings and, in the 49th minute, came the game's defining moment as referee Barry Knight pointed to the spot after a clumsy challenge on Nicolau by Chris Willmott.

That enabled Eastwood to confidently step forward and send Harper the wrong way from the resulting penalty which rolled into the bottom left hand corner of the South Stand net.

Blues then almost doubled their advantage in bizarre circumstances as a harmless, sliced left wing cross somehow bounced back off the underside of the cross-bar, with Harper just a bemused spectator. Another break from the Shrimpers soon resulted with Willmott bravely blocking a well struck shot from Nicolau but, after the introduction of Eric Sabin, Northampton began to pose Southend more problems.

The speedy striker was a constant threat to the Seasiders and, in the 80th minute, he set up a chance for Hearn whose left foot shot was deflected for a corner by Barrett.

With the Cobblers pushing hard for a late leveller, David Hunt then curled a 25-yard free kick over the cross bar but, in a rare break forward, Blues had strong shouts for a penalty turned down in the 89th minute as Luke Chambers' tackle on a goalbound Eastwood went unpunished.

And with play immediately switching to the other end of the field, Knight was then forced to wave away further appeals for a spot kick – this time from the Cobblers – as Duncan Jupp appeared to push Sabin to the floor in the penalty area.

But, after a collective sigh of relief from the vociferous Shrimpers supporters, there was still time for further drama as, in the 94th minute, Flahavan pulled off one of the saves of the season as he dived full length to his left to somehow tip a header from McGleish around the right post.

SOUTHEND UNITED: Flahavan, Jupp, Prior, Barrett, Wilson, Pettefer, Maher, Bentley, Nicolau, Dudfield (Gray 72), Eastwood (Guttridge 90). Subs. not used: Griemink, Edwards, Gower.

NORTHAMPTON TOWN: Harper, Chambers, Willmott, Murray (Hunt 65), Kirk, Low, McGleish, Rowson (Richards 79), Hearn, Smith (Sabin 56), Togwell. Subs. not used: Bunn, Williamson.

Referee: Barry Knight (Kent).
Attendance: 9,152.

CHAPTER SEVENTEEN

Finals 1912-2005

Tuesday, April 30th, 1912
Southern Counties Charity Cup Final (at White Hart Lane)
SOUTHEND UNITED (0) 1 (Bradshaw 85), COVENTRY CITY (0) 0. Gate: 586

On the ground of the Tottenham Hotspur F.C., on Tuesday evening, Southend United won the Southern Counties Charity Cup competition trophy, by beating Coventry City in the final. It was an exciting encounter, for it was not until exactly five minutes from the end that Bradshaw obtained the winning goal. The point was received with much enthusiasm from the small crowd that was present, for they were sympathetic towards the Seasiders all through. It looked very much as though extra time would have to be played, for the point was rather unexpected.

In the remaining time the City made a desperate effort to equalise but Southend were equal to the occasion and ran out winners. The game was good, bad and indifferent; the latter quality prevailing for a considerable length of time. There were numberless mistakes on both sides, but the winners can be said to have deserved their victory. Whereas Coventry for a long period were the attacking party, their chronic weakness in front of goal accounted for their failure to score. Time and again when right on the goal the forwards shot over or wide. The van kept Southend on the defensive for a long time, but the poor shooting was hardly worthy of a Southern League team. It must be said, however, that the United's defence gave them little rest and time for steadying themselves. On the other hand, the considerable majority of really dangerous attempts at scoring came from Southend.

In the first half they were not so able in field work as their opponents, but after the interval they improved greatly. For really artistic football they were the superior side and had they had a really capable centreforward might have won by two or three goals. At the last moment it was decided to place McNaught as leader of the van, with Wilson and Wileman on the wing. The ex-Ranger was very much below form and did not accustom himself to the position as he had done previously. He failed to secure possession of the ball and distribute to his wings. He was also unable to accept several scoring opportunities.

With this disadvantage the strong and well-combined eleven from Coventry were seen more in the limelight, but for really good football Southend were the better team. When in their stride they outwitted Coventry individually and with some nice collective movements. The poorness of the centre-forward, however, spoiled several chances of scoring. Their goal was the result of a brilliant manoeuvre on the part of Arnold, Bradshaw and Parke, which left the inside left in possession about eighteen yards out. With a clever shot he put the ball over the keeper's head. Previously there had been little exertion by the players, but now tremendous energy was imparted into the exchanges.

There was intense excitement lest Coventry should, in the last minute or two, get a point and compel extra time to be played. Very slowly the minutes were ticked off and on one occasion it seemed almost certain the equaliser would come. The City left winger centred beautifully into the goalmouth, where there were three Coventry forwards waiting. There was a scramble while the hearts of Southend spectators almost stood still, but Arnold was seen to emerge with possession and clear amid applause.

Upon the teams lining up it was found the colours of the jerseys clashed very much and Southend had to retire, coming out very quickly in salmon and pink stripes. Coventry won the toss, but there was little to be gained thereby. They were first away and Bradley was in a good position when Emery neatly dispossessed him. Following one or two good centres by the City wingers, Southend got away and Harwood put just outside. Play was very indifferent and there were a lot of mid-field exchanges.

For Southend Harwood again came near scoring and at the other end Nurthen saved finely from Bradley. There was hot pressure on the United's citadel, but the shooting was so poor that it did not become dangerous. A clever piece of work by Parke brought relief, but, when about to centre, Thomson beat him. Holmes centred splendidly, but Bradley headed right out of goal. Gaining possession again, however, he adroitly passed to Jones and Emery was applauded for robbing him when he was in a capital scoring position. A terrific shot by Parkes shook the rigging of the Southend goal. The stripes managed to beat down the pressure of the City and a foul on Wileman just outside the penalty area gave them a free kick. The inside right took it and almost scored. Evans was only able to push the ball away and it rolled round the post.

Play continued to be uninteresting, and it was infrequently that there was an incident worthy of note. When within the twelve yards area Bradley put right over the bar. A shot from Chaplin was, however, a real teaser and Nurthen did remarkably well to clear the ball from the bottom corner of the net. In the last ten minutes of the half Southend showed up much better. They displayed more combination, and the half-backs got into capital form. Immediately upon the resumption a hard drive by Feebery looked very businesslike, for it was sailing just under the bar when Nurthen cleverly fisted it over.

From the ensuing corner Bradley put Jones in possession and his shot went only a few inches wide. Southend made a sudden breakaway, and, by a fine dash, Wileman beat Evans in a race for the ball and put in the net, just after the whistle went for off-side. After this Southend assisted themselves and they made some pretty movements. Wilson became irresistible on the wing and cleverly beating both Chaplin and Barnacle, he gave to McNaught, but he failed to gather the ball. The opposite wing also became a potent force, and by the clever work of the half-backs the United were enabled to hold the upper hand. Although they made several very praiseworthy attempts at scoring, it hardly seemed as if they would at the end of ninety minutes.

In the final ten minutes, notwithstanding Southend's monopoly of the play, Coventry were very troublesome; one dropping shot by the centre-forward being extremely dangerous, but the Southend custodian again distinguished himself in saving. Southend had a complete command of the game, mainly owing to the fine work of the half-back line, yet it seemed too late to be of avail. Success came with perseverance, and the Manager was very vigorously congratulated upon obtaining the winning point.

Upon the blowing of the final whistle, numbers of Southend supporters rushed on the ground and shook hands with the players. They immediately came up on to the grandstand where Miss Hazel Dawn, who is playing in 'The Pink Lady' at the Globe Theatre, presented Thomson with the handsome cup. She remarked upon the pleasure it gave her to see the first football match of her life. She had seen baseball in America, but not football. She thanked Southend for the entertainment they had given her, also Coventry, for, she thought, they had played a good game. There were several cries of 'Speech, Jerry.' 'Now, you've done me,' replied the Southend captain, 'but I hope I shall have the pleasure of receiving the cup again next year from the lady. I thank her on behalf of the players for her kind remarks.'

The Southend defence was in great form. Nurthen did finely in goal, three or four of his saves being really brilliant. Thomson and Layzell were very safe at back, while the halfbacks were the stay of the team. Emery made a welcome re-appearance and was in his best form. Harwood was a tireless worker and clever, perhaps the most effective player on the field. Arnold was also in fine trim and executed some masterful touches. The forwards sadly lacked a capable pivot. Bradshaw was below par but it was his third match in four days, he having played at full back at Swindon the previous evening. Wilson and Wileman were good, but Parke was hardly as successful as usual. The Coventry defence was also sound, hardly one member being weak. Their failure lay with the forwards, who were singularly inept in front of goal. From a financial point of view the game was a failure. Only 586 persons paid for admission, and the receipts were £16 14s. 3d.

SOUTHEND: Nurthen; Thomson and Layzell; Emery, Harwood and Arnold; Wilson, Wileman, McNaught, Bradshaw and Parke.

COVENTRY: Evans; Thomson and Barnacle; Yates, Feebery and Chaplin; Parkes, Turnbull, Bradley, Jones and Holmes.

Referee: Mr. A.W. McQue. Linesmen: Messrs. Fred. Wright and Robert Hale.

Sunday, March 21st, 2004
Football League Trophy Final, Sponsored as Football League LDV Vans Trophy Final
BLACKPOOL (1) 2 (Murphy 2, Coid 55), SOUTHEND UNITED (0) 0
(at Millennium Stadium, Cardiff)
Gate: 34,031

Southend United's first ever cup final ended in desperate disappointment at the Millennium Stadium yesterday afternoon as Second Division Blackpool cruised to a comfortable and convincing 2-0 victory. An offside-looking goal from Seasiders striker John Murphy set Steve McMahon's side on their way after just 90 seconds as the former Chester City forward drilled home a fine 12-yard half-volley.

And a neat finish from Danny Coid doubled the Bloomfield Road side's deserved advantage at the start of the second half as the Tangerines secured yet another win at the impressive Welsh ground.

Blackpool have now won three times in the past four seasons at the Millennium Stadium and, in truth, they were never really troubled by a Southend side who failed to continue their recent revival in this eagerly-anticipated clash.

But, despite falling at the final hurdle, Blues can be proud of their efforts and endeavour in the LDV Vans Trophy this season, as they surprisingly brushed aside a trio of high-flying Second Division sides to set up a never-to-be-forgotten final for the Roots Hall faithful. Close to 20,000 fans roared on Steve Tilson's side from the stands and they were all on their feet mid-way through the second half as Shrimpers' top scorer Leon Constantine seemed set to score.

With just Lee Jones left to beat however, the former Leyton Orient forward could only muster a tame, 10-yard volley which was easily gathered by the stranded Blackpool shot stopper.

That aside though, the Shrimpers failed to carve open the opposing back four and lacked the cutting edge to hurt the well-organised Bloomfield Road side where it mattered.

Blues wing wizard, Mark Gower, was, once again, the Shrimpers' main source of creation – despite struggling with a knee injury which had almost prevented him from playing at all. The 25-year-old midfielder was eventually forced to limp out of the action five minutes from time as Neil Jenkins came off a defensive-minded substitutes bench, which strangely did not include Michael Kightly, to figure on the left flank.

The Shrimpers started slowly in the battle of the Seaside teams – conceding the game's opening goal after just 90 seconds. The early Blackpool breakthrough came when an offside-looking John Murphy raced onto a deflected Tony Dinning shot to smash a well-taken half-volley into the bottom right hand corner of the net from 12 yards.

Carl Pettefer's 14-yard effort, at the other end of the field, was then smart-ly blocked by Tommy Jaszczun, and, in the fourth minute of the match, a curl-ing Mark Gower cross just evaded the on-rushing Drewe Broughton.

In reply, Leon Cort then did well to divert a Mike Sheron shot to safety after Martin Bullock had raced past Che Wilson on the right wing and, after 11 minutes, the Blues hit back with Lewis Hunt firing a 25-yard effort straight at Lee Jones.

The on-loan Derby County youngster then stabbed a dangerous Kevin Maher free-kick into the grateful gloves of the Blackpool custodian, before Darryl Flahavan raced off his goal-line to smartly stop Danny Coid convert-ing a fine ball from the lively Bullock.

A 25-yard free kick from Mark Gower was then easily gathered by the well-positioned Jones and, in the 26th minute, the former Stockport shot-stopper punched away a looping Drewe Broughton header while under pressure from Leon Constantine.

Having survived the scare however, the Second Division side soon nearly doubled their narrow advantage – with Martin Bullock again the orchestrator on the right wing. The pacey midfielder ran half the length of the pitch but, with Flahavan grounded, John Murphy strangely elected to square the ball back to Mike Sheron who was brilliantly tackled by a sliding Mark Warren.

With 33 minutes on the clock, Leon Constantine headed a Mark Gower free kick wide of the right post and, seven minutes later, Kevin Maher curled a 25-yard set piece well off target. An inviting centre from Blackpool's Martin Bullock then fizzed across the Shrimpers six yard box before the half drew to a close with Duncan Jupp's right wing cross straight at Lee Jones.

Immediately after the interval, Mike Sheron blasted another Bullock for-ward ball inches over the Shrimpers cross bar from 12 yards and, in the 48th minute, Leon Constantine just failed to reach Drewe Broughton's header from a Kevin Maher corner.

Danny Coid then drilled a well-hit cross shot wide of Blues' right post but, in the 55th minute, Steve McMahon's men finally doubled their lead as Mike Sheron's right wing cross eventually reached Coid at the back post, who fired home a low 12-yard shot into the bottom right hand corner of the net.

Mark Warren then bravely blocked a fierce effort from Sheron and, in the 61st minute, Blues winger Mark Gower fired a 25-yard shot just over the Blackpool bar. Two minutes later, Darryl Flahavan smartly blocked a low shot from Sheron with his legs and, in the very next attack of the afternoon, Carl Pettefer blocked a well-struck effort from Tony Dinning.

The Shrimpers soon began to carve out chances of their own however and after 69 minutes they should have halved the Blackpool lead.

But, having beaten the Seasiders offside trap and neatly controlled a Mark Gower free kick, Leon Constantine could only volley a tame 10-yard effort into the grateful gloves of Lee Jones when a goal seemed certain.

The Blackpool keeper then collected a routine header from Tes Bramble before Drewe Broughton nodded a Gower corner over the crossbar from seven yards. Lewis Hunt then fired Kevin Maher's pass straight at Jones and, following a neatly-constructed counter attack from the Second Division side, John Murphy's close-range shot was tipped around the right post by Darryl Flahavan in the closing action of the game.

Southend United manager Steve Tilson reckoned his Shrimpers side were second best in Sunday's 2-0 defeat against Second Division Blackpool.

'It was a fair result,' said the former Blues midfielder. 'Blackpool's quality shone through in the end and their attacking players were very lively. We had quite a bit of possession, we passed it around well but our final ball into the box was poor – we kept on hitting the first man.'

And Tilson was also quick to express his disgust at John Murphy's controversial, early opener – after the striker slammed home a debatable half volley in just the second minute of the match.

'He was at least two yards offside,' blasted Tilson. 'There's no doubt about that and from then on we were chasing the game against a very good footballing team.'

Tilson added he had been disappointed with a sub-standard Shrimpers showing and had expected his resurgent Third Division outfit to produce a more pleasing performance. 'Before the game I really thought we had a good chance of winning the final,' he said. 'We had been playing well. We've got a great team spirit at the moment and Blackpool were without Scott Taylor, who has scored a lot of goals for them so far this season.

'It was disappointing, but after they scored the second goal we went to a 3-4-3 formation and we started to pin them back a little bit.'

During that period of pressure, Southend striker Leon Constantine wasted a golden opportunity to bring Blues back into the game and Tilson admitted the former Leyton Orient forward should have done better with a tame, ten-yard volley.

'He should have scored,' said Tilson. 'Whether he thought he was offside or not I'm not sure, but he should have put it in and it was very disappointing.

'I would have loved us to get a goal, for the fans too as they were fantastic. We had nearly 20,000 people behind us and they were superb.

'It was a shame we couldn't give them a bit more to cheer, but hopefully they will all be here when we play Scunthorpe next Friday – although we would have to lock half of them outside!'

SOUTHEND UNITED: Flahavan; Jupp, Cort; Warren; Wilson (Bramble); Pettefer; Maher; Hunt; Gower (Jenkins); Broughton; Constantine.
Subs not used: Emberson, Stuart and McSweeney.

BLACKPOOL: Jones; Grayson; Jaszczun; Flynn; Wellens (McMahon); Sheron (Blinkhorn); Murphy; Bullock (Richardson); Coid; Dinning; Elliott.
Subs not used: Barnes and Davis.

Sunday, April 10th, 2005
Football League Trophy Final, Sponsored as Football League LDV Vans Trophy Final
WREXHAM (0) 2 (Ugarte 99, Ferguson 118), SOUTHEND UNITED (0) 0
(at Millennium Stadium, Cardiff)
Gate: 36, 216

Southend United's huge travelling contingent of supporters were again left with just tears for souvenirs in Cardiff on Sunday as the Shrimpers suffered a 2-0 defeat in the final of the LDV Vans Trophy for the second successive season. Goals from Wrexham's Juan Ugarte and Darren Ferguson in extra time ensured it was the Welshmen who triumphed from a close fought clash to leave Blues and their 18,000 fans inside the Millennium Stadium heartbroken.

The Shrimpers had previously come close to opening the scoring with both Adam Barrett and Mark Bentley being denied by Ben Foster and Freddy Eastwood hitting the woodwork from 25 yards.

But that was in stark contrast to a slow start from the Seasiders, as Wrexham began the brighter of the sides with a dangerous Chris Llewellyn cross from the left being well cleared for a corner by Adam Barrett after just six minutes. Darryl Flahavan then smothered Dennis Lawrence's header from the resulting Darren Ferguson flag-kick and, in the 11th minute, only the selfishness of Ugarte stopped Llewellyn racing clean through on goal.

With both the Dragons strikers up against just Che Wilson, the Spaniard inexplicably ignored his unmarked team-mate to fire a 20-yard shot against the Shrimpers full back's legs.

With Wrexham continuing to pile on the pressure, a last ditch challenge from Spencer prior then stopped Llewellyn converting from close range and, in the 21st minute, Ugarte curled a 20-yard shot just inches over the cross bar after collecting a fine through ball from Lawrence. In an attempt to stop the Welshmen breaking down their right flank, Southend midfielders Mark Gower and Carl Pettefer soon switched wings.

And, just moments after the alteration, Steve Tilson's side almost opened the scoring as a Spencer Prior header from Kevin Maher's left wing corner was tipped over the cross bar by Ben Foster. The young custodian then rushed off his goal-line to stop Wayne Gray reaching a deflected Andy Holt attempt.

But with play soon switching back to the other end of the field, Mark Jones saw his curling 25-yard shot flash just inches past the left upright. Having survived the scare however, the Shrimpers hit back and, in the 31st minute, they also came within a whisker of breaking the deadlock as star striker Freddy Eastwood fired a stinging long range effort against the foot of the left post. Eastwood was soon at it again and only seconds later he sent a left-foot shot, from 20 yards, fizzing just over the Dragons goal.

Blues were now beginning to force their way into the game with Wrexham substitute Shaun Pejic doing well to stop the speedy Gray reaching Gower's through ball and Foster superbly tipping away a powerful long range strike from Mark Bentley.

In reply and, on the stroke of half-time, Wrexham striker Ugarte volleyed straight at Flahavan from 20 yards, but after the interval it was Southend creating the chances with Bentley shooting into Foster's grateful gloves with a low drive. The shot stopper then acrobatically prevented Prior reaching a left wing cross from Pettefer and, after 66 minutes, he was again called into action as he parried away a 10 yard shot from Bentley when the midfielder seemed certain to score after some fine approach play from both Eastwood and Gray.

But Bentley then almost netted at the wrong end too as his looping and misdirected header bounced back off the bar with Flahavan doing well to claw away Ugarte's follow up effort from the subsequent rebound in an intense goal-mouth scramble.

With only minutes remaining both teams then began to push for a late winner, with Gray just failing to reach an intelligent through ball from Eastwood and a long clearance from Flahavan which was bizarrely left by Pejic.

Wrexham again replied though, with Jones warming the gloves of Flahavan from 25 yards before the entertaining clash headed into extra time where the first action saw Eastwood shoot at Foster after cutting in off the left flank in the 98th minute. The Dragons keeper easily held the scorching shot and within 60 seconds his side were celebrating the game's opening goal as the 6' 7" tall Lawrence headed Ferguson's left wing corner into the path of Ugarte to nod home his 19th goal of the season from six yards. The close range effort stunned the Shrimpers supporters into silence, but they were almost on their feet in the 105th minute as Barrett dived full length to powerfully head Bentley's right wing cross into the gloves of Foster.

That proved to be Southend's last clear cut chance and, in the 118th minute, their misery was compounded even further when the Dragons doubled their advantage as Ferguson raced past a dithering Che Wilson to convert from six yards after Flahavan had palmed away a low effort from Ugarte. Blues boss Steve Tilson was left cursing the quality of his side's final ball after the 2-0 defeat to Wrexham. 'Although the result was the same as when we came to Cardiff last season the performance we gave was certainly a lot better,' he said. 'What let us down was our final ball and I would have to say Wrexham probably deserved to edge what I thought was a good game of football. They're a good team and we would have loved to have come here and won. But their keeper made some good saves and it was a frustrating day for us.'

SOUTHEND: Flahavan, Jupp, Prior, Barrett, Wilson, Pettefer (Guttridge 109), Bentley, Maher, Gower (McCormack 81), Eastwood (Dudfield 103), Gray. Subs not used: Holloway and Edwards.

WREXHAM: Foster, Roberts (Pejic 14), Lawrence, Morgan, Edwards, Ferguson, Crowell (Bennett 105), Jones (Williams 100), Holt, Llewellyn, Ugarte. Subs not used: Harrison and Sam.

Saturday, May 28th, 2005
Football League Two, Promotion Play-offs Final
SOUTHEND UNITED (0) 2 (Eastwood 105, Jupp 110), LINCOLN CITY (0) 0
(at Millennium Stadium, Cardiff).
Gate: 19,602

Extra time strikes from Freddy Eastwood and Duncan Jupp handed Southend United a memorable 2-0 victory over Lincoln City on Saturday and ensured the Shrimpers will be playing in League One next season. The duo both clinically converted from close range as Steve Tilson's side deservedly won the final of the play-offs at the Millennium Stadium to make it third time lucky in the Welsh capital. Blues had previously suffered two defeats in Cardiff, both in the final of the LDV Vans Trophy.

But there was to be no tears shed this time around as Southend, who were roared on by around 6,000 noisy supporters, enjoyed one of the greatest moments in the club's history.

That was despite a tentative start from the Seasiders who began slowly, with City's Francis Green heading a long throw from Gary Taylor-Fletcher wide of the right post after just three minutes.

In reply and, as the Shrimpers soon hit back, Kevin Sandwith diverted a goal-bound shot from Carl Pettefer to safety after Imps keeper Alan Marriott had flapped a curling left wing cross from Nicky Nicolau.

The former Arsenal trainee then sent a long range effort wide of the left upright from 25 yards before Lincoln came close to opening the scoring in the 26th minute.

The free-scoring Simon Yeo raced onto a flick from Green but his cool lob from 10 yards was harshly ruled out for offside with TV replays suggesting the goal should have been given.

The Shrimpers were then almost undone just seconds later as Darryl Flahavan's attempt to punch clear rebounded back off Ben Futcher. But, with the ball heading towards the back of the net and, with Yeo in close attendance, Mark Bentley raced back to brilliantly volley the effort off the goal-line.

Adam Barrett then did exceptionally well to block efforts from Yeo and Richard Butcher in quick succession and, immediately after the half time break, Green fired a tame long range drive straight at Flahavan.

Blues soon began to work their way back into the game however and, after 51 minutes, a well struck shot from Freddy Eastwood was scrambled for a corner by Gareth McAuley. Bentley then sent a long range strike over the crossbar before Eastwood slipped when attempting to reach a through ball from Nicolau.

With the game starting to stretch, Flahavan then did well to push away a vicious left foot shot from Yeo but, 30 seconds later, Bentley curled a long range shot into the grateful gloves of Marriott from 20 yards.

Having survived the scare, Lincoln soon replied and, in the 71st minute, Keith Alexander's men almost broke the deadlock as Flahavan fumbled a deep right wing cross from Kevin Sandwith.

That enabled Futcher to tee up Green but the forward's low shot was cleared off the line by the well positioned Che Wilson to spare his keeper's blushes.

With play switching back to the other end of the field, a dangerous low cross from skipper Kevin Maher then fizzed across the face of goal, before the Imps again hit back with Flahavan brilliantly fisting away a looping over-head kick from Green while under pressure from Yeo. A 25 yard shot from Butcher then fizzed just past the left post and, in the 90th minute, the Shrimpers shouts for a penalty fell on deaf ears as Bentley crashed to the floor following a challenge from Paul Morgan.

With the tie locked level, the match headed into extra time. And, as the Seasiders began to take control, a fierce Eastwood shot appeared to be han-dled by McAuley. Referee Martin Atkinson again waved away the protests and, in the 98th minute, Nicolau sent a right foot shot trickling just wide of the left post.

But Blues finally made their relentless pressure count in the 105th minute as a left wing corner from Nicolau was flicked towards his own net by Futcher – only for Bloomer to block the header on the goal-line.

The resulting rebound landed at the feet of substitute Lawrie Dudfield, who teed up his strike colleague Eastwood to slam the ball home from five yards.

Blues were now in cruise control and they doubled their advantage just five minutes later as Eastwood turned provider. The in-form forward raced half the length of the pitch before teeing up the on-rushing Jupp with a perfect square ball.

The former Fulham full back then neatly strolled a shot into the bottom left hand corner of the net to make sure of promotion for the Shrimpers. His first goal in a decade sparked wild celebrations from the Southend players and supporters who will never ever forget their first triumph at the Millennium Stadium.

Southend United manager, Steve Tilson, was overjoyed with the win.

He said: 'This is the greatest moment of my footballing career. I thought we deserved to win and the players and fans have been fantastic all season. It's great that they have got this reward. It's brilliant and although I won two back-to-back promotions as a player with Southend this tops the lot. It's fantastic and I'm so pleased. The players have been different class and I thought we deserved to beat Lincoln as well.'

SOUTHEND UNITED: Flahavan, Jupp, Barrett, Prior, Wilson, Pettefer, Maher, Bentley, Nicolau (Gower), Gray (Dudfield), Eastwood (Edwards). Subs. not used: Griemink and Guttridge.

LINCOLN CITY: Marriott, McAuley, Sandwith, McCombe, Morgan, Futcher, Butcher, Yeo (Asamoah), Taylor-Fletcher (Bloomer), Green (Beevers), Gain. Subs. not used: Rayner and Hanlon.

CHAPTER EIGHTEEN

'International' Match Reports 1931-2006

Wednesday, April 22nd, 1931
Friendly match
HOLLAND 'B' 1 SOUTHEND UNITED 3

The visit of Southend United to Rotterdam, on Wednesday, aroused no less interest than has the visit of several other English Football League teams, and the fact that the United won by 3-1 did not detract from the value of the visit to the Dutchmen, who were sporting enough to admit, after the match, that the result flattered the homesters.

The team to which the United were opposed was the Dutch 'B' eleven, a side in the nature of a reserve international one. Continental countries make a practice of forming 'B' international teams, and this might well be followed by the football authorities in other countries. It enables the selectors to form a second line of defence, on which they can readily draw if any of the first line fail them.

Southend were referred to as 'The Guests.' Such is the courtesy of the Dutch and their sense of hospitality. The Guests did not play convincing football at the opening of the match, but after leading at the interval by 1-0, they took charge of the game, and the inferiority of the Dutchmen was marked. In fact, it was evident that the United did not need to go all out to win. From the kick-off the Dutchmen took the initiative and Moore was tested with a very hot shot. Play ranged round about midfield for a quarter of an hour and then Southend set up a series of onslaughts, in which the forwards, admirably supported by the half-backs, combined perfectly and fired in shots at the Dutch goal-keeper from all angles. He withstood the onslaught, however, but it was only a matter of time before Southend scored. They did so after half an hour's play, Shankly sending in a fine drive, which the Dutch goalkeeper was unable to hold. The home team retaliated and caused Southend to go on the defensive, but they could not score, and at the interval Southend led 1-0.

The United, continues our special representative, had obviously reserved the second half in which to show their mettle. In some incisive attacks on the Dutch goal, they showed clever passing, and their ball control and positioning were lessons to the Dutchmen. Barnett raced down the wing to send in a shot which beat the Dutch goalkeeper to place Southend two up, but the Dutchmen fought back strenuously and they were eventually rewarded when their centre-forward beat Moore.

Just to convince the home team that they could win with ease, the United redoubled their efforts, and Shankly, receiving a pass from Crompton, obtained a third goal. From then until the final whistle, it was touch and go for the Dutchmen as to whether their citadel would fall again.

The game was watched by a large crowd, and altogether it was a most enjoyable meeting.

Wednesday, March 18th, 1936
Friendly match
DUTCH INTERNATIONAL XI 4, SOUTHEND UNITED 0

Under the brilliant white light which flooded the field from fifty 1,000-watt electric lamps, Southend United met a representative Dutch eleven at the Haarlem Stadium, twelve miles from Amsterdam, on Wednesday night, and were decisively and deservedly beaten in an extremely fast match by 4-0. The United players, usually sound in defence, were left floundering by the rapid quickfire tactics of the Dutchmen, whose open game and fine work were much ahead of their English rivals. The only excuse Southend could offer for the defeat was that they had difficulty throughout in judging the white light and the extremely lively white ball.

The international eleven are trained by Bob Glendenning, the former Barnsley and Bolton half-back, now in his thirteenth season with the Dutch F.A., and his influence was marked on the display of the homesters, as the teams played distinct types of football. The United, as usual, adopted the third back game and close passing methods, whereas the Dutchmen played the old-fashioned but very effective style with an attacking centre-half, and thus kept the exchanges very open as a result. It was quite refreshing to watch Schoemaker moving up with his forwards and only one back down the field. It was a lesson to modern English sides in tactics.

There was a last-minute change in the Dutch eleven, L.R.J. Vente having to withdraw owing to a leg injury, and H. Vegte, of the Haarlem Club, deputized for him. The game opened at a great pace before 8,000 spectators, with each side attacking in turn. The Dutch representatives revealed a surprisingly good standard of combination.

The light ball travelled very fast on the dry and sandy pitch. Although the Dutch forwards always looked likely to score, two defensive errors assisted them to open their account in the twelfth minute. Smith, who deputized for Turner at centre-half, made his only error of the match when he failed to clear a loose ball, and it was swung out to the right wing, where Kammeijer sent over a first-time centre. MacKenzie ran out to catch it, but the next second was bundled over by the fast-moving centre-forward, de Hoed. Both men fell to the ground and the ball went into the net.

The Southend players still found difficulty in judging the white ball in the artificial light, but the Dutch team seemed to have an exact knowledge of just where it would bounce and their combination and understanding throughout were excellent. Crisp first-time passing, particularly by de la Mar and Bool, had the United on tenterhooks and the visitors did not dictate the play until half an hour had passed.

Then Wilders, the right-back, dropped back and kicked out from under the bar a shot from Willshaw. Just before half-time the Dutchmen gained their second success. MacKenzie ran out and caught a dropping centre and then lost hold of the lively ball, dropped it and fell over. This left Kammeijer the simple task of tapping it into an empty net. The Dutch team, although they had obtained two lucky goals, well deserved their lead at half-time and their quick passing and moving into position were little short of ideal pattern-weaving football.

Their only fault, perhaps, was that the swift speed at which they played often defeated its own object in that they failed to keep control of the ball. They proved themselves, however, a clever side, with little to learn in tactics. Mul did not have much to do until the second half, when he brought off one outstanding save, Wilders and Plenter stemming most of the United attacks, with Plenter the better of the pair. They were assisted in their work by the failure of the Blues to forsake the futile close passing game – an old but persistent fault. There was not a good forward on the Southend side. Lane being one of the chief culprits in holding on to the ball too long. Schoemaker and his wing halves were generally able to break up all the United's efforts without undue trouble.

In the second half Southend's defence went all to pieces after ten minutes, when Vegte scored an excellent goal. Two minutes later the backs were again in trouble and Woltjes added the fourth point. In the closing stages Southend played a little better, but Smith and Robinson were about the two best men in a poor side.

The Dutch eleven, which was not the full international side that was only beaten 1-0 by England last season, was composed of players who were after positions in the senior side. They were out to impress their own authority that they should go into the first eleven, and this brought a crispness into their game that brought their football to a very high level. It was rather interesting to note that the old style of open game has paid this team very handsomely, for they have beaten Gillingham and Swindon by nine and seven goals respectively, through such tactics. The visit of Southend broke fresh ground in that it was the first representative match to be played at the Haarlem Stadium, which has only been completed six months. The Haarlem team itself contributed three players, and, judging by their form, Jack Bollington, the old Southend and Brighton footballer, who is their trainer, has made a very good job of things.

Of the Dutch forwards, the chief danger always came from Vrauwdeunt and Kammeijer, the two wingers, and den Hoed, a dashing leader, outshone Fryar by reason of his ball control and the way he kept the game open. It was a weird and new experiment for Englishmen to see a game played under flood-lighting conditions, with a white ball. The teams were:–

DUTCH XI: E.G. Mul (H.B.S.); C. Wilders (Blauw-Wit), H.A. Plenter (Be-Quick); H. de la Mar (Haarlem), A.H. Schoemaker (Quick), G.R. Bool (H.V.V.); H.L.W. Vrauwdeunt (Feyenoord), H. Vegte (Haarlem), P. den Hoed (M.V.V.), Jb. Woltjes (Veendam), R. Kammeijer (Haarlem).

SOUTHEND UNITED: MacKenzie; Nelson and Robinson; Deacon, Smith and Carr; Oswald, Firth, A. Fryar, Lane and Willshaw.

Wednesday, May 15th, 1957
Friendly match
AUSTRIA 'B' 2, SOUTHEND UNITED 1

Southend United were beaten 2-1 at Vienna on Wednesday week by Austria's national 'B' side. The Austrians led 2-0 at half-time in a match which provided few thrills. Baron, easily the best of the Southend forwards, got the Blues only goal in the 66th minute.

Frequently during the match he made openings, but poor support from the rest of the front line, which included ex-Aldershot amateur centre-forward 'Lou' Costello and Jimmy Smith, on loan from Leyton Orient. Weak shooting prevented them from taking full advantage of the shakiness of the Austrian defence.

The entire Southend team looked slow and undecided in the first half and goals by inside right Tamandi (seven minutes) and inside-left Huberts (10 minutes) gave the Austrians a good start. Southend improved after the interval, but poor finishing spoiled their attacking efforts. Team:–

SOUTHEND UNITED: Threadgold; Williamson, Anderson; Duthie, Stirling, Duffy; Smith, McCrory, Costello, Baron and McGuigan.

Wednesday, May 14th, 1958
Friendly match
AUSTRIA 'B' 4, SOUTHEND UNITED 3

A disputed goal ten seconds from the final whistle gave Austria 'B' an unde-served win over Southend United at Vienna on Wednesday week. Over 30,000 fans saw the Blues give a great display against a side which included seven full internationals.

It was the general opinion among the sporting Austrian fans that poor ref-ereeing was responsible for Blues' first defeat of the tour. After an early Austrian attack, in which Threadgold made a magnificent save from Knoll, the Blues settled down and amazed the fans by more than holding their own.

Hollis, Price, Baron and McCrory all came close with good efforts before the home side surprisingly took the lead in the 15th minute.

After an appeal for offside had been ignored, Kaltenbrunner ran on to beat Threadgold. Fighting back grimly, Blues regained the initiative, Hollis had a shot saved at the expense of a corner and a Duthie drive grazed the post. A nice Crossan, McCrory and Price move saw Sam shoot inches past the upright.

Blues equalised in the 37th minute, when Duthie moved down the wing and sent over an accurate centre for McCrory to net a nice goal. Before the Austrians had time to recover from this shock, the Blues were ahead. Baron started the move, slipped the ball to Hollis, who put Price through to score from close range.

After Hollis just failed to connect with a Baron pass in the opening minutes of the second half, both goals ran narrow escapes before Kaltenbrunner headed the equaliser. Back came the Blues for Price to head inches over from a free-kick, while at the other end Threadgold brought off three magnificent saves in quick succession.

The Austrians brought on the first of four substitutes in an all-out attempt to force the pace, but the Blues, although tiring in the heat, were always dangerous. Fifteen minutes from time the Blues went ahead when Hollis veered to the left and centred for McCrory to steer the ball just out of the 'keeper's reach.

This was the signal for a terrific Austrian attack, and after Stirling had cleverly stopped Kaltenbrunner, who looked set to score, Dr. Schleger was allowed to carry on from an offside position to equalise.

In the final stages, McCrory twice hit an upright with the 'keeper beaten, but then came the last vital seconds. From a Ninaus corner Knoll forced the ball into the net with Threadgold obstructed by Kaltenbrunner. Despite strong protests the goal was allowed to stand, and Blues suffered their first defeat.

Southend gave a really tip-top display, worthy of a First Division side. Threadgold was a brilliant 'keeper, with stop-gap backs, Morrison and Duffy tireless workers. Stirling dominated the centre of the field, while Crossan and Price were speedy wingers. Hollis had one of his best games of the season.

UNITED: Threadgold; Morrison, Duffy; Duthie, Stirling, Smith; Crossan, McCrory, Hollis, Baron, Price.

Sunday, November 12th, 1972
Friendly match
GUERNSEY 2, SOUTHEND UNITED 8

Despite very poor conditions – heavy rain and a strong wind – the Blues provided some entertaining soccer at the Cycling Ground in Guernsey on Sunday during their four-day stay in the island.

The Blues soon opened the scoring but then the islanders equalised. However the Blues were in command and at half-time led 3-1.

They continued to provide grand football throughout the second period and added five more goals, goalkeeper Derek Bellotti getting one from the penalty spot. Billy Best (2) and Dave Elliott scored in the first half, and Gary Moore (2), Peter Taylor, Bobby Bennett (who replaced Best) and Bellotti netted in the second.

The Guernsey goals were scored by Laurence Graham, a former Burnley trialist, and Colin Loveridge, a former Manchester City trialist.

SOUTHEND UNITED: Bellotti, Booth, Ternent (Harrison), Elliott, Barnett, Moody, Johnson, Best (Bennett), Moore, Woods, Taylor.

The bad weather cut the crowd to only 244.

Monday, August 25th, 1975
Friendly match
SOUTHEND UNITED 3, QATAR 1

It was a reporter's nightmare. Southend's opponents, from the Sheikdom of Qatar on the Persian Gulf, had numbers on their backs alright, but nobody could understand them. They were in Arabic. But their football made up for that. The national coach is Frank Wignall, the former England striker whose League career spanned Nottingham Forest, Derby County and Everton.

Wignall, who has been in Qatar for nearly a year, said before the match: 'We can't play in our country at the moment because the temperature is getting on for 130 degrees.

This side is only young and they have a lot to learn but they are coming on very well. It hasn't taken them long to grab the basics of the game – which is growing a tremendous amount in the gulf area.'

The men from Qatar are quick and agile, good on the ball, and capable of neat passing. Perhaps their only downfall is lack of concentration. Southend made sure they suffered. First, Steve Lamb's header should have been safely gathered by the goalkeeper but he took his eye off the ball and dropped it over his head. Then the goalkeeper again lost the ball and Lamb was on hand to pounce.

Qatar pulled a goal back, but an over-enthusiastic defender brought Dave Cunningham down in the penalty area and Willie Coulson made it 3-1.

Southend's man-of-the-match – Willie Coulson.

Friday, August 12th, 1983
Friendly match
SOUTHEND UNITED 0, JAPAN 1

Blues supporters who went to Roots Hall for the pre-season friendly between Southend United and the Japan national team saw that a start had been made to rebuild the squad depleted by transfers and allowing some players to go free.

But they also saw that manager Peter Morris still has a lot to do as he aims to try and get the Blues into the Second Division. The Japanese side won 1-0, but the Blues had six times as many chances of scoring goals and should have had the game won within the first fifteen minutes.

It was a good workout and quite entertaining. The United, in an unfamiliar all-red strip, included newcomers Steve Collins, Greig Shepherd, Glen Skivington and Roy McDonough, and the pitch was in perfect condition, a fine illustration of the hard work obviously put in by the groundsman and his staff during the difficult dry weather of past weeks.

The visitors were in an all-blue strip, and were comparatively small players. Naturally, they kept the ball on the ground and were soon impressing with their man-to-man passing all along the ground.

Shepherd and McDonough were much taller than the visitors tallest defender and the two new strikers were soon laying the ball off to Steve Phillips. He had only the 'keeper to beat early on, but shot over the bar, and then, when McDonough made a chance, the usually reliable goal-poacher sent in such a poor shot that the 'keeper had no difficulty in saving. And after Paul Clark had stopped lively striker Nobutoshi Kaneda at the expense of a corner Steve Collins lofted the ball to McDonough, who headed it into the path of Phillips, but this time he hit the bar.

So within 11 minutes the Blues had wasted three good chances. And as the game continued so the Blues had the upper hand. McDonough headed just wide and after Ron Pountney had crossed the ball well Shepherd sent it over the bar.

At the other end a fine run by Kazushi Kimura led to another unproductive corner and soon after both Yahito Kazama and Kaneda went close. Kazama produced some clever footwork and fast runs which always spelt danger, but Mervyn Cawston was seldom really troubled.

The visitors attacked after the interval and Hiroma Hara missed a chance to open the scoring. But soon after the visitors did grab the lead. They made a fast break and Masafumi Yokoyama beat Cawston with a good drive from inside the box.

This proved to be the only goal, and as the game progressed so the Blues took command again. But they then found the visitors had a very capable goalkeeper in Mitsuhisa Taguchi.

With Skivington getting through a lot of work in midfield, the Blues set up a series of raids. McDonough had a fine header well saved, Micky Stead had a powerful low drive well taken, the 'keeper raced from his goal to kick clear as Shepherd threatened, then pushed the ball around the post as McDonough sent in another worthwhile header. But at the end the Blues had nothing to show for their efforts.

It had been a good workout against unusual opposition; the Blues will not meet many teams with this particular style of ground play.

Tuesday, May 22nd, 1984
Friendly match
SRI LANKA PRESIDENT'S XI 1, SOUTHEND UNITED 1

Thursday, May 24th, 1984
Friendly match
SRI LANKA PRESIDENT'S XI 2, SOUTHEND UNITED 12

Southend United returned from their tour of Sri Lanka with some lovely silver trophies, secretary Keith Holmes describing the trip as really fantastic, a wonderful, unforgettable experience. The Blues played four games. All the matches were played in Colombo, in a beautiful stadium built a couple of years ago by public donations, a stadium capable of handling a crowd of 20,000 all seated.

The Blues did some coaching while there, which was much appreciated, and also donated a set of shirts to be given to a deserving club. In addition, some small boy kits were left to be distributed to deserving youngsters.

The first match was against the President's XI, and this ended 1-1 with Glenn Pennyfather getting the Blues goal. The second match was won 12-2 and ended more of an exhibition. Keeper John Keeley played up front and scored twice, as did Pennyfather and Trevor Whymark. Steve Phillips hit four and Greig Shepherd and Brian Ferguson one each.

Keith Holmes added: 'The hospitality was out of this world and I think we left a good enough impression to be invited out there again.'

Wednesday, February 5th, 1992
Friendly match
SOUTHEND UNITED 4, NEW ZEALAND 2

Southend United refused to be overawed when they took on the New Zealand World Cup squad in front of a pathetically small turnout at Roots Hall last night.

Less than 700 fans turned up but they missed a memorable night with Blues at times toying with the opposition and running out comfortable 4-2 winners. The Kiwis had seen off a Celtic side containing five Scottish Internationals 1-0 just 24 hours earlier and understandably looked a little leg weary as they found Southend a much tougher proposition.

Boss David Webb was delighted with the result although he admitted his men made hard work of it at times.

'The big pity was that a few more people didn't come along – it's not every day that we get an International side at Roots Hall.'

Southend went into action without four men who played in Saturday's 1-0 win over Watford.

Spencer Prior, Steve Tilson, Andy Ansah and top marksman Brett Angell were all missing with various injuries and Webb called up Andy Edwards, Keith Jones, Kevin O'Callaghan and Andy Sussex to plug the gaps.

Blues did not let the lack of atmosphere worry them as they got off to a cracking start with a goal after only two minutes – and from the penalty spot! O'Callaghan jinked his way into the penalty area before being upended by Mike Ridenton. Great Wakering League referee David Axcell immediately pointed to the spot and skipper Ian Benjamin coolly blasted home to prove Blues can score from 12 yards following their recent nightmares.

And there was even better to come for Southend after 15 minutes when the industrious John Cornwell was on hand to score from close in after Dean Austin's cross was touched on by Benjamin.

Blues continued to run the show with Jones firing just wide and Benjamin forcing a world class save out of 'keeper Clint Gosling before the Kiwis reduced the arrears after 35 minutes. Paul Sansome tipped a fierce shot from Vaughan Coveny over the bar and from the flag kick the defence was caught napping as Harry Ngata was allowed time and space to hook the ball home.

Any fears that Southend might throw away their advantage were quickly dispelled when two goals within six minutes of the restart put them firmly back in charge. First Sussex stabbed in after Benjamin flicked on Jones' left-wing corner and then Benjamin worked an opening for Jones to squeeze the ball under the 'keeper.

Webb made several second-half substitutions in an effort to give a number of players a run-out and they continued to cruise along until another lapse in the dying minutes presented New Zealand substitute Jason New with a gift he accepted with relish.

Friday, June 30th, 2006
Friendly match
BERMUDA 2, SOUTHEND UNITED 3

The match was billed as a tribute to The Goat and a thank-you from Southend to the striker who helped them win promotion to the Championship last season. And fittingly it was the man of the moment that took centre stage.

Goater struck the most unusual hat-trick of his career, opening the scoring for Bermuda, before swapping sides at half-time and banging in two for the Shrimpers. Goater broke the deadlock on the brink of half-time playing a neat one-two with Janhai Raynor before crashing home a low drive from the edge of the box to give Bermuda the lead. Only minutes into the second half he scored a second – this time for Southend. Left unmarked in the box he latched onto a Frank Moussa cross to head home the equaliser. Midfield powerhouse Kwame Steede restored Bermuda's lead before The Goat completed his hat-trick, volleying home from the edge of the box.

He was subbed with around 20 minutes remaining to a standing ovation from the sparse crowd (982), after which the match lost some of its momentum. Southend grabbed a third though, with the impressive James Lawson bundling home the winner from close range after a goalmouth scramble in the dying minutes of the game (87).

The match, a casual introduction to pre-season training for Southend and a mid-summer workout for Bermuda, was played at a friendly pace with rolling subs. But it turned out to be a tougher workout than the Shrimpers had expected with Bermuda pushing them all the way.

After the game Goater thanked the few hundred fans who had turned out at the island's national stadium for the game and paid tribute to his former Southend team-mates.

CHAPTER NINETEEN

Testimonial Match for Steve Tilson

Monday, March 31st, 2003
SOUTHEND UNITED 8, ENGLAND XI 2

The people of Southend and star names from the soccer world turned out in force to pay tribute to one of their favourite sons – Steve Tilson – at Roots Hall last night.

Tilson, 36, has clocked up 274 appearances for Blues during a long, long affiliation with the Shrimpers, having made his first team debut back in 1989, and was rightly finally awarded with a fitting testimonial by the club he loves.

An official attendance of 4,555 spectators turned out to salute their hero, although there looked to be a far bigger crowd inside the Roots Hall terraces.

Tilson must have felt like he had stepped back in time as he ran out for an England XI, rubbing shoulders with the likes of Dennis Wise, Ray Wilkins and Clive Allen, at the ground which has become his second home.

The Roots Hall North Bank was opened to home fans for the first time in nearly a decade and the Blues fans sitting there sang out Tilson's name, just as they did when he played such a key role in Southend's tremendous rise from the old Fourth to Second Division during the early 90s. And there were so many other reminders of the great times at Roots hall during those heady First Division days. Tilson's defensive support down the left flank in those great Southend sides, Chris Powell, returned to reform his partnership with his old team mate in the England XI. Former Shrimpers boss Barry Fry was also in town, as was undoubtedly Blues' most famous player ever, striker Stan Collymore, who returned to Roots Hall, following spells with Premiership giants Liverpool and Aston Villa, much to the delight of autograph hungry fans. Rob Newman, sacked by Southend as manager last week, also turned out for the England XI in support of Tilson, and was given a warm reception by the Shrimpers supporters.

The match was a real cracker with ten goals shared by the current Southend team and the England team, led by Tilson. Blues' opponents gave them an early scare when Millwall midfielder Wise flashed a header over the south stand goal after just five minutes. Shrimpers forward Tes Bramble hit back soon after, drilling wide of the left upright from the edge of the box, before Southend goalkeeper Darryl Flahavan pulled off a stunning save, parrying Warren Barton's point-blank header from Wise's centre.

Barrington Belgrave's appearance came to a premature end after 11 minutes when midfielder Wilkins clattered the Blues forward in front of the Seasiders dug-out.

And it was Belgrave's replacement, Mark Rawle, who fed Bramble to open the scoring two minutes later, with a crisp 15-yard finish past Brighton's veteran custodian Dave Beasant. Both Rawle and Southend winger Brett Darby tested Beasant from other openings, before man of the night Tilson netted a stunning 25th minute equaliser. Wise was the architect, chipping over a pinpoint free-kick, which Tilson broke free to meet and stab past a flat-footed Flahavan from a couple of yards.

But it was only a brief respite, as Blues, led by Bramble, hit the ageing Three Lions with a three goal blitz in nine minutes. Bramble got his second of the night on 29 minutes, crashing an unstoppable volley in off the underside of the crossbar, before finishing off Steven Clark's low cross for his hat-trick three minutes later.

Wideman Clark got in on the act himself on 35 minutes driving through the centre of the park, taking a return pass from Bramble, and dribbling the ball inside the left hand post after dumping Beasant on his backside. And within another three minutes, Southend grabbed a fifth. Bramble was again the provider, picking out Brett Darby, who burst down the right-hand side of the England penalty area and curled a 12-yard effort inside the near post.

Blues made six changes at half-time, which included a rest for loan Spurs centre-half Ronnie Henry, making his first appearance in a Southend shirt, but they still carried on looking for more goals.

Bramble hit an effort straight at substitute England goalkeeper Tim Flowers, before side-footing Neil Jenkins' left-wing cross wide from six yards Fellow Blues hitman Rawle raced clear and rounded Flowers, but his angled drive was blocked on the goal-line by ex-AC Milan and Manchester United star Wilkins.

England reduced the heavy deficit on 51 minutes with a goal of the highest quality, when former Spurs and West Ham forward Allen chipped a stunning 35-yard effort over Southend's substitute goalkeeper Danny Gay. However, Clark conjured up another Southend goal after 55 minutes, supplying Darby with a right-wing pass which the diminutive winger blasted past old Leicester City team mate Flowers.

Derby County midfielder Rob Lee fired two long range efforts just over the Shrimpers crossbar, before Wise's vicious cross-shot was pushed past the left upright by Gay. Young Southend substitute Michael Kightly forced Flowers into a solid save after riding a typical strong challenge from old West Ham and Canvey Island defender Julian Dicks.

And Rawle completed the rout with two late goals, shooting across Flowers from a tight angle, before intercepting a Wilkins pass in the very last minute before drilling an unstoppable 18-yard effort inside the left post. Newcastle United favourites Peter Beardsley and Chris Waddle pulled out of the England XI at the last minute. Beardsley got injured playing in the Football Masters tournament at the weekend and Waddle cried off with a badly bruised foot.

SOUTHEND: Flahavan (Gay), Searle (Jenkins), Henry (Jordan), McSweeney (Cort), Darby, Maher (Thurgood), Clark, Sutch, Beard (Broad), Belgrave (Rawle), Bramble (Kightly).

ENGLAND XI: Beasant (Flowers), Parker, Powell, Osman, Dicks, Wilkins, Lee (Beasant), Barton (Newman), Wise (Greaves), Allen, Tilson.

'It was a cracking night and I want to thank everybody, the fans and players, for coming here and supporting me,' said Tilson. 'I was really nervous when I got on the pitch and I must admit there were a few tears in my eyes – it was an emotional evening. But it was great to get out there and play for the fans who have stuck by me during all the years I have been with the club. And it was amazing to play with all the England players like Dennis Wise and Ray Wilkins. I even got a goal, and they didn't just let me have it, it was a proper one. At least I can say I've scored for England now. I was so worried when I turned up, because I didn't know how many people were going to come,' he said. 'I was more nervous than I was before my wedding day, but I feel like I've been married to Blues all these years and I hope we stay together for a lot, lot longer.'

Tilson also thanked former Blues boss Rob Newman for turning out, just seven days after getting sacked by the club.

'It was brilliant to see everyone here, all the England players and all the old boys, especially Stan Collymore and Chris Powell, but I can't thank Rob enough for turning up,' he added. 'Despite what has happened to him he never once suggested he wouldn't come and I'm glad the fans gave him such a good reception because he deserves it.'

From the *Southend Echo* of 18th May, 2005

Southend United boss Steve Tilson today expressed his delight at being named League Two manager of the year by the League Managers' Association. The former Shrimpers midfielder has turned a previously relegation threatened side into promotion play-off qualifiers, while also reaching the final of the LDV Vans Trophy for the second successive season. He has also made a number of key signings, including Adam Barrett and Freddy Eastwood. That terrific progress has now been recognised by the LMA at their annual awards ceremony and the Wickford born chief admitted he was honoured to have won. 'I'm obviously delighted to have won this award, but this is for everyone, not just me,' said Tilson.

'The players have been fantastic, they deserve the most credit, but all my staff and everyone at the club have been brilliant as well.'

From the *Echo* of 23rd January, 2006

Southend United boss Steve Tilson has been named assistant manager of the Football League's Under-21 side. The 39-year-old boss will work alongside former Shrimpers chief Peter Taylor when their team, which will consist of the best young players outside the Premiership, take on their Italian counterparts at Hull City's KC Stadium on Tuesday, February 21. Tilson said he was shocked by the news but is looking forward to linking up with the squad. 'It was a massive surprise for me but it will be a great experience,' he said. 'I get on well with Peter Taylor and it will be good to see what goes on at International level.'

From the *Echo* of 21st February, 2006

Steve Tilson is hoping to enhance his managerial credentials this evening as he strives to secure victory for the Football League's Under-21 side against their Italian counterparts at Hull City's KC Stadium. 'I have really enjoyed being part of the set up going into the game and I'm looking forward to the game starting now,' said Tilson, who drove up to meet the squad after Saturday's 4-3 victory at Chesterfield.

'It's obviously been a real honour to be involved with this game. I didn't really have much to do with the actual selection of the squad other than a couple of calls from Pete who asked me about some players. But it's interesting to see how he works and he's obviously someone you can learn things from so it's going to be a really good experience.'

From the *Echo* of 22nd February, 2006

Manager Steve Tilson aims to apply the tricks of the trade he picked up from Peter Taylor to his Southend United side. Tilson said he learned some valuable lessons from the Hull City boss as they helped the Football League's Under-21 side secure a 1-0 victory over their Italian counterparts at the Tigers' KC Stadium last night. A close range effort from Southampton striker Dexter Blackstock settled the tie and left Tilson delighted at the final whistle.

'In terms of management I'm still a puppy so it was great to see how Pete approached the game and what he did during it as well,' he said. 'I did some of the ball work and warm ups but it was Pete who worked on the shape and I learnt a lot. I will take the best of what he did and bring that back to Southend. This has been such a fantastic experience for me and is certainly something I will always remember,' added Tilson.

'It was obviously nice to win the game but it wasn't just the match that was memorable for me, it was the whole build up and the three days training we had together as well.'

Boss Taylor, who also coaches the England Under-21 side, was also pleased with Tilson's contributions. 'I was delighted to have Tilly as my assistant,' he said. 'He's someone I've known for many years now and was a very reliable and honest player when I was his manager at Southend.

'He's showing the same qualities now. He is doing a fantastic job and I really hope he guides Blues to another promotion this season.'

From the *Echo* of 9th May, 2006

Southend United boss Steve Tilson was named League One Manager of the Season by the League Managers' Association in Nottingham last night.

The Shrimpers chief was rewarded by his fellow bosses after guiding the Shrimpers to the title with the smallest squad in the division. Tilson was delighted to clinch the award after also winning League Two Manager of the Year last season.

'It's fantastic to win the award and is a real honour for me,' said Tilson. 'I didn't think I was going to win it either, so it came as a bit of a surprise to be honest. But it's an award for the whole of Southend United, not just me. My coaching staff and players have been fantastic, as have the fans and this is another nice moment from what has proved to be another great season for us.'

The side which beat Bristol City on Saturday to seal the League One title was assembled for just £105,000 and included eight free transfers.

'A few of the sides splashed the cash in our league to try and get up there but we managed to see them all off,' said Tilson. 'It's been brilliant and now we can't wait to go on and challenge in the Championship next season.'

CHAPTER TWENTY

A Selection of Match Reports 2003-2006

Saturday, January 3rd, 2004
F.A. Challenge Cup, 3rd Round
SOUTHEND UNITED 1, SCARBOROUGH 1

Southend United face a tricky trip to the McCain Stadium next Wednesday following a disappointing 1-1 draw with Conference club Scarborough in the third round of the F. A. Cup at Roots Hall on Saturday.

In front of a near-7,000 crowd, the Blues began brightly and opened the scoring after just ten minutes as in-form midfielder Jay Smith volleyed home an acrobatic effort from a well-worked Mark Gower corner.

Following the former Aston Villa man's fourth goal of the season however, the game quietened down – with neither side creating any clear-cut chances during a fairly uneventful opening half. But, after the break, the two seaside teams both started to look more dangerous during a quicker and strongly contested second period, which saw substitute striker Drewe Broughton miss a glorious chance to seal Southend's passage to the fourth round.

The shot-shy forward, who has netted two goals in 27 games since signing from Kidderminster Harriers during the summer, frustratingly failed to convert a fine Neil Jenkins through ball which sent him clean through on goal – firing a tame, low effort straight at Leigh Walker's legs.

And, 20 minutes later, the wasted opportunity was to increase in significance as Seadogs midfielder Scott Kerr cancelled out Smith's early opener with a well-directed, low volley that flew into the bottom right-hand corner of the net. As a result, the two sides will do battle again in nine days time, when the Shrimpers will attempt to reach the fourth round stage for the first time in 11 years.

The Shrimpers started the brighter of the two sides with a stretching Leon Cort heading Mark Gower's drilled corner wide of the left post after just three minutes. And, just six minutes later, the Roots Hall faithful were celebrating the game's opening goal as Leon Constantine flicked another Gower corner into the path of Jay Smith, who fired an acrobatic, vicious volley past Leigh Walker from ten yards. Tes Bramble then just failed to control Constantine's well hit through ball, before Mark Quayle's header at the other end of the field was scrambled to safety by Neil Jenkins.

Having survived the scare, a last-ditch Mark Hotte challenge then stopped Mark Gower striking a fine Kevin Maher pass towards goal, before Duncan Jupp bravely beat Quayle to Ashley Sestanovich's curling right wing cross in a well-constructed counter attack from the visitors.

With 32 minutes on the clock and, following a prolonged period of inactivity, Wayne Gill then struck a long range shot over the South Stand crossbar. Gower also skied a similar effort minutes later after impressive approach play from Neil Jenkins and Tes Bramble had created the chance. Scarborough midfielder Scott Kerr then fired another wayward effort well wide of the right post, before Gower replied with a delicate 20-yard chip that just cleared the Conference club's crossbar. Seconds later, Gill hit a 25-yard drive over Darryl Flahavan's goal. And then Tes Bramble limped out of the action to be replaced by Drewe Broughton on the stroke of half-time.

After the interval, Broughton headed Leon Constantine's right wing cross straight into the grateful gloves of Walker. Then Scarborough's Sestanovich saw his well-directed 16-yard shot brilliantly palmed around the right post by a diving Darryl Flahavan. Minutes later, Glint Marcelle's dangerous left wing cross was deflected just wide of the Southend goal and Sestanovich's cheeky 65th minute effort was ruled out for a foul on Flahavan.

The on-loan Sheffield United winger, who has been earning rave reviews so far this season, raced from behind the Shrimpers shot stopper to kick the ball from the keeper's hands, but the controversial effort was quickly disallowed by referee Brian Curson. The Blues then wasted a golden opportunity to double their advantage as Drewe Broughton collected Neil Jenkins' through ball to race clean through on goal.

But, with just Walker left to beat, the goal-shy striker fired a low, right foot shot straight at the Scarborough custodian, with Jay Smith's deflected drive from the subsequent rebound flying wide of the right post. Broughton's header from the resulting Mark Gower corner was then well cleared by Steve Baker. But then Russell Slade's men drew back level in the 74th minute as Sestanovich and Marcelle combined to set up the on-rushing Scott Kerr, who volleyed a low 14-yard effort into the bottom right-hand corner of the net.

The shell-shocked Shrimpers quickly replied with Leon Constantine firing a 20-yard drive straight at Walker, before Steve Tilson threw young Michael Kightly into the action in place of Neil Jenkins.

The Basildon-born winger soon crossed for Jay Smith to volley another acrobatic effort over the crossbar, and then lively Scarborough substitute Tristan Whitman fired a blistering 18-yard shot inches over the Southend goal.

The former Doncaster Rovers forward then warmed Flahavan's gloves with another stinging shot. Broughton then fired a sliced 16-yard effort way off target in the closing action of an evenly-contested encounter.

'It was disappointing from our point of view,' said Smith. 'We started off well, and appeared to be in control, but Scarborough came back into it during the second half, and although we could have won, a draw was probably a fair result.' Smith, who netted twice during the opening round derby victory over Canvey Island, admitted he was delighted to work his way onto the scoresheet once again. 'It was good for me to get another goal because I hadn't got one for a while, and I was happy with that finish,' he said. 'We should have gone on from there though and converted more of our chances to tie the game up.' But Smith was also quick to praise the performance of a spirited Scarborough side, who came close to upsetting the Shrimpers. 'They gave us a good game and were playing some good stuff,' said the former Aston Villa youngster. 'We found it quite hard at times, but now we've got to stick together and go to their place to try and win the replay. It's going to be hard; I'm sure they will have a lot of support behind them, but we're confident of doing a job up there.'

And Blues caretaker-boss Steve Tilson was again left ruing his side's wastefulness in front of goal. 'We didn't capitalise on our early goal but, similar to our last two home games, we didn't take our chances,' said the 37-year-old.

'We need to start killing teams off, but full credit to Scarborough, they worked hard and got bodies behind the ball to hit us on the break. After they scored they went close on a couple of other occasions, but we're still in the cup and now we've got another bite of the cherry back at their place.'

BLUES (4-4-2 formation): Flahavan, Jupp, Cort, Hunt, Stuart, Gower, Maher, Smith, Jenkins (Kightly), Bramble (Broughton), Constantine. Subs, not used: Emberson, S. Clark, Fullarton.

SCARBOROUGH: Walker, Lyth, Cryan, Hotte, Baker, Sestanovich, Kerr, Kelly, Gill (Whitman), Marcelle (Williams), Quayle. Subs, not used: Senior, Capper, Downey.

Ref: B. Curson (Leicestershire). Att: 6,902

Saturday, October 16th, 2004
Football League Two
SOUTHEND UNITED 4, SWANSEA CITY 2

A superb hat-trick from debutant Shrimpers striker Fredy Eastwood knocked a stunned Swansea City off the top of the League Two table on Saturday, as Steve Tilson's side ran riot at Roots Hall and beat the Welshmen 4-2.

Eastwood hit home a terrific trio of strikes and continually terrorised a bemused Swansea back four in another immensely exciting encounter. In fact, Eastwood took just 7.7 seconds to open his League goalscoring account as, following some impressive approach play from both Mark Gower and Wayne Gray, the latter curled over a fine left wing cross for the highly-rated 20-year-old to head into the North Bank net from point blank range.

In reply, Adam Barrett then scrambled a Bradley Maylett centre, which had been fumbled by the Shrimpers stand-in keeper Ryan Clarke, off the goal-line before the lively Lee Trundle headed Paul Connor's left wing cross well wide.

Having survived the double scare, the home-side soon hit back with an unmarked Gower tamely heading a deep Duncan Jupp cross off target and, as the electric opening continued, visiting shot-stopper Willy Gueret parried away a low drive from Gray after previously failing to hold a Kevin Maher corner.

The Frenchman then denied both Gower and Gray from 25 yards but, with 11 minutes on the clock, his Swans drew back level – courtesy of a series of sublime skills from Lee Trundle. The goal-getting Scouser bamboozled both Jupp and Maher to slide a fine pass into the path of his strike-partner Connor, who duly lifted the ball over the advancing Clarke for his third goal of the season. Trundle was at it again soon after – curling a 20-yard shot straight at the new Shrimpers custodian and, as play soon switched back to the other end of the field, Lewis Hunt lashed an effort, from a similar distance, over the Swans crossbar. With Blues beginning to get back on top, Carl Pettefer's shot, from another Gray cross, was then diverted to safety by City centre-back Alan Tate.

But, from the resulting Maher, left wing corner, the Shrimpers restored their advantage as former Cardiff City defender Spencer Prior leapt high to head an eight-yard effort into the bottom left hand corner of the net on 42 minutes. Swansea soon replied with Trundle sending an audacious 25-yard chip only inches over the South Stand net, before Gray stabbed a diagonal pass from Maher into the grateful gloves of Gueret in the closing action of the opening half.

Immediately after the interval, Paul Connor nodded Sam Ricketts' inviting cross past the right post and, in the 56th minute, Lee Trundle turned outside Adam Barrett to fire an angled drive off target. Two minutes later however, Blues extended their lead as Gray again curled over a fantastic cross, this time from the right, enabling a well positioned Eastwood to plant a six-yard header past the helpless Gueret. The shell-shocked Swans immediately responded with Roberto Martinez fizzing a ferocious 25-yard shot inches wide of the right post before another powerful effort from Andy Robinson was tipped around the opposite upright by Ryan Clarke.

But, in the 82nd minute, the Blues rearguard was finally breached once again as substitute winger Adrian Forbes set up a grandstand finish by neatly dispatching Trundle's right wing cross with a well-placed header.

The Shrimpers, and Eastwood in particular, were not to be denied though and, just three minutes from time, the on-loan Grays front-runner completed his hat-trick with a deflected low drive from 25 yards which skimmed into the centre of the net. Still the excitement was not over as, straight from the resulting kick-off, Trundle struck the Seasiders crossbar from fully 50 yards, with Scott Fitzgerald somehow side-footing the rebound wide of the right post to sum up a miserable afternoon for the Swans.

SOUTHEND: Clarke, Jupp, Prior, Barrett, Wilson, Pettefer, Maher, Hunt, Gower (Corbett 30), Gray, Eastwood (Kightly 90). Subs not used: Morgan, Edwards and Nicolau.

SWANSEA: Gueret, Monk, Tate, Austin, Ricketts, Maylett (Forbes 59), O'Leary, Martinez, Robinson, Connor (Fitzgerald 70), Trundle. Subs not used: Murphy, Britton and Nugent.

Referee: Mick Russell (Herts.). Attendance: 4,940

Sunday, October 9th, 2005
Football League One
SOUTHEND UNITED 1, NOTTINGHAM FOREST 0

Rampant Southend United surged to the top of the League One table with a
1-0 victory over Nottingham Forest – thanks to a late strike from super sub
Freddy Eastwood.

The goal-getting youngster, who was surprisingly omitted from the starting
line-up, fired home a six-yard shot just nine minutes from time to send a
packed Roots Hall wild and ensure the current Shrimpers side's entrance into
the record books.

Never before had Blues won eight games in succession but the forward's
fine finish secured the feat as Steve Tilson's side continued their impressive
sequence of successful score-lines.

But it was Forest who carved open the first chance of the game as Nicky
Southall's well-struck 25-yard half-volley was superbly pushed away by a diving Darryl Flahavan after just seven minutes. Jack Lester then volleyed a flick
from fellow forward David Johnson over the North Bank roof but the effort
sparked Southend into life as Mark Bentley headed a Kevin Maher free kick,
from the right flank, straight at the visitors' custodian Russell Hoult.

Bentley – again appearing on the right hand side of midfield – then turned
provider as his curling cross found the head of Shaun Goater whose aerial
effort was smartly stopped by Hoult from eight yards.

The hosts were now beginning to pile on the pressure after enduring a
tense and tentative start. And with 31 minutes on the clock they came agonisingly close to opening the scoring as a low, long-range drive from the lively
Luke Guttridge bounced back off the outside of the left post.

Wayne Gray then dragged a left foot shot wide of the opposite upright following a half-cleared Che Wilson free kick and, moments after a female streak-
er had sped across the pitch, it was the Shrimpers who started the second half
strongly too. Maher – after bring teed up by Gray – shot woefully wide of the
target from 25 yards before the Southend skipper went closer with a powerful
effort which flew just wide of the right post from a similar distance.

The former Tottenham Hotspur trainee then delivered a right-wing cross
for Bentley to head over the cross bar in the 65th minute and, just seconds
later, he wasted an even better chance to score.

This time another intelligent pass from Guttridge saw Bentley presented
with a free shot at goal but, with Roots Hall ready to celebrate, the hard-working winger – who had netted three goals in his previous three games – flashed
a 10-yard shot agonisingly wide of the left post.

Andy Edwards then curled a 20-yard shot tamely over the cross bar from
a short Maher free-kick and, in the 73rd minute, Tilson threw both Eastwood
and Jamal Campbell-Ryce into the action in a double substitution.

It was Forest's replacement striker Gareth Taylor who then forced Flahavan into action though as his screaming 20-yard shot was well held by the former Southampton shot-stopper.

But after surviving that slight scare Blues were soon back on top as the sublime skills of Eastwood began to cause problems for the visitors. After 78 minutes, the forward almost broke the deadlock as he delightfully controlled a through-ball from Edwards and jinked his way past a bemused Wes Morgan, only to fire well wide of the left post with a mis-cued finish.

Campbell-Ryce had also been well positioned inside the area had Eastwood elected to pass. But, with 81 minutes on the clock, he atoned for the error as he fired home what proved to be the only goal of the game.

Maher was again instrumental as his deep left wing cross was headed back across goal by Bentley which, via a slight flick on from Adam Barrett, landed at the feet of Eastwood who duly finished from close range, despite Hoult's best efforts. Eastwood then delivered a left-wing cross for Goater to shoot wide of the target before the final whistle sparked yet more lengthy celebrations from the Shrimpers and their supporters.

Boss Tilson, who collected his manager of the month award before kick-off, must decide whether to recall Eastwood for next weekend's trip to Doncaster Rovers. But while he ponders who will lead the line the Wickford-born chief was delighted to see the striker work his way onto the scoresheet.

'Freddy could have had a hat-trick in the time he was on but I can't complain if he keeps on scoring,' said the former Blues midfielder. 'We dug in again and I thought we played well in the second half. That makes it eight wins in a row and we want to keep it going for as long as possible.'

SOUTHEND: Flahavan, Hunt, Edwards, Barrett, Wilson, Bentley, Guttridge, Maher, Cole (Campbell-Ryce 63), Goater, Gray (Eastwood 73). Subs not used: Griemink, Lawson and Smith.

NOTTINGHAM FOREST: Hoult, Eaden, Breckin, Morgan, Thompson, Southall, Perch, Friio (Bopp 62), Commons, Lester (Weir-Daley 89), Johnson (Taylor 64). Subs not used: Gerrard and Gardner.

Attendance: 10,104.

Saturday, May 6th, 2006
Football League One
SOUTHEND UNITED 1, BRISTOL CITY 0

Super Southend United clinched the League One Championship on a memorable afternoon of action at Roots Hall on Saturday.

Substitute striker Wayne Gray bagged the only goal of the game just three minutes from time to start some wild celebrations which went on long into the night as more than 11,000 supporters danced and sang with delight to create a carnival atmosphere inside the stadium.

Results elsewhere – with fierce Essex rivals Colchester only drawing at Yeovil Town – were enough to guarantee Blues a table-topping finish, but they wanted to finish their stunning season in style and started the stronger of the two sides.

Mark Gower shot wide of the left post after only two minutes before City – who went into the game having lost just one of their last 13 matches – began to work their way into the game. Mark McCammon headed wide of the right post from 14 yards and, in the 14th minute, Blues defender Lewis Hunt did well to race back and volley Richard Keogh's looping aerial effort off the goal-line.

In reply, a stretching Lee Bradbury headed Gower's right wing cross straight at Adriano Basso, but just moments later the visitors almost opened the scoring when the lively David Cotterill sped past Che Wilson on the right flank - only to see his inviting centre flash agonisingly across the face of goal with McCammon unable to convert. Cotterill then volleyed a Bradley Orr cross just wide of the left post from 12 yards but, with 40 minutes on the clock, Blues hit back as Freddy Eastwood beat two defenders on the edge before unleashing a low 20-yard drive which Basso smartly gathered.

But, with play immediately switching back towards the South Stand, City again almost broke the deadlock as David Noble's 25 yard shot was superbly pushed onto the right post by Darryl Flahavan, with the onrushing McCammon embarrassingly failing to convert the resulting rebound from close range as he could only scuff a seven-yard shot with the goal gaping.

After the break, Blues were brighter with Luke Guttridge forcing Basso into action with a low half-volley from 20 yards and, in the 55th minute, Gower wastefully fired wide of the left post after being teed up by Eastwood inside the area.

City again hit back with Adam Barrett blocking Steve Brooker's well struck shot and Flahavan impressively tipping a curling Luke Wilkshire free kick around the left upright.

But Southend, who brought on Mitchell Cole to replace Gower in the 69th minute, continued to push for the winner as they slowly began to pile on the pressure as Guttridge shot just wide of the target from long range. Cole then blazed wildly wide of the left post from 20 yards but, after 77 minutes, his well-struck shot from a similar distance was tipped over the cross-bar by Nathan Abbey – a second half replacement for the injured Basso.

The match was then held up for close to three minutes for the Shrimpers' next change which signalled the end of Shaun Goater's amazing career. The Bermudan left the field to a rapturous reception and was replaced by Gray, who proved to be the match winner.

Just four minutes after his introduction the striker collected a pass from Kevin Maher to fire a deflected 20-yard shot into the bottom left-hand corner of the net to send the Shrimpers supporters wild.

Their cheers were even louder when Maher was presented with the trophy in the centre of the park as the skipper lifted the club's first League title in a quarter of a century to underline their amazing achievement in a fitting end to an unexpected season of success.

'Winning the League at home in front of our own fans is as good as it gets. The players and fans have been fantastic and I feel great as well because everyone knows just how much I love Southend United,' said Blues boss Steve Tilson.

SOUTHEND UNITED: Flahavan; Jupp, Barrett, Hunt and Wilson; Bradbury, Maher, Guttridge (Bentley 83) and Gower (Cole 69); Goater (Gray 83) and Eastwood. Subs. not used: Lawson and Pettefer.

BRISTOL CITY: Basso (Abbey 65); Orr, Carey, Keogh and Woodman; Cotterill, Noble, Skuse and Wilkshire (Brown 75); Brooker and McCammon (Williams 61). Subs. not used: Savage and Wilson.

Referee: Keith Stroud (Hants.)

Attendance: 11,387.

Champions

Football League One		2005-06
Football League Div 4		1980-81
Southern League Div 2	1906-07	1907-08
South Eastern League Div 2		1906-07

Runner-up

Football League Div 3		1990-91
Football League Div 4	1971-72	1977-78
Southern League Div 2		1912-13
United League		1907-08

Third Place

Football League Div 3 (S)	1931-32	1949-50
Football League Div 4	1986-87	1989-90

Fourth Place

Football League Div 3 (S)	1955-56
Football League Two	2004-05
Southern League Div 2	1911-12
United League (S)	1908-09
Football League South (Group 'D')	1939-40
Football League South	1940-41

Cup Winners

Southern Counties Charity Cup	1911-12

Cup Finalists

Football League Trophy	2003-04	2004-05

Cup Semi-finalists

Football League Trophy	2000-01
Anglo - Italian Cup	1993-94

Cup Quarter-finalists

Football League Associate Members' Cup		1990-91
Football League Div 3 (S) Cup		1935-36
Southern Counties Charity Cup	1909-10	1910-11

Best Home Wins   (nine goals or more)

13-0	v Chesham Generals	SE Lge 2	1906-07
12-0	v Royal Engineers	Southern Lge 2	1906-07
10-1	v Golders Green	FA Cup 1	1934-35
10-1	v Brentwood Town	FA Cup 2	1968-69
10-1	v Aldershot	FL AMC Prelim	1990-91
9-0	v King's Lynn	FA Cup 1	1968-69
9-2	v Newport	FL 3 (S)	1936-37
9-3	v Clapton Orient	S Regional Div	1940-41

Best Away Wins   (eight goals or more)

9-0	v Chesham Town	Southern Lge 2	1911-12
9-2	v Barnet	FA Cup 2	1946-47
8-0	v Chesham Generals	SE Lge 2	1906-07
8-0	v Cwm Albion	Southern Lge 2	1911-12

Highest Scoring Draw

4-4	A	v Luton	FL 3 (S)	1923-24
4-4	H	v Bournemouth	FL 3 (S)	1928-29
4-4	A	v Mansfield	FL 3 (S)	1931-32
4-4	A	v Tottenham	FA Cup 3	1935-36
4-4	H	v Exeter	FL 3 (S)	1936-37
4-4	H	v Northampton	FA Cup 2	1986-87
4-4	H	v York	FL 2	1997-98

Worst Home Defeats   (six goals or more)

1-7	v Arsenal	S Regional Div	1940-41
0-6	v West Ham	Southern Lge 1	1910-11
1-6	v Birmingham City	FA Cup 4	1956-57
2-6	v Portsmouth	Southern Lge 1	1908-09

Worst Away Defeats   (nine goals or more)

0-11	v West Ham	S Regional Div	1940-41
1-11	v Northampton	Southern Lge 1	1909-10
0-9	v Brighton reserves	SE Lge 1	1911-12
1-9	v Brighton	FL 3	1965-66

SEASON BY SEASON LEAGUE RESULTS: 1906-07 to 2005-06

1906-07
Southern League Div 2

	H	A
Fulham II	3-0	1-1
Hastings	2-0	2-1
Portsmouth II	4-1	2-0
Reading II	6-2	0-2
Royal Engineers	12-0	5-1
Salisbury City	4-2	1-0
Southampton II	1-0	2-4
Southern United		7-0
Swindon II	0-1	0-0
Tunbridge WR	2-1	2-2
West Ham II	2-2	2-1
Wycombe	3-0	2-2

1906-07
South Eastern League Div 2

	H	A
Chesham Gen	13-0	8-0
Chesham Town	4-0	5-0
Clapton Orient II	2-0	5-1
Depot Batt RE	4-0	5-0
Eastbourne	5-0	5-1
Hastings	2-0	3-0
Redhill	7-0	5-1
Tunbridge Wells	5-0	5-1
Tunbridge WR	2-1	0-1
W Hampstead	5-1	

1907-08
Southern League Div 2

	H	A
Brighton II	3-1	3-2
Croydon Com	2-0	3-0
Hastings	2-1	2-0
Portsmouth II	1-3	0-0
Salisbury	3-2	1-1
Southampton II	7-0	2-1
Swindon II	2-0	5-1
Tunbridge WR	0-1	2-2
Wycombe	5-0	4-1

1907-08
South Eastern League Div 1

	H	A
Chelsea II	0-1	1-2
Clapton Orient II	2-1	0-1
Croydon Com	2-0	1-7
Fulham II	5-0	1-2
Hastings	0-0	0-5
Hitchin	2-1	1-1
Leyton II	4-1	3-2
Luton II	1-1	2-1
Maidstone	2-1	0-4
Norwich II	2-1	2-4
QPR II	4-2	1-2
Sittingbourne	5-4	1-1
Tottenham II	2-1	1-3
Tunbridge WR	4-0	1-1
Watford II	2-0	2-4
West Ham II	5-1	1-0
W' Arsenal II	3-0	1-2

1907-08 United League

	H	A
Brentford	0-0	2-5
Croydon Com	4-0	2-5
Hastings	3-2	2-0
New Brompton	2-2	1-2

1908-09
Southern League Div 1

	H	A
Brentford	1-0	1-4
Brighton	0-2	0-2
Bristol Rovers	2-1	0-1
Coventry	4-0	5-2
Crystal Palace	1-0	3-1
Exeter	0-0	1-2
Leyton	0-0	0-0
Luton	2-0	0-3
Millwall	3-0	1-3
New Brompton	1-0	0-1
Northampton	2-2	1-2
Norwich	3-0	0-2
Plymouth	2-1	1-2
Portsmouth	2-6	0-2
QPR	0-0	1-2
Reading	0-0	0-0
Southampton	2-0	1-1
Swindon	6-2	2-4
Watford	2-0	2-2
West Ham	0-0	0-4

1908-09
United League (South)

	H	A
Brentford	4-3	1-1
Croydon Com	5-0	1-2
Gravesend	*	*
Hastings	1-1	1-2
New Brompton	2-2	0-7

* Gravesend resigned mid-season; record expunged

1909-10
Southern League Div 1

	H	A
Brentford	0-3	1-4
Brighton	2-0	1-1
Bristol Rovers	0-0	0-2
Coventry	0-1	2-0
Croydon Com	3-1	2-3
Crystal Palace	3-0	0-6
Exeter	2-0	1-3
Leyton	1-0	3-7
Luton	4-1	3-3
Millwall	1-0	2-1
New Brompton	3-0	0-5
Northampton	1-2	1-11
Norwich	2-5	0-3
Plymouth	0-0	0-3
Portsmouth	0-0	1-1
QPR	0-1	2-2
Reading	1-0	2-3
Southampton	2-0	2-6
Swindon	1-1	1-6
Watford	0-1	1-3
West Ham	0-1	0-0

1910-11
Southern League Div 1

	H	A
Brentford	0-2	1-3
Brighton	0-1	0-4
Bristol Rovers	1-1	0-1
Coventry	4-1	1-5
Crystal Palace	0-0	0-0
Exeter	1-2	0-1
Leyton	1-1	1-1
Luton	1-4	1-3
Millwall	7-0	1-3
New Brompton	2-2	2-1
Northampton	2-0	0-0
Norwich	1-0	1-0
Plymouth	3-2	1-0
Portsmouth	2-0	2-3
QPR	1-2	1-1
Southampton	0-1	4-2
Swindon	0-1	0-4
Watford	2-0	1-2
West Ham	0-6	3-3

1911-12
Southern League Div 2

	H	A
Aberdare	7-1	2-0
Cardiff	0-1	2-0
Chesham Town	7-0	9-0
Croydon Com	3-0	2-0
Cwm Albion	7-0	8-0
Kettering	5-0	1-3
Mardy	4-0	2-3
Merthyr Town	0-1	0-5
Pontypridd	1-0	0-3
Portsmouth	0-0	0-2
Ton Pentre	4-0	1-2
Treharris	2-0	3-1
Walsall	2-0	1-2

1911-12
South Eastern League Div 1

	H	A
Brighton II	1-1	0-9
Bristol City II	2-0	2-3
Chelsea II	1-2	3-2
Clapton Orient II	1-1	0-2
Coventry II	1-0	1-3
Croydon Com	3-3	0-3
Fulham II	1-0	1-5
Leyton II	2-1	1-0
Luton II	6-0	1-3
Northampton II	3-0	1-3
Norwich II	2-1	1-0
Peterborough C	1-2	0-8
Reading II	3-0	0-4
Swindon II	2-0	1-0
Tottenham II	2-1	0-2
Tunbridge WR	7-4	1-3
Watford II	1-1	0-3
West Ham II	2-2	2-2
Wlwch Arsenal II	3-0	2-3

1912-13
Southern League Div 2

	H	A
Aberdare	1-0	2-1
Cardiff	1-1	0-1
Croydon Com	3-1	1-1
Llanelly	2-2	1-4
Luton	1-1	3-4
Mardy	2-0	3-1
Mid-Rhondda	1-0	1-1
Newport	1-0	2-0
Pontypridd	2-1	1-0
Swansea	3-1	0-1
Ton Pentre	7-2	2-0
Treharris	3-0	0-0

1912-13 Southern Alliance

	H	A
Brentford	2-0	0-4
Brighton	0-1	0-4
Cardiff	1-0	1-1
Croydon Com	1-1	0-0
Luton	5-1	0-4
Millwall	4-3	1-5
Portsmouth	3-0	0-4
Southampton	0-3	1-1

1913-14
Southern League Div 1

	H	A
Brighton	0-1	1-1
Bristol Rovers	2-2	0-0
Cardiff	2-1	0-3
Coventry	1-1	0-3
Crystal Palace	3-3	0-0

Exeter	1-0	0-0
Gillingham	2-3	2-4
Merthyr Town	2-2	0-1
Millwall	1-3	1-2
Northampton	1-3	0-2
Norwich	2-2	0-6
Plymouth	2-1	1-0
Portsmouth	3-2	2-4
QPR	1-2	0-0
Reading	2-1	0-2
Southampton	0-0	2-4
Swindon	2-0	0-5
Watford	1-0	2-1
West Ham	1-1	1-0

1913-14 Southern Alliance

	H	A
Brentford	1-1	0-2
Brighton	2-4	1-3
Cardiff	1-1	1-3
Croydon Com	1-0	0-3
Luton	1-0	1-7
Newport	2-0	0-3
Portsmouth	3-1	0-2
Southampton	1-1	0-4

1914-15
Southern League Div 1

	H	A
Brighton	2-2	0-1
Bristol Rovers	2-0	1-4
Cardiff	2-1	0-3
Croydon Com	2-0	1-1
Crystal Palace	2-3	1-1
Exeter	0-2	1-7
Gillingham	1-1	0-1
Luton	1-0	4-3
Millwall	0-0	4-1
Northampton	1-2	0-1
Norwich	4-1	1-1
Plymouth	3-1	0-1
Portsmouth	0-2	0-1
QPR	1-1	2-4
Reading	0-2	0-3
Southampton	4-0	0-2
Swindon	2-1	0-4
Watford	0-0	1-2
West Ham	0-1	1-3

1919-20
Southern League Div 1

	H	A
Brentford	3-1	0-2
Brighton	0-0	0-3
Bristol Rovers	1-1	1-4
Cardiff	1-1	0-1
Crystal Palace	1-1	0-0
Exeter	2-0	0-3
Gillingham	0-1	1-0
Luton	3-0	1-1
Merthyr Town	2-1	1-1

Millwall	1-0	1-2
Newport	3-0	0-0
Northampton	0-0	1-2
Norwich	2-1	1-1
Plymouth	1-0	0-0
Portsmouth	0-2	1-0
QPR	2-2	2-2
Reading	2-2	0-0
Southampton	2-1	0-4
Swansea	2-2	1-0
Swindon	0-1	2-3
Watford	4-1	1-1

1920-21
Football League Div 3 (S)

	H	A
Brentford	4-1	2-2
Brighton	2-0	0-1
Bristol Rovers	1-0	1-2
Crystal Palace	0-2	3-2
Exeter	0-0	0-0
Gillingham	1-0	1-1
Grimsby	3-1	0-1
Luton	1-1	0-4
Merthyr Town	0-1	0-2
Millwall	1-2	2-4
Newport	2-1	1-1
Northampton	1-2	0-1
Norwich	3-1	1-3
Plymouth	2-1	0-0
Portsmouth	2-1	0-3
QPR	1-0	0-2
Reading	1-0	1-1
Southampton	1-0	0-3
Swansea	1-2	0-2
Swindon	1-3	0-3
Watford	4-1	0-3

1921-22
Football League Div 3 (S)

	H	A
Aberdare	3-2	1-1
Brentford	1-1	0-1
Brighton	1-2	0-0
Bristol Rovers	3-0	0-1
Charlton	1-1	0-4
Exeter	0-1	1-4
Gillingham	2-0	0-1
Luton	0-1	0-3
Merthyr Town	2-1	2-2
Millwall	1-1	0-1
Newport	0-1	1-2
Northampton	1-1	2-0
Norwich	0-1	1-1
Plymouth	1-0	0-4
Portsmouth	1-2	0-6
QPR	1-2	0-1
Reading	2-0	0-4
Southampton	0-0	0-5
Swansea	1-0	1-1
Swindon	1-2	1-6
Watford	1-4	1-4

1922-23
Football League Div 3 (S)

	H	A
Aberdare	4-0	1-1
Brentford	1-2	0-0
Brighton	0-0	1-0
Bristol City	0-3	0-5
Bristol Rovers	0-0	0-2
Charlton	0-0	1-5
Exeter	5-0	1-2
Gillingham	1-1	0-1
Luton	1-3	0-2
Merthyr Town	1-1	1-2
Millwall	4-0	1-1
Newport	3-1	2-0
Northampton	1-2	2-5
Norwich	3-1	1-2
Plymouth	2-1	1-1
Portsmouth	0-0	0-0
QPR	2-0	0-0
Reading	3-1	1-1
Swansea	0-1	0-1
Swindon	2-0	0-3
Watford	2-1	1-1

1923-24
Football League Div 3 (S)

	H	A
Aberdare	1-1	2-5
Bournemouth	1-1	1-0
Brentford	3-1	1-3
Brighton	1-0	0-2
Bristol Rovers	1-0	1-3
Charlton	2-2	1-4
Exeter	0-0	0-2
Gillingham	3-2	2-3
Luton	1-1	4-4
Merthyr Town	3-1	2-3
Millwall	0-0	0-0
Newport	2-0	0-5
Northampton	5-1	0-8
Norwich	3-1	1-3
Plymouth	0-2	1-7
Portsmouth	0-1	0-3
QPR	4-2	0-0
Reading	2-1	0-1
Swansea	0-0	1-2
Swindon	0-2	0-3
Watford	3-0	1-4

1924-25
Football League Div 3 (S)

	H	A
Aberdare	2-1	0-3
Bournemouth	3-0	0-1
Brentford	6-1	2-2
Brighton	2-0	1-2
Bristol City	2-0	0-5
Bristol Rovers	2-1	3-1
Charlton	0-3	0-0
Exeter	3-0	1-0

Gillingham	4-0	1-3
Luton	2-1	0-4
Merthyr Town	2-1	0-1
Millwall	1-0	0-2
Newport	0-1	1-1
Northampton	0-1	1-0
Norwich	0-1	1-0
Plymouth	0-3	0-6
QPR	1-0	1-3
Reading	3-0	2-2
Swansea	1-0	0-4
Swindon	0-0	0-3
Watford	0-4	3-0

1925-26
Football League Div 3 (S)

	H	A
Aberdare	0-1	0-2
Bournemouth	3-0	2-1
Brentford	3-1	3-1
Brighton	4-0	2-3
Bristol City	1-2	4-1
Bristol Rovers	3-1	0-2
Charlton	1-2	0-5
Crystal Palace	5-1	0-3
Exeter	3-1	1-0
Gillingham	1-1	1-3
Luton	2-0	0-2
Merthyr Town	5-1	1-5
Millwall	0-2	1-8
Newport	4-1	0-1
Northampton	6-1	3-3
Norwich	0-1	2-1
Plymouth	2-0	2-6
QPR	2-1	2-2
Reading	2-2	0-1
Swindon	3-0	0-2
Watford	0-1	4-1

1926-27
Football League Div 3 (S)

	H	A
Aberdare	5-1	0-1
Bournemouth	0-3	0-3
Brentford	3-1	1-3
Brighton	0-1	1-2
Bristol City	0-1	1-5
Bristol Rovers	2-1	1-5
Charlton	5-0	0-1
Coventry	3-1	1-1
Crystal Palace	3-1	3-5
Exeter	1-2	0-2
Gillingham	1-0	3-2
Luton	2-1	0-0
Merthyr Town	3-1	1-0
Millwall	1-1	0-2
Newport	5-0	0-3
Northampton	2-0	1-2
Norwich	3-3	1-1
Plymouth	1-2	1-2
QPR	0-3	2-3
Swindon	2-2	1-5

	H	A
Watford	2-0	2-4

1927-28
Football League Div 3 (S)

	H	A
Bournemouth	3-0	3-2
Brentford	3-2	2-2
Brighton	0-1	0-1
Bristol Rovers	2-1	3-1
Charlton	1-2	2-1
Coventry	3-2	1-6
Crystal Palace	6-1	1-4
Exeter	1-2	2-3
Gillingham	1-2	0-1
Luton	1-0	0-0
Merthyr Town	2-1	3-2
Millwall	0-1	1-5
Newport	5-1	2-3
Northampton	2-0	1-2
Norwich	1-1	1-2
Plymouth	3-0	2-3
QPR	7-0	2-3
Swindon	1-1	1-0
Torquay	1-0	3-3
Walsall	2-1	1-0
Watford	3-0	1-1

1928-29
Football League Div 3 (S)

	H	A
Bournemouth	4-4	2-2
Brentford	1-1	0-1
Brighton	1-1	1-2
Bristol Rovers	1-0	2-3
Charlton	1-3	2-3
Coventry	0-0	1-1
Crystal Palace	3-0	2-3
Exeter	1-0	2-1
Fulham	0-1	4-2
Gillingham	2-0	2-0
Luton	5-0	2-4
Merthyr Town	5-1	1-2
Newport	4-2	2-2
Northampton	2-2	3-2
Norwich	5-3	5-2
Plymouth	1-1	1-1
QPR	0-3	1-3
Swindon	1-1	1-3
Torquay	3-0	1-4
Walsall	3-1	1-4
Watford	1-3	1-4

1929-30
Football League Div 3 (S)

	H	A
Bournemouth	4-1	0-0
Brentford	2-0	1-2
Brighton	0-0	0-1
Bristol Rovers	6-0	2-4
Clapton Orient	4-1	1-1
Coventry	1-2	1-5
Crystal Palace	3-2	2-1
Exeter	1-0	1-3
Fulham	1-2	2-2
Gillingham	0-0	0-1
Luton	1-1	3-0
Merthyr Town	6-0	2-2
Newport	2-1	0-0
Northampton	1-2	1-5
Norwich	1-1	1-1
Plymouth	1-1	0-1
QPR	1-0	5-2
Swindon	3-1	1-5
Torquay	1-1	1-1
Walsall	1-0	3-1
Watford	1-3	1-2

1930-31
Football League Div 3 (S)

	H	A
Bournemouth	4-0	0-0
Brentford	0-1	1-3
Brighton	0-2	2-1
Bristol Rovers	4-0	3-2
Clapton Orient	2-0	1-3
Coventry	2-0	0-0
Crystal Palace	2-4	1-3
Exeter	5-1	1-1
Fulham	2-4	0-1
Gillingham	3-2	0-1
Luton	0-2	1-2
Newport	6-2	1-3
Northampton	2-1	0-4
Norwich	2-0	1-0
Notts County	2-1	1-1
QPR	2-0	2-0
Swindon	5-3	1-1
Thames	1-0	0-3
Torquay	6-3	1-3
Walsall	2-0	3-1
Watford	1-0	3-1

1931-32
Football League Div 3 (S)

	H	A
Bournemouth	1-3	0-0
Brentford	1-0	3-2
Brighton	2-0	2-1
Bristol Rovers	4-1	0-0
Cardiff	1-1	3-2
Clapton Orient	1-3	4-2
Coventry	4-0	2-0
Crystal Palace	1-0	2-3
Exeter	0-1	0-3
Fulham	4-1	1-1
Gillingham	2-0	0-4
Luton	1-1	3-1
Mansfield	5-2	4-4
Northampton	0-1	2-1
Norwich	2-0	1-1
QPR	0-0	1-2
Reading	1-1	1-3
Swindon	3-0	2-1
Thames	1-1	3-1
Torquay	4-2	1-2
Watford	3-0	1-1

1932-33
Football League Div 3 (S)

	H	A
Aldershot	5-1	2-1
Bournemouth	2-1	0-4
Brentford	0-1	1-3
Brighton	2-1	2-1
Bristol City	3-1	1-5
Bristol Rovers	2-2	1-3
Cardiff	2-2	0-2
Clapton Orient	3-3	0-0
Coventry	1-3	3-2
Crystal Palace	1-2	1-4
Exeter	1-2	0-3
Gillingham	2-2	2-3
Luton	2-1	3-3
Newport	3-0	3-1
Northampton	1-0	0-0
Norwich	2-1	0-1
QPR	0-1	1-6
Reading	3-1	1-1
Swindon	0-0	2-2
Torquay	2-1	1-8
Watford	2-1	2-2

1933-34
Football League Div 3 (S)

	H	A
Aldershot	1-0	0-2
Bournemouth	1-2	4-1
Brighton	0-0	0-1
Bristol City	3-0	1-5
Bristol Rovers	2-2	1-3
Cardiff	1-1	1-1
Charlton	1-0	3-1
Clapton Orient	2-1	2-5
Coventry	2-1	0-2
Crystal Palace	0-4	1-1
Exeter	3-1	0-2
Gillingham	1-2	0-0
Luton	0-1	1-3
Newport	3-5	0-3
Northampton	2-0	0-2
Norwich	0-0	0-0
QPR	0-2	0-4
Reading	2-2	0-5
Swindon	4-1	4-1
Torquay	3-1	0-3
Watford	1-1	1-2

1934-35
Football League Div 3 (S)

	H	A
Aldershot	2-1	2-3
Bournemouth	0-0	1-2
Brighton	3-2	2-2
Bristol City	6-0	0-2
Bristol Rovers	5-1	1-2
Cardiff	2-1	0-2
Charlton	0-3	0-3
Clapton Orient	0-2	0-3
Coventry	1-1	3-6
Crystal Palace	1-4	0-1
Exeter	1-2	3-4
Gillingham	0-0	2-2
Luton	3-3	1-1
Millwall	2-1	0-1
Newport	0-1	5-0
Northampton	2-1	1-1
QPR	2-0	1-1
Reading	6-1	2-3
Swindon	2-0	0-5
Torquay	2-3	0-2
Watford	0-2	1-3

1935-36
Football League Div 3 (S)

	H	A
Aldershot	2-2	1-1
Bournemouth	3-3	1-2
Brighton	0-0	3-1
Bristol City	0-1	1-2
Bristol Rovers	1-1	2-3
Cardiff	3-1	1-1
Clapton Orient	2-1	0-3
Coventry	0-0	0-3
Crystal Palace	7-1	0-3
Exeter	4-0	0-1
Gillingham	4-2	1-2
Luton	0-1	2-1
Millwall	6-0	2-1
Newport	1-2	1-3
Northampton	0-1	0-2
Notts County	0-0	2-1
QPR	0-1	1-2
Reading	1-2	1-2
Swindon	1-0	3-1
Torquay	2-1	1-1
Watford	1-1	0-5

1936-37
Football League Div 3 (S)

	H	A
Aldershot	2-2	2-1
Bournemouth	0-0	0-1
Brighton	2-1	0-1
Bristol City	3-0	1-0
Bristol Rovers	2-3	2-1
Cardiff	8-1	1-1
Clapton Orient	0-0	0-3
Crystal Palace	2-1	1-1
Exeter	4-4	2-2
Gillingham	0-2	0-1
Luton	3-0	0-1
Millwall	0-0	2-1
Newport	9-2	2-6
Northampton	2-0	3-4
Notts County	2-3	1-2
QPR	3-2	2-7

Reading	1-1	3-2
Swindon	2-0	0-4
Torquay	0-0	4-1
Walsall	3-0	0-3
Watford	1-1	3-1

1937-38
Football League Div 3 (S)

	H	A
Aldershot	4-1	0-1
Bournemouth	1-0	1-7
Brighton	2-1	1-3
Bristol City	5-0	2-4
Bristol Rovers	1-1	1-2
Cardiff	3-1	0-5
Clapton Orient	1-2	1-1
Crystal Palace	2-2	1-2
Exeter	1-1	1-1
Gillingham	2-0	1-2
Mansfield	0-1	2-2
Millwall	1-2	0-1
Newport	0-2	0-2
Northampton	4-2	2-0
Notts County	2-1	2-0
QPR	2-1	0-1
Reading	4-2	2-3
Swindon	0-0	1-1
Torquay	5-1	3-3
Walsall	1-0	5-1
Watford	2-2	1-3

1938-39
Football League Div 3 (S)

	H	A
Aldershot	2-1	0-1
Bournemouth	2-2	4-0
Brighton	1-1	0-3
Bristol City	2-0	0-1
Bristol Rovers	3-2	1-4
Cardiff	2-0	0-1
Clapton Orient	1-0	0-5
Crystal Palace	3-1	3-4
Exeter	0-1	3-3
Ipswich	0-0	2-4
Mansfield	2-0	1-3
Newport	5-0	0-3
Northampton	2-0	2-2
Notts County	1-0	1-4
Port Vale	0-0	2-2
QPR	2-1	1-1
Reading	2-0	0-3
Swindon	2-3	1-2
Torquay	1-1	0-2
Walsall	2-0	2-0
Watford	3-0	0-3

1939-40
Football League Div 3 (S)

	H	A
Clapton Orient		0-0
Reading		0-1

Walsall	3-2
Season abandoned	
due to hostilities	

1939-40 Football League
South Division (Group 'A')

	H	A
Arsenal	0-5	1-5
Charlton	0-2	1-8
Clapton Orient	7-0	1-5
Crystal Palace	3-1	2-4
Millwall	1-2	1-6
Norwich	2-4	2-3
Tottenham	1-2	4-2
Watford	1-2	0-4
West Ham	3-2	0-4

1939-40 Football League
South Division (Group 'D')

	H	A
Aldershot	2-2	0-1
Bournemouth	2-1	1-6
Brighton	8-2	3-1
Clapton Orient	3-0	1-5
Crystal Palace	3-0	2-5
Norwich	3-0	3-1
QPR	0-1	1-3
Reading	4-2	1-1
Watford	2-2	2-4

1940-41 Football League
South Regional Division

	H	A
Arsenal	1-7	0-7
Clapton Orient	9-3	2-1
Crystal Palace		2-1
and		0-7
Fulham		2-8
Norwich	3-0	4-8
and	3-3	0-3
Portsmouth		0-0
Tottenham		3-2
Watford	1-3	1-1
West Ham	3-1	0-11

1940-41 Football League
South Division

	H	A
Bournemouth		0-3
Brighton	2-0	2-2
Luton	4-2	
Norwich	3-2	3-5
Portsmouth	2-1	3-1
Southampton	6-4	
and		1-4
Watford	2-3	2-8

1945-46 Football League
Div 3 (S) (North of Thames)

	H	A
Clapton Orient	1-1	2-2
Ipswich	2-0	1-3
Mansfield	1-1	2-2
Northampton	0-1	2-6
Norwich	1-4	1-6
Notts County	7-3	1-4
Port Vale	2-0	1-1
QPR	1-2	1-4
Walsall	0-1	0-6
Watford	6-2	1-0

1946-47
Football League Div 3 (S)

	H	A
Aldershot	2-1	0-0
Bournemouth	2-2	1-3
Brighton	0-0	1-2
Bristol City	4-1	0-2
Bristol Rovers	2-3	3-1
Cardiff	0-2	1-3
Crystal Palace	2-0	3-0
Exeter	2-2	5-1
Ipswich	1-1	0-1
Leyton Orient	0-0	1-1
Mansfield	1-1	1-0
Northampton	4-0	3-2
Norwich	3-0	5-1
Notts County	3-0	2-0
Port Vale	1-1	1-5
QPR	1-3	0-1
Reading	0-2	2-7
Swindon	2-0	1-2
Torquay	0-2	1-0
Walsall	3-1	2-2
Watford	5-0	0-4

1947-48
Football League Div 3 (S)

	H	A
Aldershot	4-0	1-1
Bournemouth	0-2	1-0
Brighton	2-2	0-1
Bristol City	4-0	0-6
Bristol Rovers	1-0	2-1
Crystal Palace	2-1	0-0
Exeter	2-0	0-0
Ipswich	3-2	0-4
Leyton Orient	2-1	0-2
Newport	1-0	5-1
Northampton	3-1	0-2
Norwich	0-0	0-1
Notts County	1-2	1-2
Port Vale	1-1	1-2
QPR	0-0	2-3
Reading	1-1	3-1
Swansea	1-1	0-3
Swindon	1-0	0-0
Torquay	1-0	1-4

Walsall	1-1	0-6
Watford	1-1	2-2

1948-49
Football League Div 3 (S)

	H	A
Aldershot	1-0	0-1
Bournemouth	0-0	2-3
Brighton	0-0	0-1
Bristol City	1-0	1-2
Bristol Rovers	0-1	0-0
Crystal Palace	0-1	1-2
Exeter	0-0	0-0
Ipswich	1-1	3-1
Leyton Orient	2-2	0-2
Millwall	2-1	0-1
Newport	0-1	2-4
Northampton	0-1	2-2
Norwich	2-2	0-3
Notts County	3-2	0-0
Port Vale	0-0	2-0
Reading	0-0	1-2
Swansea	0-0	2-2
Swindon	3-4	1-2
Torquay	1-1	3-0
Walsall	2-0	3-0
Watford	0-1	0-0

1949-50
Football League Div 3 (S)

	H	A
Aldershot	3-0	1-1
Bournemouth	1-0	0-3
Brighton	3-2	1-2
Bristol City	2-0	1-1
Bristol Rovers	3-1	1-1
Crystal Palace	0-0	1-2
Exeter	1-0	1-1
Ipswich	2-2	3-1
Leyton Orient	2-0	2-2
Millwall	3-0	2-1
Newport	6-0	1-2
Northampton	1-2	0-2
Norwich	1-0	0-0
Nottingham For	2-3	2-1
Notts County	2-0	0-2
Port Vale	1-0	0-0
Reading	3-2	0-5
Swindon	2-0	2-2
Torquay	2-0	4-2
Walsall	2-2	1-1
Watford	1-1	0-1

1950-51
Football League Div 3 (S)

	H	A
Aldershot	4-2	2-2
Bournemouth	6-1	1-3
Brighton	3-1	1-2
Bristol City	1-1	3-0
Bristol Rovers	1-1	1-4

Colchester	4-2	3-1
Crystal Palace	5-2	2-0
Exeter	5-1	0-1
Gillingham	4-0	0-0
Ipswich	1-0	0-1
Leyton Orient	0-1	1-1
Millwall	0-3	1-1
Newport	3-0	1-6
Northampton	3-0	1-1
Norwich	0-2	0-3
Nottingham For	3-2	0-3
Plymouth	1-0	0-2
Port Vale	1-1	1-3
Reading	3-3	2-0
Swindon	8-2	1-4
Torquay	3-0	2-2
Walsall	0-1	2-1
Watford	5-1	3-1

1951-52
Football League Div 3 (S)

	H	A
Aldershot	7-1	2-2
Bournemouth	1-0	1-2
Brighton	2-0	0-5
Bristol City	5-1	0-6
Bristol Rovers	2-1	0-2
Colchester	3-2	0-1
Crystal Palace	4-0	0-1
Exeter	0-0	2-2
Gillingham	3-1	0-2
Ipswich	5-0	1-4
Leyton Orient	1-0	4-1
Millwall	0-1	0-2
Newport	2-1	0-3
Northampton	2-0	3-4
Norwich	2-1	0-1
Plymouth	1-1	0-2
Port Vale	0-0	0-0
Reading	2-0	2-5
Shrewsbury	2-2	1-1
Swindon	2-2	0-1
Torquay	2-2	3-1
Walsall	3-0	0-2
Watford	5-1	0-0

1952-53
Football League Div 3 (S)

	H	A
Aldershot	1-1	1-1
Bournemouth	0-0	1-5
Brighton	1-2	2-2
Bristol City	0-4	0-5
Bristol Rovers	2-1	1-2
Colchester	4-0	3-3
Coventry	1-0	1-2
Crystal Palace	2-2	0-0
Exeter	1-1	2-0
Gillingham	3-1	1-1
Ipswich	2-0	0-0
Leyton Orient	1-0	0-3
Millwall	2-1	1-4

Newport	1-0	1-0
Northampton	3-1	3-4
Norwich	1-2	1-3
QPR	2-0	2-3
Reading	3-1	0-1
Shrewsbury	2-2	1-7
Swindon	3-0	3-1
Torquay	3-1	2-4
Walsall	2-1	1-1
Watford	1-0	1-1

1953-54
Football League Div 3 (S)

	H	A
Aldershot	2-1	0-4
Bournemouth	2-1	1-0
Brighton	2-0	2-3
Bristol City	0-1	1-4
Colchester	3-0	1-0
Coventry	2-2	0-1
Crystal Palace	1-2	2-4
Exeter	0-1	1-1
Gillingham	1-1	1-3
Ipswich	3-1	1-1
Leyton Orient	2-1	1-1
Millwall	1-2	1-2
Newport	0-1	2-3
Northampton	2-0	0-5
Norwich	5-2	0-1
QPR	4-1	0-1
Reading	1-2	0-2
Shrewsbury	3-0	1-2
Southampton	2-1	5-3
Swindon	3-1	0-3
Torquay	1-0	1-1
Walsall	3-1	0-2
Watford	3-0	2-2

1954-55
Football League Div 3 (S)

	H	A
Aldershot	0-1	0-1
Bournemouth	2-2	1-2
Brentford	3-2	2-2
Brighton	4-0	1-2
Bristol City	3-2	2-3
Colchester	4-2	0-2
Coventry	1-0	4-1
Crystal Palace	3-2	2-2
Exeter	0-0	1-2
Gillingham	3-1	1-1
Leyton Orient	1-2	1-5
Millwall	1-0	4-1
Newport	1-1	2-3
Northampton	4-1	2-6
Norwich	4-1	3-3
QPR	2-2	1-1
Reading	0-0	1-1
Shrewsbury	4-1	3-2
Southampton	0-1	0-3
Swindon	4-1	1-0
Torquay	1-2	1-4

Walsall	2-1	1-4
Watford	1-3	1-1

1955-56
Football League Div 3 (S)

	H	A
Aldershot	3-2	3-3
Bournemouth	4-1	1-4
Brentford	2-2	1-2
Brighton	1-2	0-4
Colchester	4-0	6-3
Coventry	3-0	0-0
Crystal Palace	4-3	2-1
Exeter	6-0	1-0
Gillingham	2-2	3-2
Ipswich	2-3	0-3
Leyton Orient	0-0	0-3
Millwall	3-1	0-5
Newport	4-1	0-2
Northampton	2-0	1-1
Norwich	3-1	2-7
QPR	5-1	2-1
Reading	1-0	1-4
Shrewsbury	1-0	1-1
Southampton	2-1	0-0
Swindon	0-0	1-1
Torquay	2-3	2-2
Walsall	3-2	1-3
Watford	1-0	2-3

1956-57
Football League Div 3 (S)

	H	A
Aldershot	2-4	3-5
Bournemouth	2-1	1-1
Brentford	1-0	2-3
Brighton	3-1	1-1
Colchester	3-2	2-3
Coventry	1-2	0-2
Crystal Palace	1-1	0-2
Exeter	2-0	1-6
Gillingham	5-0	2-0
Ipswich	2-0	3-3
Millwall	1-0	0-0
Newport	3-3	1-2
Northampton	0-1	2-2
Norwich	0-0	2-1
Plymouth	0-1	0-0
QPR	3-0	0-3
Reading	4-0	2-3
Shrewsbury	1-2	0-0
Southampton	1-2	2-1
Swindon	1-0	2-3
Torquay	2-0	3-3
Walsall	2-0	1-0
Watford	2-0	1-1

1957-58
Football League Div 3 (S)

	H	A
Aldershot	1-2	2-0

Bournemouth	2-0	1-2
Brentford	0-0	2-4
Brighton	0-2	1-3
Colchester	2-3	0-1
Coventry	5-1	0-1
Crystal Palace	1-1	0-2
Exeter	2-0	5-0
Gillingham	2-0	0-2
Millwall	2-0	2-1
Newport	1-1	0-1
Northampton	6-3	3-1
Norwich	5-2	2-0
Plymouth	2-1	3-2
Port Vale	1-1	3-1
QPR	6-0	1-1
Reading	2-1	1-1
Shrewsbury	5-1	1-1
Southampton	3-2	2-2
Swindon	2-3	1-2
Torquay	0-0	2-2
Walsall	4-1	1-1
Watford	2-1	1-1

1958-59
Football League Div 3

	H	A
Accrington	4-2	0-3
Bournemouth	2-0	4-1
Bradford City	1-1	1-6
Brentford	2-0	1-6
Bury	1-0	3-2
Chesterfield	2-5	0-4
Colchester	1-1	1-0
Doncaster	5-0	1-2
Halifax	3-2	0-1
Hull	1-1	2-3
Mansfield	5-1	4-1
Newport	1-0	1-3
Norwich	1-0	0-4
Notts County	5-2	4-1
Plymouth	0-0	1-3
QPR	4-0	3-1
Reading	2-2	0-3
Rochdale	3-1	1-1
Southampton	1-1	2-3
Stockport	3-1	1-0
Swindon	0-2	1-2
Tranmere	1-3	1-1
Wrexham	4-1	1-3

1959-60
Football League Div 3

	H	A
Accrington	6-1	4-0
Barnsley	2-2	1-4
Bournemouth	3-0	0-3
Bradford City	2-1	1-3
Brentford	2-0	1-3
Bury	0-4	0-3
Chesterfield	1-2	0-1
Colchester	1-0	3-2
Coventry	1-0	0-2

Team	H	A
Grimsby	3-0	1-1
Halifax	3-0	1-2
Mansfield	0-2	1-1
Newport	3-2	1-1
Norwich	1-0	3-4
Port Vale	2-1	1-3
QPR	3-2	0-0
Reading	2-0	1-4
Shrewsbury	2-1	3-1
Southampton	2-4	1-3
Swindon	1-3	0-2
Tranmere	7-1	0-1
Wrexham	1-1	1-3
York	1-1	3-2

1960-61
Football League Div 3

Team	H	A
Barnsley	2-0	1-2
Bournemouth	0-0	2-3
Bradford City	0-0	1-2
Brentford	1-1	1-1
Bristol City	1-0	0-2
Bury	0-3	0-2
Chesterfield	1-1	3-0
Colchester	2-1	0-2
Coventry	4-1	0-3
Grimsby	1-1	0-1
Halifax	2-2	2-6
Hull	3-1	1-0
Newport	4-2	2-1
Notts County	3-1	2-1
Port Vale	2-1	0-4
QPR	0-0	1-2
Reading	0-1	0-3
Shrewsbury	1-1	2-2
Swindon	0-2	1-1
Torquay	3-2	1-2
Tranmere	1-2	1-2
Walsall	1-2	1-5
Watford	6-1	0-3

1961-62
Football League Div 3

Team	H	A
Barnsley	1-2	1-1
Bournemouth	0-0	0-3
Bradford PA	2-1	0-4
Brentford	0-0	0-0
Bristol City	1-0	2-3
Coventry	2-0	3-3
Crystal Palace	2-2	2-2
Grimsby	2-0	1-3
Halifax	2-1	2-0
Hull	2-1	0-0
Lincoln	0-0	0-2
Newport	1-0	3-0
Northampton	1-3	1-3
Notts County	3-2	0-2
Peterborough	1-1	1-4
Portsmouth	2-2	0-1
Port Vale	4-1	0-0
QPR	2-3	3-5
Reading	0-2	1-3
Shrewsbury	1-1	1-1
Swindon	0-2	0-0
Torquay	2-1	2-2
Watford	0-1	3-1

1962-63
Football League Div 3

Team	H	A
Barnsley	0-0	2-2
Bournemouth	0-1	0-0
Bradford PA	3-1	2-2
Brighton	1-1	0-0
Bristol City	2-2	3-6
Bristol Rovers	3-2	2-1
Carlisle	2-0	2-1
Colchester	2-3	1-3
Coventry	1-1	4-3
Crystal Palace	1-0	3-2
Halifax	1-1	1-0
Hull	0-1	2-1
Millwall	2-1	1-3
Northampton	5-1	3-5
Notts County	1-2	1-2
Peterborough	2-1	3-1
Port Vale	2-0	1-5
QPR	1-3	0-1
Reading	2-0	3-1
Shrewsbury	3-1	0-6
Swindon	1-1	1-4
Watford	1-1	1-3
Wrexham	2-0	1-1

1963-64
Football League Div 3

Team	H	A
Barnsley	4-1	1-0
Bournemouth	1-1	0-1
Brentford	2-1	0-3
Bristol City	1-1	2-2
Bristol Rovers	3-4	1-3
Colchester	0-0	3-3
Coventry	1-2	5-2
Crewe	1-1	2-1
Crystal Palace	2-1	0-3
Hull	1-1	0-1
Luton	0-1	1-4
Mansfield	2-1	1-4
Millwall	1-1	1-1
Notts County	3-1	1-1
Oldham	2-2	3-0
Peterborough	2-0	0-3
Port Vale	1-1	1-4
QPR	1-3	5-4
Reading	2-0	2-4
Shrewsbury	7-1	2-2
Walsall	1-1	0-2
Watford	3-0	1-3
Wrexham	1-1	3-1

1964-65
Football League Div 3

Team	H	A
Barnsley	2-0	4-1
Bournemouth	2-1	1-2
Brentford	0-1	1-2
Bristol City	0-4	0-4
Bristol Rovers	6-3	2-2
Carlisle	1-0	3-4
Colchester	6-3	1-3
Exeter	0-0	1-1
Gillingham	3-1	0-1
Grimsby	4-0	0-1
Hull	2-1	0-0
Luton	5-0	1-0
Mansfield	1-4	1-6
Oldham	6-1	2-0
Peterborough	2-0	2-4
Port Vale	2-1	2-2
QPR	0-0	0-2
Reading	2-2	0-2
Scunthorpe	0-1	1-2
Shrewsbury	1-0	3-1
Walsall	0-0	3-2
Watford	0-1	1-2
Workington	3-0	1-3

1965-66
Football League Div 3

Team	H	A
Bournemouth	1-2	0-0
Brentford	1-0	0-2
Brighton	0-0	1-9
Bristol Rovers	2-0	1-3
Exeter	4-2	1-1
Gillingham	5-2	0-1
Grimsby	3-1	0-1
Hull	0-2	0-1
Mansfield	1-0	0-2
Millwall	0-2	0-2
Oldham	0-2	0-1
Oxford	2-1	2-3
Peterborough	2-0	0-4
QPR	1-3	1-2
Reading	2-1	0-1
Scunthorpe	0-1	0-0
Shrewsbury	2-0	0-3
Swansea	2-0	0-5
Swindon	4-2	0-4
Walsall	5-3	0-3
Watford	1-0	1-4
Workington	3-1	1-3
York	2-3	3-0

1966-67
Football League Div 4

Team	H	A
Aldershot	4-0	2-5
Barnsley	3-0	2-1
Barrow	1-3	0-1
Bradford City	2-1	1-2
Bradford PA	4-0	2-1
Brentford	3-0	1-1
Chester	5-1	1-1
Chesterfield	4-1	1-2
Crewe	1-1	0-1
Exeter	0-0	1-0
Halifax	1-0	2-2
Hartlepools	2-0	2-1
Lincoln	3-0	2-2
Luton	2-0	0-1
Newport	1-0	0-3
Notts County	1-0	0-1
Port Vale	4-1	3-1
Rochdale	0-0	2-1
Southport	0-1	0-1
Stockport	0-1	1-4
Tranmere	0-0	2-1
Wrexham	1-1	0-2
York	2-1	1-2

1967-68
Football League Div 4

Team	H	A
Aldershot	1-1	3-1
Barnsley	4-1	1-1
Bradford City	1-1	1-2
Bradford PA	2-1	1-0
Brentford	1-0	2-1
Chester	5-1	0-0
Chesterfield	1-1	1-3
Crewe	0-0	0-1
Darlington	2-2	1-1
Doncaster	1-2	1-2
Exeter	1-0	2-0
Halifax	2-2	2-1
Hartlepools	2-1	1-0
Lincoln	2-1	2-4
Luton	3-0	1-3
Newport	2-2	0-2
Notts County	0-1	3-4
Port Vale	1-1	2-1
Rochdale	3-1	1-0
Swansea	1-0	2-2
Workington	7-0	2-2
Wrexham	3-1	1-4
York	0-1	2-2

1968-69
Football League Div 4

Team	H	A
Aldershot	4-2	1-2
Bradford City	2-0	2-3
Bradford PA	5-0	3-0
Brentford	4-0	1-1
Chester	1-2	2-1
Chesterfield	2-2	0-0
Colchester	3-1	0-4
Darlington	1-1	3-2
Doncaster	2-0	0-2
Exeter	6-1	2-1
Grimsby	0-1	0-0
Halifax	2-1	1-1

Lincoln	3-0	1-2
Newport	1-0	1-4
Notts County	4-0	2-2
Peterborough	2-1	0-1
Port Vale	1-1	1-1
Rochdale	1-3	0-3
Scunthorpe	0-3	1-4
Swansea	4-0	2-2
Workington	1-0	0-0
Wrexham	1-0	3-3
York	1-2	1-1

1969-70
Football League Div 4

	H	A
Aldershot	2-2	1-2
Bradford PA	1-1	0-1
Brentford	2-2	1-3
Chester	4-2	0-2
Chesterfield	0-0	0-0
Colchester	2-1	2-0
Crewe	2-0	3-5
Darlington	2-0	2-0
Exeter	1-1	0-3
Grimsby	1-3	2-2
Hartlepool	0-2	1-2
Lincoln	2-2	3-3
Newport	3-2	0-4
Northampton	2-2	0-2
Notts County	2-5	0-2
Oldham	1-0	0-3
Peterborough	2-0	4-3
Port Vale	1-1	0-3
Scunthorpe	3-0	0-2
Swansea	2-1	0-2
Workington	3-1	0-5
Wrexham	1-0	0-4
York	1-0	0-1

1970-71
Football League Div 4

	H	A
Aldershot	2-2	2-2
Barrow	2-3	0-2
Bournemouth	1-2	0-4
Brentford	4-3	2-4
Cambridge	1-1	3-0
Chester	1-1	0-2
Colchester	1-1	1-1
Crewe	0-2	2-1
Darlington	0-0	4-0
Exeter	0-0	0-2
Grimsby	1-1	0-2
Hartlepool	2-0	1-0
Lincoln	1-1	2-1
Newport	3-0	0-3
Northampton	1-0	2-0
Notts County	1-0	1-2
Oldham	3-0	0-2
Peterborough	1-2	0-4
Scunthorpe	2-2	0-3
Southport	1-1	0-3

Stockport	2-1	0-0
Workington	1-1	1-1
York	1-0	0-3

1971-72
Football League Div 4

	H	A
Aldershot	1-0	0-0
Barrow	1-0	1-2
Brentford	3-1	2-1
Bury	0-0	0-2
Cambridge	1-2	1-1
Chester	4-2	1-1
Colchester	1-4	0-1
Crewe	4-1	2-1
Darlington	3-0	3-2
Doncaster	2-1	2-0
Exeter	3-0	1-0
Gillingham	2-2	0-0
Grimsby	3-1	1-4
Hartlepool	3-1	2-2
Lincoln	2-1	0-0
Newport	3-1	0-2
Northampton	4-1	1-1
Peterborough	2-1	0-2
Reading	4-1	4-1
Scunthorpe	2-3	1-1
Southport	2-1	1-0
Stockport	4-2	2-2
Workington	2-0	1-3

1972-73
Football League Div 3

	H	A
Blackburn	0-1	1-2
Bolton	1-1	1-1
Bournemouth	2-2	0-2
Brentford	4-0	2-1
Bristol Rovers	0-0	2-1
Charlton	1-1	0-0
Chesterfield	5-1	4-2
Grimsby	2-0	1-3
Halifax	1-1	1-2
Notts County	2-1	0-2
Oldham	0-1	1-0
Plymouth	3-1	0-3
Port Vale	5-0	1-3
Rochdale	1-2	2-3
Rotherham	1-0	0-1
Scunthorpe	1-0	0-0
Shrewsbury	2-0	0-1
Swansea	3-1	1-1
Tranmere	1-0	1-3
Walsall	2-0	1-3
Watford	0-0	0-1
Wrexham	0-1	2-4
York	3-0	0-2

1973-74
Football League Div 3

	H	A
Aldershot	2-1	3-3
Blackburn	1-1	0-1
Bournemouth	2-2	3-1
Brighton	0-2	2-0
Bristol Rovers	0-0	0-4
Cambridge	3-1	2-3
Charlton	2-0	1-2
Chesterfield	1-3	0-0
Grimsby	4-1	1-2
Halifax	1-2	0-0
Hereford	2-1	2-1
Huddersfield	5-2	1-0
Oldham	2-2	0-2
Plymouth	2-0	1-1
Port Vale	1-0	0-0
Rochdale	1-2	1-1
Shrewsbury	2-0	2-1
Southport	0-1	0-0
Tranmere	1-1	0-2
Walsall	2-1	2-1
Watford	2-3	0-1
Wrexham	1-1	1-5
York	3-3	0-1

1974-75
Football League Div 3

	H	A
Aldershot	1-1	0-3
Blackburn	2-2	0-1
Bournemouth	0-0	0-0
Brighton	1-0	0-2
Bury	1-0	1-0
Charlton	2-1	1-2
Chesterfield	2-1	1-1
Colchester	1-1	1-1
Crystal Palace	0-1	1-1
Gillingham	2-2	1-2
Grimsby	3-0	0-0
Halifax	4-0	1-3
Hereford	0-0	0-1
Huddersfield	1-0	1-4
Peterborough	1-2	0-1
Plymouth	2-1	0-1
Port Vale	1-3	0-0
Preston	1-1	4-1
Swindon	2-0	0-2
Tranmere	1-0	1-2
Walsall	3-0	0-3
Watford	0-0	0-2
Wrexham	1-1	1-1

1975-76
Football League Div 3

	H	A
Aldershot	0-2	1-2
Brighton	4-0	0-2
Bury	2-0	0-1
Cardiff	0-2	1-3

Chester	2-0	1-1
Chesterfield	1-1	2-1
Colchester	2-0	1-2
Crystal Palace	1-2	1-1
Gillingham	2-2	2-1
Grimsby	5-2	2-2
Halifax	4-1	0-1
Hereford	1-3	1-2
Mansfield	2-2	1-3
Millwall	0-0	1-2
Peterborough	0-0	2-3
Port Vale	3-3	1-1
Preston	0-2	1-5
Rotherham	1-2	0-2
Sheffield Wed	2-1	1-2
Shrewsbury	1-3	1-3
Swindon	3-0	0-0
Walsall	2-2	3-2
Wrexham	2-1	2-2

1976-77
Football League Div 4

	H	A
Aldershot	5-0	0-0
Barnsley	1-1	1-3
Bournemouth	2-2	0-2
Bradford City	4-1	0-2
Brentford	2-1	0-1
Cambridge	0-1	3-2
Colchester	0-0	1-0
Crewe	1-0	1-1
Darlington	0-0	0-0
Doncaster	2-1	3-0
Exeter	2-0	1-3
Halifax	1-1	1-3
Hartlepool	1-0	1-1
Huddersfield	1-1	1-1
Newport	1-1	0-3
Rochdale	3-0	0-0
Scunthorpe	1-1	0-1
Southport	3-2	0-0
Stockport	0-0	0-0
Swansea	1-2	0-2
Torquay	0-3	0-0
Watford	2-1	1-1
Workington	2-0	3-0

1977-78
Football League Div 4

	H	A
Aldershot	3-1	0-3
Barnsley	0-0	1-1
Bournemouth	5-1	3-0
Brentford	2-1	0-1
Crewe	1-0	1-0
Darlington	2-0	0-2
Doncaster	4-0	0-2
Grimsby	1-1	0-2
Halifax	5-0	1-0
Hartlepool	1-1	0-1
Huddersfield	1-3	0-2
Newport	4-2	2-1

Northampton	0-0	0-0
Reading	0-2	1-0
Rochdale	3-1	2-1
Scunthorpe	2-0	2-1
Southport	4-2	0-0
Stockport	0-2	0-1
Swansea	2-1	0-0
Torquay	4-0	1-0
Watford	1-0	1-1
Wimbledon	1-0	3-1
York	0-0	2-1

1978-79
Football League Div 3

	H	A
Blackpool	4-0	2-1
Brentford	1-1	0-3
Bury	0-0	3-3
Carlisle	1-1	0-0
Chester	0-1	1-0
Chesterfield	2-0	2-3
Colchester	1-1	1-1
Exeter	0-1	0-0
Gillingham	0-1	0-1
Hull	3-0	0-2
Lincoln	2-0	1-1
Mansfield	1-1	1-1
Oxford	2-0	0-0
Peterborough	1-0	1-0
Plymouth	2-1	1-1
Rotherham	2-1	1-2
Sheffield Wed	2-1	2-3
Shrewsbury	0-1	0-2
Swansea	0-2	2-3
Swindon	5-3	0-1
Tranmere	0-1	2-1
Walsall	1-0	1-1
Watford	1-0	0-2

1979-80
Football League Div 3

	H	A
Barnsley	2-1	2-1
Blackburn	0-1	1-1
Blackpool	1-2	0-1
Brentford	3-2	0-2
Bury	0-0	1-1
Carlisle	1-0	0-4
Chester	4-1	1-2
Chesterfield	0-0	0-1
Colchester	0-1	1-2
Exeter	4-0	2-4
Gillingham	0-3	0-1
Grimsby	1-0	0-1
Hull	3-0	0-1
Mansfield	1-1	1-3
Millwall	1-0	2-1
Oxford	1-1	0-1
Plymouth	4-1	0-0
Reading	2-2	1-1
Rotherham	0-2	1-2
Sheffield Utd	2-1	0-2

Sheffield Wed	1-1	0-2
Swindon	1-0	0-1
Wimbledon	1-3	1-0

1980-81
Football League Div 4

	H	A
Aldershot	3-0	2-1
Bournemouth	2-1	1-2
Bradford City	3-1	1-2
Bury	1-0	2-1
Crewe	3-0	1-1
Darlington	1-0	2-0
Doncaster	0-0	0-1
Halifax	5-1	5-1
Hartlepool	4-0	3-1
Hereford	2-0	0-0
Lincoln	0-0	1-2
Mansfield	2-0	1-0
Northampton	0-0	0-2
Peterborough	1-0	2-5
Port Vale	5-1	0-1
Rochdale	1-1	2-0
Scunthorpe	2-0	1-2
Stockport	2-0	0-1
Torquay	3-1	3-0
Tranmere	2-0	2-2
Wigan	1-0	1-0
Wimbledon	1-0	1-0
York	3-0	1-0

1981-82
Football League Div 3

	H	A
Brentford	1-1	1-0
Bristol City	3-0	2-0
Bristol Rovers	1-0	1-2
Burnley	1-4	5-3
Carlisle	1-1	2-3
Chester	2-0	1-1
Chesterfield	0-2	2-1
Doncaster	1-1	1-1
Exeter	2-1	1-1
Fulham	0-0	1-2
Gillingham	3-0	0-2
Huddersfield	4-0	2-3
Lincoln	0-2	1-1
Millwall	2-2	1-1
Newport	0-4	2-3
Oxford	0-1	2-0
Plymouth	3-0	0-0
Portsmouth	2-0	0-0
Preston	2-2	0-1
Reading	2-0	2-0
Swindon	0-0	0-0
Walsall	3-2	1-0
Wimbledon	2-0	0-3

1982-83
Football League Div 3

	H	A
Bournemouth	0-0	2-0
Bradford City	1-1	0-1
Brentford	4-2	2-4
Bristol Rovers	1-0	2-2
Cardiff	1-2	1-4
Chesterfield	2-0	2-0
Doncaster	3-2	0-0
Exeter	1-1	3-4
Gillingham	1-1	0-1
Huddersfield	0-1	1-2
Lincoln	2-0	1-0
Millwall	1-1	1-3
Newport	1-4	1-1
Orient	1-1	1-1
Oxford	1-2	0-1
Plymouth	3-1	0-1
Portsmouth	4-0	0-2
Preston	2-3	1-1
Reading	4-2	1-1
Sheffield Utd	3-1	1-0
Walsall	1-1	3-1
Wigan	2-0	0-4
Wrexham	2-2	2-3

1983-84
Football League Div 3

	H	A
Bolton	0-1	0-2
Bournemouth	0-0	0-1
Bradford City	2-1	1-1
Brentford	6-0	0-0
Bristol Rovers	1-2	1-2
Burnley	2-2	0-3
Exeter	0-3	3-3
Gillingham	3-1	1-5
Hull	2-2	1-2
Lincoln	2-0	2-1
Millwall	3-2	0-4
Newport	3-1	1-1
Orient	3-0	0-1
Oxford	0-1	1-2
Plymouth	1-1	0-4
Port Vale	1-2	1-2
Preston	1-1	1-4
Rotherham	2-2	0-0
Scunthorpe	0-0	6-1
Sheffield Utd	0-1	0-5
Walsall	0-0	0-4
Wigan	1-0	0-1
Wimbledon	1-1	2-3

1984-85
Football League Div 4

	H	A
Aldershot	1-0	2-6
Blackpool	1-4	0-1
Bury	3-3	0-2
Chester	1-1	1-5

Chesterfield	0-1	1-2
Colchester	2-5	3-3
Crewe	3-1	2-0
Darlington	1-1	1-3
Exeter	1-0	1-2
Halifax	2-1	0-1
Hartlepool	1-1	1-2
Hereford	0-0	0-3
Mansfield	1-3	0-1
Northampton	2-1	2-1
Peterborough	2-1	4-1
Port Vale	1-1	1-4
Rochdale	0-2	2-2
Scunthorpe	1-1	1-2
Stockport	1-1	2-1
Swindon	3-2	0-2
Torquay	1-0	2-2
Tranmere	2-3	0-2
Wrexham	0-1	2-1

1985-86
Football League Div 4

	H	A
Aldershot	2-0	3-1
Burnley	2-3	3-1
Cambridge	1-0	2-1
Chester	1-1	0-2
Colchester	2-4	0-2
Crewe	0-1	1-1
Exeter	2-0	2-0
Halifax	2-1	3-2
Hartlepool	3-2	2-3
Hereford	3-1	1-2
Mansfield	3-1	0-3
Northampton	0-4	0-0
Orient	5-1	0-3
Peterborough	0-1	1-1
Port Vale	2-1	0-4
Preston	2-1	2-3
Rochdale	5-0	1-2
Scunthorpe	2-1	0-2
Stockport	0-0	1-2
Swindon	0-0	1-2
Torquay	1-2	2-2
Tranmere	2-2	1-1
Wrexham	3-0	0-0

1986-87
Football League Div 4

	H	A
Aldershot	2-0	1-0
Burnley	2-1	1-2
Cambridge	3-1	2-1
Cardiff	2-0	2-0
Colchester	1-1	2-1
Crewe	3-1	1-2
Exeter	2-1	0-0
Halifax	2-3	1-0
Hartlepool	1-1	0-1
Hereford	2-0	1-0
Lincoln	1-0	3-1
Northampton	0-4	1-2

	H	A
Orient	2-1	0-1
Peterborough	2-2	0-2
Preston	1-2	0-2
Rochdale	5-3	2-1
Scunthorpe	3-1	0-3
Stockport	0-0	2-0
Swansea	1-2	0-1
Torquay	4-0	1-2
Tranmere	3-0	3-1
Wolves	1-0	2-1
Wrexham	0-3	0-4

1987-88
Football League Div 3

	H	A
Aldershot	0-1	1-0
Blackpool	4-0	1-1
Brentford	2-3	0-1
Brighton	2-1	0-0
Bristol City	2-0	2-3
Bristol Rovers	4-2	0-0
Bury	1-0	2-2
Chester	2-2	1-1
Chesterfield	3-0	1-3
Doncaster	4-1	1-0
Fulham	0-2	1-3
Gillingham	1-3	1-8
Grimsby	0-0	3-1
Mansfield	2-1	0-1
Northampton	1-1	0-4
Notts County	1-2	2-6
Port Vale	3-3	1-4
Preston	1-2	1-1
Rotherham	1-1	1-1
Sunderland	1-4	0-7
Walsall	1-1	1-2
Wigan	3-2	0-1
York	3-1	3-0

1988-89
Football League Div 3

	H	A
Aldershot	1-1	2-2
Blackpool	2-1	2-3
Bolton	2-0	0-0
Brentford	1-1	0-4
Bristol City	1-2	2-0
Bristol Rovers	2-2	1-1
Bury	1-1	1-3
Cardiff	0-0	0-2
Chester	1-0	4-2
Chesterfield	3-1	1-2
Fulham	0-0	0-1
Gillingham	2-1	1-1
Huddersfield	2-4	2-3
Mansfield	1-1	0-4
Northampton	2-1	2-2
Notts County	1-1	1-1
Port Vale	1-1	0-2
Preston	2-1	2-3
Reading	2-1	0-4
Sheffield Utd	2-1	2-1

	H	A
Swansea	0-2	0-2
Wigan	1-2	0-3
Wolves	3-1	0-3

1989-90
Football League Div 4

	H	A
Aldershot	5-0	5-0
Burnley	3-2	0-0
Cambridge	0-0	1-2
Carlisle	2-0	0-3
Chesterfield	0-2	1-1
Colchester	0-2	2-0
Doncaster	2-0	1-0
Exeter	1-2	1-2
Gillingham	2-0	0-5
Grimsby	0-2	0-2
Halifax	2-0	2-1
Hartlepool	3-0	1-1
Hereford	2-0	3-0
Lincoln	2-0	0-2
Maidstone	0-1	0-3
Peterborough	0-0	2-1
Rochdale	3-2	1-0
Scarborough	1-0	1-1
Scunthorpe	0-0	1-1
Stockport	2-0	0-1
Torquay	1-0	0-3
Wrexham	2-1	3-3
York	2-0	1-2

1990-91
Football League Div 3

	H	A
Birmingham City	2-1	1-1
Bolton	1-1	0-1
Bournemouth	2-1	1-3
Bradford City	1-1	1-2
Brentford	0-1	1-0
Bury	2-1	1-0
Cambridge	0-0	4-1
Chester	1-1	0-1
Crewe	3-2	2-0
Exeter	2-1	2-1
Fulham	1-1	3-0
Grimsby	2-0	0-1
Huddersfield	0-1	2-1
Leyton Orient	1-1	1-0
Mansfield	2-1	1-0
Preston	3-2	1-2
Reading	1-2	4-2
Rotherham	2-1	1-0
Shrewsbury	2-1	1-0
Stoke	1-0	0-4
Swansea	4-1	4-1
Tranmere	1-0	1-3
Wigan	0-2	1-4

1991-92
Football League Div 2

	H	A
Barnsley	2-1	0-1
Blackburn	3-0	2-2
Brighton	2-1	2-3
Bristol City	1-1	2-2
Bristol Rovers	2-0	1-4
Cambridge	1-1	1-0
Charlton	1-1	0-2
Derby	1-0	2-1
Grimsby	3-1	2-3
Ipswich	1-2	0-1
Leicester	1-2	0-2
Middlesbrough	0-1	1-1
Millwall	2-3	0-2
Newcastle	4-0	2-3
Oxford	2-3	1-0
Plymouth	2-1	2-0
Portsmouth	2-3	1-1
Port Vale	0-0	0-0
Sunderland	2-0	2-1
Swindon	3-2	1-3
Tranmere	1-1	1-1
Watford	1-0	2-1
Wolves	0-2	1-3

1992-93
Football League Div 1

	H	A
Barnsley	3-0	1-3
Birmingham City	4-0	0-2
Brentford	3-0	1-2
Bristol City	1-1	1-0
Bristol Rovers	3-0	2-0
Cambridge	1-1	1-3
Charlton	0-2	1-1
Derby	0-0	0-2
Grimsby	1-0	0-1
Leicester	3-1	1-4
Luton	2-1	2-2
Millwall	3-3	1-1
Newcastle	1-1	2-3
Notts County	3-1	0-4
Oxford	0-3	1-0
Peterborough	0-1	0-1
Portsmouth	0-0	0-2
Sunderland	0-1	4-2
Swindon	1-1	2-3
Tranmere	1-2	0-3
Watford	1-2	0-0
West Ham	1-0	0-2
Wolves	1-1	1-1

1993-94
Football League Div 1

	H	A
Barnsley	0-3	3-1
Birmingham City	3-1	1-3
Bolton	0-2	2-0
Bristol City	0-1	1-2

	H	A
Charlton	4-2	3-4
Crystal Palace	1-2	0-1
Derby	4-3	3-1
Grimsby	1-2	0-4
Leicester	0-0	0-3
Luton	2-1	1-1
Middlesbrough	1-0	0-1
Millwall	1-1	4-1
Nottingham For	1-1	0-2
Notts County	1-0	1-2
Oxford	6-1	1-2
Peterborough	3-0	1-3
Portsmouth	2-1	1-2
Stoke	0-0	1-0
Sunderland	0-1	2-0
Tranmere	1-2	1-1
Watford	2-0	0-3
WBA	0-3	2-2
Wolves	1-1	1-0

1994-95
Football League Div 1

	H	A
Barnsley	3-1	0-0
Bolton	2-1	0-3
Bristol City	2-1	0-0
Burnley	3-1	1-5
Charlton	2-1	1-3
Derby	1-0	2-1
Grimsby	0-0	1-4
Luton	3-0	2-2
Middlesbrough	0-2	2-1
Millwall	0-1	1-3
Notts County	1-0	2-2
Oldham	1-0	2-0
Portsmouth	1-2	1-1
Port Vale	1-2	0-5
Reading	4-1	0-2
Sheffield Utd	1-3	0-2
Stoke	4-2	1-4
Sunderland	0-1	1-0
Swindon	2-0	2-2
Tranmere	0-0	2-0
Watford	0-4	0-1
WBA	2-1	0-2
Wolves	0-1	0-5

1995-96
Football League Div 1

	H	A
Barnsley	0-0	1-1
Birmingham City	3-1	0-2
Charlton	1-1	3-0
Crystal Palace	1-1	0-2
Derby	1-2	0-1
Grimsby	1-0	1-1
Huddersfield	0-0	1-3
Ipswich	2-1	1-1
Leicester	2-1	3-1
Luton	0-1	1-3
Millwall	2-0	0-0
Norwich	1-1	1-0

Oldham	1-1	1-0
Portsmouth	2-1	2-4
Port Vale	2-1	1-2
Reading	0-0	3-3
Sheffield Utd	2-1	0-3
Stoke	2-4	0-1
Sunderland	0-2	0-1
Tranmere	2-0	0-3
Watford	1-1	2-2
WBA	2-1	1-3
Wolves	2-1	0-2

1996-97
Football League Div 1

	H	A
Barnsley	1-2	0-3
Birmingham City	1-1	1-2
Bolton	5-2	1-3
Bradford City	1-1	0-0
Charlton	0-2	0-2
Crystal Palace	2-1	1-6
Grimsby	1-0	0-4
Huddersfield	1-2	0-0
Ipswich	0-0	1-1
Manchester City	2-3	0-3
Norwich	1-1	0-0
Oldham	1-1	0-0
Oxford	2-2	0-5
Portsmouth	2-1	0-1
Port Vale	0-0	1-2
QPR	0-1	0-4
Reading	2-1	2-3
Sheffield Utd	3-2	0-3
Stoke	2-1	2-1
Swindon	1-3	0-0
Tranmere	1-1	0-3
WBA	2-3	0-4
Wolves	1-1	1-4

1997-98
Football League Div 2

	H	A
Blackpool	2-1	0-3
Bournemouth	5-3	1-2
Brentford	3-1	1-1
Bristol City	0-2	0-1
Bristol Rovers	1-1	0-2
Burnley	1-0	0-1
Carlisle	1-1	0-5
Chesterfield	0-2	0-1
Fulham	1-0	0-2
Gillingham	0-0	2-1
Grimsby	0-1	1-5
Luton	1-2	0-1
Millwall	0-0	1-3
Northampton	0-0	1-3
Oldham	1-1	0-2
Plymouth	3-0	3-2
Preston	3-2	0-1
Walsall	0-1	1-3
Watford	0-3	1-1
Wigan	1-0	3-1

Wrexham	1-3	1-3
Wycombe	1-2	1-4
York	4-4	1-1

1998-99
Football League Div 3

	H	A
Barnet	2-3	2-0
Brentford	1-4	1-4
Brighton	3-0	2-0
Cambridge	0-1	0-3
Cardiff	0-1	0-2
Carlisle	0-1	0-3
Chester	0-1	1-1
Darlington	2-1	1-2
Exeter	0-0	1-2
Halifax	0-0	1-3
Hartlepool	1-1	4-2
Hull	0-1	1-1
Leyton Orient	2-2	3-0
Mansfield	1-2	0-0
Peterborough	2-0	1-1
Plymouth	1-0	3-0
Rochdale	1-1	0-1
Rotherham	3-0	2-2
Scarborough	1-0	2-1
Scunthorpe	0-1	1-1
Shrewsbury	2-1	1-3
Swansea	2-0	1-3
Torquay	0-0	0-2

1999-2000
Football League Div 3

	H	A
Barnet	1-3	1-2
Brighton	2-1	0-1
Carlisle	2-0	1-1
Cheltenham	2-1	1-2
Chester	3-1	0-0
Darlington	1-2	0-1
Exeter	1-2	1-0
Halifax	4-1	0-0
Hartlepool	2-1	2-1
Hull	1-2	0-0
Leyton Orient	1-1	1-2
Lincoln	2-2	0-1
Macclesfield	1-0	2-1
Mansfield	1-0	1-3
Northampton	2-2	0-2
Peterborough	0-1	0-1
Plymouth	2-1	1-3
Rochdale	3-3	0-2
Rotherham	1-2	0-0
Shrewsbury	3-2	1-2
Swansea	2-1	1-3
Torquay	0-2	1-0
York	0-0	2-2

2000-01
Football League Div 3

	H	A
Barnet	2-0	1-2
Blackpool	0-3	2-2
Brighton	2-0	2-0
Cardiff	1-1	2-2
Carlisle	1-1	1-3
Cheltenham	0-1	1-2
Chesterfield	3-2	1-1
Darlington	0-2	1-1
Exeter	1-1	2-2
Halifax	0-3	1-0
Hartlepool	2-1	0-1
Hull	1-1	1-1
Kidderminster	1-1	1-2
Leyton Orient	0-1	2-0
Lincoln	1-0	0-3
Macclesfield	3-1	0-1
Mansfield	3-1	1-1
Plymouth	2-2	3-3
Rochdale	3-0	1-0
Scunthorpe	1-0	1-1
Shrewsbury	0-0	1-0
Torquay	1-1	1-1
York	1-0	0-1

2001-02
Football League Div 3

	H	A
Bristol Rovers	2-1	1-2
Carlisle	3-2	0-0
Cheltenham	0-1	1-1
Darlington	1-0	2-2
Exeter	3-1	1-2
Halifax	4-1	1-1
Hartlepool	0-0	1-5
Hull	2-0	0-0
Kidderminster	1-0	0-2
Leyton Orient	1-2	1-2
Lincoln	1-1	1-0
Luton	1-2	0-2
Macclesfield	3-0	0-0
Mansfield	1-0	0-0
Oxford	2-2	0-2
Plymouth	0-1	0-0
Rochdale	1-1	1-0
Rushden	4-2	1-0
Scunthorpe	2-0	0-2
Shrewsbury	0-2	0-2
Swansea	4-2	2-3
Torquay	1-1	1-2
York	0-1	1-2

2002-03
Football League Div 3

	H	A
Boston	4-2	0-1
Bournemouth	0-1	0-1
Bristol Rovers	2-2	1-0
Bury	1-2	3-1

Cambridge	2-1	1-1
Carlisle	0-1	0-1
Darlington	2-0	1-2
Exeter	1-0	0-1
Hartlepool	0-1	1-2
Hull	3-0	2-2
Kidderminster	0-2	0-1
Leyton Orient	1-0	1-2
Lincoln	0-1	1-2
Macclesfield	1-0	1-2
Oxford	2-1	1-0
Rochdale	1-0	2-1
Rushden	2-1	0-3
Scunthorpe	1-2	1-4
Shrewsbury	2-3	1-0
Swansea	0-2	0-1
Torquay	3-0	1-3
Wrexham	0-1	0-3
York	1-0	0-2

2003-04
Football League Div 3

	H	A
Boston	0-2	2-0
Bristol Rovers	0-1	1-1
Bury	1-0	1-1
Cambridge	1-0	1-0
Carlisle	2-2	2-1
Cheltenham	2-0	1-1
Darlington	3-2	0-0
Doncaster	0-2	0-2
Huddersfield	1-2	0-1
Hull	2-2	2-3
Kidderminster	3-0	2-1
Leyton Orient	2-3	1-2
Lincoln	0-2	2-2
Macclesfield	1-0	2-1
Mansfield	0-3	0-1
Northampton	0-1	2-2
Oxford	0-1	0-2
Rochdale	4-0	1-1
Scunthorpe	4-2	1-1
Swansea	1-1	3-2
Torquay	1-2	0-3
Yeovil	0-2	0-4
York	0-0	0-2

2004-05
Football League Two

	H	A
Boston	2-1	0-2
Bristol Rovers	2-0	1-2
Bury	1-0	1-0
Cambridge	0-0	2-0
Cheltenham	0-2	3-0
Chester	1-0	2-2
Darlington	2-0	0-4
Grimsby	1-1	1-1
Kidderminster	1-0	3-1
Leyton Orient	0-1	2-2
Lincoln	1-1	1-1
Macclesfield	2-1	2-1

Mansfield	0-1	1-1						
Northampton	2-1	2-1						
Notts County	0-0	2-1						
Oxford	4-0	1-2						
Rochdale	3-0	0-2						
Rushden	3-0	4-1						
Scunthorpe	0-0	2-3						
Shrewsbury	1-0	1-1						
Swansea	4-2	1-1						
Wycombe	1-2	1-0						
Yeovil	0-1	1-3						

Promotion Play-offs

Semi-final

Northampton	1-0	0-0

Final

Lincoln *	2-0

* Played at Millennium Stadium, Cardiff

2005-06

Football League One

	H	A
Barnsley	1-1	2-2
Blackpool	2-1	2-1
Bournemouth	2-1	1-1
Bradford City	1-1	2-0
Brentford	4-1	0-2
Bristol City	1-0	3-0
Chesterfield	0-0	4-3
Colchester	2-1	3-0
Doncaster	0-1	0-2
Gillingham	0-1	2-1

(cont from previous column)

Hartlepool	3-0	2-1
Huddersfield	1-1	0-0
Milton Keynes	0-0	1-2
Nottingham For	1-0	0-2
Oldham	2-1	0-0
Port Vale	1-2	1-2
Rotherham	2-0	4-2
Scunthorpe	3-0	0-1
Swansea	1-2	2-2
Swindon	2-0	2-1
Tranmere	3-1	0-0
Walsall	0-0	2-2
Yeovil	4-1	2-0

FA CHALLENGE CUP

1907-08
Round	Opponent	Venue	Score
Prelim.	East Ham	H	3-0
Qual 1	Clapton	A	1-0
Qual 2	Ilford	H	3-1
Qual 3	Clapton Orient	A	1-1
Re-play	Clapton Orient	H	3-1
Qual 4	4th King's R Rifles	H	6-0
Qual 5	Carlisle	A	0-4

1908-09
Round	Opponent	Venue	Score
Prelim.	London Cale	A	4-0
Qual 1	Leyton	A	1-0
Qual 2	Shoeburyness Ga	H	4-0
Qual 3	Ilford	A	3-1
Qual 4	Cromer	H	2-0
Qual 5	Luton	A	1-1
Re-play	Luton	H	2-4

1909-10
Round	Opponent	Venue	Score
Qual 4	Barnet	H	5-2
Qual 5	Hastings	H	4-2
1st Rd	Gainsborough	A	1-1
Re-play	Gainsborough	H	1-0
2nd Rd	QPR	H	0-0
Re-play	QPR	A	2-3

1910-11
Round	Opponent	Venue	Score
Qual 4	Enfield	A	3-3
Re-play	Enfield	H	3-1
Qual 5	Tunbridge WR	H	1-0
1st Rd	Blackburn *	H	1-5

* played at Ewood Park

1911-12
Round	Opponent	Venue	Score
Qual 4	London Cale	A	3-1
Qual 5	Brentford	H	0-1

1912-13
Round	Opponent	Venue	Score
Prelim.	Southend Am	H	5-0
Qual 1	Walthamstow Gr *	A	6-2

* played at Roots Hall

Round	Opponent	Venue	Score
Qual 2	Leytonstone	A	5-0
Qual 3	Custom House	A	1-0
Qual 4	Clapton	A	2-1
Qual 5	Cardiff	A	3-0
1st Rd	Chelsea	A	2-5

1913-14
Round	Opponent	Venue	Score
Qual 4	Tunbridge WR *	A	3-0

* played at Roots Hall

Round	Opponent	Venue	Score
Qual 5	Brentford	A	1-1
Re-play	Brentford	H	2-0
1st Rd	Birmingham	A	1-2

1914-15
Round	Opponent	Venue	Score
1st Rd	Bristol Rovers	A	0-0
Re-play	Bristol Rovers	H	3-0
2nd Rd	Burnley	A	0-6

1919-20
Round	Opponent	Venue	Score
Qual 6	Watford	H	1-0
1st Rd	Sheffield Utd *	H	0-3

* played at Bramall Lane

1920-21
Round	Opponent	Venue	Score
Qual 6	Hednesford	H	3-1
1st Rd	Eccles	H	5-1
2nd Rd	Blackpool	H	1-0
3rd Rd	Tottenham	H	1-4

1921-22
Round	Opponent	Venue	Score
1st Rd	Worksop	A	2-1
2nd Rd	Swansea	H	0-1

1922-23
Round	Opponent	Venue	Score
Qual 4	Sittingbourne	A	0-0
Re-play	Sittingbourne	H	4-2
Qual 5	Norwich	H	2-2
Re-play	Norwich	A	1-2

1923-24
Round	Opponent	Venue	Score
Qual 4	King's Lynn	H	1-0
Qual 5	Clapton *	A	3-1

* played at Boleyn Castle Ground

Round	Opponent	Venue	Score
Qual 6	Llanelly	A	1-2

1924-25
Round	Opponent	Venue	Score
Qual 4	London Cale	H	3-3
Re-play	London Cale	A	4-1
Qual 5	Reading	A	1-2

1925-26
Round	Opponent	Venue	Score
1st Rd	Dulwich Hamlet	H	5-1
2nd Rd	Gillingham	H	1-0
3rd Rd	Southport	H	5-2
4th Rd	Derby	H	4-1
5th Rd	Nottingham For	H	0-1

1926-27
Round	Opponent	Venue	Score
1st Rd	Dulwich Hamlet	A	4-1
2nd Rd	Reading	A	2-3

1927-28
Round	Opponent	Venue	Score
1st Rd	Wellington	H	1-0
2nd Rd	Gillingham	A	0-2

1928-29
Round	Opponent	Venue	Score
1st Rd	Luton	A	1-5

1929-30
Round	Opponent	Venue	Score
1st Rd	Brentford	H	1-0
2nd Rd	York	H	1-4

1930-31
Round	Opponent	Venue	Score
1st Rd	Torquay	H	0-1

1931-32
Round	Opponent	Venue	Score
1st Rd	Torquay	A	3-1
2nd Rd	Northampton	A	0-3

1932-33
Round	Opponent	Venue	Score
1st Rd	Exeter	H	1-1
Re-play	Exeter	A	1-0
2nd Rd	Scarborough	H	4-1
3rd Rd	Watford	A	1-1
Re-play	Watford	H	2-0
4th Rd	Derby	H	2-3

1933-34
Round	Opponent	Venue	Score
1st Rd	London PM	A	1-0
2nd Rd	Chester	H	2-1
3rd Rd	Tranmere	A	0-3

1934-35
Round	Opponent	Venue	Score
1st Rd	Golders Green	H	10-1
2nd Rd	Wimbledon	A	5-1
3rd Rd	Sheffield Utd	H	0-4

1935-36
Round	Opponent	Venue	Score
1st Rd	Newport	A	1-0
2nd Rd	Burton Town	H	5-0
3rd Rd	Tottenham	A	4-4
Re-play	Tottenham	H	1-2

1936-37
Round	Opponent	Venue	Score
1st Rd	Crystal Palace	A	1-1
Re-play	Crystal Palace	H	2-0
2nd Rd	York	H	3-3
Re-play	York	A	1-2

1937-38
Round	Opponent	Venue	Score
1st Rd	Corinthian	A	2-0
2nd Rd	Walthamstow Ave	A	1-0
3rd Rd	Barnsley	H	2-2
Re-play	Barnsley	A	1-2

1938-39
Round	Opponent	Venue	Score
1st Rd	Corinthian	H	3-0
2nd Rd	Port Vale	A	1-0
3rd Rd	Chesterfield	A	1-1
Re-play	Chesterfield	H	4-3
4th Rd	Blackburn	A	2-4

1945-46
Round	Opponent	Venue	Score
1st Rd			
1st Leg	Watford	A	1-1
2nd Leg	Watford	H	0-3

1946-47
Round	Opponent	Venue	Score
1st Rd	Brush Sports	A	6-1
2nd Rd	Barnet	A	9-2
3rd Rd	Everton	A	2-4

1947-48
Round	Opponent	Venue	Score
1st Rd	Newport	A	2-3

1948-49
Round	Opponent	Venue	Score
1st Rd	Swansea	H	1-2

1949-50
Round	Opponent	Venue	Score
1st Rd	Leyton Orient	A	2-0
2nd Rd	Wrexham	A	2-2
Re-play	Wrexham	H	2-0
3rd Rd	Blackpool	A	0-4

1950-51
Round	Opponent	Venue	Score
1st Rd	Swindon	H	0-3

1951-52
Round	Opponent	Venue	Score
1st Rd	Bournemouth	H	6-1
2nd Rd	Oldham	H	5-0
3rd Rd	Southampton	H	3-0
4th Rd	Bristol Rovers	H	2-1
5th Rd	Sheffield Utd	H	1-2

1952-53
Round	Opponent	Venue	Score
1st Rd	Bath	A	1-3

1953-54
Round	Opponent	Venue	Score
1st Rd	Finchley	A	3-1
2nd Rd	Chesterfield	H	1-2

1954-55
Round	Opponent	Venue	Score
1st Rd	Bristol City	A	2-1
2nd Rd	Bradford PA	A	3-2
3rd Rd	Everton	A	1-3

1955-56
Round	Opponent	Venue	Score
1st Rd	QPR	H	2-0
2nd Rd	Weymouth	A	1-0
3rd Rd	Lincoln	A	3-2
4th Rd	Manchester City	H	0-1

1956-57
Round	Opponent	Venue	Score
1st Rd	Colchester	A	4-1
2nd Rd	Hereford	A	3-2
3rd Rd	Liverpool	H	2-1

1956-57
Round	Opponent	Venue	Score
4th Rd	Birmingham City	H	1-6

1957-58
Round	Opponent	Venue	Score
1st Rd	Trowbridge	A	2-0
2nd Rd	Torquay	A	1-1
Re-play	Torquay	H	2-1
3rd Rd	Liverpool	A	1-1
Re-play	Liverpool	H	2-3

1958-59
Round	Opponent	Venue	Score
1st Rd	Yeovil	H	0-0
Re-play	Yeovil	A	0-1

1959-60

1st Rd	Oswestry	H	6-0
2nd Rd	Southampton	A	0-3
1960-61			
1st Rd	Clacton	A	3-1
2nd Rd	Gillingham	A	2-3
1961-62			
1st Rd	Watford	H	0-2
1962-63			
1st Rd	Brighton	H	2-1
2nd Rd	Watford	H	0-2
1963-64			
1st Rd	Yeovil	A	0-1
1964-65			
1st Rd	Luton	A	0-1
1965-66			
1st Rd	Notts County	H	3-1
2nd Rd	Watford	H	2-1
3rd Rd	Rotherham	A	2-3
1966-67			
1st Rd	Watford	A	0-1
1967-68			
1st Rd	Brighton	A	0-1
1968-69			
1st Rd	King's Lynn	H	9-0
2nd Rd	Brentwood Town	H	10-1
3rd Rd	Swindon	A	2-0
4th Rd	Mansfield	A	1-2
1969-70			
1st Rd	Gillingham	H	0-0
Re-play	Gillingham	A	1-2
1970-71			
1st Rd	Weymouth	H	7-0
2nd Rd	Dagenham	H	1-0
3rd Rd	Carlisle	H	0-3
1971-72			
1st Rd	Aston Villa	H	1-0
2nd Rd	Bournemouth	A	0-2
1972-73			
1st Rd	Aldershot	H	0-2
1973-74			
1st Rd	Boreham Wood	H	3-0
2nd Rd	Reading	H	2-0
3rd Rd	Peterborough	A	1-3
1974-75			
1st Rd	AP Leamington	A	2-1
2nd Rd	Ilford	A	2-0
3rd Rd	QPR	H	2-2
Re-play	QPR	A	0-2
1975-76			
1st Rd	Swansea	H	2-0
2nd Rd	Dover	H	4-1
3rd Rd	Brighton	H	2-1
1975-76			
4th Rd	Cardiff	H	2-1
5th Rd	Derby	A	0-1
1976-77			
1st Rd	Exeter	A	1-1
Re-play	Exeter	H	2-1
2nd Rd	Newport	H	3-0
3rd Rd	Chester	H	0-4
1977-78			
1st Rd	Torquay	A	2-1
2nd Rd	AP Leamington	A	0-0
Re-play	AP Leamington	H	4-0

3rd Rd	Derby	A	2-3
1978-79			
1st Rd	Peterborough	H	3-2
2nd Rd	Watford	A	1-1
Re-play	Watford	H	1-0
3rd Rd	Liverpool	H	0-0
Re-play	Liverpool	A	0-3
1979-80			
1st Rd	Wealdstone	A	1-0
2nd Rd	Harlow	H	1-1
Re-play	Harlow	A	0-1
1980-81			
1st Rd	Hereford	H	0-1
1981-82			
1st Rd	Hereford	A	1-3
1982-83			
1st Rd	Bournemouth	A	2-0
2nd Rd	Yeovil	H	3-0
3rd Rd	Sheffield Wed	H	0-0
Re-play	Sheffield Wed	A	2-2
Re-play	Sheffield Wed	A	1-2
1983-84			
1st Rd	Plymouth	H	0-0
Re-play	Plymouth	A	0-2
1984-85			
1st Rd	Colchester	H	2-2
Re-play	Colchester	A	2-3
1985-86			
1st Rd	Newport	H	0-1
1986-87			
1st Rd	Halesowen	H	4-1
2nd Rd	Northampton	H	4-4
Re-play	Northampton	A	2-3
1987-88			
1st Rd	Walsall	H	0-0
Re-play	Walsall	A	1-2
1988-89			
1st Rd	Bristol City	A	1-3
1989-90			
1st Rd	Aylesbury	A	0-1
1990-91			
1st Rd	Leyton Orient	A	2-3
1991-92			
3rd Rd	Everton	A	0-1
1992-93			
3rd Rd	Millwall	H	1-0
4th Rd	Huddersfield	A	2-1
5th Rd	Sheffield Wed	A	0-2
1993-94			
3rd Rd	Luton	A	0-1
1994-95			
3rd Rd	Southampton	A	0-2
1995-96			
3rd Rd	West Ham	A	0-2
1996-97			
3rd Rd	Leicester	A	0-2
1997-98			
1st Rd	Woking	A	2-0
2nd Rd	Fulham	A	0-1
1998-99			
1st Rd	Doncaster	H	0-1
1999-00			
1st Rd	Torquay	A	0-1
2000-01			

1st Rd	Torquay	A	1-1
Re-play	Torquay	H	2-1
2nd Rd	Canvey Island *	A	2-1
			played at Roots Hall
3rd Rd	Kingstonian	H	0-1
2001-02			
1st Rd	Luton	H	3-2
2nd Rd	Chesterfield	A	1-1
Re-play	Chesterfield	H	2-0
3rd Rd	Tranmere	H	1-3
2002-03			
1st Rd	Hartlepool	H	1-1
Re-play	Hartlepool	A	2-1
2nd Rd	Bournemouth	A	1-1
Re-play	Bournemouth	A	2-3
2003-04			
1st Rd	Canvey Island	H	1-1
Re-play	Canvey Island	A	3-2
2nd Rd	Lincoln	H	3-0
3rd Rd	Scarborough	A	1-1
Re-play	Scarborough	A	0-1
2004-05			
1st Rd	Luton	H	0-3
2005-06			
1st Rd	Barnet	A	1-0
2nd Rd	Milton Keynes	H	1-2

SOUTHERN COUNTIES CHARITY CUP

1909-10			
1st Rd	New Brompton	H	4-1
Q/F	QPR	A	1-2
1910-11			
1st Rd	Crystal Palace	H	1-1
Re-play	Crystal Palace	A	2-1
Q/F	QPR	H	1-1
Re-play	QPR	A	3-5
1911-12			
1st Rd	New Brompton	A	3-0
Q/F	QPR	H	5-4
S/F	Reading *	N	1-0
			played at White Hart Lane, Tottenham Hotspur FC
Final	Coventry *	N	1-0
			played at White Hart Lane, Tottenham Hotspur FC
1912-13			
1st Rd	Crystal Palace	H	0-2

FOOTBALL LEAGUE THIRD DIV SOUTHERN SECTION CUP

1933-34			
1st Rd	bye		
2nd Rd	Coventry	A	1-3
1934-35			
1st Rd	Brighton	H	1-1
Re-play	Brighton	A	1-3
1935-36			
1st Rd	Newport	H	3-0
2nd Rd	bye		
Q/F	Crystal Palace	A	2-3
1936-37			

1st Rd	bye	
2nd Rd	Clapton Orient	H 0-2
1937-38		
1st Rd	Exeter	H 1-2
1938-39		
1st Rd	Northampton	A 1-1
Re-play	Northampton	H 2-3
1945-46 Qualifying Competition		
	Northampton	H 4-3
	Northampton	A 1-0
	Ipswich	H 2-1
	Ipswich	A 1-2
	QPR	A 0-4
	Norwich	H 1-0
	Norwich	A 1-0
	Walsall	H 2-2
	Walsall	A 0-2
	Clapton Orient	H 2-1
	Clapton Orient	A 3-0
	Brighton	A 2-2
	Brighton	H 1-1
	QPR	H 0-0
	Port Vale	A 1-2
	Port Vale	H 1-1

FOOTBALL LEAGUE (WAR) CUP

1939-40		
Prelim.	QPR	H 1-0
1st Rd		
1st Leg	Watford	H 3-1
2nd Leg	Watford	A 3-1
2nd Rd		
1st Leg	Nottingham For	A 1-3
2nd Leg	Nottingham For	H 0-1
1940-41		
1st Rd		
1st Leg	Millwall	H 3-1
2nd Leg	Millwall	A 1-2
2nd Rd		
1st Leg	West Ham	H 2-1
2nd Leg	West Ham	A 1-3

SOUTHERN PROFESSIONAL FLOODLIGHT CHALLENGE CUP

1959-60		
1st Rd	bye	
2nd Rd	Coventry	H 0-0
Re-play	Coventry	A 0-4

FOOTBALL LEAGUE CUP

1960-61		
1st Rd	bye	
2nd Rd	Rochdale	A 2-5
1961-62		
1st Rd	Stoke	H 0-1
1962-63		
1st Rd	bye	
2nd Rd	Notts County	H 2-3
1963-64		
1st Rd	bye	
2nd Rd	Port Vale	H 2-1
3rd Rd	Swindon	A 0-3
1964-65		
1st Rd	Brentford	A 2-0
2nd Rd	Hull	A 0-0
Re-play	Hull	H 3-1
3rd Rd	Stoke	A 1-3
1965-66		
1st Rd	Newport	A 2-2
Re-play	Newport	H 3-1
2nd Rd	Reading	A 1-5
1966-67		
1st Rd	Gillingham	H 0-0
Re-play	Gillingham	A 0-2
1967-68		
1st Rd	Brentford	H 1-0
2nd Rd	Darlington	H 1-2
1968-69		
1st Rd	Bournemouth	A 6-1
2nd Rd	Wolves	A 0-1
1969-70		
1st Rd	Brentford	H 2-2
Re-play	Brentford	A 0-0
Re-play	Brentford *	N 3-2
	played at The Den	
2nd Rd	Shrewsbury	A 2-2
Re-play	Shrewsbury	H 2-0
3rd Rd	Bradford City	A 1-2
1970-71		
1st Rd	Charlton	A 0-3
1971-72		
1st Rd	Aldershot	A 1-1
Re-play	Aldershot	H 1-2
1972-73		
1st Rd	Aldershot	H 2-1
2nd Rd	Chelsea	H 0-1
1973-74		
1st Rd	Portsmouth	A 1-2
1974-75		
1st Rd	Cambridge	H 2-0
2nd Rd	Colchester	H 0-2
1975-76		
1st Rd		
1st Leg	Peterborough	H 2-0
2nd Leg	Peterborough	A 0-3
1976-77		
1st Rd		
1st Leg	Brighton	H 1-1
2nd Leg	Brighton	A 1-2
1977-78		
1st Rd		
1st Leg	Northampton	H 2-3
2nd Leg	Northampton	A 1-2
1978-79		
1st Rd		
1st Leg	Wimbledon	H 1-0
2nd Leg	Wimbledon	A 1-4
1979-80		
1st Rd		
1st Leg	Brentford	H 2-1
2nd Leg	Brentford	A 4-1
2nd Rd		
1st Leg	Bolton	A 2-1
2nd Leg	Bolton	H 0-0
3rd Rd	West Ham	A 1-1
Re-play	West Ham	H 0-0
Re-play	West Ham	A 1-5
1980-81		
1st Rd		
1st Leg	Oxford	H 1-0
2nd Leg	Oxford	A 0-2
1981-82		
1st Rd		
1st Leg	Portsmouth	H 0-0
2nd Leg	Portsmouth	A 1-4
1982-83		
1st Rd		
1st Leg	Fulham	H 1-0
2nd Leg	Fulham	A 2-4
1983-84		
1st Rd		
1st Leg	Wimbledon	H 1-0
2nd Leg	Wimbledon	A 4-6
1984-85		
1st Rd		
1st Leg	Orient	A 1-2
2nd Leg	Orient	H 0-0
1985-86		
1st Rd		
1st Leg	Gillingham	H 1-1
2nd Leg	Gillingham	A 0-2
1986-87		
1st Rd		
1st Leg	Brentford	H 1-0
2nd Leg	Brentford	A 3-2
2nd Rd		
1st Leg	Manchester City	H 0-0
2nd Leg	Manchester City	A 1-2
1987-88		
1st Rd		
1st Leg	Brentford	A 1-2
2nd Leg	Brentford	H 4-2
2nd Rd		
1st Leg	Derby	H 1-0
2nd Leg	Derby	A 0-0
3rd Rd	Ipswich	A 0-1
1988-89		
1st Rd		
1st Leg	Brighton	H 2-0
2nd Leg	Brighton	A 1-0
2nd Rd		
1st Leg	Derby	A 0-1
2nd Leg	Derby	H 1-2
1989-90		
1st Rd		
1st Leg	Colchester	A 4-3
2nd Leg	Colchester	H 2-1
2nd Rd		
1st Leg	Tottenham	A 0-1
2nd Leg	Tottenham	H 3-2
	3-3 on aggregate score; Tottenham win on the 'away goals' rule	
1990-91		
1st Rd		
1st Leg	Aldershot	H 2-1
2nd Leg	Aldershot	A 2-2
2nd Rd		
1st Leg	Crystal Palace	A 0-8
2nd Leg	Crystal Palace	H 1-2

1991-92			
1st Rd			
1st Leg	Watford	A	0-2
2nd Leg	Watford	H	1-1
1992-93			
1st Rd			
1st Leg	Derby	H	1-0
2nd Leg	Derby	A	0-7
1993-94			
1st Rd			
1st Leg	Barnet	H	0-2
2nd Leg	Barnet	A	1-1
1994-95			
1st Rd			
1st Leg	Watford	H	0-0
2nd Leg	Watford	A	0-1
1995-96			
1st Rd			
1st Leg	Crystal Palace	H	2-2
2nd Leg	Crystal Palace	A	0-2
1996-97			
1st Rd			
1st Leg	Fulham	H	0-2
2nd Leg	Fulham	A	2-1
1997-98			
1st Rd			
1st Leg	Cardiff	A	1-1
2nd Leg	Cardiff	H	3-1
2nd Rd			
1st Leg	Derby	H	0-1
2nd Leg	Derby	A	0-5
1998-99			
1st Rd			
1st Leg	Gillingham	H	1-0
2nd Leg	Gillingham	A	1-0
2nd Rd			
1st Leg	Coventry	A	0-1
2nd Leg	Coventry	H	0-4
1999-00			
1st Rd			
1st Leg	Oxford	H	0-2
2nd Leg	Oxford	A	0-1
2000-01			
1st Rd			
1st Leg	Birmingham City	H	0-5
2nd Leg	Birmingham City	A	0-0
2001-02			
1st Rd	Birmingham City	A	0-3
2002-03			
1st Rd	Wimbledon	H	1-4
2003-04			
1st Rd	Swindon	H	2-3
2004-05			
1st Rd	West Ham	A	0-2
2005-06			
1st Rd	Southampton	H	0-3

FOOTBALL LEAGUE GROUP CUP

1981-82			
Group	Orient	A	0-2
Group	Gillingham	A	0-0
Group	Wimbledon	H	1-2

FOOTBALL LEAGUE TROPHY

1982-83			
Group	Colchester	A	1-3
Group	Orient	H	1-1
Group	Watford	H	1-4

FOOTBALL LEAGUE ASSOCIATE – MEMBERS' CUP

1983-84			
1st Rd	Reading	H	5-0
2nd Rd	Colchester	A	2-0
3rd Rd	Bristol Rovers	H	1-2
1984-85			
1st Rd			
1st Leg	Millwall	H	0-2
2nd Leg	Millwall	A	1-3
1985-86			
Group	Colchester	A	1-4
1985-86			
Group	Northampton	H	1-3
1986-87			
Group	Cambridge	H	5-4
Group	Fulham	A	2-1
2nd Rd	Bristol City	A	0-1
1987-88			
Group	Fulham	H	1-0
Group	Brighton	A	2-3
2nd Rd	Brighton	A	2-4
1988-89			
Group	Lincoln	H	2-1
Group	Colchester	A	1-2
1st Rd	Northampton	A	1-2
1989-90			
Group	Gillingham	H	1-0
Group	Cambridge	A	3-3
1st Rd	Northampton	H	2-1
2nd Rd	Walsall	A	1-4
1990-91			
Group	Aldershot	H	10-1
Group	Reading	A	4-1
1st Rd	Maidstone	H	2-0
2nd Rd	Torquay	H	7-0
Quarter-final *(Southern Semi-final)*			
	Brentford	H	0-3

FOOTBALL LEAGUE FULL – MEMBERS' CUP

1991-92			
1st Rd	Watford	A	1-0
2nd Rd	Crystal Palace	A	2-4

ANGLO – ITALIAN CUP

1992-93			
Group	Bristol Rovers	A	0-3
Group	West Ham	H	0-3
1993-94			
Group	Luton	A	1-1
Group	Watford	H	3-0
International Round			
	Fiorentina	A	0-3
	Cosenza	A	2-1
	Pescara	H	1-3
	Padova	H	5-2
Semi-final			
1st Leg	Notts County	H	1-0
2nd Leg	Notts County	A	0-1
1-1 on aggregate score;			
County win 4-3 on penalties			
1995-96			
International Round			
	Brescia	H	0-0
	Reggiana	A	1-1
	Salernitana	A	1-2
	Foggia	H	1-2

FOOTBALL LEAGUE TROPHY

1997-98			
1st Rd	Wycombe	H	0-1
1998-99			
1st Rd	Exeter	A	1-3
1999-00			
1st Rd	Cheltenham	H	0-1
2000-01			
1st Rd	Cheltenham	H	2-0
2nd Rd	Cambridge	H	3-1
3rd Rd	Bristol Rovers	H	1-0
Quarter-final *(Southern Semi-final)*			
	Swindon	H	2-1
Semi-final *(Southern Final)*			
1st Leg	Brentford	H	1-2
2nd Leg	Brentford	A	1-2
2001-02			
1st Rd	Stevenage	A	4-1
2nd Rd	Bristol City	H	0-2
2002-03			
1st Rd	Swindon	A	1-6
2003-04			
1st Rd	Bristol Rovers	H	2-1
2nd Rd	Swansea	A	2-1
3rd Rd	Luton	H	3-0
Quarter-final *(Southern Semi-final)*			
	QPR	H	4-0
Semi-final *(Southern Final)*			
1st Leg	Colchester	A	3-2
2nd Leg	Colchester	H	1-1
Final	Blackpool *	N	0-2
* played at Millennium Stadium			
2004-05			
1st Rd	Colchester	A	1-1
Southend win 5-3 on penalties			
2nd Rd	Shrewsbury	H	4-1
3rd Rd	Northampton	A	2-0
Quarter-final *(Southern Semi-final)*			
	Swindon	H	2-0
Semi-final *(Southern Area Final)*			
1st Leg	Bristol Rovers	A	2-1
2nd Leg	Bristol Rovers	H	2-2
Final	Wrexham *	N	0-2
* played at Millennium Stadium			
2005-06			
1st Rd	Rushden	A	0-1

CLUB BY CLUB

Leagues
SL Southern League
SEL South Eastern League
UL United League
SA Southern Alliance
FL Football League
PO Football League Play-offs
War Leagues
South South Division
South A South Division Group 'A'
South D South Division Group 'D'
South R South (Regional) Division
Cups
FAC F. A. Challenge Cup
SCC Southern Counties
 Charity Cup
D3SC Football League Third Div
 (Southern Section) Cup
FLWC Football League (War) Cup
SPFC Southern Professional
 Floodlight Challenge Cup
FLC Football League Cup
FLGC Football League Group Cup
FLT Football League Trophy
AMC Football League
 Associate Members' Cup
FMC Football League Full
 Members' Cup
AIC Anglo-Italian Cup

ABERDARE ATHLETIC

Season	Comp.	H	A
1911-12	SL2	7-1	2-0
1912-13	SL2	1-0	2-1
1921-22	FL3S	3-2	1-1
1922-23	FL3S	4-0	1-1
1923-24	FL3S	1-1	2-5
1924-25	FL3S	2-1	0-3
1925-26	FL3S	0-1	0-2
1926-27	FL3S	5-1	0-1

ACCRINGTON STANLEY
old club

1958-59	FL3	4-2	0-3
1959-60	FL3	6-1	4-0

ALDERSHOT

1932-33	FL3S	5-1	2-1
1933-34	FL3S	1-0	0-2
1934-35	FL3S	2-1	2-3
1935-36	FL3S	2-2	1-1
1936-37	FL3S	2-2	2-1
1937-38	FL3S	4-1	0-1
1938-39	FL3S	2-1	0-1
1939-40	South D	2-2	0-1
1946-47	FL3S	2-1	0-0
1947-48	FL3S	4-0	1-1
1948-49	FL3S	1-0	0-1
1949-50	FL3S	3-0	1-1

1950-51	FL3S	4-2	2-2
1951-52	FL3S	7-1	2-2
1952-53	FL3S	1-1	1-1
1953-54	FL3S	2-1	0-4
1954-55	FL3S	0-1	0-1
1955-56	FL3S	3-2	3-3
1956-57	FL3S	2-4	3-5
1957-58	FL3S	1-2	2-0
1966-67	FL4	4-0	2-5
1967-68	FL4	1-1	3-1
1968-69	FL4	4-2	1-2
1969-70	FL4	2-2	1-2
1970-71	FL4	2-2	2-2
1971-72	FL4	1-0	0-0
1971-72	FLC	1-2	1-1
1972-73	FAC	0-2	
1972-73	FLC	2-1	
1973-74	FL3	2-1	3-3
1974-75	FL3	1-1	0-3
1975-76	FL3	0-2	1-2
1976-77	FL4	5-0	0-0
1977-78	FL4	3-1	0-3
1980-81	FL4	3-0	2-1
1984-85	FL4	1-0	2-6
1985-86	FL4	2-0	3-1
1986-87	FL4	2-0	1-0
1987-88	FL3	0-1	1-0
1988-89	FL3	1-1	2-2
1989-90	FL4	5-0	5-0
1990-91	FLC	2-1	2-2
1990-91	AMC	10-1	

H	27	9	7	104	46
A	9	15	16	54	68

AP LEAMINGTON

1974-75	FAC		2-1
1977-78	FAC	4-0	0-0

ARSENAL
as Woolwich Arsenal

1907-08	SEL1 *	3-0	1-2
1911-12	SEL1 *	3-0	2-3

 * Arsenal reserves
as Arsenal

1939-40	South A	0-5	1-5
1940-41	South R	1-7	0-7

ASTON VILLA

1971-72	FAC	1-0	

AYLESBURY UNITED

1989-90	FAC		0-1

BARNET
as Barnet Alston

1909-10	FAC	5-2	

as Barnet

1946-47	FAC		9-2

1993-94	FLC	0-2	1-1
1998-99	FL3	2-3	2-0
1999-00	FL3	1-3	1-2
2000-01	FL3	2-0	1-2
2005-06	FAC		1-0

BARNSLEY

1937-38	FAC	2-2	1-2
1959-60	FL3	2-2	1-4
1960-61	FL3	2-0	1-2
1961-62	FL3	1-2	1-1
1962-63	FL3	0-0	2-2
1963-64	FL3	4-1	1-0
1964-65	FL3	2-0	4-1
1966-67	FL4	3-0	2-1
1967-68	FL4	4-1	1-1
1976-77	FL4	1-1	1-3
1977-78	FL4	0-0	1-1
1979-80	FL3	2-1	2-1
1991-92	FL2	2-1	0-1
1992-93	FL1	3-0	1-3
1993-94	FL1	0-3	3-1
1994-95	FL1	3-1	0-0
1995-96	FL1	0-0	1-1
1996-97	FL1	1-2	0-3
2005-06	FL1	1-1	2-2

H	9	7	3	33	18
A	5	7	7	25	30

BARROW

1966-67	FL4	1-3	0-1
1970-71	FL4	2-3	0-2
1971-72	FL4	1-0	1-2

BATH CITY

1952-53	FAC		1-3

BIRMINGHAM CITY
as Birmingham

1913-14	FAC		1-2

as Birmingham City

1956-57	FAC	1-6	
1990-91	FL3	2-1	1-1
1992-93	FL1	4-0	0-2
1993-94	FL1	3-1	1-3
1995-96	FL1	3-1	0-2
1996-97	FL1	1-1	1-2
2000-01	FLC	0-5	0-0
2001-02	FLC		0-3

BLACKBURN ROVERS

1910-11	FAC *	1-5	

 * played at Ewood Park

1938-39	FAC		2-4
1972-73	FL3	0-1	1-2
1973-74	FL3	1-1	0-1
1974-75	FL3	2-2	0-1
1979-80	FL3	0-1	1-1

1991-92	FL2	3-0	2-2

BLACKPOOL

1920-21	FAC	1-0	
1949-50	FAC		0-4
1978-79	FL3	4-0	2-1
1979-80	FL3	1-2	0-1
1984-85	FL4	1-4	0-1
1987-88	FL3	4-0	1-1
1988-89	FL3	2-1	2-3
1997-98	FL2	2-1	0-3
2000-01	FL3	0-3	2-2
2003-04	FLT		0-2

played at The Millennium Stadium

2005-06	FL1	2-1	2-1

BOLTON WANDERERS

1972-73	FL3	1-1	1-1
1979-80	FLC	0-0	2-1
1983-84	FL3	0-1	0-2
1988-89	FL3	2-0	0-0
1990-91	FL3	1-1	0-1
1993-94	FL1	0-2	2-0
1994-95	FL1	2-1	0-3
1996-97	FL1	5-2	1-3

BOREHAM WOOD

1973-74	FAC	3-0	

BOSTON UNITED

2002-03	FL3	4-2	0-1
2003-04	FL3	0-2	2-0
2004-05	FL2	2-1	0-2

AFC BOURNEMOUTH

as Bournemouth and
Boscombe Athletic

1923-24	FL3S	1-1	1-0
1924-25	FL3S	3-0	0-1
1925-26	FL3S	3-0	2-1
1926-27	FL3S	0-3	0-3
1927-28	FL3S	3-0	3-2
1928-29	FL3S	4-4	2-2
1929-30	FL3S	4-1	0-0
1930-31	FL3S	4-0	0-0
1931-32	FL3S	1-3	0-0
1932-33	FL3S	2-1	0-4
1933-34	FL3S	1-2	4-1
1934-35	FL3S	0-0	1-2
1935-36	FL3S	3-3	1-2
1936-37	FL3S	0-0	0-1
1937-38	FL3S	1-0	1-7
1938-39	FL3S	2-2	4-0
1939-40	South D	2-1	1-6
1940-41	South		0-3
1946-47	FL3S	2-2	1-3
1947-48	FL3S	0-2	1-0
1948-49	FL3S	0-0	2-3
1949-50	FL3S	1-0	0-3

1950-51	FL3S	6-1	1-3
1951-52	FL3S	1-0	1-2
1951-52	FAC	6-1	
1952-53	FL3S	0-0	1-5
1953-54	FL3S	2-1	1-0
1954-55	FL3S	2-2	1-2
1955-56	FL3S	4-1	1-4
1956-57	FL3S	2-1	1-1
1957-58	FL3S	2-0	1-2
1958-59	FL3	2-0	4-1
1959-60	FL3	3-0	0-0
1960-61	FL3	0-0	2-3
1961-62	FL3	0-0	0-3
1962-63	FL3	0-1	0-0
1963-64	FL3	1-1	0-1
1964-65	FL3	2-1	1-2
1965-66	FL3	1-2	0-0
1968-69	FLC		6-1
1970-71	FL4	1-2	0-4

as AFC Bournemouth

1971-72	FAC		0-2
1972-73	FL3	2-2	0-2
1973-74	FL3	2-2	3-1
1974-75	FL3	0-0	0-0
1976-77	FL4	2-2	0-2
1977-78	FL4	5-1	3-0
1980-81	FL4	2-1	1-2
1982-83	FL3	0-0	2-0
1982-83	FAC		2-0
1983-84	FL3	0-0	0-1
1990-91	FL3	2-1	1-3
1997-98	FL2	5-3	1-2
2002-03	FL3	0-1	0-1
2002-03	FAC	1-1	2-3
2005-06	FL1	2-1	1-1

H	24	20	8	95	54
A	13	10	32	61	98

BRADFORD CITY

1958-59	FL3	1-1	1-6
1959-60	FL3	2-1	1-3
1960-61	FL3	0-0	1-2
1966-67	FL4	2-1	1-2
1967-68	FL4	1-1	1-2
1968-69	FL4	2-0	2-3
1969-70	FLC		1-2
1976-77	FL4	4-1	0-2
1980-81	FL4	3-1	1-2
1982-83	FL3	1-1	0-1
1983-84	FL3	2-1	1-1
1990-91	FL3	1-1	1-2
1996-97	FL1	1-1	0-0
2005-06	FL1	1-1	2-0

BRADFORD PARK AVENUE

old club

1954-55	FAC		3-2
1961-62	FL3	2-1	0-4
1962-63	FL3	3-1	2-2
1966-67	FL4	4-0	2-1
1967-68	FL4	2-1	1-0

1968-69	FL4	5-0	3-0
1969-70	FL4	1-1	0-1

BRENTFORD

1907-08	UL	0-0	2-5
1908-09	SL1	1-0	1-4
1908-09	UL	4-3	1-1
1909-10	SL1	0-3	1-4
1910-11	SL1	0-2	1-3
1911-12	FAC	0-1	
1912-13	SA	2-0	0-4
1913-14	SA	1-1	0-2
1913-14	FAC	2-0	1-1
1919-20	SL1	3-1	0-2
1920-21	FL3S	4-1	2-2
1921-22	FL3S	1-1	0-1
1922-23	FL3S	1-2	0-0
1923-24	FL3S	3-1	1-3
1924-25	FL3S	6-1	2-2
1925-26	FL3S	3-1	3-1
1926-27	FL3S	3-1	1-3
1927-28	FL3S	3-2	2-2
1928-29	FL3S	1-1	0-1
1929-30	FL3S	2-0	1-2
1929-30	FAC	1-0	
1930-31	FL3S	0-1	1-3
1931-32	FL3S	1-0	3-2
1932-33	FL3S	0-1	1-3
1954-55	FL3S	3-2	2-2
1955-56	FL3S	2-2	1-2
1956-57	FL3S	1-0	2-3
1957-58	FL3S	0-0	2-4
1958-59	FL3	2-0	1-6
1959-60	FL3	2-0	1-3
1960-61	FL3	1-1	1-1
1961-62	FL3	0-0	0-3
1963-64	FL3	2-1	0-3
1964-65	FL3	0-1	1-2
1964-65	FLC		2-0
1965-66	FL3	1-0	0-2
1966-67	FL4	3-0	1-1
1967-68	FL4	1-0	2-1
1967-68	FLC	1-0	
1968-69	FL4	4-0	1-1
1969-70	FL4	2-2	1-3
1969-70	FLC	2-2	0-0
1969-70	FLC *		3-2

played at The Den

1970-71	FL4	4-3	2-4
1971-72	FL4	3-1	2-1
1972-73	FL3	4-0	2-1
1976-77	FL4	2-1	0-1
1977-78	FL4	2-1	0-1
1978-79	FL3	1-1	0-3
1979-80	FL3	3-2	0-2
1979-80	FLC	2-1	4-1
1981-82	FL3	1-1	1-0
1982-83	FL3	4-2	2-4
1983-84	FL3	6-0	0-0
1986-87	FLC	1-0	3-2
1987-88	FL3	2-3	0-1
1987-88	FLC	4-2	1-2
1988-89	FL3	1-1	0-4

1990-91	FL3	0-1	1-0
1990-91	AMC	0-3	
1992-93	FL1	3-0	1-2
1997-98	FL2	3-1	1-1
1998-99	FL3	1-4	1-4
2000-01	FLT	1-2	1-2
2005-06	FL1	4-1	0-2

H	38	13	12	121	66
A	11	14	36	67	125

BRENTWOOD TOWN
old club

1968-69	FAC	10-1

BRESCIA

1995-96	AIC	0-0

BRIGHTON & HOVE ALBION

1907-08	SL2 *	3-1	3-2
	* Albion reserves		
1908-09	SL1	0-2	0-2
1909-10	SL1	2-0	1-1
1910-11	SL1	0-1	0-4
1911-12	SEL1 *	1-1	0-9
	* Albion reserves		
1912-13	SA	0-1	0-4
1913-14	SL1	0-1	1-1
1913-14	SA	2-4	1-3
1914-15	SL1	2-2	0-1
1919-20	SL1	0-0	0-3
1920-21	FL3S	2-0	0-1
1921-22	FL3S	1-2	0-0
1922-23	FL3S	0-0	1-0
1923-24	FL3S	1-0	0-2
1924-25	FL3S	2-0	1-2
1925-26	FL3S	4-0	2-3
1926-27	FL3S	0-1	1-2
1927-28	FL3S	0-1	0-1
1928-29	FL3S	1-1	1-2
1929-30	FL3S	0-0	0-1
1930-31	FL3S	0-2	2-1
1931-32	FL3S	2-0	2-1
1932-33	FL3S	2-1	2-1
1933-34	FL3S	0-0	0-1
1934-35	FL3S	3-2	2-2
1934-35	D3SC	1-1	1-3
1935-36	FL3S	0-0	3-1
1936-37	FL3S	2-1	0-1
1937-38	FL3S	2-1	1-3
1938-39	FL3S	1-1	0-3
1939-40	South D	8-2	3-1
1940-41	South	2-0	2-2
1945-46	D3SC	1-1	2-2
1946-47	FL3S	0-0	1-2
1947-48	FL3S	2-2	0-1
1948-49	FL3S	0-0	0-1
1949-50	FL3S	3-2	1-2
1950-51	FL3S	3-1	1-2
1951-52	FL3S	2-0	0-5
1952-53	FL3S	1-2	2-2

1953-54	FL3S	2-0	2-3
1954-55	FL3S	4-0	1-2
1955-56	FL3S	1-2	0-4
1956-57	FL3S	3-1	1-1
1957-58	FL3S	0-2	1-3
1962-63	FL3	1-1	0-0
1962-63	FAC	2-1	
1965-66	FL3	0-0	1-9
1967-68	FAC		0-1
1973-74	FL3	0-2	2-0
1974-75	FL3	1-0	0-2
1975-76	FL3	4-0	0-2
1975-76	FAC	2-1	
1976-77	FLC	1-1	1-2
1987-88	FL3	2-1	0-0
1987-88	AMC		2-3
1987-88	AMC		2-4
1988-89	FLC	2-0	1-0
1991-92	FL2	2-1	2-3
1998-99	FL3	3-0	2-0
1999-00	FL3	2-1	0-1
2000-01	FL3	2-0	2-0

H	29	17	13	90	51
A	11	10	39	57	121

BRISTOL CITY

1911-12	SEL1 *	2-0	2-3
	* City reserves		
1922-23	FL3S	0-3	0-5
1924-25	FL3S	2-0	0-5
1925-26	FL3S	1-2	4-1
1926-27	FL3S	0-1	1-5
1932-33	FL3S	3-1	1-5
1933-34	FL3S	3-0	1-5
1934-35	FL3S	6-0	0-2
1935-36	FL3S	0-1	1-2
1936-37	FL3S	3-0	1-0
1937-38	FL3S	5-0	2-4
1938-39	FL3S	2-0	0-1
1946-47	FL3S	4-1	0-2
1947-48	FL3S	4-0	0-6
1948-49	FL3S	1-0	1-2
1949-50	FL3S	2-0	1-1
1950-51	FL3S	1-1	3-0
1951-52	FL3S	5-1	0-6
1952-53	FL3S	0-4	0-5
1953-54	FL3S	0-1	1-4
1954-55	FL3S	3-2	2-3
1954-55	FAC		2-1
1960-61	FL3	1-0	0-2
1961-62	FL3	1-0	2-3
1962-63	FL3	2-2	3-6
1963-64	FL3	1-1	2-2
1964-65	FL3	0-4	0-4
1981-82	FL3	3-0	2-0
1986-87	AMC		0-1
1987-88	FL3	2-0	2-3
1988-89	FL3	1-2	2-0
1988-89	FAC		1-3
1991-92	FL2	1-1	2-2
1992-93	FL1	1-1	1-0
1993-94	FL1	0-1	1-2

1994-95	FL1	2-1	0-0
1997-98	FL2	0-2	0-1
2001-02	FLT	0-2	
2005-06	FL1	1-0	3-0

H	20	5	11	63	35
A	8	4	26	44	97

BRISTOL ROVERS

1908-09	SL1	2-1	0-1
1909-10	SL1	0-0	0-2
1910-11	SL1	1-1	0-1
1913-14	SL1	2-2	0-0
1914-15	SL1	2-0	1-4
1914-15	FAC	3-0	0-0
1919-20	SL1	1-1	1-4
1920-21	FL3S	1-0	1-2
1921-22	FL3S	3-0	0-1
1922-23	FL3S	0-0	0-2
1923-24	FL3S	1-0	1-3
1924-25	FL3S	2-1	3-1
1925-26	FL3S	3-1	0-2
1926-27	FL3S	2-1	1-5
1927-28	FL3S	2-1	3-1
1928-29	FL3S	1-0	1-4
1929-30	FL3S	6-0	2-4
1930-31	FL3S	4-0	3-2
1931-32	FL3S	4-1	0-0
1932-33	FL3S	2-2	1-3
1933-34	FL3S	2-2	1-3
1934-35	FL3S	5-1	1-2
1935-36	FL3S	1-1	2-3
1936-37	FL3S	2-3	2-1
1937-38	FL3S	1-1	1-2
1938-39	FL3S	3-2	1-4
1946-47	FL3S	2-3	3-1
1947-48	FL3S	1-0	2-1
1948-49	FL3S	0-1	0-0
1949-50	FL3S	3-1	1-1
1950-51	FL3S	1-1	1-4
1951-52	FL3S	2-1	0-2
1951-52	FAC	2-1	
1952-53	FL3S	2-1	1-2
1962-63	FL3	3-2	2-1
1963-64	FL3	3-4	1-3
1964-65	FL3	6-3	2-2
1965-66	FL3	2-0	1-3
1972-73	FL3	0-0	2-1
1973-74	FL3	0-0	0-4
1981-82	FL3	1-0	1-2
1982-83	FL3	1-0	2-2
1983-84	FL3	1-2	1-2
1983-84	AMC	1-2	
1987-88	FL3	4-2	0-0
1988-89	FL3	2-2	1-1
1991-92	FL2	2-0	1-4
1992-93	FL1	3-0	2-0
1992-93	AIC		0-3
1997-98	FL2	1-1	0-2
2000-01	FLT	1-0	
2001-02	FL3	2-1	1-2
2002-03	FL3	2-2	1-0
2003-04	FL3	0-1	1-1

2003-04	FLT	2-1	
2004-05	FL2	2-0	1-2
2004-05	FLT	2-2	2-1

H	33	16	7	110	56
A	11	10	32	56	104

BRUSH SPORTS

1946-47	FAC	6-1	

BURNLEY

1914-15	FAC	0-6	
1981-82	FL3	1-4	5-3
1983-84	FL3	2-2	0-3
1985-86	FL4	2-3	3-1
1986-87	FL4	2-1	1-2
1989-90	FL4	3-2	0-0
1994-95	FL1	3-1	1-5
1997-98	FL2	1-0	0-1

BURTON TOWN

1935-36	FAC	5-0	

BURY

1958-59	FL3	1-0	3-2
1959-60	FL3	0-4	0-3
1960-61	FL3	0-3	0-2
1971-72	FL4	0-0	0-2
1974-75	FL3	1-0	1-0
1975-76	FL3	2-0	0-1
1978-79	FL3	0-0	3-3
1979-80	FL3	0-0	1-1
1980-81	FL4	1-0	2-1
1984-85	FL4	3-3	0-2
1987-88	FL3	1-0	2-2
1988-89	FL3	1-1	1-3
1990-91	FL3	2-1	1-0
2002-03	FL3	1-2	3-1
2003-04	FL3	1-0	1-1
2004-05	FL2	1-0	1-0

H	8	5	3	15	14
A	6	4	6	19	24

CAMBRIDGE UNITED

1970-71	FL4	1-1	3-0
1971-72	FL3	1-2	1-1
1973-74	FL3	3-1	2-3
1974-75	FLC	2-0	
1976-77	FL4	0-1	3-2
1985-86	FL4	1-0	2-1
1986-87	FL4	3-1	2-1
1986-87	AMC	5-4	
1989-90	FL4	0-0	1-2
1989-90	AMC		3-3
1990-91	FL3	0-0	4-1
1991-92	FL2	1-1	1-0
1992-93	FL1	1-1	1-3
1998-99	FL3	0-1	0-3

2000-01	FLT	3-1	
2002-03	FL3	2-1	1-1
2003-04	FL3	1-0	1-0
2004-05	FL2	0-0	2-0

H	8	6	3	24	15
A	8	3	4	27	21

CANVEY ISLAND

2000-01	FAC *		2-1

played at Roots Hall

2003-04	FAC	1-1	3-2

CARDIFF CITY

1911-12	SL2	0-1	2-0
1912-13	SL2	1-1	0-1
1912-13	SA	1-0	1-1
1912-13	FAC		3-0
1913-14	SL1	2-1	0-3
1913-14	SA	1-1	1-3
1914-15	SL1	2-1	0-3
1919-20	SL1	1-1	0-1
1931-32	FL3S	1-1	3-2
1932-33	FL3S	2-2	0-2
1933-34	FL3S	1-1	1-1
1934-35	FL3S	2-1	0-2
1935-36	FL3S	3-1	1-1
1936-37	FL3S	8-1	1-1
1937-38	FL3S	3-1	0-5
1938-39	FL3S	2-0	0-1
1946-47	FL3S	0-2	1-3
1975-76	FL3	0-2	1-3
1975-76	FAC	2-1	
1982-83	FL3	1-2	1-4
1986-87	FL4	2-0	2-0
1988-89	FL3	0-0	0-2
1997-98	FLC	3-1	1-1
1998-99	FL3	0-1	0-2
2000-01	FL3	1-1	2-2

H	11	8	5	39	24
A	4	6	14	21	44

CARLISLE UNITED

1907-08	FAC		0-4
1962-63	FL3	2-0	2-1
1964-65	FL3	1-0	3-4
1970-71	FAC	0-3	
1978-79	FL3	1-1	0-0
1979-80	FL3	1-0	0-4
1981-82	FL3	1-1	2-3
1989-90	FL4	2-0	0-3
1997-98	FL2	1-1	0-5
1998-99	FL3	0-1	0-3
1999-00	FL3	2-0	1-1
2000-01	FL3	1-1	1-3
2001-02	FL3	3-2	0-0
2002-03	FL3	0-1	0-1
2003-04	FL3	2-2	2-1

CHARLTON ATHLETIC

1921-22	FL3S	1-1	0-4
1922-23	FL3S	0-0	1-5
1923-24	FL3S	2-2	1-4
1924-25	FL3S	0-3	0-0
1925-26	FL3S	1-2	0-5
1926-27	FL3S	5-0	0-1
1927-28	FL3S	1-2	2-1
1928-29	FL3S	1-3	2-3
1933-34	FL3S	1-0	3-1
1934-35	FL3S	0-3	0-3
1939-40	South A	0-2	1-8
1970-71	FLC		0-3
1972-73	FL3	1-1	0-0
1973-74	FL3	2-0	1-2
1974-75	FL3	2-1	1-2
1991-92	FL2	1-1	0-2
1992-93	FL1	0-2	1-1
1993-94	FL1	4-2	3-4
1994-95	FL1	2-1	1-3
1995-96	FL1	1-1	3-0
1996-97	FL1	0-2	0-2

H	6	6	8	25	29
A	3	3	15	20	54

CHELSEA

1907-08	SEL1 *	0-1	1-2
1911-12	SEL1 *	1-2	3-2

* Chelsea reserves

1912-13	FAC		2-5
1972-73	FLC	0-1	

CHELTENHAM TOWN

1999-00	FL3	2-1	1-2
1999-00	FLT	0-1	
2000-01	FL3	0-1	1-2
2000-01	FLT	2-0	
2001-02	FL3	0-1	1-1
2003-04	FL3	2-0	1-1
2004-05	FL2	0-2	3-0

CHESHAM UNITED

Formed from the merger of Chesham Generals and Chesham Town

as Chesham Generals

1906-07	SEL2	13-0	8-0

as Chesham Town

1906-07	SEL2	4-0	5-0
1911-12	SL2	7-0	9-0

CHESTER CITY

as Chester

1933-34	FAC	2-1	
1966-67	FL4	5-1	1-1
1967-68	FL4	5-1	0-0
1968-69	FL4	1-2	2-1
1969-70	FL4	4-2	0-2
1970-71	FL4	1-1	0-2

1971-72	FL4	4-2	1-1
1975-76	FL3	2-0	1-1
1976-77	FAC	0-4	
1978-79	FL3	0-1	1-0
1979-80	FL3	4-1	1-2
1981-82	FL3	2-0	1-1
as Chester City			
1984-85	FL4	1-1	1-5
1985-86	FL4	1-1	0-2
1987-88	FL3	2-2	1-1
1988-89	FL3	1-0	4-2
1990-91	FL3	1-1	0-1
1998-99	FL3	0-1	1-1
1999-00	FL3	3-1	0-0
2004-05	FL2	1-0	2-2

H	11	5	4	40	23
A	3	9	6	17	25

CHESTERFIELD

1938-39	FAC	4-3	1-1
1953-54	FAC	1-2	
1958-59	FL3	2-5	0-4
1959-60	FL3	1-2	0-1
1960-61	FL3	1-1	3-0
1966-67	FL4	4-1	1-2
1967-68	FL4	1-1	1-3
1968-69	FL4	2-2	0-0
1969-70	FL4	0-0	0-3
1972-73	FL3	5-1	4-2
1973-74	FL3	1-3	0-0
1974-75	FL3	2-1	1-1
1975-76	FL3	1-1	2-1
1978-79	FL3	2-0	2-3
1979-80	FL3	0-0	0-1
1981-82	FL3	0-2	2-1
1982-83	FL3	2-0	2-0
1984-85	FL4	0-1	1-2
1987-88	FL3	3-0	1-3
1988-89	FL3	3-1	1-2
1989-90	FL4	0-2	1-1
1997-98	FL2	0-2	0-1
2000-01	FL3	3-2	1-1
2001-02	FAC	2-0	1-1
2005-06	FL1	0-0	4-3

H	10	7	8	40	33
A	6	7	11	29	37

CLACTON TOWN

1960-61	FAC	3-1

CLAPTON

1907-08	FAC	1-0
1912-13	FAC	2-1
1923-24	FAC *	3-1

* played at Boleyn Castle Ground

COLCHESTER UNITED

1950-51	FL3S	4-2	3-1

1951-52	FL3S	3-2	0-1
1952-53	FL3S	4-0	3-3
1953-54	FL3S	3-0	1-0
1954-55	FL3S	4-2	0-2
1955-56	FL3S	4-0	6-3
1956-57	FL3S	3-2	2-3
1956-57	FAC		4-1
1957-58	FL3S	2-3	0-1
1958-59	FL3	1-1	1-0
1959-60	FL3	1-0	3-2
1960-61	FL3	2-1	0-2
1962-63	FL3	2-3	1-3
1963-64	FL3	0-0	3-3
1964-65	FL3	6-3	1-3
1968-69	FL4	3-1	0-4
1969-70	FL4	2-1	2-0
1970-71	FL4	1-1	1-1
1971-72	FL4	1-4	0-1
1974-75	FL3	1-1	1-1
1974-75	FLC	0-2	
1975-76	FL3	2-0	1-2
1976-77	FL4	0-0	1-0
1978-79	FL3	1-1	1-1
1979-80	FL3	0-1	1-2
1982-83	FLT		1-3
1983-84	AMC		2-0
1984-85	FL4	2-5	3-3
1984-85	FAC	2-2	2-3
1985-86	FL4	2-4	0-2
1985-86	AMC		1-4
1986-87	FL4	1-1	2-1
1988-89	AMC		1-2
1989-90	FL4	0-2	2-0
1989-90	FLC	2-1	4-3
2003-04	FLT	1-1	3-2
2004-05	FLT		1-1
2005-06	FL1	3-1	3-0

H	15	9	8	63	48
A	14	7	16	61	64

CORINTHIAN – CASUALS
Formed from the merger of the
Corinthian and Casuals FCs

as Corinthian

1937-38	FAC		2-0
1938-39	FAC	3-0	

COSENZA

1993-94	AIC	2-1

COVENTRY CITY

1908-09	SL1	4-0	5-2
1909-10	SL1	0-1	2-0
1910-11	SL1	4-1	1-5
1911-12	SEL1 *	1-0	1-3

* City reserves

1911-12	SCC **		1-0

** played at White Hart Lane

1913-14	SL1	1-1	0-3
1926-27	FL3S	3-1	1-1

1927-28	FL3S	3-2	1-6
1928-29	FL3S	0-0	1-1
1929-30	FL3S	1-2	1-5
1930-31	FL3S	2-0	0-0
1931-32	FL3S	4-0	2-0
1932-33	FL3S	1-3	3-2
1933-34	FL3S	2-1	0-2
1933-34	D3SC		1-3
1934-35	FL3S	1-1	3-6
1935-36	FL3S	0-0	0-3
1952-53	FL3S	1-0	1-2
1953-54	FL3S	2-2	0-1
1954-55	FL3S	1-0	4-1
1955-56	FL3S	3-0	0-0
1956-57	FL3S	1-2	0-2
1957-58	FL3S	5-1	0-1
1959-60	FL3	1-0	0-2
1959-60	SPFC	0-0	0-4
1960-61	FL3	4-1	0-3
1961-62	FL3	2-0	3-3
1962-63	FL3	1-1	4-3
1963-64	FL3	1-2	5-2
1998-99	FLC	0-4	0-1

H	15	7	6	49	26
A	8	5	17	40	67

CREWE ALEXANDRA

1963-64	FL3	1-1	2-1
1966-67	FL4	1-1	0-1
1967-68	FL4	0-0	0-1
1969-70	FL4	2-0	3-5
1970-71	FL4	0-2	2-1
1971-72	FL4	4-1	2-1
1976-77	FL4	1-0	1-1
1977-78	FL4	1-0	1-0
1980-81	FL4	3-0	1-1
1984-85	FL4	3-1	2-0
1985-86	FL4	0-1	1-1
1986-87	FL4	3-1	1-2
1990-91	FL3	3-2	2-0

CROMER TOWN

as Cromer

1908-09	FAC	2-0

CROYDON COMMON

1907-08	SL2	2-0	3-0
1907-08	SEL1	2-0	1-7
1907-08	UL	4-0	2-5
1908-09	UL	5-0	1-2
1909-10	SL1	3-1	2-3
1911-12	SL2	3-0	2-0
1911-12	SEL1	3-3	0-3
1912-13	SL2	3-1	1-1
1912-13	SA	1-1	0-0
1913-14	SA	1-0	0-3
1914-15	SL1	2-0	1-1

CRYSTAL PALACE

1908-09	SL1	1-0	3-1
1909-10	SL1	3-0	0-6
1910-11	SL1	0-0	0-0
1910-11	SCC	1-1	2-1
1912-13	SCC	0-2	
1913-14	SL1	3-3	0-0
1914-15	SL1	2-3	1-1
1919-20	SL1	1-1	0-0
1920-21	FL3S	0-2	3-2
1925-26	FL3S	5-1	0-3
1926-27	FL3S	3-1	3-5
1927-28	FL3S	6-1	1-4
1928-29	FL3S	3-0	2-3
1929-30	FL3S	3-2	2-1
1930-31	FL3S	2-4	1-3
1931-32	FL3S	1-0	2-3
1932-33	FL3S	1-2	1-4
1933-34	FL3S	0-4	1-1
1934-35	FL3S	1-4	0-1
1935-36	FL3S	7-1	0-3
1935-36	D3SC		2-3
1936-37	FL3S	2-1	1-1
1936-37	FAC	2-0	1-1
1937-38	FL3S	2-2	1-2
1938-39	FL3S	3-1	3-4
1939-40	South A	3-1	2-4
1939-40	South D	3-0	2-5
1940-41	South R		2-1
1940-41	South R		0-7
1946-47	FL3S	2-0	3-0
1947-48	FL3S	2-1	0-0
1948-49	FL3S	0-1	1-2
1949-50	FL3S	0-0	1-2
1950-51	FL3S	5-2	2-0
1951-52	FL3S	4-0	0-1
1952-53	FL3S	2-2	0-0
1953-54	FL3S	1-2	2-4
1954-55	FL3S	3-2	2-3
1955-56	FL3S	4-3	2-1
1956-57	FL3S	1-1	0-2
1957-58	FL3S	1-1	0-2
1961-62	FL3	2-2	2-2
1962-63	FL3	1-0	3-2
1963-64	FL3	2-1	0-3
1974-75	FL3	0-1	1-1
1975-76	FL3	1-2	1-1
1990-91	FLC	1-2	0-8
1991-92	FMC		2-4
1993-94	FL1	1-2	0-1
1995-96	FL1	1-1	0-2
1995-96	FLC	2-2	0-2
1996-97	FL1	2-1	1-6

H	23	12	13	96	66
A	9	13	29	59	118

CUSTOM HOUSE

1912-13	FAC		1-0

CWM ALBION

1911-12	SL2	7-0	8-0

DAGENHAM & REDBRIDGE

*Ilford and Leytonstone merged in
1979 to form Leytonstone/Ilford.
In 1988 Walthamstow Avenue was
incorporated.
In 1989 Leytonstone/ Ilford
(incorporating Walthamstow Avenue)
changed name to Redbridge Forest
who, in 1992, merged with Dagenham
to form the present club*

as Ilford (old club)

1907-08	FAC	3-1	
1908-09	FAC		3-1
1974-75	FAC		2-0

as Leytonstone

1912-13	FAC		5-0

as Walthamstow Avenue (old club)

1937-38	FAC		1-0

as Dagenham

1970-71	FAC	1-0	

DARLINGTON

1967-68	FL4	2-2	1-1
1967-68	FLC	1-2	
1968-69	FL4	1-1	3-2
1969-70	FL4	2-0	2-0
1970-71	FL4	0-0	4-0
1971-72	FL4	3-0	3-2
1976-77	FL4	0-0	0-0
1977-78	FL4	2-0	0-2
1980-81	FL4	1-0	2-0
1984-85	FL4	1-1	1-3
1998-99	FL3	2-1	1-2
1999-00	FL3	1-2	0-1
2000-01	FL3	0-2	1-1
2001-02	FL3	1-0	2-2
2002-03	FL3	2-0	1-2
2003-04	FL3	3-2	0-0
2004-05	FL2	2-0	0-4

H	9	5	3	24	13
A	5	5	6	21	22

DEPOT BATTALION, ROYAL ENGINEERS

1906-07	SEL2	4-0	5-0

DERBY COUNTY

1925-26	FAC	4-1	
1932-33	FAC	2-3	
1975-76	FAC		0-1
1977-78	FAC		2-3
1987-88	FLC	1-0	0-0
1988-89	FLC	1-2	0-1
1991-92	FL2	1-0	2-1
1992-93	FL1	0-0	0-2
1992-93	FLC	1-0	0-7
1993-94	FL1	4-3	3-1
1994-95	FL1	1-0	2-1
1995-96	FL1	1-2	0-1
1997-98	FLC	0-1	0-5

DONCASTER ROVERS

1958-59	FL3	5-0	1-2
1967-68	FL4	1-2	1-2
1968-69	FL4	2-0	0-2
1971-72	FL4	2-1	2-0
1976-77	FL4	2-1	3-0
1977-78	FL4	4-0	0-2
1980-81	FL4	0-0	0-1
1981-82	FL3	1-1	1-1
1982-83	FL3	3-2	0-0
1987-88	FL3	4-1	1-0
1989-90	FL4	2-0	1-0
1998-99	FAC	0-1	
2003-04	FL3	0-2	0-2
2005-06	FL1	0-1	0-2

DOVER

1975-76	FAC	4-1	

DULWICH HAMLET

1925-26	FAC	5-1	
1926-27	FAC		4-1

EASTBOURNE TOWN

as Eastbourne

1906-07	SEL2	5-0	5-1

EAST HAM

1907-08	FAC	3-0	

ECCLES UNITED

1920-21	FAC	5-1	

ENFIELD

1910-11	FAC	3-1	3-3

EVERTON

1946-47	FAC		2-4
1954-55	FAC		1-3
1991-92	FAC		0-1

EXETER CITY

1908-09	SL1	0-0	1-2
1909-10	SL1	2-0	1-3
1910-11	SL1	1-2	0-1
1913-14	SL1	1-0	0-0
1914-15	SL1	0-2	1-7
1919-20	SL1	2-0	0-3
1920-21	FL3S	0-0	0-0

Season	Comp.	H	A
1921-22	FL3S	0-1	1-4
1922-23	FL3S	5-0	1-2
1923-24	FL3S	0-0	0-2
1924-25	FL3S	3-0	1-0
1925-26	FL3S	3-1	1-0
1926-27	FL3S	1-2	0-2
1927-28	FL3S	1-2	2-3
1928-29	FL3S	1-0	2-1
1929-30	FL3S	1-0	1-3
1930-31	FL3S	5-1	1-1
1931-32	FL3S	0-1	0-3
1932-33	FL3S	1-2	0-3
1932-33	FAC	1-1	1-0
1933-34	FL3S	3-1	0-2
1934-35	FL3S	1-2	3-4
1935-36	FL3S	4-0	0-1
1936-37	FL3S	4-4	2-2
1937-38	FL3S	1-1	1-1
1937-38	D3SC	1-2	
1938-39	FL3S	0-1	3-3
1946-47	FL3S	2-2	5-1
1947-48	FL3S	2-0	0-0
1948-49	FL3S	0-0	0-0
1949-50	FL3S	1-0	1-1
1950-51	FL3S	5-1	0-1
1951-52	FL3S	0-0	2-2
1952-53	FL3S	1-1	2-0
1953-54	FL3S	0-1	1-1
1954-55	FL3S	0-0	1-2
1955-56	FL3S	6-0	1-0
1956-57	FL3S	2-0	1-6
1957-58	FL3S	2-0	5-0
1964-65	FL3	0-0	1-1
1965-66	FL3	4-2	1-1
1966-67	FL4	0-0	1-0
1967-68	FL4	1-0	2-0
1968-69	FL4	6-1	2-1
1969-70	FL4	1-1	0-3
1970-71	FL4	0-0	0-2
1971-72	FL4	3-0	0-0
1976-77	FL4	2-0	1-3
1976-77	FAC	2-1	1-1
1978-79	FL3	0-1	0-0
1979-80	FL3	4-0	2-4
1981-82	FL3	2-1	1-1
1982-83	FL3	1-1	3-4
1983-84	FL3	0-3	3-3
1984-85	FL4	1-0	1-2
1985-86	FL4	2-0	2-0
1986-87	FL4	2-1	0-0
1989-90	FL4	1-2	1-2
1990-91	FL3	2-1	2-1
1998-99	FL3	0-0	1-2
1998-99	FLT		1-3
1999-00	FL3	1-2	1-0
2000-01	FL3	1-1	2-2
2001-02	FL3	3-1	1-2
2002-03	FL3	1-0	0-1

H	31	18	15	103	50
A	14	20	30	72	106

FIORENTINA
old club

1993-94	AIC		0-3

FOGGIA

1995-96	AIC	1-2	

4th KING'S ROYAL RIFLES

1907-08	FAC	6-0	

FULHAM

1906-07	SL2 *	3-0	1-1
1907-08	SEL1 *	5-0	1-2
1911-12	SEL1 *	1-0	1-5
	* Fulham reserves		
1928-29	FL3S	0-1	4-2
1929-30	FL3S	1-2	2-2
1930-31	FL3S	2-4	0-1
1931-32	FL3S	4-1	1-1
1940-41	South R		2-8
1981-82	FL3	0-0	1-2
1982-83	FLC	1-0	2-4
1986-87	AMC		2-1
1987-88	FL3	0-2	1-3
1987-88	AMC	1-0	
1988-89	FL3	0-0	0-1
1990-91	FL3	1-1	3-0
1996-97	FLC	0-2	2-1
1997-98	FL2	1-0	0-2
1997-98	FAC		0-1

H	7	3	5	20	13
A	4	3	10	23	37

GAINSBOROUGH TRINITY

1909-10	FAC	1-0	1-1

GILLINGHAM
as New Brompton

1907-08	UL	2-2	1-2
1908-09	SL1	1-0	0-1
1908-09	UL	2-2	0-7
1909-10	SL1	3-0	0-5
1909-10	SCC	4-1	
1910-11	SL1	2-2	2-1
1911-12	SCC		3-0

as Gillingham

1913-14	SL1	2-3	2-4
1914-15	SL1	1-1	0-1
1919-20	SL1	0-1	1-0
1920-21	FL3S	1-0	1-1
1921-22	FL3S	2-0	0-1
1922-23	FL3S	1-1	0-1
1923-24	FL3S	3-2	2-3
1924-25	FL3S	4-0	1-3
1925-26	FL3S	1-1	1-3
1925-26	FAC	1-0	
1926-27	FL3S	1-0	3-2

1927-28	FL3S	1-2	0-1
1927-28	FAC		0-2
1928-29	FL3S	2-0	2-0
1929-30	FL3S	0-0	0-1
1930-31	FL3S	3-2	0-1
1931-32	FL3S	2-0	0-4
1932-33	FL3S	2-2	2-3
1933-34	FL3S	1-2	0-0
1934-35	FL3S	0-0	2-2
1935-36	FL3S	4-2	1-2
1936-37	FL3S	0-2	0-1
1937-38	FL3S	2-0	1-2
1950-51	FL3S	4-0	0-1
1951-52	FL3S	3-1	0-2
1952-53	FL3S	3-1	1-1
1953-54	FL3S	1-1	1-3
1954-55	FL3S	3-1	1-1
1955-56	FL3S	2-2	3-2
1956-57	FL3S	5-0	2-0
1957-58	FL3S	2-0	0-2
1960-61	FAC		2-3
1964-65	FL3	3-1	0-1
1965-66	FL3	5-2	0-1
1966-67	FLC	0-0	0-2
1969-70	FAC	0-0	1-2
1971-72	FL4	2-2	0-0
1974-75	FL3	2-2	1-2
1975-76	FL3	2-2	2-1
1978-79	FL3	0-1	0-1
1979-80	FL3	0-3	0-1
1981-82	FL3	3-0	0-2
1981-82	FLGC		0-0
1982-83	FL3	1-1	0-1
1983-84	FL3	3-1	1-5
1985-86	FLC	1-1	0-2
1987-88	FL3	1-3	1-8
1988-89	FL3	2-1	1-1
1989-90	FL4	2-0	0-5
1989-90	AMC	1-0	
1997-98	FL2	0-0	2-1
1998-99	FLC	1-0	1-0
2005-06	FL1	0-1	2-1

H	28	19	9	100	55
A	11	9	37	47	105

GRAVESEND ATHLETIC

Season	Comp.	H	A
1908-09	UL	*	*

not played; Gravesend resigned mid-December, 1908, shortly before the teams were due to meet

GRIMSBY TOWN

1920-21	FL3S	3-1	0-1
1959-60	FL3	3-0	1-1
1960-61	FL3	1-1	0-1
1961-62	FL3	2-0	1-3
1964-65	FL3	4-0	0-1
1965-66	FL3	3-1	0-1
1968-69	FL4	0-1	0-0
1969-70	FL4	1-3	2-2

1970-71	FL4	1-1	0-2
1971-72	FL4	3-1	1-4
1972-73	FL3	2-0	1-3
1973-74	FL3	4-1	1-2
1974-75	FL3	3-0	0-0
1975-76	FL3	5-2	2-2
1977-78	FL4	1-1	0-2
1979-80	FL3	1-0	0-1
1987-88	FL3	0-0	3-1
1989-90	FL4	0-2	0-2
1990-91	FL3	2-0	0-1
1991-92	FL2	3-1	2-3
1992-93	FL1	1-0	0-1
1993-94	FL1	1-2	0-4
1994-95	FL1	0-0	1-4
1995-96	FL1	1-0	1-1
1996-97	FL1	1-0	0-4
1997-98	FL2	0-1	1-5
2004-05	FL2	1-1	1-1

H	16	5	5	46	19
A	1	7	19	18	53

HALESOWEN TOWN

1986-87	FAC	4-1	

HALIFAX TOWN

1958-59	FL3	3-2	0-1
1959-60	FL3	3-0	1-2
1960-61	FL3	2-2	2-6
1961-62	FL3	2-1	2-0
1962-63	FL3	1-1	1-0
1966-67	FL4	1-0	2-2
1967-68	FL4	2-2	2-1
1968-69	FL4	2-1	1-1
1972-73	FL3	1-1	1-2
1973-74	FL3	1-2	0-0
1974-75	FL3	4-0	1-3
1975-76	FL3	4-1	0-1
1976-77	FL4	1-1	1-3
1977-78	FL4	5-0	1-0
1980-81	FL4	5-1	5-1
1984-85	FL4	2-1	0-1
1985-86	FL4	2-1	3-2
1986-87	FL4	2-3	1-0
1989-90	FL4	2-0	2-1
1998-99	FL3	0-0	1-3
1999-00	FL3	4-1	0-0
2000-01	FL3	0-3	1-0
2001-02	FL3	4-1	1-1

H	14	6	3	53	25
A	9	5	9	29	31

HARLOW TOWN

1979-80	FAC	1-1	0-1

HARTLEPOOL UNITED

as Hartlepools United

1966-67	FL4	2-0	2-1

1967-68	FL4	2-1	1-0

as Hartlepool

1969-70	FL4	0-2	1-2
1970-71	FL4	2-0	1-0
1971-72	FL4	3-1	2-2
1976-77	FL4	1-0	1-1

as Hartlepool United

1977-78	FL4	1-1	0-1
1980-81	FL4	4-0	3-1
1984-85	FL4	1-1	1-2
1985-86	FL4	3-2	2-3
1986-87	FL4	1-1	0-1
1989-90	FL4	3-0	1-1
1998-99	FL3	1-1	4-2
1999-00	FL3	2-1	2-1
2000-01	FL3	2-1	0-1
2001-02	FL3	0-0	1-5
2002-03	FL3	0-1	1-2
2002-03	FAC	1-1	2-1
2005-06	FL1	3-0	2-1

H	11	6	2	32	14
A	8	3	8	27	28

HASTINGS UNITED

as Hastings and St. Leonards United

1906-07	SL2	2-0	2-1
1906-07	SEL2	2-0	3-0
1907-08	SL2	2-1	2-0
1907-08	SEL1	0-0	0-5
1907-08	UL	3-2	2-0
1908-09	UL	1-1	1-2
1909-10	FAC	4-2	

HEDNESFORD TOWN

1920-21	FAC	3-1	

HENDON

as Golders Green

1934-35	FAC	10-1	

HEREFORD UNITED

1956-57	FAC		3-2
1973-74	FL3	2-1	2-1
1974-75	FL3	0-0	0-1
1975-76	FL3	1-3	1-2
1980-81	FL4	2-0	0-0
1980-81	FAC	0-1	
1981-82	FAC		1-3
1984-85	FL4	0-0	0-3
1985-86	FL4	3-1	1-2
1986-87	FL4	2-0	1-0
1989-90	FL4	2-0	3-0

HITCHIN TOWN

1907-08	SEL1	2-1	1-1

HUDDERSFIELD TOWN

1973-74	FL3	5-2	1-0
1974-75	FL3	1-0	1-4
1976-77	FL4	1-1	1-1
1977-78	FL4	1-3	0-2
1981-82	FL3	4-0	2-3
1982-83	FL3	0-1	1-2
1988-89	FL3	2-4	2-3
1990-91	FL3	0-1	2-1
1992-93	FAC		2-1
1995-96	FL1	0-0	1-3
1996-97	FL1	1-2	0-0
2003-04	FL3	1-2	0-1
2005-06	FL1	1-1	0-0

HULL CITY

1958-59	FL3	1-1	2-3
1960-61	FL3	3-1	1-0
1961-62	FL3	2-1	0-0
1962-63	FL3	0-1	2-1
1963-64	FL3	1-1	0-1
1964-65	FL3	2-1	0-0
1964-65	FLC	3-1	0-0
1965-66	FL3	0-2	0-1
1978-79	FL3	3-0	0-2
1979-80	FL3	3-0	0-1
1983-84	FL3	2-2	1-2
1998-99	FL3	0-1	1-1
1999-00	FL3	1-2	0-0
2000-01	FL3	1-1	1-1
2001-02	FL3	2-0	0-0
2002-03	FL3	3-0	2-2
2003-04	FL3	2-2	2-3

H	8	5	4	29	17
A	2	8	7	12	18

IPSWICH TOWN

1938-39	FL3S	0-0	2-4
1945-46	FL3S(N)	2-0	1-3
1945-46	D3SC	2-1	1-2
1946-47	FL3S	1-1	0-1
1947-48	FL3S	3-2	0-4
1948-49	FL3S	1-1	3-1
1949-50	FL3S	2-2	3-1
1950-51	FL3S	1-0	0-1
1951-52	FL3S	5-0	1-4
1952-53	FL3S	2-0	0-0
1953-54	FL3S	3-1	1-1
1955-56	FL3S	2-3	0-3
1956-57	FL3S	2-0	3-3
1987-88	FLC		0-1
1991-92	FL2	1-2	0-1
1995-96	FL1	2-1	1-1
1996-97	FL1	0-0	1-1

H	9	5	2	29	14
A	2	5	10	17	32

KETTERING TOWN

as Kettering

1911-12	SL2	5-0	1-3

KIDDERMINSTER HARRIERS

2000-01	FL3	1-1	1-2
2001-02	FL3	1-0	0-2
2002-03	FL3	0-2	0-1
2003-04	FL3	3-0	2-1
2004-05	FL2	1-0	3-1

KING'S LYNN

1923-24	FAC	1-0
1968-69	FAC	9-0

KINGSTONIAN

2000-01	FAC	0-1

LEEDS UNITED

Season	Comp.	H	A

LEICESTER CITY

1991-92	FL2	1-2	0-2
1992-93	FL1	3-1	1-4
1993-94	FL1	0-0	0-3
1995-96	FL1	2-1	3-1
1996-97	FAC		0-2

LEYTON

1907-08	SEL1 *	4-1	3-2
1908-09	SL1	0-0	0-0
1908-09	FAC		1-0
1909-10	SL1	1-0	3-7
1910-11	SL1	1-1	1-1
1911-12	SEL1 *	2-1	1-0

* Leyton reserves

LEYTON ORIENT

as Clapton Orient

1906-07	SEL2 *	2-0	5-1
1907-08	SEL1 *	2-1	0-1
1907-08	FAC	3-1	1-1
1911-12	SEL1 *	1-1	0-2

* Orient reserves

1929-30	FL3S	4-1	1-1
1930-31	FL3S	2-0	1-3
1931-32	FL3S	1-3	4-2
1932-33	FL3S	3-3	0-0
1933-34	FL3S	2-1	2-5
1934-35	FL3S	0-2	0-3
1935-36	FL3S	2-1	0-3
1936-37	FL3S	0-0	0-3
1936-37	D3SC	0-2	
1937-38	FL3S	1-2	1-1
1938-39	FL3S	1-0	0-5
1939-40	FL3S		0-0
1939-40	South A	7-0	1-5
1939-40	South D	3-0	1-5
1940-41	South R	9-3	2-1
1945-46	FL3S(N)	1-1	2-2
1945-46	D3SC	2-1	3-0

as Leyton Orient

1946-47	FL3S	0-0	1-1
1947-48	FL3S	2-1	0-2
1948-49	FL3S	2-2	0-2
1949-50	FL3S	2-0	2-2
1949-50	FAC		2-0
1950-51	FL3S	0-1	1-1
1951-52	FL3S	1-0	4-1
1952-53	FL3S	1-0	0-3
1953-54	FL3S	2-1	1-1
1954-55	FL3S	1-2	1-5
1955-56	FL3S	0-0	0-3

as Orient

1981-82	FLGC		0-2
1982-83	FL3	1-1	1-1
1982-83	FLT	1-1	
1983-84	FL3	3-0	0-1
1984-85	FLC	0-0	1-2
1985-86	FL4	5-1	0-3
1986-87	FL4	2-1	0-1

as Leyton Orient

1990-91	FL3	1-1	1-0
1990-91	FAC		2-3
1998-99	FL3	2-2	3-0
1999-00	FL3	1-1	1-2
2000-01	FL3	0-1	2-0
2001-02	FL3	1-2	1-2
2002-03	FL3	1-0	1-2
2003-04	FL3	2-3	1-2
2004-05	FL2	0-1	2-2

H	21	13	10	77	45
A	9	12	25	52	88

LINCOLN CITY

1955-56	FAC		3-2
1961-62	FL3	0-0	0-2
1966-67	FL4	3-0	2-2
1967-68	FL4	2-1	2-4
1968-69	FL4	3-0	1-2
1969-70	FL4	2-2	3-3
1970-71	FL4	1-1	2-1
1971-72	FL4	2-1	0-0
1978-79	FL3	2-0	1-1
1980-81	FL4	0-0	1-2
1981-82	FL3	0-2	1-1
1982-83	FL3	2-0	1-0
1983-84	FL3	2-0	2-1
1986-87	FL4	1-0	3-1
1988-89	AMC	2-1	
1989-90	FL4	2-0	0-2
1999-00	FL3	2-2	0-1
2000-01	FL3	1-0	0-3
2001-02	FL3	1-1	1-0
2002-03	FL3	0-1	1-2
2003-04	FL3	0-2	2-2
2003-04	FAC	3-0	
2004-05	FL2	1-1	1-1

2004-05	PO *	2-0

* played at The Millennium Stadium

H	12	7	3	32	15
A	7	7	8	29	33

LIVERPOOL

1956-57	FAC	2-1	
1957-58	FAC	2-3	1-1
1978-79	FAC	0-0	0-3

LLANELLI

as Llanelly

1912-13	SL2	2-2	1-4
1923-24	FAC		1-2

LONDON CALEDONIAN

1908-09	FAC		4-0
1911-12	FAC		3-1
1924-25	FAC	3-3	4-1

LONDON PAPER MILLS

1933-34	FAC		1-0

LUTON TOWN

1907-08	SEL1 *	1-1	2-1
1908-09	SL1	2-0	0-3
1908-09	FAC	2-4	1-1
1909-10	SL1	4-1	3-3
1910-11	SL1	1-4	1-3
1911-12	SEL1 *	6-0	1-3

* Town reserves

1912-13	SL2	1-1	3-4
1912-13	SA	5-1	0-4
1913-14	SA	1-0	1-7
1914-15	SL1	1-0	4-3
1919-20	SL1	3-0	1-1
1920-21	FL3S	1-1	0-4
1921-22	FL3S	0-1	0-3
1922-23	FL3S	1-3	0-2
1923-24	FL3S	1-1	4-4
1924-25	FL3S	2-1	0-4
1925-26	FL3S	2-0	0-2
1926-27	FL3S	2-1	0-0
1927-28	FL3S	1-0	0-0
1928-29	FL3S	5-0	2-4
1928-29	FAC		1-5
1929-30	FL3S	1-1	3-0
1930-31	FL3S	0-2	1-2
1931-32	FL3S	1-1	3-1
1932-33	FL3S	2-1	3-3
1933-34	FL3S	0-1	1-3
1934-35	FL3S	3-3	2-1
1935-36	FL3S	0-1	2-1
1936-37	FL3S	3-0	0-1
1940-41	South	4-2	
1963-64	FL3	0-1	1-4
1964-65	FL3	5-0	1-0
1964-65	FAC		0-1

1966-67	FL4	2-0	0-1
1967-68	FL4	3-0	1-3
1992-93	FL1	2-1	2-2
1993-94	FL1	2-1	1-1
1993-94	FAC		0-1
1993-94	AIC		1-1
1994-95	FL1	3-0	2-2
1995-96	FL1	0-1	1-3
1997-98	FL2	1-2	0-1
2001-02	FL3	1-2	0-2
2001-02	FAC	3-2	
2003-04	FLT	3-0	
2004-05	FAC	0-3	

H	23	7	12	81	45
A	6	12	24	48	95

MACCLESFIELD TOWN

1999-00	FL3	1-0	2-1
2000-01	FL3	3-1	0-1
2001-02	FL3	3-0	0-0
2002-03	FL3	1-0	1-2
2003-04	FL3	1-0	2-1
2004-05	FL2	2-1	2-1

MAIDSTONE UTD
old club

1907-08	SEL1	2-1	0-4
1989-90	FL4	0-1	0-3
1990-91	AMC	2-0	

MANCHESTER CITY

1955-56	FAC	0-1	
1986-87	FLC	0-0	1-2
1996-97	FL1	2-3	0-3

MANSFIELD TOWN

1931-32	FL3S	5-2	4-4
1937-38	FL3S	0-1	2-2
1938-39	FL3S	2-0	1-3
1945-46	FL3S(N)	1-1	2-2
1946-47	FL3S	1-1	1-0
1958-59	FL3	5-1	4-1
1959-60	FL3	0-2	1-1
1963-64	FL3	2-1	1-4
1964-65	FL3	1-4	1-6
1965-66	FL3	1-0	0-2
1968-69	FAC		1-2
1975-76	FL3	2-2	1-3
1978-79	FL3	1-1	1-1
1979-80	FL3	1-1	1-3
1980-81	FL4	2-0	1-0
1984-85	FL4	1-3	0-1
1985-86	FL4	3-1	0-3
1987-88	FL3	2-1	0-1
1988-89	FL3	1-1	0-4
1990-91	FL3	2-1	1-0
1998-99	FL3	1-2	0-0
1999-00	FL3	1-0	1-3
2000-01	FL3	3-1	1-1

2001-02	FL3	1-0	0-0
2003-04	FL3	0-3	0-1
2004-05	FL2	0-1	1-1

H	12	6	7	39	31
A	4	9	13	26	49

MARDY

1911-12	SL2	4-0	2-3
1912-13	SL2	2-0	3-1

MERTHYR TOWN

1911-12	SL2	0-1	0-5
1913-14	SL1	2-2	0-1
1919-20	SL1	2-1	1-1
1920-21	FL3S	0-1	0-2
1921-22	FL3S	2-1	2-2
1922-23	FL3S	1-1	1-2
1923-24	FL3S	3-1	2-3
1924-25	FL3S	2-1	0-1
1925-26	FL3S	5-1	1-5
1926-27	FL3S	3-1	1-0
1927-28	FL3S	2-1	3-2
1928-29	FL3S	5-1	1-2
1929-30	FL3S	6-0	2-2

MIDDLESBROUGH

1991-92	FL2	0-1	1-1
1993-94	FL1	1-0	0-1
1994-95	FL1	0-2	2-1

MID-RHONDDA

1912-13	SL2	1-0	1-1

MILLWALL

1908-09	SL1	3-0	1-3
1909-10	SL1	1-0	2-1
1910-11	SL1	7-0	1-3
1912-13	SA	4-3	1-5
1913-14	SL1	1-3	1-2
1914-15	SL1	0-0	4-1
1919-20	SL1	1-0	1-2
1920-21	FL3S	1-2	2-4
1921-22	FL3S	1-1	0-0
1922-23	FL3S	4-0	1-1
1923-24	FL3S	0-0	0-0
1924-25	FL3S	1-0	0-2
1925-26	FL3S	0-2	1-8
1926-27	FL3S	1-1	0-2
1927-28	FL3S	0-1	1-5
1934-35	FL3S	2-1	0-1
1935-36	FL3S	6-0	2-1
1936-37	FL3S	0-0	2-1
1937-38	FL3S	1-2	0-1
1939-40	South A	1-2	1-6
1940-41	FLWC	3-1	1-2
1948-49	FL3S	2-1	0-1
1949-50	FL3S	3-0	2-1
1950-51	FL3S	0-3	1-1

1951-52	FL3S	0-1	0-2
1952-53	FL3S	2-1	1-4
1953-54	FL3S	1-2	1-2
1954-55	FL3S	1-0	4-1
1955-56	FL3S	3-1	0-5
1956-57	FL3S	1-0	0-0
1957-58	FL3S	2-0	2-1
1962-63	FL3	2-1	1-3
1963-64	FL3	1-1	1-1
1965-66	FL3	0-2	0-2
1975-76	FL3	0-0	1-2
1979-80	FL3	1-0	2-1
1981-82	FL3	2-2	1-1
1982-83	FL3	1-1	1-3
1983-84	FL3	3-2	0-4
1984-85	AMC	0-2	1-3
1991-92	FL2	2-3	0-2
1992-93	FL1	3-3	1-1
1992-93	FAC	1-0	
1993-94	FL1	1-1	4-1
1994-95	FL1	0-1	1-3
1995-96	FL1	2-0	0-0
1997-98	FL2	0-0	1-3

H	22	12	13	72	47
A	9	9	28	48	99

MILTON KEYNES DONS
as Wimbledon

1934-35	FAC		5-1
1977-78	FL4	1-0	3-1
1978-79	FLC	1-0	1-4
1979-80	FL3	1-3	1-0
1980-81	FL4	1-0	1-0
1981-82	FL3	2-0	0-3
1981-82	FLGC	1-2	
1983-84	FL3	1-1	2-3
1983-84	FLC	1-0	4-6
2002-03	FLC	1-4	

as Milton Keynes Dons

2005-06	FL1	0-0	1-2
2005-06	FAC	1-2	

NEWCASTLE UNITED

1991-92	FL2	4-0	2-3
1992-93	FL1	1-1	2-3

NEWPORT COUNTY
old club

1912-13	SL2	1-0	2-0
1913-14	SA	2-0	0-3
1919-20	SL1	3-0	0-0
1920-21	FL3S	2-1	1-1
1921-22	FL3S	0-1	1-2
1922-23	FL3S	3-1	2-0
1923-24	FL3S	2-0	0-5
1924-25	FL3S	0-1	1-1
1925-26	FL3S	4-1	0-1
1926-27	FL3S	5-0	0-3
1927-28	FL3S	5-1	2-3
1928-29	FL3S	4-2	2-2

Season	Comp.	H	A
1929-30	FL3S	2-1	0-0
1930-31	FL3S	6-2	1-3
1932-33	FL3S	3-0	3-1
1933-34	FL3S	3-5	0-3
1934-35	FL3S	0-1	5-0
1935-36	FL3S	1-2	1-3
1935-36	FAC		1-0
1935-36	D3SC	3-0	
1936-37	FL3S	9-2	2-6
1937-38	FL3S	0-2	0-2
1938-39	FL3S	5-0	0-3
1947-48	FL3S	1-0	5-1
1947-48	FAC		2-3
1948-49	FL3S	0-1	2-4
1949-50	FL3S	6-0	1-2
1950-51	FL3S	3-0	1-6
1951-52	FL3S	2-1	0-3
1952-53	FL3S	1-0	1-0
1953-54	FL3S	0-1	2-3
1954-55	FL3S	1-1	2-3
1955-56	FL3S	4-1	0-2
1956-57	FL3S	3-3	1-2
1957-58	FL3S	1-1	0-1
1958-59	FL3	1-0	1-3
1959-60	FL3	3-2	1-1
1960-61	FL3	4-2	2-1
1961-62	FL3	1-0	3-0
1965-66	FLC	3-1	2-2
1966-67	FL4	1-0	0-3
1967-68	FL4	2-2	0-2
1968-69	FL4	1-0	1-4
1969-70	FL4	3-2	0-4
1970-71	FL4	3-0	0-3
1971-72	FL4	3-1	0-2
1976-77	FL4	1-1	0-3
1976-77	FAC	3-0	
1977-78	FL4	4-2	2-1
1981-82	FL3	0-4	2-3
1982-83	FL3	1-4	1-1
1983-84	FL3	3-1	1-1
1985-86	FAC	0-1	

H	35	5	11	122	55
A	10	9	31	57	106

NORTHAMPTON TOWN

Season	Comp.	H	A
1908-09	SL1	2-2	1-2
1909-10	SL1	1-2	1-11
1910-11	SL1	2-0	0-0
1911-12	SEL1 *	3-0	1-3

* Town reserves

Season	Comp.	H	A
1913-14	SL1	1-3	0-2
1914-15	SL1	1-2	0-1
1919-20	SL1	0-0	1-2
1920-21	FL3S	1-2	0-1
1921-22	FL3S	1-1	2-0
1922-23	FL3S	1-2	2-5
1923-24	FL3S	5-1	0-8
1924-25	FL3S	0-1	1-0
1925-26	FL3S	6-1	3-3
1926-27	FL3S	2-0	1-2
1927-28	FL3S	2-0	1-2
1928-29	FL3S	2-2	3-2

Season	Comp.	H	A
1929-30	FL3S	1-2	1-5
1930-31	FL3S	2-1	0-4
1931-32	FL3S	0-1	2-1
1931-32	FAC		0-3
1932-33	FL3S	1-0	0-0
1933-34	FL3S	2-0	0-2
1934-35	FL3S	2-1	1-1
1935-36	FL3S	0-1	0-2
1936-37	FL3S	2-0	3-4
1937-38	FL3S	4-2	2-0
1938-39	FL3S	2-0	2-2
1938-39	D3SC	2-3	1-1
1945-46	FL3S(N)	0-1	2-6
1945-46	D3SC	4-3	1-0
1946-47	FL3S	4-0	3-2
1947-48	FL3S	3-1	0-2
1948-49	FL3S	0-1	2-2
1949-50	FL3S	1-2	0-2
1950-51	FL3S	3-0	1-1
1951-52	FL3S	2-0	3-4
1952-53	FL3S	3-1	3-4
1953-54	FL3S	2-0	0-5
1954-55	FL3S	4-1	2-6
1955-56	FL3S	2-0	1-1
1956-57	FL3S	0-1	2-2
1957-58	FL3S	6-3	3-1
1961-62	FL3	1-3	1-3
1962-63	FL3	5-1	3-5
1969-70	FL4	2-2	0-2
1970-71	FL4	1-0	2-0
1971-72	FL4	4-1	1-1
1977-78	FL4	0-0	0-0
1977-78	FLC	2-3	1-2
1980-81	FL4	0-0	0-2
1984-85	FL4	2-1	2-1
1985-86	FL4	0-4	0-0
1985-86	AMC	1-3	
1986-87	FL4	0-4	1-2
1986-87	FAC	4-4	2-3
1987-88	FL3	1-1	0-4
1988-89	FL3	2-1	2-2
1988-89	AMC		1-2
1989-90	AMC	2-1	
1997-98	FL2	0-0	1-3
1999-00	FL3	2-2	0-2
2003-04	FL3	0-1	2-2
2004-05	FL2	2-1	2-1
2004-05	PO	1-0	0-0
2004-05	FLT		2-0

H	31	11	20	114	77
A	12	16	35	75	144

NORWICH CITY

Season	Comp.	H	A
1907-08	SEL1 *	2-1	2-4
1908-09	SL1	3-0	0-2
1909-10	SL1	2-5	0-3
1910-11	SL1	1-0	0-1
1911-12	SEL1 *	2-1	1-0

* City reserves

Season	Comp.	H	A
1913-14	SL1	2-2	0-6
1914-15	SL1	4-1	1-1
1919-20	SL1	2-1	1-1
1920-21	FL3S	3-1	1-3
1921-22	FL3S	0-1	1-1
1922-23	FL3S	3-1	1-2
1922-23	FAC	2-2	1-2
1923-24	FL3S	3-1	1-3
1924-25	FL3S	0-1	1-0
1925-26	FL3S	0-1	2-1
1926-27	FL3S	3-3	1-1
1927-28	FL3S	1-1	1-2
1928-29	FL3S	5-3	5-2
1929-30	FL3S	1-1	1-1
1930-31	FL3S	2-0	1-0
1931-32	FL3S	2-0	1-1
1932-33	FL3S	2-1	0-1
1933-34	FL3S	0-0	0-0
1939-40	South A	2-4	2-3
1939-40	South D	3-0	3-1
1940-41	South R	3-0	4-8
1940-41	South R	3-3	0-3
1940-41	South	3-2	3-5
1945-46	FL3S(N)	1-4	1-6
1945-46	D3SC	1-0	1-0
1946-47	FL3S	3-0	5-1
1947-48	FL3S	0-0	0-1
1948-49	FL3S	2-2	0-3
1949-50	FL3S	1-0	0-0
1950-51	FL3S	0-2	0-3
1951-52	FL3S	2-1	0-1
1952-53	FL3S	1-2	1-3
1953-54	FL3S	5-2	0-1
1954-55	FL3S	4-1	3-3
1955-56	FL3S	3-1	2-7
1956-57	FL3S	0-0	2-1
1957-58	FL3S	5-2	2-0
1958-59	FL3	1-0	0-4
1959-60	FL3	1-0	3-4
1995-96	FL1	1-1	1-0
1996-97	FL1	1-1	0-0

H	26	12	8	91	56
A	11	10	25	56	96

NOTTINGHAM FOREST

Season	Comp.	H	A
1925-26	FAC	0-1	
1939-40	FLWC	0-1	1-3
1949-50	FL3S	2-3	2-1
1950-51	FL3S	3-2	0-3
1993-94	FL1	1-1	0-2
2005-06	FL1	1-0	0-2

NOTTS COUNTY

Season	Comp.	H	A
1930-31	FL3S	2-1	1-1
1935-36	FL3S	0-0	2-1
1936-37	FL3S	2-3	1-2
1937-38	FL3S	2-1	2-0
1938-39	FL3S	1-0	1-4
1945-46	FL3S(N)	7-3	1-4
1946-47	FL3S	3-0	2-0
1947-48	FL3S	1-2	1-2
1948-49	FL3S	3-2	0-0
1949-50	FL3S	2-0	0-2

1958-59	FL3	5-2	4-1
1960-61	FL3	3-1	2-1
1961-62	FL3	3-2	0-2
1962-63	FL3	1-2	1-2
1962-63	FLC	2-3	
1963-64	FL3	3-1	1-1
1965-66	FAC	3-1	
1966-67	FL4	1-0	0-1
1967-68	FL4	0-1	3-4
1968-69	FL4	4-0	2-2
1969-70	FL4	2-5	0-2
1970-71	FL4	1-0	1-2
1972-73	FL3	2-1	0-2
1987-88	FL3	1-2	2-6
1988-89	FL3	1-1	1-1
1992-93	FL1	3-1	0-4
1993-94	FL1	1-0	1-2
1993-94	AIC	1-0	0-1
1994-95	FL1	1-0	2-2
2004-05	FL2	0-0	2-1

H	20	3	7	61	35
A	6	6	16	33	53

OLDHAM ATHLETIC

1951-52	FAC	5-0	
1963-64	FL3	2-2	3-0
1964-65	FL3	6-1	2-0
1965-66	FL3	0-2	0-1
1969-70	FL4	1-0	0-3
1970-71	FL4	3-0	0-2
1972-73	FL3	0-1	1-0
1973-74	FL3	2-2	0-2
1994-95	FL1	1-0	2-0
1995-96	FL1	1-1	1-0
1996-97	FL1	1-1	0-0
1997-98	FL2	1-1	0-2
2005-06	FL1	2-1	0-0

OXFORD UNITED

1965-66	FL3	2-1	2-3
1978-79	FL3	2-0	0-0
1979-80	FL3	1-1	0-1
1980-81	FLC	1-0	0-2
1981-82	FL3	0-1	2-0
1982-83	FL3	1-2	0-1
1983-84	FL3	0-1	1-2
1991-92	FL2	2-3	1-0
1992-93	FL1	0-3	1-0
1993-94	FL1	6-1	1-2
1996-97	FL1	2-2	0-5
1999-00	FLC	0-2	0-1
2001-02	FL3	2-2	0-2
2002-03	FL3	2-1	1-0
2003-04	FL3	0-1	0-2
2004-05	FL2	4-0	1-2

H	6	3	7	25	21
A	4	1	11	10	22

PADOVA

1993-94	AIC	5-2

PESCARA

1993-94	AIC	1-3

PETERBOROUGH CITY
old club

1911-12	SEL1	1-2	0-8

PETERBOROUGH UNITED

1961-62	FL3	1-1	1-4
1962-63	FL3	2-1	3-1
1963-64	FL3	2-0	0-3
1964-65	FL3	2-0	2-4
1965-66	FL3	2-0	0-4
1968-69	FL4	2-1	0-1
1969-70	FL4	2-0	4-3
1970-71	FL4	1-2	0-4
1971-72	FL4	2-1	0-2
1973-74	FAC		1-3
1974-75	FL3	1-2	0-1
1975-76	FL3	0-0	2-3
1975-76	FLC	2-0	0-3
1978-79	FL3	0-0	1-0
1978-79	FAC	3-2	
1980-81	FL4	1-0	2-5
1984-85	FL4	2-1	4-1
1985-86	FL4	0-1	1-1
1986-87	FL4	2-2	0-2
1989-90	FL4	0-0	2-1
1992-93	FL1	0-1	0-1
1993-94	FL1	3-0	1-3
1998-99	FL3	2-0	1-1
1999-00	FL3	0-1	0-1

H	13	5	5	32	16
A	5	2	16	25	52

PLYMOUTH ARGYLE

1908-09	SL1	2-1	1-2
1909-10	SL1	0-0	0-3
1910-11	SL1	3-2	1-0
1913-14	SL1	2-1	1-0
1914-15	SL1	3-1	0-1
1919-20	SL1	1-0	0-0
1920-21	FL3S	2-1	0-0
1921-22	FL3S	1-0	0-4
1922-23	FL3S	2-1	1-1
1923-24	FL3S	0-2	1-7
1924-25	FL3S	0-3	0-6
1925-26	FL3S	2-0	2-6
1926-27	FL3S	1-2	1-2
1927-28	FL3S	3-0	2-3
1928-29	FL3S	1-1	1-1
1929-30	FL3S	1-1	0-1
1950-51	FL3S	1-0	0-2
1951-52	FL3S	1-1	0-2
1956-57	FL3S	0-1	0-0

1957-58	FL3S	2-1	3-2
1958-59	FL3	0-0	1-3
1972-73	FL3	3-1	0-2
1973-74	FL3	2-0	1-1
1974-75	FL3	2-1	0-1
1978-79	FL3	2-1	1-1
1979-80	FL3	4-1	0-0
1981-82	FL3	3-0	0-0
1982-83	FL3	3-1	0-1
1983-84	FL3	1-1	0-4
1983-84	FAC	0-0	0-2
1991-92	FL2	2-1	2-0
1997-98	FL2	3-0	3-2
1998-99	FL3	1-0	3-0
1999-00	FL3	2-1	1-3
2000-01	FL3	2-2	3-3
2001-02	FL3	0-1	0-0

H	23	8	5	58	30
A	6	11	19	29	66

PONTYPRIDD

1911-12	SL2	1-0	0-3
1912-13	SL2	2-1	1-0

PORTSMOUTH

1906-07	SL2 *	4-1	2-0
1907-08	SL2 *	1-3	0-0

* Pompey reserves

1908-09	SL1	2-6	0-2
1909-10	SL1	0-0	1-1
1910-11	SL1	2-0	2-3
1911-12	SL2	0-0	0-2
1912-13	SA	3-0	0-4
1913-14	SL1	3-2	2-4
1913-14	SA	3-1	0-2
1914-15	SL1	0-2	0-1
1919-20	SL1	0-2	1-0
1920-21	FL3S	2-1	0-3
1921-22	FL3S	1-2	0-6
1922-23	FL3S	0-0	0-0
1923-24	FL3S	0-1	0-3
1940-41	South R	0-0	
1940-41	South	2-1	3-1
1961-62	FL3	2-2	0-1
1973-74	FLC		1-2
1981-82	FL3	2-0	0-0
1981-82	FLC	0-0	1-4
1982-83	FL3	4-0	0-2
1991-92	FL2	2-3	1-1
1992-93	FL1	0-0	0-2
1993-94	FL1	2-1	1-2
1994-95	FL1	1-2	1-1
1995-96	FL1	2-1	2-4
1996-97	FL1	2-1	0-1

H	12	7	8	40	32
A	3	6	18	18	52

PORT VALE

1938-39	FL3S	0-0	2-2

Season	Comp	H	A
1938-39	FAC		1-0
1945-46	FL3S(N)	2-0	1-1
1945-46	D3SC	1-1	1-2
1946-47	FL3S	1-1	1-5
1947-48	FL3S	1-1	1-2
1948-49	FL3S	0-0	2-0
1949-50	FL3S	1-0	0-0
1950-51	FL3S	1-1	1-3
1951-52	FL3S	0-0	0-0
1957-58	FL3S	1-1	3-1
1959-60	FL3	2-1	1-3
1960-61	FL3	2-1	0-4
1961-62	FL3	4-1	0-0
1962-63	FL3	2-0	1-5
1963-64	FL3	1-1	1-4
1963-64	FLC	2-1	
1964-65	FL3	2-1	2-2
1966-67	FL4	4-1	3-1
1967-68	FL4	1-1	2-1
1968-69	FL4	1-1	1-1
1969-70	FL4	1-1	0-3
1972-73	FL3	5-0	1-3
1973-74	FL3	1-0	0-0
1974-75	FL3	1-3	0-0
1975-76	FL3	3-3	1-1
1980-81	FL4	5-1	0-1
1983-84	FL3	1-2	1-2
1984-85	FL4	1-1	1-4
1985-86	FL4	2-1	0-4
1987-88	FL3	3-3	1-4
1988-89	FL3	1-1	0-2
1991-92	FL2	0-0	0-0
1994-95	FL1	1-2	0-5
1995-96	FL1	2-1	1-2
1996-97	FL1	0-0	1-2
2005-06	FL1	1-2	1-2

H	14	18	4	57	35
A	5	11	20	32	72

PRESTON NORTH END

Season	Comp	H	A
1974-75	FL3	1-1	4-1
1975-76	FL3	0-2	1-5
1981-82	FL3	2-2	0-1
1982-83	FL3	2-3	1-1
1983-84	FL3	1-1	1-4
1985-86	FL4	2-1	2-3
1986-87	FL4	1-2	0-2
1987-88	FL3	1-2	1-1
1988-89	FL3	2-1	2-3
1990-91	FL3	3-2	1-2
1997-98	FL2	3-2	0-1

QUEEN'S PARK RANGERS

Season	Comp	H	A
1907-08	SEL1 *	4-2	1-2

* QPR reserves

Season	Comp	H	A
1908-09	SL1	0-0	1-2
1909-10	SL1	0-1	2-2
1909-10	FAC	0-0	2-3
1909-10	SCC		1-2
1910-11	SL1	1-2	1-1
1910-11	SCC	1-1	3-5
1911-12	SCC	5-4	
1913-14	SL1	1-2	0-0
1914-15	SL1	1-1	2-4
1919-20	SL1	2-2	2-2
1920-21	FL3S	1-0	0-2
1921-22	FL3S	1-2	0-1
1922-23	FL3S	2-0	0-1
1923-24	FL3S	4-2	0-0
1924-25	FL3S	1-0	1-3
1925-26	FL3S	2-1	2-2
1926-27	FL3S	0-3	2-3
1927-28	FL3S	7-0	2-3
1928-29	FL3S	0-3	1-3
1929-30	FL3S	1-0	5-2
1930-31	FL3S	2-0	2-0
1931-32	FL3S	0-0	1-2
1932-33	FL3S	0-1	1-6
1933-34	FL3S	0-2	0-4
1934-35	FL3S	2-0	1-1
1935-36	FL3S	0-1	1-2
1936-37	FL3S	3-2	2-7
1937-38	FL3S	2-1	0-1
1938-39	FL3S	2-1	1-1
1939-40	South D	0-1	1-3
1939-40	FLWC	1-0	
1945-46	FL3S(N)	1-2	1-4
1945-46	D3SC	0-0	0-4
1946-47	FL3S	1-3	0-1
1947-48	FL3S	0-0	2-3
1952-53	FL3S	2-0	2-3
1953-54	FL3S	4-1	0-1
1954-55	FL3S	2-2	1-1
1955-56	FL3S	5-1	2-1
1955-56	FAC	2-0	
1956-57	FL3S	3-0	0-3
1957-58	FL3S	6-0	1-1
1958-59	FL3	4-0	3-1
1959-60	FL3	3-2	0-0
1960-61	FL3	0-0	1-2
1961-62	FL3	2-3	3-5
1962-63	FL3	1-3	0-1
1963-64	FL3	1-3	5-4
1964-65	FL3	0-0	0-2
1965-66	FL3	1-3	1-2
1974-75	FAC	2-2	0-2
1996-97	FL1	0-1	0-4
2003-04	FLT	4-0	

H	24	12	17	90	61
A	5	11	34	60	115

READING

Season	Comp.	H	A
1906-07	SL2 *	6-2	0-2
1908-09	SL1	0-0	0-0
1909-10	SL1	1-0	2-3
1911-12	SEL1 *	3-0	0-4

* Reading reserves

Season	Comp	H	A
1911-12	SCC **		1-0

** played at White Hart Lane

Season	Comp	H	A
1913-14	SL1	2-1	0-2
1914-15	SL1	0-2	0-3
1919-20	SL1	2-2	0-0
1920-21	FL3S	1-0	1-1
1921-22	FL3S	2-0	0-4
1922-23	FL3S	3-1	1-1
1923-24	FL3S	2-1	0-1
1924-25	FL3S	3-0	2-2
1924-25	FAC		1-2
1925-26	FL3S	2-2	0-1
1926-27	FAC		2-3
1931-32	FL3S	1-1	1-3
1932-33	FL3S	3-1	1-1
1933-34	FL3S	2-2	0-5
1934-35	FL3S	6-1	2-3
1935-36	FL3S	1-2	1-2
1936-37	FL3S	1-1	3-2
1937-38	FL3S	4-2	2-3
1938-39	FL3S	2-0	0-3
1939-40	FL3S		0-1
1939-40	South D	4-2	1-1
1946-47	FL3S	0-2	0-3
1947-48	FL3S	1-1	3-1
1948-49	FL3S	0-0	1-2
1949-50	FL3S	3-2	0-5
1950-51	FL3S	3-3	2-0
1951-52	FL3S	2-0	2-5
1952-53	FL3S	3-1	0-1
1953-54	FL3S	1-2	0-2
1954-55	FL3S	0-0	1-1
1955-56	FL3S	1-0	1-4
1956-57	FL3S	4-0	2-3
1957-58	FL3S	2-1	1-1
1958-59	FL3	2-2	0-3
1959-60	FL3	2-0	1-4
1960-61	FL3	0-1	0-3
1961-62	FL3	0-2	1-3
1962-63	FL3	2-0	3-1
1963-64	FL3	2-0	2-4
1964-65	FL3	2-2	0-2
1965-66	FL3	2-1	0-1
1965-66	FLC		1-5
1971-72	FL4	4-1	4-1
1973-74	FAC	2-0	
1977-78	FL4	0-2	1-0
1979-80	FL3	2-2	1-1
1981-82	FL3	2-0	2-0
1982-83	FL3	4-2	1-1
1983-84	AMC	5-0	
1988-89	FL3	2-1	0-4
1990-91	FL3	1-2	4-2
1990-91	AMC		4-1
1994-95	FL1	4-1	0-2
1995-96	FL1	0-0	3-3
1996-97	FL1	2-1	2-3

H	32	14	8	111	55
A	10	12	36	66	129

REDHILL

Season	Comp	H	A
1906-07	SEL2	7-0	5-1

REGGIANA

Season	Comp	H	A
1995-96	AIC		1-1

ROCHDALE

1958-59	FL3	3-1	1-1
1960-61	FLC		2-5
1966-67	FL4	0-0	2-1
1967-68	FL4	3-1	1-0
1968-69	FL4	1-3	0-3
1972-73	FL3	1-2	2-3
1973-74	FL3	1-2	1-1
1976-77	FL4	3-0	0-0
1977-78	FL4	3-1	2-1
1980-81	FL4	1-1	2-0
1984-85	FL4	0-2	2-2
1985-86	FL4	5-0	1-2
1986-87	FL4	5-3	2-1
1989-90	FL4	3-2	1-0
1998-99	FL3	1-1	0-1
1999-00	FL3	3-3	0-2
2000-01	FL3	3-0	1-0
2001-02	FL3	1-1	1-0
2002-03	FL3	1-0	2-1
2003-04	FL3	4-0	1-1
2004-05	FL2	3-0	0-2

H	11	5	4	45	23
A	9	5	7	24	27

ROTHERHAM UNITED

1965-66	FAC		2-3
1972-73	FL3	1-0	0-1
1975-76	FL3	1-2	0-2
1978-79	FL3	2-1	1-2
1979-80	FL3	0-2	1-2
1983-84	FL3	2-2	0-0
1987-88	FL3	1-1	1-1
1990-91	FL3	2-1	1-0
1998-99	FL3	3-0	2-2
1999-00	FL3	1-2	0-0
2005-06	FL1	2-0	4-2

ROYAL ENGINEERS

1906-07	SL2	12-0	5-1

RUSHDEN & DIAMONDS

2001-02	FL3	4-2	1-0
2002-03	FL3	2-1	0-3
2004-05	FL2	3-0	4-1
2005-06	FLT		0-1

SALERNITANA

1995-96	AIC		1-2

SALISBURY CITY
old club

1906-07	SL2	4-2	1-0
1907-08	SL2	3-2	1-1

SCARBOROUGH

1932-33	FAC	4-1	
1989-90	FL4	1-0	1-1
1998-99	FL3	1-0	2-1
2003-04	FAC	1-1	0-1

SCUNTHORPE UNITED

1964-65	FL3	0-1	1-2
1965-66	FL3	0-1	0-0
1968-69	FL4	0-3	1-4
1969-70	FL4	3-0	0-2
1970-71	FL4	2-2	0-3
1971-72	FL4	2-3	1-1
1972-73	FL3	1-0	0-0
1976-77	FL4	1-1	0-1
1977-78	FL4	2-0	2-1
1980-81	FL4	2-0	1-2
1983-84	FL3	0-0	6-1
1984-85	FL4	1-1	1-2
1985-86	FL4	2-1	0-2
1986-87	FL4	3-1	0-3
1989-90	FL4	0-0	1-1
1998-99	FL3	0-1	1-1
2000-01	FL3	1-0	1-1
2001-02	FL3	2-0	0-2
2002-03	FL3	1-2	1-4
2003-04	FL3	4-2	1-1
2004-05	FL2	0-0	2-3
2005-06	FL1	3-0	0-1

H	10	6	6	30	19
A	2	7	13	20	38

SHEFFIELD UNITED

1919-20	FAC *	0-3	

*played at Bramall Lane

1934-35	FAC	0-4	
1951-52	FAC	1-2	
1979-80	FL3	2-1	0-2
1982-83	FL3	3-1	1-0
1983-84	FL3	0-1	0-5
1988-89	FL3	2-1	2-1
1994-95	FL1	1-3	0-2
1995-96	FL1	2-1	0-3
1996-97	FL1	3-2	0-3

SHEFFIELD WEDNESDAY

1975-76	FL3	2-1	1-2
1978-79	FL3	2-1	2-3
1979-80	FL3	1-1	0-2
1982-83	FAC	0-0	2-2
1982-83	FAC		1-2
1992-93	FAC		0-2

SHOEBURYNESS GARRISON

1908-09	FAC	4-0	

SHREWSBURY TOWN

1951-52	FL3S	2-2	1-0
1952-53	FL3S	2-2	1-7
1953-54	FL3S	3-0	1-2
1954-55	FL3S	4-1	3-2
1955-56	FL3S	1-0	1-1
1956-57	FL3S	1-2	0-0
1957-58	FL3S	5-1	1-1
1959-60	FL3	2-1	3-1
1960-61	FL3	1-1	2-2
1961-62	FL3	1-1	1-1
1962-63	FL3	3-1	0-6
1963-64	FL3	7-1	2-2
1964-65	FL3	1-0	3-1
1965-66	FL3	2-0	0-3
1969-70	FLC	2-0	2-2
1972-73	FL3	2-0	0-1
1973-74	FL3	2-0	2-1
1975-76	FL3	1-3	1-3
1978-79	FL3	0-1	0-2
1990-91	FL3	2-1	1-0
1998-99	FL3	2-1	1-3
1999-00	FL3	3-2	1-2
2000-01	FL3	0-0	1-0
2001-02	FL3	0-2	0-2
2002-03	FL3	2-3	1-0
2004-05	FL2	1-0	1-1
2004-05	FLT	4-1	

H	17	5	5	56	27
A	8	8	10	30	46

SITTINGBOURNE

1907-08	SEL1	5-4	1-1
1922-23	FAC	4-2	0-0

SOUTHAMPTON

1906-07	SL2 *	1-0	2-4
1907-08	SL2 *	7-0	2-1

* Saints reserves

1908-09	SL1	2-0	1-1
1909-10	SL1	2-0	2-6
1910-11	SL1	0-1	4-2
1912-13	SA	0-3	1-1
1913-14	SL1	0-0	2-4
1913-14	SA	1-1	0-4
1914-15	SL1	4-0	0-2
1919-20	SL1	2-1	0-4
1920-21	FL3S	1-0	0-3
1921-22	FL3S	0-0	0-5
1940-41	South	6-4	
1940-41	South	1-4	
1951-52	FAC	3-0	
1953-54	FL3S	2-1	5-3
1954-55	FL3S	0-1	0-3
1955-56	FL3S	2-1	0-0
1956-57	FL3S	1-2	2-1
1957-58	FL3S	3-2	2-2
1958-59	FL3	1-1	2-3
1959-60	FL3	2-4	1-3
1959-60	FAC		0-3

1994-95	FAC		0-2
2005-06	FLC	0-3	

H	12	4	7	41	29
A	4	4	13	26	57

SOUTHEND AMATEUR

1912-13	FAC	5-0

SOUTHERN UNITED

1906-07	SL2	*	7-0

*not played; Southern resigned
from the League; record expunged*

SOUTHPORT

1925-26	FAC	5-2	
1966-67	FL4	0-1	0-1
1970-71	FL4	1-1	0-3
1971-72	FL4	2-1	1-0
1973-74	FL3	0-1	0-0
1976-77	FL4	3-2	0-0
1977-78	FL4	4-2	0-0

STEVENAGE BOROUGH

2001-02	FLT		4-1

STOCKPORT COUNTY

1958-59	FL3	3-1	1-0
1966-67	FL4	0-1	1-4
1970-71	FL4	2-1	0-0
1971-72	FL4	4-2	2-2
1976-77	FL4	0-0	0-0
1977-78	FL4	0-2	0-1
1980-81	FL4	2-0	0-1
1984-85	FL4	1-1	2-1
1985-86	FL4	0-0	1-2
1986-87	FL4	0-0	2-0
1989-90	FL4	2-0	0-1

STOKE CITY

1961-62	FLC	0-1	
1964-65	FLC		1-3
1990-91	FL3	1-0	0-4
1993-94	FL1	0-0	1-0
1994-95	FL1	4-2	1-4
1995-96	FL1	2-4	0-1
1996-97	FL1	2-1	2-1

SUNDERLAND

1987-88	FL3	1-4	0-7
1991-92	FL2	2-0	2-1
1992-93	FL1	0-1	4-2
1993-94	FL1	0-1	2-0
1994-95	FL1	0-1	1-0
1995-96	FL1	0-2	0-1

SWANSEA CITY

as Swansea Town

1912-13	SL2	3-1	0-1
1919-20	SL1	2-2	1-0
1920-21	FL3S	1-2	0-2
1921-22	FL3S	1-0	1-1
1921-22	FAC	0-1	
1922-23	FL3S	0-1	0-1
1923-24	FL3S	0-0	1-2
1924-25	FL3S	1-0	0-4
1947-48	FL3S	1-1	0-3
1948-49	FL3S	0-0	2-2
1948-49	FAC	1-2	
1965-66	FL3	2-0	0-5
1967-68	FL4	1-0	2-2
1968-69	FL4	4-0	2-2
1969-70	FL4	2-1	0-2

as Swansea City

1972-73	FL3	3-1	1-1
1975-76	FAC	2-0	
1976-77	FL4	1-2	0-2
1977-78	FL4	2-1	0-0
1978-79	FL3	0-2	2-3
1986-87	FL4	1-2	0-1
1988-89	FL3	0-2	0-2
1990-91	FL3	4-1	4-1
1998-99	FL3	2-0	1-3
1999-00	FL3	2-1	1-3
2001-02	FL3	4-2	2-3
2002-03	FL3	0-2	0-1
2003-04	FL3	1-1	3-2
2003-04	FLT		2-1
2004-05	FL2	4-2	1-1
2005-06	FL1	1-2	2-2

H	15	5	10	46	32
A	4	8	16	28	53

SWINDON TOWN

1906-07	SL2 *	0-1	0-0
1907-08	SL2 *	2-0	5-1
1908-09	SL1	6-2	2-4
1909-10	SL1	1-1	1-6
1910-11	SL1	0-1	0-4
1911-12	SEL1 *	2-0	1-0

* Town reserves

1913-14	SL1	2-0	0-5
1914-15	SL1	2-1	0-4
1919-20	SL1	0-1	2-3
1920-21	FL3S	1-3	0-3
1921-22	FL3S	1-2	1-6
1922-23	FL3S	2-0	0-3
1923-24	FL3S	0-2	0-3
1924-25	FL3S	0-0	0-3
1925-26	FL3S	3-0	0-2
1926-27	FL3S	2-2	1-5
1927-28	FL3S	1-1	1-0
1928-29	FL3S	1-1	1-3
1929-30	FL3S	3-1	1-5
1930-31	FL3S	5-3	1-1
1931-32	FL3S	3-0	2-1
1932-33	FL3S	0-0	2-2
1933-34	FL3S	4-1	4-1
1934-35	FL3S	2-0	0-5
1935-36	FL3S	1-0	3-1
1936-37	FL3S	2-0	0-4
1937-38	FL3S	0-0	1-1
1938-39	FL3S	2-3	1-2
1946-47	FL3S	2-0	1-2
1947-48	FL3S	1-0	0-0
1948-49	FL3S	3-4	1-2
1949-50	FL3S	2-0	2-2
1950-51	FL3S	8-2	1-4
1950-51	FAC	0-3	
1951-52	FL3S	2-2	0-1
1952-53	FL3S	3-0	3-1
1953-54	FL3S	3-1	0-3
1954-55	FL3S	4-1	1-0
1955-56	FL3S	0-0	1-1
1956-57	FL3S	1-0	2-3
1957-58	FL3S	2-3	1-2
1958-59	FL3	0-2	1-2
1959-60	FL3	1-3	0-2
1960-61	FL3	0-2	1-1
1961-62	FL3	0-2	0-0
1962-63	FL3	1-1	1-4
1963-64	FLC		0-3
1965-66	FL3	4-2	0-4
1968-69	FAC		2-0
1974-75	FL3	2-0	0-2
1975-76	FL3	3-0	0-0
1978-79	FL3	5-3	0-1
1979-80	FL3	1-0	0-1
1981-82	FL3	0-0	0-0
1984-85	FL4	3-2	0-2
1985-86	FL4	0-0	1-2
1991-92	FL2	3-2	1-3
1992-93	FL1	1-1	2-3
1994-95	FL1	2-0	2-2
1996-97	FL1	1-3	0-0
2000-01	FLT	2-1	
2002-03	FLT		1-6
2003-04	FLC	2-3	
2004-05	FLT	2-0	
2005-06	FL1	2-0	2-1

H	33	13	16	114	69
A	10	13	38	57	138

TELFORD UNITED

as Wellington Town

1927-28	FAC	1-0

THAMES

1930-31	FL3S	1-0	0-3
1931-32	FL3S	1-1	3-1

THE NEW SAINTS

merger of Llansantffraid and Oswestry Town in 2003. They initially played under the name Llansantffraid, then their sponsored title of Total Network Solutions. They changed name again in 2006 to become The New Saints.

As Oswestry Town

1959-60	FAC	6-0	

TON PENTRE
old club

1911-12	SL2	4-0	1-2
1912-13	SL2	7-2	2-0

TORQUAY UNITED

1927-28	FL3S	1-0	3-3
1928-29	FL3S	3-0	1-2
1929-30	FL3S	1-1	1-1
1930-31	FL3S	6-3	1-3
1930-31	FAC	0-1	
1931-32	FL3S	4-2	1-2
1931-32	FAC		3-1
1932-33	FL3S	2-1	1-8
1933-34	FL3S	3-1	0-3
1934-35	FL3S	2-3	0-2
1935-36	FL3S	2-1	1-1
1936-37	FL3S	0-0	4-1
1937-38	FL3S	5-1	3-3
1938-39	FL3S	1-1	0-2
1946-47	FL3S	0-2	1-0
1947-48	FL3S	1-0	1-4
1948-49	FL3S	1-1	3-0
1949-50	FL3S	2-0	4-2
1950-51	FL3S	3-0	2-2
1951-52	FL3S	2-2	3-1
1952-53	FL3S	3-1	2-4
1953-54	FL3S	1-0	1-1
1954-55	FL3S	1-2	1-4
1955-56	FL3S	2-3	2-2
1956-57	FL3S	2-0	3-3
1957-58	FL3S	0-0	2-2
1957-58	FAC	2-1	1-1
1960-61	FL3	3-2	1-2
1961-62	FL3	2-1	2-2
1976-77	FL4	0-3	0-0
1977-78	FL4	4-0	1-0
1977-78	FAC		2-1
1980-81	FL4	3-1	3-0
1984-85	FL4	1-0	2-2
1985-86	FL4	1-2	2-2
1986-87	FL4	4-0	1-2
1989-90	FL4	1-0	0-3
1990-91	AMC	7-0	
1998-99	FL3	0-0	0-2
1999-00	FL3	0-2	1-0
1999-00	FAC		0-1
2000-01	FL3	1-1	1-1
2000-01	FAC	2-1	1-1
2001-02	FL3	1-1	1-2
2002-03	FL3	3-0	1-3
2003-04	FL3	1-2	0-3

TOTTENHAM HOTSPUR

1907-08	SEL1 *	2-1	1-3
1911-12	SEL1 *	2-1	0-2
	* Spurs reserves		
1920-21	FAC	1-4	
1935-36	FAC	1-2	4-4
1939-40	South A	1-2	4-2
1940-41	South R	3-2	
1989-90	FLC	3-2	0-1

TRANMERE ROVERS

1933-34	FAC		0-3
1958-59	FL3	1-3	1-1
1959-60	FL3	7-1	0-1
1960-61	FL3	1-2	1-2
1966-67	FL4	0-0	2-1
1972-73	FL3	1-0	1-3
1973-74	FL3	1-1	0-2
1974-75	FL3	1-0	1-2
1978-79	FL3	0-1	2-1
1980-81	FL4	2-0	2-2
1984-85	FL4	2-3	0-2
1985-86	FL4	2-2	1-1
1986-87	FL4	3-0	3-1
1990-91	FL3	1-0	1-3
1991-92	FL2	1-1	1-1
1992-93	FL1	1-2	0-3
1993-94	FL1	1-2	1-1
1994-95	FL1	0-0	2-0
1995-96	FL1	2-0	0-3
1996-97	FL1	1-1	0-3
2001-02	FAC	1-3	
2005-06	FL1	3-1	0-0

H	8	6	7	32	23
A	4	6	11	19	36

TREHARRIS

1911-12	SL2	2-0	3-1
1912-13	SL2	3-0	0-0

TROWBRIDGE TOWN
old club

1957-58	FAC		2-0

TUNBRIDGE WELLS
old club

1906-07	SEL2	5-0	5-1

TUNBRIDGE WELLS RANGERS

1906-07	SL2	2-1	2-2
1906-07	SEL2	2-1	0-1
1907-08	SL2	0-1	2-2
1907-08	SEL1	4-0	1-1
1910-11	FAC	1-0	

1911-12	SEL1	7-4	1-3
1913-14	FAC *		3-0
	* played at Roots Hall		

WALSALL

1911-12	SL2	2-0	1-2
1927-28	FL3S	2-1	1-0
1928-29	FL3S	3-1	1-4
1929-30	FL3S	1-0	3-1
1930-31	FL3S	2-0	3-1
1936-37	FL3S	3-0	0-3
1937-38	FL3S	1-0	5-1
1938-39	FL3S	2-0	2-0
1939-40	FL3S	3-2	
1945-46	FL3S(N)	0-1	0-6
1945-46	D3SC	2-2	0-2
1946-47	FL3S	3-1	2-2
1947-48	FL3S	1-1	0-6
1948-49	FL3S	2-0	3-0
1949-50	FL3S	2-2	1-1
1950-51	FL3S	0-1	2-1
1951-52	FL3S	3-0	0-2
1952-53	FL3S	2-1	1-1
1953-54	FL3S	3-1	0-2
1954-55	FL3S	2-1	1-4
1955-56	FL3S	3-2	1-3
1956-57	FL3S	2-0	1-0
1957-58	FL3S	4-1	1-1
1960-61	FL3	1-2	1-5
1963-64	FL3	1-1	0-2
1964-65	FL3	0-0	3-2
1965-66	FL3	5-3	0-3
1972-73	FL3	2-0	1-3
1973-74	FL3	2-1	2-1
1974-75	FL3	3-0	0-3
1975-76	FL3	2-2	3-2
1978-79	FL3	1-0	1-1
1981-82	FL3	3-2	1-0
1982-83	FL3	1-1	3-1
1983-84	FL3	0-0	0-4
1987-88	FL3	1-1	1-2
1987-88	FAC	0-0	1-2
1989-90	AMC		1-4
1997-98	FL2	0-1	1-3
2005-06	FL1	0-0	2-2

H	24	11	4	70	32
A	13	6	20	50	83

WALTHAMSTOW GRANGE

1912-13	FAC *		6-2
	* played at Roots Hall		

WATFORD

Season	Comp.	H	A
1907-08	SEL1 *	2-0	2-4
1908-09	SL1	2-0	2-2
1909-10	SL1	0-1	1-3
1910-11	SL1	2-0	1-2
1911-12	SEL1 *	1-1	0-3
	* Watford reserves		

1913-14	SL1	1-0	2-1
1914-15	SL1	0-0	1-2
1919-20	SL1	4-1	1-1
1919-20	FAC	1-0	
1920-21	FL3S	4-1	0-3
1921-22	FL3S	1-4	1-4
1922-23	FL3S	2-1	1-1
1923-24	FL3S	3-0	1-4
1924-25	FL3S	0-4	3-0
1925-26	FL3S	0-1	4-1
1926-27	FL3S	2-0	2-4
1927-28	FL3S	3-0	1-1
1928-29	FL3S	1-3	1-4
1929-30	FL3S	1-3	1-2
1930-31	FL3S	1-0	3-1
1931-32	FL3S	3-0	1-1
1932-33	FL3S	2-1	2-2
1932-33	FAC	2-0	1-1
1933-34	FL3S	1-1	1-2
1934-35	FL3S	0-2	1-3
1935-36	FL3S	1-1	0-5
1936-37	FL3S	1-1	3-1
1937-38	FL3S	2-2	1-3
1938-39	FL3S	3-0	0-3
1939-40	South A	1-2	0-4
1939-40	South D	2-2	2-4
1939-40	FLWC	3-1	3-1
1940-41	South R	1-3	1-1
1940-41	South	2-3	2-8
1945-46	FL3S(N)	6-2	1-0
1945-46	FAC	0-3	1-1
1946-47	FL3S	5-0	0-4
1947-48	FL3S	1-1	2-2
1948-49	FL3S	0-1	0-0
1949-50	FL3S	1-1	0-1
1950-51	FL3S	5-1	3-1
1951-52	FL3S	5-1	0-0
1952-53	FL3S	1-0	1-1
1953-54	FL3S	3-0	2-2
1954-55	FL3S	1-3	1-1
1955-56	FL3S	1-0	2-1
1956-57	FL3S	2-0	1-1
1957-58	FL3S	2-1	1-1
1960-61	FL3	6-1	0-3
1961-62	FL3	0-1	3-1
1961-62	FAC	0-2	
1962-63	FL3	1-1	1-3
1962-63	FAC	0-2	
1963-64	FL3	3-0	1-3
1964-65	FL3	0-1	1-2
1965-66	FL3	1-0	1-4
1965-66	FAC	2-1	
1966-67	FAC		0-1
1972-73	FL3	0-0	0-1
1973-74	FL3	2-3	0-1
1974-75	FL3	0-0	0-2
1976-77	FL4	2-1	1-1
1977-78	FL4	1-0	1-1
1978-79	FL3	1-0	0-2
1978-79	FAC	1-0	1-1
1982-83	FLT	1-4	
1991-92	FL2	1-0	2-1
1991-92	FLC	1-1	0-2
1991-92	FMC		1-0

1992-93	FL1	1-2	0-0
1993-94	FL1	2-0	0-3
1993-94	AIC	3-0	
1994-95	FL1	0-4	0-1
1994-95	FLC	0-0	0-1
1995-96	FL1	1-1	2-2
1997-98	FL2	0-3	1-1

H	37	15	22	118	81
A	11	23	36	77	137

WEALDSTONE

1979-80	FAC		1-0

WEST BROMWICH ALBION

1993-94	FL1	0-3	2-2
1994-95	FL1	2-1	0-2
1995-96	FL1	2-1	1-3
1996-97	FL1	2-3	0-4

WEST HAMPSTEAD

1906-07	SEL2 *	5-1	*

* not played. West Hampstead did not complete their fixtures; record expunged

WEST HAM UNITED

1906-07	SL2 *	2-2	2-1
1907-08	SEL1 *	5-1	1-0
1908-09	SL1	0-0	0-4
1909-10	SL1	0-1	0-0
1910-11	SL1	0-6	3-3
1911-12	SEL1 *	2-2	2-2

* Hammers reserves

1913-14	SL1	1-1	1-0
1914-15	SL1	0-1	1-3
1939-40	South A	3-2	0-4
1940-41	South R	3-1	0-11
1940-41	FLWC	2-1	1-3
1979-80	FLC	0-0	1-1
1979-80	FLC		1-5
1992-93	FL1	1-0	0-2
1992-93	AIC	0-3	
1995-96	FAC		0-2
2004-05	FLC		0-2

H	5	5	4	19	21
A	3	4	9	13	43

WEYMOUTH

1955-56	FAC		1-0
1970-71	FAC	7-0	

WIGAN ATHLETIC

1980-81	FL4	1-0	1-0
1982-83	FL3	2-0	0-4
1983-84	FL3	1-0	0-1
1987-88	FL3	3-2	0-1

1988-89	FL3	1-2	0-3
1990-91	FL3	0-2	1-4
1997-98	FL2	1-0	3-1

WINGATE & FINCHLEY

Formed from the merger of the Wingate and Finchley FCs

as Finchley

1953-54	FAC		3-1

WOKING

1997-98	FAC		2-0

WOLVERHAMPTON WANDERERS

1968-69	FLC		0-1
1986-87	FL4	1-0	2-1
1988-89	FL3	3-1	0-3
1991-92	FL2	0-2	1-3
1992-93	FL1	1-1	1-1
1993-94	FL1	1-1	1-0
1994-95	FL1	0-1	0-5
1995-96	FL1	2-1	0-2
1996-97	FL1	1-1	1-4

WORKINGTON

1964-65	FL3	3-0	1-3
1965-66	FL3	3-1	1-3
1967-68	FL4	7-0	2-2
1968-69	FL4	1-0	0-0
1969-70	FL4	3-1	0-5
1970-71	FL4	1-1	1-1
1971-72	FL4	2-0	1-3
1976-77	FL4	2-0	3-0

WORKSOP TOWN

1921-22	FAC		2-1

WREXHAM

1949-50	FAC	2-0	2-2
1958-59	FL3	4-1	1-3
1959-60	FL3	1-1	1-3
1962-63	FL3	2-0	1-1
1963-64	FL3	1-1	3-1
1966-67	FL4	1-1	0-2
1967-68	FL4	3-1	1-4
1968-69	FL4	1-0	3-3
1969-70	FL4	1-0	0-4
1972-73	FL3	0-1	2-4
1973-74	FL3	1-1	1-5
1974-75	FL3	1-1	1-1
1975-76	FL3	2-1	2-2
1982-83	FL3	2-2	2-3
1984-85	FL4	0-1	2-1
1985-86	FL4	3-0	0-0
1986-87	FL4	0-3	0-4
1989-90	FL4	2-1	3-3
1997-98	FL2	1-3	1-3

2002-03	FL3	0-1	0-3
2004-05	FLT *		0-2

* played at The Millennium Stadium

H	9	6	5	28	20
A	2	7	12	26	54

WYCOMBE WANDERERS

1906-07	SL2	3-0	2-2
1907-08	SL2	5-0	4-1
1997-98	FL2	1-2	1-4
1997-98	FLT	0-1	
2004-05	FL2	1-2	1-0

YEOVIL TOWN

1958-59	FAC	0-0	0-1
1963-64	FAC		0-1
1982-83	FAC	3-0	
2003-04	FL3	0-2	0-4
2004-05	FL2	0-1	1-3
2005-06	FL1	4-1	2-0

YORK CITY

1929-30	FAC	1-4	
1936-37	FAC	3-3	1-2
1959-60	FL3	1-1	3-2
1965-66	FL3	2-3	3-0
1966-67	FL4	2-1	1-2
1967-68	FL4	0-1	2-2
1968-69	FL4	1-2	1-1
1969-70	FL4	1-0	0-1
1970-71	FL4	1-0	0-3
1972-73	FL3	3-0	0-2
1973-74	FL3	3-3	0-1
1977-78	FL4	0-0	2-1
1980-81	FL4	3-0	1-0
1987-88	FL3	3-1	3-0
1989-90	FL4	2-0	1-2
1997-98	FL2	4-4	1-1
1999-00	FL3	0-0	2-2
2000-01	FL3	1-0	0-1
2001-02	FL3	0-1	1-2
2002-03	FL3	1-0	0-2
2003-04	FL3	0-0	0-2

H	9	7	5	32	24
A	5	4	11	22	29

Season	Competition	Pos.	Pl.	W.	D.	L.	F.	A.	Pts.
1906-07	Southern League, Second Division	1	22	14	5	3	58	23	33
1906-07	South Eastern League, Second Division	1	18	17	0	1	85	6	34
1907-08	Southern League, Second Division	1	18	13	3	2	47	16	29
1907-08	South Eastern League, First Division	6	34	17	5	12	64	57	39
1907-08	United League	2	8	3	2	3	16	16	8
1908-09	Southern League, First Division	12	40	14	10	16	52	54	38
1908-09	United League, Southern Section	4	8	2	3	3	15	18	7
1909-10	Southern League, First Division	20	42	12	9	21	51	90	33
1910-11	Southern League, First Division	19	38	10	9	19	47	64	29
1911-12	Southern League, Second Division	4	26	16	1	9	73	24	33
1911-12	South Eastern League, First Division	11	38	16	6	16	61	77	38
1912-13	Southern League, Second Division	2	24	14	6	4	43	23	34
1912-13	Southern Alliance	6	16	5	4	7	19	32	14
1913-14	Southern League, First Division	16	38	10	12	16	41	66	32
1913-14	Southern Alliance	9	16	4	3	9	15	35	11
1914-15	Southern League, First Division	18	38	10	8	20	44	64	28
1919-20	Southern League, First Division	11	42	13	17	12	46	48	43

Season	Competition	Pos.	Pl.	W.	D.	L.	F.	A.	Pts.
1920-21	Football League Third Division (Southern Section)	17	42	14	8	20	44	61	36
1921-22	Football League Third Division (Southern Section)	22	42	8	11	23	34	74	27
1922-23	Football League Third Division (Southern Section)	15	42	12	13	17	49	54	37
1923-24	Football League Third Division (Southern Section)	19	42	12	10	20	53	84	34
1924-25	Football League Third Division (Southern Section)	10	42	19	5	18	51	61	43
1925-26	Football League Third Division (Southern Section)	11	42	19	4	19	78	73	42
1926-27	Football League Third Division (Southern Section)	19	42	14	6	22	64	77	34
1927-28	Football League Third Division (Southern Section)	7	42	20	6	16	80	64	46
1928-29	Football League Third Division (Southern Section)	12	42	15	11	16	80	75	41
1929-30	Football League Third Division (Southern Section)	11	42	15	13	14	69	59	43
1930-31	Football League Third Division (Southern Section)	5	42	22	5	15	76	60	49
1931-32	Football League Third Division (Southern Section)	3	42	21	11	10	77	53	53
1932-33	Football League Third Division (Southern Section)	13	42	15	11	16	65	82	41
1933-34	Football League Third Division (Southern Section)	16	42	12	10	20	51	74	34
1934-35	Football League Third Division (Southern Section)	21	42	11	9	22	65	78	31
1935-36	Football League Third Division (Southern Section)	18	42	13	10	19	61	62	36
1936-37	Football League Third Division (Southern Section)	10	42	17	11	14	78	67	45
1937-38	Football League Third Division (Southern Section)	12	42	15	10	17	70	68	40
1938-39	Football League Third Division (Southern Section)	12	42	16	9	17	61	64	41
1939-40	Football League Third Division (Southern Section)	14	3	1	1	1	3	3	3

season abandoned due to outbreak of hostilities

Season	Competition	Pos.	Pl.	W.	D.	L.	F.	A.	Pts.
1939-40	Football League South Division (Group 'A')	10	18	4	0	14	30	61	8
1939-40	Football League South Division (Group 'D')	4	18	8	3	7	41	37	19
1940-41	Football League South Regional Division	28	15	6	3	6	32	51	0.628

position decided by goal average

Season	Competition	Pos.	Pl.	W.	D.	L.	F.	A.	Pts.
1940-41	Football League South Division	4	12	6	1	5	30	35	13

At the end of the 1940-41 season it was decided that the results of the South Regional Division and South Division would be amalgamated; this gave a final record of:-

Season	Competition	Pos.	Pl.	W.	D.	L.	F.	A.	Pts.
1940-41	Football League South Regional Division	31	29	12	4	13	64	101	0.633

position decided by goal average

This final record includes two South Regional Division games played outside of the scheduled season (August – December,1940); these were the 0-7 loss at Crystal Palace on 17th May and a 2-8 defeat at Fulham on 24th May

Season	Competition	Pos.	Pl.	W.	D.	L.	F.	A.	Pts.
1945-46	Football League Third Division (Southern Section)								
	(North of Thames Region)	10	20	5	5	10	33	49	15
1946-47	Football League Third Division (Southern Section)	8	42	17	10	15	71	60	44
1947-48	Football League Third Division (Southern Section)	9	42	15	13	14	51	58	43
1948-49	Football League Third Division (Southern Section)	18	42	9	16	17	41	46	34
1949-50	Football League Third Division (Southern Section)	3	42	19	13	10	66	48	51
1950-51	Football League Third Division (Southern Section)	7	46	21	10	15	92	69	52
1951-52	Football League Third Division (Southern Section)	9	46	19	10	17	75	66	48
1952-53	Football League Third Division (Southern Section)	8	46	18	13	15	69	74	49
1953-54	Football League Third Division (Southern Section)	16	46	18	7	21	69	71	43
1954-55	Football League Third Division (Southern Section)	10	46	17	12	17	83	80	46
1955-56	Football League Third Division (Southern Section)	4	46	21	11	14	88	80	53
1956-57	Football League Third Division (Southern Section)	7	46	18	12	16	73	65	48
1957-58	Football League Third Division (Southern Section)	7	46	21	12	13	90	58	54
1958-59	Football League Third Division	8	46	21	8	17	85	80	50
1959-60	Football League Third Division	12	46	19	8	19	76	74	46
1960-61	Football League Third Division	20	46	14	11	21	60	76	39
1961-62	Football League Third Division	16	46	13	16	17	57	69	42
1962-63	Football League Third Division	8	46	19	12	15	75	77	50
1963-64	Football League Third Division	14	46	15	15	16	77	78	45
1964-65	Football League Third Division	12	46	19	8	19	78	71	46
1965-66	Football League Third Division	21	46	16	4	26	54	83	36

Season	Competition	Pos.	Pl.	W.	D.	L.	F.	A.	Pts.
1966-67	Football League Fourth Division	6	46	22	9	15	70	49	53
1967-68	Football League Fourth Division	6	46	20	14	12	77	58	54
1968-69	Football League Fourth Division	7	46	19	13	14	78	61	51
1969-70	Football League Fourth Division	17	46	15	10	21	59	85	40
1970-71	Football League Fourth Division	18	46	14	15	17	53	66	43
1971-72	Football League Fourth Division	2	46	24	12	10	81	55	60
1972-73	Football League Third Division	14	46	17	10	19	61	54	44
1973-74	Football League Third Division	12	46	16	14	16	62	62	46
1974-75	Football League Third Division	18	46	13	16	17	46	51	42
1975-76	Football League Third Division	23	46	12	13	21	65	75	37
1976-77	Football League Fourth Division	10	46	15	19	12	52	45	49
1977-78	Football League Fourth Division	2	46	25	10	11	66	39	60
1978-79	Football League Fourth Division	13	46	15	15	16	51	49	45
1979-80	Football League Third Division	22	46	14	10	22	47	58	38
1980-81	Football League Fourth Division	1	46	30	7	9	79	31	67
1981-82	Football League Third Division	7	46	18	15	13	63	51	69
1982-83	Football League Third Division	15	46	15	14	17	66	65	59
1983-84	Football League Third Division	22	46	10	14	22	55	76	44
1984-85	Football League Fourth Division	20	46	13	11	22	58	83	50
1985-86	Football League Fourth Division	9	46	18	10	18	69	67	64
1986-87	Football League Fourth Division	3	46	25	5	16	68	55	80
1987-88	Football League Third Division	17	46	14	13	19	65	83	55
1988-89	Football League Third Division	21	46	13	15	18	56	75	54
1989-90	Football League Fourth Division	3	46	22	9	15	61	48	75
1990-91	Football League Third Division	2	46	26	7	13	67	51	85
1991-92	Football League Second Division	12	46	17	11	18	63	63	62
1992-93	Football League First Division	18	46	13	13	20	54	64	52
1993-94	Football League First Division	15	46	17	8	21	63	67	59
1994-95	Football League First Division	13	46	18	8	20	54	73	62
1995-96	Football League First Division	14	46	15	14	17	52	61	59
1996-97	Football League First Division	24	46	8	15	23	42	86	39
1997-98	Football League Second Division	24	46	11	10	25	47	79	43
1998-99	Football League Third Division	18	46	14	12	20	52	58	54
1999-00	Football League Third Division	16	46	15	11	20	53	61	56
2000-01	Football League Third Division	11	46	15	18	13	55	53	63
2001-02	Football League Third Division	12	46	15	13	18	51	54	58
2002-03	Football League Third Division	17	46	17	3	26	47	59	54
2003-04	Football League Third Division	17	46	14	12	20	52	64	54
2004-05	Football League Two	4	46	22	12	12	65	46	78
2005-06	Football League One	1	46	23	13	10	72	43	82